Shooter's Bible

ABOUT OUR COVER

The handsome Browning shotguns featured on this year's cover are the famed Auto-5 Classic models issued during the mid-1980s in limited edition. The Auto-5 Gold Classic (top) is a 12-gauge model with 28-inch barrel and Modified choke. The Gold Classic Superposed (bottom) is a 20-gauge over/under with 26-inch barrels choked Imp. Cyl./Mod. The mallard duck studies and Labrador retriever engraved on these guns commemorate the unfailing reliability of the Auto-5 since its introduction in 1903. A portrait of John Moses Browning is engraved on each of these classics.

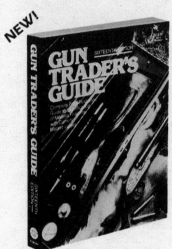

Shooter's Bible

NO. 85
1994 EDITION

EDITOR:
William S. Jarrett

PRODUCTION & DESIGN:
Charlene Cruson Step

FIREARMS CONSULTANTS:
Bill Meade
Vincent A. Pestilli
Paul Rochelle
Robert A. Scanlon

COVER PHOTOGRAPHER:
Ray Wells

PUBLISHER:
Robert E. Weise
PRESIDENT
Brian T. Herrick

STOEGER PUBLISHING COMPANY

Published by Stoeger Publishing Company
55 Ruta Court
South Hackensack, New Jersey 07606

Library of Congress Catalog Card No.: 63-6200
International Standard Book No.: 0-88317-168-6
Manufactured in the United States of America

In the United States:
Distributed to the book trade and to the sporting goods trade by
Stoeger Industries, 55 Ruta Court
South Hackensack, New Jersey 07606

In Canada:
Distributed to the book trade and to the sporting goods trade by
Stoeger Canada Ltd.
1801 Wentworth Street, Unit 16
Whitby, Ontario, L1N 8R6, Canada

Contents

FOREWORD

As we launch the 85th edition of SHOOTER'S BIBLE, we once again begin with the latest in a series of reprints from editions published exactly 50 years ago. This popular feature leads off the article section, providing readers with a new perspective on the products and prices that existed in 1944, the year our Armed Forces finally established a foothold in Europe after D-day.

The articles that follow include several by writers who have become steady contributors—Ralph Quinn (rifle stocks), Steve Irwin (the Kentucky Rifle), Wayne van Zwoll (elk hunting), Jim Casada (the sporting life of Nash Buckingham), Wilf Pyle (how to buy a rifle for your son or daughter), and Sam Fadala (reloading, from his new book, *Rifle Guide*). As always, we are introducing a few new writers as well, namely, Gary Brown, who covers the evolution of Colt's legendary Peacemaker, and Don Henry, who shows you how easy it is to handle the big bores.

Next, we revisit the Manufacturers' Showcase, which made its debut last year. We invite you to browse through this unique marketplace of outdoor-related products. The Showcase, in turn, flows right into the Specifications section, which leads off with nearly 100 illustrated pages packed with facts and figures on handguns. Highlighted are such vital statistics as caliber, barrel length, overall length, weight, price, special features and much more. In the Handgun section, you will note a number of new manufacturers—European American Armory, Para-Ordnance, Brno, Coonan Arms, Hammerli U.S.A., Heritage and McMillan. The Rifle segment includes more than 100 pages this year, augmented by a few new entrants: JagerSports (which takes over the Heym and Voere lines as a subsidiary of Swarovski) and European American Armory.

In the Shotgun section, we introduce AYA, Connecticut Valley Classics, Rizzini, Imperial and Magtech. The Black Powder section covers the A to Zs of muzzleloading arms, including classic replicas as well as modern high-tech entries. The Sights & Scopes section encompasses the latest state-of-the-art sighting equipment, including laser and red dot sights. The Specifications section concludes with nearly 75 pages of cartridges, ballistics data, bullets, powder and reloading equipment. All in all, this section of SHOOTER'S BIBLE gives readers over 450 fact-filled pages of firearms-related information.

Last, but by no means least, readers will profit greatly by using our Reference section. It offers an extensive look at current gun-related books, a listing of discontinued models from last year's book, and the names and complete addresses of all the major manufacturers and suppliers. Perhaps the most useful features of all, though, are the Caliberfinder™ and Gunfinder™ pages. In the former, every model, whether handgun, rifle or muzzleloader, is listed according to caliber, from the 17 (T/C's Contender pistol) to the 600 Nitro Express (Heym's Express Rifle).

That wraps up this 85th milestone edition of SHOOTER'S BIBLE. We invite your comments and suggestions as we strive to make this the best possible book of its kind. Good reading—and good shooting.

William S. Jarrett
Editor

Articles

50 YEARS AGO IN SHOOTER'S BIBLE

Half a century ago, in 1944, America was in the process of liberating Europe and bringing Japan to its knees in the Pacific. On the following pages, we've reprinted a dozen pages from that year's edition of SHOOTER'S BIBLE (#36) to give our readers a new slant on an old era. With each reprint, we've added a few of the major news and sports events on a month-by-month basis. Most of our professional athletes were in military service in 1944, but still the World Series was played, the NFL had its championship game in December, and

Byron Nelson kept on winning golf tournaments.

You'll also note that Winchester's Model 52 sold for $56.95 that year ($66.95 with a Lyman sight), whereas Remington's Model 141 cost $69.95 ($350.45 for the "Premier" Grade). A Browning Auto-5 (featured on our front cover) went for $68.65—without the gold engravings—and a High Standard pistol, with its "new long handle and automatic slide lock," was priced at $35.35.

We hope you enjoy this nostalgic glance at world happenings 50 years ago.

COLT AUTOMATIC PISTOLS

In every part of the world Colt Automatic Pistols are known and used. The speed with which they may be fired, their power and dependability, have made them popular for every type of service requiring an arm of absolute dependability and complete safety. Colt Automatic Pistols are equipped with both manual and automatic safety features—they are the safest automatic pistols that can be purchased. There is a Colt model for every purpose.

WOODSMAN TARGET MODEL

CALIBER: .22 Long Rifle
6½ Inch Barrel

The Colt Woodsman Model is the most popular .22 Caliber automatic pistol ever produced. Thousands of shooters have found it ideal for all around shooting—and for target shooting. Graceful in appearance and beautifully finished. It is furnished with an unusually comfortable grip that fits the hand snugly and securely. Checked walnut stocks make slipping impossible. Fast and certain action—a trigger pull that is smooth and crisp. Ten shot magazine, and slide lock safety. Target sights, either Bead or Patridge.

Price $34.50

SPECIFICATIONS

Ammunition: .22 Long Rifle Greased cartridges. Regular or High Speed.
Magazine Capacity: 10 cartridges
Length of Barrel: 6½ inches.
Length Over All: 10½ inches.
Distance Between Sights: 9 inches.
Weight: 29 ounces.
Sights: Adjustable, Bead or Patridge. Stippled.
Trigger: Grooved, set-back type.
Stocks: Checked Walnut. Finish: Blued.

Extra Magazine $2.40

Price $34.50

SPECIFICATIONS

Ammunition: .22 Long Rifle Greased cartridges. Regular or High Speed.
Magazine Capacity: 10 cartridges.
Length of Barrel: 4½ inches.
Length Over All: 8½ inches.
Distance Between Sights: Fixed Front sight—7½ inches. Adjustable front sight—7 inches.
Weight: 27 ounces.
Stocks: Checked Walnut.
Sights: Front sight fixed, ramp type with serrated face, or adjustable front sight. Rear sight adjustable for windage. Both stippled.
Trigger: Grooved, set-back type. Finish: Blued.

WOODSMAN SPORT MODEL

CALIBER: .22 Long Rifle
4½ Inch Barrel

The same as the standard model described above, except for length of barrel. It can now be furnished with either fixed or adjustable front sight. Ramp type front sight is sturdy and rugged, built to stand up under hard service and abuse. Adjustable type front sight is same as on target model. Rear sight is adjustable for windage. This model was produced for use in the woods and on the trail, where compactness is essential. Unusually accurate and a thoroughbred Colt in every way. Uses either Regular or High Speed cartridges, including hollow point type. Ten shot magazine.

WOODSMAN HIGH SPEED MAIN SPRING HOUSING

The new Main Spring Housing, built of hardened steel and adapting the Woodsman for use with the new High Speed Cartridges.

Those who may wish to change over their present Woodsman to handle the High Speed Cartridges need simply replace their old housing with the new type.

Price $2.40

POCKET MODEL AUTOMATIC PISTOL

CALIBER: .25

The .25 Caliber Colt Automatic Pistol is designed for personal protection. Because of its small size and light weight it can be easily carried in vest pocket or ladies hand bag. Shoots the hard-hitting .25 Automatic cartridge, with magazine having six shot capacity. Makes a beautiful gift when finished in nickel with pearl or ivory stocks. Three safety features make it absolutely safe to handle.

SPECIFICATIONS

Ammunition: 25 Automatic cartridge. Magazine Capacity: 6 cartridges. Length of Barrel: 2 inches. Length Over All: 4½ inches. Weight: 13 ounces. Stocks: Checked Walnut. Finish: Blued or Nickel.

Price $20.50
Extra Magazine $1.00

Colt Grip Safety and Magazine Disconnector

To doubly insure absolute safety in handling Colt Automatic Pistols, all models (with the exception of the Woodsman Model) are fitted with the world famed Colt Grip Safety—in addition to the Slide Lock Safety. The Colt Grip Safety operates automatically and requires the grip safety to be squeezed simultaneously with pulling the trigger in order to discharge the Arm. The arm cannot be fired by simply pulling the trigger.

Colt Automatic Pistol models in calibers .32, .380 and .25 are also equipped with the Colt Magazine Safety Disconnector.

Price $26.50
Extra Magazine. 1.20

This is the favorite model for personal and home protection. Ready always for instant action.

POCKET MODEL AUTOMATIC PISTOL

CALIBERS: .32 and .380

This pocket model Automatic Pistol can be furnished in either .32 or .380 caliber. Large magazine capacity, powerful, rugged and dependable. Flat construction takes up minimum room in pocket, bag or dresser drawer. Three safety features, both manual and automatic.

SPECIFICATIONS

Ammunition: .32 Automatic cartridge. .380 Automatic cartridge.
Magazine Capacity: .32 caliber, 8 cartridges. .380 caliber, 7 cartridges.
Length of Barrel: 3¾ inches. Length Over All: 6¾ inches.
Weight: 24 ounces. Stocks: Checked Walnut.
Finish: Blued or Nickel.

NEW STYLE ARCHED MAIN SPRING HOUSING

NEW STYLE SHORT CHECKERED TRIGGER

STOEGER'S 25-SHOT MAGAZINE

AVAILABLE AGAIN AFTER THE WAR

GENUINE BROWNING AUTOMATIC SHOTGUNS

**12, 16 AND 20 GAUGES
5 OR 3 SHOT**

5-Shot is adjustable to 3-Shot with Browning Magazine Adaptor furnished at no extra cost with all new 5-shot guns.

GRADE 1

SPECIAL

BROWNING QUALITY

All Browning Guns are painstakingly fitted, assembled, and tested by specialized craftsmen. Decorated receiver, hand-checkered stocks and forearms and drop-forged receivers add to the appearance, durability and satisfactory performance of the gun and to the safety and convenience of the shooter.

PRICES
12, 16 OR 20 GAUGE—5 OR 3 SHOT

Grade 1—Either Gauge, 5- or 3-shot without rib*	$68.65
Browning Special, either gauge, 5- or 3-shot with raised matted rib*	78.45
Browning Special, either gauge, 5- or 3-shot with ventilated rib*	86.05
Extra barrel, either gun, without rib*	26.30
Extra barrel, either gun, with raised matted rib*	36.05
Extra barrel, either gun, with ventilated rib*	43.70
Extra for Standard Grade American Walnut stock made to special dimensions on new gun, any grade	19.80
Extra for high-grade curly selected American Walnut stock made to special dimensions on new gun, any grade	28.50
Extra for Circassian Walnut stock made to special dimensions on new gun, any grade	40.00
Extra for Recoil Pad, most any standard type fitted, (no extra charge for shortening stock)	6.75
Extra for Sights, ivory or red fitted, per set, front and middle on ribbed barrel guns only	2.65

*When ordering be sure to state Gauge, Barrel Length, Choke or Bore and whether 5- or 3-Shot desired.

NEW FEATURES

● **Non-Glare Receiver.** Top of receiver is specially processed, giving it a beautiful dull grain finish that completely eliminates sun glare. This finish is very durable and does not become marred.

● **Chambered for 2¾" Shells.** All three gauges will handle 2¾" shells.

● **Matted Sighting Plane.** All plain barrels have a matting on top which eliminates sun glare and affords quicker alignment in sighting— Result, Better Shooting.

● **Browning Ribs.** Raised matted and ventilated ribs are correctly designed and are milled in one piece with the barrel from one solid forging.

● **Magazine Cut-Off.** Added feature for carrying gun in car— greater convenience in quickly changing loads in duck blind or elsewhere.

● **Cross Bolt Safety.** Located behind the trigger, is simply constructed and can be pushed off safe or on safe by a flip of the finger.

STANDARD SPECIFICATIONS ALL GAUGES— 5 AND 3 SHOT

In design, material, quality of workmanship and ornamentation, 12, 16 and 20 Gauge Browning Automatics are identical—all have walnut stocks and forearms, nicely finished and hand checkered, and specially prepared steel barrels and action parts. The only differences are in size and weight. All guns are chambered for 2¾-inch shells. Weight: 20 Gauge about 6⅞ pounds, 16 Gauge about 7¼ pounds, 12 Gauge about 8 pounds. Stock specifications for all three gauges are—half pistol grip, drop at comb 1⅝ inches, drop at heel 2½ inches, length 14¼ inches.

	Striped	Matted Barrel Without Rib, or Raised Matted or Ventilated Rib	
12 Gauge			
Full choke	32",	30",	28"
Modified choke	30",	28",	26"
Improved cylinder	28",	26"	
Skeet bore	28",	26"	
Cylinder	28",	26"	
16 Gauge			
Full choke	30",	28"	
Modified choke	28",	26"	
Improved cylinder	28",	26"	
Skeet bore	28",	26"	
Cylinder	28",	26"	
20 Gauge			
Full choke	30",	28",	26"
Modified choke	28",	26"	
Improved cylinder	28",	26"	

ORDER IT FROM STOEGER

THE FOX SHOTGUN

A SUPREME ACHIEVEMENT IN SHOTGUN BUILDING

It has been said that to the true lover of the beautiful in a gun, there is nothing more beautiful in all the realm of mechanics than the rhythmic speed and action of a perfectly designed gun lock.

From the old flint lock, down through the muzzle-loaders and the breech-loader with external-hammers, to the present highly developed "hammerless," the lock has always been a subject of keen interest to the true sportsman.

In spite of some popular belief to the contrary, the tendency has been toward a steady simplification in design. For instance, the flint lock contained twenty-two parts, including lock plate. The muzzle-loading lock consisted of fifteen parts. The breech-loading hammer gun lock contains seventeen parts.

The Fox Lock, simplest gun-firing mechanism ever devised, contains but *three principal working parts*—the coil spring, the one-piece hammer, including as part of it the firing pin, and the sear. No other gun made operates so simply or with so few parts. In some cases the firing pin is still a separate part from the hammer, which alone adds several extra delicate parts, such as bushings, etc., to the lock. In other cases as high as ten or fifteen additional parts are required to do no more than is accomplished by the wonderful simplicity of the Fox Lock.

12, 16 AND 20 GAUGE

GRADE AE

SPECIFICATIONS

Barrels, high quality alloy forged steel, adapted to smokeless or black powders. Selected walnut stock; checkered and engraved; half pistol grip; 12, 16 and 20 gauge: 26, 28, 30 and 32 inch barrels. Full pistol or straight grip to order at no extra charge. Weight, 12 gauge, 6⅞ to 8 pounds; 16 gauge, 6 to 7 pounds; 20 gauge, 5¾ to 6¾ pounds; various drops and lengths of stocks.

A.E. with Selective Automatic Ejectors......................$103.50

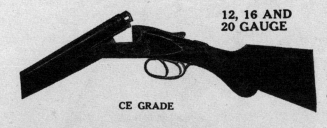

12, 16 AND 20 GAUGE

CE GRADE

This is the grade that is making good everywhere. In every respect it is unusual—a high grade gun—at a very modest price. It's a beauty in looks and finish. No gun will stand up better to hard work. Its every detail is perfect. And at the price it is in a class absolutely by itself.

High Quality, alloy forged Steel Barrels, figured and dark finished, selected walnut stock; artistic engraving, well covered with scroll and picture work. Half pistol grip; made in 12, 16 and 20 gauge; 26, 28, 30 and 32 inch barrels. Full pistol or straight grip to order at no extra charge. Weight, 12 gauge, 6⅞ to 8 pounds; 16 gauge, 6 to 7 pounds; 20 gauge, 5¾ to 6¾ pounds.

CE with Automatic Shell Ejector.........................$171.00

High quality alloy forged Steel Barrels, especially bored and tested by hand for evenness of pattern for trap shooting. Stock of beautifully figured Walnut straight, half or full pistol grip, all at the same price. Beautiful engraving of new style. Equipped with Silver's Recoil Pad, Automatic Ejector and Lyman sights. Weight, 12 gauge, 6⅞ to 8 pounds; 16 gauge, 6 to 7 pounds; 20 gauge, 5¾ to 6¾ pounds. Barrels 26, 28, 30 and 32 inch.

Grade XE $227.90
Grade DE 347.25
Grade FE 612.75

(Any extras may be had on FE Grade at no extra cost.)

12, 16 AND 20 GAUGE

XE GRADE

EXTRAS, FITTED TO NEW GUNS

Fox-Kautzky Selective Single Trigger $27.50	Set of Ivory Bead Sights—any grade $1.45	Beavertail Forend—CE Grade $26.25
Ventilated Rib—any grade 45.20	Soft Rubber Recoil Pad—any grade 4.60	Beavertail Forend—A, AE, or HE Grade .. 17.65
Drop of stock changed ⅜" either way 7.25	Beavertail Forend—DE Grade 33.90	Beavertail Forend—SP or SPE Grade 17.65
Stock cut off to any length and refinished .. 2.85	Beavertail Forend—XE Grade 28.12	Beavertail Forend—Sterlingworth 14.45

© **FOX GUNS ARE TRADITIONALLY FINE**

Remington
REG. U.S. PAT. OFF.

GAMEMASTER—MODEL 141
HIGH-POWER SLIDE ACTION RIFLE

Made in Calibers
.30 Remington   .32 Remington
.35 Remington

THE ONLY HIGH POWER SLIDE ACTION RIFLE
Fast! Powerful! Accurate!

Here is a high power big game rifle with a repeating action that is smooth as silk, swift as lightning, dependable as government time—an action that helps you throw six bullets at your target with the least effort. The "Gamemaster" combines accuracy with speed of operation, and its beautiful, graceful lines make it superior in appearance. The twenty-four inch barrel, large stock, semi-beavertail fore-end, front sight ramp, and suitability for all North American big game are outstanding features.

Specifications of "Gamemaster" Model 141A

"Standard" Grade. Slide action, takedown, hammerless, solid breech. .30, .32 and .35 Remington calibers, all center fire and rimless. 24-inch barrel. American walnut stock and fore-end. Stock with half pistol grip and shotgun style steel butt plate, deeply checkered to prevent slipping. Semi-beavertail fore-end. Step adjustable rear sight. White metal bead front sight mounted on non-glare matted ramp. Magazine holds five cartridges which, with one in the chamber, gives a capacity of six shots. Cross bolt safety. Length over-all, 42¾"; taken down, 29½", weight about 7¾ pounds.

No. 141A "STANDARD" GRADE	$ 69.95
No. 141B "SPECIAL" GRADE	81.15
No. 141D "PEERLESS" GRADE	184.35
No. 141F "PREMIER" GRADE	350.45
⅞-inch Sling Strap (leather, Whelen type, with hooks and eyes) extra	3.75

REMINGTON OVER AND UNDER SHOTGUNS

MODEL 32A 12 GAUGE

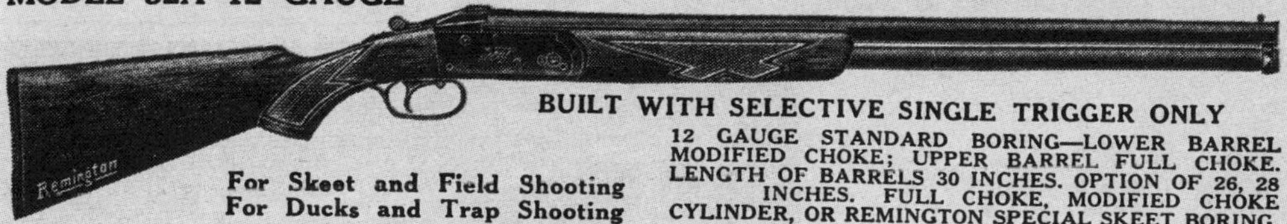

For Skeet and Field Shooting
For Ducks and Trap Shooting

BUILT WITH SELECTIVE SINGLE TRIGGER ONLY

12 GAUGE STANDARD BORING—LOWER BARREL MODIFIED CHOKE; UPPER BARREL FULL CHOKE. LENGTH OF BARRELS 30 INCHES. OPTION OF 26, 28, INCHES. FULL CHOKE, MODIFIED CHOKE CYLINDER, OR REMINGTON SPECIAL SKEET BORING.

The first American-made Over-and-Under gun. No finer or stronger gun of this type available. Has exclusive features not found in imported Over-and-Under guns at considerably higher prices. Its attractive appearance, smooth graceful lines and superb balance will appeal to discriminating sportsmen. Smaller, stronger and better looking frame. Simple but sturdy construction. Upper and lower tangs made in one piece with frame. Special mounting of barrels to allow for uneven expansion and to insure shooting on center. Absence of side ribs eliminates heat waves and permits better pointing. Mechanism readily accessible. Automatic ejectors. Selective three-way safety—automatic, manual or inoperative. Heat treated frame for greater strength. Both sides of frame handsomely decorated. Grip and fore-end beautifully checkered.

One barrel above the other gives the advantage of a single sighting plane; straight line recoil reduces recoil and whip of gun. Simple take-down. Narrow-grip—more natural. Ideal for Trap and Skeet shooting, especially on doubles.

SPECIFICATIONS

No. 32A Standard Grade. Take-down, hammerless, automatic ejectors, 12 gauge only. Standard length barrels 30 inches; also furnished in 26, 28, inches. Full choke, modified choke, improved cylinder or true cylinder bore. Option of any combination desired. Selective single trigger. Walnut pistol-grip stock and fore-end, both handsomely checkered. Top of main bolt is matted and both sides of frame are decorated. Regular stock dimensions 14 inches long, 2½ inches drop at heel, and 1⅝ inches drop at comb. Bakelite butt plate. Weight about 7½ lbs.

No. 32A—"Standard" Grade $153.55
    Extra pair of barrels 73.15

*Standard stock dimensions, 14 inches long, 2½ inches drop at heel, 1⅝ inches drop at comb. Half pistol grip. Any other dimensions, subject to extra charge of 18.30
No. 32D—"Tournament" Grade 336.85
No. 32E—"Expert" Grade 397.80
No. 32F—"Premeir" Grade 501.35

Nos. 32D, E, F also supplied with any grip, length or drop desired without additional charge.
Raised solid matted rib, extra 9.75

MODEL 32 SKEET GUN

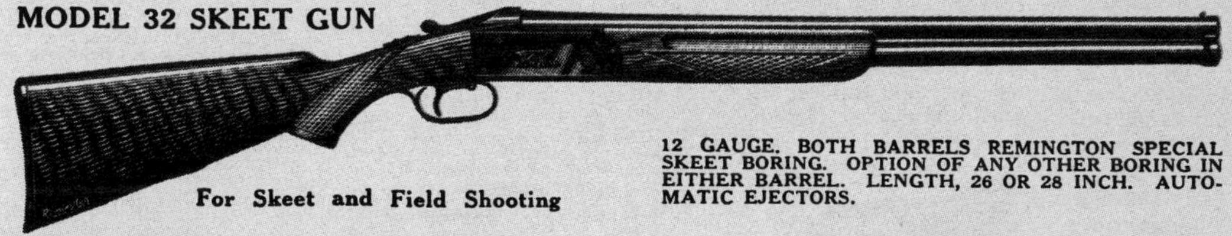

For Skeet and Field Shooting

12 GAUGE. BOTH BARRELS REMINGTON SPECIAL SKEET BORING. OPTION OF ANY OTHER BORING IN EITHER BARREL. LENGTH, 26 OR 28 INCH. AUTO-MATIC EJECTORS.

This is the coming gun for Skeet shooting. Its popularity is rapidly increasing. Particularly fine on Skeet "doubles" shots. Straight line recoil of lower barrel leaves the shooter ready without disturbance for his second shot immediately after breaking the first target. Single sighting plane permits the most accurate pointing. Perfect balance. Remington Selective Single Trigger absolutely dependable. Remington Special Skeet Boring in both barrels assures well distributed shot patterns at all Skeet ranges. Lower barrel is marked "out" for use on outgoing target. Upper barrel is marked "in" for use on incoming target.
No. 32. "Skeet" Grade with plain barrel $157.15
No. 32. "Skeet" Grade with raised solid rib 166.90
No. 32. "Skeet" Grade with ventilated rib 182.00
Shortening regular stock up to 1 inch, extra 5.35
Special drop or greater length of stock, extra 18.30

SPECIFICATIONS

No. 32 Skeet Grade (26-inch barrels). Take-down, hammerless, automatic ejectors, 12 gauge only. Standard length barrels 26 inches; also furnished in 28, inches. Standard boring, both barrels Remington Special Skeet Boring. Lower barrel marked "out" for use on outgoing target, upper barrel marked "in" for incoming target. Option of any other combination of borings desired. Single trigger. Selected, high-grade walnut pistol-grip stock and fore-end, both handsomely checkered. Top of main bolt is matted and both sides of frame are decorated. Regular stock dimensions 14 inches long from front trigger, 2½ inches drop at heel, and 1⅝ inches drop at comb. Bakelite butt plate. Weight about 7½ pounds. Half pistol grip. Beaver tail fore-end.

MODEL 32TC 12 GAUGE
WITH VENTILATED RIB

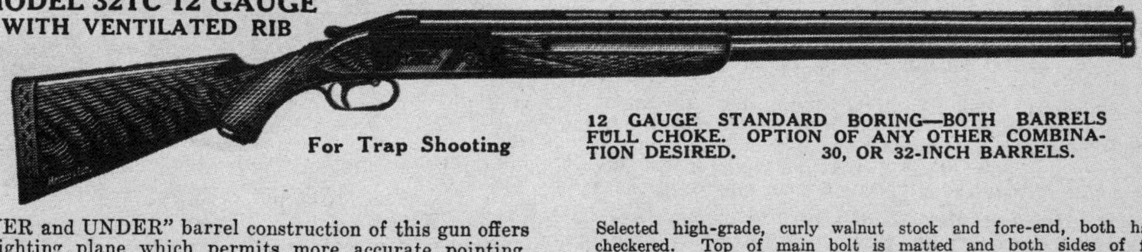

For Trap Shooting

12 GAUGE STANDARD BORING—BOTH BARRELS FULL CHOKE. OPTION OF ANY OTHER COMBINATION DESIRED. 30, OR 32-INCH BARRELS.

The "OVER and UNDER" barrel construction of this gun offers a single sighting plane which permits more accurate pointing. Straight line recoil of the lower barrel eliminates barrel whip.

SPECIFICATIONS

Model 32TC Target Grade with raised ventilated matted rib. Take-down, hammerless, automatic ejectors, 12 gauge only. Choice of 30 or 32-inch barrels. Standard boring—both barrels full choke. Option of any other combination desired. Front and rear sights. Hawkins recoil pad.

Selected high-grade, curly walnut stock and fore-end, both handsomely checkered. Top of main bolt is matted and both sides of frame are decorated. Standard stock dimensions 14⅜ inches long over all, 1⅞ inches drop at heel and 1½ inches drop at comb. Full pistol grip with rubber cap; option of straight grip. Will furnish made-to-order lengths from 13½ to 15 inches without extra charge. Weight about 8¼ pounds.

No. 32TC—"Target" Grade with Ventilated rib, Selective Single Trigger and Beaver Tail Fore-end (as illustrated) $188.70

Stock with dimensions outside of prescribed limits, No. 32T, extra .. 18.30

SMITH & WESSON

The Most Powerful Handgun Ever Made

The S & W
".357" MAGNUM*

THE S & W ".357" MAGNUM* shown with 8⅜" barrel. Coupled with its tremendous speed and power, this amazing gun is capable of less than 1 inch diameter machine rest groups at 20 yards. And at 100, 200, 500 yards, and even beyond, the inherent power and accuracy continue to exist.

1510 foot-seconds muzzle velocity! Greater bullet speed by far than ever before achieved in handguns. 800 foot-pounds muzzle energy! No hand arm cartridge ever manufactured has come within hundreds of pounds of this terrific power.

And with this speed and power — accuracy. Never, except for those made with other Smith & Wesson revolvers, have there been published machine rest groups made by a large caliber hand arm that can in any way compare with those made with the S & W ".357" Magnum*.

Its square-shouldered Sharpe-type lead bullet will shoot through steel plates that are only dented by other cartridges, yet the S & W ".357" Magnum* bullet will upset to .50 caliber in 8 inches of soft paraffin; other bullets pass through practically unchanged in form. **The S & W ".357" Magnum* Has Far Greater Shock Power Than Any .38, .44, or .45 Ever Tested.**

While this revolver is chambered especially for the ultra-powerful S & W ".357" Magnum* cartridge, its accuracy and effectiveness with all the .38 Specials (Mid-Range, Regular and High-Speeds) is actually amazing, and make it the greatest all-purpose hand arm ever developed.

*Registered U. S. Patent Office

SUPER UNDERCOVER SERVICE GUN

The S & W ".357" Magnum* with short 3½" barrel, and Baughman Quick-Draw Sight on King Plain Ramp. Favorite shoulder-holster gun with leading Federal and State peace officers.

SPECIFICATIONS

CALIBER: ".357" (Actual bullet diameter .38 S & W Special)

NUMBER OF SHOTS: 6

BARREL: 3½, 5, 6, 6½, or 8⅜ inches

LENGTH: With 6-inch barrel, 11⅜ inches

WEIGHT: With 8⅜-inch barrel, 47 oz. — 6½-inch barrel, 44½ oz. — 6-inch barrel, 44 oz. — 5-inch barrel, 42½ oz. — 3½-inch barrel, 41 oz.

SIGHTS: Choice of any standard target sights

STOCKS: Checkered Circassian walnut with S & W Monograms — choice of square or Magna type

FINISH: S & W Blue or Nickel

FRAME: ".357" Magnum*, with finely checkered top strap matching barrel rib. Front and rear straps, S & W grooving

CYLINDER: Heat-treated chrome-nickel steel. Recessed head space and patented burnished chamber walls

HAMMER: Full surface of thumb piece checkered to prevent slipping in rapid fire. Concentric relief cuts on sides. Hammer fall weighed and timed for uniform ignition and least disturbance of arm

TRIGGER: S & W grooving. Glass-hard point engaging hammer notch

TRIGGER PULL: Single action, 3 to 4 lbs. Double action, 10 lbs.

AMMUNITION
S & W ".357" Magnum*
.38 S & W Special High-Speed
.38 S & W Special
.38 S & W Special Super Police
.38 S & W Special Mid-Range
.38 Colt Special

$60.00
Including Federal Excise Tax

ENTIRE S & W PRODUCTION NOW DEVOTED TO VICTORY

.38 SPECIAL CALIBER

MILITARY AND POLICE SQUARE BUTT

AMERICA'S LARGEST SELLING QUALITY REVOLVER

$33.00

Over 1,250,000 Made to Date . . . the Smith & Wesson Military and Police Revolver has stood as the criterion of quality in service arms for over a quarter of a century. Its extreme accuracy and rugged dependability have made it the choice of top-ranking police departments everywhere.

Made throughout from drop forgings, with chrome-nickel steel, heat-treated cylinder, ground and polished lock-work parts, hammer and trigger case-hardened to give glass-hard wearing surfaces. It has a fine full grip, beautifully tapered barrel and is finished in heavy nickel or Smith & Wesson's famous high-polished deep blue.

The perfect gun for municipal police and sheriffs. Incorporates all the famous features of design that make Smith & Wesson revolvers the world's most reliable sidearms.

SPECIFICATIONS

CALIBER: .38 S & W Special

NUMBER OF SHOTS: 6

BARREL: 2, 4, 5, or 6 inches

LENGTH: With 6-inch barrel, 11⅜ inches

WEIGHT: With 6-inch barrel, 31 ounces

SIGHTS: Fixed, 1/10-inch service type front; square notch rear

STOCKS: Checkered Circassian walnut with S & W Monograms. Choice of square or Magna type

FINISH: S & W Blue or Nickel

AMMUNITION
.38 S & W Special
.38 S & W Special Super Police
.38 S & W Special Mid-Range
.38 Colt Special
.38 Short Colt
.38 Long Colt

HIGH STANDARD AUTOMATIC PISTOLS

SPECIAL FEATURES OF MODELS A, D & E

New Long Handle

We have felt that the shooter wants more room for the grip on an automatic, and have developed a longer grip that provides more room for the hand. The grips are of walnut, nicely shaped, and finely checked.

NEW AUTOMATIC SLIDE LOCK A Double Feature

We have provided an automatic lock to lock the action open when the last cartridge has been fired from the magazine. This also operates as a lock on the action when the magazine is empty, and holds the slide open when the pistol is used at the target as a single shot.

HAMMERLESS

MODEL D .22 L.R.

Barrel 4½" or 6¾"

With extra heavy Barrel and adjustable Rear Sight

Price $35.35

Thumb Rest Grips, Extra $3.05

HAMMER

MODEL H-D .22 L.R.

Barrel 4½" or 6¾"

With extra heavy Barrel and adjustable Rear Sight

Price $35.35

Thumb Rest Grips, Extra $3.05

MODELS D AND H-D

The target shooters have long wanted a heavier barrel on a pistol and in designing our new long handle we had particularly in view the fact that we would need additional weight in the handle to balance the additional weight of the barrel. We therefore have gone to the extra expense of getting out new forging dies so that the metal in the handle would come all the way to the bottom.

The result was most gratifying and we have plenty of weight in the handle to balance the heavier barrel. The Model "D" has a barrel of medium weight, an adjustable rear sight, automatic slide lock, and trigger pull that undoubtedly will satisfy the most exacting requirements. Regular model has straight grip but can be fitted with thumb rest for the target shooter on special order and at an extra cost.

SPECIFICATIONS

Barrel—Heavy barrel weighing 4 ounces more than on the model A.

Sights—Patridge front with wide blade and special adjustable rear sight.

Safety—Positive.

Grips—Walnut, finely checkered.

Finish—Blued.

Takedown—Slide removed without the use of any tools for inspection and cleaning of barrel from the breech end. No loose parts, pins or screws to fall out.

Weight of Pistol—40 oz. **Extra Magazine, $1.50.**

MODELS E AND H-E

With the same qualifications as to smoothness of operation and trigger pull as the Model "D" but with an extra heavy barrel, this Model "E" is built to meet the demand from that class of shooters who want all the weight possible in a pistol. Here again the long metal handle, extending all of the way to the bottom of the grip provides the necessary weight for a perfect balance. The Model "E" as well as the Model "D" is highly recommended by experts and its users number some of the best nationally known shooters. Regularly furnished with thumb rest grip that is said to be one of the best ever designed for average shooters.

SPECIFICATIONS

Barrel—Extra heavy, barrel, slide and frame giving a straight line effect along the entire top of the pistol.

Sights—Patridge front with wide blade and special adjustable rear sight.

Safety—Positive.

Grips—Full walnut grips with thumb rest, finely checkered.

Finish—Blued.

Takedown—The same as model A or D.

Weight of Pistol—42 oz. **Extra Magazine, $1.50.**

HAMMERLESS

MODEL E .22 L.R.

Barrel 4½" or 6¾"

with extra heavy Barrel and Target Grips with Thumb Rest

Price $40.40

HAMMER

MODEL H-E .22 L.R.

Barrel 4½" or 6¾"

with extra heavy Barrel and Target Grips with Thumb Rest

Price $40.40

WINCHESTER MODEL 52
TRADE MARK

COMES IN THESE STYLES

Standard Weight Target Rifle—Bolt Action Box Magazine with Winchester Speed Lock

28 inch standard weight round barrel, tapered, of Winchester Proof-Steel. Telescope sight bases spaced 7.2" center to center. These barrels have a ramp (lug) front sight base forged on the barrel.

Pistol grip target stock of walnut with a chromium plated, satin finish metal forearm adjustment base and a composition hand support, located on the underside of the front portion of the forearm.

This stock is used with standard height sight combinations. Standard dimensions are:

Length of pull, 13¼; Drop of stock from center of bore, (at comb) .63", (at heel) .98"; Drop of stocks from line of sights with sights set for 25 yards, (at comb) 1⁹⁄₁₆, (at heel) 2"; Down pitch, 3". Convenient triple locking safety. Weight, approximately 10 pounds.

PRICES
(Please Order By Symbol Number)
FLAT TOP RECEIVER

Symbol	Front Sight	Rear Sight	Receiver Sight	Price
*G5217R	None	None	None	$56.95
G5207R	Winchester 93-B	Win. 82A	None	64.00
G5237R	Lyman 17-A	Win. 82A	None	66.95
G5269R	Lyman 17-AG	None	Vaver WS2 Lt. Ext. Marble Goss MG52	80.35
G5279R	Lyman 17-A	None	Ext. Low Base	76.30

*Front sight cut in barrel filled with blank piece.

ROUND TOP RECEIVER

Symbol	Front Sight	Rear Sight	Receiver Sight	Price
†G5210R	Lyman 17-A	None	Lyman 57-F	68.30
G5209R	Winchester 93-B	None	Lyman 48-F	72.75
G5239R	Lyman 17-A	None	Lyman 48-F	75.65
G5289R	Lyman 17-A	None	Lyman 52-F Ext.	77.70

†Will be furnished if order does not specify sight combination desired.

Heavy Weight Target Rifle—Bolt Action Box Magazine with Winchester Speed Lock

BARREL—28 inch heavy weight, round, tapered of Winchester Proof Steel. New type barrel band. Telescope sight bases spaced 7.2" center to center. STOCK—Marksman stock of selected walnut with full pistol grip, full fluted comb and wide beavertail fore-end. Chromium plated, satin finish metal forearm adjustment base and a composition hand support, located on the under side of the front portion of the forearm.

STOCK DIMENSIONS

Length of Pull .... 13¼"   Drop at Heel .... 1⅞"
Drop at Comb .... 1⁹⁄₁₆"   Pitch .... 3"

Drop of stock from center of bore .50" at comb and .83" at heel. Steel butt plate checked. WEIGHT—About 12 lbs. Other details same as described for Standard Weight Barrel model.

PRICES
(Please Order By Symbol Number)
28" RD. HEAVY WEIGHT BARREL
Flat Top Receiver — Marksman No. 1 Stock (High Comb) High Sights

Symbol	Front Sight	Rear Sight	Receiver Sight	Price
G5245R	None	None	None	66.00

No receiver sight cut in stock. Receiver drilled and tapped on left side, holes filled with plug screws. Front sight cut filled with blank piece. Win. 82A Rear Sight Seat Cut (Dovetail) on Receiver, filled with blank piece. Winchester Comb. Telescope Sight Bases attached.

G5264R	Vaver 36 F.S. with 35E Barrel Band	None	Vaver 35 Mielt Ext.	96.90
G5274R	Lyman 77	None	Marble Goss M.G.—52 M.S.—Ext.	87.45
†G5225R	Lyman 77	None	None	71.40
†G5235R	Redfield 63	None	None	70.75

†Win. 82A Sight Cut on Receiver filled with blank piece.

28" HEAVY WEIGHT BARREL

G5255R	None	None	None	66.00

No receiver sight cut in stock. Receiver drilled and tapped on left side, holes filled with plug screws. Front sight filled with blank piece. Winchester Comb. Telescope Sight Bases attached.

†G5265R	None	None	None	66.00

†No receiver sight cut in stock. No sight cut on barrel or receiver, except disc clearance cut on rear of receiver. Receiver drilled and tapped on left side, holes filled with plug screws. Winchester Comb. Telescope Sight Bases attached.

*G5234R	Lyman 77	None	Lyman 48 F.H.	86.85
G5284R	Lyman 77	None	Lyman 52 F.H. Ext.	88.85
G5294R	Vaver W11AT	None	Vaver R5237—Ext.	94.20

*Will be furnished if order does not specify sight combination desired.

A NEW GUN GIVES NO REGRETS

Thumb-lever safety. Firing pin uncocked, thumb lever forward, safety inactive.

Forearm of Marksman stock, showing new adjustable barrel band (adjustable screw on right side, not shown), and adjustable hand support and sling swivel.

Showing how receiver is stiffened by additional steel at left side of leading well. Does not interfere with convenient hand loading. Cartridge is shown on tray of single-shot adaptor.

Bolt closed, firing pin cocked, safety in rear or safe position, triple locking the action.

IDEAL SHOTSHELL RELOADING TOOLS

The reloading of shotshells is safe, economical, and simple, enabling the reloader to load shells which will give better results than the factory product in his particular gun. The skeet shooter, trap shooter or hunter will find that he can save enough in a short time in reloading his fired cases to pay for a good set of reloading tools besides providing himself with a most fascinating pastime or hobby.

STRAIGHTLINE RE- and DE-CAPPER

Furnished for All Gauges from 10 to .410

Expels plain or battery cup primers but will be furnished for battery cup primers unless otherwise specified. For plain primers, a different Stud "A" and Crosshead "D" is required. It can be adapted to any gauge by purchasing extra Guide Bushings "H."

This tool combines the operations of re- and decapping in a highly satisfactory manner. In priming shotgun cartridges, it is of the utmost importance to seat primers to a uniform depth. The IDEAL Straight Line Re- and De-Capper is the *only* tool that will seat plain primers to an absolutely uniform depth.

Price $3.00

Weight 1¼ lb.

Extra Guide Bushing..........50c.   Extra Crosshead..........50c.

LOADING MACHINE FOR SHOT SHELLS

Made for 10, 12, 16 and 20 Gauges Only

This machine is designed to perform the operations of charging shells with powder, ramming the over-powder and filler wads, and measure the shot charge with only one handling of the shell. It is the only machine that will handle fired cases and measure all kinds of powders in either drams or grains. It can be set to throw charges of many powders by the graduations alone but, in common with all mechanical measures, the setting should be checked with a scale when dense powders are used.

The shot measure is graduated in ounces and is easily and accurately adjustable.

The powder measure can be used for charging rifle and pistol cases as it can be swung to one side and used independently of the charging tube. For this purpose the funnel "R" will be required which can be supplied at small additional cost.

The method of adjusting the measuring slide is the same as for the IDEAL No. 5 Powder Measure except that the slide takes the place of the "D" and "E" slides of the No. 5 Measure.

The arrangement of the charging cavities is such that one is in the charging position when the other is in the discharging position. There is a stop so located that the charging handle can be left in a half-way position with the cavities cut off from the powder and shot reservoirs, eliminating any possibility of irregular charges settling in the cavities from the jarring due to ramming the wads.

The operation of the machine is simple and convenient.

Ideal Loading Machine No. 1 price.............................$17.00
Ideal Loading Machine No. 2.................................. 18.00
Attachments (10-20 ga.) No. 1...............................   3.00
Attachments (10-20 ga.) No. 2...............................   4.00
Rammer Tube 10-20 ga. No. 1.................................   .85
Rammer Guide Bushing 10-20 ga. No. 1........................   .75

IDEAL Pocket and Shot Measure $.50
IDEAL Pocket Closer $1.00

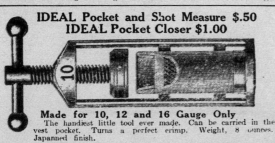

Made for 10, 12 and 16 Gauge Only

The handiest little tool ever made. Can be carried in the vest pocket. Turns a perfect crimp. Weight, 8 ounces. Japanned finish.

IDEAL SHELL TRIMMER

PRICE $2.75

No outfit for reloading paper shot shells is complete without this implement. With it the soft and frayed ends of shells that have been fired a number of times, may be ironed at the mouth or cut off to any length. These implements will be made for 10, 12, 16, 20, 24 and 28 gauge only. They will cut shells any length from 3½ to 2 inches. They are light and strong, made of malleable iron. The finish is japan, with nickel trimmings. The cutter is of the best quality of tool steel, hardened properly, tempered and ground. Will last a lifetime. The plug G and the Shell Holder D may be purchased for different gauges so that one Shell Trimmer may be used for all or any of the gauges listed. Weight about 1½ lb.

Extra shell Holder.............50c.   Extra Plug.............50c.

STRAIGHTLINE HAND LOADER

Those who do not load in sufficient quantities to warrant the purchase of a complete loading machine, will find this implement all that they desire. The illustration shows it is a handy portable hand loader that may be used by being fastened to a bench or not, as desired. The "Straightline" Hand Loader will be made for 10, 12, 16, 20, 28 gauge only. Parts "A" and "B" are different for each gauge; the part "C" is the same for all gauges. Those having an Ideal Loading Machine, desiring a portable hand implement to take with them on a trip, may purchase only the parts "A," "C" and "D" and use the chamber that is with the loading machine, for the part "B" in the "Straightline" Hand Loader is the same as chamber No. 2 in the Loading Machine.

Shipping weight about 1¼ lbs.

10-28 gauge $4.00

IDEAL Pocket Loader $1.50

Weight 6 oz.

Loader for Paper and Brass Shot Shells.
Capper, De-Capper, Rammer and Extractor.

EUREKA SHOTGUN SHELL LOADING SET

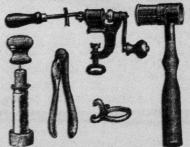

No. 160—Brass and Paper Shell Set in partitioned box—comprising No. 189 Loader, No. 0 Closer, No. 1180B Recapper, No. 20R Powder and Shot Measure and No. X Extractor—10 to 28 gauge.

Price, each........$1.75
410 (12 M-M) and 32 gauge (14 M-M), each.... 2.25
Loading Block No. 75, 10 to 28 gauge, each...... 1.10

SAVAGE MODEL 99 HIGH POWER RIFLES

This is the famous repeating rifle that first introduced the hammerless, solid breech design and rotary type magazine. Its popularity in every hunting field is tremendous—for it embodies all the technical superiority and mechanical perfection of tested Savage methods.

An extra margin of safety is built into the Model 99 mechanism. The breech bolt has an unusually large locking area, wedging solidly against the receiver. The cycle of operation is quick and positive—permitting easy firing from the shoulder. All Savage Model 99 rifles are made with barrels of "Hi-Pressure" steel, especially adapted to modern smokeless powder high power cartridges. Sportsmen around the world know the Savage reputation for barrel accuracy.

GENERAL SPECIFICATIONS

Hammerless, solid breech, lever action. Hi-Pressure steel barrel, polished breech bolt, case hardened lever, blued receiver. Varnished American Walnut stock and forearm. Steel butt plate. White metal bead front sight on raised ramp base and adjustable semi-buckhorn sporting rear sight. Six shots, magazine capacity five cartridges. Magazine rotary box type with numerical indicator. Hammer indicator showing automatically cocked or fired position of hammer. Made in 8 styles and 5 calibers.

CALIBERS OF THE 99 MODELS

.250-3000 Savage Hi-Power—Noted for its high speed and accuracy, this cartridge is powerful enough for any animal in North America. Excellent for mountain sheep, goats, deer, etc. For use in Savage Rifles: Models 99-EG and 99-G.

.300 Savage Hi-Power—For biggest American game, this is a super-modern cartridge, similar in ballistics to the .30 Springfield-Government Cartridge. Ideal for Alaskan bear, moose, and elk. For use in Savage Rifles: Models 99-EG, 99-G, 99-R and 99-RS.

MODELS 99-G & EG
24" BBL.

FOR BIG GAME

CALIBERS
.250-3000 SAVAGE
.300 SAVAGE

Model 99-G. Takedown. Tapered round barrel. Raised ramp front sight base. Shotgun butt, full pistol grip, checkered stock and forearm, checkered trigger and corrugated steel butt plate. Matted trigger. Weight about 7¾ pounds.

The Savage Model 99, Style G is our most popular rifle and is selected by sportsmen who desire a rifle of moderate weight, fine finish and extreme efficiency. Especially adapted to high concentration cartridges because of the exceptional strength and safety of the action. Ideal for all American game.

Model 99-EG is same as the Model 99-G, but solid frame and without checkering.

Model 99-G, Takedown $71.90
Model 99-EG, Solid Frame—No Checkering 61.75

MODEL 99-R
24" BBL.

CALIBER
.300 SAVAGE ONLY

THE IDEAL DEER RIFLE

Model 99-R—Solid Frame. Tapered medium weight round barrel. Raised ramp front sight base. Special large stock and forearm of selected walnut, oil finish, corrugated steel butt plate of shotgun design. Full pistol grip stock. Fine checkering on grip and forearm. Adjustable Semi-Buckhorn rear sight and gold bead front sight. Matted trigger. Weight about 7¼ pounds.

The Model 99-R has been designed to meet the demands of expert riflemen requiring a solid frame rifle of extreme accuracy. An ideal deer rifle.

Model 99-R, solid frame $70.00

MODEL 99-RS
24" BBL.

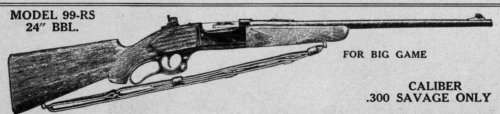

FOR BIG GAME

CALIBER
.300 SAVAGE ONLY

Model 99-RS. Solid Frame. Same specifications as Model 99-R with following refinements: Redfield windgauge and elevation adjustment rear peep sight and gold bead front sight. Also equipped with ⅞ inch combined adjustable leather sling and carrying strap with quick release swivels and screw studs. Weight about 7½ pounds.

The Model 99-RS is the same rifle as the Model 99-R, with additional equipment consisting of special sights, with accurate windage and elevation adjustments and a sling strap, which is provided for ease in carrying and as an aid to steady holding.

Model 99-RS, solid frame $83.00

.410 BORE SHOTGUN BARREL FOR MODEL 99 TAKEDOWN RIFLE

.410 Bore Auxiliary Shotgun Barrel—Interchangeable with all caliber rifle barrels on Savage Model 99 Takedown Rifles.

Weight about 2 pounds. Length 22 or 24 inches.
Price $10.20

SAVAGE OVER AND UNDER SHOTGUNS

MODEL 420
MODEL 430

The Savage Over-and-Under Double has filled the long felt demand for such a gun. It is beautifully designed, of safe construction and has fine balance, especially recommended for Field and Skeet shooting. Once you use one of these new Over-and-Under guns you will find a different reaction of the recoil; no side whip, therefore much faster to fire your second shot. For the hunter used to shooting a rifle it will appeal instantly, doing away with the side by side vision always found to interfere with the sighting of a double barrel shotgun.

Model 420—Hammerless, Takedown made in 12, 16 and 20 Gauge. Stock of selected oil finished walnut with full pistol grip. (No checkering.)

Barrels to be had 12 and 16 Gauge in 26 inch, 28 inch and 30 inch length and in 20 Gauge, 26 inch and 28 inch.

Chokes: Modified and Full or Open cylinder and Improved cylinder for skeet shooting.

Action with automatic top tang safety, hammerless with unbreakable coil springs, all working parts are made to give long wearing service. The front trigger fires the lower barrel and the rear trigger the upper barrel.

Stock dimensions on all guns are 14 inch length, drop at heel 2¾ inch, at comb 1⅝ inch.

Weight—12 Ga./28 inch about 7 lbs. 12 oz.
Weight—16 Ga./28 inch about 7 lbs. 6 oz.
Weight—20 Ga./28 inch about 6 lbs. 13 oz.

Price **$46.95**

Model 430—Hammerless, Takedown made in 12 16 and 20 Gauge. Same specifications as Model 420 with following extras:

Barrel with matted side line on top barrel.

Stock of selected Fancy Crotch Walnut with full pistol grip beautifully checkered and fitted with Jostam Anti-Flinch Recoil Pad.

Price **$52.50**

Extras for Models 420 and 430:
Non-selective Single Trigger . . . . Price **$12.65**
Extra set of barrels for Model 420 . . . . **23.25**
Extra set of barrels for Model 430 . . . . **26.60**

STEVENS REPEATING SHOTGUNS

MODEL 620

This gun has many features well liked by those who have used it. The take-down is one of the simplest ever constructed and is based on the Browning patents. This gun will stand heavy loads when used for Field shooting or in the Duck blind, and when given proper care it will last a life time. As a Riot gun it is used for guard duty and stands rough handling. In price it is the cheapest, but in quality it counts among the best.

Model 620 Repeating Shotgun to be had in 12 Ga. 28, 30 and 32 inch full choked, 28 and 30 inch modified, 26 and 28 inch cylinder bored;

12 Ga. 28 inch full, modified or cylinder bored, 26 inch cylinder bored; 20 Ga. 26 and 28 inch cylinder, modified or full choke.

Action Hammerless, visible locking bolt, safety firing pin, independent safety side ejection, take down and solid breech drop forged.

Stock of American walnut with checkered full pistol grip and checkered slide handle, rubber buttplate. Length 13¾ inches. Drop at heel 2¾ inches.

Weight: 12 Ga., about 7¾ lbs., 16 Ga. 7¼ lbs., 20 Ga. about 6 lbs.

Magazine capacity—Six Shots. A plug is furnished to cut down magazine capacity to 3 shots to conform with Government regulations on migratory birds.

Model 620 . . . . **$47.75**
Model 620P—Same as above but equipped with Poly-Choke. Barrel 12 Gauge, 28" or 30"; 16 or 20 Gauge, 28" only **53.95**
Model 621 the same as Model 620 with raised matted solid rib **51.95**

STEVENS DOUBLE BARREL HAMMERLESS SHOTGUNS

MODEL 530

The Stevens factory has been making shotguns for a good many years and knows how to make them to stand up under any and all conditions. Here is a model designed according to the most modern ideas, nothing forgotten to make these guns as wanted by the shooter for field and skeet.

Model 530 comes with blued compressed forged steel barrels tested with Nitro Powder. Length: 12 Ga. 26, 28, 30 and 32 inches; 16 Ga. 26, 28 and 30 inches; 20 Ga. 26 and 28 inches; 410 Ga. 26 inches with matted rib and 2 Lyman ivory bead sights. All 12 Ga. 32 inch and 410 Ga.

Model 530M with Tenite Stock **$29.25**
Model 530 MST with Tenite Stock **33.00**
Double Guns are furnished with full choke in both barrels, all others have right barrel modified and left barrel full choke.

Stock selected American walnut with full pistol grip checkered and fitted with Jostam Anti-flinch recoil pad. Length 14 inches, drop about 2¾ inches. Frame is polished and case hardened. Action is hammerless with coil springs of new design.

Weight: 12 Ga. 7½ to 8 lbs., 16 Ga. 7 to 7½ lbs., 20 Ga. 6½ to 6¾ lbs., 410 Ga. 5¾ to 6 lbs.

Model 530 . . . . **$30.75**
Model 530ST Same specifications as Model 530 except fitted with non-selective single trigger.
Price **$34.55**

STOEGER

OLD CONNECTICUT GUN BLUER

AMERICA'S MOST POPULAR BLUER

Old Connecticut Bluer is a real boon to the average gunsmith or private party who has occasion to undertake reblueing. It is particularly valuable for the gunsmith who is desirous of giving a first-class factory-like finish, but who for reasons of time or economy cannot afford to take the time that our regular Gunsmith's Bluer requires, Old Connecticut Bluer has proven itself over many years to be the most practical rapid bluer on the market and the process which in brief consists of cleaning, applying solution, rusting and brushing, is almost identical to that of our Gunsmith's Bluer except that the rust occurs in a few minutes instead of many hours and permits a high class blueing job in little more than an hour. Old Connecticut is unique amongst rapid bluers because of its great permanency and richness of color and has the advantage that this solution will not easily burn the hands and is therefore very easy to work with. Complete instructions included with each bottle.

Price, per 4 oz. bottle $1.00

Utility pint size bottle 3.00

DAMASCUS BROWNER

THE ONLY COMMERCIAL BROWNER FOR DAMASCUS, TWIST, OR LAMINATED BARRELS

Up to the general introduction of smokeless powder about the time of the Spanish-American War, Damascus or "Twist" barrels represented the best.

Because of the method of manufacture of Damascus which is made up by twisting from one to three bars or rods of iron together and hand welding, the grain of the metal is so arranged that it appears on the outside of the finished barrel in the form of irregular links or spirals. These variations in the steel account for the beautiful design which many Damascus barrels show and which pattern is brought forth in its full beauty by browning, NOT blueing. Stoeger Damascus Browner is especially prepared according to a very old London formula.

Each bottle is accompanied with detailed instructions for the successful use of the Browner and if carefully followed a beautiful effect can be achieved. With a little experience the tone or shade may be varied from brown-black to copper-red.

Price per 4 oz. bottle $2.50

Shop size, one pint 7.50

WHAT IT TAKES TO HUNT ELK SUCCESSFULLY

by Wayne van Zwoll

Elk rifles are like breakfast cereals and pickup trucks: you can buy one and forget about the rest. The only difference is that most of us can eat and drive without taking extra time to practice.

Gun magazines and catalogs are full of advice for elk hunters. In fact, they cover just about everything anyone needs to know on the subject. Several decades ago, though, Elmer Keith and Jack O'Connor, legendary writers and hunters of the past, fueled a debate about elk rifles that still rages. Hunters who had never even seen an elk staked out a position. Others who had killed a bull with one shot to the neck claimed broad experience, while magazine articles by Keith and O'Connor fanned the flames of controversy for fun and profits.

O'Connor, who had shot several bulls across open meadows, wrote that cartridges like the .270 and .30-06 worked just fine. Keith, who liked to hunt in Idaho's 'pole thickets, argued in favor of heavier, slower bullets. Rejecting foot-pounds as a measure of killing power, he advocated pounds-feet instead. Essentially, both methods produce enough kinetic energy to do the job. But using the foot-pounds formula—$E=V^2(W)/450,240$—squaring the velocity gives fast bullets an edge over slow ones. According to hunters who favor fat, heavy bullets, that edge doesn't always translate effectively from paper to elk.

Actually, there is logic to be found in both arguments. A fast, light bullet has a flat trajectory; hence, it is easier to shoot accurately at long range. It generates less recoil than a beefier bullet from a case of the same capacity, so there is less danger of flinching. Given proper construction, a small bullet will expand to at least twice its diameter, yet hold together sufficiently to drive deep into the vitals from the side.

Large-caliber bullets cannot be driven as fast or as flat, but their extra weight helps them penetrate and open wider wound channels. They can also lose big pieces to fragmentation without losing their ability to plow a lethal wound. Moreover, they are just as accurate as smaller, faster bullets at the ranges most elk are shot; and given identical shape, they are slightly less vulnerable to deflection by twigs.

For many years, most fat bullets—those of more than 30 caliber—had blunt noses. Because they lost speed and energy in flight, they were deemed inappropriate for shots beyond 200 yards. But today, pointed (spitzer) bullets in 8mm, .338, .358. and .375 have stretched the range of big-bore cartridges. Nosler's 250-grain .338 Partition bullet, for example, has a ballistic coefficient of .473, the same as a 180-grain 30-caliber or 160-grain 7mm Spitzer. In terms of sectional density (essentially, this is the ratio of length to caliber, or the ballistic

These superb deer cartridges suffice for elk most of the time, but some hunters prefer more punch in an all-around elk cartridge.

coefficient minus form factor), the .338 edges Nosler's 200-grain .308 spitzer and its 175-grain 7mm. When it comes to long shooting, the big-bores are certainly in the race.

FIVE CARTRIDGES FAVORED BY ELK HUNTERS

Which cartridge you select depends largely on what kind of shooting you expect to do. For all-around elk hunting, the middle ground in bore diameter ranges from 7mm (.284) to .338. Of the five cartridges most favored by elk hunters (according to four annual surveys taken among members of the Rocky Mountain Elk Foundation) only one—the .270 Winchester—came from outside that bracket. Conceived in 1925, the .270 became a hit almost immediately and is now widely used for big game, even if it is not the best elk cartridge. It remains popular partly because it is loaded to reasonably high pressures, doesn't kick hard, and generally turns in fine accuracy with factory-loaded bullets of 130, 140 and 150 grains.

In three of the surveys, the .30-06 topped the list of elk cartridges; and it barely lost to the perennial runner-up, Remington's 7mm Magnum, in the fourth. The other two contenders—Winchester's .300 and .338 Magnums—shifted places from year to year with the .270. No other cartridge came close to these five in popularity.

The three belted magnums all appeared as recently as the 1960s, but the .30-06 dates back to 1906, when it replaced the .30-03 (with its slightly longer case) as the U.S. infantry round. Its longevity gave it an edge in the surveys. The availability of surplus rifles, a wide selection of bullets, and well-distributed factory ammunition helped the '06 from the start. It has survived, however, mainly because of its versatility. Factories now load it with hunting-style bullets in weights from 150 to 220 grains.

In 1958, Winchester's .338 Magnum became the first in a series of short bottle-necked magnums fashioned from the .458 case. Winchester put a red recoil pad and 25-inch barrel on its first Model .338 and called this version the "Alaskan." The round is indeed powerful enough for big bears, but current interest arises mostly from the ranks of elk hunters, who have boosted sales of .338 rifles considerably. Factory loads, with bullets of 200 to 250 grains, generate nearly two tons of muzzle energy.

In 1962, the same year Remington introduced its new Model 700 rifle, the company brought out its 7mm Magnum. Combining the long reach of a .30 magnum with the manageable recoil of a .30-06, the belted 7mm caught on quickly. It was especially popular in the West, thanks largely to Wyoming outfitter Les Bowman, who helped de-

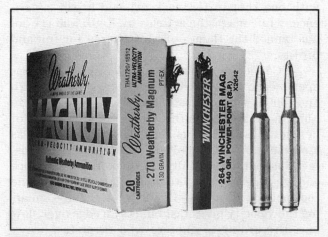

These magnums shoot flat and generate plenty of energy for elk. But bigger bores mean heavier bullets, which prove useful on raking shots.

sign and promote the cartridge. Factory loads now feature big-game bullets in weights of 140 to 175 grains. Nearly every domestic rifle built for a magnum cartridge has been chambered for this one—including Browning's BLR and BAR lever-action and autoloading rifles.

Following right behind the 7mm Remington Magnum came the .300 Winchester Magnum in 1963. Designed to work in standard-length actions, this .300 measures 2.62 inches, rim to case mouth—.12 inch longer than the .458, .338 and 7mm magnums, or the .30-338 wildcat many shooters thought Winchester would copy. The short neck of Winchester's .300 doesn't appeal to handloaders. American ammunition firms load this round with bullets weighing 150 to 220 grains. It will launch 180-grain spitzers faster than a .30-06 drives 150s.

These five rounds share the following attributes found useful in an elk cartridge:

1. They all work through standard-length bolt actions.

2. Rifles and ammunition (or handloading components, including bullets suitable for elk) are readily available.

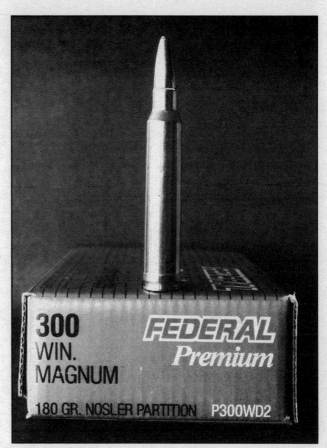

It is hard to imagine better cartridges for elk than those using Nosler Partition bullets, which are now available in factory loads.

Of these potent .30 magnums (from left to right)—.30-06, .308 Norma, .300 Winchester, .300 Weatherby—the .30-06 has killed more elk than any other.

3. Each delivers at least 1,800 foot-pounds of energy at 200 yards with bullets weighing at least 150 grains.

4. Recoil doesn't exceed 30 foot-pounds in eight-pound rifles.

By knocking out the .270, requisite bullet energy can be boosted to 2,000 foot-pounds at 200 yards; although this may not provide an advantage at that range, it could help considerably farther out. On the back end of a rifle, shooters may have trouble with the .338. A potent round, it is effective only if the recoil does not cause the shooter to flinch.

Short .30 magnums—the Winchester, certainly, but also the .308 Norma and wildcats like the .300 Mashburn—offer an ideal compromise for elk. With sectional densities of .270 to .300 and ballistic coefficients of .470 to .550, 180- and 200-grain bullets for the belted .30s have lots of push for close-up penetration; they also have the right

Of the five most popular elk rounds, the .338 Winchester Magnum (right) is the most powerful. Remington's Safari Grade ammunition offers the Swift A-frame bullet in .338 and .375. (and .416, not shown).

shape to retain energy well downrange. The .300 Winchester heaves a 180-grain bullet as fast as Remington's 7mm Magnum kicks out a 160, And it delivers 530 foot-pounds more energy than the .30-06 at 300 yards, plus its 180-grain bullet can scribe a trajectory as flat as the .270s 130-grain.

The .300 Holland & Holland almost matches the Winchester ballistically but requires a magnum action. Weatherby's brawny .300 offers considerably more speed and energy, but again a long action is needed. Factory loads for these leggy .30s are limited; until recently, Weatherby's was pro-

prietary. Now Remington loads Weatherby ammunition, but at different listed velocities, presumably because Remington rifles chambered for this .300 have shorter throats than Weatherby rifles. Remington also uses 24-inch test barrels, whereas Weatherby employs 26-inch barrels.

Small-bore magnums—the .264 Winchester and the Weatherby .257 and .270—show flat bullet trajectories and plenty of energy for elk, but their lighter bullets make them less effective than belted .30s. The .264 and .270 magnums are almost on a par with the 7mms.

Bigger bullets give the .338 a better reception in the Keith camp, where the 8mm Remington, .340 Weatherby, .358 Norma and .375 H&H Magnums are all preferred. The giant .378 Weatherby necked to .338 has a following among shooters who "set up" on a ridge for cross-canyon shots at elk. But these rounds, besides limiting rifle and bullet choices (and draining ammunition budgets), kick hard. They make sense only in heavy, long-barreled guns. If the shooter flinches because of recoil, or he can't get into action quickly because his gun comes up like an irrigation pipe, he might miss a

together during upset in heavy muscle and bone and track straight to the vitals.

For those who prefer standard rimless cases, a .35 Whelen is a better choice. Though its bullets sag a handbreadth more than their 25-caliber counterparts at 300 yards, they reach that mark with 200 foot-pounds more energy and twice the bullet weight. The .35 Whelen Improved is even better; wildcatters like the .35 Brown-Whelen, the .338-06 and .338-06 Improved. The .284 Winchester and .280 Remington match .270 performance. Short-action rounds like the .308 Winchester, 7mm-

The recovered bullet jacket at right lost its core in an elk, compromising penetration. Though the Nosler Partition at left got mutilated up front, the protected rear portion drove deep.

chance at a bull that could have been killed with a .30-06.

Recently, a hunter described his favorite elk rifle as a .25-06 that he handloads with 117-grain Hornady Spire Points. He claims deep penetration and has made several one-shot kills without losing an animal. A good and deliberate marksman who has taken a lot of elk, he does not mind passing up a shot. His rifle will kill elk as far away as he can shoot accurately—which is as far as any belted magnum will kill them. Its weakness is on raking shots that test the bullet's ability to hold

08 Remington and 7×57 Mauser can stretch to that level. The .358 and .348 Winchester kill well up close.

One thing that's seldom mentioned in discussing elk cartridges is the size of the animal. The ones hunters dream about are big-boned, solid, tenacious fellows, but most elk shot today are young. There is as much difference in weight between full-grown elk and yearling bulls as there exists between the mature buck mule deer and yearlings. Muley rounds that work on elk work better on some than on others.

Among the preferred elk rifles are Remington's Model 700 (top, this one is the Safari Classic), Winchester's Model 70 (middle, the Sporter Wintuff), and Ruger's Model 77RS (bottom).

Nosler Partition bullets have become standard for handloaders who build elk cartridges. But Nosler is getting fresh competition from small firms, including Jensen, Blue Mountain, Hawk, Armfield and Northern Precision. All offer elk bullets in weights and styles not available from big bullet companies. Although Hornady, Sierra and Speer share with Nosler the bulk of the market, offering proven bullets at modest cost, many hunters like to load something special—a Barnes or Bitterroot early on, now a Trophy-Bonded or Swift. The demand for premium-quality bullets has prompted Federal to list factory-loaded Partitions and Remington to offer Swifts in some big-game ammunition. A-Square, which made its mark with guns and bullets for heavy African game, now sells .338 soft-nose ammo to elk hunters.

A LOOK AT ELK RIFLES

In our survey, Remington's Model 700 and Winchester's 70 earned equal billing as top choices among elk hunters, with the Ruger 77 clinching third place. The remaining hunters used other bolt guns: the Weatherby Mark V, Savage 110, Browning A-Bolt, various Mausers and 1903 Springfields. The lever-action Savage 99 and Winchester 88, the autoloading Browning BAR and Remington 740-series rifles, all showed about the same modest support as Ruger's Number One single-shot and Remington's 760 pump.

Generally, bolt rifles can be made to shoot tighter groups than the others; and with single-shots, they have proven most trouble-free. They handle hot handloads and out-sized cases best and offer great primary extracting leverage. They have

No matter how sophisticated your ammunition, it won't work if it does not hit. Here the author demonstrates the proper use of a sling in the erect kneeling posture. It is important to practice shooting from each hunting position.

the best triggers, come in the broadest assortment of chamberings and are easiest to re-stock.

Although most bolt guns are ready to shoot from the box, their performance is improved simply by adjusting the trigger. The threat of lawsuits has moved manufacturers to supply triggers that would test a team of Clydesdales. If you or your gunsmith can not make your trigger break cleanly and consistently at 3 pounds, then buy one from Timney or Canjar.

Unlike triggers, factory-engineered rifle stocks are better than they used to be. They are straighter, putting the eye squarely in line with the scope; they are shaped to fit the hands better; and, for the most part, they are tastefully checkered. Some come glass-bedded in the recoil-lug mortise; if yours is not, the job can be handled easily with Brownell's Acraglas. As Acraglas sets, the barrel can be floated by leaving a thin brass shim under the forend tip. Should your groups tighten with increased forend pressure, the shim can always be replaced.

Synthetic stocks make sense on elk rifles. Unlike wood stocks, they do not "walk" when wet, ruining accuracy. They are rugged, too, and most are lightweight. Brown, Clifton, McMillan, H-S

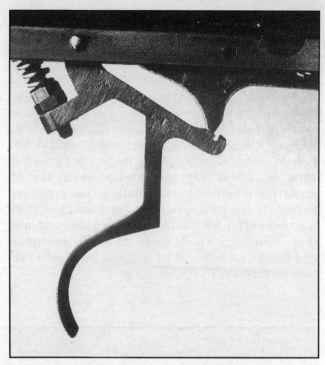

A properly adjusted trigger can improve anyone's performance. This Model 70 trigger is harder to tune than most others, but once it has been set properly you can forget about it.

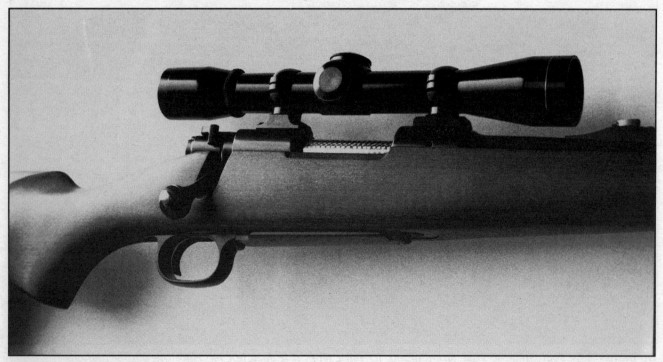

This Winchester Model 70 Ranger is a great bargain for elk hunters. Although the compact scope shown here is a 6X, a 4X would be better.

The author zeroes a modified Springfield in .30-06 Improved—a first-class elk rifle—at 200 yards. The scope is a 3X Leupold in Conetrol mounts.

Precision and Intermountain Arms offer excellent synthetic stocks. Bell & Carlson's are great bargains, among others. "Drop-In" stocks fit best when glass-bedded like semi-inletted stocks.

SCOPES AND BINOCULARS; MUST-HAVES FOR SERIOUS ELK HUNTERS

More than 40 percent of the elk hunters surveyed by the author use 3-9X or 3.5-10X variable scopes. Leupolds account for nearly half of all scopes specified, a testament to its products and marketing program. Redfield, Burris, Nikon and Bausch & Lomb scopes also offer good service, while the optics and adjustments on a 4X Zeiss are without peer, although its high price may deter some buyers.

A bright, dependable scope is a smart investment for any serious hunter. For elk hunters, the relative simplicity, compactness, light weight and low price of a fixed-power scope are definite assets. There is rarely a need for more than 4X magnification on any big game—2.5 or 3X suffices most of the time. Through a 4X glass, most hunters can distinguish ¼-inch grid patterns at 100 yards.

If your target is a bull elk measuring three feet through from back to brisket, and you are having a problem quartering its chest with a 4X scope, then the target is simply too far for a clean shot.

Other advantages of low-power scopes include a wide field of view, generous eye relief, and a big exit pupil. The last-named determines how much light reaches the eye. In bright daylight, when the pupils in the eye shrink, there is a need for a big exit pupil. But at dawn and dusk, when the pupils dilate to let in more light, high-scope magnification reduces light transmission. In dim shooting light, the eye normally dilates to about 6mm. Because a 4X scope with a 40mm objective lens has an exit pupil (objective lens diameter/magnification) of 10, it should provide more than enough light. But a 3-9X variable with the same objective size cuts available light at magnifications above 6.5. Even at noon on a sunny day, a big exit pupil makes head placement less critical, enabling the shooter to find—and keep—the sight picture quicker and easier.

The most popular scope reticle by far is the "plex" crosswire. Its thick outer bars allow fast aim in dim light, while the fine sections at the center permit precise aim at small targets. By measuring the bottom thin section of vertical wire where it subtends, this reticle becomes a rangefinder. For example, if you know it covers 8 inches at 100 yards, then an elk appearing that deep must be roughly 400 yards away. With most elk cartridges, where the range is unknown, the tip of the bottom bar can also be used as an aiming point—assuming the thin wire subtends 8 inches—by keeping it at belly line. The intersection of the crosswire will automatically rise in relation to the elk as range and bullet drop increase.

It is wise to mount all scopes as low as possible. That way, the gun's balance won't be unduly affected; moreover, the chin can then be drawn firmly into the stock. Conetrol, Redfield JR, and Leupold's Dual Dovetail are excellent choices for mounts. An ancient but still useful mount is Weaver's Tip-Off, improved now with better-shaped clamp screws. These mounts are about the lightest and least expensive available, and they hold scopes securely.

Scope covers are a good idea, whether or not you hunt in the rain. Dust can cloud the lenses, causing damage when they are wiped off. Rifles slung vertically in saddle scabbards can pick up all manner of debris in exposed lenses. Butler Creek offers caps that pop open with a thumb button; it also carries "bikini" scope covers that look better than a strip of inner tube but are essentially the same. In any event, good lenses cost a lot and are worth protecting.

Just as important as a rifle and ammunition are to experienced elk hunters, so are a good sling and binoculars. The right kind of sling can help you shoot and carry a rifle. Brownell's "Latigo" mode, a one-inch leather strap with a single brass ring and one brass button, is an excellent choice. Both ring and button are shielded from the rifle

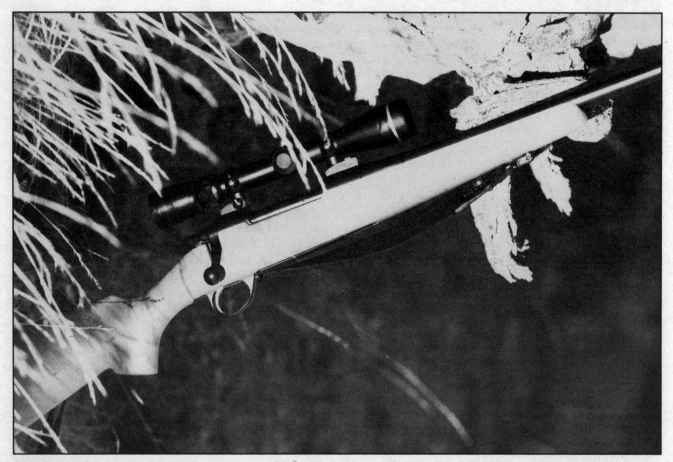

This Sako rifle wears a synthetic stock, a useful addition to any elk rifle. The 3.5-10X Leupold scope it carries has a great following among hunters.

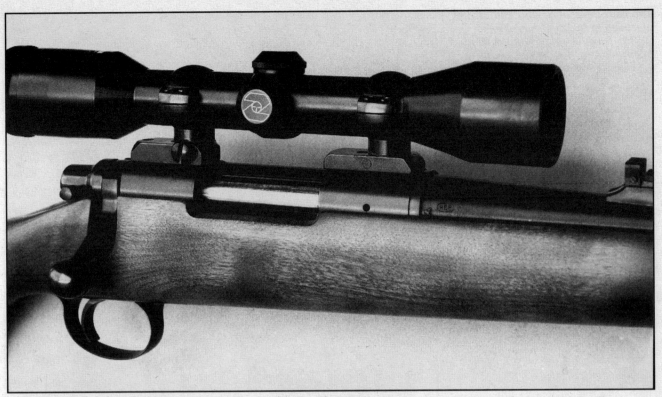

Another excellent elk rifle is this discontinued Model 78, a plain-Jane Remington Model 700 that features a 4X Zeiss scope.

stock by the sling's clever design. A quick tug adjusts sling length and loop to any shooting position.

Like a scope, binoculars can be expensive when one insists on top-grade glass. But you will spend a lot more time looking for elk through your binoculars than looking at them through a scope. Buy the best you can afford—roof-prism or porroprism—and stick with full-size glasses that provide a 5mm exit pupil (such as 7X35s or 8X40s). If you are hunting primarily in open country, where magnification is more important than light transmission, try 9X35s or 10X40s. The best woods glass may be a 7X42. Objective lenses bigger than 42mm make binoculars too unwieldy. Center-focus adjustments are preferable to individual-focus because they are quicker to use. On the other hand, individual adjustments are probably more foolproof.

Most elk hunters observed by the author have been as well equipped to kill elk as the elk have been to escape them. The trouble is, few hunters have practiced with their rifles or conditioned their legs and lungs sufficiently, thus, the advantage lay with the elk. While there is still time, it is important to refine your rifle's zero, so every

shot from a clean, cold barrel strikes point of aim at 200 yards. Leave enough time as well for practice shooting—from the sitting, kneeling and offhand postions—and also to hike or jog yourself into proper shape. When the chance finally comes to stalk or shoot a bull, you will be ready. And with that, you will begin to realize that your choice of an elk rifle did not really matter at all.

WAYNE VAN ZWOLL is a journalist and book author known for his work on big-game hunting and the technical aspects of shooting. He has written for most of the major sporting magazines. His first book, *Mastering Mule Deer,* appeared in 1988. His second book, *America's Great Gunmakers,* was published in 1992 by Stoeger Publishing Company. Wayne's most recent book, *Elk Rifles, Cartridges and Hunting Tactics,* from which this article was adapted, combines technical and historical information on guns and is loaded with practical tips for elk hunters.

The best binoculars you can afford are usually the best buy. These 9X35s from Leupold work well in open country; for timber choose 7X35s, 7X42s or 8X40s.

The biggest reward is just being there... in the woods, the swamp, the high country, wherever. But, once in a while, if you've scouted well and the weather is right, with a little luck, your hard work can pay off.

At Swarovski we have come up with some additional rewards of our own for you. When you purchase one of our premium optical products like binoculars or scopes, you'll receive a coupon entitling you to a discount off the purchase price of selected Swarovski premium items. Your Swarovski dealer even has a reward poster with a list of these most wanted items like premium watches, knives, books, apparel and other quality outdoor accessories.

See your local dealer for details on our premium optics and information on how you can save on the purchase of one or more of our "Rewards" or call 800-426-3089.

SWAROVSKI
O P T I K

The Ultimate Hunting Glasses

Swarovski Optik North America, Limited, One Wholesale Way, Cranston, Rhode Island 02920

FINLAND
sako
WORLD CLASS RIFLES

COMMITMENT TO EXCELLENCE—A SAKO TRADITION

Go Straight to the Main Course.

VENISON
LOW IN FAT
100% NATURAL

BAR Mark II Safari
(Scope not included)

A-Bolt Medallion

Model 81 BLR Long Action

Sitting down to a delicious wild game dinner is one of hunting's greatest rewards. Unfortunately, obtaining the main course is not always an easy task. Put the odds in your favor with the exceptional accuracy of a Browning rifle.

The secret behind the BAR's accuracy is its strong, multiple lug, rotary bolt head. This bolt head locks solidly and precisely into mating recesses in the barrel — a combination that spells accuracy. **The design of the new BAR Mark II Safari further enhances accuracy.** A new, more rigid action bar/inertia block eliminates inaccuracy from barrel vibration. A new bolt release lever allows faster and easier operation.

The Browning A-Bolt is known for its "out of the box" accuracy. Precise rifling, a free floating barrel and sound engineering preserve this accuracy. All Browning rifles have a crowned muzzle as final assurance to their precision.

The Browning BLR is the only lever action chambered for belted magnums. Its modern design incorporates a strong locking system — consisting of a rotary, multiple lug bolt head — and a durable rack and pinion gearing mechanism. Together they give the BLR exceptional strength, silky smooth, trouble-free operation and outstanding accuracy.

For more information on highly accurate Browning rifles and other firearms, shooting equipment, clothing, boots, knives and gun safes please send $2.00 for our 124 page catalog. Send to Browning, Dept. M024, One Browning Place, Morgan, Utah 84050-9326. For the Browning dealers near you, call 1-800-333-3288.

The Best There Is.
BROWNING

THE KENTUCKY RIFLE: ART AT WORK

by R. Stephen Irwin, M.D.

The best piece of meat found on a squirrel is the jowl, so you don't want to ruin it by shooting a hole through it. For that matter, there's no need to waste any of the rest of the squirrel either. The solution is simple: a rifle ball fired at just the right place in the limb below a squirrel's head—not too high and not too low—can splinter the bark with enough force to daze the squirrel, causing it to fall to the ground with nary a bullet hole.

The best time to "bark" squirrels this way is at midday. Stuffed and lazy from their early morning feed, they like to stretch out flat on a limb to snooze in the warm sun. Daniel Boone was a master at barking squirrels, as were many other frontiersmen. They did it not only to conserve meat, but also because of the pride they had in their marksmanship. Such feats were not, however, the result of a sharp eye and steady aim alone. The frontiersman had at his disposal a magnificent firearm seemingly developed for just this purpose—the Kentucky Rifle. For the eastern half of the country, at least, it was the supreme American hunting rifle, flourishing in the century between 1750 and 1850.

Born of necessity, the Kentucky Rifle was designed to meet the specific requirements of hunting in a new and vast wilderness area. Its roots lay in the Jaeger, a rifle brought to this country by early Swiss and German gunsmiths. When it came to gunmaking, these men were steeped in the traditions of their homelands. But the American frontiersman was obstinate enough to have his own ideas about what was needed in a rifle. What might have worked admirably in the civilized forests of Europe, he reckoned, was not necessarily right for the wilderness of the New World.

No hunter in those days wanted to carry a heavy weapon on his long treks in the woods, so the weight was steadily reduced until the average Kentucky Rifle weighed between 9 and 10 pounds. This was accomplished largely by reducing the bore from that of the German Jaegers (.65–.75) to .40–.45 for most Kentucky rifles. The American frontiersman had no need for a rifle that could penetrate armor. Besides, the smaller caliber conserved lead and powder, both of which were usually in short supply along the frontier.

The straight, thick European stock gradually gave way to a slender design with a graceful droop and a crescent-shaped buttplate that fit the shooter's shoulder and permitted the rifle to "hang" steady for offhand shooting. The stocks, which were hewn by hand from native maple that was especially selected for the curl and beauty of its grain, extended all the way out the barrel to the muzzle. Indeed, craftsmanship may have reached its apex in the carving of the stock. For a gunstock that was scheduled for carving, the wood was left

The work and style of Kentucky Rifle gunsmiths, as in these examples, was distinctive. Most frontiersmen knew each other's rifles by sight, name and reputation.

purposely oversized wherever carving was indicated. Patterns—including scrolls, animals and geometric figures—were then carved in bas-relief on the cheek side and other appropriate areas. Frequently inlays of brass, pewter or silver were added.

Another artistic focal point of the Kentucky Rifle was the patchbox on its butt. The sliding covers made of wood, bone or horn on the earlier rifles were without expression; moreover, these covers were easily dropped and lost in the woods. Eventually, they were replaced by hinged patchboxes made of brass, often consisting of three or four pieces whose graceful curves and cutouts were inlaid in the curly maple stocks.

IMPROVING THE BARREL AND LOADING TECHNIQUES

Perhaps nothing contributed more to the success of the Kentucky Rifle than did the lengthening of its barrel. This change was probably influenced most by the long-barreled smoothbore English fowling pieces of the Scotch-Irish. Not only did the longer sighting radius increase accuracy, but also the longer barrel ensured that the powder charge was completely consumed and the noise of the firing deadened accordingly.

Unlike barrels forged by hand and laboriously rifled by the gunsmith, the Kentucky's lock mechanisms were usually imported from Germany and England. For that reason, the name on the lock plate rarely had any connection with the maker of the gun in question. If a gunmaker signed his work at all it was on the barrel, but few early pieces were signed for fear of reprisal from the British. Besides, most gunsmiths were well known in their own localities, if not beyond them. Their work and styles were so distinctive that no signatures were needed.

Long before the advent of the Kentucky, it was accepted that a spinning bullet gained greater distance and was more accurate than one shot without rotation of any kind. Rifling in the barrel caused a bullet to spin and, therefore, like the Jaeger before it, the Kentucky featured a rifled barrel as well. But problems persisted. For example, any ball that fit loosely into the barrel created "windage"; that is, the escape of propelling gases through the rifling grooves. For the ball to be tightly sealed in the barrel, it had to be as large as the bore of the grooves. This meant pounding

it home when loading with a metal rod and mallet—a lengthy (and noisy) undertaking. Whether one anticipated hunting game or defending oneself against marauding Indians, this was a distinct disadvantage in the wilderness. Moreover, as the lands—the ridges between the rifling grooves—cut into the lead of the bullet, they distorted it so that its flight was often erratic.

These problems were alleviated when some unknown genius invented the patch method of loading, a technique first used widely with the Kentucky Rifle. To patch load a rifle, a piece of dressed buckskin or a bit of old felt, about the size of a fifty-cent piece and well-greased with tallow, was slipped under the ball as it was suspended over the muzzle. Then, as the ball was rammed down the barrel, the greased patch enabled it to slide along with relative ease. Finally, the noisy hammering had become a thing of the past; moreover, the grooves of the rifling now cut into the

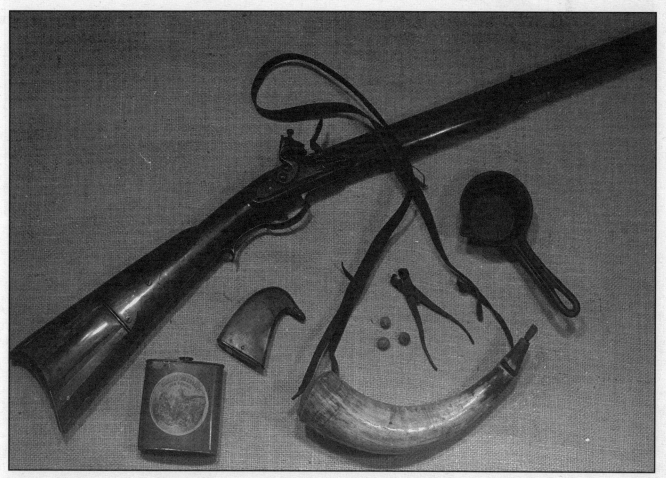

To ensure proper bore, bullet molds were usually custom made by the gunsmith. Lead, considered a precious commodity on the frontier, was extracted from fallen game to be melted and reused.

patch, not the ball, which remained unmarked and undistorted. Thanks to this discovery, reloading time was shortened significantly, allowing many hunters to get off their second shot in less than half a minute.

ITS ORIGINS AND DOWNFALL

Kentucky may have been where the legend of this famous rifle was established, hence, its name; but it was in Pennsylvania, specifically Lancaster County, where the Kentucky Rifle was born. Its creators there were the Pennsylvania Dutch, from whose ingenuity the famous Kentucky style

the American legend, these men treasured the long rifle as their favorite weapon. So the name "Kentucky Rifle" stuck.

Except for the lock, the Kentucky is a completely handcrafted firearm. It has no interchangeable parts. Most rifles were built to each buyer's specifications or in accordance with the maker's latest innovations. While there existed certain regional trends or "schools," still, no two firearms were ever exactly alike. It's important to recognize that the improvements made in the Kentucky Rifle did not evolve all at once, but were spread over many years.

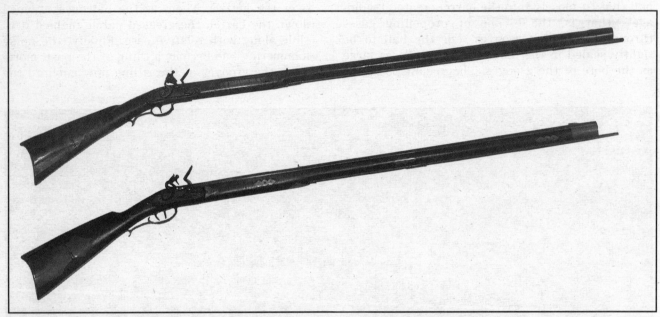

The barrel of the .45-caliber Kentucky Flintlock Rifle (top) is signed by gunsmith G. G. Oter. The bottom flintlock is unusually thick at the wrist and of larger than normal caliber. Note the brass patchboxes in each of the rifle's stocks.

evolved. From Lancaster County, these early gunmakers spread in all directions, first to York and Reading counties, then east to Philadelphia and west to Pittsburgh. Later, rifles were also made in New York, Maryland, North Carolina, Virginia, Ohio and Tennessee.

Actually, the name "Kentucky Rifle" was coined after a phrase from a ballad extolling Andrew Jackson's riflemen at the Battle of New Orleans during the War of 1812. Daniel Boone and other adventurers had crossed the Cumberland Mountains some years earlier into an ill-defined wilderness known as Kentucky. Already a part of

Kentucky rifles truly represent the individualistic expressions of many superb gunsmiths, who valued beauty no less than firing accuracy. These men believed that a man's rifle was his finest possession. Thus, the silver inlays, the brass furniture, the carved stocks, all were like signatures in themselves. Likewise, the relationship of the American frontiersman to his rifle was intimate and unique. With it, he protected himself, his family and his livestock, mostly from Indians; thus, it was never far from his grasp. With it, he also killed the game that provided most of the meat for his table, as well as skins to sell or trade for those

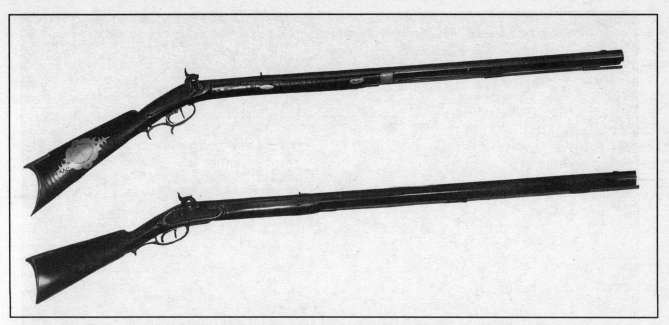

Note the dramatic drop in the stock of the .38-caliber percussion rifle (top) with its half-stock ornately decorated with German silver inlays. The .40-caliber full-stock Kentucky Rifle at bottom has a percussion lock marked "J. Golcher."

commodities he could not produce himself.

Even the frontiersman's amusement and prestige were garnered from his rifle. Turkey shoots were a popular frontier sport, and the marksmanship exhibited at these affairs was amazing even by modern standards. In this competition, a turkey was tethered behind a log some 250 feet or more away. The shooters then tried to coax the bird into showing its head by clucking at it. The moment its head appeared from behind the log, the shooter would get off a quick shot at the tiny target.

Frequently, a frontiersman expressed endearment for his rifle by giving it a name—"Old Sure Fire," "Indian Lament," and Davy Crockett's infamous "Ol' Betsy" are examples. Neighbors lived far apart on the frontier, yet most men knew each other's rifles by sight, name and reputation. The American frontiersman and his rifle were indeed a rare combination unparalleled anywhere in the world.

The death knell for the Kentucky Rifle was first sounded in 1807 in, of all places, the British Isles. That was the year a Scotch Presbyterian minister named Alexander Forsyth received a patent for his percussion ignition system. By 1830, the flintlock mechanism was considered obsolete, with many of the earlier rifles being converted to the percussion form. The rifles built solely as percussion pieces, however, lacked many of the refinements shared by the old flintlocks. Patchboxes

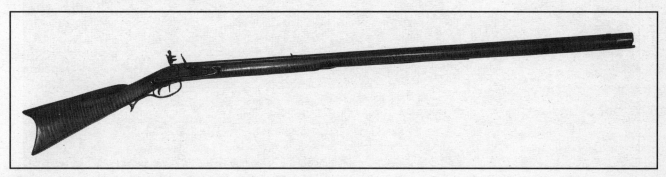

Although it lacks a patchbox, this rifle, which has been traced to a Tennessee gunsmith, is absolutely classic in line. Note the exquisite grain in its curly maple stock.

Kentucky Rifle gunsmiths valued beauty as well as accuracy. They believed that a man's rifle should be his finest possession.

This Southern-stlye rifle in .36 caliber has an unusually long barrel. Its lock was make by H. E. Dimick & Company of St. Louis. Instead of the usual brass, the trigger guard on this model was blacksmith forged.

became ovate in shape; fine relief carvings gave way to mere incised lines; and the new rifles tended to be more elaborate and overdecorated, ruining the flintlock's delicacy of line. Wealthy rifle owners of this later era, who preferred silver over brass inlay, decorated their guns with everything from Chinese yin-yang emblems to various fraternal symbols. The frontiersman of old would have deplored these gaudy additions, if only because they might reflect the sun and thus alert wild game or nearby unfriendly Indians to their whereabouts.

Anyone fortunate enough to possess a good, early Kentucky Rifle understands the talent and care required to build it in the first place, and how much it must have meant to its original owner. The Kentucky Rifle was nothing less than art at work. Representing a rare balance of line and symmetry, with its tasteful inlays of brass and the rich, raised carving on its mellow hand-rubbed stock, the Kentucky is still recognized by many as the most beautiful firearm ever produced. It has earned its place as America's own rifle, the proud symbol of an era and, yes, an entire nation.

DR. STEPHEN IRWIN is an avid big-game hunter and sport fisherman in his home state of Montana. For many years, he has written on the history of hunting and fishing, including such specialized areas as antique fishing lures, duck decoys and firearms. His articles have appeared in most of the major outdoor publications. He has also authored a book, *The Providers: Hunting and Fishing Methods of the Indians and Eskimos.* This is the fifth in a series of articles by Dr. Irwin to appear in SHOOTER'S BIBLE.

THE .357 MAGNUM MODEL P: COLT'S "TOP GUN"

by Gary M. Brown

When Douglas Wesson, of the famous Smith & Wesson firm, introduced his .357 Magnum cartridge and revolver to the shooting world in 1935, the company's monopoly on the round was short-lived. Colt's Firearms Division was quick to realize the advantage of the shell and chambered it in their Single Action Army revolver (known at the factory as the Model P) that same year. Colt also adapted the powerful Magnum to its large frame New Service revolvers.

The .357 Magnum is basically a "hopped-up" .38 Special, with both rounds sharing a projectile of identical diameter. The case of the .357 was lengthened by about 1/10", thus making its insertion in the chambers of older (and presumably weaker) .38 Special revolvers difficult. Nevertheless, the magnum shell could still be placed in some older, unaltered .38 Special pistols, thus presenting a potentially explosive situation.

From its inception, the Smith & Wesson .357 Magnum revolver was touted as "the most powerful handgun ever made." This was only partly true. Elmer Keith and other handgun pioneers had for years handloaded hot .44 Special shells that absolutely dwarfed the .357 in energy and approached its velocity levels. Velocity is what made the 158-grain, Keith-style semi-wadcutter factory load "most powerful" by quite a margin over any other commercial fodder.

In his book, *Fighting Handguns*, Jeff Cooper reported in 1958 the velocity of the original .357 at a sizzling 1430 feet per second (fps) from a 6 1/2" barrel. Cooper also noted, however, that the factories had reduced the velocity to a somewhat less impressive 1370 fps during this time, presumably to extend the life of guns subjected to extensive firing of the magnum loading. Cooper lists ballistics for the full load from an 8 3/8" barrel at 1510 fps (1450 fps for the 1958 version of the round). By extrapolation, the original shell would clock a conservative 1475 fps from the barrel of a 7 1/2" .357 SAA, making it easily the most powerful standard factory production version of its kind (with commercial ammo or its handloaded equivalent).

The Colt Single Action Army revolver holds a unique place in the annals of American firearms history. Adopted in 1873 by the U.S. military in .45 Long Colt with a 7 1/2" barrel, the combination served with distinction until 1892. That year marked the approval of a Colt "hand ejecting" (swing-out cylinder) revolver in .38 Long Colt, a decision that is widely regarded as one of the greatest blunders in U.S. military sidearms history. Countless thousands of SAAs in a myriad of calibers were employed by persons on both sides of the law from its introduction, until long after its "official" discontinuation in 1940, just prior to World War II. In all, more than 356,000 original

First Generation SAAs were produced.

At the end of hostilities, Colt fought tooth and nail against reintroduction of the Model P. Various reasons were cited for refusing to revive the model. Supposedly, some or all of the tooling required for its manufacture had been altered, lost or discarded to facilitate wartime production of other, more modern weapons. When pressed on this matter, the firm responded that the cost of the revolver placed it in the $75 price range, about twice that of the gun's list price in 1940. Even "junk" Colt SAA originals were being scalped then at astronomical prices.

Enter William Ruger, who had been successful in marketing his first firearm, the .22 LR semiautomatic pistol. With the name "Ruger"—only one consonant removed from "Luger"—and with an external silhouette remarkably similar to the "P-08," the popularity of this pistol was predictable. An excellent modifier of existing designs, Ruger also possessed an uncanny knack of perceiving what the gun-buying public wanted. Thus, he introduced in the early 1950s his .22 rimfire "Single-Six," a somewhat miniaturized version of the Single Action Army. The little gun was a smash hit.

Still, Colt stubbornly refused to recant its decision never to build the "original." Around 1955, Ruger scooped Colt with his centerfire look-alike of the Model P. This new Ruger Blackhawk, although mostly investment cast (as was its predecessor, the Single-Six), featured real mechanical improvements over the original Colt. Adjustable target sights, coil music-wire springs and frame-mounted, floating firing pins were among them. All in all, these Ruger single-actions were much better shooters. Still, the mystique and natural handling characteristics of the Colt continued to be sought by the traditionalists.

COLT REINTRODUCES THE MODEL P

Finally, in 1956, Colt reintroduced its Model P at the hefty price of $125.00. With the exception of a new serial-number range, ending with an "SA" suffix (beginning at 0001SA), and a slight alteration of the front sight, the gun was identical to the prewar model. Absolutely no substantial improvements, with the possible exception of improved metallurgy, had been made, and there were only two choices of chamberings. One was the .45

This rare First Generation (prewar) SAA in .38 WCF is in near-mint condition. Note the color-casehardened hammer, a common feature on earlier prewar Model Ps. The gun is also fitted with "Rampant Colt Only" (non-Eagle) black, hard rubber grips.

The author's .357 Magnum Model P is in the high 69XXXSA serial-number range. It features vivid color casehardening and "Eagle" black composition grips.

Long Colt, which had been by far the most popular caliber for the original prewar First Generation model. The second round was the pipsqueak .38 Special that Jeff Cooper wrote of in *Fighting Handguns*: "Any .38 Special, except the flyweight models, should be bored to take the .357 load if necessary."

What Colt's thinking was concerning the .38 chambering remains a matter of mystery and speculation. As noted, Colt had offered the .357 in the Model P from the earliest days of the round; in fact, 525 prewar SAAs had been chambered for the "hot".357 Magnum cartridge prior to the discontinuation of the model in 1940. Although the prewar .357s apparently possessed cylinders of strengthened "special steel"—as indicated by a five-pointed star stamped on the cylinder face—the gun was virtually identical to other calibers available. Many of the postwar .38 Special SAAs had their chambers deepened to accept the .357 Magnum shell. Ironically, because of their relative scarcity, these original and unaltered "Second Generation" (i.e., postwar) SAA .38 Specials now command a top-dollar collector's value. Those who buy one of these guns, however, are well advised to try placing a .357 round in each chamber before parting with their funds.

According to Colt historian M.S. "Marty"

Huber, the only reason for the inclusion of the .38 Special as an initial chambering for the new SAA was the vast popularity of the round at that time. Huber makes a valid point, for it was then considered the No. 1 revolver target cartridge. Moreover, the great majority of U.S. police organizations then considered the .38 Special as "standard"; in fact, there was considerable resistance to arming America's police officers with the "overly powerful" .357 Magnum round.

In 1960, with no apparent safety or mechanical reasons preventing Colt from offering the .357 shell in its early Second Generation guns, the company decided to go ahead. According to Colt's announcement in that year's SHOOTER'S BIBLE, "The .357 Magnum Single Action Army. . . combines the western handgun with modern service ballistics." The accompanying photo depicts a 7½″ barreled Model P with wooden grips. For a time, an apparent overlap existed between availability of the .357 and the .38 Special, at least until barrels rollmarked with the latter designation were exhausted. During this transition period, the Colt factory may have fitted a few of these late .38 Specials with cylinders chambered for the Magnum round. A fourth caliber—the relatively short-lived .44 Special—shared billing during this time.

Eventually, Colt standardized on the .357

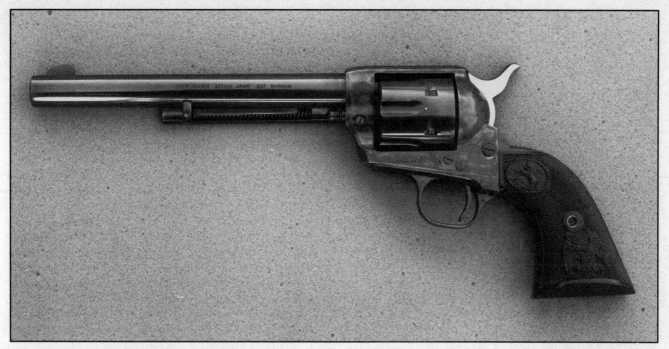

This Second Generation Single Action Army revolver, Model P-1670, with a 7½" barrel gets the author's vote as "Colt's Most Powerful Peacemaker."

Magnum and the .45 Colt. These were the only choices being offered when the Second Generation guns were discontinued (or modified) in late 1975. Second Generation standard barrel lengths were 4¾", 5½", 7½", and the superlong 12" "Buntline Special" (in .45 Colt only). Ballistically, the 7½" Second Generation Model P in .357 Magnum joined its prewar cousins as the most powerful, original production Colt Single Action Army ever offered by the factory.

The final Second Generation SAA was produced at a serial number in the 75000SA range, with a gap of about 5,000 purposely built in. At approximately 80000SA, Colt introduced the Third Generation variation of Single Action Army in 1976. Externally, these Third Generation guns appeared virtually identical to the late Second Generation models. The original machinery used to produce the initial run of postwar guns had worn out, and in the process of retooling Colt made some minor changes. The most noticeable of these was the placement of the removable, full-length cylinder "base pin bushing" with a short cylinder bushing pressed permanently in place. Slight modification of the weapon's hand and its cylinder "star" or ratchet was also made. For reasons unknown, barrel-to-frame thread pitch was changed

to 11/16×24 TPI (Threads per Inch), which meant that if anyone wished to install a Third Generation barrel on a First Generation (prewar) gun or a Second Generation (postwar) version, it had to be "crush fit" into the earlier frame, thus becoming essentially non-removable.

THE THIRD GENERATION ARRIVES

Third Generation calibers were .45 Colt, .357 Magnum (including the 7½" gun) and the .44 Special. Such notable gun writers of the period as Charles Skelton convinced Colt to offer the classic .44-40 as the fourth standard caliber. Third Generation regular production barrel lengths included 4¾", 5½" and 7½" versions. These latter-day examples of the SAA also provided good availability of 3" barreled Sheriff's Models, devoid of an extractor rod assembly, in .44-40, .44-40/.44 Special convertible, and .45 Colt. Many other non-standard barrel lengths were incorporated during this generation's final "parts cleanup" period.

By late 1981, rapidly accelerating production costs, coupled with increased product liability concerns, caused Colt to announce its "complete and final" discontinuance of the Single Action Army. Actually, this was only partially true; until quite recently, enough were retained by Colt's

Custom Shop to assure availability of Special Order Third Generation SAAs.

Whether Colt itself knows the actual Third Generation production total is doubtful, especially considering the large numbers of parts cleanup and Special Order pieces made. Sometime in the early 1980s, this writer bought a late standard production 7½" Blue/Casehardened SAA .44-40 (P-1970) in the SA61XXX serial-number range. Considering that some 20,000 early Third Generation guns were made with an "SA" suffix, it follows that Third Generation production had already exceeded Second Generation totals by the time my .44-40 was built. I also have a letter dated April 13, 1981, from C. E. Warner, then president of Colt Firearms, in which he explained the final decision to drop the SAA. Warner's closing statement in that letter was perhaps prophetic: "Although we cannot foresee when," he stipulated, "we are hopeful that at some point in the future we will be able to resume production of this famous gun."

Beginning in 1991, Colt finally acceded to Warner's prediction. Chamberings at first included 9mm Luger, .45 ACP, .45 Colt and .44-40 (the .357 Magnum was not listed as being available). Whether or not these latest Colt factory SAAs will be technically classified by collectors as "Fourth Generation" guns remains speculative; the only apparent difference between them and their Third Generation cousins are the roughly finished "smooth" walnut grips and Bright "Royal Blue"/ Casehardened or Bright Nickel finishes. Regardless of their suggested retail prices, which start at more than $1,200, purists are happy just to have renewed access to the SAA. Caliber choices in 1992 were limited to the .45 Colt and the .44-40

THE SAA IN .357 MAGNUM

Who were the people that bought the Model P in .357 Magnum? Why would they turn their backs on the traditional big-bore calibers of the SAA? Although the SAA revolver was available in underpowered chamberings like the .32-20 (.32 WCF), its fame was made with such large diameter favorites as the .45 Long Colt and the .44-40. In the 1951 *Gun Digest*, Charles Askins is shown with an altered 7½" prewar Single Action Army in .357 Magnum. In that same photo, Askins proudly displays the remains of a jackrabbit whose rear end has been virtually destroyed. Was Askins suggesting that his gun-cartridge combination was suitable only for small-game animals of jackrabbit size? Hardly. He was simply pointing out the flat trajectory and massive destructive power of the cartridge, combined with the versatility of the original SAA design. But for its slow-to-reload

A late Second Generation P-1840, with a 4³/4" barrel is shown housed in its "Stagecoach" box. This configuration is considered one of the SAA's most popular variations. This example, which falls in the 62XXXSA range, is equipped with black "Eagle" composition grips.

Colt's Third Generation Single Action revolver for the first time provided widespread availability of 3″ barreled Sheriff's Models like this P-1932 .44-40. Most blued Third Generation guns were fitted with "Eagle Pattern" black plastic grips (as were many late Second Generation SAAs).

mechanism, the Model P in .357 Magnum could have been applied equally to law enforcement use, as well as by hunters of medium-sized game up to, and including, white-tailed deer. The .357 SAA doubtless found favor with some law enforcement officers who wanted the traditional "feel" and pointability of the SAA, plus the advanced ballistics of the magnum round. Not only was the cartridge spectacular in the energy and velocity departments, but also it succeeded from the penetration viewpoint as well. In fact, penetration may well have been the shell's primary appeal to these officers, whether stationed on the Mexican border or along desolate stretches of western highways. These men fervently desired the uncomplicated design of the Colt single-action revolver, along with its capability of driving a powerful projectile to its maximum possible depth into the target.

As for those who favored the postwar magnum version of the SAA, Colt's own descriptive literature of 1960 seems to provide the key. That combination of "western handgun" featuring "modern service ballistics" undoubtedly appealed to many contemporary shooters. Besides, Bill Ruger was already selling tons of Blackhawks in .357 Magnum. The Blackhawk, in fact, wasn't even offered in a traditional caliber until it appeared about 1970 in .45 Long Colt, near the end of "Old Model" production. Regardless, those who chose the .357 Magnum Model P from 1960 on preferred its original design and handling characteristics—chambered for the most powerful round ever offered in the venerable piece—over the vastly improved, less costly Ruger model of identical caliber.

The author's .357 Magnum Colt Single Action Army revolver (pictured on page 45) is factory new and unturned in its original wood-grained box with all papers, including instructional manual and warranty card, intact. The box end label identifies it as a Model P-1670, which is Colt's factory code for the standard Blue/Casehardened .357 Magnum with 7½″ barrel. The revolver bears a serial number in the high 69XXXSA range, making it a late

The "Stagecoach" box (bottom) was used throughout much of the SAA's Second Generation. Late Second Generation and most Third Generation Model Ps were housed in wood-grained boxes (top).

These .357 Magnum shells (c. 1958) 158-grain factory rounds (lead SWC and round-nose FMJ), although somewhat reduced, still enabled the 7¹/₂" barreled SAA to claim in .357 the title "Top Gun."

(1974) Second Generation gun, complete with removable base pin bushing, barrel thread pitch, and unaltered hand and ratchet.

One thing my 69XXXSA shares with most Third Generation guns is its "Eagle Pattern" black plastic grips. These were incorporated on late Second Generation pieces in the 60XXXSA (1970-71) range, replacing the earlier "Rampant Colt Only" grips of the black-checkered, hard-rubber type used on most First and Second Generation guns produced in this century. Inside both grips are scratched the guns' serial numbers. The front face of the cylinders are marked with the serial number's last three digits. Overall fit and finish are nearly perfect.

It is unlikely that my 69XXXSA will ever be fired. If it were to be shot (with factory ammunition), it would be—at least on paper—an ex-

ample of the most powerful version of the Colt Single Action Army ever produced: truly, the Model P's "Top Gun."

GARY M. BROWN is a full-time freelance writer and photographer who resides in Florida. While his preferred weapons of interest are classic cartridge firearms of the pre-World War II era, his areas of expertise extend, quite literally, from matchlocks to automatic weapons. His articles have appeared in such publications as *Man at Arms* and *Machine Gun News.* This article marks Brown's first appearance in SHOOTER'S BIBLE.

RIFLE STOCK STYLES: PROs AND CONs

by Ralph Quinn

Reams of copy have been written on the design and function of rifle stocks, and in the last decade hundreds of custom gunmakers have sprung up to supply shooters everywhere with the kind of rifle they want. Predictably, one man's notion of a purely functional rifle stock does not always suit another's, and so the debate rages on.

Nevertheless, the functional rifle stock has several features in common with others of its kind: it is properly designed, it fits the person using it, and it has trim lines, cleanly proportioned forends, grips and sparse adornment. Its shape, proportion and balance ideally permit the shooter to get on target quickly and steadily; and, most important, it should minimize recoil. If by chance it also boasts crisp lines and graceful curves, so much the better.

Since the end of World War II, some rather exotic features have been added to hunting stocks that are better suited to other types of rifles. For example, target and bench rifles with sharply curved, vertical grips may be great for timed trigger let-offs, but for the big-game hunter who has only fractions of a second to make the shot with his sporter, they are a royal pain in the neck.

Another unusual design adopted from the ranks of target shooters is the thumbhole stock. Again, for silhouette or Schuetzen matches, where a rifler has time to lock into a position, they are

hard to beat. Beyond this, however, such designs hinder rather than help. On a recent late-season deer hunt in Wyoming, one hunter, while attempting to bring down a rutting whitetail buck, got his glove tangled up in the thumbhole stock. During the confusion, his rifle went off and shot the outfitter's truck parked a few yards away.

Other nonfunctional stock features include beavertail, flat-bottomed and slab-sided forends. Because the human hand is naturally curved when grasping the forend of a rifle, it follows that the wood in this area should be similarly shaped; that is, round or slightly pear-shaped. Although these features may admittedly have a place on larger stocks, they are of little use on a hunting rifle. Moreover, the grip section of the stock should be round on cross-section and sized to fit the hand. It should sweep cleanly to the grip and not be adorned with an odd-shaped cap.

The buttstock of the functional rifle should aid the hunter in shooting quickly and accurately. And it should be long enough to prevent the thumb from hitting the shooter's nose when the rifle recoils. Also, the comb should be comfortably rounded so it does not bruise the cheek. Finally, the comb and cheekpiece should support the face in direct line with the scope or iron sights, allowing a steadier hold on the target.

To get on target quickly and accurately, a hunting rifle stock should have balance, proportion and fit, especially when hunting big game in tight covers where fractions of a second can make a difference.

HOW THE MANUFACTURERS WENT WRONG

Shooters who have been around since the late 1930s are quick to point out how much straighter rifle stocks are today compared to the "good old days." Apparently, the introduction of scopes and heavy recoil cartridges, plus changing shooting styles, forced manufacturers to modify their stocks dimensionally or lose sales. Even so, the industry was slow to move. A look at a 1930 Winchester catalog reveals that most of the sporting rifles, including the popular Model 95, had curved butt-plates and were chambered for powerful smokeless cartridges, such as the .35 W.C.F, .30-40 Krag, .30-06 and the .405 Winchester. Drop at both comb and heel (1⅓ inches) for the Model 95 was excessive—and painful.

Despite the fact that stock shape and size are crucial to the performance of both rifle and man, gunmakers in the early 1900s produced rifle stocks with poor lines and atrocious dimensions. Starting with muskets made at the Springfield Armory around 1795, and continuing through the Winchester Model 1873 and 1903 Springfield, United States arms makers clung to outdated government specifications in their pursuit of the "ideal" stock. The net result: most rifles manufactured prior to and after World War II were designed to fit everyone and thus they fit no one.

In the mid-1930s, Winchester made a serious attempt to improve its Model 54 bolt-action, and hired the late, great Bob Owen to redesign the rifle's forend contours. Owen succeeded in this instance, but when it came to creating a true classic, the company chose the outdated, overdropped buttstock. A similar story occurred in the 1960s when Bill Ruger hired Len Brownell to design the stock for his company's M77R bolt. Without question, that rifle remains one of the best looking of the "classic" designs offered today; but once again, it represents a compromise in the drop department.

The thumbhole silhouette stock (top) and straight-grip target designs have found their way into hunting stocks. Although both allow for controlled trigger releases, they are ill-equipped for fast shooting.

THE PROBLEM OF TOO MUCH DROP

Because a higher percentage of cartridges in use today develop recoil than did those made 40 to 50 years ago, namely, the .416 Remington, .458 Winchester, .460 Weatherby and others, it makes sense from the shooter's standpoint to equip such rifles with straight-comb stocks. Aside from positioning the eye directly in line with the scope, a stock with zero drop has the added advantage of directing recoil straight back, rather than upward.

A bullet leaving the barrel creates an equal and opposite reaction. Because the buttplate is below the line of recoil, a pivotal motion causes the rifle to jump. The more drop at heel a stock has in relation to the bore, the greater the tendency for the rifle to jump up and smack the shooter in the face. A rifle with little or no drop at heel is less apt to pivot upward when recoiling. But if it does rise, the shooter's face remains in firm contact with the comb and felt recoil is lessened.

Over the years various attempts have been made to reduce recoil. Perhaps the most notable of these was a stock style incorporating the Monte

Carlo comb. Shortly after World War II, the design was widely copied by rifle manufacturers on the West Coast. Actually, these stocks magnified recoil rather than reduced it. The comb was high, thin and slanted downward toward the tang. Drop at heel was about 3¼ inches; and to align the eye with the scope, cheekpieces were made very thick.

Advocates insisted this stock design reduced felt recoil. If a rifle recoiled straight back, that claim might be valid; but as we know, rifles recoil upward. Because the Monte Carlo did not change drop at heel, rifles sporting these out-of-date measurements were real thumpers.

A better compromise could have been to straighten the existing buttstock, raise the comb (so the bolt cleared the wood) and reduce drop at heel. Using such a simple modification could have reduced recoil. Moreover, it could have enabled the shooter to align his eye with the scope faster.

One popular stock incorporating this design was created in the 1950s by Keith Stegall, whose

Stock design is important where accurate shooting is demanded. The top two rifles shown here have Monte Carlo combs. The bottom rifle is a classic with swept grip and straight comb. The grip on the middle rifle curves too sharply.

A full, well-rounded forend helps a shooter absorb recoil with his left hand. The checkering provides a positive grip.

work was classic in every respect. His raised combs sloped forward, while maintaining minimal drop at heel. The aft section of Stegall's comb was finely sculpted to shed unwanted weight. By combining the best of both worlds, Stegall's stock pointed quickly, supported the cheek nicely, and was comfortable to shoot.

Numerous ways exist to reduce apparent recoil. Armed with a full, rounded forend, a shooter can absorb some of the kick with his left hand. Another way is to use a large buttplate for distributing recoil over a broader area. Also, a comb that is full and rounded will not gouge into the cheek. Perhaps the best idea, though, is to use a straight stock—one with the same drop at heel and comb. Such a design has a tendency to bring recoil straight back, not up. Remember, the greater the distance between drop at comb and heel, the greater the recoil felt.

THE CLASSIC LOOK

Perhaps the first and most celebrated of the so-called classic rifle designs was the Ruger Model 77 flat bolt introduced in 1968. Based on an im-

proved Mauser action, the stock was, nevertheless, pure classic, created by ace riflesmith Len Brownell. For the first time in commercial history, the shooting public had a rifle that looked great, pointed naturally, and was comfortable to shoot. Predictably, gun fanciers flocked to its side in droves. At last count, no less than 13 "classics" were listed in the 1993 SHOOTER'S BIBLE, with doubtless more to come in 1994.

The "classic" label is generally bestowed on rifles with high, relatively thick combs, zero drop at heel, and a cheekpiece merging into the comb nose some 2¾ inches from the action's tang. For the most part, the classic comb is well-rounded in cross-section and provides excellent face support. The pistol grip has a slightly parabolic curve and is "swept" to the rear. The forward edge of the grip cap is usually 3½ to 3⅝ inches from the center of the trigger, whereas grip circumference is typically 3½ inches on standard calibers and 4¾ inches on big bores. Although length of pull varies with caliber selected, it usually runs 13½ to 14 inches on big-bore rifles (up to .338 caliber) used in warm weather hunting.

Even though many rifle companies are now offering "classic" stocks with measurements close to the above numbers, most leave too much wood on the stock. Grips are generally too large, buttstocks too thick, and forends too bulky. Part of this problem stems from a misguided attempt to offer a stock that fits everyone, which usually translates into baseball-sized grips and clumsy forends. An exception to this trend is the rifle produced by Dakota Arms (Sturgis, SD). Their customers can select any number of custom features, with higher prices reflecting the additional labor required to produce the work. For those who desire an essentially made-to-measure stock without waiting forever, this could be the answer.

Shooters who are on a budget have the choice of buying blanks turned to general dimensions, with final measurements completed by the customer. Some stock carving companies offer such duplicating services and their prices are reasonable—usually $60 to $70 to turn a pattern (plus the cost of wood). Shooting associate Pete Belding has built a thriving business around such services, and he is now paring down his standard factory stocks to custom dimensions. The net result in either case is a functional stock that fits the buyer

to a tee and handles like a dream.

Ideally, the forend of a hunting rifle should be full enough to keep the hand away from the barrel. It should also provide a firm hold while the shooter follows a running target. Distance from the recoil lug to forend tip should be 10 to 10 1/2 inches for barrels measuring 22–24 inches. The author's favorite .257 Roberts, which was fit and finished in tiger maple by custom stocker Dale Tuttle, has a diameter of 4 7/8 inches just forward of the receiver ring and measures 1 5/16 inches deep and 1 3/8 inches wide. The forend is slightly pear-shaped at the bottom, but nearly round. Rifles with heavy recoil—.458s and .416s—should have fuller forends with which to take up the recoil of the left hand. The buttplate for a rifle in the .30-06 class should be almost flat and measure about 5 1/4 inches in length and 1 5/8 inches in width.

THE SHOOTER'S PERFECT PITCH

Over the years, shotgunners have paid particular attention to specifications on "pitch" (or angle of buttplate attachment). But for some reason, riflers have ignored the issue, even though they know that too much down (or negative) pitch leads to undershooting. Why this disinterest remains a

The function of a well-proportioned cheekpiece, as shown on this classic, is to align the shooter's eye with the scope. A trim grip and flowing lines give the stock an elegant look.

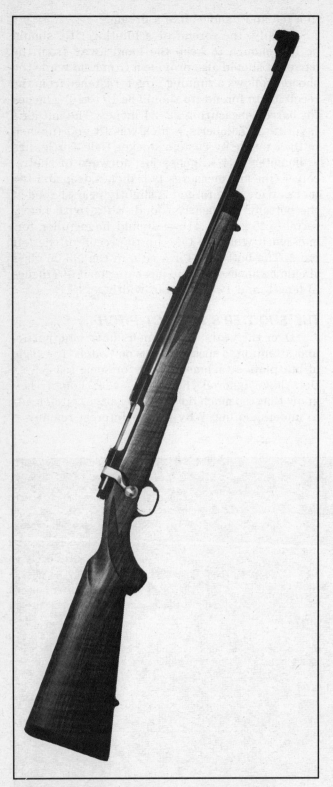

Ruger's M-77 Mark II Deluxe rifle is of classic design with an integral solid steel sighting rib and an upgraded walnut stock. Attention to fit and finish put rifles like these in the semicustom class.

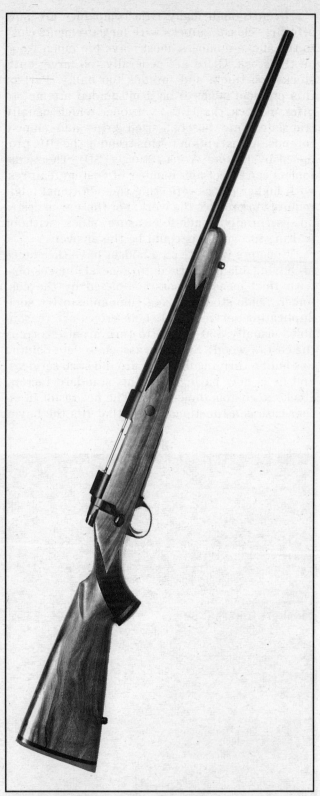

European manufacturers have added the classic look to their rifle lineups. Sako's new Classic is designed with clean, graceful lines and is available in both regular and magnum calibers.

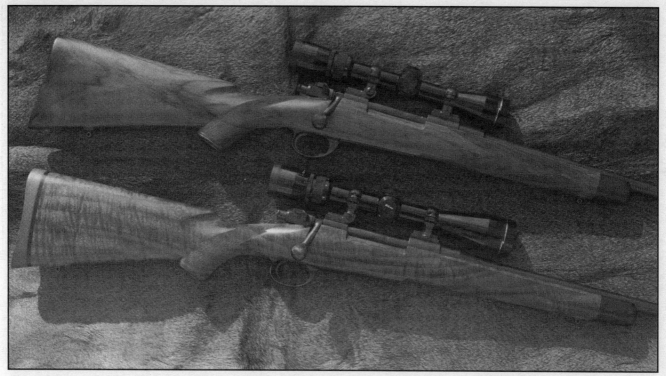

This pair of classic sporters features a severe classic style with swept grips and straight combs. The top rifle has a steel buttplate. The bottom one has a solid recoil pad to absorb kick. The ebony tips have no real function but are a nice touch.

mystery, because pitch does indeed make a difference in the fit and pointability of a rifle. Often rifles must be fired as fast as scatterguns, and with a single bullet at work the margin for error becomes slim indeed.

Factory rifles almost always have a slight negative pitch or angle, whereby the toe of the buttplate is farther ahead than the heel. The theory is that this feature tends to hold the muzzle down when the rifle recoils upward. But many shooters find that no angle—with buttplate or pad

at 90 degrees to the bore—serves best, especially on calibers with 48 or more foot-pounds of recoil.

Buttplates for the hunting rifle vary from rubber to checkered steel. On classic rifles of light recoil the preference is for curved steel. But unless the wood-to-metal fit is perfect or glassed, steel buttplates are subject to breakage, particularly in the toe region. For rifles used primarily in mountainous terrain, the best choice is a solid rubber recoil pad of good quality. These are available in varying thicknesses and, when made of "high

The Dakota Arms 76 is a true custom rifle available direct from the factory. The straight classic comb on this African series helps reduce recoil on heavy recoil cartridges.

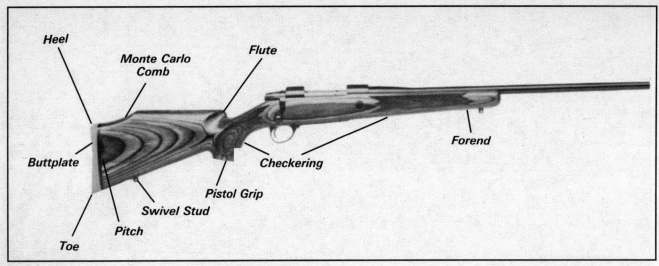

Nomenclature of a modern rifle stock (Sako Laminated).

tech'' sorbothane rubber, are capable of taming magnum calibers. Be sure they are smooth on all the edges, however, so they will not catch on any loose clothing.

CHECKERING: THE FINAL TOUCH

The crowning glory of any functional rifle stock is *checkering*, or, as the wood monger says, *scratching*. The primary function of checkering is to keep the hand from slipping on both forend and grip; its secondary function is simply as ornamentation to break up large expanses of wood. When properly executed with each diamond identical to each other and brought to a point, the checkered stock is not only functional, but is also a joy to behold.

For hunting purposes, 18 lines per inch (l.p.i.) is standard. Occasionally, manufacturers will use 20 to 22 l.p.i. to dress up better grades of walnut, but the best checkering on show guns usually runs 26 l.p.i. Even though this takes a great deal of talent, skill and care to create, its function is purely decorative.

With the exception of a few select-grade classic rifles—including Sako's Classic, Ruger's MKII Deluxe, Dakota's 76, McMillan's Signature Rifles, Weatherby's Classic Mark, and Remington's Safari Grade—most American and European factory stocks come standard with computer-cut checkering. At first glance, these patterns look acceptable, but close examination shows the diamonds to be poorly formed and structurally weak. An inexpensive job of ''hand'' checkering with power driven tools (like the MMC or DemBart) takes less than an hour, but a top-rate job can take 10 to 25 hours depending on the area to be covered and the complexity of the design, all of which can add $500 or more to the cost of a rifle.

Many rifle stocks sold today come equipped with black forend tips of ebony or rosewood. While this feature is really nonfunctional, some owners do believe it adds to the ''exclusive'' quality of a firearm. The practice was started by some gun builders in England who used water buffalo horns to cap their stocks of fine walnut. To this day, many custom shops in the United States refuse to produce a piece without a forend tip. But most Americans prefer to let the grain of the wood and lines of the stock do the talking, and let those angled tips of plastic, ivory and exotic carving go their separate ways.

RALPH QUINN is an award-winning, full-time freelance writer and film maker with credits in most of the major outdoor publications, including *Rifle, Wing & Shot, Field & Stream, Petersen's Hunting, Bow & Arrow Hunting* and others. As a dedicated big-game hunter and rifle fancier, he regularly travels throughout the U.S. in search of timely shooting topics. Quinn, who lives what he teaches, bases the advice offered in this article concerning functional stocks on more than 28 years of stockmaking experience.

NASH BUCKINGHAM: AMERICA'S TRUE "SHOOTINEST GENT'MAN"

by Jim Casada

To most lovers of fine sporting literature, Nash Buckingham's enduring story, "De Shootinest Gent'man," is one of the best-known tales among the annals of American outdoor writing. Among waterfowlers and quail hunters in particular, and wing shooters in general, Buckingham has become almost a cult figure. He remains, without question, one of the finest writers ever to grace the American sporting scene. Buckingham's world was populated by great coveys of quail, myriads of waterfowl, and gentlemen sportsmen. The indescribable bond between a dog and its master, the simple pleasures of good food and company, the seasons of the earth and the mind—these were the values he held nearest and dearest.

Buckingham was also a superb athlete, who ranked among the outstanding shots of his day. He was a fixture at National Field Trials for several decades, a man who appreciated dogs and fine dog work as few others have before or since. An ardent conservationist, he became a leading spokesman for sound sporting ethics and sensible bag limits long before holding such views became fashionable. But most of all, this stalwart Tennessean was a kind of Renaissance man of sport. He savored the smell of burned gunpowder, the camaraderie of the hunting field, and the recounting of the day's events before an evening fire. As a masterful storyteller, he left a rich legacy in the form of a small library of books and articles.

AN ATHLETE AND A GENTLEMAN

Born in Memphis, Tennessee, on May 31, 1880, Theophilus Nash Buckingham was the son of a fervent sportsman, who conveyed to young Nash the ideals of gentility and humanity that characterized Southern society at its best. During Buckingham's teen-age years, Memphis was the commercial heart of a region where cotton had long been king. But close by, one could find first-rate duck and goose hunting along the Mississippi flyway. From his writings, we know that Buckingham spent countless hours afield and astream during those formative years. In his many boyhood haunts, he would await the whistling wings at dawn at the Beaver Dam Club, or he sought quail in the remote corners of west Tennessee farms. From the moment he received his first shotgun at the age of eight, sport was central to Buckingham's life.

Blessed with a powerful intellect, young Nash was admitted to Harvard in 1898, but homesickness after a year there brought him back to Southern soil and the campus of the University of Tennessee. While at Harvard, though, he met and befriended James J. Corbett, the renowned heavyweight boxing champion, who taught Nash the elements of the pugilistic art. Indeed, Buckingham took justifiable pride in the fact that he earned heavyweight championship laurels in the Amateur Athletic Union's Southern Open Tournament held

Long considered one of the country's finest wing shots, Buckingham is shown here quail hunting in his prime.

in New Orleans a decade later, in 1910.

During his college days at Tennessee, Buckingham won varsity letters in four sports: boxing, baseball, track and football. The same abilities that served him so well as a college athlete stood Nash in equally good stead in the duck blind or field. Accounts of his extraordinary ability in this regard have been passed on by some contemporaries, including Henry Davis, Remington Arms' public relations director. "He was the best field shot on any kind of game I ever saw," Davis wrote. Another noted authority, Horace Lytle, echoed that sentiment in 1929: "I regard Nash Buckingham as the best all-around marksman in America. No man can beat Nash in the field, whether it be on wildfowl or upland game."

Once, while visiting New York, Buckingham shot skeet for the first time. Using a borrowed gun he had not fired until he called "pull" on the first clay pigeon, he proceeded to break 99 out of 100 birds. Harold P. Sheldon, a close friend of Buck-

ingham's and chief conservation officer for the Fish and Wildlife Service as well as a noted outdoor writer, said he once saw Nash bring down a limit of 15 ducks with 17 shells using a 12-gauge Burt Becker magnum. "I sincerely doubt if any duck was closer than 50 yards," Sheldon recalled, "and the two extra loads were used to second-shot badly winged mallards."

Buckingham's gun, built by Becker on a Fox action and chambered for three-inch shells, came to be known as "Bo Whoop" after the resounding noise it made when fired. According to Sheldon, the magnum had a ringing, two-note sound, "exactly like two, deep solo notes from the bass horn in a symphony orchestra." Buckingham stridently advocated use of such weapons, which he called "Big 'Uns." He once commented to the noted outdoor writer John Madson: "I never gamble when I shoot waterfowl, sir. I believe in taking a bird close and hitting him very, very hard with big shot from a big gun."

THE WRITER EMERGES

As masterful with the shotgun as Buckingham was, he eventually made even more of a mark as a writer. His apprenticeship came immediately after college, when he joined the staff of the Memphis *Commercial Appeal* as a sports writer, a job that ended when he married Irma Lee Jones in 1910. Thereafter, no doubt because of his new marital status and the responsibilities it brought, Buckingham tried his hand at a number of occupations over the next two decades, including ownership of a sporting goods business in Memphis (1917–1925), an advisory position with the Western Cartridge Company, and an associate editor's position with *Field & Stream* magazine.

Meanwhile, Buckingham sold his first outdoor magazine story to *Recreation* in 1909, and soon his pieces were appearing regularly in *Field & Stream*, *National Sportsman*, *Outdoor Life* and other major sporting periodicals. His single, most famous effort, however, was "De Shootinest

Gent'man," a story about Captain Harold Money. It first appeared in *Recreation* in 1916 and subsequently in various editions of the book for which it served as the title piece. The tale gave Buckingham a national reputation and made him realize in time just how much the sporting life meant to him. Accordingly, he lived that life precisely as he wished, something precious few of us can claim. He moved in the best sporting circles, saw and judged the finest bird dogs in the country, enjoyed countless hours afield, and lived for more than 90 years until his death on March 10, 1971.

Both the man and the books he left behind reflected a deeper, more meaningful approach to sport and life itself. John Madson once told me of the indelible impression Buckingham created from the moment they were first introduced, an imprint that went straight to the heart of what made Nash's prose so powerful. "He was a writer who had read a great many very good things," Madson explained, "and who listened to a great many good

Nash Buckingham (left) and Colonel Harold Sheldon, chief conservation officer, on a Tennessee quail hunt in 1928.

Buckingham, who loved good food and wrote about it frequently, prepares a field lunch.

and thoughtful conversations. It was all reflected in a certain kind of grace, a courtliness of style that is somehow lost to us in this age of careless and hasty writing."

EXCERPTS FROM THE MASTER

Whether it was working trained gun dogs, simple conversation with good friends, or the endless flow of correspondence that poured forth from his battered typewriter, Buckingham never seemed hurried. This same quality is mirrored in his writing. It is as though the reader could accompany him as a hunting companion along overgrown fence rows, amidst brooms-edge, or as an awe-struck witness to a covey rise. Join him as a youth partnering an old hunter in his twilight years, a man whom Nash revered:

With a dynamic buzz and swirl, a bevy exploded just beyond Don's pop-eyed stare. I couldn't shoot; I just had to watch Mister Arthur. Up came his weapon—hitched quickly, but steadily. His eyes handled the covey, the gun itself. A husky cock-bird, skimming the briars. For an opening higher up, wilted at the fringe of mock-orange and tumbled into the weed tops. A second fugitive, arching over sassafras tippets, was sent hurtling. A clean, beautiful double. Would that I could see him now—just as he stood there! Boot tops flipped with frost dribble from the sedge. Stained, bottle-green shooting coat sharp against the brilliant sunlight. Hair, mustache, weatherbeaten tan. 'My boy''—

there was an excited quaver in his voice—
"my boy, I'm a very, very lucky old dog;
I have made a sure enough, old-time
double."

With such passages, Buckingham evoked a sporting
world we no longer know. His description of what
he called a "red letter" day evokes all that is grand
about being afield in autumn. When he writes, "I
looked out upon night frost and over a string of
bobwhites hanging high against the moonlight,"
the reader is entranced.

Amidst his rare knack for capturing the ro-
mance of hunting, there remained a streak of
practicality in "Mr. Buck," who felt that the hunt

should always be approached in a frame of mind
"aloof from mere heft of the game bag." As he
once wrote:

Frankly, I do not agree with blurbings
which suggest that starry-eyed straying
through scented countrysides is ample reward for a birdless gunner. If one's mind
is receptive to the beauties of frosted
pumpkins and vivid sunsets beyond pur-
pling ridges, so much the better. . . In a
vast majority of us lurks an urge for action, an ear for trigger music, and a nose
for skillet savor. When those blessings are
decently earned, good luck and amen!

*Buckingham, in his later years,
admires a cock pheasant he shot
at Winchester's Nilo Farms. The
hat he is shown wearing here,
bedecked with medals, was a
familiar trademark of his.*

Today, the best way to sample and savor Nash Buckingham's haunting, harmonious words is through his full-length works. Far from diminishing with the passage of time, his books come through the years as a clarion call from days gone by. It is in the printed word that any writer seeks immortality, and in that regard "Mr. Buck" was quite successful. His first four volumes were published originally by the Derrydale Press in limited editions; today, along with first or special editions of his other works, they are quite rare. His books, in the order of the years in which they were pub-

personal papers have surfaced and provided the raw material for two books. The first is called *"Mr. Buck:" The Autobiography of Nash Buckingham* (1990). In many ways this work is a disappointment, for it fails to present either the man or his abilities in the best possible light. The other book is *"Once Upon a Time,"* a collection of stories Buckingham put together in his final years. Dr. William "Chubby" Andrews, who was probably Buckingham's closest friend in his later years, is also busy at work on the final stages of a book of reminiscences.

Buckingham's second Bert Becker magnum ("Bo Whoop"), which friends gave to him along with a gun case, is shown here with other memorabilia.

lished, are:

> *De Shootinest Gent'man and Other Tales* (1934)
> *Mark Right!* (1936)
> *Ole Miss'* (1937)
> *Blood Lines* (1938)
> *Tattered Coat* (1944)
> *Game Bag* (1945)
> *Hallowed Years* (1953)

All these books represent collections of Nash Buckingham's stories, the vast majority of which first appeared in magazines. More recently, his

HONORS TO AN HONORABLE MAN

In the fullness of time, Buckingham's writings, along with his tireless advocacy of game conservation, earned him national recognition. He played an important role as executive secretary of the American Wildfowlers (now Ducks Unlimited) from 1928 to 1932. And in 1947 *Field & Stream* made him their first recipient of a special award for "Outstanding service to conservation." In 1960, the Outdoor Writers Association of America, of which Buckingham had been a founding member, recognized him with its prestigious "Jade of Chiefs Award" in support of the principles of conservation. The Tennessee Conservation League also heralded his work, and Louis J. Williams rightly styled him, "Dean of Tennessee Conservation."

The most treasured of all his honors came when Mr. Buck's fellow outdoor writers and conservationists honored him in 1962 as the "Outdoorsman of the Year." His acceptance speech on that occasion was vintage Buckingham, made all the more impressive because the then octogenarian delivered it without benefit of a single written note. To the assembled audience, which included the likes of Jack O'Connor, Warren Page, Elmer

arts and their honorable traditions. He took us from the rockbound Pilgrim coast down to the Blue Ridge and beyond, through the Cumberland Gap and past the 'Dark and Bloody Ground' into the fathomless grasslands that reached to the lofty Sierra Nevada and down into a golden land that ended in a vast and pacific sea. Through all this great westering odyssey, men were brothers-in-arms, and brothers *to* their arms, and still are.

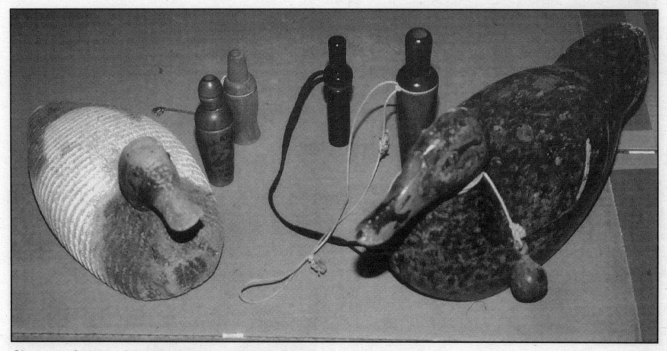

Close-up of some of Buckingham's collection of bird calls and duck decoys.

Keith and Jim Carmichel, all great names in the outdoor writing field, he traced the history of America through the "marching song of powder, lead, and steel," reminding those present that they should "be proud of the company we have kept."

John Madson described Buckingham's speech as follows:

> He spoke of the gunmakers [the 'armorers,' he called them] and their role in the establishment of our republican government, our defense of freedom, the settlement of wilderness, and the preservation of rural

In his speech, Buckingham also looked toward the future of sport, calling to mind his young great-grandson by urging all to support "the dawn of a better understanding" in conservation and in sport. Whether we have truly seen that dawn may be questionable, but there is no doubt that through his literary genius Mr. Buck placed us squarely in touch with the pulse of the wild world and those who are privileged enough to walk through it as hunters.

Nash Buckingham told tales of real people, making them both credible and likable. And through him, we are able to journey through time

Nash Buckingham at 85—the Tennessean who was a kind of ''Renaissance man of sport.''

Nash Buckingham studies a copy of Louis J. Williams' book Tennessee's Conservation Revolution, *in which the author extols Buckingham as ''the dean of Tennessee conservation.'' He received many other honors as well, including the most treasured of all from his fellow outdoor writers—''Outdoorsman of the Year'' for 1962.*

"Nash Buckingham, noted author and conservationist, was honored recently by a trapshooter who has admired his writings and accomplishments for years. Lyman McLallen III (standing right) presented Buckingham (seated center) with a complete set of duck stamps issued by the government since 1934. McLallen's son, Lyman IV (standing), and his wife Ruth (seated right) also attended the presentation at the Memphis (Tenn.) Gun Club. Mrs. Irma Buckingham, wife of the recipient, is seated on the left."—From the cover of *Trap & Field, February 1963.*

Dr. William ''Chubby'' Andrews displays a treasured photo of Buckingham taken during a duck hunt.

to endless days dominated by sporting ways. Such a journey alongside this great man is one every sportsman and lover of great sporting literature is bound to enjoy—and savor.

JIM CASADA, a frequent contributor to SHOOTER'S BIBLE, teaches history at Winthrop University (Rock Hill, SC) and writes for several outdoor publications on a wide variety of subjects. He is currently senior editor for *Sporting Classics,* field editor for *Sporting Clays,* and coeditor of *Turkey & Turkey Hunting.* He also writes three weekly newspaper columns and recently edited a trilogy of books featuring the collected hunting tales of Archibald Rutledge. Jim is now at work on a book about the great African hunter, Fred Selous.

What's New To Shoot For In '93.

This year, there's a whole lot of good news from Remington.
Our all-new Peerless™ over-and-under shotgun. The new Model 522™ Viper,™
"the first 22 from the 21st Century." Absolutely Wetproof™ Nitro-Steel™
and Express-Steel™ shotshells. Golden Saber,™ the high-tech standard
in handgun ammunition. And the Premier® Copper Solid™ sabot,
the new benchmark for accuracy in rifled slugs.
See everything you've been shooting for, at your Remington retailer.

IT'S WHAT YOU'RE SHOOTING FOR.

STOEGER IGA
SHOTGUNS

RUGGED. RELIABLE. PERFORMANCE AT AN AFFORDABLE PRICE!

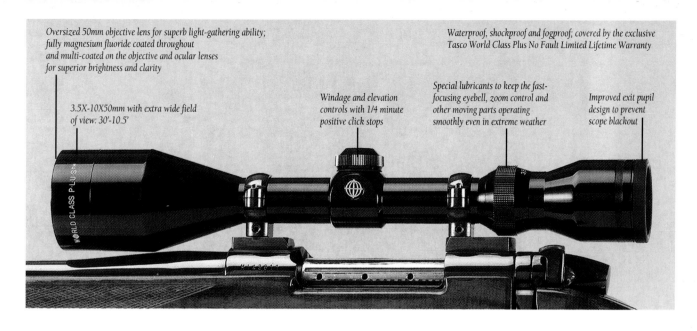

Oversized 50mm objective lens for superb light-gathering ability; fully magnesium fluoride coated throughout and multi-coated on the objective and ocular lenses for superior brightness and clarity

3.5X-10X50mm with extra wide field of view: 30'-10.5'

Windage and elevation controls with 1/4 minute positive click stops

Special lubricants to keep the fast-focusing eyebell, zoom control and other moving parts operating smoothly even in extreme weather

Waterproof, shockproof and fogproof; covered by the exclusive Tasco World Class Plus No Fault Limited Lifetime Warranty

Improved exit pupil design to prevent scope blackout

"SATISFACTION GUARANTEED"

"If our Tasco World Class Plus™ riflescopes don't meet your expectations for quality, performance and value, we'll give you your money back."

I founded Tasco in 1951 and we've been designing, refining and improving binoculars and scopes year after year ever since. Now I'd like you to share my pride and a little of the excitement that I've experienced in the creation of our Tasco World Class Plus™ line.

Building on the proven record of performance and customer satisfaction enjoyed by our World Class™ line, our research and development department set out to take that quality to a new level of excellence and they succeeded. The result is Tasco World Class *PLUS*, a line with a *Performance Level Uniquely Superior*. But don't take my word for it. Experience Tasco World Class Plus™ first hand. And I'll help you do just that with the following personal offer from me to you.

Buy any Tasco World Class Plus™ riflescope. If you don't like it, return it with your receipt from your local authorized Tasco World Class Plus™ dealer for a full refund. Yes, you read it right. I'll give you your money back if you buy a Tasco World Class Plus™ riflescope and don't agree with my enthusiasm for this exceptional line of optics. It's that simple.

See your authorized Tasco World Class Plus™ dealer today and look into Tasco World Class Plus.™ Discover a line that demonstrates edge-to-edge sharpness, complete clarity and unusual brightness. Add to this the Tasco World Class Plus™ No Fault Warranty which guarantees that should the product be damaged and fail to operate, it will be repaired or replaced free of charge (except for a nominal handling charge)...and you'll be sold. On Tasco World Class Plus.™ A uniquely superior product. You've got my word on that...and the guarantee of complete satisfaction or your money back.

George G. Rosenfield

Founder and President

tasco®

P.S. For more information on purchasing Tasco World Class Plus™ products and how to get in on this offer, contact your sporting goods dealer or write/call Tasco, Dept. 000, P.O. Box 520080, Miami, FL 33152/(305) 591-3670, ext. 315.

©1993 Tasco Sales, Inc.

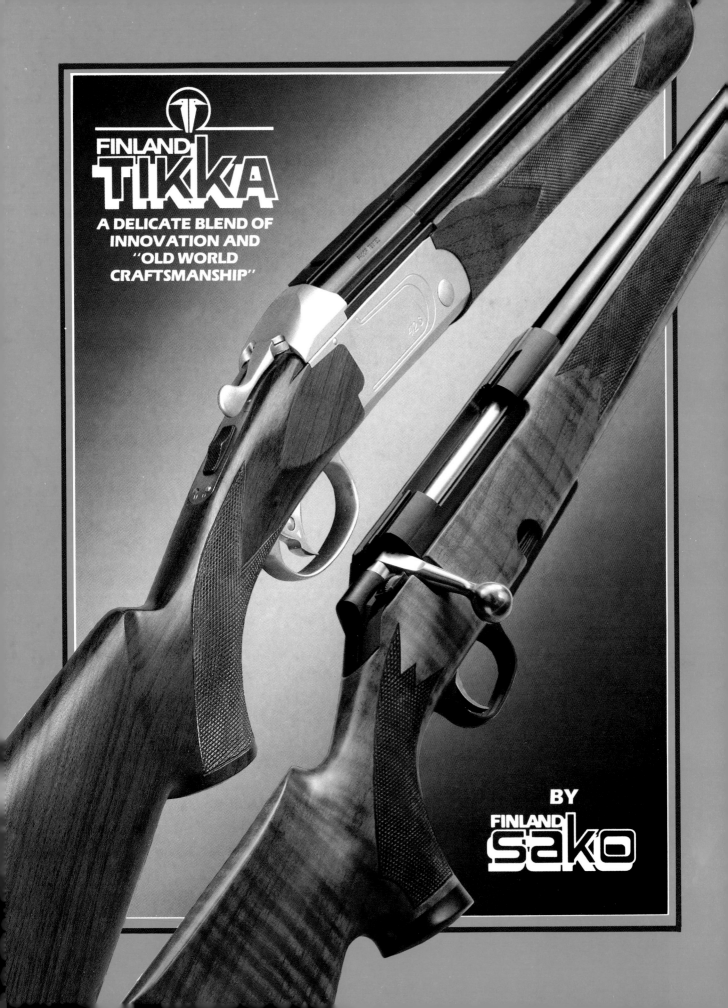

HANDLING THE BIG BORES: JUST DO IT!

by Don L. Henry

There is no mathematical formula to tell us what recoil feels like. Mathematics is a kind of virtual reality that, according to the dictionary, is not real at all. It is a mythical system with an imprecise relation to actual experience; by its inherent nature, it distorts reality. If one unit of anything—say, an apple—were like all others, it would not matter which one you picked.

Gun writers and shooters have fallen victim to the cult of scientism which decrees that all comparisons must be numerical. But human shoulders are not fitted with digital readouts. If truth be desired, you will have to do your own shooting. If you are not overweight, and if you do not beat yourself against the butt by flinching forward in anticipation, and if you do not give it a running start by flinching backward—which is like outrunning a bear in the alders—you'll survive to smile again sooner than you may think.

Bob Hagel, in his book *Guns, Loads and Hunting Tips* (1986), says the following:

Some gun buffs seem inclined to make too much fuss over recoil and believe that no one can handle it effectively, whereas others think that if you are not hairy-chested enough to handle it you have no business hunting. . . I have seen plenty of fellows who took one look at big cartridges and started mentally flinching before they picked up the rifle.

Handling recoil may be a psychological problem made worse by mathematics; but for those with a desire to shoot big bores, it is mostly no problem at all. Big cartridges (and gun writers with an axe to grind) have incited fear all out of proportion to any pain inflicted. It took several rounds for the author to master the trigger, quit flinching, and then hit a generously-sized paper with my first .375 H&H. Before the afternoon ended, 30 rounds had been fired from a rest and groups had shrunk to 2¼ inches. That a .375 could be so painless to shoot ran contrary to everything I had read since I was a youngster.

The Lyman Reloading Handbook (43d edition) states that the .375 generates 44 foot-pounds of recoil from a nine-pound rifle, whereas the .30-06 kicks 20 pounds from an eight-pound piece. A .270 weighing around eight pounds stabs far worse than the 9.3×74R (.366 caliber), the 10.3×60R Swiss (.406 caliber), or the .375. Ten rounds from the .270 at the bench are plenty.

In *African Rifles and Cartridges* (1946), John Taylor attests to this as follows: "Personally, I have always been punished more seriously by the vicious jab of some medium and small bores than I ever have by large bores. . . I sometimes wonder

Unfazed by the critics, Jeanne Henry (the author's wife) takes aim. This petite lady, who loves shooting big bores, scoffs at those who claim big-bore recoil hurts. "And I bruise easily," she says.

While there is no denying the .375s recoil energy works out to approximately twice that of a typical .30-06 with 180-grain bullet loads, some mitigating circumstances generally tend to narrow the margin of difference. . . Recoil velocity—the speed at which the rifle kicks back—is lower with the .375 than with the big .300s and the new 8mm Magnum, giving the shooter a chance to roll with the punch. I for one attach more importance to recoil velocity than to recoil energy alone.

"Recoil," writes John Taylor, "is a direct con-

just how much of this recoil nuisance is fact and how much is due to an overactive imagination."

When the first .375 shot failed to punch paper because of excessive flinch, I mistook the mild report and low recoil for a dud round. This obviously was not the case when a 300-grain Silvertip nicked the target, causing so much damage to the target frame that it had to be completely rebuilt. In general, I would liken the difference in recoil between the .375 and the .270 to being bumped by a 440-pound man as opposed to being punched by a 170-pound athlete.

In his book *Pet Loads* (1980), Ken Waters makes this comforting analysis:

I personally think the recoil. . . of this cartridge has frequently been exaggerated.

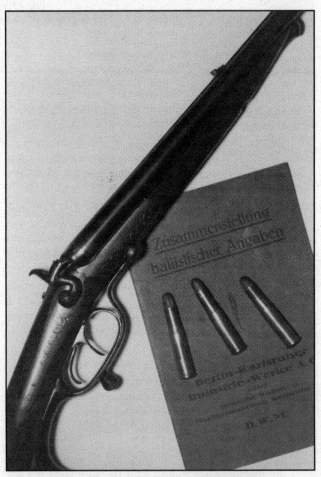

This under-lever double rifle by Miller and Val. Greiss (Munich, Germany) is over 100 years old. It is chambered for the 10.3×60R Swiss cartridge—a powerful round that can push a 300-grain bullet ahead of 95 grains of black powder. Jeanne Henry calls this firearm her "Little Big Bore."

Big game in the big timber is a great place for a big-bore rifle like this one. Recoil is no more noticeable when shooting big game than it is when shooting at targets with a .22.

sequence of the Law of Motion: the force that drives the expanding powder grains and projectile out of the muzzle is employed equally in driving the rifle against your shoulder.''

Perhaps that's why the high-intensity small bores with so much clout downrange also smack the shooter. I once fired 100 rounds of .243 from a Winchester Model 70 that weighed slightly over nine pounds. The load of 46 grains of 4831 zipped the 75-grain Sierra hollow-points along at about 3300 feet per second. But after 40 rounds of dime-hole accuracy, the groups suddenly opened. A cleaned bore did not help, and the mild report and minuscule poke provided no clue that I had developed a flinch. Only later did I discover the .243 had broken several blood vessels in my shoulder.

MEASURING FELT RECOIL

Nowhere in my collection of arms-related books has any writer explained adequately the measurement of shooter-felt recoil. Nor have several late-night conversations with Ph.D.-types and long-distance calls to expert ballisticians. The closest we came goes something like this: The faster the mass (bullet and powder) is accelerated, the more power (powder) is required. The slightly increased velocity obtained from disproportionate charges of powder in overbore capacity cartridges comes at a price: an increase in recoil. At some point, the recoil velocity is increased disproportionately faster than the recoil energy of the rifle mass. Like putting a 455-horsepower engine in an old roadster, it would really pop your neck—that is, until the whole thing came unglued.

In short, the foot-pounds theory fails to address the discrepancy between the sharp recoil of a high-velocity small-bore and the felt push of the larger and more powerful—but slower—calibers. Powder-burning characteristics alter recoil significantly when other variables are identical. Elmer Keith tested his .333 O.K.H. extensively with 60 grains of 4350 and Winchester '06 cases with every available 250- to 300-grain bullet. "With a duplex load," he wrote in *Hell, I Was There* (1979), "in-

This 9.3 rifle is fitted with a Leupold variable in quick-attachable claw mounts hand-filed to fit the original bases. The scope takes advantage of the cartridge's flat trajectory.

The difference in recoil between the .375 and .270 is like being bumped by a 440-pound man compared to a quick but healthy punch thrown by a 170-pound athlete.

stead of a sharp crack it was more of a 'ker-whooom' sound, and the recoil was different too. It was not as sharp."

All things being equal, the longer the pressure curve, the slower the distribution of recoil energy; or, the more gradually a bullet is accelerated from breech to muzzle, the longer the lapsed time for recoil absorption. This explains how recoil pads and in-stock recoil reducing devices work. They distribute shock time, thereby reducing felt recoil.

A variation on this theme illustrates why no reliable formula is possible: the British gunmaker uses a faster powder to cure the recoil headache. Although this may sound like "hair of the dog," it works, partly because the weight of the powder charge, which contributes to recoil, is reduced. High velocity means sharp kick. Even though the foot-pounds of recoil may be less, the speed with which the recoil is delivered to the shooter more than makes up the difference. Velocity increases only mathematically when the powder charge (or the energy it contains) increases geometrically. Recoil intensity then increases logarithmically— in principle, but not according to any precise formula.

Recoil intensity is not the product of some mathematical equation that computes velocity and mass (bullet + powder weight) as it reacts on the mass of the rifle and shooter. By the same token, the "foot-pounds of energy" equation does little more than approximate relative kinetic energy. Recoil calculators have long confused shooters. The point is, current numerical formulae cannot tell what a shooter will feel. Until such a formula is devised, one that is current for a vast range of variables and for a wide range of calibers and car-

With foot-pounds of recoil energy almost half her body weight, as some theorists claim, Jeanne Henry should fall down or at least be forced to take a step back. This photo, taken at full recoil, shows why she was quickly on target for the second shot as well.

The 10.3×60R Swiss double express rifle (left) was designed for shooting boar and stag. The 9.3×74R Nitro rifle on the right was popular with affluent German sportsmen and African settlers. Comparable in power to the .375 H&H, the 9.3×74R makes a good hole in both sides of a bull elk, even with a soft-point. Both rifles have push-forward set triggers for precision shooting, a feature that would be negated if the shooter were to flinch.

tridges, a lot of time can be saved by just taking the rifle to the range and shooting it.

After firing the first ten rounds of .375 in an eight-pound rifle, I sensed that I had been lied to. Now after many more shots, I am sure of it. I was lied to first by certain shooting authorities, one of whom owned a .375 and had been to Africa, affirming my illusion that this was truly a macho character. Considering the man's bulk—he weighed over 300 pounds—I can understand why he whined so when he shot it.

O'CONNOR VS. KEITH: LEGENDARY HUNTERS WITH OPPOSING VIEWS

Jack O'Connor and Elmer Keith did not enjoy each other's company, partly because O'Connor preferred to hunt the open country with his flat-shooting .270, while Keith found his game in the timber where heavier bullets performed best. The articles and books they wrote are evidence of a tacit agreement to hunt opposite sides of the hill and kick out targets for their respective type-writers. Every columnist needs a foil; it's also better to argue ballistics in print, where it pays.

O'Connor never lied about the .270, which is still my favorite caliber. Perhaps he loved it to excess, but one cannot expect a man to whip a pup that delivers game and fame to hand. He once admitted that he had no quarrel with hyperbole—so long as he was not expected to swallow it. He also pronounced the .375 the world's most versatile hunting cartridge, capable of shooting as flat as a .30-06 to 300 yards, even though, in his words, "recoil is a bit severe." He never said in print that the .375 felt as though it had less recoil than a .270—which, from the author's experience, is true (if not a mathematical fact).

Back in the 1960s, a few magnums were built with a thumbhole stock based on a prototype of mine, which I naturally calculated was essential to taming big-bore recoil. It worked well, was not altogether ugly, and now reposes in my gun rack. Elmer Keith's unprinted comments about the piece left no doubt that he wanted nothing to do with my thumbhole stock. It was too slow in the black timber, and besides, he claimed, his magnums did not kick. He even sent me a "Keith Pattern" profile

During his younger days, the author (shown here with his .270 rifle) was more afraid of recoil than he was of bears in the alder. Once enlightened, he was glad to replace the .270 with a more effective and shooter-friendly big bore.

One look at the .374 H&H cartridge can induce a serious flinch in those who have never tried it. Shooter-felt recoil with big-bore cartridges has been grossly exaggerated.

style and attitude. Yes, attitude is important. Many shooters hurt themselves from sheer fright alone.

A .375 may recoil between two and three times as much as a .270, depending on whose typewriter it is fired from, but the bottom line is this: It just does not hurt as much, because big bores do not kick as fast. As John Taylor advises: "There is the answer to the recoil bug-bear—forget about it. Given a well-balanced weapon that fits you, just concentrate on putting your bullets where you want them and leave your rifle to take care of its own recoil."

My 101-pound wife, Jeanne, favors a handy little 7½-pound Miller and Greiss 10.3×60R Swiss double express rifle with a steel trap buttplate. It can push a 300-grain bullet ahead of 95 grains of powder through a railroad tie. How much farther we have not yet discovered. Jeanne now prefers a J.P. Sauer 9.3×74R double rifle—Germany's answer to the .375 H&H flanged cartridge. With scope, sling and two cartridges, it weighs in at 8½ pounds. This rifle fires a 270-grain bullet at 2878 fps and recently made a good hole in both sides of a mule deer buck and a bull elk.

So, to those who have wished to shoot a big-bore rifle but were afraid, my best advice is this: Just do it!

for his promotional rifle. Elmer had been trying to tell the world all along that magnums do not hurt, but his advice was mistaken as boasting.

I have watched a disproportionate number of smallish hunters shoot big bores. One paraplegic shoots heavy magnums with his wheelchair brakes unlocked and grins with the spin. Felt recoil is increased by resistance. Ignore recoil computation—the results are misleading at best. No formula can calculate all essential objective factors, much less such subjective variables as the shooter's weight,

DON L. HENRY has served as a guide and outfitter for more than 35 years and is currently Executive Secretary of the Mannlicher Collectors Association, for which he edits *The Mannlicher Collector,* their quarterly journal. He is also a member of the Board of Directors of the National Rifle Association. Don is a frequent contributor to various outdoor publications, including the *1994 Handloader's Digest, American Rifleman, Rifle* and the *Australian Shooters Journal.* He holds a Master's degree in Clinical Psychology with equivalency in English Psycholinguistics. This is his first appearance in SHOOTER'S BIBLE.

RIFLES AND THE YOUNG SHOOTER

by Wilf E. Pyle

The rifle is more than simply a tool used for hunting or recreational target practice, and it is more than a defensive weapon that spits lead and makes loud, jarring noises. From its blue-steeled barrel to its walnut stock, the modern rifle is the embodiment of the fierce individualism that has characterized our nation's history. In our forefathers' stubborn battle against the elements, the rifle became the primary instrument with which they tamed a harsh environment and gained some measure of prosperity. Unlike the elegant shotgun, the timeless blackpowder gun, or the hapless handgun, the rifle has become part of our heritage and our system of values—the same values we all want to pass on to our children.

As a boy, I recall with fondness those many Sunday afternoons when my father drove me and my brother to a nearby gravel pit, set up a few tin cans, and taught us how to shoot. Included in our treasure chest of firearms were a Canadian-made Cooey .22 single-shot, a Stevens 12-gauge bolt shotgun, a Model '94 Winchester .30-30, and a marvelously accurate Eddystone P14 .303 British. These informal target sessions were followed by leisurely hunts that had us casting about for unwary Richardson's ground squirrels and other small game. It was all very recreational and done in a pastoral setting not available to many youths of today.

THE THREE STAGES OF A YOUNG SHOOTER'S EDUCATION

The best way to get a youngster started is probably through membership in a good shooting and hunting club. It is also a good way for adults to ease their concerns about safety and responsible firearms handling. Memberships in shooting-oriented organizations, such as the American Rifle Association, are also recommended along with books and magazines on shooting and hunting subjects.

Each youth must pass through three distinct stages—beginning, intermediate and advanced—on the path to gaining firearm competence and experience. Each stage includes a type of firearm that best suits the immediate needs, interests and capability level of the youth. The actual chronological age is relatively unimportant, but interest and experience levels must change and grow at each passage. Some young shooters will remain at a particular level for an extended period, perhaps years, while others will move through two or three stages in one season of intense activity.

The beginning stage is characterized by much questioning and requests by the novices to experiment with firearms. It is critical here to communicate the basics of safety and respect for the power that any firearm is capable of delivering. Once the trigger is pulled, there's no turning back.

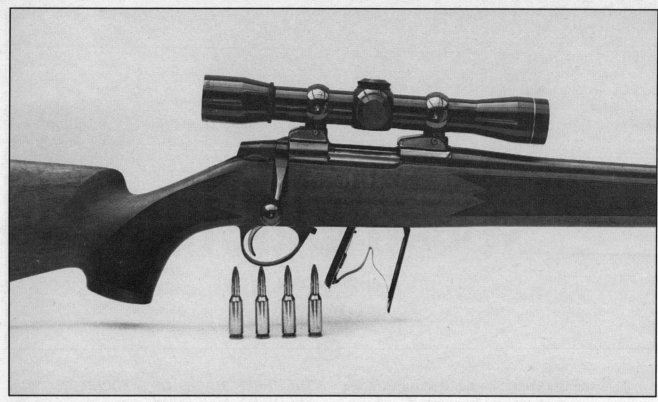

The 6mm PPC in the Sako Hunter is an excellent training cartridge in a lightweight, youth-sized rifle.

The BB rifle remains an excellent training rifle for kids who are just beginning to learn the basics.

In the intermediate stage, each youth develops actual skills and familiarity with firearms. Now is the time when a boy or girl might ask if he/she can try a few shots with Dad's .300 Winchester Magnum.

In the final advanced stage, the young shooter must be prepared to handle most firearms. He must also understand the rigorous concerns about safety as expressed by his instructors and parents. Only then can he begin some shooting activities on his own. These include small-game hunting trips, visits to an outdoor range, or the start of competition with whatever firearm suits his fancy.

to the family farm, we were ready to take on any kind of field shooting available.

Safety training is also best accomplished with a pellet or BB rifle. Developing good field habits, such as controlling where the muzzle points at all times, is best handled with a pellet gun. The same can be said for ensuring adequate backstops for each shot, loading and unloading, and developing the ability to discern legal targets from their surroundings. With a pellet gun, young shooters can also learn how a rifle should feel and fit. In fact, modern rifles provide sight training and many other features comparable to sporting rifles.

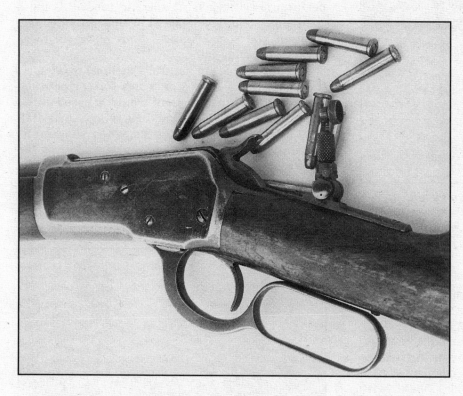

Old cartridges like these .32-20s in a Model 52 Winchester make excellent small-game cartridges and are perfect for training youths.

Most beginners are urged to confine their early experimentation and learning to the use of BB rifle and pellet guns. No better piece of advice was ever given, especially at a time when most gun owners live in urban areas, with no opportunities to sit on a back step in open country and shoot a few rounds at empty tin cans. My brother and I began by shooting a Sheridan Silver Streak 5mm or .20-caliber air rifle in the basement of our house. We also had a Daisy Model 1000 BB rifle that taught us a lot about firearms. That gun held 1,000 tiny BBs, giving new meaning to the term "muzzle heavy." When it came time for our weekend trip

CHOOSING A FIREARM

When it comes to selecting firearms for kids, several excellent choices present themselves. IGA, for example, now offers a Youth Model shotgun with a 22-inch barrel in 20 gauge and .410 bore. Winchester makes a Model 70 bolt-action rifle—the Ranger—with a scaled-down stock for youths and ladies. Since 1990, Precision Sports has been importing an Anschutz Model 1449D bolt-action rifle in .22 rimfire. Lightweight rifles have grown in popularity in recent years and are now recommended for youths and women, including the Sako Hunter and Remington's Model 7 bolt-action.

Lightweight rifles are the current favorite among young shooters. Cartridges that produce low recoil and low muzzle blast should be used with these rifles.

For intermediate shooters, the .22 rimfire is often recommended because of its low report and mild kick. For advanced young hunters, Winchester's venerable Model 94 lever rifle in .30-30 remains a good choice for any boy or girl who is ready for that first deer hunt—accompanied by a knowledgeable adult, of course. The .30-30, with a 170-grain bullet and a muzzle velocity of 2200 fps, still has 989 foot-pounds of striking energy at 200 yards. That is enough to take any white-tailed deer cleanly and humanely under most hunting conditions.

The lever rifle is also compact, lightweight, easy to get onto a moving target, while providing ample opportunity for quick second shots. Today's choices in lever rifles for less experienced, smaller-sized shooters cover the entire shooting spectrum, for small to big game. Marlin's Model 1894 Classic weighs only 6¼ pounds and is available in two excellent cartridges—the .25-20 and .32-20.

When choosing firearms for the young shooter,

do not forget those old reliable guns. Many families have firearms that were passed down from previous generations and are frequently attached emotionally to one's family history. These guns can be very useful for beginners, carrying with them the added excitement of being family heirlooms.

BECOMING A "GOOD SHOT"

In the past, people who lived in rural areas learned to shoot out of simple necessity—protecting their resources—while learning important facts about cartridge economy. This process—sometimes called the "tool approach" to shooting—treats the rifle as a specialized tool used to perform specific jobs at specific times. "Being a good shot" is a developed skill that provides recognition and social status—both powerful motivators for young minds.

Young people are naturally inclined to organize themselves into groups or teams for competition, using firearms just as they would a baseball bat or hockey stick. Always anxious to test their abilities, they are especially keen when shooting is encouraged in a positive environment. Setting the proper stage for such controlled challenges is the responsibility of the adults. This applies to both target shooting and hunting. Later on, as adults,

Young shooters should always be outfitted with hearing protection when plinking and target shooting.

Do not let old guns like this one prevent a youngster from shooting. Many such heirlooms make good, serviceable firearms during the learning period.

these same competitors may strive to become world-class target shooters or perhaps globe-trotting big-game hunters.

For intermediate shooters who are largely unfamiliar with firearms, and for more advanced shooters who want to develop competitive shooting to its highest possible degree, the .22-rimfire rifle remains the No. 1 choice. It offers all the basics needed to become an above-average shot in a short period. Moreover, this traditional cartridge is of mild report, provides good short-range accuracy, offers no recoil, and leaves no muzzle blast. It is about the closest thing we have to the perfect training round.

One of the best training rifles ever produced in the United States was Mossberg's Model 340B. It featured a walnut pistol grip on a sporting-style Monte Carlo stock and one of the nicest cheek-pieces ever put on an American-made rifle. The rifling on this model, which was of the eight-groove variety, contributed to its excellent accuracy. The crowning feature was a Mossberg-made

S331 receiver sight with ¼-minute adjustments for windage and elevation, and an S320 hooded ramp front sight with interchangeable post and peep.

Because of declining interest in indoor sport-target shooting, brought about by a growing emphasis on Olympic-style shooting, Mossberg's rifle disappeared form the marketplace around 1983. This shift in shooting preference did sport shooting no good and contributed to a decline in skill levels that remains today. Olympic-style shooting is an elitist game limited to those with very specific range designs, not to mention expensive and uncommon rifles available only to those with access to special coaching.

Today, the Lakefield Model 90B approaches the kind of .22 rifle considered adequate for training on the range. Safe, reliable and accurate, this rifle conforms to the requirements of most indoor ranges. Outfitted with excellent iron sights, Lakefield's model boasts a full-sized stock that nearly compares with the Olympic-style rifles; as such, it prepares young shooters for the weight and heft of a full-sized Olympic competitive rifle.

Training with an iron sight, by the way, is still strongly recommended, because it allows the shooter to concentrate on other skills, such as correct breath and trigger control, relaxed sighting, and sight picture development. Any young shooter who masters these basics and then moves to the scope will discover new rewards in shooting. Naturally, many young shooters wonder how much better it would be if they had a full-fledged scope sitting atop their rifles. Scope sighting is best left, however, until after training with the iron sight. Modern scopes are above reproach as aids for shooting, but young shooters require practice if they are to establish the target quickly, align the eye with the objective lens, position the head properly along the comb, and then confirm the target. That is why the use of iron sights is highly encouraged for beginning and intermediate shooters.

For those who have real difficulty lining up iron sights with a target and find a scope much easier to use, Aimpoint offers a 2-power electronic red dot sight. It has a fixed low power, so that one simply needs to place the red dot on the target. The device looks like a regular scope and mounts any Weaver-type base. Although more popular with high-power pistol shooters, it is an excellent training aid and fits any rifle capable of taking a standard scope.

Lever-action rifles are the top choice for youngsters who are prepared to take on limited big-game hunting (when accompanied by an adult, of course).

Brendan Pyle is old enough now to take on some hunting trips. His Winchester Model 94 in .30-30 is an excellent lightweight choice for a youthful shooter about to go after his first deer.

CHOOSING THE RIGHT CARTRIDGE

Cartridge selection is a critical element in successful youth training and directly influences rifle selection. For some years, rimfire cartridges were recognized as the single best training cartridges available today as they were at the turn of the century. But modern centerfire cartridges are also excellent for training, provided they are selected with three factors in mind: (1) the report created, which is considered a significant factor in teaching the techniques of shooting (low-powered cartridges generally produce less noise in an average sporter than do high-velocity kinds); (2) the amount of re-

coil generated (a .30-caliber magnum is obviously not recommended as a youth-training cartridge); and (3) the availability of a particular cartridge for a specific rifle, which may not always be possible.

For some years, the .243 Winchester was considered an excellent youth or lady's cartridge. It is still a wise choice as an intermediate training round and offers mid-range power with mild recoil. Hunting applications come to mind, but the .243 is also a good Sunday afternoon plinker and has a reputation as a reasonable small-bore competitor. Experienced youths who select a 6¼-pound Remington Model 7 or a 7-pound Winchester Model 70 are definitely on the right track.

While the 6mm PPC has never been characterized as a youth cartridge, but mainly as a competitive round for the International Bench Rest crowd, it performs well as a small-game and plinking number. Its accuracy, low recoil and light muzzle blast make it an ideal training cartridge for youths in the intermediate to advanced level of shooting skills. Rifle selection is not as broad as it could be, but the Sako Hunter in 6mm PPC produces fine accuracy for the average trainee.

Another cartridge popular with young shooters is the .257 Roberts. Combined with a Ruger Model 77RL Ultra Light, it provides any youth going after deer and antelope with an advantage. Ruger's rifle weighs only six pounds (seven pounds with a scope) and is ideal for any youth interested in hunting. But perhaps the greatest boons of all to youth shooting since the invention of the .22 rimfire are the .222 and .223 centerfire cartridges, which feature low report, no recoil and high ac-

curacy. Even a physically small child can handle these rounds with some basic training. In fact, all ages and skill levels can handle these centerfires well while developing good plinking skills in the process. The number and styles of rifles that feature the .223 are greater now than ever before; indeed, every major United States and foreign rifle manufacturer offers at least one .223 rifle in its line.

THE CRITICAL ELEMENTS OF SAFETY

The bottom line in dealing with kids and guns is, of course, safety. Experience gained from many lectures and shooting sessions is necessary to get the right information out to young shooters and build the kind of understanding needed to ensure their safe handling of all firearms. Adults should also encourage the use of hearing protection devices and shooting glasses. The average rifle produces 40 decibels of sound and damage to the human ear can occur with as little as 24 decibels.

Here are some of the safety points every

The author poses with his three sons as evidence that "the family that shoots together, stays together."

youngster should learn:

1. How to handle a supposedly empty rifle
2. How to proceed when cleaning a rifle
3. How to load and unload various rifle actions safely
4. How to carry a rifle properly
5. How to know when it is safe to shoot in a given area
6. How to judge distances from 10 to 300 yards within a 20 percent margin of error

Above all else, parents are an essential element in the shooting equation. They are the primary educators, and they must choose the right firearms for their children based on personal knowledge and their own sense of responsibility. With the decline in numbers of adults who are interested in the shooting sports, proper adult supervision becomes ever more critical. Only then can we produce responsible hunters and top-notch outdoorsmen and women of the future.

WILF PYLE is an avid sportsman who has hunted nearly all game species with a broad variety of firearms. A well-known authority on sporting firearms and reloading, he shoots often and actively with his three sons, whose shooting abilities and outdoor skills improve daily. Pyle's recent books include *Small Game and Varmint Hunting* and *Hunting Predators for Hides and Profit,* both Stoeger publications. He has also co-authored *The Hunter's Book of the Pronghorn Antelope* (New Century) and regularly writes ''The Hunting Handbook'' column for *Outdoor Edge* magazine.

HANDLOADING FOR RIFLES

by Sam Fadala

In effect, handloading predates the cartridge. Every load fired from a muzzleloader was put together "by hand." The tradition never died.

The practice of handloading cartridges is only slightly younger than the cartridge itself. Rifle companies such as Winchester sold handloading tools to match their rifles, so that a sportsman could reload the expensive brass case. Reloading components—bullets, powder, empty brass cases, primers—were available from the start for the rifleman who wanted to put together his own ammo.

In blackpowder days, reloading was a simpler matter because of the nature of the propellant. The handloader didn't need a scale. He simply poured powder into the resized case with a dipper, leaving enough room to seat the bullet. Smokeless powder changed all that. Carefully weighing the smokeless charge became essential due to increased pressure created by the new powder.

WHY RELOAD?

Factory ammo is powerful, accurate, reliable and available. Then why reload? There are at least seven good reasons.

1. *Economy.* Reloading enables a rifleman to enjoy his sport at a considerable savings.

2. *Cartridge versatility.* A wide range of factory ammunition is available, but not nearly as wide as home-rolled fodder. For example, factory loads for the 30-06 Springfield cartridge offer bullet weights from 110 to 220 grains—a wide selection. However, the handloader can prepare 30-06 ammo with lighter or heavier bullets. Moreover, he can create 30-06 loads with greater-than-factory power or far lower power. He can cast his own projectiles, loading them, if he wants, to mere 22 Long Rifle muzzle velocity for plinking, practice, or even small-game hunting.

3. *Pet loads.* The handloader can experiment (using a loading manual only) until he finds the specific combination of bullet, powder type, charge weight, case and primer that his particular rifle shoots best. The handloader can also prepare rounds for rifles that would otherwise serve only as wall-hangers.

4. *The ability to make ammo that is either obsolete or otherwise difficult to buy in factory form.* A good example is the 32-40 Winchester cartridge. Ammunition is not entirely obsolete for this old-timer, but it is difficult to locate. Not long ago, a fine Model 94 Winchester rifle was lying fallow until handloads of mine brought it back to usefulness. A set of RCBS dies; Hornady and Speer 32-caliber, 170-grain bullets; IMR-4064 powder; and standard rifle primers provided the right equipment, fuel and spark for ignition.

But what about 32-40 cartridge cases? No cases were for sale in my area. So I formed some

It all begins with a loading manual, such as this two-volume set by Hornady. All information in the manual must be strictly adhered to for safety as well as for the best results.

from 30-30 brass by running them one time through a resizing die. Now the 32-40 rides again—in style.

5. *Power.* Some factory ammunition is loaded to full potential, but much of it is not. This is not a black mark against ammo companies; they do so because they have no control over the guns in which their products are used. The 30-06, for example, is loaded with a 180-grain bullet to about 2700 fps mv by most factories. A careful handloader who owns a strong bolt-action rifle in perfect condition can boost the punch of the '06 with a 180-grain bullet to over 2800 fps mv.

Sometimes the difference in power between factory ammo and handloads is even more pronounced. For example, some factory 300 H&H Magnum ammunition gains only a little bullet speed over the 30-06, while the handloader can turn the 300 H&H into a true magnum.

6. *Accuracy.* Although factory ammunition is now available in super-accurate loads, it is impossible for the factory to provide "personal" ammo for a given rifle. A pet load allows the shooter to build ammo that works well in his particular rifle. In some instances, increased accuracy for reloads is substantial.

7. *Enjoyment.* It's a hobby in its own right. Thousands of reloading fans in this and other countries would continue to make their own ammunition even if it was more expensive than buying factory loads. Handloading is rewarding because it's relaxing, and it's also a science unto

itself. Without handloading, there would be no wildcat ammunition. The research invested in that field has brought about some of the finest factory rounds we enjoy today.

TOOLING UP

Reloading Manual. The reloading manual is vital to the reloading process. Manuals contain all pertinent details to the load. Perfect agreement between loading manuals is impossible because of variations in the exact firearm or testing device used to gather velocity information. It is wise to own several manuals and study them for loads that may work especially well in a particular rifle.

The Reloading Bench. One of the first considerations when reloading is finding a place to work and a surface on which to work. A reloading bench is ideal. Those who would reload thousands of rounds a year should consider a first-class, heavyduty, permanent bench. The casual reloader can get by with a less rigid surface.

The Press. A reloading press is the basic tool of reloading. It supplies the mechanical force to resize cases and seat bullets. Compact loading tools are an exception, in that no press is required. However, extended reloading, case forming and other operations demanding considerable application of force call for a press. There are many different kinds of presses; check the Reloading Section in the back of this book or manufacturers' catalogs available at sporting goods stores.

Shell Holder. A shell holder that matches the cartridge head size is necessary to stabilize the cartridge case in the press.

Priming Tool. Cases can generally be reprimed on the reloading press. Some hand-held priming

Every detail in the manual should be followed. These two powders, for example, bear the same number, 4831, but not the same name. They do not produce the same results in handloads.

One way to get started in handloading is with a complete outfit like this RCBS Rock Chucker Master Reloading Kit.

tools also do an excellent job.

Dies. A set of dies is necessary to reform the case to near-original dimensions so it will once again fit the chamber of the rifle and allow the bullet to seat at the correct depth. Some die sets offer the ability to crimp the mouth of the case into a bullet cannelure.

Scale. With some basic reloads that use certain powders, it is possible to reload by volume using a dipper. But the serious reloader should have a scale, a precision instrument designed to weigh powder to $1/10$ grain or so (there are 7000 grains in 1 pound). Some scales are electronic, such as the RCBS Model 90, which offers a display window and readout of the powder charge weight.

Powder Measure. A precision powder measure is a time-saving device and can produce remark-

ably accurate loads. Benchrest loads are usually built with the use of a powder measure. Of course a scale is necessary to set the measure, so the powder measure doesn't preclude the need for an accurate scale.

Funnel. Simple as it is, the funnel is vital for introducing the weighed powder charge into the cartridge case. Of course, the powder measure will have a built-in funnel, while loads from a scale are put into the case with a separate funnel.

Case Block. A case block is simply a device used to hold cartridge cases during the reloading process. It prevents powder spillage.

Trimmer. The trimmer is used to reduce the neck length of a cartridge case. Cases that stretch beyond the acceptable limit can produce high pressures, because the mouth of the case can pinch

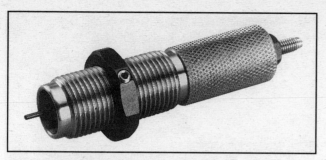

The reloading die set provides case resizing, case forming, decapping and bullet seating operations. A close look at an RCBS Decap Die reveals superb workmanship with extremely precise tolerances.

the bullet in the leade or throat of the chamber, thus retarding the bullet's normal escape from the case. Too much friction at this particular juncture can cause trouble. Trimming maintains cases at a safe length.

Trim Die. Rather than use a trimmer to tailor cases, a special trim die can be inserted in the reloading press and the case run up into that die. Any portion of the case mouth that protrudes beyond the top of the die is removed with a file, then the mouth of the case is deburred and chamfered to make it uniform.

Deburring Tool. This small tool is used to chamfer the mouth of the cartridge case to ease bullet entry and to make the brass in this area of the case uniform in thickness.

Primer Pocket Cleaner. As the name suggests, this tool cleans powder residue from the primer pocket.

Bullet Puller. A bullet puller of some kind is necessary to withdraw a bullet from a loaded round. The puller is useful when the handloader wishes to break down a round for any reason.

Tumbler. The tumbler is used to clean cartridge cases, mostly for cosmetic reasons but also to remove powder fouling from within the case.

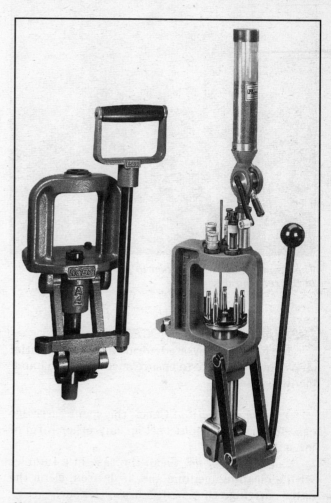

Uncomplicated and extremely powerful, the RCBS press (left) will form cases and handle many reloading operations. A modern sophisticated unit like the Hornady Pro-7 Progressive Press (right) performs several loading operations automatically.

Case Lube. Vital to resizing the fired brass case is a special lube that prevents galling, or sticking of the case in the die. Some dies of carbide material do not require case lube.

Stuck Case Remover. Should a cartridge case become stuck in the die, this device serves to withdraw the stuck case.

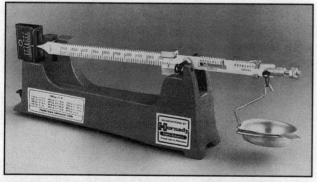

A reloader's bullet/powder scale is essential to creating accurate loads. This is a standard scale with high reliability in the 1/10-grain domain. Electronic scales are also available to today's handloaders.

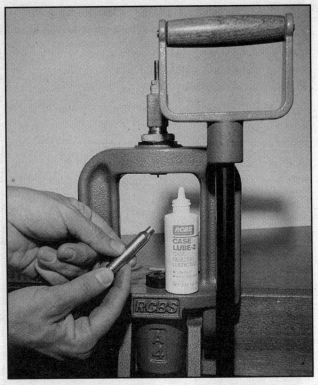

The empty case is first lubed to prevent galling in the resizing die.

The case is resized by running it up all the way into the resize die.

THE HANDLOADING PROCESS

Here, in abbreviated form, are the essential steps you must take to ensure success in the handloading process:

1. *Case inspection.* Check the spent cartridge case for cracks, a split neck or any other form of brass fatigue.

2. *Case cleaning.* Clean the case in a tumbler with a cleaning medium and, if desired, clean the outer cartridge case with a brass cleaner.

3. *Lubrication.* Lube the outside of the case using a case lube pad treated with lubricant; this prevents galling of the case in the resizing die.

4. *Decapping/resizing.* This is done in the press, where the case is returned to near-original dimensions (never perfect) and the spent primer is expelled by a decapping pin.

5. *Trimming.* Do this with a trim die or trimming tool; with the trim die, any portion of the case resting above the top of it is filed away.

6. *Deburring.* This step guarantees a beveled case mouth, which makes bullet seating easier and provides a more uniform case neck.

7. *Cleaning the primer pocket.* Using a primer

pocket tool, fouling is quickly cleared from the primer pocket.

8. *Repriming and charging the case.* Done in the press as part of the resize/decap step, or with a separate priming tool.

9. *Bullet seating.* In the press, the seater die now replaces the resize die; carefully insert a bullet, base down, into the neck of the cartridge case. As you work the ram, the case is pushed up into the seater die while the bullet is guided into the opening of the die.

10. *Setting the bullet seater die.* Seat the bullet deeply enough so that the cartridge will fit the magazine of the rifle; use a factory round to compare lengths.

11. *Choosing the load.* Always consult a good loading manual. Never exceed a recommended maximum load, and never reduce powder charges below the minimum recommended levels for large-capacity cartridges that use slow-burning powder. Preferably, start below the maximum recommended load, because rifle variation plays a role in load compatibility. A rifle of tight chamber and/or bore dimensions, for example, may need lighter loads than a rifle with larger dimensions.

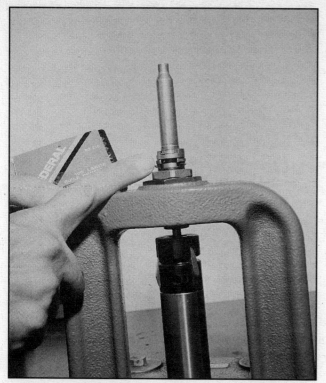

After depriming, the brass case is fitted with a new primer. On this press, the operation is accomplished at the top of the unit.

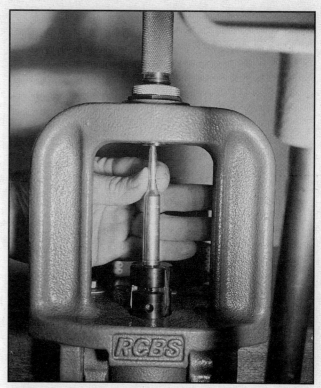

After the correct powder charge has been weighed and introduced to the case, the bullet is seated. The finished product is a professionally reloaded cartridge.

12. *Selecting the primers.* Primers do make a difference, so use one that best fits your load.

13. *Testing with a chronograph.* The only real way to know how a given load performs in a specific rifle is to chronograph that load in that rifle.

14. *Making a dry run.* To ensure proper fit, load the round into the magazine and feed the round into the rifle chamber to see that it feeds properly and fits the chamber.

THE HANDLOADER'S DIARY

Trusting results to memory is foolish and can be dangerous. Every handloader should keep a diary of his range work. Every nuance of reload behavior must be recorded, including accuracy and how the load functioned in the rifle. Then the shooter can go back to his records to find out what loads worked best in a specific rifle. That's how pet loads are born. A recipe box is useful as a shooting diary, each card representing a particular date with weather conditions and range elevation.

Handloading is and always has been an important aspect of rifle shooting. Custom loads expand the range of usefulness of any centerfire rifle, while also providing a savings that translates into

more shooting for the money. Several top companies provide a long list of high-grade reloading equipment, and the components for handmaking ammunition are better than ever, with more useful powders than ever before, precision bullets in hundreds of variations, the finest in brass cartridge cases, more primer types than existed in the past and a huge body of reloading data. There has never been a better time to be a handloader.

SAM FADALA is an experienced and highly regarded author of articles and books on firearms and related subjects. This article is excerpted from his latest book, *Rifle Guide* (1993, Stoeger Publishing Co.). Sam is currently Technical Editor for *Handloader* and *Rifle,* Feature Editor for *Muzzleloader,* and Special Projects Editor for *Guns Magazine.* A frequent contributor to SHOOTER'S BIBLE, he also writes regularly for several national publications, including *Gun World, Outdoor Life, Sports Afield* and *Bow and Arrow Hunter.*

MANUFACTURERS' SHOWCASE

In the following pages, readers will find a rich assortment of products available to shooters of all kinds. These range from guns to reloading equipment, scopes, ammunition and sporting publications. We invite you to browse through this marketplace of sorts and take advantage of the offers you will discover along the way.

SWIFT INSTRUMENTS, INC. SCOPE MODEL 666 SHOTGUN 1X, 20mm

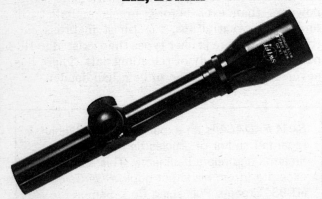

At last, a high-quality shotgun scope with SWIFT's special features of multi-coating, waterproof integrity, and the popular Quadraplex reticle. The Model 666 is lightweight (9.6 oz.), has an eye relief of 3.2, a field of 113 feet at 100 yards, is 7.5 inches long, and is equally good for use on shotguns and bows. Black anodized one-inch tube and shockproof. Gift boxed.

SWIFT INSTRUMENTS, INC.
952 Dorchester Ave., Boston, MA 02025 or
P.O. Box 562, San Jose, CA 95106

NEW "93 MATCH" SIGHT FROM LYMAN

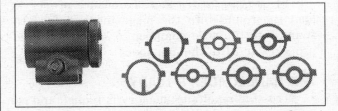

LYMAN, the company that has been making quality gun sights for over 100 years, introduces the new "93 Match." A globe sight with 7/8-inch diameter, the 93 Match adapts to any rifle with a standard dovetail mounting block. The sight comes complete with seven target inserts and accepts most of the popular line of Anschutz accessories. For target shooters who travel with sights disassembled from their rifles, the 93 Match has a hooked locking bolt and nut, allowing quick removal or installation. Bases are available in .860 (European) and .562 (American) hole spacing. Sight height is .550. Suggested retail price: $45.00. For more information, write to:

Ed Schmitt, LYMAN PRODUCTS
Dept. 400/401, Route 147, Middlefield, CT 06455
or call toll free: 1-800-22-LYMAN

NATIONAL HOME GUARD SHOTGUN

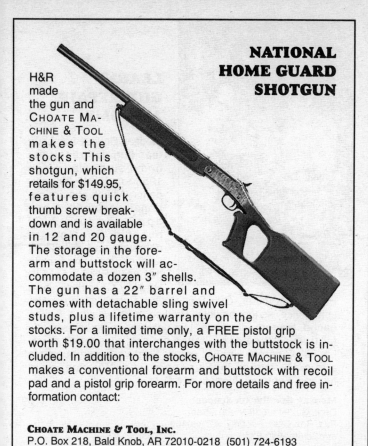

H&R made the gun and CHOATE MACHINE & TOOL makes the stocks. This shotgun, which retails for $149.95, features quick thumb screw breakdown and is available in 12 and 20 gauge. The storage in the forearm and buttstock will accommodate a dozen 3″ shells. The gun has a 22″ barrel and comes with detachable sling swivel studs, plus a lifetime warranty on the stocks. For a limited time only, a FREE pistol grip worth $19.00 that interchanges with the buttstock is included. In addition to the stocks, CHOATE MACHINE & TOOL makes a conventional forearm and buttstock with recoil pad and a pistol grip forearm. For more details and free information contact:

CHOATE MACHINE & TOOL, INC.
P.O. Box 218, Bald Knob, AR 72010-0218 (501) 724-6193

ACTION ARMS' NEW CZ-75 COMPACT 9mm

ACTION ARMS expands its line of famed Czech CZ pistols to include the CZ-75 Compact. At only 32 oz. with features not found on its full-sized counterpart, the new CZ-75 Compact has the advantages of a custom pocket pistol at a factory-made price. The CZ-75 Compact has the same smooth trigger pull and choices of carry modes and finishes as the standard model, but also features a non-glare, ribbed slide top, squared, serrated trigger guard, round combat hammer, firing pin block and walnut grips. Its double-column, 13-round magazine means high capacity. Suggested retail price: under $500. For a full-color catalog of CZ-Brno firearms from Czechoslovakia, send $3.00 to:

ACTION ARMS LTD.
P.O. Box 9573, Philadelphia, PA 19124

MANUFACTURERS' SHOWCASE

TRIUS TRAPS

TRIUS has set the standard for the industry. From "behind the barn" shooters to upstart Sporting/Hunters' Clay ranges, the easy-cocking, lay-on loading make TRIUS Traps easy to operate. Singles, doubles plus piggy-back doubles offer unparalleled variety. **Birdshooter**—quality at a budget price. **Model 92**—a best seller with high-angle clip and can thrower. **Trapmaster**—sit-down comfort plus pivoting action. **SC-92**—permanent heavy-duty trap for all sporting clay targets except battue and rabbit. **BAT2**—same as SC92 plus will throw single/double battue targets. **Rabbitmaster**—designed to throw "rabbit disc" clay targets along the ground. **Squirrelmaster**—a magazine to hold 5 "rabbit disc" clay targets that when released will roll down a ramp and across the ground.

TRIUS PRODUCTS, INC. P.O. Box 25, Cleves, Ohio 45002

HARRIS ENGINEERING, INC. BIPODS

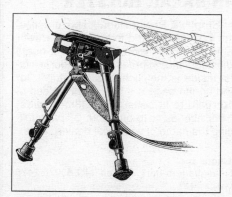

HARRIS bipods clamp securely to most stud-equipped bolt action rifles and are quick-detachable. With adapters, they can fit other guns as well. HARRIS bipods are the result of time-proven design and quality, and are made with heat-treated steel and hard alloys. Folding legs on the bipods have completely adjustable spring-return extensions (except Model LM). The sling swivel attaches to the clamp. Series S Bipods rotate 45 degrees for instant leveling on uneven ground. The hinged base has tension adjustment and buffer springs to eliminate tremor or looseness in the crotch area of the bipod. Otherwise, all Series S models are similar to the non-rotating Series 1A2.

HARRIS ENGINEERING, INC.
Barlow, Kentucky 42024 (502) 334-3633

GLASER/CHEROKEE FEATHERWEIGHT BIPOD

At less than six ounces—half the usual weight—the GLASER/CHEROKEE bipod offers the discriminating shooter the ultimate in strength and sleek beauty. A frontal area 4½ times smaller than other bipods greatly reduces snag hazards. Uneven terrain is automatically compensated for up to 33 degrees. Deployment and retraction require only single and silent one-hand movements that take less than a second. The bipod fits all sporter, varmint and most paramilitary firearms. The basic mount permits front or rear mounting to the forearm, rather than the barrel, for target accuracy. Hidden or quick-detachable, customized mounting accessories are available. For a free brochure contact:

GLASER SAFETY SLUG, INC.
P. O. Box 8223, Foster City, CA 94404

LEARN GUN REPAIR AT HOME

MODERN SCHOOL has been teaching gun repair the home study way since 1956 to over 45,000 students. All courses are nationally accredited and approved for VA/GI benefits. Courses are complete and include all lessons (including how to get your FFL), tool kit, Powley Calculator and Powley Computer, *Gun Digest, Gun Parts Catalog,* mainspring vice, school binders, *Brownell's Catalog,* pull & drop gauge, trigger pull gauge, two parchment diplomas ready for framing, free consultation service, plus much more. Launch a career you will enjoy. Start your own business and make money in your spare time. No experience needed. For free information, write:

MODERN GUN REPAIR SCHOOL
Dept. GJZ94, 2538 N. 8th Street
P.O. Box 5338, Phoenix, AZ 85010
or call: 602-990-8346

MANUFACTURERS' SHOWCASE

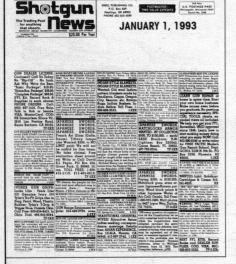

THE SHOTGUN NEWS

Established in 1946, THE SHOTGUN NEWS offers some of the finest gun buys in the United States. Published three times each month, with over 150,000 readers, this national publication has helped thousands of gun enthusiasts locate, buy, trade and sell antique, modern, military and sporting firearms and accessories. As the cover says, SHOTGUN NEWS is "The Trading Post for Anything That Shoots." Call TOLL FREE 1-800-345-6923 and receive a one-year subscription (36 issues) for just $20.00 (use your Master or Visa card). For more information, call 1-402-463-4589 or write:

THE SHOTGUN NEWS
P. O. Box 669, Hastings, NE 68902

NEW ADVANCED BELT THUMB-BREAK HOLSTER

With Nichols Sight Strip™ & Power Band™ This practical concealment holster is re-engineered to include the Power Band™ for adjustable drawing tension, plus a trigger-guard buffer. The fully-adjustable thumb-break includes our exclusive strap keepers. Inside is the Nichols Sight Strip™ for sight protection, and on the back is a belt panel molded of tough engineering resin to fit belts 1.5;" (38mm) wide. Weighs only 5 oz. For queries or to order our 24-page full-line catalog (including the name of your local dealer), write:

SHOOTING SYSTEMS GROUP INC.
Dept. B-HG, 1075 Headquarters Park, Fenton, MO 63026-2478
or call toll free: 1-800-325-3049

wideview
NEW BLACK POWDER MOUNT

The new WIDEVIEW Black Powder Mount pictured above fits the Thompson/Center Renegade and Hawken rifles with no drilling or tapping. The barrel still comes off for easy cleaning, and the original iron sight is used. With Wideview's Ultra Precision See-Thru mounts included, you may use a scope or iron sights. No hammer modification is needed.

WIDEVIEW SCOPE MOUNT CORP.
26110 Michigan Ave., Inkster, MI 38141 (313) 274-1238

BEEMAN KODIAK RIFLE

The BEEMAN Kodiak—the world's most powerful, conventional mainspring air rifle. A true breakthrough! With just one cocking stroke, this simple mechanism lays out an astonishing 28–30 ft. lbs. of energy—double the power of previous high-power adult airguns. No pumping, no CO_2, no valves, no external or internal air tanks—cock and shoot in 5 seconds! Such a powerhouse theoretically could produce 1400+ fps in .177", but that is too small a bore to handle all this power! BEEMAN recommends only .25 caliber, providing maximum effective range, best accuracy and great impact. For a free catalog and more information write:

BEEMAN PRECISION ARMS
3440-C16 Airway Drive, Santa Rosa, CA 95403
or call: 707-578-7900

MANUFACTURERS' SHOWCASE

BELL & CARLSON COMPOSITE GUN STOCKS

Carbelite® stocks are composed of hand-placed layers of Kevlar, fiberglass, and graphite and bound by a unique filler throughout the stock. Both the Carbelite® and the new upscale Premier line are offered in six finishes, including the award-winning woodgrain and camouflage. BELL & CARLSON has a fully staffed custom-fitting department for each customer's unique requirements. For a free color brochure and list of available models, write:

BELL & CARLSON, INC. Dept. SB, 509 N. Fifth, Atwood, Kansas 67730

SWIFT INSTRUMENTS

MODEL 664 4-12X, 40mm

Spot that mountain goat with 4X, then bring him 12 times closer for the kill. Because of its parallax adjustment from 5mm to infinity, this SWIFT scope is highly adaptable. It is also excellent for use in gas-powered air rifles. Externally adjustable caps amplify corrections in elevation and drift. Self-centering Quadraplex reticle and multi-coated optics bring you on the target with clarity. Hard anodized 1" tube. Fogproof. Gift boxed.

SWIFT INSTRUMENTS, INC. 952 Dorchester Ave., Boston, MA 02025 or P.O. Box 562, San Jose, CA 95106

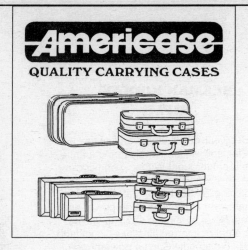

Americase
QUALITY CARRYING CASES

Known worldwide for its superior quality airline duty carrying cases, the AMERICASE catalog offers more than 75 different shapes and sizes of gun and accessory cases. All AMERICASE products feature extruded tempered aluminum frames, hand-anodized finish, and the finest hardware available. If you are looking for more than a plain aluminum box, one that is "beauty" as well as "beast," choose AMERICASE. Custom sizes are easily available. Send $2 for our 24-page color catalog:

AMERICASE INC.
P.O. Box 271, Waxahachie, TX 75165
or call toll free: 1-800-972-2737

FORT KNOX SECURITY PRODUCTS

FORT KNOX, the most trusted name in security, offers a full line of quality safes. The Chuck Yeager series features concealed hinges, reinforced door, 1200Ω certified fire protection, corner bolts, and a patented rack-and-pinion locking mechanism. Our Executive, Guardian and Protector series offer similar security advantages, including a UL Listing and lifetime warranty. For more information write:

FORT KNOX
1051 North Industrial Park Road, Orem, UT 84057
or call toll free: 1-800-821-5216

MANUFACTURERS' SHOWCASE

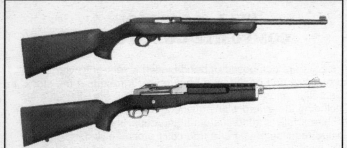

NEW RUGER 10/22* & MINI 14/30* SPORTER STOCKS

BUTLER CREEK'S new featherweight Ruger Sporter Stocks will dress up your favorite semiauto rifles. They offer a slimmer, more comfortable pistol-grip area with double palm swells that fit both right- or left-handed shooters. Able to withstand the toughest heat or cold without warpage or swelling, these stocks are made with space-age polymers that give maximum quietness and unsurpassed strength. Each full-length stock is designed for a fast drop-in right at home. Complete with buttpad and swivel studs. The 10/22* comes with raised checkering and schnabel forend. The Mini 14/30* fits all 181 series and newer guns. * Registered trademark of Sturm, Ruger & Co.

Butler Creek Corporation
290 Arden Drive, Belgrade, MT 59714
Phone: 406-388-1356 Fax: 406-388-7204

SWIFT INSTRUMENTS, INC.

SCOPE MODEL 656
3-9X, 40mm

Universally useful, the SWIFT Model 656 has proven to be a most popular scope. It has a maximum field of 40 feet at 100 yards at 3X, and a field of 14 feet at the highest power—9X. Maximum R.L.E. 266 to 30 is provided by a 40mm objective lens. The optical system has 11 lens elements and Quadraplex reticle. Model 656 is waterproof, sports a wide angle field of view and is multi-coated.

SWIFT INSTRUMENTS, INC.
952 Dorchester Ave., Boston, MA 02025 or
P.O. Box 562, San Jose, CA 95106

Aimpoint® 2X RED DOT SIGHT

AIMPOINT introduces its new 30mm AIMPOINT 500 2 Power, a fixed, low-power electronic sight with a floating red dot. It's the only unit of its kind with built-in magnification. The shooter now has the speed and accuracy of a red dot sight combined with the advantages of a low-power scope. Because the magnification is in the objective lens instead of the ocular lens (as with previous screw-in attachments), the dot covers only 1.5″ at 200 yards. The 5000 2 Power can be used on all types of firearms and comes complete with 30mm rings and all accessories. Suggested retail price is $399.95. For more information write:

AIMPOINT
580 Herndon Pkwy., Suite 500, Dept. SB, Herndon, VA 22070
703-471-6828

GLASER SAFETY SLUG AMMO

GLASER SAFETY SLUG'S state-of-the-art, professional-grade personal defense ammunition is now offered in two bullet styles: BLUE uses a #12 compressed shot core for maximum ricochet protection, and SILVER uses a #6 compressed shot core for maximum penetration. The manufacturing process results in outstanding accuracy, with documented groups of less than an inch at 100 yards! That's why Glaser has been the top choice of professional and private law enforcement agencies worldwide for over 15 years. Currently available in every caliber from 25 ACP through 30-06, including 40 S&W, 10mm, 223 and 7.62×39. For a free brochure contact:

GLASER SAFETY SLUG, INC.,
P.O. Box 8223, Foster City, CA 94404

MANUFACTURERS' SHOWCASE

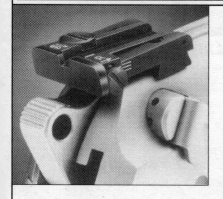

NEW LOW-PROFILE PISTOL SIGHTS

Built in Italy, this new sight boasts a remarkably low profile. While other low-profile designs extend the rear sight back past the pistol slide and down, PACHMAYR'S new sight fits into the standard sight groove and stays ahead of the slide end. Radiused corners on the sight blade itself further enhance the unique design. As a result, the pistol is far less likely to grab or catch on a holster or garment when it is drawn. The sight is CNC machined from solid steel for superior strength and true target-pistol sight accuracy. Microadjustable windage and elevation click-screws ensure ultimate accuracy. Sight blade available in plain black/target, white outline, or twin white dot for 3-dot systems. For further information, contact:

PACHMAYR LTD.
1875 South Mountain Ave., Monrovia, CA. 91016
Phone: 818-357-7771 or TOLL FREE: 1-800-423-9704

AMT's DA ONLY 380 BACKUP

The innovative, action engineering that spurred development of its acclaimed AUTOMAG series is demonstrated again in AMT's new Double Action Only .380 Backup. Foremost in the development of Backups, AMT proudly introduces this new pistol, featuring the company's exclusive Backup Double Action Only engineering. Professionals in the shooting industry have extolled the pistol's smooth and reliable performance. Constructed of stainless steel with black carbon fiber grips, this extremely compact handgun measures 5 inches long, weighs 18 ounces, and holds 5 rounds of .380 ammo.

ARCADIA MACHINE & TOOL INC. (AMT)
6226 Santos Diaz St., Irwindale, CA 91702 or call: 818-334-6629

93

LYMAN'S LEFT-HANDED GREAT PLAINS RIFLE

Left-handed muzzleloaders will be pleased to learn that Lyman's famous Great Plains Rifle is now available in a left-hand version. The Great Plains Rifle offers the authentic style of the rifle carried by Western pioneers and fur trappers, including such high-quality features as a walnut stock, double-set triggers, Hawken-style percussion "snail" and 32″ octagon barrel with 1 in 60″ twist. The left-hand Great Plains Rifle is available in either percussion or flintlock in calibers 50 or 54. In 1991, Lyman introduced a full compliment of left-handed models to its popular Deerstalker Rifle and carbine lines, and has since added more. For more information, write to:

Ed Schmitt, **LYMAN PRODUCTS** Dept. 400/401, Route 147, Middlefield, CT 06455 or call toll free: 1-800-22-LYMAN

GUN LIST

GUN LIST is the nationwide firearms marketplace publication. In each of its 26 annual issues, it presents over 10,000 listings of quality firearms, related products and services from gun dealers, shops and individuals. You can profit from this vast selection of great bargains. Alphabetically indexed for easy use, GUN LIST puts you instantly in touch with your collecting, hunting, reloading, shooting or other firearms specialty, as well as national gun show information. More than 120,000 enthusiasts love GUN LIST—you will too! Sample issue: $1.00. One-year subscription: $24.95. Money-back guarantee.

GUN List
Dept. ABAF8C, 700 E. State Street, Iola, WI 54990-0001

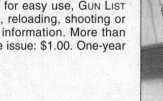

MANUFACTURERS' SHOWCASE

The Original L. Thomas Variable Rifle Support is a reliable, easy-to-use rifle support. Made of space-age plastic, it is sturdy, compact and comes with a telescoping aluminum pod. It adjusts to hunters of any height and is available in a regular model (11.5 oz.) as well as for hunters in the over-six-foot-tall category (13.5 oz.). Hand-crafted in America, this ingenious device improves accuracy, is a model of simplicity, and works well with shotgun as well as rifle. It is even said to produce fantastic results when used in bow hunting!

For further information, contact:

THE ORIGINAL L. THOMAS VARIABLE RIFLE SUPPORT
P.O. Box 126, Katy, TX 77492
or call: 713-530-7298

CARBIDE PRIMER POCKET UNIFORMERS FROM SINCLAIR INTERNATIONAL

SINCLAIR INTERNATIONAL has introduced a new line of primer pocket uniformers designed for the precision handloader. The 8000 Series Uniformers are designed to cut primer pockets to a uniform depth. The cutters can be used under power (drill or drill press) or by hand with the optional accessory handle. These uniformers are precision ground from solid tungsten carbide. Uniformers are available in small rifle/small pistol, large rifle, or large pistol for $18.50 each. The optional handle sells for $7.50. For a free catalog of other precision reloading equipment write:

SINCLAIR INTERNATIONAL
2330 Wayne Haven St., Fort Wayne, Indiana 46803
or call: 219-493-1858

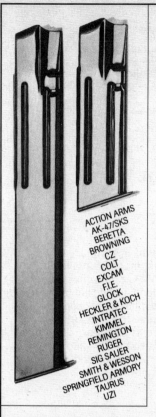
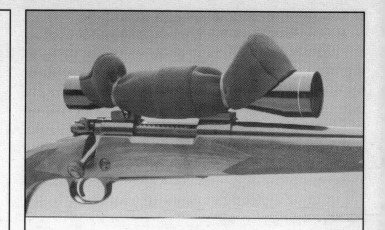

95

NEW HASTINGS HQC MUZZLE BRAKE

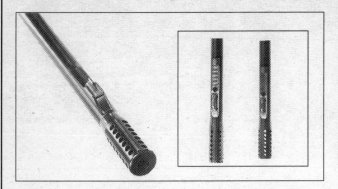

The innovative HASTINGS Quick-Change Muzzle Brake is at home on the range or in the woods. It tames recoil and muzzle jump by deflecting expanding gases perpendicular to the bore. That reduces the pounding you take during extended shooting sessions and helps eliminate flinching. Any effective muzzle brake tends to increase noise to the shooter; the HQC is unique in that a quick rotation of the outer sleeve seals the gas ports, deactivating the brake and returning noise levels to normal for hunting. HASTINGS installs the HQC, in stainless steel or blued finish, on most centerfire rifles. For complete details, contact:

HASTINGS BARRELS
P.O. Box 224, Clay Center, Kansas 67432

K.B.I./FEG
SINGLE ACTION PISTOL
MODEL PJK-9HP

All FEG pistols are manufactured in Hungary by skilled craftsmen using the finest material available. The 9mm single action pistol PJK-9HP is patterned after the military pistol of most NATO nations. In addition to its high luster, blued steel frame and slide, hand-checkered walnut grips and manual slide release, the PJK-9HP has a rounded combat-serrated external hammer, ramp front sight and rear dovetail sight adjustable for windage. This model comes with two 13-round magazines and a cleaning rod. Barrel length is 4³⁄₄″ and weight is 32 oz.

K.B.I.
P.O. Box 6346, Harrisburg, PA 17112

MANUFACTURERS' SHOWCASE

For Traditional Personal Protection

Model number D1425

The New Colt Detective Special®

America's classic revolver returns.

Introduced in 1927, the Colt Detective Special has earned a legendary reputation in the law enforcement field and for personal protection. Now, this classic compact 38 Special revolver resumes its honored place in the Colt line.

Retaining the familiar appearance of its predecessors, the Colt Detective Special is finished in Colt blue with 2" barrel and glare-proof ramp front sight, and features a grooved trigger and black composition grips. The shrouded, free-floating ejector rod won't catch on clothing or holster. Unlike many competitive snubnosed revolvers, the Detective Special will accommo-

date six rounds of 38 Special ammunition.

Constructed of forged, high-strength alloy steel, today's Colt Detective Special is based on the tough, dependable Colt "D" frame, the basis for such respected products as the Colt Police Positive, Agent, Cobra, Viper, and Diamondback.

If you've admired the proven reliability, easy handling, and familiar feel of this timeless design, wait no longer. The Detective Special is back on the case. See one today at your Colt dealer.

Colt's Manufacturing Company, Inc. P.O. Box 1868, Hartford, CT 06144-1868

Warning: Be a safe shooter – never chamber a round until you are ready to shoot. Always read and follow the instruction manual which accompanies each firearm. Free instruction manuals are available upon request.

Foolproof Safety and Double Action Readiness...

HIGH CONTRAST SIGHTS for rapid target acquisition even in low light conditions. Unique dovetail sights are easily interchangeable. Betalight night sights available on some models.

STEEL-TO-STEEL LOCKUP and hard coat, anodized frame for outstanding durability.

PATENTED AUTOMATIC FIRING PIN SAFETY BLOCK permits carrying of loaded, decocked pistol. Pistol will not fire until trigger is pulled.

DECOCKING LEVER puts hammer in perfect register with safety intercept notch in one smooth motion. Tactical advantage over two-step slide mounted decocking levers.

THUMB-LEVEL MAGAZINE RELEASE for rapid magazine changes can be easily switched to accommodate both left- and right-handed shooters.

ERGONOMICALLY-DESIGNED GRIP DIMENSIONS and grip angle for easy, thumb-level manipulation of all controls including decocking lever. Ideal weight distribution for maximum shooting comfort.

SIG SAUER: The Tactical Edge

All SIG SAUER Small Arms are distinguished by their dependable performance in the field, and double action readiness for enhanced first shot potential.

For over 125 years, the SIG name has been synonymous with highly accurate, safe handling firearms. We build the finest guns in the world because we build safety, reliability and accuracy into every firearm we manufacture.

Contact SIGARMS today for the name of your local SIG SAUER Dealer. He's anxious to show you how SIG SAUER Handguns give you the tactical edge.

SIG SAUER HANDGUNS...THE TACTICAL EDGE!

SIGARMS

SIGARMS INC.
Industrial Drive
Exeter, NH 03833

SIG SAUER P 220: 7 + 1 ROUND, .45 ACP
SIG SAUER P 225: 8 + 1 ROUND 9mm PARA
SIG SAUER P 226: 15 + 1 ROUND (20 + 1 OPTIONAL) 9mm PARA
SIG SAUER P 230: 7 + 1 ROUND .380 ACP STAINLESS or BLUED

SIG encourages safe shooting. Consult your local District Attorney's office or police authorities for rules and regulations governing firearms ownership in your area. When handling firearms, follow safety guidelines in owner's manual. If a manual is not accompanied with your weapon, please contact SIGARMS for a replacement manual.

The only thing we can't hide is the value!

More Popular Patterns...

Turkey hunters know the importance of having the right camo. So do the hunters at Mossberg. With 12 camo guns and camo combo sets, Mossberg offers more choices than anyone. The Model 835 Pump in popular RealTree® camo and the New Model 9200 Autoloader in Mossy Oak® camo patterns are good examples. They are two of the most popular and effective patterns hunters can select.

Mossberg has even developed their own pattern. It's designed to work with a wide variety of patterns, including Mother Nature's originals, without adding a lot to the price of the shotgun. This OFM Camo comes on the popular Model 500, the Model 835 and the new Model 9200.

More Innovative Features...

Nobody has developed more innovations for shotgunners than Mossberg. They introduced Factory Camo Shotguns. The Model 835 introduced the 3 1/2 inch 12 gauge magnum. For the first time, turkey hunters could get true 10 gauge performance in a gun that shoots all the traditional 12 gauge loads as well. As a Mossberg Hard Case Combo, the Model 835 offers the versatility of both a turkey barrel and a fully rifled slug barrel.

The Model 9200 Autoloader handles everything from light target loads up to 3 inch magnums and it comes with a Lifetime Limited Warranty.

More Value...
because they're Mossbergs

Ask knowledgeable hunters about the best shotgun value for the money. Most will say "get a Mossberg." Mossberg Turkey Guns come packed with values like: an extra full "Turkey" choke tube, a sling, Q.D. studs, recoil pads, plus wide vent ribs with mid and front beads.

The Model 500 introduced money saving, multi-barrel Combos that let the hunter simply change barrels with the seasons.

In addition, there is always a wide selection of inexpensive interchangeable barrels available for every Mossberg model.

We're changing the way America thinks about shotguns.

O.F. Mossberg & Sons, Inc. • 7 Grasso Ave. • P.O. Box 497 • North Haven, CT 06473-9844

Safety and safe firearms handling is everyone's responsibility.

© 1993, O.F. Mossberg & Sons, Inc.

FINLAND SAKO

CLASSIC GRADE

THE SAKO CLASSIC GRADE MODEL...
THE UNDERSTATED ELEGANCE OF
A TRADITIONALLY STYLED RIFLE.
THE TRUE RIFLEMAN'S RIFLE.

CLASSIC ELEGANCE CAN
BEST DESCRIBE SAKO'S LATEST
MODEL—THE CLASSIC GRADE.
CONSTRUCTED WITH OLD WORLD
CRAFTSMANSHIP THAT THROUGHOUT THE
YEARS HAS BECOME A SAKO TRADITION.
A TRUE SAKO MASTERPIECE.

Handguns

For addresses and phone numbers of manufacturers and distributors included in this section, turn to *DIRECTORY OF MANUFACTURERS AND SUPPLIERS* at the back of the book.

ACTION ARMS/BRNO PISTOLS

MODEL CZ-75 STANDARD

SPECIFICATIONS
Caliber: 9mm
Capacity: 15 rounds
Barrel length: 4.7″
Overall length: 8.1″
Weight: 34.3 oz. (unloaded)
Sights: Fixed blade front; drift adjustable rear
Safety: Thumb safety; cocked and locked or double action
Stock: Polymer or walnut
Finish: Mil-spec enamel (matte or gloss blue)
Price: $629.00 ($729.00 w/gold appointments or chrome finish)

MODEL CZ-75 COMPACT

SPECIFICATIONS
Caliber: 9mm
Capacity: 13 + 1
Barrel length: 3.9″
Overall length: 7.3″
Weight: 32.1 oz. (unloaded)
Sights: Fixed blade front (white line front sight pinned in place); drift adjustable rear
Grips: Walnut
Finish: Mil-spec black polymer (matte or gloss blue)
Safety: Thumb safety; cocked and locked or double action
Features: Square trigger guard; rounded hammer; non-glare ribbed sighting
Price: $495.00 ($516.00 matte; **$535.00** polished blue)

MODEL CZ-83

SPECIFICATIONS
Caliber: 380 ACP
Capacity: 12 rounds
Barrel length: 3.8″
Overall length: 6.8″
Weight: 27.9 oz. (unloaded)
Safety: Thumb safety; cocked and locked or double action
Sights: Fixed blade front; drift adjustable rear
Stock: Polymer
Finish: Blue
Price: $509.00 ($665.00 w/gold appointments or chrome finish)

MODEL CZ-85 STANDARD

SPECIFICATIONS
Calibers: 9mm and 9×21mm
Capacity: 15 rounds
Barrel length: 4.7″
Overall length: 8.1″
Weight: 35.7 oz. (unloaded)
Sights: Fixed blade front; drift adjustable rear
Safety: Thumb safety; cocked and locked or double action
Stock: Walnut
Finish: Mil-spec enamel (matte or gloss blue)
Features: Ambidextrous controls; squared-off, finger-rest trigger guard; non-glare serrated slide top; trigger stop
Price: $675.00 ($779.00 w/gold appointments or chrome finish)
Also available:
MODEL CZ-85 COMBAT w/fully adjustable rear sight, round combat-style hammer, walnut grip; free-dropping magazine.
Price: $595.00

AMERICAN ARMS PISTOLS

MODEL PK-22 DA SEMIAUTO
$198.00

SPECIFICATIONS
Caliber: 22 LR
Capacity: 8-shot clip
Barrel length: 3¹/₃"
Overall length: 6¹/₃"
Weight: 22 oz. (empty)
Sights: Fixed; blade front, "V"-notch rear
Grip: Black polymer

MODEL P-98 CLASSIC SEMIAUTO
$213.00

SPECIFICATIONS
Caliber: 22 LR
Capacity: 8-shot clip
Barrel length: 5"
Overall length: 8¹/₈"
Weight: 26 oz. (empty)
Sights: Fixed blade front; adjustable square-notch rear
Grip: Black polymer

MODEL CX-22 DA SEMIAUTO
$198.00

SPECIFICATIONS
Caliber: 22 LR
Capacity: 8-shot clip
Barrel length: 3¹/₃"
Overall length: 6¹/₃"
Weight: 22 oz. (empty)
Sights: Fixed; blade front, "V"-notch rear
Grip: Black polymer
Also available:
MODEL PX-22 (7-shot magazine) $193.00

REGULATOR SINGLE ACTION REVOLVER
$305.00
TWO-CYLINDER SET $349.00

SPECIFICATIONS
Calibers: 45 Long Colt, 44-40, 357 Mag.
Barrel lengths: 4³/₄", 5¹/₂" and 7¹/₂"
Action: Single Action
Sights: Fixed
Safety: Half cock
Features: Brass trigger guard and back strap; two-cylinder combinations available (45 L.C./45 ACP and 44-40/44 Special)
Also available:
BUCKHORN SA. Same as Regulator but with stronger frame for 44 Mag $320.00

AMERICAN DERRINGER PISTOLS

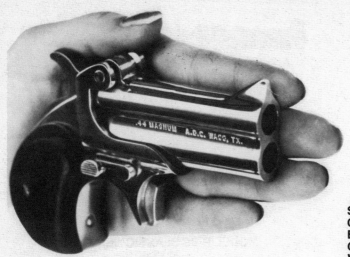

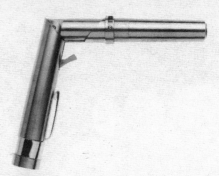

MODEL 1

SPECIFICATIONS
Overall length: 4.82″
Barrel length: 3″
Weight: 15 oz. (in 45 Auto)
Action: Single action w/automatic barrel selection
Number of shots: 2

Calibers	Prices
22 Long Rifle	$212.50
22 Magnum Rimfire	225.00
32 Magnum/32 S&W Long	222.00
32-20	222.00
357 Magnum	250.00
357 Maximum	265.00
38 Special	219.00
38 Super	235.00
38 Special +P+ (Police)	225.00
38 Special Shot Shells	235.00
380 Auto, 9mm Luger	215.00
10mm Auto, 40 S&W, 45 Auto, 30 M-1 Carbine	250.00
45-70 (single shot)	312.00
45 Colt, 2¹/₂″ Snake (45 cal.rifled barrel), 44-40 Win., 44 Special	320.00
45 Win. Mag., 44 Magnum, 41 Magnum, 30-30 Win., 223 Rem. Comm. Ammo dual calibers	375.00
Engraved	855.00

MODEL 3
Stainless Steel Single Shot Derringer
(not shown)

SPECIFICATIONS
Calibers: 32 Magnum, 38 Special
Barrel length: 2.5″
Overall length: 4.9″
Weight: 8.5 oz.
Safety: Manual ''Hammer-Block''
Grips: Rosewood

Price:	$120.00

Also available:
LADY DERRINGER (Stainless Steel Double)

38 Special, 32 Magnum, 32 S&W	$235.00
Engraved	750.00

MODEL 2 STEEL "PEN" PISTOL

SPECIFICATIONS
Calibers: 22 LR, 25 Auto, 32 Auto
Barrel length: 2″
Overall length: 5.6″ (4.2″ in pistol format)
Weight: 5 oz.

Price:	$177.00-187.50

Also available:
MODEL 7 Ultra Lightweight (7¹/₂ oz.) Single Actions

22 Long Rifle	$200.00
22 Magnum Rimfire	215.00
32 Magnum, 32 S&W Long	202.50
38 Special	202.50
380 Auto	199.95
44 Special	500.00

MODEL 10 (10 oz.)

45 Colt	$320.00
45 Auto	250.00

MODEL 11 Lightweight (11 oz.) Double Derringer

38 Special	$205.00

38 DOUBLE ACTION DERRINGER (14.5 oz.)

38 Special	$250.00
38 Special Lady Derringer w/syn. ivory grips	265.00
9mm Luger	275.00
357 Magnum	244.00
40 S&W	300.00

AMERICAN DERRINGER PISTOLS

MODEL 4

MODEL 4
Stainless Steel Double Derringer

SPECIFICATIONS
Calibers: 45 Colt or 3″ .410
Barrel length: 4.1″
Overall length: 6″
Weight: 16.5 oz.
Number of shots: 2
Finish: Satin or high polish stainless steel
Price: **$352.00**
    With oversize grips 382.00
Also available:
In 45 Auto, 45 Colt, 357 Mag., 357 Maximum **$369.00**
In 45-70 .... 495.00
Alaskan Survival Model in 45-70, 44 Mag. 387.50
    With oversize grips 422.00

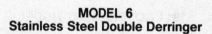
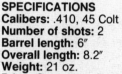

MODEL 6

MODEL 6
Stainless Steel Double Derringer

SPECIFICATIONS
Calibers: .410, 45 Colt
Number of shots: 2
Barrel length: 6″
Overall length: 8.2″
Weight: 21 oz.
Price: Grey matte finish **$350.00**
    Satin finish 362.50
    High polish finish 387.50
    W/oversize grips **add** 35.00

COP AND MINI-COP 4-SHOT DA DERRINGERS
(not shown)

22 Magnum Rimfire (Mini-Cop) **$312.50**
357 Mag. or 38 Special (Cop) 375.00

125th ANNIVERSARY DOUBLE DERRINGER
COMMEMORATIVE (1866–1991)

38 Special **$215.00**
44-40 or 45 Colt 320.00
Engraved models 750.00

**SEMMERLING
LM-4 DOUBLE ACTION**

SEMMERLING LM-4 DOUBLE ACTION

SPECIFICATIONS
Caliber: 45 ACP or 9mm
Action: Double action
Capacity: 5 rounds
Overall length: 5″
Price: Blued finish (manual repeating) **$1750.00**
    Stainless steel 1875.00

AMT PISTOLS

1911 GOVERNMENT

AMT 380 BACKUP II

1911 GOVERNMENT MODEL
$475.95

SPECIFICATIONS
Caliber: 45 ACP
Capacity: 7 shots
Barrel length: 5″
Overall length: 8 1/2″
Weight: 38 oz.
Width: 1 1/4″
Sights: Fixed
Features: Long grip safety; rubber wraparound Neoprene grips; beveled magazine well; wide adjustable trigger
Also available:
1911 HARDBALLER. Same specifications as Standard Model, but with Millett adjustable sights and matte rib. **Price: $575.95**

AMT 380 BACKUP II
$295.99 (Single or Double Action)

SPECIFICATIONS
Caliber: 380
Capacity: 5 shots
Barrel length: 2 1/2″
Overall length: 5″
Weight: 18 oz.
Width: 11/16″
Sights: Open
Grips: Carbon fiber

ON DUTY DOUBLE ACTION PISTOL
(not shown)
$469.95 ($529.99 in 45 ACP)

SPECIFICATIONS
Caliber: 40 S&W, 45 ACP and 9mm Luger
Capacity: 13 rounds
Barrel length: 4 1/2″
Overall length: 7 3/4″
Weight: 32 oz.
Features: Stainless steel slide and barrel; carbon fiber grips; inertia firing pin; steel recoil shoulder; white 3 dot sighting system; trigger disconnector safety; light let-off double action.
Also available: **Decocker model** (same price).

45 ACP LONGSLIDE (not shown)
$575.95

SPECIFICATIONS
Caliber: 45 ACP
Capacity: 7 shots
Barrel length: 7″
Overall length: 10 1/2″
Weight: 46 oz.
Sights: Millett adjustable
Features: Wide adjustable trigger; Neoprene wraparound grips
Also available:
45 ACP Government $475.95
45 ACP Hardballer 529.99
Conversion Kit (5″ Hardballer) 279.99
  For 7″ Longslide 299.99

AMT PISTOLS

22 AUTOMAG II RIMFIRE MAGNUM
$375.95

The only production semiautomatic handgun in this caliber, the Automag II is ideal for the small-game hunter or shooting enthusiast who wants more power and accuracy in a light, trim handgun. The pistol features a bold open-slide design and employs a unique gas-channeling system for smooth, trouble-free action.

SPECIFICATIONS
Caliber: 22 Rimfire Magnum
Barrel lengths: $3^3/8''$, $4^1/2''$ or $6''$
Magazine capacity: 9 shots ($4^1/2''$ & $6''$), 7 shots ($3^3/8''$)
Weight: 32 oz.
Sights: Millett adjustable (white outline rear; red ramp)
Features: Squared trigger guard; grooved carbon fiber grips

22 AUTOMAG II

AUTOMAG III
$465.95

SPECIFICATIONS
Caliber: 30 M1 Carbine, 9mm Win. Mag.
Capacity: 8 shots
Barrel length: $6^3/8''$
Overall length: $10^1/2''$
Weight: 43 oz.
Sights: Millett adjustable
Grips: Carbon fiber
Finish: Stainless steel

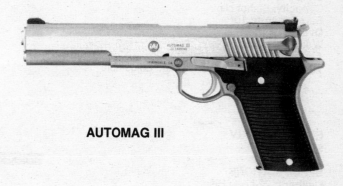

AUTOMAG III

AUTOMAG IV
$679.99

SPECIFICATIONS
Caliber: 45 Win. Mag., 10mm
Capacity: 7 shots
Barrel lengths: $6^1/2''$ and $8^5/8''$
Overall length: $10^1/2''$
Weight: 46 oz.
Sights: Millett adjustable
Grips: Carbon fiber
Finish: Stainless steel

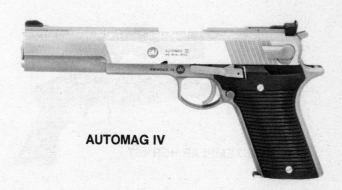

AUTOMAG IV

ANSCHUTZ PISTOLS

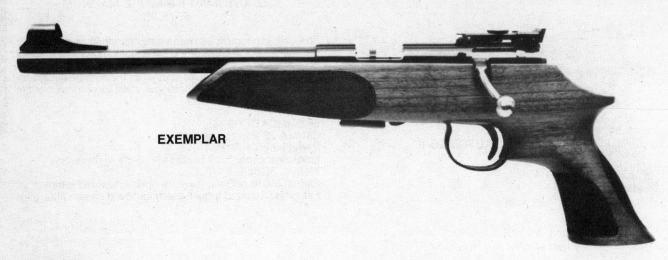

EXEMPLAR

EXEMPLAR
$499.50

SPECIFICATIONS
Calibers: 22 Long Rifle
Capacity: 5-shot clip
Barrel length: 10″
Overall length: 19″
Weight: 3⅓ lbs.
Action: Match 64
Trigger pull: 9.85 oz., two-stage adjustable

Safety: Slide
Sights: Hooded ramp post front; open notched rear; adjustable for windage and elevation
Stock: European walnut

Also available:
EXEMPLAR LEFT featuring right-hand operating bolt.
Price: **$499.50**

EXEMPLAR XIV
$522.00

SPECIFICATIONS
Calibers: 22 Long Rifle
Barrel length: 14″
Overall length: 23″
Weight: 4.15 lbs.
Action: Match 64
Trigger pull: 9.85 oz., two-stage
Safety: Slide

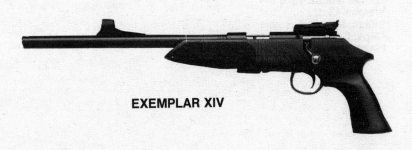

EXEMPLAR XIV

EXEMPLAR HORNET

EXEMPLAR HORNET
$822.00

A centerfire version with Match 54 action.

SPECIFICATIONS
Caliber: 22 Hornet
Trigger pull: 19.6 oz.
Barrel: 10″
Overall length: 20″
Weight: 4.35 lbs.
Features: Tapped and grooved for scope mounting; wing safety

AUTO-ORDNANCE PISTOLS

MODEL 1911A1 THOMPSON

SPECIFICATIONS
Calibers: 45 ACP, 9mm and 38 Super; also 10mm, 40 S&W
Capacity: 9 rounds (9mm & 38 Super); 7 rounds (45 ACP)
Barrel length: 5″
Overall length: 8¹/₂″
Weight: 39 oz.
Sights: Blade front; rear adjustable for windage
Stock: Checkered plastic with medallion
Prices:
In 9mm and 38 Super $415.00
In 10mm 420.95
In 40 S&W 427.95
In 45 ACP 388.95
Satin nickel finish (45 cal. only) 405.00
PIT BULL MODEL (45 ACP w/3¹/₂″ barrel) 420.95
WW II PARKERIZED PISTOL (45 cal. only) 379.25

**MODEL 1911A1 THOMPSON
(9mm)**

MODEL 1911 "THE GENERAL"
(not shown)

SPECIFICATIONS
Caliber: 45 ACP
Capacity: 7 rounds
Barrel length: 4¹/₂″
Overall length: 7³/₄″
Weight: 37 oz.
Stock: Black textured, rubber wraparound with medallion
Feature: Full-length recoil guide system
Price: $427.95

Also available:
1911A1 DUO-TONE PISTOL (45 cal. only) $405.00

**MODEL 1911A1
DUO-TONE**

MODEL 1927A5

SPECIFICATIONS
Caliber: 45 ACP
Capacity: 30 rounds
Barrel length: 13¹/₂″ (finned)
Overall length: 26″
Weight: 7 lbs.
Sights: Blade front; adjustable open rear
Stock: Walnut rear grip, vertical forend
Price: $704.00

**MODEL 1927A5
(Shown w/50-round
L-Type Drum)**

BERETTA PISTOLS
SMALL FRAME

MODEL 21

MODEL 21 DA SEMIAUTOMATIC
$235.00 ($260.00 Nickel)

A safe, dependable, accurate small-bore pistol in 22 LR or 25 Auto. Easy to load with its unique barrel tip-up system.

SPECIFICATIONS
Caliber: 22 LR or 25 Auto. **Magazine capacity:** 7 rounds (22 LR); 8 rounds (25 Auto). **Overall length:** 4.9″. **Barrel length:** 2.4″. **Weight:** 11.5 oz. (25 ACP); 11.8 oz. (22 LR) **Sights:** Blade front; V-notch rear. **Safety:** Thumb operated. **Grips:** Walnut. **Frame:** Special alloy.
Also available:
Model 21 Engraved **$285.00**
W/Plastic Matte Finish **185.00**

MODEL 950 BS

MODEL 950 BS
SINGLE ACTION SEMIAUTOMATIC

SPECIFICATIONS
Caliber: 25 ACP. **Barrel length:** 2¹/₂″. **Overall length:** 4¹/₂″. **Overall height:** 3.4″. **Safety:** External, thumb-operated. **Magazine capacity:** 8 rounds. **Sights:** Blade front; V-notch rear. **Weight:** 9.9 oz. **Frame:** Special alloy.

Model 950 BS **$180.00**
Model 950 BS Nickel **210.00**
Model 950 EL Engraved **260.00**
Model 950 BS Plastic Matte Finish **150.00**

MEDIUM FRAME

MODEL 84F

This pistol is pocket size with a large magazine capacity. The lockwork is of double-action type. The first shot (with hammer down, chamber loaded) can be fired by a double-action pull on the trigger without cocking the hammer manually.

The pistol also features a favorable grip angle for natural pointing, positive thumb safety (uniquely designed for both right- and left-handed operation), quick takedown (by means of special takedown button) and a conveniently located magazine release. Black plastic grips. Wood grips available at extra cost.

MODEL 84F

SPECIFICATIONS
Caliber: 380 Auto (9mm Short). **Weight:** 1 lb. 7 oz. (approx.). **Barrel length:** 3³/₄₄″. (approx.) **Overall length:** 6¹/₂″. (approx.) **Sights:** Fixed front and rear. **Magazine capacity:** 13 rounds. **Height overall:** 4¹/₄″ (approx.).

Model 84F w/Plastic **$525.00**
Model 84F w/Wood **555.00**
Model 84F w/Wood Nickel **600.00**

BERETTA PISTOLS

MEDIUM FRAME PISTOLS
Calibers 22 LR and 380

MODEL 85F

This double-action semiautomatic pistol features walnut or plastic grips, matte black finish on steel slide, barrel and anodized alloy frame, ambidextrous safety, and a single line 8-round magazine.

SPECIFICATIONS
Caliber: 380 Auto. **Barrel length:** 3.82″. **Weight:** 21.8 oz. (empty). **Overall length:** 6.8″. **Overall height:** 4.8″. **Capacity:** 8 rounds. **Sights:** Blade integral with slide (front); square notched bar, dovetailed to slide (rear).
Prices:
Model 85 w/Plastic (8 rounds) $485.00
Model 85 w/Wood 510.00
Model 85 w/Wood Nickel 550.00
Model 87 w/Wood (22 LR) 490.00
Model 87 (Long barrel, SA) 510.00

MODEL 85F

MODEL 86

MODEL 86

SPECIFICATIONS
Caliber: 380 Auto. **Barrel length:** 4.33″. **Overall length:** 7.33″. **Capacity:** 8 rounds. **Weight:** 23 oz. **Sight radius:** 5.0″. **Overall height:** 4.8″. **Overall width:** 1.4″. **Grip:** Walnut or plastic. **Features:** Same as other Medium Frame, straight blow-back models, plus safety and convenience of a tip-up barrel (rounds can be loaded directly into chamber without operating the slide).
Price: $510.00

MODEL 89 STANDARD TARGET

This sophisticated single-action, target pistol features an 8-round magazine, adjustable target sights, and target-style contoured walnut grips with thumb rest.

SPECIFICATIONS
Caliber: 22 LR. **Barrel length:** 6″. **Overall length:** 9½″. **Height:** 5.3″. **Weight:** 41 oz.
Price: $735.00

MODEL 89 TARGET

BERETTA PISTOLS
LARGE FRAME

MODEL 92FS (9mm)

This 9mm Parabellum semiautomatic pistol is specifically designed for use by law enforcement agencies. It has also been adopted as the official sidearm of the U.S. Armed Forces. Its 15-round firepower combines with flawless reliability and safety to make it the ideal police and military sidearm. Its firing mechanism will handle thousands of rounds without malfunction. And the ambidextrous triple-safety mechanism features a passive firing pin catch, a slide safety that acts as a decocking lever, plus a unique firing pin to ensure that a falling hammer can never break safety and discharge accidentally. Available in two compact versions; 3-dot and tritium night sights available.

SPECIFICATIONS
Caliber: 9mm Parabellum. **Overall length:** 8.54″. **Height:** 5.4″. **Barrel length:** 4.9″. **Weight** (empty): 34 oz. **Magazine:** 15 rounds, removable floorplate. **Sights:** Front, blade integral with slide; rear, square-notched bar, dovetailed to slide. **Slide stop:** Holds slide open after last round, manually operable.

Model 92FS Plastic	$ 625.00
(Wood grips **$20.00** additional)	
Model 92F Stainless	755.00
Model 92FS Compact (13 rounds)	625.00
With wood grips	645.00
Model 92FS Plastic Centurion (9mm or 40 cal.)	
w/3-Dot Sight	625.00
Model 92D (DA only) w/Bobbed Hammer and	
3-Dot Sight	585.00
w/Trijicon Sight	650.00
Deluxe Gold-plated Engraved	5430.00

Optional: 3-Dot Sights (same price) and Trijicon Sights ($75.00 additional)

MODEL 92F (9mm)

MODEL 92D

MODEL 92FS CENTURION

MODEL 92F-EL

This deluxe version of the 92FS features exquisite gold trim on the safety levers, trigger, magazine release and grip screws. Top of barrel has Beretta logo with gold inlay. Richly grained walnut grips are ergonomically designed and also have engraved Beretta logo. High polish, blued finish on barrel, slide and frame. All other specifications same as the standard 92F.

Model 92F-EL Stainless $1240.00

MODEL 96

MODEL 96

Same specifications as the Model 92FS, except in 40 caliber with a 10-shot magazine capacity (9 shot in Compact version).

Model 96	$640.00
w/Trijicon Sight	710.00
Model 96D (DA only)	605.00
w/Trijicon Sight	670.00
Model 96 Centurion (Compact Barrel and	
Slide on Full-size Frame)	640.00

BERSA AUTOMATIC PISTOLS

THUNDER 9 DOUBLE ACTION
$414.95

SPECIFICATIONS
Caliber: 9mm
Capacity: 15
Action: Double
Barrel length: 4″
Overall length: 7³/₈″
Weight: 30 oz.
Height: 5¹/₂″
Sights: Blade front (integral w/slide); fully adjustable rear
Safety: Manual, firing pin, and decocking lever
Grips: Black polymer
Finish: Matte blue
Features: Reversible extended magazine release; adjustable trigger release; ''Link-Free'' design system (ensures positive lockup); instant disassembly; ambidextrous slide release

THUNDER 9 DOUBLE ACTION

MODEL 23 DOUBLE ACTION (not shown)
$281.95 ($314.95 in Nickel)

SPECIFICATIONS
Caliber: 22 LR
Capacity: 10 shots
Action: Blowback
Barrel length: 3¹/₂″
Weight: 24¹/₂ oz.
Sights: Blade front; notch-bar dovetailed rear, adjustable for windage
Grips: Walnut
Finish: Blue or satin nickel

MODEL 83 DOUBLE ACTION

MODEL 83 DOUBLE ACTION
$281.95 ($314.95 in Nickel)

SPECIFICATIONS
Caliber: 380 Auto
Capacity: 7 shots
Action: Blowback
Barrel length: 3¹/₂″
Weight: 25³/₄ oz.
Sights: Front blade sight integral on slide; rear sight square notched adjustable for windage
Grips: Custom wood

MODEL 85 DOUBLE ACTION
$331.95 ($391.95 in Nickel)

SPECIFICATIONS
Caliber: 380 Auto
Capacity: 13 shots
Barrel length: 3¹/₂″
Overall length: 6⁵/₈″
Weight: 26.45 oz.

Also available:
MODEL 86 CUSTOM UNDERCOVER DA. Same specifications as Model 85, except with military non-glare matte finish and 3-dot sight system. **$366.95 ($399.95 in Nickel)**

MODEL 85 DOUBLE ACTION

BROWNING AUTOMATIC PISTOLS

**9mm HI-POWER
SINGLE ACTION**

9mm HI-POWER SINGLE ACTION

The Browning 9mm Parabellum, also known as the 9mm Browning Hi-Power, is now available in 40 S&W. Both come with either a fixed-blade front sight and a windage-adjustable rear sight or a non-glare rear sight, screw adjustable for both windage and elevation. The front sight is an 1/8-inch-wide blade mounted on a ramp. The rear surface of the blade is serrated to prevent glare. All models have an ambidextrous safety. See table below for specifications.

Prices:

Standard Mark III w/matte finish, molded grip	**$493.95**
Same model in 40 S&W	**612.95**
Polished blue with adjustable sights	**571.95**
Polished blue with fixed sights	**524.95**
Practical	
w/fixed sights, molded rubber grip	**569.95**
w/adjustable sights	**612.95**
Silver chrome w/adj. sights, molded rubber grip	**581.95**
Capitan w/polished blue finish, tangent sights, walnut grip	**619.95**

9mm SEMIAUTOMATIC PISTOL

	SINGLE ACTION FIXED SIGHTS	SINGLE ACTION ADJUSTABLE SIGHTS
Finish	Polished Blue, Matte, or Nickel	Polished Blue
Capacity of Magazine	13 (10 in 40 S&W)	13 (10 in 40 S&W)
Overall Length	7 3/4″	7 3/4″
Barrel Length	4 21/32″	4 21/32″
Height	5″	5″
Weight (Empty)	32 oz. (35 oz. in 40 S&W)	32 oz. (33 oz. w/tangent sight) and 35 oz. in 40 S&W
Sight Radius	6 5/16″	6 3/8″
Ammunition	9mm Luger (Parabellum) or 40 S&W	9mm Luger (Parabellum) or 40 S&W
Grips	Checkered Walnut or Contoured Molded	Checkered Walnut or Contoured Molded
Front Sights	1/8″	1/8″ wide on ramp
Rear Sights	Drift adjustable for windage and elevation.	Drift adjustable for windage and elevation. Square Notch.

MODEL BDM 9mm DOUBLE ACTION

Browning's Model BDM (for Browning Double Mode) pistol brings shooters into a new realm of convenience and safety by combining the best advantages of double-action pistols with those of the revolver. In just seconds, the shooter can set the BDM to conventional double-action "pistol" mode or to the all-new double-action "revolver" mode.

**MODEL BDM
9mm DOUBLE ACTION**

SPECIFICATIONS
Caliber: 9mm Luger
Capacity: 15 rounds
Barrel length: 4.73″
Overall length: 7.85″
Weight: 31 oz. (empty)
Sight radius: 6.26″
Sights: Low-profile front (removable); rear screw adjustable for windage; includes 3-dot sight system
Finish: Matte blue
Features: Dual-purpose ambidextrous decocking lever/safety designed with a short stroke for easy operation (also functions as slide release); contoured grip is checkered on all four sides
Price: **$559.95**

BROWNING AUTOMATIC PISTOLS

MODEL BDA-380

BUCK MARK 5.5 TARGET

MODEL BDA-380

A high-powered, double-action semiautomatic pistol with fixed sights in 380 caliber. See specifications on preceding page.

SPECIFICATIONS
Capacity: 13 shots
Barrel length: 3 13/16″
Overall length: 6 3/4″
Weight: 32 oz.
Grips: Walnut
Prices:
Nickel Finish $624.95
Standard Finish 592.95

MICRO BUCK MARK

Features light weight, Pro Target Sight, bull barrel and black molded composite grips.

BUCK MARK SEMIAUTOMATIC PISTOL SPECIFICATIONS

	MICRO BUCK MARK	BUCK MARK STD. BUCK MARK PLUS	BUCK MARK* 5.5 TARGET/FIELD	BUCK MARK* SILHOUETTE	BUCK MARK* VARMINT	BUCK MARK* UNLTD. SILHOUETTE
Capacity	10	10	10	10	10	10
Overall length	8″	9 1/2″	9 5/8″	14″	14″	18 11/16″
Barrel length	4″	5 1/2″	5 1/2″	9 7/8″	9 7/8″	14″
Height	5 3/8″	5 3/8″	5 5/16″	5 15/16″	5 5/16″	5 15/16″
Weight (empty)	32 oz.	32 oz.	35 oz.	53 oz.	48 oz.	64 oz.
Sight radius	6 1/2″	8″	8 1/4″	13″	—	15″
Ammunition	22 LR	22 LR	22 LR	22 LR	22 LR	22 LR
Grips	Laminated Wood	Black, Molded; Impregnated Hardwood	Contoured Walnut	Contoured Walnut	Contoured Walnut	Contoured Walnut
Front Sights	Ramp front	1/8″ wide	Interchangeable Post*	Interchangeable Post*	None*	Interchangeable Post*
Rear Sights	Pro Target Sight	Pro Target Sight	Pro Target Sight	Pro Target Sight	None*	Pro Target Sight
Prices:	$234.95 (Std.) $274.95 (Nickel) $284.95 (Plus)	$234.95 $284.95 (Buck Mark Plus) $274.95 (Nickel)	$374.95 ($399.95 Gold Target)	$394.95	$354.95	$469.95

* Bark Mark Target, Silhouette and Varmint models supplied with full length top rib designed to accept most standard clamp style scope rings. Additional accessories for the Silhouette and Target models are available. Finger-groove grip option on all target models.

CHARTER ARMS REVOLVERS

BULLDOG PUG 44 SPECIAL

SPECIFICATIONS
Caliber: 44 Special. **Type of action:** 5-shot, single- and double-action. **Barrel length:** 3″. **Overall length:** 7³/₄″. **Height:** 5″. **Weight:** 19 oz. **Grips:** Neoprene or American walnut hand-checkered bulldog grips. **Sights:** Patridge-type, ⁹/₆₄″ wide front; square-notched rear. **Finish:** High-luster Service Blue or stainless steel.

Prices:
Blue finish Pug $278.75
Stainless steel Pug 334.50

**BULLDOG PUG
44 SPECIAL**

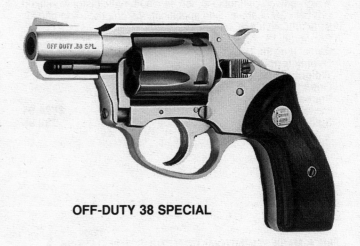

OFF-DUTY 38 SPECIAL

SPECIFICATIONS
Calibers: 22 LR and 38 Special. **Type of action:** 5-shot, single and double action. **Barrel length:** 2″. **Overall length:** 6¹/₄″. **Height:** 4¹/₄″. **Weight:** 16 oz. (matte black); 17 oz. (stainless). **Grips:** Select-a-grip (9 colors) or Neoprene. **Sights:** Patridge-type ramp front (with "red dot" feature); square-notch rear on stainless.

Prices:
Matte black finish $208.75
Stainless steel 267.75

OFF-DUTY 38 SPECIAL

POLICE UNDERCOVER

SPECIFICATIONS
Caliber: 32 H&R Magnum and 38 Special. **Type of action:** 6-shot, single and double action. **Barrel length:** 2″. **Height:** 4¹/₂″. **Weight:** 17¹/₂ oz. (2″ barrel) and 19 oz. (4″ barrel.) **Grips:** Checkered walnut panel. **Sights:** Patridge-type ramp front; square-notch rear. **Finish:** Blue.

Price $250.00
Stainless steel and checkered walnut panel 275.75

POLICE UNDERCOVER

CHARTER ARMS REVOLVERS

UNDERCOVER 38 SPECIAL

SPECIFICATIONS
Caliber: 38 Special (Mid-Range & Standard). **Type of Action:** 5-shot, single and double action. **Barrel length** (with shroud): 2″. **Overall length:** 6¼″. **Height:** 4¼″. **Weight:** 16 oz. **Grips:** American walnut hand-checkered. **Sights:** Patridge-type or standard ramp front, square-notched rear. **Finish:** Stainless steel.

Price:. **$304.25**

UNDERCOVER 38 SPECIAL

BONNIE

CLYDE

BONNIE AND CLYDE

This matching pair of handguns in 32 Magnum and 38 Special are designed for couples who like to go to the shooting range together. Both guns come with their own "gun rug" identified by name. Each model also offers a scrolled name on the barrel and features Select-A-Grip color-coordinated grips. The fully shrouded barrels are 2½″ long with an attractive blue finish.

Price: (each) **$256.00**

COLT AUTOMATIC PISTOLS

DOUBLE EAGLE MK SERIES 90

Model	Caliber	Barrel Length (inches)	Finish	Sights	Approx. Weight (ozs.)	Overall Length (inches)	Sight Radius (inches)	Rounds	Price
Double Eagle	45ACP	5	STS	WDS	39	8¹/₂	6¹/₂	8	$695.95
Double Eagle	45ACP	5	STS	AS	39	8¹/₂	6³/₄	8	725.95
Double Eagle	10mm Auto	5	STS	WDS	39	8¹/₂	6¹/₂	8	715.95
Double Eagle	10mm Auto	5	STS	AS	39	8¹/₂	6³/₄	8	745.95
D.E. Combat Com.	40 S&W	4¹/₄	STS	WDS	36	7³/₄	5³/₄	8	695.95
D.E. Combat Com.	45ACP	4¹/₄	STS	WDS	36	7³/₄	5³/₄	8	695.95
D.E. Officer's ACP	45ACP	3¹/₂	STS	WDS	35	7¹/₄	5¹/₄	8	695.95
D.E. Officer's L.W.	45ACP	3¹/₂	B	WDS	25	7¹/₄	5¹/₄	8	695.95

COMBAT COMMANDER
4¹/₄″ barrel only

DOUBLE EAGLE

COMBAT COMMANDER MKIV SERIES 80

The semiautomatic Combat Commander, available in 45 ACP and 38 Super, features an all-steel frame that supplies the pistol with an extra measure of heft and stability. This Colt pistol also offers 3-Dot high-profile sights, lanyard-style hammer and thumb and beavertail grip safety. Also available in lightweight version with alloy frame (45 ACP only).

SPECIFICATIONS

Caliber	Weight	Overall Length	Magazine Rounds	Finish	Price
45 ACP	36 oz.	7³/₄″	8	Blue	$673.95
45 ACP	36 oz.	7³/₄″	8	Stainless	728.95
45 ACP LW	27¹/₂ oz.	7³/₄″	8	Blue	673.95
38 Super	37 oz.	7³/₄″	9	Stainless	727.95

MODEL M1991 A1

MODEL M1991A1 PISTOL

SPECIFICATIONS
Caliber: 45 ACP
Capacity: 7 rounds
Barrel length: 5″
Overall length: 8¹/₂″
Sight radius: 6¹/₂″
Grips: Black composition
Finish: Parkerized
Features: Custom-molded carry case
Price: $499.95

Also available:
COMPACT M1991A1 with 3¹/₂″ barrel $499.95
COMMANDER M1991A1 with 4¹/₄″ barrel and
7-round capacity 499.95

COLT AUTOMATIC PISTOLS

MKIV SERIES 80

GOLD CUP NATIONAL MATCH

SPECIFICATIONS
Caliber: 45 ACP
Capacity: 8 rounds
Barrel length: 5″
Weight: 39 oz.
Overall length: 8¹/₂″
Sights: Colt Elliason sights; adjustable rear for windage and elevation
Hammer: Serrated rounded hammer
Stock: Rubber combat
Finish: Colt blue, stainless or "Ultimate" bright stainless steel
Prices: $860.95 Blue
      920.95 Stainless steel
      989.95 Bright stainless
Also available:
COMBAT ELITE 45 ACP and 38 Super; features Accro Adjustable sights, beavertail grip safety. **Prices: $816.95** in 45 ACP; **$826.95** in 38 Super.

GOLD CUP NATIONAL MATCH

GOVERNMENT MODEL

GOVERNMENT MODEL SERIES 80 SEMIAUTOMATIC

These full-size automatic pistols, available exclusively with 5-inch barrels, may be had in 45 ACP, 40 S&W and 38 Super. The Government Model's special features include high-profile 3 dot sights, grip and thumb safeties, and rubber combat stocks.

SPECIFICATIONS
Calibers: 40 S&W, 38 Super and 45 ACP
Barrel length: 5″
Overall length: 8¹/₂″
Capacity: 9 rds.; 7 rds. (45 ACP)
Weight: 38 oz.
Prices: $718.95 40 S&W
      673.95 45 ACP blue
      717.95 45 ACP stainless
      790.95 45 ACP bright stainless
      684.95 38 Super blue
      727.95 38 Super stainless
      795.95 38 Super bright stainless

GOVERNMENT MODEL 380 MKIV SERIES 80 SEMIAUTOMATIC

This scaled-down version of the 1911 A1 Colt Government Model does not include a grip safety. It incorporates the use of a firing pin safety to provide for a safe method to carry a round in the chamber in a "cocked and locked" mode. Available in matte stainless steel finish with black composition stocks.

SPECIFICATIONS
Caliber: 380 ACP
Magazine capacity: 7 rounds
Barrel length: 3.25″
Overall length: 6″
Height: 4.4″
Weight (empty): 21.75 oz., 14³/₄ oz. (Lightweight)
Sights: Fixed ramp blade front; fixed square notch rear
Grip: Composition stocks
Prices: $419.95 Blue
      469.95 Satin Nickel
      449.95 Stainless steel
Also available:
POCKETLITE MODEL (14³/₄ oz.), blue finish only. **$419.95**

380 GOVERNMENT POCKETLITE

COLT AUTOMATIC PISTOLS

MKIV SERIES 80

DELTA ELITE AND DELTA GOLD CUP

The proven design and reliability of Colt's Government Model has been combined with the powerful 10mm auto cartridge to produce a highly effective shooting system for hunting, law enforcement and personal protection. The velocity and energy of the 10mm cartridge make this pistol ideal for the serious handgun hunter and the law enforcement professional who insist on down-range stopping power.

SPECIFICATIONS
Type: 0 Frame, semiautomatic pistol
Caliber: 10mm
Magazine capacity: 8 rounds
Barrel length: 5″
Overall length: 8½″
Weight (empty): 38 oz.
Sights: 3-dot, high-profile front and rear combat sights; Accro rear sight adj. for windage and elevation (on Delta Gold Cup only)
Sight radius: 6½″ (3 dot sight system), 6¾″ (adjustable sights)
Grips: Rubber combat stocks with Delta medallion
Safety: Trigger safety lock (thumb safety) is located on left-hand side of receiver; grip safety is located on backstrap; internal firing pin safety

DELTA ELITE

Rifling: 6 groove, left-hand twist, one turn in 16″
Prices: **$743.95** Blue
   754.95 Stainless steel
   832.95 "Ultimate" Bright Stainless
Also available:
DELTA GOLD CUP. Same specifications as Delta Elite, except 39 oz. weight and 6¾″ sight radius. Stainless. **$947.95**

COLT MUSTANG .380

This backup automatic has four times the knockdown power of most 25 ACP automatics. It is a smaller version of the 380 Government Model.

SPECIFICATIONS
Caliber: 380 ACP
Capacity: 6 rounds
Weight: 18.5 oz.
Overall length: 5.5″
Height: 3.9″
Prices: **$419.95** Standard blue
   469.95 Nickel
   449.95 Stainless steel
Also available:
MUSTANG POCKETLITE 380 with aluminum alloy receiver; ½″ shorter than standard Govt. 380; weighs only 12.5 oz.
Price: $419.95; $449.95 in Nickel.
MUSTANG PLUS II features full grip length (Govt. 380 model only) with shorter compact barrel and slide (Mustang .380 model only). **Price: $419.95** Blue; **$449.95** Stainless steel.

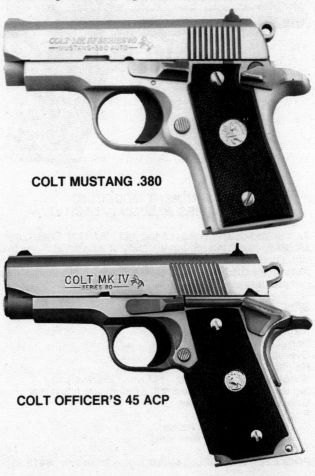

COLT MUSTANG .380

COLT OFFICER'S 45 ACP

COLT OFFICER'S 45 ACP

SPECIFICATIONS
Caliber: 45 ACP
Barrel length: 3½″
Overall length: 7¼″
Weight: 34 oz.
Prices: **$717.95** Stainless steel
   673.95 Standard blue
   790.95 Ultimate stainless
Also available:
OFFICER'S LW w/aluminum alloy frame (24 oz.) and blue finish. **Price: $673.95.**

COLT AUTOMATIC PISTOLS

ALL AMERICAN MODEL 2000
(Right view)

COLT ALL AMERICAN MODEL 2000

Colt's 9mm semiautomatic pistol combines a 15-round magazine capacity with the smooth double action and simple operation of a revolver. The All American shares important technology with the famous Colt M16 military rifle: locked breech; recoil-operated action with locking lugs integral to the barrel; barrel and slide lock together and work as a unit. This precise rotary action reduces felt recoil by slowing down the unlocking cycle. Also available with 3³/₄" barrel and matched barrel bushing kit.

SPECIFICATIONS
Caliber: 9mm
Capacity: 15 + 1 standard
Barrel length: 4¹/₂"
Overall length: 7¹/₂" w/4¹/₂" barrel
Weight: 29 oz. (approx., empty)
Sights: Fixed, ramp blade (glare-proof) front; square notch (glare-proof) rear, Tritium 3-Dot system
Sight radius: 6³/₈"
Rifling: 6 grooves, left-hand twist, 1 turn in 14"
Safety system: Internal striker block
Magazine: Can be fired without magazine; magazine release located behind trigger guard and readily reversible
Finish: Non-glare carbon steel blue slide; electroless nickel-plated carbon steel barrel, polymer or aluminum frame
Price: $575.00
Also available: Optional 3³/₄" barrel and matched barrel bushing kit (same price).

Rotary barrel action reduces recoil and straightline design promotes shot-to-shot accuracy.

Three-dot sight system allows rapid target acquisition even under low light conditions.

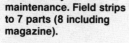

Safe, simple operation with internal striker block safety and no external safety or decocking lever—simplifies and reduces training time.

Roller-bearing mounted trigger features smooth, straight double action pull with no overtravel.

Checkered trigger guard and grip improve handling and pointability during firing.

Magazine release is reversible for left- or right-handed shooters, and is operated without shifting your grip.

Slide release operates easily without shifting grip.

Easy assembly and disassembly for field maintenance. Field strips to 7 parts (8 including magazine).

The All American can be fired without a magazine.

ALL AMERICAN MODEL 2000
(Left view)

COLT REVOLVERS

DETECTIVE SPECIAL

Introduced in 1927, the Colt Detective Special has earned a legendary reputation in the law enforcement field and for personal protection. This classic compact 38 Special revolver retains the familiar appearance of its predecessors, with a 2" barrel and glare-proof ramp front sight, grooved trigger, black composition grips, and shrouded free-floating ejector rod. The Detective Special accommodates six 38 Special rounds. Constructed of forged, high-strength alloy steel, the updated Detective Special is based on the Colt "D" frame, the basis for such respected products as the Colt Police Positive, Agent, Cobra, Viper and Diamondback.

SPECIFICATIONS
Caliber: 38 Special
Capacity: 6 rounds
Weight: 27½ oz.
Barrel length: 2"
Finish: Blue

DETECTIVE SPECIAL
$383.95

SINGLE ACTION ARMY
(Nickel Finish)

SINGLE ACTION ARMY REVOLVER

Colt's maintains the tradition of quality and innovation that Samuel Colt began more than a century and a half ago. Single Action Army revolvers continue to be highly prized collectible arms and are offered in full nickel finish or in Royal Blue with color casehardened frame, without engraving unless otherwise specified by the purchaser. Grips are American walnut.
Price: **$1273.95**

SINGLE ACTION ARMY SPECIFICATIONS

Caliber	Bbl. Length (inches)	Finish	Approx. Weight (ozs.)	O/A Length (inches)	Grips	Medallions
45LC	4¾	CC/B	40	10¼	Walnut	Gold
45LC	4¾	N	40	10¼	Walnut	Nickel
45LC	5½	CC/B	42	11	Walnut	Gold
45LC	5½	N	42	11	Walnut	Nickel
45LC	7½	CC/B	43	13	Walnut	Gold
44-40	4¾	CC/B	40	10¼	Walnut	Gold
44-40	4¾	N	40	10¼	Walnut	Nickel
44-40	5½	CC/B	42	11	Walnut	Gold
44-40	5½	N	42	11	Walnut	Nickel

—Overall   N—Nickel   CC/B—Colorcase frame, Royal Blue cylinder & barrel

SINGLE ACTION ARMY
(Royal Blue Finish)

COLT REVOLVERS

KING COBRA DOUBLE ACTION

This "snake" revolver features a solid barrel rib, full-length ejector rod housing, red ramp front sight, white outline adjustable rear sight, and "gripper" rubber combat grips.

SPECIFICATIONS
Calibers: 357 Magnum and 38 Special
Capacity: 6 rounds
Barrel lengths: 2¹/₂″, 4″, 6″, 8″ (stainless and "Ultimate" bright stainless)
Overall length: 8″ (2¹/₂″ bbl.); 9″ (4″ bbl.); 11″ (6″ bbl.); 13″ (8″ bbl.)
Weight: 36 oz. (2¹/₂″), 42 oz. (4″), 46 oz. (6″), 48 oz. (8″)
Prices: $409.95 Blue
　　　　434.95 Stainless
　　　　469.95 "Ultimate" Bright Stainless

KING COBRA (8″ barrel) in "Ultimate" Bright Stainless Steel

ANACONDA (6″ barrel)

ANACONDA DOUBLE ACTION

SPECIFICATIONS
Calibers: 44 Magnum, 44 Special and 45 Colt (6″ barrel only)
Capacity: 6 rounds
Barrel lengths: 4″, 6″, 8″
Overall length: 9⁵/₈″, 11⁵/₈″, 13⁵/₈″
Weight: 47 oz. (4″), 53 oz. (6″), 59 oz. (8″)
Sights: Red insert front; adjustable white outline rear
Sight radius: 5³/₄″ (4″), 7³/₄″ (6″), 9³/₄″ (8″)
Grips: Black neoprene combat-style with finger grooves
Finish: Matte stainless steel
Price: $569.95 All barrel lengths

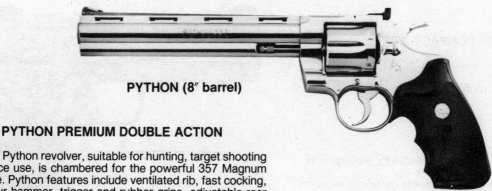

PYTHON (8″ barrel)

PYTHON PREMIUM DOUBLE ACTION

The Colt Python revolver, suitable for hunting, target shooting and police use, is chambered for the powerful 357 Magnum cartridge. Python features include ventilated rib, fast cocking, wide-spur hammer, trigger and rubber grips, adjustable rear and ramp-type front sights, grooved.

SPECIFICATIONS
Calibers: 357 Mag. and 38 Special
Barrel lengths: 2¹/₂″, 4″, 6″, 8″
Overall length: 8″ to 13¹/₂″
Weight: 33 oz. (2¹/₂″), 38 oz. (4″), 43¹/₂ oz. (6″), 48 oz. (8″)
Stock: Rubber combat (2¹/₂″, 4″) or rubber target (6″, 8″)

Finish: Colt high-polish royal blue, stainless steel and "Ultimate" bright stainless steel
Prices: $775.95 Royal Blue
　　　　864.95 Stainless steel
　　　　894.95 "Ultimate" Bright Stainless Steel

COONAN ARMS

357 MAGNUM PISTOL
5″ Barrel (Top)
6″ Barrel (Middle)
Compensated Barrel (Bottom)

COONAN 357 MAGNUM

SPECIFICATIONS
Caliber: 357 Magnum
Magazine capacity: 7 rounds + 1
Barrel length: 5″ (6″ or Compensated barrel optional)
Overall length: 8.3″
Weight: 48 oz. (loaded)
Height: 5.6″

Width: 1.3″
Sights: Ramp front; fixed rear, adjustable for windage only
Grips: Smooth black walnut (checkered grips optional)
Finish: Stainless steel and alloy steel
Features: Linkless barrel; recoil-operated; extended slide catch and thumb lock
Prices: With 5″ barrel $720.00
With 6″ barrel 755.00
With Compensated barrel 999.00

"CADET" COMPACT MODEL

SPECIFICATIONS
Caliber: 357 Magnum
Magazine capacity: 6 rounds + 1
Barrel length: 3.9″
Overall length: 7.8″
Weight: 39 oz.
Height: 5.3″
Width: 1.3″
Sights: Ramp front; fixed rear, adjustable for windage only
Grips: Smooth black walnut
Features: Linkless bull barrel; full-length guide rod; recoil-operated (Browning falling-block design); extended slide catch and thumb lock for one-hand operation
Price: $841.00

"CADET" COMPACT

DAEWOO PISTOL

MODEL DP51 9mm PISTOL
$349.50

SPECIFICATIONS
Caliber: 9mm Parabellum
Capacity: 13 rounds
Barrel length: 4 1/8″
Overall length: 7 1/2″
Weight: 28 oz.
Muzzle velocity: 1150 fps
Sights: Blade front (1/8″) with self-luminous dot (optional); square notch rear, drift adjustable with 2 self-luminous dots
Safety: Ambidextrous manual safety, half-cocking and automatic firing pin block
Finish: Sand-blasted black or polished
Also available in 22 LR (Model DP-52), 40 S&W (Model DH-40) and 45 ACP (Model DH-45). Contact U.S. distributor for specifications and prices (see Directory of Manufacturers and Suppliers).

DAVIS PISTOLS

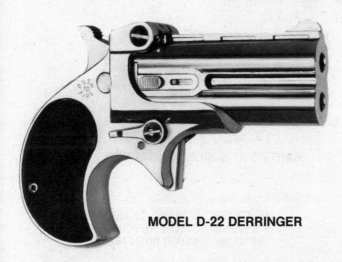

MODEL D-22 DERRINGER

D-SERIES DERRINGERS
$64.90

SPECIFICATIONS
Calibers: 22 LR, 22 Mag., 25 Auto, 32 Auto
Barrel length: 2.4″
Overall length: 4″
Height: 2.8″
Weight: 9.5 oz.
Capacity: 2 shot
Grips: Laminated wood
Finish: Black teflon or chrome
Also available:
BIG BORE 38 SPECIAL D-SERIES. Barrel length: 2.75″.
Overall length: 4.65″. **Weight:** 11.5 oz. **Price:** . . **$87.90**

MODEL P-380 (not shown)
$98.00

SPECIFICATIONS
Caliber: 380 Auto
Magazine capacity: 5 rounds
Barrel length: 2.8″
Overall length: 5.4″
Height: 4″
Weight: 22 oz. (empty)

MODEL P-32
$87.50

SPECIFICATIONS
Caliber: 32 Auto
Magazine capacity: 6 rounds
Barrel length: 2.8″
Overall length: 5.4″
Height: 4″
Weight (empty): 22 oz.
Grips: Laminated wood
Finish: Black teflon or chrome

MODEL P-32

EMF/DAKOTA

SINGLE ACTION REVOLVERS

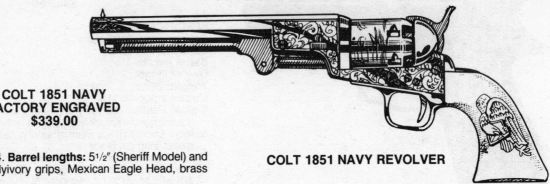

COLT 1851 NAVY
FACTORY ENGRAVED
$339.00

SPECIFICATIONS
Calibers: 36 and 44. **Barrel lengths:** 5¹/₂″ (Sheriff Model) and
7¹/₂″. **Features:** Polyivory grips, Mexican Eagle Head, brass
or steel.

COLT 1851 NAVY REVOLVER

HARTFORD MODEL

HARTFORD MODELS
$600.00   ($760.00 in Nickel)

EMF's Hartford Single Action revolvers are available in the
following calibers: 32-20, 38-40, 44-40, 44 Special and 45 Long
Colt. **Barrel lengths:** 4³/₄″, 5¹/₂″ and 7¹/₂″. All models feature
steel back straps, trigger guards and forged frame. Identical
to the original Colts.

HARTFORD SCROLL ENGRAVED

HARTFORD SCROLL ENGRAVED
SINGLE ACTION REVOLVER
$840.00   ($1000.00 in Nickel)

SPECIFICATIONS
Calibers: 22, 45 Long Colt, 357 Magnum, 44-40. **Barrel
lengths:** 4⁵/₈″, 5¹/₂″ and 7¹/₂″. **Features:** Classic original-type
scroll engraving.

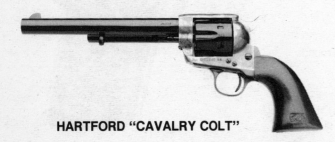

HARTFORD "CAVALRY COLT"

HARTFORD MODELS
"CAVALRY COLT" AND "ARTILLERY"
$655.00

The Model 1873 Government Model Cavalry revolver is an
exact reproduction of the original Colt made for the U.S. Cavalry in caliber 45 Long Colt with barrel length of 7¹/₂″. The
Artillery Model has 5¹/₂″ barrel.

EMF/DAKOTA

MODEL 1873 (With Extra Cylinder)
$665.00

SPECIFICATIONS
Calibers: 32-20, 38-40, 44-40, 357 Mag., 45 Long Colt, 30 M1 Carbine. **Barrel lengths:** 4³/₄″, 5¹/₂″, 7¹/₂″. **Finish:** Engraved models, blue or nickel. **Special feature:** Each gun is fitted with second caliber.

DAKOTA TARGET
$500.00

SPECIFICATIONS
Calibers: 45 Long Colt, 357 Magnum, 22 LR. **Barrel lengths:** 5¹/₂″ and 7¹/₂″. **Finish:** Polished blue. **Special features:** Case-hardened frame, one-piece walnut grips, brass back strap, ramp front blade target sight and adjustable rear sight.

1873 DAKOTA SINGLE
ACTION REVOLVER
$490.00   ($636.00 in Nickel)

SPECIFICATIONS
Calibers: 357 Mag., 44-40, 45 Long Colt. **Barrel lengths:** 4³/₄″, 5¹/₂″ and 7¹/₂″. **Finish:** Blued, casehardened frame. **Grips:** One-piece walnut. **Features:** Set screw for cylinder pin release; parts are interchangeable with early Colts.

MODEL 1875 "OUTLAW"
$465.00 ($550.00 in Nickel)

SPECIFICATIONS
Calibers: 44-40, 45 Long Colt, 357 Magnum. **Barrel length:** 7¹/₂″. **Finish:** Blue or nickel. **Special features:** Casehardened frame, walnut grips; an exact replica of the Remington No. 3 revolver produced from 1875 to 1889.
Factory Engraved Model **$600.00**
  In nickel **710.00**

MODEL 1890 REMINGTON POLICE
$470.00   ($560.00 in Nickel)

SPECIFICATIONS
Calibers: 44-40, 45 Long Colt and 357 Magnum. **Barrel length:** 5³/₄″. **Finish:** Blue or nickel. **Features:** Original design (1891–1894) with lanyard ring in buttstock; casehardened frame; walnut grips.
Engraved Model **$620.00**
  In nickel **725.00**

ERMA TARGET ARMS

MODEL 777 SPORTING REVOLVER

SPECIFICATIONS
Caliber: 357 Magnum
Capacity: 6 cartridges
Barrel length: 4″ and 5½″
Overall length: 9.7″ and 11.3″
Weight: 43.7 oz. w/5½″ barrel
Sight radius: 6.4″ and 8″
Grip: Checkered walnut
Price: **$1200.00**

Also available:
MODEL 773 MATCH (32 S&W Wadcutter).
   Same specifications as Model 777 (5½″ barrel), but with adjustable match grip and 6″ barrel. **Weight:** 47.3 oz. **$1345.00; $1265.00** in Standard Model.
MODEL 772 MATCH (22 Long Rifle).
   Same specifications as Model 773, except weight is 47¼ oz. **$1345.00; $1265.00** in Standard Model.
Both Match revolvers feature micrometer rear sights (adjustable for windage and elevation), interchangeable front and rear sight blades, adjustable triggers, polished blue finish and 6-shot capacity.

MODEL 777 STANDARD

**MODEL 777
(With Match Grip)**

MODEL ESP 85A

MODEL ESP 85A SPORTING PISTOL

SPECIFICATIONS
Caliber: 22 LR or 32 S&W Wadcutter (interchangeable)
Action: Semiautomatic
Capacity: 5 cartridges (8 in 22 LR optional)
Barrel length: 6″
Overall length: 10″
Weight: 40 oz.
Sight radius: 7.8″
Sights: Micrometer rear sight; fully adjustable interchangeable front and rear sight blade (3.5mm/4.0mm)
Grip: Checkered walnut grip with thumbrest

Prices:
ESP 85A SPORTING 22 LR	**$1228.00**
Target adjustable grip, **add**	169.50
Left hand, **add**	199.00
ESP 85A CHROME SPORTING (22 LR)	1449.00
ESP 85A MATCH 22 LR	1345.00
Left hand	1375.00
ESP 85A CHROME MATCH 22 LR	1568.00
In 32 S&W	1400.00
Conversion Units 22 LR	689.00
In 32 S&W	746.00

EUROPEAN AMERICAN ARMORY

ASTRA MODEL A-70
$325.00 (Blue)
$351.00 (Nickel)

SPECIFICATIONS
Calibers: 9mm and 40 S&W
Capacity: 8 rounds
Barrel length: 3½″
Overall length: 6½″
Weight: 23.3 oz.
Finish: Blue or nickel

**ASTRA MODEL A-70
BLUED**

**ASTRA MODEL A-75
BLUED**

ASTRA MODEL A-75
$377.00 (Blue)
$403.00 (Nickel)

SPECIFICATIONS
Calibers: 9mm and 40 S&W
Capacity: 8 rounds (7 in 40 S&W)
Barrel length: 3½″
Overall length: 6½″
Weight: 29.3 oz.
Finish: Blue or nickel

ASTRA MODEL A-100
$403.00 (Blue)
$429.00 (Nickel)

SPECIFICATIONS
Calibers: 9mm, 40 S&W and 45 ACP
Capacity: 15 rounds (9 in 45 ACP)
Barrel length: 3.75″
Overall length: 7″
Weight: 48 oz.
Finish: Blue or nickel

**ASTRA MODEL A-100
BLUED**

EUROPEAN AMERICAN ARMORY

WITNESS DOUBLE ACTION PISTOLS

WITNESS SUBCOMPACT

SPECIFICATIONS
Calibers: 9mm and 40 S&W
Capacity: 13 rounds (9mm); 9 rounds (40 S&W)
Barrel length: 3.66″
Overall length: 7.24″
Weight: 30 oz.
Finish: Blue, chrome, blue/chrome
Prices:
9mm Blue $370.00
Chrome or blue/chrome 396.00
40 S&W Blue 396.00
Chrome or blue/chrome 422.00

WITNESS SUBCOMPACT

WITNESS BASIC (not shown)

SPECIFICATIONS
Calibers: 9mm, 40 S&W and 45 ACP
Capacity: 16 rounds (9mm); 12 rounds (40 S&W); 10 rounds (45 ACP)
Barrel length: 4¹/₂″
Overall length: 8.1″
Weight: 33 oz.
Finish: Blue, chrome, blue/chrome, stainless steel

Prices:
9mm Blue $370.00
Chrome or blue/chrome 396.00
Stainless steel 435.00
40 S&W Blue 396.00
Chrome or blue/chrome 422.00
Stainless steel 461.00
45 ACP Blue 474.00
Chrome or blue/chrome 500.00
Stainless steel 539.00

WITNESS GOLD TEAM

SPECIFICATIONS
Calibers: 9mm, 40 S&W and 38 Super
Capacity: 19 rounds (9mm); 14 rounds (40 S&W); 13 rounds (38 Super)
Barrel length: 5¹/₄″
Overall length: 10¹/₂″
Weight: 38 oz.
Finish: Hard chrome
Features: Triple chamber comp, S/A trigger, extended safety, competition hammer, checkered front strap and backstrap, low-profile competition grips, square trigger guard
Price: $1560.00

WITNESS GOLD TEAM

EUROPEAN AMERICAN ARMORY

**WINDICATOR · TARGET
GRADE REVOLVER**

WINDICATOR DOUBLE ACTION
(STANDARD GRADE)

SPECIFICATIONS
Calibers: 22 LR, 22 LR/22 WMR, 32 H&R, 38 Special, 357
   Mag.
Capacity: 6 rounds (38 Special only); 7 rounds (32 H&R only);
   8 rounds (22 LR and 22 LR/22 WMR)
Barrel lengths: 2″, 4″ and 6″
Finish: Blue only
Features: Swing-out cylinder; competition-style grips; hammer
   block safety

Prices:

22 LR w/4″ barrel	$181.50
22 LR w/6″ barrel	191.75
22 LR/22 WMR w/4″ barrel	233.00
22 LR/22 WMR w/6″ barrel	243.00
32 H&R w/2″ barrel	179.00
38 Special w/2″ barrel	179.00
38 Special w/4″ barrel	188.50
Also available:	
TARGET GRADE	$351.00
TACTICAL GRADE	240.00

**BIG BORE BOUNTY HUNTER
SINGLE ACTION**

BIG BORE BOUNTY HUNTER SA

SPECIFICATIONS
Calibers: 357 Mag., 45 Long Colt and 44 Mag.
Capacity: 6 rounds
Barrel lengths: 4¹/₂″, 5¹/₂″ and 7¹/₂″
Sights: Adjustable rear sight; scope mounts
Finish: Blue, blue/gold, color casehardened, gold or chrome
Features: Transfer bar safety, 3-position hammer; hammer-
   forged barrel; walnut grips

Prices:

4¹/₂″ or 5¹/₂″ barrel, blued	$284.70
7¹/₂″ barrel, blued	287.30
4¹/₂″ or 5¹/₂″ bbl., case colored receiver	295.00
7¹/₂″ bbl., color casehardened receiver	297.70
4¹/₂″ or 5¹/₂″ barrel, blue/gold	297.70
7¹/₂″ barrel, blue/gold finish	300.30
7¹/₂″ barrel, gold finish	348.40
4¹/₂″ or 5¹/₂″ barrel, chrome finish	327.60
7¹/₂″ barrel, chrome finish	330.20

FREEDOM ARMS

454 CASULL FIELD GRADE

**MODEL 353 REVOLVER
FIELD GRADE 7¹/₂″ BARREL**

454 CASULL PREMIER & FIELD GRADES

SPECIFICATIONS
Calibers: 454 Casull, 44 Rem. Mag.
Action: Single action
Capacity: 5 rounds
Barrel lengths: 4³/₄″, 6″, 7¹/₂″, 10″
Overall length: 14″ (w/7¹/₂″ barrel)
Weight: 3 lbs. 2 oz. (w/7¹/₂″ barrel)
Safety: Patented sliding bar
Sights: Notched rear; blade front (optional adjustable rear and replaceable front blade)
Grips: Impregnated hardwood
Finish: Brushed stainless
Features: Patented interchangeable forcing cone bushing (optional); Bo-Mar silhouette, Millett competition and express sights are optional; SSK T'SOB 3-ring scope mount optional
Prices:
MODEL FA-454AS (Premier Grade)
W/adjustable sights **$1385.00**
W/fixed sights (7¹/₂″ barrel only) **1298.00**
44 Remington w/adjustable sights
   (7¹/₂″ or 10″ barrel only) **1385.00**
MODEL FA-454FGAS (Field Grade)
With stainless steel matte finish, adj. sight,
   Pachmayr presentation grips **1115.00**
W/fixed sights (4³/₄″ barrel only) **1035.00**
44 Remington w/adjustable sights **1115.00**
MODEL FA-454ASM U.S. Deputy Marshall
With adjustable sights (3″ barrel only) **1558.00**
With fixed sights **1475.00**
HUNTER PAKS available: . . . . **$1408.85 to $1611.00**

MODEL 353

SPECIFICATIONS
Caliber: 357 Magnum
Action: Single action
Capacity: 5 shots
Barrel lengths: 4³/₄″, 6″, 7¹/₂″, 9″
Sights: Removable front blade; adjustable rear
Grips: Pachmayr Presentation grips (Premier Grade has impregnated hardwood grips
Finish: Non-glare Field Grade (standard model); Premier Grade finish (all stainless steel)
Prices:
Field Grade **$1115.00**
Premier Grade **1385.00**

**MODEL 252 REVOLVER
SILHOUETTE CLASS 10″ BARREL**

COMPETITION MODELS
(not shown)

SPECIFICATIONS
Calibers: 357 Magnum and 44 Rem. Mag.
Barrel lengths: 9″ (357 Mag.) and 10″ (44 Rem. Mag.)
Sights: Adjustable ISGW rear sight; removable Patridge front blade
Grips: Pachmayr Presentation
Trigger: Pre-set stop; trigger overtravel screw
Finish: Matte
Price: **$1213.80**

MODEL 252

SPECIFICATIONS
Caliber: 22 LR (optional 22 Magnum cylinder)
Barrel lengths: 5¹/₈″, 7¹/₂″ (Varmint Class) and 10″ (Silhouette Class)
Sights: Silhouette competition sights (Silhouette Class); adjustable rear express sight; removable front express blade
Grips: Black micarta (Silhouette Class); black and green laminated hardwood (Varmint Class)
Finish: Stainless steel
Features: Dual firing pin; lightened hammer; pre-set trigger stop; accepts all sights and/or scope mounts
Prices:
Silhouette Class **$1295.00**
Varmint Class **1248.00**

GLOCK PISTOLS

MODEL 17
$579.95

MODEL 17L COMPETITION
$768.25

SPECIFICATIONS
Caliber: 9mm Parabellum
Magazine capacity: 17 rounds (19 rounds optional)
Barrel length: 4¹/₂″ (hexagonal profile with right-hand twist
Overall length: 7.28″
Weight: 22 oz. (without magazine)
Sights: Fixed or adjustable rear sights

Also available:
MODEL 21 in 45 ACP (13 round capacity). **Price: $638.49**
MODEL 22 (Sport and Service models) in 40 S&W. **Overall length:** 7.28″. **Capacity:** 15 rounds. **Price: $579.95**

SPECIFICATIONS
Caliber: 9mm Parabellum
Magazine capacity: 17 rounds
Barrel length: 6.02″
Overall length: 8.85″
Weight: 23.35 oz. (without magazine)
Sights: Fixed or adjustable rear sights

Also available:
MODEL 23 (Compact Sport and Service models) in 40 S&W. **Overall length:** 6.85″. **Capacity:** 13 rounds. **Price: $579.95**

MODEL 19 COMPACT
$579.95

MODEL 20
$638.49

SPECIFICATIONS
Caliber: 9mm Parabellum
Magazine capacity: 15 rounds
Barrel length: 4″
Overrall length: 6.85″
Weight: 21 oz. (without magazine)
Sights: Fixed or adjustable rear sights

SPECIFICATIONS
Caliber: 10mm
Magazine capacity: 15 rounds
Action: Double action
Barrel length: 4.6″
Overall length: 7.59″
Height: 5.47″ (w/sights)
Weight: 26.35 oz. (empty)
Sights: Fixed or adjustable
Features: 3 safeties, "safe action" system, polymer frame

GRENDEL PISTOLS

MODEL P-30
$225.00

SPECIFICATIONS
Caliber: 22 WRF Magnum
Capacity: 30 rounds
Barrel length: 5″
Overall length: 8¹/₂″
Weight: 21 oz. (empty)
Sight radius: 7.2″
Features: Fixed barrel, flat trajectory, low recoil, ambidextrous safety levers, front sight adjustable for windage.
Also available:
Model P-30M (w/removable muzzle brake); **barrel length:** 5.6″; **overall length:** 10″. **Price: $235.00**
Model P-31 with 11″ barrel; **weight:** 48 oz. **Price: $345.00**

MODEL P-30

MODEL P-12
$175.00   ($195.00 in Nickel)

SPECIFICATIONS
Caliber: 380 ACP
Capacity: 12 rounds
Barrel length: 3″
Overall length: 5.3″
Weight: 13 oz. (empty)
Sight radius: 4¹/₂″
Features: Low inertia safety hammer system; glass reinforced Zytel magazine; solid steel slide w/firing pin and extractor; polymer DuPont ST-800 grip

MODEL P-12

HÄMMERLI U.S.A. PISTOLS

MODEL 280 SPORT PISTOL

MODEL 280 SPORT PISTOL
$1465.00 ($1650.00 in 32 S&W)

SPECIFICATIONS
Calibers: 22 LR and 32 S&W
Capacity: 6 rounds (22 LR); 5 rounds (32 S&W)
Barrel length: 4.58″
Weight: (excluding counterweights) 34.92 oz. (22 LR); 38.8 oz. (32 S&W)
Sight radius: 8.66″

HÄMMERLI U.S.A. PISTOLS

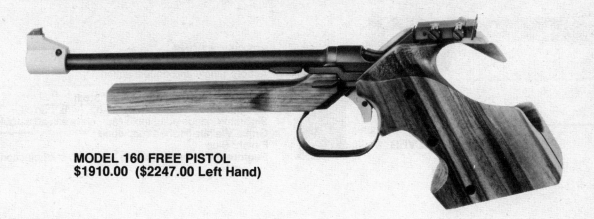

MODEL 160 FREE PISTOL
$1910.00 ($2247.00 Left Hand)

SPECIFICATIONS
Caliber: 22 LR
Overall length: 17.2"
Weight: 45.6 oz.
Trigger action: Infinitely variable set trigger weight; cocking lever located on left of receiver; trigger length variable along weapon axis
Sights: Sight radius 14.8"; micrometer rear sight adj. for windage and elevation
Locking action: Martini-type locking action w/side-mounted locking lever
Barrel: Free floating, cold swaged precision barrel w/low axis relative to the hand
Ignition: Horizontal firing pin (hammerless) in line w/barrel axis; firing pin travel 0.15"
Grips: Selected walnut w/adj. hand rest for direct arm to barrel extension

MODEL 162 ELECTRONIC PISTOL (not shown)
$2095.00 ($2419.00 Left Hand)

SPECIFICATIONS:
Same as **Model 160** except trigger action is electronic. Features short lock time (1.7 milliseconds between trigger actuation and firing pin impact), light trigger pull, and extended battery life.

MODEL 208S TARGET PISTOL
$1695.00

SPECIFICATIONS:
Caliber: 22 LR
Barrel length: 6"
Overall length: 10.2"
Weight: 37.3 oz. (w/accessories)
Capacity: 9 rounds
Sight radius: 8.3"
Sights: Micrometer rear sight w/notch width; standard front blade

MODEL 212 TARGET PISTOL
$1500.00

SPECIFICATIONS
Caliber: 22 LR
Barrel length: 5"
Overall length: 8.6"
Weight: 31 oz.
Capacity: 8 rounds
Sights: Blade front; notched rear

HARRINGTON & RICHARDSON

SPORTSMAN 999 REVOLVER
$229.95

SPECIFICATIONS
Calibers: 22 Short, Long, Long Rifle
Action: Single and double action
Capacity: 9 rounds
Barrel lengths: 4″ and 6″ (both fluted)
Weight: 30 oz. (w/4″ barrel); 34 oz. (w/6″ barrel)
Sights: Windage adjustable rear; elevation adjustable front
Grips: Walnut-finished hardwood
Finish: Blue
Features: Top-break loading with auto shell ejection

HECKLER & KOCH PISTOLS

MODEL HK USP
$624.00
($644.00 w/Control Lever on Right)

The Heckler & Koch USP (Universal Self-loading Pistol) is the first H&K pistol designed especially for the demanding needs of the American shooter. It can be safely carried "cocked and locked." The control lever—a combination safety and de-cocking lever—is frame-mounted and quickly accessible (unlike the slide-mounted safeties found on many pistols). The USP control lever has a positive stop and returns to the "fire" position after decocking. The USP also has an ambidextrous magazine release that is shielded by the trigger guard to prevent inadvertent firing. The grip is stepped at the rear and combined with the tapered magazine well, making magazine releases fast and precise. An extended slide release lever is positioned to allow easy operation without changing the grip of the shooting hand. Other features include: a mechanical recoil reduction system; universal mounting grooves in the frame; extra-large trigger guard for use with gloved hands; metal reinforced polymer frame; bobbed hammer (DA only); and adjustable 3-dot sights (tritium sights optional).

SPECIFICATIONS
Calibers: 9mm and 40 S&W
Capacity: 13 rounds (40 S&W); 16 rounds (9mm)
Operating system: Short recoil, modified Browning action
Barrel length: 4.13″
Overall length: 7.64″
Weight: 1.74 lbs. (40 S&W); 1.66 lbs. (9mm)
Height: 5.35″
Sights: 3-Dot
Grips/stock: Polymer receiver and integral grips

HECKLER & KOCH PISTOLS

MODEL P7M8
SELF-LOADING PISTOL
$1059.00 (Blue or Nickel)

SPECIFICATIONS
Caliber: 9mm × 19 (Luger)
Capacity: 8 rounds
Barrel length: 4.13″
Overall length: 6.73″
Weight: 1.75 lbs. (empty)
Sight radius: 5.83″
Sights: Adjustable rear
Finish: Blue or nickel
Also available: **MODEL P7M13** with same barrel length, but
  slightly longer overall, heavier and 13-round capacity
  $1284.00 (Blue or nickel)

MODEL P7M10
$1314.00 (Blue or Nickel)

SPECIFICATIONS
Caliber: 40 S&W
Capacity: 10 rounds
Barrel length: 4.13″
Overall length: 6.9″
Weight: 2.69 lbs. (empty)
Sights: Adjustable rear
Finish: Blue or nickel
Operating system: Recoil operated;
  retarded inertia bolt

MODEL P7K3
$1059.00

SPECIFICATIONS
Calibers: 22 LR, 380
Capacity: 8 rounds
Barrel length: 3.8″
Overall length: 6.3″
Weight: 1.65 lbs. (empty)
Sight radius: 5.5″
Sights: Adjustable rear
Also available: 22 LR Conversion Kit **$529.00**; Tritium Sights
  (orange, yellow or green rear with green front) **$59.00**

MODEL SP89
$1324.00

This multi-purpose sporting/security pistol features a rotary-
aperture rear sight adjustable for windage and elevation; a
hooded front sight; and a shape designed to accept H&K clawlock mounts for adding a telescopic sight.

SPECIFICATIONS
Caliber: 9mm
Action: Semiautomatic, recoil-operated, delayed roller-locked
  bolt system
Capacity: 15 rounds
Barrel length: 4$\frac{1}{2}$″
Overall length: 13″
Weight: 4.4 lbs.

HERITAGE MANUFACTURING

**ROUGH RIDER
SINGLE ACTION**

ROUGH RIDER SINGLE ACTION

SPECIFICATIONS
Caliber: 22 LR or 22 LR/22 WMR
Capacity: 6 rounds
Barrel lengths: 3″, 4³/₄″, 6¹/₂″, 9″
Weight: 31 to 38 oz.
Sights: Blade front
Finish: Blue with gold accents
Features: Smooth walnut grips; rotating hammer block safety
Prices:
22 LR (3¹/₄″, 4³/₄″, 6¹/₂″ barrel) $104.95
   With 9″ barrel 111.95
22 Magnum (3¹/₄″ barrel only) 134.95
   With 9″ barrel only 139.95
   With 4³/₄″ or 6¹/₂″ barrel 119.95

SENTRY DOUBLE ACTION
$104.95 – $129.95

SPECIFICATIONS
Calibers: 38 S&W Special
Capacity: 6 rounds
Barrel length: 2″ or 4″
Finish: Blue or chrome
Features: Checkered composition grips; internal hammer block; additional safety plug in cylinder

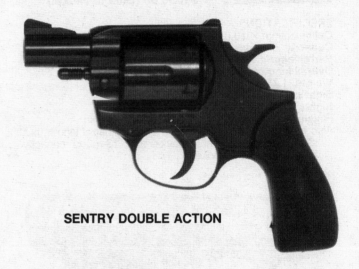

SENTRY DOUBLE ACTION

EAGLE SEMIAUTOMATIC
$146.95 (Blue)
$169.95 (Chrome)
$219.95 (Stainless)

SPECIFICATIONS
Caliber: 380 ACP
Barrel length: 3¹/₄″
Overall length: 6¹/₂″
Weight: 25 oz.
Capacity: 7 shots
Finish: Blue or chrome
Grip: European walnut
Sights: Integral tapered post front sight; windage adjustable rear sight

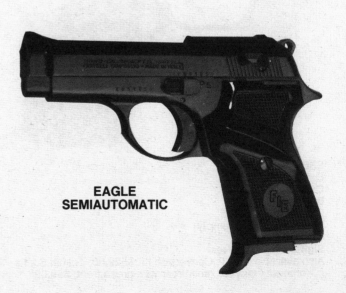

**EAGLE
SEMIAUTOMATIC**

KBI PISTOLS

MODEL PSP-25
$249.00   ($299.00 Hard Chrome)

SPECIFICATIONS
Caliber: 25 ACP
Barrel length: 2¹/₈″
Overall length: 4¹/₈″
Weight: 9.5 oz. (empty)
Height: 2⁷/₈″
Features: Dual safety system; all-steel construction; honed, polished and blued.

FEG MODEL PJK-9HP
$329.00

SPECIFICATIONS
Caliber: 9mm Para.
Magazine capacity: 13 rounds
Barrel length: 4³/₄″
Overall length: 8″
Weight: 32 oz.
Action: Single
Grips: Hand-checkered walnut
Safety: Thumb safety
Features: Two 13-round magazines; cleaning rod; high-lustre blued all-steel construction

FEG MODEL PMK-380
$249.00

SPECIFICATIONS
Caliber: 380 ACP
Capacity: 6 rounds
Action: Double
Barrel length: 3¹/₂″
Overall length: 6.1″
Weight: 18¹/₂ oz.
Safety: Thumb safety
Grips: Black composite
Features: High-lustre blued steel slide; blue anodized aluminum alloy frame; two 7-round magazines; cleaning rod

L.A.R. GRIZZLY

MARK I
GRIZZLY 45 WIN MAG $920.00
(357 Magnum $933.00)

This semiautomatic pistol is a direct descendant of the tried and trusted 1911-type .45 automatic, but with the added advantage of increased caliber capacity.

SPECIFICATIONS
Calibers: 45 Win. Mag., 45 ACP, 357 Mag., 10mm
Barrel lengths: 5.4″ and 6¹/₂″
Overall length: 10¹/₂″
Weight (empty): 48 oz.
Height: 5³/₄″
Sights: Fixed, ramped blade (front); fully adjustable for elevation and windage (rear)

Magazine capacity: 7 rounds
Grips: Checkered rubber, nonslip, combat-type
Safeties: Grip depressor, manual thumb, slide-out-of-battery disconnect
Materials: Mil spec 4140 steel slide and receiver with non-corrosive, heat-treated, special alloy steels for other parts

Also available:
Grizzly 44 Magnum Mark 4 w/adj. sights **$933.00**
Grizzly Win Mag Conversion Units **214.00**
  In 357 Magnum **228.00**
Win Mag Compensator **110.00**

**GRIZZLY WIN MAG
6¹/₂″ BARREL**

MARK 4 GRIZZLY 44 MAG.

**GRIZZLY WIN MAG
8″ BARREL**

GRIZZLY 50 MARK 5

**GRIZZLY 50 MARK 5
$1060.00**

Also available:
GRIZZLY WIN MAG (8″ and 10″)
Model G-WM8 (8″ barrel in 45 Win. Mag., 45 ACP
  or 357/45 Grizzly Win. Mag. **$1313.00**
Model G357M8 (8″ barrel in 357 Magnum) **1337.50**
Model G-WM10 (10″ barrel in 45 Win Mag, 45 ACP
  or 357/45 Grizzly Win. Mag. **1375.00**
Model G357M10 (10″ barrel in 357 Magnum) **1400.00**

SPECIFICATIONS
Caliber: 50 AE
Capacity: 6 rounds
Barrel lengths: 5.4″ and 6.5″
Overall length: 10⁵/₈″
Sights: Fixed front; fully adjustable rear

LLAMA REVOLVERS

COMANCHE
$274.95

SPECIFICATIONS
Calibers: 22 LR and 357 Magnum
Capacity: 6 shots
Action: Double
Barrel length: 4″ (357 Mag. only); 6-inch
Overall length: 9¼″ (w/4-inch barrel); 11″ (w/6-inch barrel)
Weight: 2 lbs. 4 oz. (w/4″ barrel); 2 lbs. 7 oz. (w/6″ barrel)
Frame: Forged high-tensile strength steel; serrated front and back strap
Trigger: Wide-grooved target trigger

Hammer: Wide-spur target hammer with serrated gripping surface
Sights: Square notch rear sight with windage and elevation adjustments; serrated quick-draw front sight on ramp
Sight radius: 5¾″ (w/4-inch barrel); 7¾″ (w/6-inch barrel)
Grips: Oversized target, checkered walnut
Finish: High-polished, deep blue
Safety feature: Hammer is mounted on an eccentric cam (position is controlled by trigger); firing pin contacts the primer only when trigger is fully depressed

SUPER COMANCHE 44 MAGNUM
$366.95

SPECIFICATIONS
Caliber: 44 Magnum
Number of Shots: 6
Barrel Length: 6″ and 8½″
Overall Length: 11¾″ or 14½″
Weight: 3 lbs. 2 oz. (6″ barrel); 3 lbs. 8 oz. (8½″ barrel)
Frame: Forged high-tensile strength steel

Trigger: Smooth extra wide
Hammer: Wide spur, deep positive serrations
Sights: Rear, click-adjustable for windage and elevation, leaf serrated to reduce glare; ramped-blade front
Sight Radius: 8″ (6″ barrel); 10⅜″ (8½″ barrel)
Grips: Oversized target, checkered walnut

LLAMA AUTOMATIC PISTOLS

SMALL-FRAME AUTOMATIC PISTOL
(Satin Chrome Finish)
22 and 380 Caliber
$399.00

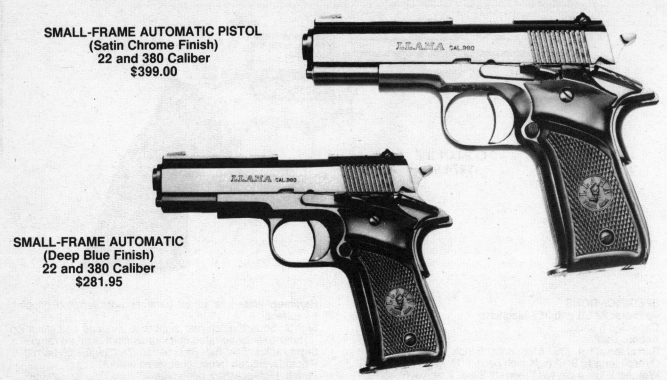

SMALL-FRAME AUTOMATIC
(Deep Blue Finish)
22 and 380 Caliber
$281.95

LLAMA AUTOMATIC PISTOL SPECIFICATIONS

Type:	Small-Frame Auto Pistols		Compact-Frame Auto Pistols			Large-Frame Auto Pistols
Calibers:	22 LR	380 Auto	9mm Parabellum	40 S&W	45 Auto	9mm, 38 Super, 40 S&W, 45 Auto
Frame:	Precision machined from high-strength steel; serrated front strap, checkered (curved) backstrap		Precision machined from high-strength steel; serrated front strap, checkered (curved) backstrap			Precision machined from high-strength steel; plain front strap, checkered (curved) backstrap
Trigger:	Serrated		Serrated			Serrated
Hammer:	External; wide spur, serrated		External; wide spur, serrated			External; wide spur, serrated
Operation:	Straight blow-back		Locked breech			Locked breech
Loaded Chamber Indicator:	No	Yes	No	No	No	Yes
Safeties:	Side lever thumb safety, grip safety		Side lever thumb safety, grip safety			Side lever thumb safety, grip safety
Grips:	Modified thumbrest black plastic grips		Matte black polymer			Matte black polymer
Sights:	Patridge-type front; square-notch rear adjustable for windage		Patridge-type front; square-notch rear adjustable for windage			Patridge-type front; square-notch rear adjustable for windage
Sight Radius:	4 1/4″		6 1/4″			6 1/4″
Magazine Capacity:	8-shot	7-shot	9-shot	8-shot	7-shot	7-shot
Weight:	23 oz.		37 oz.	37 oz.	34 oz.	36 oz.
Barrel Length:	3 11/16″		4 1/4″			5 1/8″
Overall Length:	6 1/2″		7 7/8″			8 1/2″
Height:	4 3/8″		5 7/16″			5 5/16″
Finish:	Std. models: High-polished, deep blue. Deluxe models: Satin chrome (22 & 380 Auto)		Std. models: High-polished, deep blue. Deluxe models: Satin chrome (9mm, 40 S&W & 45 Auto)			Std. models: High-polished, deep blue. Deluxe models: Satin chrome (9mm 38 Super, 40 S&W, 45)

LLAMA AUTOMATIC PISTOLS

COMPACT 9mm, 40 S&W and 45
$324.95

9mm, 40 S&W and 45
STANDARD BLUE
$314.95

MODEL M-82 DOUBLE ACTION
$584.95

SPECIFICATIONS
Caliber: 9mm Parabellum and 40 S&W
Magazine: 15 cartridges (15 + 1 shot)
Barrel length: 4¹/₄″
No. of barreling grooves: 6
Overall length: 8″
Height: 5⁵/₁₆″
Maximum width: 1³/₈″
Weight: 39 oz. (empty)
Sights: High visibility, 3-dot sights; rear sight drift adj.
Sight radius: 6″
Grips: Matte black polymer
Stocks: Plastic
Finish: Blued satin
Features: Positive safety mechanism; twin lug lockup; full-length guide rails; recessed breech face; ambidextrous safety; articulated firing pin; enlarged ejection port; changeable magazine release; instant disassembly

M-82 Double Action

LARGE-FRAME AUTOMATIC
(Deep Blue Finish)
9mm, 38 Super, 40 S&W, 45 Auto
$324.95

LARGE-FRAME AUTOMATIC
(Satin Chrome Finish)
45 Auto Caliber
$363.95

MAGNUM RESEARCH

DESERT EAGLE PISTOLS

SPECIFICATIONS	357 MAGNUM	41/44 MAGNUM
Length, with 6-inch barrel	10.6 inches	10.6 inches
Height	5.6 inches	5.7 inches
Width	1.25 inches	1.25 inches
Trigger reach	2.75 inches	2.75 inches
Sight radius (wh 6-inch barrel)	8.5 inches	8.5 inches
Additional available barrels	14 inch	14 inch & 10 inch
Weight	See below	See below
Bore rifling — Six rib	Polygonal: 1 turn in 14 inches	Polygonal: 1 turn in 18 inches
Method of operation	Gas operated	Gas operated
Method of locking	Rotating bolt	Rotating bolt
Magazine capacity	9 rounds (plus one in chamber)	8 rounds (plus one in chamber)

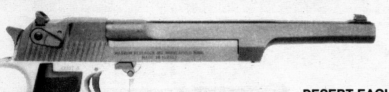

**DESERT EAGLE MARK I
(10″ Barrel)**

DESERT EAGLE MARK VII (not shown)
44 Magnum w/polished chrome finish, 6″ barrel, walnut target grip **$899.00**
357 Magnum w/14″ barrel, walnut ''Skinny'' grip **$949.00**

DESERT EAGLE — WEIGHT TABLES
357 Magnum

Frame	Without Magazine		With Empty Magazine	
	6″ Barrel	14″ Barrel	6″ Barrel	14″ Barrel
	ounces	ounces	ounces	ounces
Aluminum	47.8	55.0	51.9	59.1
Steel	58.3	65.5	62.4	96.6
Stainless	58.3	65.5	62.4	69.6

41/44 Magnum

Frame	Without Magazine		With Empty Magazine	
	6″ Barrel	14″ Barrel	6″ Barrel	14″ Barrel
	ounces	ounces	ounces	ounces
Aluminum	52.3	61.0	56.4	65.1
Steel	62.8	71.5	66.9	75.6
Stainless	62.8	71.5	66.9	75.6

DESERT EAGLE PISTOLS

357 MAGNUM
$789.00 Standard Parkerized Finish (6″ Barrel)
  839.00 Stainless Steel (6″)
  939.00 Standard (10″ barrel)
  989.00 Stainless (10″ barrel)
  949.00 Standard (14″ barrel)
  999.00 Stainless (14″ barrel)

41 MAGNUM (6″ & 14″ Barrels)
$799.00 Std. Parkerized Finish
  849.00 Stainless Steel

44 MAGNUM (6″, 10″, 14″ Barrels)
$ 899.00 Standard Parkerized Finish
  949.00 Stainless Steel (6″ Barrel)
 1099.00 Standard (10″ Barrel)
 1159.00 Stainless (10″ Barrel)
 1119.00 Standard (14″ Barrel)
 1169.00 Stainless (14″ Barrel)
  839.00 Alloy Frame

**DESERT EAGLE 50 MAGNUM
$1249.00**

Features 10½″ barrel; **weight:** 72.4 oz.; **height:** 5.9″; **sight radius:** 8.3″

MAGNUM RESEARCH

MOUNTAIN EAGLE

MOUNTAIN EAGLE
$239.00

This affordable, lightweight triangular barreled pistol with minimum recoil is ideal for plinkers, target shooters and varmint hunters. The barrel is made of hybrid injection-molded polymer and steel, and the standard 15-round magazine is made of high-grade, semi-transparent polycarbonate resin. It uses a constant force spring to load all 15 rounds easily. The receiver is made of machined T-6 alloy.

SPECIFICATIONS
Caliber: 22 LR
Barrel length: 6¹/₂″
Overall length: 10.6″
Weight: 21 oz.
Sights: Standard orange in front, black in rear (adjustable for windage and elevation
Grip: One-piece injection-molded, checkered conventional contour side panels, horizontally textured front and back panels
Also available:
TARGET EDITION with 8″ barrel, 2-stroke target trigger, jeweled bolt, adj. sights, range case. **$279.00**

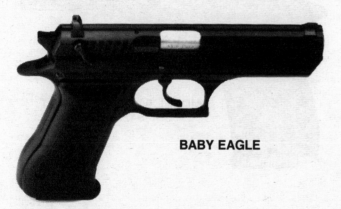

BABY EAGLE

BABY EAGLE PISTOL
$569.00

SPECIFICATIONS
Calibers: 9mm, 40 S&W, 41 AE
Capacity: 10 rounds (40 S&W), 11 rounds (41 AE), 16 rounds (9mm)
Barrel length: 4.72″
Overall length: 8.14″
Weight: 35.37 oz. (empty)
Sights: Combat
Features: Extra-long slide rail; combat-style trigger guard; decocking safety; polygonal rifling; ambidextrous thumb safety; all-steel construction; double action
Also available:
Conversion Kit (9mm to 41 AE). **$239.00**
GT Model with green tea finish. **$169.00**
Tritium Sights (fixed or adjustable)

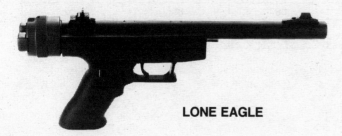

LONE EAGLE

LONE EAGLE SINGLE SHOT PISTOL
$344.00

This specialty pistol is designed for hunters, silhouette enthusiasts, long-range target shooters and other marksmen. The pistol can fire 15 different calibers of ammunition. Available with interchangeable 14-inch barreled actions, the gun is accurate and engineered to handle the high internal pressures of centerfire rifle ammunition. The design of the grip and its placement toward the center of the barrel provide the Lone Eagle with balance, reduced actual and felt recoil, and a high level of comfort for the shooter. **Calibers:** 22-250, 223 Rem., 22 Hornet, 22 Win. Mag., 243 Rem., 30-30, 30-06, 308 Win., 357 Maximum, 358 Win., 35 Rem., 44 Mag., 444 Marlin, 7mm-08, 7mm Bench Rest.

MAUSER PISTOLS

MODEL 80-SA
$372.00

HIGH POWER 9mm PISTOLS

These three models from Mauser are basic Hi-power designs. Available in caliber 9mm Parabellum only, with blued finish, wooden grips and fixed sights, they are each packaged with an extra magazine and cleaning rod. See specifications in the chart below.

MODEL 90-DA
$399.00

MODEL 90-DAC COMPACT
$425.00

SPECIFICATIONS

Model	Action	Capacity	Barrel Length	Overall Length	Weight
Model 80-SA	Single	13 rounds	4.67″	8″	31.5 oz.
Model 90-DA	Double	14 rounds	4.67″	8″	35 oz.
Model 90-DAC Compact	Double	14 rounds	4.13″	7.4″	33.25 oz.

McMILLAN

WOLVERINE PISTOL
$1600.00

This competition-ready pistol is built and designed around the 1911 Colt auto pistol frame. Two models—the **Combat** and **Competition Match**—are available with metal finish options (electroless nickel, NP³, black Teflon and deep blue), plus wood or Pachmayr grips. Other features include: a compensator integral to the barrel; round burr-style hammer; oversized button-style catch for quick clip release; high grip system to reduce muzzle rise and felt recoil; knurled backstrap and low-profile adjustable sights; skeletonized aluminum trigger with hand-tuned medium weight pull.

SPECIFICATIONS
Calibers: 45 ACP, 45 Italian, 38 Super, 38 Wadcutter, 9mm, 10mm
Action: Single
Barrel length: 6″ (5″ in Officer's Model)

MITCHELL ARMS

SINGLE ACTION ARMY REVOLVERS

The Mitchell Arms Single Action Army Model Revolver is a modern version of the original ''gun that won the West,'' adopted by the U.S. Army in 1873. Faithful to the original design, these revolvers—Bat Masterson, Cowboy, U.S. Army and U.S. Cavalry—are made of modern materials and use up-to-date technology.

SINGLE ACTION ARMY MODEL
(44 Magnum)

SPECIFICATIONS
Calibers: 357 Mag., 44 Mag., 45 Colt/45 ACP dual cylinder
Barrel lengths: 4³/₄″, 5¹/₂″, 6¹/₂″ and 7¹/₂″
Frame: Forged steel, fully machined with traditional color case-hardening; two-piece style backstrap made of solid brass
Action: Traditional single action with safety position and half-cock position for loading and unloading
Sights: Rear sight is fully adjustable for windage and elevation. Front sight is two-step ramp style with non-glare serrations. Fixed sight models feature deep notch with fixed blade front sight.
Grip: One-piece solid walnut grip built in the style of the old blackpowder revolvers
Accuracy: High-grade steel barrel honed for accuracy with smooth lands and grooves; precise alignment between cylinder and barrel. Fully qualified for big game hunting or silhouette shooting.

Prices:
Fixed and Adjustable Sight Models **$399.00–494.00**

MITCHELL ARMS

PISTOL PARABELLUM '08
AMERICAN EAGLE

SPECIFICATIONS
Caliber: 9mm Parabellum
Barrel length: 4″
Features: Stainless steel frame; American walnut grips; loaded
 chamber indicator; American Eagle engraving
Price: $695.00

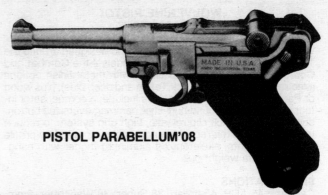

PISTOL PARABELLUM '08

MITCHELL HIGH STANDARD PISTOLS

VICTOR II

SPECIFICATIONS
Caliber: 22 LR
Barrel lengths: 4½″ (full-length vent rib only) and 5½″
Sights: Rib-mounted
Grips: Military-style with thumb rest; full checkered American
 walnut
Frame: Stippled grip, front and rear
Trigger: Adjustable for both travel and weight; gold-plated
Features: Push-button barrel takedown; gold-filled marking;
 safety, magazine and slide lock; left- or right-hand styles
Prices:
W/full-length dovetail rib $594.00
W/full-length vent rib 554.00
W/full-length vent rib/Weaver-style base 633.00
Detachable barrel weights (2 or 3 oz.) **add** 20
Also available: **CITATION II.** Same specifications as Victor II
 except finish is satin stainless or satin blue. **Price: $454.00**

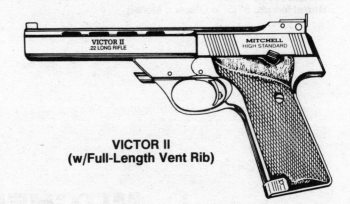

VICTOR II
(w/Full-Length Vent Rib)

TROPHY II

SPECIFICATIONS
Caliber: 22 LR
Barrel length: 5½″ (Bull) or 7½″ (Fluted)
Sights: Bridge rear; frame mounted on rails
Grips: Military-style
Trigger: Adjustable for travel and weight; gold-plated
Features: Full checkered American walnut thumbrest grips;
 push-button barrel takedown; all roll marks gold filled; stip-
 pled grip frame (front and rear)
Price: Blue or stainless $479.00
Weaver scope base 29.95

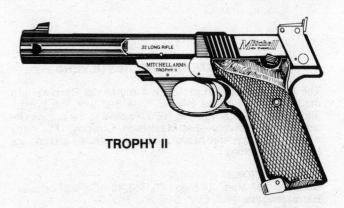

TROPHY II

OLYMPIC I.S.U. MODEL (not shown)

SPECIFICATIONS
Caliber: 22 Short
Barrel length: 6¾″ w/integral stabilizer
Sights: Bridge rear sight; frame-mounted on rails
Trigger: Adjustable for travel and weight
Grips: Full checkered with thumb rest
Finish: Royal blue or stainless steel
Features: Push-button barrel takedown; stippled grip frame
 (front and rear); military-style grip; adjustable barrel weights
Price: Blue or stainless $599.00

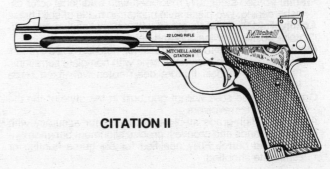

CITATION II

MOA MAXIMUM PISTOL

MAXIMUM

SPECIFICATIONS
Calibers: 22 Hornet to 358 Win.
Barrel lengths: 8½", 10½" and 14"
Weight: 3 lbs. 8 oz. (8¾" bbl.); 3 lbs. 13 oz. (10½" bbl.); 4 lbs. 3 oz. (14" bbl.)
Prices:
Stainless receiver, blued barrel **$622.00**
Stainless receiver and barrel **677.00**
Extra barrels (blue) **164.00**
For stainless, **add** **58.00**

This single-shot pistol with its unique falling-block action performs like a finely tuned rifle. The single piece receiver of stainless steel is mated to a Douglas barrel for optimum accuracy and strength.

NAVY ARMS REPLICAS

1873 SINGLE ACTION

1873 COLT-STYLE SINGLE ACTION REVOLVERS

The classic 1873 Single Action is the most famous of all the "six shooters." From its adoption by the U.S. Army in 1873 to the present, it still retains its place as America's most popular revolver. **Calibers:** 44-40 or 45 Long Colt. **Barrel lengths:** 3", 4¾", 5½" or 7½". **Overall length:** 10¾" (5½" barrel). **Weight:** 2¼ lbs. **Sights:** Blade front; notch rear. **Grips:** Walnut.
Prices: . . . . **$285.00** to **$455.00**

1895 U.S. ARTILLERY MODEL (not shown)

Same specifications as the U.S. Cavalry Model, but with a 5½" barrel as issued to Artillery units. **Caliber:** 45 Long Colt.
Price: **$455.00**

1873 U.S. CAVALRY MODEL
(not shown)

An exact replica of the original U.S. Government issue Colt Single Action Army, complete with Arsenal stampings and inspector's cartouche. **Caliber:** 45 Long Colt. **Barrel length:** 7½". **Overall length:** 13¼". **Weight:** 2 lbs. 7 oz. **Sights:** Blade front; notch rear. **Grips:** Walnut.
Price: **$455.00**

TT-OLYMPIA PISTOL

The TT-Olympia is a faithful reproduction of the famous Walther .22 target pistol that won the gold medal at the 1936 Olympics in Berlin. **Caliber:** 22 LR. **Barrel length:** 4⅝". **Overall length:** 8". **Weight:** 1 lb. 11 oz. **Sights:** Blade front; adjustable rear.
Price: **$300.00**

TT-OLYMPIA PISTOL

NEW ENGLAND FIREARMS

STANDARD REVOLVER
$119.95 ($129.95 in Nickel)

SPECIFICATIONS
Calibers: 22 S, L or LR
Capacity: 9 shots
Barrel lengths: 2¹/₂″ and 4″
Overall length: 7″ (2¹/₂″ barrel) and 8¹/₂″ (4″ barrel)
Weight: 25 oz. (2¹/₂″ bbl.) and 28 (4″ bbl.)
Sights: Blade front; fixed rear
Grips: American hardwood, walnut finish
Finish: Blue or nickel
Also available in 5-shot 32 H&R Mag. Blue **$114.95**

STANDARD MODEL
(22 LR, 2¹/₂″ Barrel)

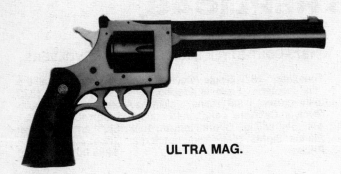

ULTRA MAG.

ULTRA MODEL (6″ Barrel)

ULTRA AND ULTRA MAG. REVOLVERS
$149.95

SPECIFICATIONS
Calibers: 22 Short, Long, Long Rifle (Ultra); 22 Win. Mag.
(Ultra Mag.)
Capacity: 9 shots (22 LR); 6 shots (22 Win. Mag.)
Barrel lengths: 4″ and 6″
Overall length: 10⁵/₈″
Weight: 36 oz. (6″ barrel)
Sights: Blade on rib front; fully adjustable rear
Grips: American hardwood, walnut finish
Also available:
LADY ULTRA in 5-shot 32 H&R Magnum. **Barrel length:** 3″.
  Overall length: 7¹/₂″. **Weight:** 31 oz. **Price:** $149.95

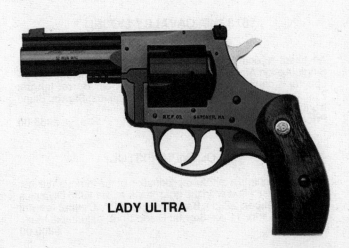

LADY ULTRA

NORTH AMERICAN ARMS REVOLVERS

22 LR MINI-REVOLVER
w/NAA Holster Grip

22 MAGNUM
MINI-REVOLVER

MINI-REVOLVERS

SPECIFICATIONS (Standard on all models)
Caliber: 22 LR and 22 Magnum
Capacity: 5-shot cylinder
Grips: Laminated rosewood
Safety: Half-cock safety
Sights: Blade front (integral w/barrel); fixed, notched rear
Material: Stainless steel
Finish: Matte with brushed sides

SPECIFICATIONS: MINI-REVOLVERS & MINI-MASTER SERIES

Model	Weight	Barrel Length	Overall Length	Overall Height	Overall Width	Prices
NAA-MMT-M	10.7 oz.	4″	7³/4″	3⁷/8″	7/8″	$267.50
NAA-MMT-L	10.7 oz.	4″	7³/4″	3⁷/8″	7/8″	267.50
*NAA-BW-M	8.8 oz.	2″	5⁷/8″	3⁷/8″	7/8″	225.50
*NAA-BW-L	8.8 oz.	2″	5⁷/8″	3⁷/8″	7/8″	225.50
NAA-22LR**	4.5 oz.	1¹/8″	4¹/4″	2³/8″	13/16″	164.50
NAA-22LLR**	4.6 oz.	1⁵/8″	4³/4″	2³/8	13/16″	164.50
*NAA-22MS	5.9 oz.	1¹/8″	5″	2⁷/8″	7/8″	184.50
*NAA-22M	6.2 oz.	1⁵/8″	5³/8″	2⁷/8″	7/8″	184.50

* Available with Conversion Cylinder chambered for 22 Long Rifle (**$260.50**)
** Available with holster grip (**$195.50**) and belt buckle combinations (**$197.50**)

MINI-MASTER NAA-MMT-M
(22 Mag. 4″ Barrel)

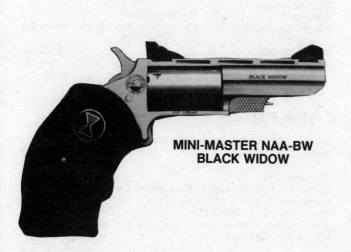

MINI-MASTER NAA-BW
BLACK WIDOW

MINI-MASTER SERIES

SPECIFICATIONS (Standard on all models)
Calibers: 22 LR (NAA-MMT-L, NAA-BW-L) and 22 Magnum
(NAA-MMT-M, NAA-BW-M)
Barrel: Heavy vent
Rifling: 8 land and grooves, 1/12 R.H. button broach twist
Grips: Oversized black rubber
Cylinder: Bull
Sights: Front integral with barrel; rear Millett adjustable white
outlined (elevation only) or low-profile fixed

PARA-ORDNANCE

MODEL P12 • 45 COMPACT
With 3¹/₂″ Barrel

SPECIFICATIONS
Caliber: 45 ACP
Capacity: 11 + 1
Barrel length: 3¹/₂″

Overall length: 7″
Weight: 24 oz. (alloy); 33 oz. (steel)
Receiver: Alloy, steel or stainless steel
Sights: 3-dot sight system
Finish: Matte black or silver
Features: Manual thumb safety; firing pin lock safety; trigger guard contoured for higher, tighter grip; flared ejection port; grooved front strap rounded smooth; rounded combat-style hammer; solid barrel bushing; ramped barrel; high-capacity double-column magazine with bumper pad; beveled magazine well

Prices:

Alloy w/13 rounds	$595.95
Alloy w/11 rounds	650.00
Steel w/13 rounds	716.25
Steel w/11 rounds	708.75

Also available:
MODEL P14 • 45. Same specifications, features and prices as the P12 with the following exceptions: **Barrel length:** 5″. **Overall length:** 8¹/₂″. **Weight:** 28 oz. (alloy) and 38 oz. (steel). **Capacity:** 13 + 1.

REMINGTON LONG-RANGE PISTOLS

MODEL XP-100
BOLT ACTION SILHOUETTE

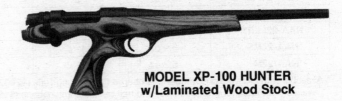

MODEL XP-100 HUNTER
w/Laminated Wood Stock

These unique single-shot centerfire, bolt-action pistols have become legends for their strength, precision, balance and accuracy. Chambered for 223 Rem., 35 Rem. and 7mm-08 Rem. with a 14¹/₂″ barrel, they are also available in 7mm BR, which many feel is the ideal factory-made metallic silhouette handgun for "unlimited" events. All XP-100 handguns have one-piece Du Pont "Zytel" nylon stocks with universal grips, two-position thumb safety switches, receivers drilled and tapped for scope mounts or receiver sights, and match-type grooved triggers.

SPECIFICATIONS
Calibers: 223 Rem., 35 Rem., 7mm BR Rem. and 7mm-08 Rem.
Barrel length: 14¹/₂″ (10¹/₂″ also in 7mm-08)
Overall length: 21¹/₄″ (17¹/₂″ w/10¹/₂″ barrel)
Weight: 4¹/₈ lbs. (3⁷/₈ lbs. w/10¹/₂″ barrel)
Stock: American walnut (10¹/₂″ barrel model) and laminated wood

Model XP-100	**$532.00**
w/10¹/₂″ barrel	**613.00**

XP-100 LONG-RANGE CUSTOM PISTOLS

Remington's Model XP-100 Custom pistol is chambered for the 22-250 Rem., 6mm BR Rem., 223 Rem., 250 Savage, 7mm BR, 7mm-08 Rem., 308 Win. and 35 Rem. All XP-100 Custom pistols are hand-crafted from select English walnut in right- and left-hand versions. All chamberings except the 35 Rem. (standard barrel only) are offered in a choice of standard 14¹/₂″ barrels with adjustable rear leaf and front bead sights or 15¹/₂″ barrels without sights. Receivers are drilled and tapped for scope mounts. **Weight** averages 4¹/₂ lbs. for standard models and 5¹/₂ lbs. for heavy barrel models.

Price:	**$945.00**

Also available:
Model XP-100 KS Custom Bolt Action Centerfire Repeater. Same specifications as the XP-100, but with Kevlar-reinforced stock and sling swivel studs. **Calibers:** 22-250, 223 Rem., 250 Savage, 7mm-08 Rem., 308 Win., 35 Rem., 350 Rem. Mag. **Price: $840.00**

ROSSI REVOLVERS

MODEL 68 "S" SERIES

SPECIFICATIONS
Caliber: 38 Special
Barrel length: 2″ and 3″
Overall length: 6½″ (2″ barrel); 7½″ (3″ barrel)
Weight: 21 oz. (2″ barrel); 23 oz. (3″ barrel)
Capacity: 5 rounds
Finish: Blue or nickel
Price: w/3″ barrel $227.00
    w/2″ barrel (wood or rubber grips) 238.00
    w/3″ barrel (nickel) 232.00

MODEL 720 (not shown)
$332.00

SPECIFICATIONS
Caliber: 44 S&W Special
Capacity: 5 shots
Barrel length: 3″
Overall length: 8″
Weight: 27½ oz.
Sights: Adjustable rear; red insert front
Finish: Stainless steel
Features: Rubber combat grips; full ejector rod shroud

MODEL 851
$280.00

SPECIFICATIONS
Caliber: 38 Special
Capacity: 6 rounds
Barrel length: 4″
Overall length: 7½″
Weight: 30 oz.
Frame: Medium
Finish: Stainless

MODEL M88 "S" SERIES
$262.00 (3″ Barrel)
$275.00 (2″ Barrel)

SPECIFICATIONS
Caliber: 38 Special
Capacity: 5 rounds, swing-out cylinder
Barrel lengths: 2″ and 3″
Overall length: 6½″ (2″ barrel); 7½″ (3″ barrel)
Weight: 21 oz. (2″); 23 oz. (3″)
Sights: Ramp front, square notch rear adjustable for windage
Finish: Stainless steel
Price: w/3″ barrel $262.00
    w/2″ barrel 275.00

MODEL 971
$280.00 Blue
$315.00 Stainless
$320.00 (2½″ barrel)

SPECIFICATIONS
Caliber: 357 Magnum
Capacity: 6 rounds
Barrel lengths: 2½″, 4″ and 6″
Overall length: 8⁵/₁₆″ w/2½″ bbl.; 9³/₁₆″ w/4″ bbl.; 11³/₁₆″ w/6″ bbl.
Weight: 22 oz. (2½″ bbl.); 35.4 oz. (4″ bbl.); 40.5 oz. (6″ bbl.)
Finish: Blue or stainless steel
Price: Blue $280.00
    Stainless 315.00
    w/2½″ barrel 320.00

MODEL 971 COMP GUN (not shown)
$320.00

SPECIFICATIONS
Caliber: 357 Magnum
Capacity: 6 rounds
Barrel length: 3¼″
Overall length: 9″
Weight: 32 oz.
Finish: Stainless steel

RUGER REVOLVERS

BLUED REDHAWK REVOLVER

STAINLESS REDHAWK REVOLVER

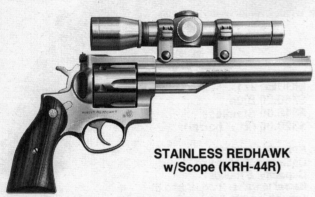

STAINLESS REDHAWK
w/Scope (KRH-44R)

SUPER REDHAWK STAINLESS
DOUBLE-ACTION REVOLVER

BLUED STEEL REDHAWK REVOLVER

The popular Ruger Redhawk® double-action revolver is available in an alloy steel model with blued finish in 44 Magnum caliber. Constructed of hardened chrome-moly and other alloy steels, this Redhawk is satin polished to a high lustre and finished in a rich blue.

Catalog Number	Caliber	Barrel Length	Overall Length	Approx. Weight (Ounces)	Price
RUGER BLUED REDHAWK REVOLVER					
RH-445	44 Mag.	5¹/₂″	11″	49	**$458.50**
RH-44	44 Mag.	7¹/₂″	13″	54	**458.50**
RH-44R*	44 Mag.	7¹/₂″	13″	54	**496.50**

* Scope model, with Integral Scope Mounts, 1″ Ruger Scope rings.

STAINLESS REDHAWK DOUBLE-ACTION REVOLVER

There is no other revolver like the Ruger Redhawk. Knowledgeable sportsmen reaching for perfection in a big bore revolver will find that the Redhawk demonstrates its superiority at the target, whether silhouette shooting or hunting. The scope sight model incorporates the patented Ruger integral Scope Mounting System with 1″ stainless steel Ruger scope rings.

Catalog Number	Caliber	Barrel Length	Overall Length	Approx. Weight (Ounces)	Price
RUGER STAINLESS REDHAWK REVOLVER					
KRH-445	44 Mag.	5¹/₂″	11″	49	**$516.75**
KRH-44	44 Mag.	7¹/₂″	13″	54	**516.75**
KRH-44R*	44 Mag.	7¹/₂″	13″	54	**557.25**

* Scope model, with Integral Scope Mounts, 1″ Stainless Steel Ruger Scope rings.

SUPER REDHAWK STAINLESS DOUBLE-ACTION REVOLVER

The **Super Redhawk** double-action revolver in stainless steel features a heavy extended frame with 7¹/₂″ and 9¹/₂″ barrels. Cushioned grip panels contain Goncalo Alves wood grip panel inserts to provide comfortable, nonslip hold. Comes with integral scope mounts and 1″ stainless steel Ruger scope rings.

SPECIFICATIONS
Caliber: 44 Magnum
Barrel length: 7¹/₂″ and 9¹/₂″
Overall length: 13″ w/7¹/₂″ bbl.; 15″ w/9¹/₂″ bbl.
Weight (empty): 53 oz. (7¹/₂″ bbl.); 58 oz. (9¹/₂″ bbl.)
Sight radius: 9¹/₂″ (7¹/₂″ bbl.); 11¹/₄″ (9¹/₂″ bbl.)
Finish: Stainless steel; satin polished

KSRH-7 (7¹/₂″ barrel) **$589.00**
KSRH-9 (9¹/₂″ barrel) **589.00**

RUGER SINGLE ACTION REVOLVERS

**VAQUERO SINGLE ACTION
$394.00 (Model BNV455)**

VAQUERO SINGLE-ACTION REVOLVER

Ruger's new Vaquero single-action centerfire revolver is based on the mechanism of the Ruger New Model Blackhawk single-action revolver, which has been in production since 1973. Vaquero's cylinder frames, fluted cylinders, triggers and hammers are all made of heat-treated steel alloys. An unbreakable coil mainspring and Nyloc screws are standard features. Grip panels are of seasoned rosewood with inletted Ruger medallions. A standard height hammer with knurled spur and an oval-shaped steel trigger guard are used.

Barrel, cylinder and grip frame are polished and blued. Stainless steel models have a polished natural finish, similar to the old nickel-plated single-actions in appearance. Vaquero revolvers are also equipped with a rounded blade front sight with no ramp and a fixed notch rear sight in a groove on the top strap. Ruger's patented transfer bar safety system and loading gate interlock to ensure security against accidental discharge.

Additional specifications and prices for the Vaquero and Ruger's other single-action Blackhawk models are detailed in the table below.

SPECIFICATIONS NEW MODEL BLACKHAWK AND BLACKHAWK CONVERTIBLE*

Catalog Number	Caliber	Finish**	Barrel Length	Overall Length	Approx. Weight (Oz.)	Price
BN31	.30 Carbine	B	7 1/2″	13 1/8″	44	$328.00
BN34	.357 Mag. + +	B	4 5/8″	10 3/8″	40	328.00
KBN34	.357 Mag. + +	SS	4 5/8″	10 3/8″	40	404.00
BN36	.357 Mag. + +	B	6 1/2″	12 1/4″	42	328.00
KBN36	.357 Mag. + +	SS	6 1/2″	12 1/2″	42	404.00
BN34X*	.357 Mag. + +	B	4 5/8″	10 3/8″	40	343.50
BN36X*	.357 Mag. + +	B	6 1/2″	12 1/4″	42	343.50
BN41	.41 Mag.	B	4 5/8″	10 1/4″	38	328.00
BN42	.41 Mag.	B	6 1/2″	12 1/8″	40	328.00
BN44	.45 Long Colt	B	4 5/8″	10 1/4″	39	328.00
KBN44	.45 Long Colt	SS	4 5/8″	10 1/4″	39	424.00
BN455	.45 Long Colt	B	5 1/2″	11 1/8″	39	328.00
BN45	.45 Long Colt	B	7 1/2″	13 1/8″	41	328.00
KBN45	.45 Long Colt	SS	7 1/2″	13 1/8″	41	424.00
BNV44	.45 Long Colt	CB	4 5/8″	10 1/4″	39	394.00
KBNV44	.45 Long Colt	SS	4 5/8″	10 1/4″	39	394.00
BNV455	.45 Long Colt	CB	5 1/2″	11 1/2″	40	394.00
KBNV455	.45 Long Colt	SS	5 1/2″	11 1/2″	40	394.00
BNV45	.45 Long Colt	CB	7 1/2″	13 1/8″	41	394.00
KBNV45	.45 Long Colt	SS	7 1/2″	13 1/8″	41	394.00

* Convertible: this model is designated by an X in the Catalog Number, and comes with an extra cylinder. The extra cylinder is 9mm Parabellum and can be instantly interchanged without the use of tools. Price of the Convertible model includes the extra cylinder.

** Finish: blued (B); stainless steel (SS); color case finish on the steel cylinder frame with blued steel grip, barrel, and cylinder (CB).

+ + Revolvers chambered for the .357 Magnum cartridge also accept factory-loaded .38 Special cartridges.

RUGER REVOLVERS

**NEW MODEL SUPER BLACKHAWK
SINGLE ACTION REVOLVER**

NEW MODEL SUPER BLACKHAWK
SINGLE ACTION REVOLVER

SPECIFICATIONS
Caliber: 44 Magnum; interchangeable with 44 Special
Barrel lengths: 5¹/₂", 7¹/₂", 10¹/₂"
Overall length: 13³/₈" (7¹/₂" barrel)
Weight: 48 oz. (7¹/₂" bbl.) and 51 oz. (10¹/₂" bbl.)
Frame: Chrome molybdenum steel or stainless steel
Springs: Music wire springs throughout
Sights: Patridge style, ramp front matted blade ¹/₈" wide; rear sight click and adjustable for windage and elevation

Grip frame: Chrome molybdenum or stainless steel, enlarged and contoured to minimize recoil effect
Trigger: Wide spur, low contour, sharply serrated for convenient cocking with minimum disturbance of grip
Finish: Polished and blued or brushed satin stainless steel

KS45N	5¹/₂" barrel, stainless steel	$413.75
KS458N	4⁵/₈" barrel, stainless steel	413.75
KS47N	7¹/₂" barrel, stainless steel	413.75
KS411N	10¹/₂" barrel, stainless steel	413.75
KSH7NH	7¹/₂" barrel, scope rings, stainless	479.50
S45N	5¹/₂" barrel, blued	378.50
S458N	4⁵/₈" barrel, blued	378.50
S47N	7¹/₂" barrel, blued	378.50
S411N	10¹/₂" bull barrel, blued	378.50

**BEARCAT SUPER
SINGLE-SIX**

NEW MODEL
SUPER SINGLE-SIX REVOLVER

SPECIFICATIONS
Caliber: 22 LR (fitted with WMR cylinder)
Barrel lengths: 4⁵/₈", 5¹/₂", 6¹/₂", 9¹/₂"; stainless steel model in 5¹/₂" and 6¹/₂" lengths only
Weight (approx.): 33 oz. (with 5¹/₂" barrel); 38 oz. (with 9¹/₂" barrel)
Sights: Patridge-type ramp front sight; rear sight click adjustable for elevation and windage; protected by integral frame ribs
Finish: Blue or stainless steel
Prices:
In blue $281.00
In stainless steel (convertible 5¹/₂" and 6¹/₂" barrels only) 354.00
Also available:
BEARCAT SINGLE ACTION with 4" barrel, walnut grips
Blue $298.00
Stainless 325.00

**NEW MODEL
SINGLE-SIX SSM™**

NEW MODEL
SINGLE-SIX SSM™ REVOLVER

SPECIFICATIONS
Caliber: 32 Magnum; also handles 32 S&W and 32 S&W Long
Barrel lengths: 4⁵/₈", 5¹/₂", 6¹/₂", 9¹/₂"
Weight (approx.): 34 oz. (with 6¹/₂" barrel)
Price: $281.00

RUGER REVOLVERS

GP-100 357 MAGNUM
6" Heavy Barrel

RUGER SPURLESS SP101

MODEL SP101
$408.00

This critically acclaimed small frame SP101 model has added 6-shot capacity in 32 Magnum and 5-shot capacity in 9mm and 357 Magnum.

SPECIFICATIONS

Catalog Number	Caliber	Capacity	Sights	Barrel Length	Approx. Wt. (Oz.)
KSP-221	22 LR	6	Adj.	2¼"	32
KSP-240	22 LR	6	Adj.	4"	33
KSP-241	22 LR	6	Adj.	4"	34
KSP-3231	32 Mag.	6	Adj.	3¹/₁₆"	30
KSP-3241	32 Mag.	6	Adj.	4"	33
KSP-921	9×19mm	5	Fixed	2¼"	25
KSP-931	9×19mm	5	Fixed	3¹/₁₆"	27
KSP-821	38 + P	5	Fixed	2¼"	25
KSP-831	38 + P	5	Fixed	3¹/₁₆"	27
KSP-321X	357 Mag.*	5	Fixed	2¼"	25
KSP-321XL	357 Mag.*	5	Fixed	2¼"	25
KSP-331X	357 Mag.*	5	Fixed	3¹/₁₆"	27

* Revolvers chambered for the .357 Magnum cartridge also accept the 38 Special cartridge.
Model KSP-240 has short shroud; all others have full.

BISLEY SINGLE ACTION
TARGET GUN (not shown)

The Bisley single-action was originally used at the British National Rifle Association matches held in Bisley, England, in the 1890s. Today's Ruger Bisleys are offered in two frame sizes, chambered from 22 LR to 45 Long Colt cartridges. These revolvers are, in effect, the target-model versions of the Ruger single-action line.
  Special features: Unfluted cylinder rollmarked with classic foliate engraving pattern (or fluted cylinder without engraving); hammer is low with smoothly curved, deeply checkered wide spur positioned for easy cocking.
Prices:
22 LR or 32 Magnum **$328.75**
357 Mag., 41 Mag., 44 Mag., 45 Long Colt **391.00**

GP-100 357 MAGNUM

The GP-100 is designed for the unlimited use of 357 Magnum ammunition in all factory loadings; it combines strength and reliability with accuracy and shooting comfort. (Revolvers chambered for the 357 Magnum cartridge also accept the 38 Special cartridge.)

SPECIFICATIONS

Catalog Number	Finish*	Sights†	Shroud††	Barrel Length	Wt. (Oz.)	Prices
GP-141	B	A	F	4"	41	**$413.50**
GP-160	B	A	S	6"	43	413.50
GP-161	B	A	F	6"	46	413.50
GPF-331	B	F	F	3"	36	397.00
GPF-340	B	F	S	4"	37	397.00
GPF-341	B	F	F	4"	38	397.00
KGP-141	S	A	F	4"	41	446.50
KGP-160	S	A	S	6"	43	446.50
KGP-161	S	A	F	6"	46	446.50
KGPF-330	S	F	S	3"	35	430.00
KGPF-331	S	F	F	3"	36	430.00
KGPF-340	S	F	S	4"	37	430.00
KGPF-341	S	F	F	4"	38	430.00
KGPF-840*	S	F	S	4"	37	430.00
KGPF-841*	S	F	F	4"	38	430.00

* B = blued; S = stainless. † A = adjustable; F = fixed. †† F = full; S = short. * 38 Special only.

BISLEY SPECIFICATIONS

Catalog Number	Caliber	Barrel Length	Overall Length	Sights	Approx. Wt. (Oz.)
RB22AW	.22 LR	6½"	11½"	Adj.	41
RB32W	.32 Mag.	6½"	11½"	Fixed*	41
RB32AW	.32 Mag.	6½"	11½"	Adj.	41
RB35W	.357 Mag.	7½"	13"	Adj.	48
RB41W	.41 Mag.	7½"	13"	Adj.	48
RB44W	.44 Mag.	7½"	13"	Adj.	48
RB45W	.45 Long Colt	7½"	13"	Adj.	48

* Dovetail rear sight adjustable for windage only.

RUGER P-SERIES PISTOLS

Ruger's P-Series pistols are now available in two Compact models—the P93 Double-Action-Only and the P93 Decock-Only. These Ruger Compacts feature a one-piece Zytel grip frame that decreases their weight to 31 ounces with a loaded 15-round magazine. The mechanism is recoil-operated, double action, and autoloading with a tilting barrel, link-actuated (as in the M1911A1).

GENERAL SPECIFICATIONS (see also table below for additional specifications and prices)
Barrel length: $3^9/_{10}''$
Overall length: $7^3/_{10}''$
Weight: 24 oz. (empty magazine)
Height: $5^1/_2''$
Width: $1^1/_2''$
Sight radius: 5″
Sights: Square notch rear, drift adjustable for windage; square post front (both sights have white dots for rapid target acquisition)

MODEL KP89DC AUTO PISTOL

MODEL KP91DAO

MODEL KP93DC

P-SERIES PISTOLS

Catalog Number	Model	Finish	Caliber	Mag. Cap.	Price
KP88X	Safety-Convertible*	Stainless	9mm & .30 Luger	15	**$497.00**
P89	Safety	Blued	9mm	15	**410.00**
KP89	Safety	Stainless	9mm	15	**452.00**
P89DC	Decock-Only	Blued	9mm	15	**410.00**
KP89DC	Decock-Only	Stainless	9mm	15	**452.00**
KP89DAO	Dbl.-Action-Only	Stainless	9mm	15	**452.00**
KP90	Safety	Stainless	.45ACP	7	**488.65**
KP90DC	Decock-Only	Stainless	.45ACP	7	**488.65**
KP91DC	Decock-Only	Stainless	.40 Auto	11	**488.65**
KP91DAO	Dbl.-Action-Only	Stainless	.40 Auto	11	**488.65**
KP93DC	Decock-Only Compact	Stainless	9mm	15	**452.00**
KP93DAO	Dbl.-Action-Only Compact	Stainless	9mm	15	**452.00**

* Safety-Convertible Model. This model comes with two interchangeable barrels: one in 9mm Luger and one in .30 Luger. The barrels can be interchanged without the use of tools. Convertible model is designated by an ''X'' in its Catalog Number; price includes both barrels.

RUGER 22 AUTOMATIC PISTOLS

MARK II STANDARD MODEL

The Ruger Mark II models represent continuing refinements of the original Ruger Standard and Mark I Target Model pistols. More than two million of this series of autoloading rimfire pistol have been produced since 1949.

The bolts on all Ruger Mark II pistols lock open automatically when the last cartridge is fired, if the magazine is in the pistol. The bolt can be operated manually with the safety in the "on" position for added security while loading and unloading. A bolt stop can be activated manually to lock the bolt open.

The Ruger Mark II pistol uses 22 Long Rifle ammunition in a detachable, 10-shot magazine (standard on all Mark II models except Model 22/45, whose 10-shot magazine is not interchangeable with other Mark II magazines). Designed for easy insertion and removal, the Mark II magazine is equipped with a magazine follower button for convenience in reloading.

For additional specifications, please see the chart on the next page.

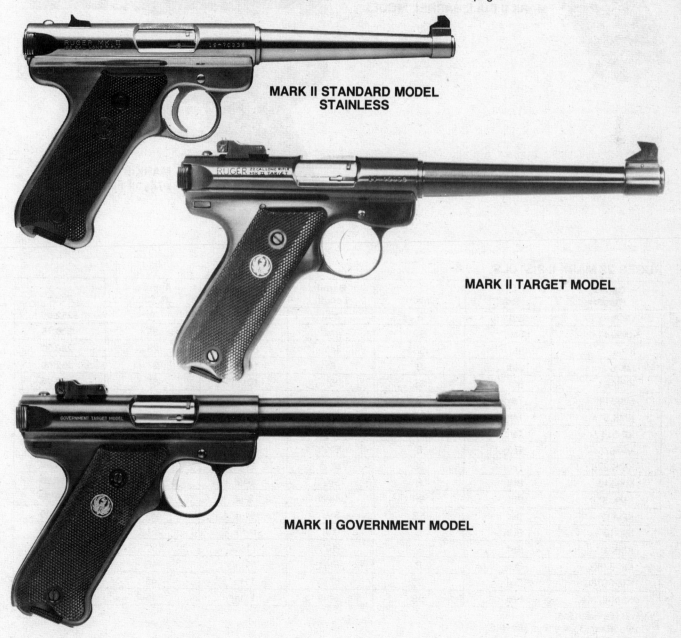

**MARK II STANDARD MODEL
STAINLESS**

MARK II TARGET MODEL

MARK II GOVERNMENT MODEL

RUGER 22 AUTOMATIC PISTOLS

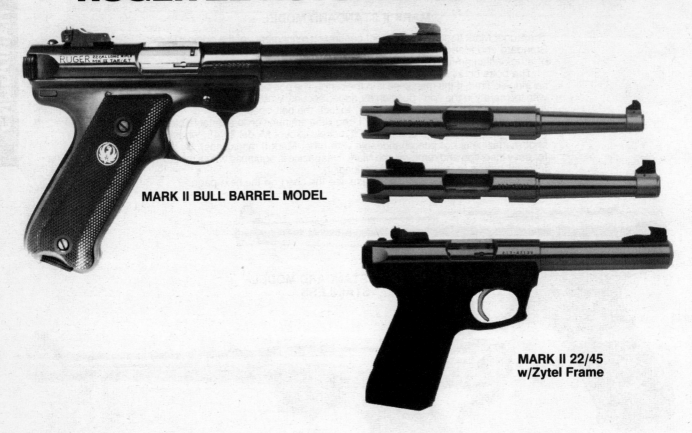

MARK II BULL BARREL MODEL

MARK II 22/45 w/Zytel Frame

RUGER 22 MARK II PISTOLS

Catalog Number	Model*	Finish**	Barrel Length	Overall Length	Approx. Wt. (Oz.)	Price
MK-4	Std.	B	4³/₄″	8⁵/₁₆″	35	$252.00
KMK-4	Std.	SS	4³/₄″	8⁵/₁₆″	35	330.25
KP-4	Std.	SS	4³/₄″	8¹³/₁₆″	28	280.00
MK-6	Std.	B	6″	10⁵/₁₆″	37	252.00
KMK-6	Std.	SS	6″	10⁵/₁₆″	37	330.25
MK-514	Target	B	5¹/₄″	9⁷/₁₆″	38	310.50
KMK-514	Target	SS	5¹/₄″	9⁷/₁₆″	38	389.00
KP-514	Target	SS	5¹/₄″	9⁵/₁₆″	32	330.00
MK-678	Target	B	6⁷/₈″	11¹/₈″	42	310.50
KMK-678	Target	SS	6⁷/₈″	11¹/₈″	42	389.00
MK-512	Bull	B	5¹/₂″	9³/₄″	42	310.50
KMK-512	Bull	SS	5¹/₂″	9³/₄″	42	389.00
KP-512	Bull	SS	5¹/₂″	9⁹/₁₆″	35	330.00
MK-10	Bull	B	10″	14⁵/₁₆″	51	294.50
KMK-10	Bull	SS	10″	14⁵/₁₆″	51	373.00
MK-678G	Bull	B	6⁷/₈″	11¹/₈″	46	356.50
KMK-678G	Bull	SS	6⁷/₈″	11¹/₈″	46	427.25
KMK-678GC	Bull	SS	6⁷/₈″	11¹/₈″	45	441.00

* Model: standard (Std.).
** Finish: blued (B); stainless steel (SS).

SIG SAUER PISTOLS

MODEL P220 "AMERICAN"

MODEL P220 "AMERICAN"

SPECIFICATIONS
Calibers: 38 Super, 9mm Parabellum, 45 ACP
Capacity: 9 rounds; 7 rounds in 45 ACP
Barrel length: 4.4″
Overall length: 7.79″
Weight (empty): 26½ oz.; 25.7 oz. in 45 ACP
Finish: Blue
Prices:
45 ACP Blued $780.00
  W/"Siglite" night sights 880.00
  W/Nickel slide 805.00
  W/Nickel slide & "Siglite" night sights 905.00
  W/K-Kote 850.00
  W/K-Kote and "Siglite" night sights 950.00

MODEL P225

SPECIFICATIONS
Caliber: 9mm Parabellum
Capacity: 8 rounds
Barrel length: 3.85″
Overall length: 7″
Weight (empty): 26.1 oz.
Finish: Blue
Prices:
Blued finish $775.00
Blued w/"Siglite" night sights 875.00
W/K-Kote. 845.00
W/K-Kote and "Siglite" night sights 945.00
W/Nickel slide 800.00
W/Nickel slide and "Siglite" night sights 900.00

MODEL P225

MODEL P226

SPECIFICATIONS
Caliber: 9mm Parabellum
Capacity: 15 rounds
Barrel length: 4.4″
Overall length: 7¾″
Weight (empty): 26.5 oz.
Finish: Blue
Prices:
Blued finish $805.00
Blued finish, nickel slide 830.00
Blued w/"Siglite" night sights 905.00
W/K-Kote. 875.00
K-Kote w/"Siglite" night sights 975.00
W/Nickel slide 830.00
W/Nickel slide & "Siglite" night sights 930.00
Blued finish, double action only 805.00
  W/"Siglite" night sight, DAO 905.00
  W/Nickel slide, DAO 830.00
  W/K-Kote, DAO 875.00
  W/K-Kote, "Siglite" night sight, DAO 975.00

MODEL P226

SIG SAUER PISTOLS

MODEL P228

MODEL P228

SPECIFICATIONS
Caliber: 9mm
Capacity: 13 rounds
Barrel length: 3.86″
Overall length: 7.08″
Weight (empty): 26.01 oz.
Finish: Blue, K-Kote or nickel
Prices:
Blued finish	**$805.00**
Blued w/"Siglite" night sights	**905.00**
W/Nickel slide	**830.00**
W/Nickel slide & "Siglite" night sights	**930.00**
W/K-Kote.	**875.00**
W/K-Kote and "Siglite" night sights	**975.00**
Double Action Only	
Blued finish	**805.00**
Blued finish, "Siglite" night sights	**905.00**
Nickel slide	**830.00**
Nickel slide, "Siglite" night sights	**930.00**

MODEL P229

MODEL P229

SPECIFICATIONS
Caliber: 40 S&W
Capacity: 12 rounds
Barrel length: 3.86″
Overall length: 7.08″
Weight (empty): 27.54 oz.
Finish: Blue
Features: Blue stainless steel slide; DA/SA or DA only; automatic firing pin lock
Prices:
Model P229	**$875.00**
W/"Siglite night sight	**975.00**

MODEL P230 SL

SPECIFICATIONS
Caliber: 380 ACP
Capacity: 7 rounds
Barrel length: 3.6″
Overall length: 6.6″
Weight (empty): 16¼ oz.; 20.8 oz. in stainless steel
Finish: Blue or stainless steel
Prices:
Blued finish	**$510.00**
Stainless steel	**595.00**

MODEL P230 SL

SMITH & WESSON COMPACT PISTOLS

MODEL 3900 COMPACT SERIES

SPECIFICATIONS
Caliber: 9mm Parabellum DA Autoloading Luger
Capacity: 8 rounds
Barrel length: 3 1/2"
Overall length: 6 7/8"
Weight (empty): 25 oz.
Sights: Post w/white dot front; fixed rear adj. for windage only w/2 white dots. Adjustable sight models include micrometer click, adj. for windage and elevation w/2 white dots. Deduct $25 for fixed sights.
Finish: Blue (Model 3914); satin stainless (Model 3913)
Prices:
MODEL 3913 . . . . $597.00
MODEL 3914 . . . . 539.00

Also available:
MODEL 3913 LADYSMITH $615.00
MODEL 3913NL (DA, stainless slide w/alloy
  frame) 597.00
MODEL 3953 (Double action only, stainless) 597.00

MODEL 3913 DA
Fixed Sight

MODEL 3914 DA
Adjustable Sight

MODEL 6900 COMPACT SERIES

SPECIFICATIONS
Caliber: 9mm Parabellum DA Autoloading Luger
Capacity: 8 rounds
Barrel length: 3 1/2"
Overall length: 6 7/8"
Weight (empty): 26 1/2 oz.
Sights: Post w/white dot front; fixed rear, adj. for windage only w/2 white dots
Stocks: Delrin one-piece wraparound, arched backstrap, textured surface
Finish: Blue (Model 6904); clear anodized/satin stainless (Model 6906)
Prices:
MODEL 6904 . . . . $590.00
MODEL 6906 . . . . 650.00
MODEL 6906 Fixed Tritium night sight 756.00
MODEL 6946 DA only, fixed sights 650.00

MODEL 6904 DA
Fixed Sight

SMITH & WESSON FULL SIZE DOUBLE ACTION PISTOLS

Smith & Wesson's double-action semiautomatic Third Generation line includes the following features: fixed barrel bushing for greater accuracy • smoother trigger pull plus a slimmer, contoured grip and lateral relief cut where trigger guard meets frame • three-dot sights • wraparound grips • beveled magazine well for easier reloading • ambidextrous safety lever secured by spring-loaded plunger • low-glare bead-blasted finish.

MODEL 1000 SERIES

SPECIFICATIONS
Caliber: 10mm
Capacity: 9 rounds
Barrel length: 4¹/₄″ and 5″
Overall length: 7⁷/₈″ and 8⁵/₈″
Weight: (w/fixed sights) 38 oz. (4¼″); 38½ oz. (5″)
Sights: Post with white dot front; fixed with white dot rear
Finish: Stainless steel
Prices:
MODEL 1006 (5″ barrel, fixed sights) $769.00
   With adjustable sights 796.00

MODEL 1026

MODEL 1076 (4¼″ barrel w/straight backstrap
   grip, frame-mounted decocking lever) 778.00

MODEL 4000 SERIES

SPECIFICATIONS
Caliber: 40 S&W
Capacity: 11 rounds
Barrel length: 4″
Overall length: 7⁷/₈″
Weight: 38½ oz. (with fixed sights)
Sights: Post w/white dot front; fixed or adjustable w/2 white
   dots rear
Stocks: Straight backstrap, Xenoy wraparound
Finish: Stainless steel
Prices:
MODEL 4003 w/fixed sights $698.00
MODEL 4006 w/fixed sights 715.00
   Same as above w/adj. sights 743.00
   w/ambidextrous safety 820.00
MODEL 4026 w/decocking lever 731.00
MODEL 4043 Double action only 698.00
MODEL 4046 w/fixed sights 715.00
   Double action only, fixed Tritium night sight 820.00

MODEL 4046

MODEL 4500 SERIES

SPECIFICATIONS
Caliber: 45 ACP Autoloading DA
Capacity: 8 rounds (Model 4506); 7 rounds (Model 4516)
Barrel length: 5″ (Model 4506); 3³/₄″ (Model 4516)
Overall length: 8⁵/₈″ (Model 4506); 7¹/₈″ (Model 4516)
Weight (empty): 38½ oz. (Model 4506); 34½ oz. (Model 4516)
Sights: Post w/white dot front; fixed rear, adj. for windage
   only. Adj. sight incl. micrometer click, adj. for windage and
   elevation w/2 white dots. Add **$29.00** for adj. sights.
Stocks: Delrin one-piece wraparound, arched backstrap, tex-
   tured surface
Finish: Satin stainless
Prices:
MODEL 4506 w/adj. sights, 5″ bbl. $773.00
   With fixed sights 742.00
MODEL 4566 w/4¹/₄″ bbl., fixed sights 742.00
MODEL 4586 DA only, 4¹/₄″ bbl., fixed sights 742.00

**MODEL 4506 DA
Fixed Sight**

SMITH & WESSON FULL SIZE DOUBLE ACTION PISTOLS

MODEL 5900 SERIES

SPECIFICATIONS
Caliber: 9mm Parabellum DA Autoloading Luger
Capacity: 15 rounds
Barrel length: 4″
Overall length: 7¹/₂″
Weight (empty): 28¹/₂ oz. (Model 5903); 26¹/₂ oz. (Model 5904); 37¹/₂ oz. (Model 5906)
Sights: Post w/white dot front; fixed rear, adj. for windage only w/2 white dots. Adjustable sight models include micrometer click, adj. for windage and elevation w/2 white dots.
Finish: Blue (Model 5904); satin stainless (Models 5903 and 5906)
Prices:
MODEL 5903 . . . . $693.00
  With fixed sights 662.00
MODEL 5904 . . . . 645.00
  With fixed sights 616.00
MODEL 5906 . . . . 711.00
  With fixed sights 679.00
  With Tritium night sight 784.00
MODEL 5946 In double action only 679.00

**MODEL 5904 DA
Fixed Sight**

MODEL 411

SPECIFICATIONS
Caliber: 40 S&W
Capacity: 11 rounds + 1
Barrel length: 4″
Overall length: 7¹/₂″
Weight: 29.4 oz.
Sights: Post w/white dot front; fixed rear
Grips: One-piece Xenoy straight backstrap
Features: Right-hand slide-mounted manual safety; decocking lever; aluminum alloy frame; blue carbon steel slide; non-reflective finish
Price: $525.00

MODEL 411

MODEL 915 9mm

SPECIFICATIONS
Caliber: 9mm
Capacity: 15 rounds
Barrel length: 4″
Overall length: 7¹/₂″
Weight: 28¹/₂ oz.
Sights: Post w/white dot front; fixed rear
Grips: One-piece Xenoy straight backstrap
Features: Right-hand slide-mounted manual safety; decocking lever; aluminum alloy frame; blue carbon steel slide; non-reflective finish
Price: $479.00

MODEL 915 9mm

SMITH & WESSON TARGET PISTOLS

MODEL 422 RIMFIRE
22 SINGLE ACTION
$225.00 (Fixed Sight)
$278.00 (Adjustable Sight)

SPECIFICATIONS
Caliber: 22 LR
Capacity: 10 rounds (magazine furnished)
Barrel lengths: 4¹/₂″ and 6″
Overall length: 7¹/₂″ (4¹/₂″ barrel) and 9″ (6″ barrel)
Weight: 22 oz. (4¹/₂″ barrel) and 23¹/₂ oz. (6″ barrel)
Stock: Plastic (field version) and checkered walnut w/S&W monogram (target version)
Front sight: Serrated ramp w/.125″ blade (field version); Patridge w/.125″ blade (target version)
Rear sight: Fixed sight w/.125″ blade (field version): adjustable sight w/.125″ blade (target version)
Hammer: .250″ internal
Trigger: .312″ serrated
Also available:
MODEL 622. Same specifications as Model 422 in stainless steel. **Price: $272.00.** (Add **$52.00** for adj. sights).

MODEL 422

MODEL 2206 (not shown)
$314.00 (Fixed Sights)
$370.00 (Adj. Sights)

SPECIFICATIONS
Caliber: 22 LR. **Capacity:** 12 rounds. **Barrel length:** 4¹/₂″ and 6″. **Overall length:** 7¹/₂″ and 9″. **Weight:** 35 oz. (4¹/₂″ bbl.); 39 oz. (6″ bbl.). **Finish:** Stainless steel.

MODEL NO. 41 RIMFIRE
$753.00 (Blue Only)

SPECIFICATIONS
Caliber: 22 Long Rifle
Magazine capacity: 12 rounds
Barrel lengths: 5¹/₂″ and 7″
Weight: 44 oz. (5¹/₂″ barrel)
Sights: Front, ¹/₈″ Patridge undercut; rear, S&W micrometer click sight adjustable for windage and elevation
Stocks: Checkered walnut with modified thumb rest, equally adaptable to right- or left-handed shooters
Finish: S&W Bright Blue
Trigger: .365″ width; with S&W grooving and an adjustable trigger stop

MODEL NO. 41

MODEL 2213/2214 RIMFIRE
"SPORTSMAN" (not shown)
$258.00 (Blue)
$302.00 (Stainless)

SPECIFICATIONS
Caliber: 22 LR. **Capacity:** 8 rounds. **Barrel length:** 3″. **Overall length:** 6¹/₈″. **Weight:** 18 oz. **Finish:** Blue carbon steel slide and alloy frame (**Model 2213** has stainless steel slide w/alloy frame)

38 MASTER MODEL NO. 52
SINGLE ACTION CENTERFIRE PISTOL
$908.00 (Bright Blue Only)

SPECIFICATIONS
Calibers: 38 S&W Special and 32 S&W Long (for Mid-Range Wadcutter only)
Magazine capacity: 5 rounds (2 five-round magazines furnished)
Barrel length: 5″
Overall length: 8⁷/₈″
Sight radius: 6¹⁵/₁₆″
Weight: 40 oz. with empty magazine
Sights: Front, ¹/₈″ Patridge on ramp base; rear, new S&W micrometer click sight with wide ⁷/₈″ sight slide
Stocks: Checkered walnut with S&W monograms
Finish: S&W Bright Blue with sandblast stippling around sighting area to break up light reflection
Trigger: .365″ width; with S&W grooving and an adjustable trigger stop

MODEL NO. 52

SMITH & WESSON REVOLVERS

SMALL FRAME

MODEL 36 LADYSMITH

MODELS 36-LS & 60-LS LADYSMITH HANDGUNS
$399.00 (36-LS)
$450.00 (60-LS Stainless)

SPECIFICATIONS
Caliber: 38
Capacity: 5 shots
Barrel length: 2″
Overall length: 6⁵/₁₆″

MODEL 36
38 CHIEFS SPECIAL
$366.00 (2″) $378.00 (3″)

SPECIFICATIONS
Caliber: 38 S&W Special
Number of shots: 5
Barrel length: 2″ or 3″
Overall length: 6¹/₂″ with 2″ barrel
Weight: 19¹/₂ oz. (2″ barrel); 21¹/₂ oz. (3″ barrel)
Sights: Serrated ramp front; fixed square notch rear
Grips: Checkered walnut Service
Finish: S&W blue carbon steel or nickel
Features: .312″ smooth combat-style trigger; .240″ service hammer
MODEL 37 AIRWEIGHT: Same as Model 36, except finish is blue or nickel aluminum alloy; wt. 13¹/₂ oz.
Blue **$394.00**
With nickel finish **410.00**

MODEL 60
38 CHIEFS SPECIAL STAINLESS
$417.00 ($443.00 w/Full Lug Barrel)

SPECIFICATIONS
Caliber: 38 S&W Special
Number of shots: 5
Barrel lengths: 2″ and 3″ (3″ full lug barrel optional)
Weight: 19¹/₂ oz. (2″ barrel); 21¹/₂ oz. (3″ barrel); 24¹/₂ oz. (3″ full lug barrel)
Sights: Micrometer click rear, adj. for windage and elevation; pinned black front (3″ full lug model only); standard sights as on Model 36
Grips: Checked walnut Service with S&W monograms; Santoprene combat-style on 3″ full lug model
Finish: Stainless steel
Features: .312″ smooth combat-style trigger (.347″ serrated trigger on 3″ full lug model); .240″ service hammer (.375″ semi-target hammer on 3″ full lug model)

MODEL 60 LADYSMITH

Weight: 20 oz.
Sights: Serrated ramp front; fixed notch rear
Grips: Contoured laminated rosewood
Finish: Glossy deep blue or stainless
Features: Both models come with soft-side LadySmith carry case

**MODEL 36
38 CHIEFS SPECIAL**

**MODEL 60
38 CHIEFS SPECIAL**

SMITH & WESSON REVOLVERS

SMALL FRAME

38 BODYGUARD "AIRWEIGHT"
MODEL 38
$418.00 Blue $433.00 Nickel

SPECIFICATIONS
Caliber: 38 S&W Special
Number of shots: 5
Barrel length: 2″
Overall length: 6³/₈″
Weight: 14 oz.
Sights: Front, fixed ¹/₁₀″ serrated ramp; rear square notch
Stocks: Checked walnut Service with S&W monograms
Finish: S&W blue or nickel aluminum alloy

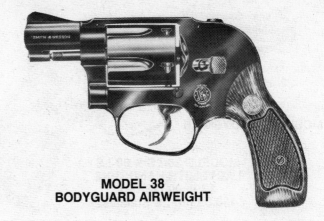

**MODEL 38
BODYGUARD AIRWEIGHT**

38 CENTENNIAL
MODEL 442 (not shown)
$418.00 (Blue) $433.00 (Nickel)

SPECIFICATIONS
Caliber: 38 Special
Capacity: 5 rounds
Barrel length: 2″
Overall length: 6⁷/₈″
Weight: 15.8 oz.
Sights: Serrated ramp front; fixed square notch rear
Finish: Matte blue or satin nickel

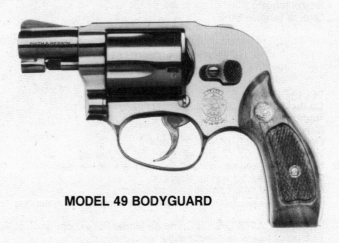

38 BODYGUARD MODEL 49
$389.00

SPECIFICATIONS
Caliber: 38 S&W Special
Number of shots: 5
Barrel length: 2″
Overall length: 6¹/₄″
Weight (empty): 20 oz.
Sights: Serrated ramp (front); fixed square notch (rear)
Finish: S&W blue

MODEL 49 BODYGUARD

MODEL 649 BODYGUARD
$441.00

SPECIFICATIONS
Caliber: 38 Special
Capacity: 5 shots
Barrel length: 2″
Overall length: 6¹/₄″
Weight: 20 oz.
Sights: Serrated ramp front, fixed square notch rear
Grips: Round butt; checkered walnut service
Finish: Stainless steel

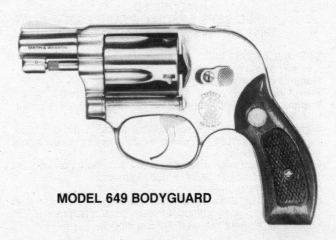

MODEL 649 BODYGUARD

SMITH & WESSON REVOLVERS

SMALL FRAME

MODEL 63
22/32 KIT GUN
$435.00

SPECIFICATIONS
Caliber: 22 Long Rifle
Number of shots: 6
Barrel lengths: 2″ and 4″
Weight: 22 oz. (2″ barrel); 24 1/2 oz. (4″ barrel)
Sights: 1/8″ red ramp front sight; rear sight is black stainless steel S&W micrometer click square-notch, adjustable for windage and elevation
Stocks: Square butt
Finish: Satin stainless

MODEL 63 22/32 KIT GUN

MODEL 640 CENTENNIAL (not shown)
$441.00

SPECIFICATIONS
Caliber: 38 S&W Special (+P))
Capacity: 5 rounds
Barrel length: 2″
Overall length: 6 7/16″
Weight: 20 oz.
Sights: Serrated ramp front; fixed square notch rear
Features: Fully concealed hammer; smooth hardwood service stock

MODEL 940 CENTENNIAL
$446.00

SPECIFICATIONS
Caliber: 9mm Parabellum
Barrel length: 2″
Overall length: 6 7/16″
Weight: 23 oz.
Sights: Serrated ramp front; fixed square notch rear
Grips: Santoprene combat grips
Feature: Fully concealed hammer

MODEL 940 CENTENNIAL

22 MAGNUM KIT GUN
MODEL 651 (not shown)
$428.00

SPECIFICATIONS
Caliber: 22 Magnum
Number of shots: 6
Barrel length: 4″
Weight: 24 1/2 oz.
Sights: Red ramp front; micrometer click rear, adjustable for windage and elevation
Grips: Checkered premium hardwood Service
Finish: Stainless steel
Features: .375″ hammer; .312″ smooth combat trigger

SMITH & WESSON REVOLVERS

MEDIUM FRAME

38 MILITARY & POLICE
MODEL 10
$361.00

SPECIFICATIONS
Caliber: 38 S&W Special
Capacity: 6 shots
Barrel length: 2″, 4″ (also 4″ heavy barrel)
Weight: 33½ oz. with 4″ barrel
Sights: Front, fixed ⅛″ serrated ramp; rear square notch
Stocks: Checkered walnut service with S&W monograms, round or square butt
Finish: S&W blue

MODEL 10

38 MILITARY & POLICE STAINLESS
MODEL 64
$402.00

SPECIFICATIONS
Calibers: 38 S&W Special, 38 S&W Special Mid Range
Capacity: 6 shots
Barrel length: 4″ heavy barrel, square butt; 3″ heavy barrel, round butt; 2″ regular barrel, round butt
Overall length: 9¼″ w/4″ barrel; 7⅞″ w/3″ barrel; 6⅞″ w/2″ barrel
Weight: With 4″ barrel, 33½ oz.; with 3″ barrel, 30½ oz.; with 2″ barrel, 28 oz.
Sights: Fixed, ⅛″ serrated ramp front; square notch rear
Stocks: Checkered walnut service with S&W monograms
Finish: Satin stainless

MODEL 64

357 MILITARY & POLICE (HEAVY BARREL)
MODEL 13
$367.00

SPECIFICATIONS
Caliber: 357 Magnum and 38 S&W Special
Capacity: 6 shots
Barrel length: 3″ and 4″
Overall length: 9¼″ (w/4″ barrel)
Weight: 34 oz. (w/4″ barrel)
Sights: Front, ⅛″ serrated ramp; rear square notch
Stocks: Checkered walnut service with S&W monograms, square butt (3″ barrel has round butt)
Finish: S&W blue

MODEL 13

357 MILITARY & POLICE (HEAVY BARREL)
MODEL 65
$402.00

Same specifications as Model 13, except Model 65 is stainless steel. Available with matte finish.
Also available:
MODEL 65 LADYSMITH. Same specifications as model 65 but with 3″ barrel only. Also features rosewood laminate stock.
Price $450.00

MODEL 65

SMITH & WESSON REVOLVERS

MEDIUM FRAME

K-38 MASTERPIECE
MODEL 14
$442.00

SPECIFICATIONS
Caliber: 38 S&W Special
Barrel length: 6″ full lug barrel
Overall length: 11 1/8″
Weight: 47 oz.
Sights: Micrometer click rear, adjustable for windage and elevation; pinned black Patridge-style front
Grips: Combat-style premium hardwood
Finish: Blue carbon steel
Features: .500 target hammer; .312″ smooth combat trigger

MODEL 14

38 COMBAT MASTERPIECE
MODEL 15
$391.00

SPECIFICATIONS
Caliber: 38 S&W Special
Number of shots: 6
Barrel length: 4″
Overall length: 9 5/16″
Weight (loaded): 32 oz.
Sights: Serrated ramp front; S&W micrometer click sight adjustable for windage and elevation
Stocks: Checkered walnut service with S&W monograms
Finish: S&W blue
Features: .375″ semi-target hammer; .312″ smooth combat-style trigger

MODEL 15

K-22 MASTERPIECE
MODEL 17
$410.00 (4″ barrel)
$449.00 (6″ full lug barrel w/target trigger, hammer)

SPECIFICATIONS
Caliber: 22 Long Rifle
Number of shots: 6
Barrel length: 4″ or 6″
Overall length: 9 1/8″ (4″ barrel); 11 1/8″ (6″ barrel)
Weight (loaded): 47 1/2 oz. with 4″ barrel; 54 oz. with 6″ barrel
Sights: Front, 1/8″ plain Patridge; rear, S&W micrometer click sight adjustable for windage and elevation
Stocks: Checkered walnut Service with S&W monograms
Finish: S&W blue
Also available:
MODEL 617. Same as Model 17 but in stainless steel.
    With 4″ or 6″ barrel **$432.00**
    W/target hammer & trigger, 6″ only **466.00**
    8 3/8″ only w/target hammer & trigger **476.00**
MODEL 648. Same as Model 617 but in 22
    Magnum **437.00**

MODEL 17

SMITH & WESSON REVOLVERS

MEDIUM FRAME

357 COMBAT MAGNUM
MODEL 19
$388.00 (2¹/₂″)
$397.00 (4″ and 6″)

SPECIFICATIONS
Caliber: 357 S&W Magnum (actual bullet dia. 38 S&W Spec.)
Number of shots: 6
Barrel length: 2¹/₂″, 4″ and 6″
Overall length: 9¹/₂″ with 4″ barrel; 7¹/₂″ with 2¹/₂″ barrel; 11¹/₂″ with 6″ barrel
Weight: 30¹/₂ oz. (2¹/₂″ barrel); 36 oz. (4″ barrel); 39 oz. (6″ barrel)
Sights: Front, ¹/₈″ Baughman Quick Draw on 2¹/₂″ or 4″ barrel, ¹/₈″ Patridge on 6″ barrel; rear, S&W micrometer click sight adjustable for windage and elevation
Stocks: Checkered Goncalo Alves Target with S&W monograms
Finish: S&W bright blue
Also available with red ramp front sight, insert and white outline rear. **$420.00**

MODEL 19

357 COMBAT MAGNUM
MODEL 66
$437.00 (2¹/₂″)
$443.00 (4″ and 6″)

SPECIFICATIONS
Caliber: 357 Magnum (actual bullet dia. 38 S&W Spec.)
Number of shots: 6
Barrel length: 6″ or 4″ with square butt; 2¹/₂″ with round butt
Length overall: 9¹/₂″ with 4″ barrel; 7¹/₂″ with 2¹/₂″ barrel; 11³/₈″ with 6″ barrel
Weight: 36 oz. with 4″ barrel; 30¹/₂ oz. with 2¹/₂″ barrel; 39 oz. with 6″ barrel
Sights: Front: ¹/₈″. Rear: S&W Red Ramp on ramp base, S&W Micrometer click sight, adjustable for windage and elevation; for white outline rear sight, add **$5.00**
Stocks: Checked Goncalo Alves target with square butt with S&W monograms
Finish: Satin stainless
Trigger: S&W grooving with an adjustable trigger stop
Ammunition: 357 S&W Magnum, 38 S&W Special Hi-Speed, 38 S&W Special, 38 S&W Special Mid Range

MODEL 66

DISTINGUISHED COMBAT MAGNUM
MODEL 586
$439.00

SPECIFICATIONS
Caliber: 357 Magnum
Capacity: 6 shots
Barrel lengths: 4″, 6″, 8³/₈″
Overall length: 9⁹/₁₆″ with 4″ barrel; 11⁵/₁₆″ with 6″ barrel; 13¹³/₁₆″ with 8³/₈″ barrel
Weight: 41 oz. with 4″ barrel; 46 oz. with 6″ barrel; 53 oz. with 8³/₈″ barrel
Sights: Front is S&W Red Ramp; rear is S&W Micrometer Click adjustable for windage and elevation; White outline notch. Option with 6″ barrel only—plain Patridge front with black outline notch; for white outline rear sight, add **$4.00**
Stocks: Checkered Goncalo Alves with speedloader cutaway
Finish: S&W Blue
MODEL 686: Same as Model 586, except also available with 2¹/₂″ barrel (weighs 35³/₄ oz.) and stainless steel finish **$457.00** (2¹/₂″) to **$499.00** (6″ w/adj. front sight)

MODEL 586

SMITH & WESSON REVOLVERS

LARGE FRAME

357 MAGNUM MODEL 27
$462.00

SPECIFICATIONS
Caliber: 357 Magnum (actual bullet dia. 38 S&W Spec.)
Number of shots: 6
Barrel length: 6″
Overall length: 11⁵/₁₆″
Weight: 45¹/₂ oz.
Sights: Front, Patridge on ramp base; rear, S&W micrometer
click sight adjustable for windage and elevation
Stocks: Checkered hardwood target
Frame: Finely checked top strap and barrel rib
Finish: Blue carbon steel

MODEL 27

44 MAGNUM MODEL 29
$526.00

SPECIFICATIONS
Caliber: 44 Magnum
Number of shots: 6
Barrel lengths: 6″ and 8³/₈″
Overall length: 11⁷/₈″ with 6″ barrel
Weight: 47 oz. with 6″ barrel; 51¹/₂ oz. with 8³/₈″ barrel
Sights: Front, Red ramp on ramp base; rear, S&W micrometer
click sight adjustable for windage and elevation; white out-
line notch
Stocks: Checkered, highly grained hardwood target type
Hammer: Checkered target type
Trigger: Grooved target type
Finish: Blue carbon steel
Also available:
MODEL 29 CLASSIC in blue carbon steel w/full lug barrel,
interchangeable front sights, Hogue combat grips.
With 5″ and 6¹/₂″ barrels $567.00
With 8³/₈″ barrels 578.00

MODEL 29

MODEL 629 (not shown)
$557.00 (4″ and 6″ Barrels)
$575.00 (8³/₈″ Barrel)

SPECIFICATIONS
Calibers: 44 Magnum, 44 S&W Special
Capacity: 6 shots
Barrel lengths: 4″, 6″, 8³/₈″
Overall length: 9⁵/₈″, 11³/₈″, 13⁷/₈″
Weight (empty): 44 oz. (4″); 47 oz. (6″ barrel); 51¹/₂ oz. (8³/₈″)
Sights: S&W red ramp front; plain blade rear w/S&W micro-
meter click; adj. for windage and elevation; scope mount
Stock: Checkered hardwood target
Finish: Stainless steel
Also available:
MODEL 629 CLASSIC w/interchangeable front sight, square
butt, synthetic grips, white outline rear sight, 5″ and 6¹/₂″
barrels $598.00
With 8³/₈″ barrel 617.00
MODEL 629 CLASSIC DX. Same features as above plus two
sets of grips and five interchangeable front sights and proof
target. With 6¹/₂″ barrel $786.00
With 8³/₈″ barrel 811.00

SMITH & WESSON REVOLVERS

LARGE FRAME

41 MAGNUM MODEL 57
$466.00

SPECIFICATIONS
Caliber: 41 Magnum
Number of shots: 6
Barrel length: 6″
Overall length: 11³/₈″
Weight: 48 oz.
Sights: Front, serrated ramp on ramp base; rear, S&W micrometer click sight adjustable for windage and elevation; white outline notch
Stocks: Checkered hardwood target
Trigger: Serrated target type
Finish: Blue carbon steel

MODEL 57

MODEL 657 STAINLESS
$497.00

SPECIFICATIONS
Caliber: 41 Magnum
Capacity: 6 shots
Barrel length: 6″
Overall length: 11³/₈″
Weight (empty): 48 oz.
Sights: Serrated ramp on ramp base (front); Blue S&W micrometer click sight adj. for windage and elevation (rear)
Finish: Satin stainless steel

MODEL 657

MODEL 625-2
$562.00

SPECIFICATIONS
Caliber: 45 ACP
Capacity: 6 shots
Barrel length: 5″ full lug barrel
Overall length: 10³/₈″
Weight (empty): 46 oz.
Sights: Front, Patridge on ramp base; S&W micrometer click rear, adjustable for windage and elevation
Stock: Pachmayr SK/GR gripper, round butt
Finish: Stainless steel

MODEL 625-2

SPRINGFIELD PISTOLS

MODEL 1911-A1 STANDARD

MODEL 1911-A1 CHAMPION

MODEL 1911-A1 STANDARD

An exact duplicate of the M1911-A1 pistol that served the U.S. Armed Forces for more than 70 years, this model has been precision manufactured from forged parts, including a forged frame, then hand-assembled.

SPECIFICATIONS
Calibers: 9mm Parabellum, 38 Super and 45 ACP
Capacity: 9 + 1 in chamber (9mm/38 Super); 8 + 1 in chamber (45 ACP)
Barrel length: 5.04″
Overall length: 8.59″
Weight: 35.62 oz.
Trigger pull: 5 to 6.5 lbs.
Sight radius: 6.281″
Rifling: 1 turn in 16; right-hand, 4-groove (9mm); left-hand, 6-groove (45 ACP)

MODEL 1911-A1

45 ACP/9mm, Blued	$489.00
45 ACP, Parkerized finish	449.00
45 ACP, Stainless finish	532.00
45 ACP/9mm, Bi-Tone finish	829.00
1911-A1 DEFENDER w/fixed combat sights, bobbed hammer, walnut grips, beveled magazine well, extended thumb safety, 45 ACP, Bi-Tone	959.00
1911-A1 CHAMPION with ½″ shortened slide and barrel, 45 ACP, stainless finish	558.00
With blued finish	513.00
With Compensator	829.00
1911-A1 38 SUPER w/blued finish	629.00
1911-A1 COMPACT w/blued finish	509.00
With stainless finish	558.00
1911-A1 FACTORY COMP 38 Super, blued	899.00
In 45 ACP	869.00

MODEL P9 DOUBLE ACTION

SPECIFICATIONS
Calibers: 9mm Parabellum, 40 S&W, 45 ACP
Capacity: 15 rounds (9mm), 11 rounds (40 S&W), 10 rounds (45 ACP)
Barrel length: 4.72″
Overall length: 8.1″
Weight: 35.3 oz.
Rifling: Right-hand; 1 turn in 10″, 4-groove
Grips: Checkered walnut
Features: Serrated front and rear frame straps; frame-mounted thumb safety, Commander-style hammer
Prices:

P9 Standard Blued in 45 ACP	$579.00
In 40 S&W	518.00
In 9mm	518.00
In 45 Ultra LSP	739.00
In 40 S&W Ultra LSP	669.00
P9 Standard Stainless Steel in 45 ACP	639.00
In 9mm	589.00
In 40 S&W	589.00
In 45 Ultra LSP, Bi-Tone	679.00
In 40 S&W Ultra LSP, Bi-Tone	649.00
In 9mm Ultra LSP, Bi-Tone	649.00

MODEL P9 DOUBLE ACTION

P9 Factory Comp 9mm Bi-Tone	$699.00
In 40 S&W, Bi-Tone	699.00
In 45 Bi-Tone	735.00

STAR AUTOMATIC PISTOLS

STAR MODELS 31P & 31PK STARFIRE
9mm Parabellum or 40 S&W

The Model 31 Starfire features a staggered 15-round button release magazine, square notch rear sight (click-adjustable for windage) and square front sight (notched to diffuse light). Removable backstrap houses complete firing mechanism. All-steel frame (Model 31PK has alloy frame).
Barrel length: 3.86″. **Overall length:** 7″. **Weight:** 39.4 oz. (Model 31P); 30 oz. (Model 31PK)
Prices:
Model 31P Blue finish, 40 S&W $643.00
   Blue finish, 9mm Para. 580.00
   Starvel finish, 40 S&W 675.00
   Starvel finish, steel frame, 9mm Para. 612.00
Model 31PK Alloy frame, 9mm Para. 580.00

MODEL 31PK

MODELS M40, M43 & M45 FIRESTAR
9mm Parabellum, 10mm, 40 S&W or 45 ACP

This pocket-sized Firestar pistol features all-steel construction, a triple-dot sight system (fully adjustable rear), and ambidextrous safety. The Acculine barrel design reseats and locks the barrel after each shot. Checkered rubber grips.
Barrel length: 3.39″. **Overall length:** 6½″. **Weight:** 30.35 oz.
Capacity: 7 rounds (6 rounds in 40 S&W).
Prices:
Firestar M40 Blue finish, 40 S&W $488.00
   Starvel finish 517.00
Firestar M43 Blue finish, 9mm Para. 460.00
   Starvel finish, 9mm Para. 492.00
Firestar M45 Blue finish, 45 ACP 525.00
   Starvel finish, 45 ACP 553.00
Megastar Blue finish, 10mm and 45 ACP 693.00
         Starvel finish, 10mm and 45 ACP 725.00

MODEL M43 FIRESTAR

TAURUS PISTOLS

MODEL PT 22

SPECIFICATIONS
Caliber: 22 LR
Action: Semiautomatic
Capacity: 9 shots
Barrel length: 2³/₄″
Overall length: 5¹/₄″
Weight: 12.3 oz.
Sights: Fixed
Grips: Brazilian hardwood
Finish: Blue
Also available:
MODEL PT 25. Same price and specifications as Model PT 22, except magazine holds 8 rounds in 25 ACP.

MODEL PT 22
$182.00

TAURUS PISTOLS

MODEL PT-58

SPECIFICATIONS
Caliber: 380 ACP
Action: Semiautomatic double action
Capacity: Staggered 13 shot
Barrel length: 4″
Overall length: 7.2″
Weight: 30 oz.
Hammer: Exposed
Sights: Front, drift adjustable; rear, notched bar dovetailed to slide, 3-dot combat
Grips: Smooth Brazilian walnut
Finish: Blue, satin nickel or stainless steel

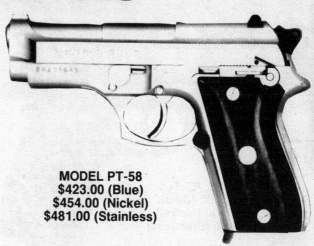

MODEL PT-58
$423.00 (Blue)
$454.00 (Nickel)
$481.00 (Stainless)

MODEL PT-92

Caliber: 9mm Parabellum
Action: Semiautomatic double action
Capacity: Staggered 15-shot magazine
Hammer: Exposed
Barrel length: 5″
Overall length: 8½″
Height: 5.39″
Width: 1.45″
Weight: 34 oz. (empty)
Rifling: R.H., 6 grooves
Sights: Front, fixed; rear, drift adjustable, 3-dot combat
Safeties: (a) Ambidextrous manual safety locking trigger mechanism and slide in locked position; (b) half-cock position; (c) inertia operated firing pin; (d) chamber loaded indicator
Slide: Hold open upon firing last cartridge
Grips: Smooth Brazilian walnut
Finish: Blue, satin nickel or stainless steel
Also available:
MODEL PT 99. Same specifications as Model PT 92, but has micrometer click-adjustable rear sight. **$512.00** (Blue); **$554.00** (Nickel); **$582.00** (Stainless).

MODEL PT-92
$473.00 (Blue)
$511.00 (Nickel)
$538.00 (Stainless)

MODEL PT-92C

SPECIFICATIONS
Caliber: 9mm Parabellum
Capacity: 13 rounds
Barrel length: 4.25″
Overall length: 7.5″
Weight: 31 oz.
Sights: Fixed front; drift-adjustable rear, 3-dot combat
Stocks: Brazilian hardwood
Slide: Last shot held open
Safety: Manual, ambidextrous hammer drop; inertia firing pin; chamber load indicator
Finish: Blue, satin nickel or stainless steel

MODEL PT-92C
$473.00 (Blue)
$511.00 (Nickel)
$538.00 (Stainless)

TAURUS PISTOLS/REVOLVERS

MODEL PT-908
$473.00 (Blue)
$511.00 (Nickel)
$538.00 (Stainless)

SPECIFICATIONS
Caliber: 9mm Parabellum
Action: Double action
Capacity: 8 shot
Barrel length: 3.8″
Overall length: 7.05″
Weight: 30 oz.
Sights: Drift adjustable front and rear, 3-dot Combat
Stock: Rubber
Finish: Blue, satin nickel or stainless steel

MODEL PT 101
$522.00 (Blue)
$564.00 (Nickel)
$592.00 (Stainless)

MODEL PT 100

SPECIFICATIONS
Caliber: 40 S&W
Capacity: 15 shots
Barrel length: 5″
Weight: 34 oz. (empty)
Sights: Fixed front; adjustable rear, 3-dot Combat
Grips: Brazilian hardwood
Finish: Blue, satin nickel or stainless steel
Prices: **$482.00** (Blue); **$521.00** (Nickel); **$547.00** (Stainless)
Also available:
MODEL PT 101. Same specifications as Model PT 100, but features micrometer click-adjustable rear sight.

MODEL 65 (2¹/₂″ Barrel)
$266.00 (Blue)
$338.00 (Stainless)

MODEL 65

SPECIFICATIONS
Caliber: 357 Magnum
Capacity: 6 shot
Barrel lengths: 2¹/₂″, 4″
Weight: 34 oz.
Sights: Rear square notch; serrated front ramp
Action: Double
Stock: Brazilian hardwood
Finish: Royal blue or stainless

MODEL 66
$292.00 (2¹/₂″ Blue)
$290.00 (4″ and 6″ Blue)

MODEL 66

SPECIFICATIONS
Caliber: 357 Magnum
Action: Double
Capacity: 6 shot
Barrel lengths: 2¹/₂″, 3″, 4″, 6″
Weight: 35 oz. (4″ barrel)
Sights: Serrated ramp front; rear micrometer click adjustable for windage and elevation
Stock: Brazilian hardwood
Finish: Royal blue or stainless steel
Features: Recoil compensator (factory installed)
Prices (add'l.): **$299.00** (4″ and 6″ Blue w/recoil compensator); **$371.00** (2¹/₂″ Stainless); **$368.00** (4″ and 6″ Stainless); **$375.00** (4″ and 6″ Stainless w/recoil compensator)

TAURUS REVOLVERS

MODEL 83
$241.00 (Blue)

SPECIFICATIONS
Caliber: 38 Special
Action: Double
Number of shots: 6
Barrel length: 4"
Weight: 34 oz.
Sights: Patridge-type front; rear micrometer click adjustable for windage and elevation
Stock: Brazilian hardwood
Finish: Blue

MODEL 86 TARGET MASTER
$326.00

SPECIFICATIONS
Caliber: 38 Special
Capacity: 6 shot
Action: Double
Barrel length: 6"
Weight: 34 oz.
Sights: Patridge-type front; micrometer click adjustable rear for windage and elevation
Stock: Brazilian hardwood
Finish: Bright royal blue

MODEL 85
$251.00 (Blue)
$315.00 (Stainless Steel)

SPECIFICATIONS
Caliber: 38 Special
Capacity: 5 shot
Action: Double
Barrel length: 2" and 3"
Weight: 21 oz. (2" barrel)
Sights: Notch rear sight, fixed sight
Stock: Brazilian hardwood
Finish: Blue or stainless steel

MODEL 85CH
$251.00 (Blue)
$315.00 (Stainless Steel)

Same specifications as Model 85, except has concealed hammer and 2" barrel only. Not available in nickel.

TAURUS REVOLVERS

MODEL 80
$229.00 (Blue)
$282.00 (Stainless)

SPECIFICATIONS
Caliber: 38 Special
Capacity: 6 shot
Action: Double
Barrel lengths: 3″, 4″
Weight: 30 oz. (4″ barrel)
Sights: Notched rear; serrated ramp front
Stock: Brazilian hardwood
Finish: Blue or stainless

MODEL 80

MODEL 82
$229.00 (Blue)
$282.00 (Stainless)

SPECIFICATIONS
Caliber: 38 Special
Capacity: 6 shot
Action: Double
Barrel lengths: 3″, 4″
Weight: 34 oz. (4″ barrel)
Sights: Notched rear; serrated ramp front
Stock: Brazilian hardwood
Finish: Blue or stainless

MODEL 82

MODEL 94
$264.00 (Blue)
$314.00 (Stainless)

SPECIFICATIONS
Caliber: 22 LR
Number of shots: 9
Action: Double
Barrel lengths: 3″ and 4″
Weight: 25 oz.
Sights: Serrated ramp front; rear micrometer click adjustable for windage and elevation
Stock: Brazilian hardwood
Finish: Blue or stainless steel

Also available:
MODEL 941 in 22 Magnum, 8-shot capacity;
  ejector shroud, blue **$290.00**
  In stainless steel **346.00**

MODEL 941

TAURUS REVOLVERS

MODEL 96
$326.00

MODEL 96

SPECIFICATIONS
Caliber: 22 LR
Number of shots: 6
Action: Double
Barrel length: 6″
Weight: 34 oz.
Sights: Patridge-type front; rear micrometer click adjustable for windage and elevation
Stock: Brazilian hardwood
Finish: Blue only

MODEL 431
$281.00 (Blue)
$351.00 (Stainless)

MODEL 431

SPECIFICATIONS
Caliber: 44 Special
Capacity: 5 shots
Action: Double
Barrel length: 3″ or 4″ w/ejector shroud; heavy, solid rib barrel
Weight: 35 oz. (4″ barrel)
Sights: Notched rear; serrated ramp front
Safety: Transfer bar
Stock: Brazilian hardwood
Finish: Blue or stainless steel

MODEL 441

SPECIFICATIONS
Caliber: 44 Special
Capacity: 5 shots
Action: Double
Barrel lengths: 3″, 4″ or 6″ w/ejector shroud; heavy, solid rib barrel
Weight: 40¼ oz. (6″ barrel)
Sights: Serrated ramp front; rear micrometer click adjustable for windage and elevation
Safety: Transfer bar
Stock: Brazilian hardwood
Finish: Blue or stainless steel

MODEL 441
$307.00 (Blue)
$386.00 (Stainless)

TAURUS REVOLVERS

MODEL 669
$301.00 (4″ and 6″ Blue)
$379.00 (4″ and 6″ Stainless)

SPECIFICATIONS
Caliber: 357 Magnum
Capacity: 6 shots
Action: Double
Barrel lengths: 4″ and 6″
Weight: 37 oz. (4″ barrel)
Sights: Serrated ramp front; rear micrometer click adjustable
   for windage and elevation
Stock: Brazilian hardwood
Finish: Royal blue or stainless
Features: Recoil compensator (optional) **$7.00** additional

MODEL 669

MODEL 689
$313.00 (Blue)
$392.00 (Stainless)

The Model 689 has the same specifications as the Model 669,
except vent rib is featured.

MODEL 689 STAINLESS

MODEL 741

MODEL 761

MODEL 741
$254.00 (Blue)
$342.00 (Stainless)

SPECIFICATIONS
Caliber: 32 H&R Magnum
Capacity: 6 shot
Action: Double
Barrel length: 3″ or 4″
Weight: 20 oz. (w/3″ barrel)
Sights: Serrated ramp front; rear micrometer click adjustable
   for windage and elevation
Stock: Brazilian hardwood
Finish: Blue or stainless steel
Also available:
MODEL 761 with 6″ barrel, weight of 34 oz., blue finish. **Price:**
   $326.00

THOMPSON/CENTER

BULL BARREL

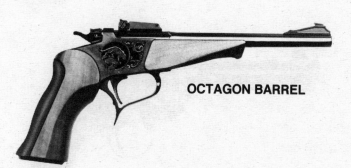

OCTAGON BARREL

CONTENDER
OCTAGON BARREL MODELS

This standard barrel is interchangeable with any model listed here. Available in 10-inch length, it is supplied with iron sights. Octagon barrel is available in 22 LR. No external choke.
Price: **$415.00**

CONTENDER SUPER "14"
STAINLESS STEEL

CONTENDER
SUPER "14" MODELS

Chambered in 11 calibers (17 Rem., 22 LR, 222 Rem., 223 Rem., 7-30 Waters, 7mm T.C.U., 30-30 Win., 35 Rem., 357 Rem. Max., 375 Win. and 44 Mag.), this gun is equipped with a 14-inch bull barrel, fully adjustable target rear sight and Patridge-style ramped front sight with 13½-inch sight radius. **Overall length:** 18¼". **Weight:** 3½ lbs.
Price: Blued. **$425.00**
    Stainless 485.00
14" Vent Rib Model in 45 Colt/.410 .... 455.00

CONTENDER
BULL BARREL MODELS

These pistols with 10-inch barrel feature fully adjustable Patridge-style iron sights. All stainless steel models (including the Super "14" and Super "16" below) are equipped with Rynite finger-groove grip with rubber recoil cushion and matching Rynite forend, plus Cougar etching on the steel frame.

Standard and Custom calibers available:
22 LR, 22 Hornet, 22 Win. Mag., 7-30 Waters, 223 Rem., 32-20 Win., 7mm T.C.U., 30-30 Win., 357 Mag., 357 Rem. Max. and 44 Mag.
Bull Barrel (less internal choke)............... **$415.00**
Bull Barrel Stainless 475.00
Standard calibers w/internal choke 45 Colt/.410 ... 420.00
Vent Rib Model............................. 435.00
With **Match Grade Barrel** (22 LR only) 425.00

CONTENDER HUNTER

Chambered in 7-30 Waters, 223 Rem., 30-30 Win., 35 Rem., 45-70 Government, 357 Rem. Max., 375 Win. and 44 Rem. Mag., the most popular commercially loaded cartridges available to handgunners. **Barrel length:** 12" or 14". **Overall length:** 16". **Weight:** 4 lbs. (approx.). **Features:** T/C Muzzle Tamer (to reduce recoil); a mounted T/C Recoil Proof 2.5X scope with lighted reticle, QD sling swivels and nylon sling, plus suede leather carrying case.
12" Barrel **$695.00**
14" Barrel 705.00

CONTENDER SUPER "16"
VENTILATED RIB/INTERNAL CHOKE MODELS
(not shown)

Featuring a raised ventilated (7/16-inch wide) rib, this Contender model is available in 45 Colt/.410 caliber. A patented detachable choke (1⅞ inches long) screws into the muzzle internally. **Barrel length:** 16¼" inches.
Price: Blued. **$460.00**
    Stainless 490.00
10" Vent Rib Model w/internal choke 435.00

A. UBERTI REPLICAS

1871 ROLLING BLOCK TARGET PISTOL
$380.00

SPECIFICATIONS
Calibers: 22 LR, 22 Hornet, 22 Magnum, 357 Magnum, 45 L.C.
Capacity: Single shot
Barrel length: 9½" (half-octagon/half-round or full round Navy Style)
Overall length: 14"
Weight: 2.75 lbs.
Sights: Fully adjustable rear; ramp front or open sight on Navy Style barrel
Grip and forend: Walnut
Trigger guard: Brass
Frame: Color casehardened steel

1871 ROLLING BLOCK TARGET PISTOL

1873 CATTLEMAN QUICK DRAW
$375.00 (Brass)
$425.00 (Steel)

SPECIFICATIONS
Calibers: 38-40, 357 Magnum, 44 Special, 44-40, 45 L.C., 45 ACP
Capacity: 6 shots
Barrel lengths: 4¾", 5½", 7½" round tapered; 10", 12", 18" (Buntline)
Overall length: 10¾" w/5½" barrel
Weight: 2.42 lbs.
Grip: One-piece walnut
Frame: Color casehardened steel; also available in charcoal blue (**$40.00** extra) or nickel (**$50.00** extra)
Also available:
45 L.C./45 ACP Convertible $455.00
In brass 415.00

1873 CATTLEMAN QUICK DRAW

1875 REMINGTON ARMY S.A. "OUTLAW"

1875 REMINGTON ARMY S.A. "OUTLAW"
$405.00

SPECIFICATIONS
Calibers: 357 Magnum, 45 Long Colt, 44-40, 45 ACP
Capacity: 6 shots
Barrel length: 7½" round tapered
Overall length: 13¾"
Weight: 2.75 lbs.
Grips: Two-piece walnut
Frame: Color casehardened steel
Also available:
In nickel plate $450.00
45 L.C./45 ACP Convertible 450.00

BUCKHORN SINGLE ACTION LARGE FRAME
$420.00

SPECIFICATIONS
Calibers: 357 Magnum, 45 Long Colt, 44-40, 44 Magnum
Capacity: 6 shots
Barrel length: 4¾", 6" or 7½"
Overall length: 11¾"
Weight: 2.5 lbs.
Sights: Open or target
Finish: Black
Also available:
In nickel plate $455.00
44-40 Mag. Convertible 460.00

BUCKHORN SINGLE ACTION LARGE FRAME

UNIQUE PISTOLS

MODEL DES 69U
$1195.00

SPECIFICATIONS
Caliber: 22 LR
Capacity: 5- or 6-shot magazine
Barrel length: 5.9″
Overall length: 11.2″
Weight: 40.2 oz. (empty)
Height: 5.5″
Width: 1.97″
Sights: Micrometric rear; lateral and vertical correction by clicks
Safety: Manual
Features: Orthopedic French walnut grip with adjustable hand rest; external hammer
Also available:
Model DES 32U in 32 S&W Long Wadcutter. Designed for centerfire U.I.T. and military rapid fire. Other specifications same as Model DES 69U. **Price: $1295.00**

MODEL I.S. INTERNATIONAL SILHOUETTE
$1095.00

SPECIFICATIONS
Calibers: 22 LR, 22 Magnum, 7mm TCU, 357 Magnum, 44 Magnum
Barrel length: 10″
Overall length: 14.5″
Weight: 38 oz.
Height: 6.5″
Width: 1.5″
Sights: Micrometric rear; lateral and vertical correction by clicks; interchangeable front sight; dovetailed grooves for scope
Features: French walnut grip; interchangeable shroud/barrel assembly; external hammer; firing adjustments

MODEL DES 2000U
$1350.00

SPECIFICATIONS
Caliber: 22 Short
Barrel length: 5.9″
Overall length: 11.4″
Weight: 43.4 oz. (empty)
Height: 5.3″
Width: 1.97″
Sights: Micrometric rear; lateral and vertical correction by clicks
Features: French walnut grips with adjustable hand rest; left-hand grips available; external hammer; dry firing device; slide stop catch; anti-recoil device
Also available:
Model DES 2000U International Sport w/light alloy frame in 22 LR and 22 Mag. **Price: $795.00**

WALTHER PISTOLS

DOUBLE-ACTION AUTOMATIC PISTOLS

The Walther double-action system combines the principles of the double-action revolver with the advantages of the modern pistol without the disadvantages inherent in either design.

Models PPK and PPK/S differ only in the overall length of the barrel and slide. Both models offer the same features, including compact form, light weight, easy handling and absolute safety. Both models can be carried with a loaded chamber and closed hammer, but ready to fire either single- or dou-

ble-action. Both models are provided with a live round indicator pin to signal a loaded chamber. An automatic internal safety blocks the hammer to prevent accidental striking of the firing pin, except with a deliberate pull of the trigger. Sights are provided with white markings for high visibility in poor light. Rich Walther blue/black finish is standard and each pistol is complete with an extra magazine with finger rest extension.

MODEL PPK & PPK/S 6-SHOT AUTOMATICS

MODEL PPK & PPK/S 6-SHOT AUTOMATICS

Caliber: 380 ACP
Barrel length: 3.2″
Overall length: 6.1″
Height: 4.28″
Weight: 21 oz. (PPK); 23 oz. (PPK/S)
Finish: Walther blue or stainless steel
Price: $627.00

MODEL TPH DOUBLE ACTION

Walther's Model TPH is considered by government agents and professional lawmen to be one of the top undercover/backup guns available. A scaled-down version of Walther's PP-PPK series.

SPECIFICATIONS
Calibers: 22 LR and 25 ACP
Capacity: 6 rounds
Barrel length: 2.3″
Overall length: 5³/₈″
Weight: 14 oz.
Finish: Walther blue or stainless steel
Price: (All models) $473.00

MODEL TPH

WALTHER PISTOLS

MODEL P-38 DOUBLE ACTION

The Walther P-38 is a double-action, locked-breech, semiautomatic pistol with an external hammer. Its compact form, light weight and easy handling are combined with the superb performance of the 9mm Luger Parabellum cartridge. The P-38 is equipped with both a manual and automatic safety, which allows it to be carried safely while the chamber is loaded.

SPECIFICATIONS
Caliber: 9mm Parabellum
Capacity: 8 rounds
Barrel length: 5"
Overall length: 8 1/2"
Weight: 28 oz.
Finish: Blue
Price: . . . . $ 627.00
Also available:
100 YEAR P-38 COMMEMORATIVE
w/Presentation case 1000.00

MODEL P-38

MODEL P-5 DA

SPECIFICATIONS
Caliber: 9mm Parabellum
Capacity: 8 rounds
Barrel length: 3 1/2"
Overall length: 7"
Weight: 28 oz.
Finish: Blue
Features: Four automatic built-in safety functions; lightweight alloy frame; supplied with two magazines
Price: $1257.00
MODEL P-5 COMPACT (3.1" barrel) 1257.00

MODEL PP DOUBLE ACTION (not shown)

SPECIFICATIONS
Caliber: 22 LR, 32 ACP or 380 ACP
Barrel length: 3.8" (32 ACP)
Overall length: 6.7" (32 ACP)
Weight: 23.5 oz. (32 ACP)
Prices:
In 22 LR . . . . $ 948.00
In 32 ACP 1448.00
In 380 ACP 1492.00
Also available:
Deluxe Engraved (22 LR only) Gold 2053.00
    Silver 1948.00

MODEL P-5 DA

MODEL P-88 DA

SPECIFICATIONS
Caliber: 9mm Parabellum
Capacity: 15 rounds
Barrel length: 4"
Overall length: 7 3/8"
Weight: 31 1/2 oz.
Finish: Blue
Sights: Rear adjustable for windage and elevation
Features: Internal safeties; ambidextrous de-cocking lever and magazine release button; lightweight alloy frame; loaded chamber indicator
Price: $1200.00
Also available:
MODEL P-88 COMPACT w/3.8" barrel. **Weight:** 29 oz. **Overall length:** 7.1". **Capacity:** 14 rounds. . . . . **Price:** $1200.00

MODEL P-88 DA

WALTHER TARGET PISTOLS

**WALTHER OSP
MATCH RAPID FIRE PISTOL
(22 Short only)
$2275.00 (with Case)
$2452.00 (Left Hand)**

MATCH RAPID FIRE PISTOL

Walther match pistols are built to conform to ISU and NRA match target pistol regulations. The model GSP, caliber 22 LR is available with either 2.2 lb. (1000 gm) or 3.0 lbs. (1360 gm) trigger, and comes with 4½-inch barrel and special hand-fitting designed walnut stock. Sights consist of fixed front and adjustable rear sight. The GSP-C 32 S&W wadcutter centerfire pistol is factory tested with a 3.0 lb. trigger. The 22 LR conversion unit for the model GSP-C consists of an interchangeable barrel, a slide assembly and two magazines.

SPECIFICATIONS
Caliber: 22 Short
Magazine capacity: 5 shots
Weight: 44.4 oz.
Overall length: 11.8″

WALTHER GSP MATCH PISTOL
22 LR & 32 S&W Wadcutter

SPECIFICATIONS GSP/GSP-C
Barrel length: 4½″
Overall length: 11.8″
Weight: 42.3 oz. (GSP); 49.4 oz. (GSP-C)
Prices:
GSP—22 Long Rifle w/carrying case $1843.00
GSP-C—32 S&W wadcutter w/carrying case 2545.00
22 LR conversion unit for GSP-C 1053.00
22 Short conversion unit for GSP-C 1495.00
32 S&W wadcutter conversion unit for GSP-C . . . 1400.00

MODEL GSP MATCH

DAN WESSON REVOLVERS

357 MAGNUM REVOLVERS

Introduced in 1935, the 357 Magnum iis still the top selling handgun caliber. It makes an excellent hunting sidearm, and many law enforcement agencies have adopted it as a duty caliber. Take your pick of Dan Wesson 357s; then, add to its versatility with an additional barrel assembly option to alter it to your other needs.

SPECIFICATIONS

Action: Slx-shot double and single action. **Ammunition:** 357 Magnum, 38 Special Hi-speed, 38 Special Mid-range. **Typical dimension:** 4″ barrel revolver, 9¼″×5¾″. **Trigger:** Smooth, wide tang (³/₈″) with overtravel adjustment. **Hammer:** Wide spur (³/₈″) with short double-action travel. **Sights: Models 14 and 714,** ¹/₈″ fixed serrated front; fixed rear integral with frame. **Models 15 and 715,** ¹/₈″ serrated interchangeable front blade; red insert standard, yellow and white available; rear notch (.125, .080, or white outline) adjustable for windage and elevation; graduated click. 10″ barrel assemblies have special front sights and instructions. **Rifling:** Six lands and grooves, right-hand twist, 1 turn in 18.75 inches (2½″ thru 8″ lengths); six lands & grooves, right-hand twist, 1 turn in 14 inches (10″ bbl.). **Note:** All 2½″ guns shipped with undercover grips. 4″ guns are shipped with service grips and the balance have oversized target grips.

Price:
Pistol Pac Models 357 Magnum . . . . . . **$615.00** (Blue) to **$888.00** (Stainless)

357 MAGNUM

Model	Caliber	Type	Barrel Lengths & Weight in Ounces					Finish
			2½″	4″	6″	8″	10″	
14-2	.357 Magnum	Service	30	34	38	NA	NA	Satin Blue
15-2	.357 Magnum	Target	32	36	40	44	50	Brite Blue
15-2V	.357 Magnum	Target	32	35	39	43	49	Brite Blue
15-2VH	.357 Magnum	Target	32	37	42	47	55	Brite Blue
714	.357 Magnum	Service	30	34	38	NA	NA	Satin Stainless Steel
715	.357 Magnum	Target	32	36	40	45	50	Satin Stainless Steel
715-V	.357 Magnum	Target	32	35	40	43	49	Satin Stainless Steel
715-VH	.357 Magnum	Target	32	37	42	49	55	Satin Stainless Steel

38 SPECIAL REVOLVER

For decades a favorite of security and law enforcement agencies, the 38 special still maintains it's reputation as a fine caliber for sportsmen and target shooters. Dan Wesson offers a choice of barrel lengths in either service or target configuration.

SPECIFICATIONS

Action: Six-shot double and single action. **Ammunition:** 38 Special Hi-speed, 38 Special Mid-range. **Typical dimension:** 4″ barrel revolver, 9¼″ × 5¾″. **Trigger:** Smooth, wide tang (³/₈″) with overtravel adjustment. **Hammer:** Wide spur (³/₈″) with short double travel. **Sights:** Models 8 and 708, ¹/₈″ fixed serrated front; fixed rear integral with frame. Models 9 and 709, ¹/₈″ serrated interchangeable front blade; red insert standard, yellow and white available; rear, standard notch (.125, .080, or white outline) adjustable for windage and elevation; graduated click. **Rifling:** Six lands and grooves, right-hand twist, 1 turn in 18.75 inches. **Note:** All 2½″ guns shipped with undercover grips. 4″ guns are shipped with service grips and the balance have oversized target grips.

Price:
Pistol Pac Models 38 Special . . . . **$615.00** (Blue) to **$888.00** (Stainless)

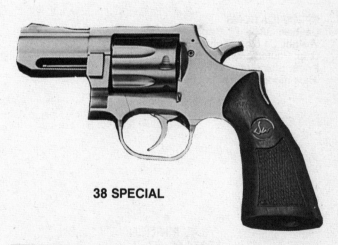

38 SPECIAL

Model	Caliber	Type	Barrel Lengths & Weight in Ounces				Finish
			2½″	4″	6″	8″	
8-2	.38 Special	Service	30	34	38	NA	Satin Blue
9-2	.38 Special	Target	32	36	40	44	Brite Blue
9-2V	.39 Special	Target	32	35	39	43	Brite Blue
9-2VH	.38 Special	Target	32	37	42	47	Brite Blue
708	.38 Special	Service	30	34	38	NA	Satin Stainless Steel
709	.38 Special	Target	32	36·	40	44	Satin Stainless Steel
709-V	.38 Special	Target	32	35	39	43	Satin Stainless Steel
709-VH	.38 Special	Target	32	37	42	47	Satin Stainless Steel

DAN WESSON REVOLVERS

22 SILHOUETTE REVOLVER

SPECIFICATIONS
This six-shot, single-action-only revolver is available with 10″ vented or vent heavy barrel assembly; incorporates a new cylinder manufacturing process that enhances the inherent accuracy of the Wesson revolver. Shipped with a combat-style grip, .080 narrow notch rear sight blade, a Patridge-style front sight blade to match. **Caliber:** 22 rimfire. **Type:** Target. **Weight:** 55 to 62 oz. **Finish:** Bright blue or stainless steel.
Price: . . . . **$459.75 to $489.00**

22 SILHOUETTE REVOLVER

FIXED BARREL REVOLVERS
$240.00–$259.00 Service Model
$248.00–$268.00 Target Model

These revolvers retain the advantages of a barrel in tension (minimal barrel whip) without the interchangeable features of earlier Wesson models.

SPECIFICATIONS
Calibers: 357 Magnum and 38 Special. **Capacity:** 6 shots. **Barrel lengths:** 3″ and 5″ (Target); 2½″ and 4″ (Service). **Overall length:** 8¾″ w/3″ barrel; 10¾″ w/5″ barrel. **Height:** 5¾″. **Weight:** 37 oz. to 42 oz. **Sight radius:** 5⅛″ (3″); 7⅛″ (5″). **Sights:** Adjustable rear target (Target model); fixed service sight (Service model). **Finish:** Brushed stainless steel or High Brite Blue (Target); brushed stainless steel or satin blue (Service).

357 MAG. FIXED BARREL REVOLVER

MODEL 738P "L'IL DAN"

SPECIFICATIONS
Caliber: 38 + P. **Capacity:** 5 shots. **Barrel length:** 6½″. **Weight:** 24.6 oz. **Sights:** Fixed. **Finish:** Stainless steel or blue. **Grip:** Pauferro wood or rubber.
Price: Stainless **$270.00**
(Blue model price not set)

MODEL 738P "L'IL DAN"

.45 PIN GUN
$654.00–$762.00

SPECIFICATIONS
Caliber: 45 Auto. **Barrel length:** 5″ (5.28″ compensated shroud). **Overall length:** 12½″. **Weight:** 54 oz. **Sight radius:** 8.375″. **Finish:** Brushed stainless steel or High Brite Blue steel.

45 PIN GUN

DAN WESSON REVOLVERS

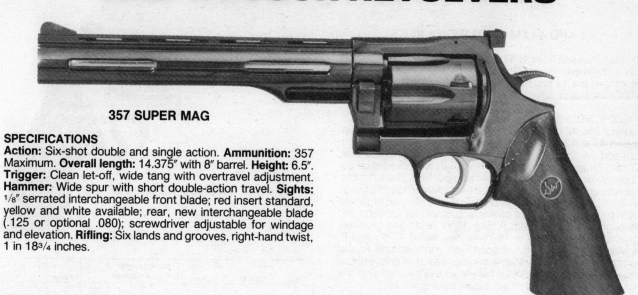

357 SUPER MAG

SPECIFICATIONS
Action: Six-shot double and single action. **Ammunition:** 357 Maximum. **Overall length:** 14.375″ with 8″ barrel. **Height:** 6.5″. **Trigger:** Clean let-off, wide tang with overtravel adjustment. **Hammer:** Wide spur with short double-action travel. **Sights:** ¹/₈″ serrated interchangeable front blade; red insert standard, yellow and white available; rear, new interchangeable blade (.125 or optional .080); screwdriver adjustable for windage and elevation. **Rifling:** Six lands and grooves, right-hand twist, 1 in 18³/₄ inches.

SPECIFICATIONS

Model	Caliber	Type	Barrel lengths & Weight (oz.)			Finish	Prices*
			6″	8″	10″		
740-V	357 Max	Target	59.5	65	69	Stainless	$550.00–$683.00
740-VH	357 Max	Target	62	72	76	Stainless	
740-V8S	357 Max	Target		64		Stainless	

*Model 40 (Blue): $488.00–575.00

32/.32-20 MAGNUM SIX SHOT

This target and small-game gun offers a high muzzle velocity and a flat trajectory for better accuracy. **Action:** Six-shot double and single. **Calibers:** 32 H&R Magnum, 32 S&W Long, 32 Colt new police cartridges interchangeable. **Barrel length:** 4″. **Overall length:** 9¹/₄″. **Trigger:** Smooth, wide tang (³/₈″) w/overtravel adjustment. **Hammer:** Wide spur (³/₈″) w/short double-action travel. **Sights:** Front—¹/₈″ serrated, interchangeable blade, red insert standard (yellow and white available); rear—interchangeable blade for wide or narrow notch sight picture (wide notch standard, narrow notch available), adj. for windage and elevation, graduated click. **Rifling:** Six lands and grooves, right-hand twist 1:18³/₄″. **Finish:** Blue or stainless steel.

SPECIFICATIONS

Model	Caliber	Type	Barrel lengths & Weight in ounces				Finish	Pistol Pac Prices*
			2¹/₂″	4″	6″	8″		
32	.32 Magnum	Target	35	39	43	48	Brite Blue	$615.00–$818.00
32V	.32 Magnum	Target	35	39	43	48	Brite Blue	
32VH	.32 Magnum	Target	35	40	46	53	Brite Blue	
732	.32 Magnum	Target	35	39	43	48	Satin Stainless Steel	$689.00–$893.00
732V	.32 Magnum	Target	35	39	43	48	Satin Stainless Steel	
732VH	.32 Magnum	Target	35	40	46	53	Satin Stainless Steel	

DAN WESSON REVOLVERS

41 AND 44 MAGNUM REVOLVERS

The Dan Wesson 41 and 44 Magnum revolvers are available with a patented "Power Control" to reduce muzzle flip. Both the 41 and the 44 have a one-piece frame and patented gain bolt for maximum strength.

SPECIFICATIONS
Action: Six-shot double- and single-action. **Ammunition:** Models 41 and 741, 41 Magnum; Models 44 and 744, 44 Magnum and 44 Special. **Typical dimension:** 6" barrel revolver, 12"×6." **Trigger:** Smooth, wide tang ($^3/_8$") with overtravel adjustment. **Hammer:** Wide checkered spur with short double-action travel. **Sights:** Front, $^1/_8$" serrated interchangeable blade; red insert standard, yellow and white available; rear, standard notch (.125, .080, or white outline) adjustable for windage and elevation; click graduated. **Rifling:** Eight lands and grooves, right-hand twist, 1 turn in 18.75 inches. **Note:** 4", 6", and 8" 44 Magnum guns will be shipped with unported and Power Control barrels. 10" 44 Magnum guns available only without Power Control. Only jacketed bullets should be used with the 44 Mag. Power Control or excessive leading will result.

Prices:
Pistol Pac Model 41 (Blue) $624.00–672.00
 Stainless Steel 690.00–739.00
Pistol Pac Model 44 (Blue) 708.00–758.00
 Stainless Steel 814.00–867.00

41/44 MAGNUM REVOLVER

Model	Caliber	Type	Barrel Lengths & Wt. in Ounces				Finish
			4"	6"	8"	10"*	
41-V	.41 Magnum	Target	48	53	58	64	Brite Blue
41-VH	.41 Magnum	Target	49	56	64	69	Brite Blue
44-V	.44 Magnum	Target	48	53	58	64	Brite Blue
44-VH	.44 Magnum	Target	49	56	64	69	Brite Blue
741-V	.41 Magnum	Target	48	53	58	64	Satin Stainless Steel
741-VH	.41 Magnum	Target	49	56	64	69	Satin Stainless Steel
744-V	.44 Magnum	Target	48	53	58	64	Satin Stainless Steel
744-VH	.44 Magnum	Target	49	56	64	69	Satin Stainless Steel

445 SUPERMAG REVOLVERS

With muzzle velocities in the 1650 fps range, and chamber pressures and recoil comparable to the 44 Magnum, the 445 Supermag has already won considerable renown in silhouette competition. As a hunting cartridge, it is more than adequate for any species of game on the American continent. **Action:** Six-shot double and single. **Type:** Target. **Caliber:** 445 Supermag. **Overall length:** 14.375" w/8" barrel. **Trigger:** Clean let-off, widg tane with overtravel adjustment. **Hammer:** Wide spur with short double-action travel. **Sights:** $^1/_8$" serrated, interchangeable front blade, red insert standard (yellow and white available); rear—interchangeable blade for wide or narrow notch sight picture, wide notch standard (narrow notch available), adj. for windage and elevation. **Rifling:** Six lands and grooves, right-hand twist 1:18$^3/_4$".

445 SUPERMAG

Model	Barrel Length & Weight in Ounces			Finish	Prices
	6"	8"	10"		
445-V	59.5	62	65	Bright Blue	
445-VH	62	72	76	Bright Blue	$516.00–$615.00
445-VHS	—	64	—	Bright Blue	
445-VS	—	60	64	Bright Blue	
7445-V	59.5	62	65	Stainless Steel	
7445-VH	62	72	76	Stainless Steel	$592.00–$683.00
7445-VHS	—	64	—	Stainless Steel	
7445-VS	—	60	64	Stainless Steel	

DAN WESSON REVOLVERS

22 RIMFIRE and 22 WIN. MAGNUM REVOLVERS

Built on the same frames as the Dan Wesson 357 Magnum, these 22 rimfires offer the heft and balance of fine target revolvers. Affordable fun for the beginner or the expert.

SPECIFICATIONS
Action: Six-shot double and single action. **Ammunition:** Models 22 & 722, 22 Long Rifle; Models 22M & 722M, 22 Win. Mag. **Typical dimension:** 4″ barrel revolver, $9\frac{1}{4}″ \times 5\frac{3}{4}″$. **Trigger:** Smooth, wide tang ($\frac{3}{8}″$) with overtravel adjustment. **Hammer:** Wide spur ($\frac{3}{8}″$) with short double-action travel. **Sights:** Front, $\frac{1}{8}″$ serrated, interchangeable blade; red insert standard, yellow and white available; rear, standard wide notch (.125, .080, or white outline) adjustable for windage and elevation; graduated click. **Rifling:** Models 22 and 722, six lands and grooves, right-hand twist, 1 turn in 12 inches; Models 22M and 722M, six lands and grooves, right-hand twist, 1 turn in 16 inches. **Note:** All $2\frac{1}{2}″$ guns are shipped with undercover grips. 4″ guns are shipped with service grips and the balance have oversized target grips.

Prices:
Pistol Pac Models 22 thru 722M . . . . **$637.00** (Blue)—
$923.00 (Stainless)

22 RIMFIRE/22 WIN. MAG.
(Blue)

22 RIMFIRE/22 WIN. MAG.
(Stainless)

Model	Caliber	Type	Barrel Lengths & Wt. in Ounces				Finish
			2¼″	4″	6″	8″	
22	.22 L.R.	Target	36	40	44	49	Brite Blue
22-V	.22 L.R.	Target	36	40	44	49	Brite Blue
22-VH	.22 L.R.	Target	36	41	47	54	Brite Blue
22-M	.22 Win Mag	Target	36	40	44	49	Brite Blue
22M-V	.22 Win Mag	Target	36	40	44	49	Brite Blue
22M-VH	.22 Win Mag	Target	36	41	47	54	Brite Blue
722	.22 L.R.	Target	36	40	44	49	Satin Stainless Steel
722-V	.22 L.R.	Target	36	40	44	49	Satin Stainless Steel
722-VH	.22 L.R.	Target	36	41	47	54	Satin Stainless Steel
722M	.22 Win Mag	Target	36	40	44	49	Satin Stainless Steel
722M-V	.22 Win Mag	Target	36	40	44	49	Satin Stainless Steel
722M-VH	.22 Win Mag	Target	36	41	47	54	Satin Stainless Steel

HUNTER PACS

Offered in all magnum calibers and include the following:
1. Gun with vent heavy 8″ shroud.
2. A vent 8″ shroud only, equipped with Burris scope mounts and Burris scope in either $1\frac{1}{2}$x4X variable or fixed 2X.
3. Barrel changing tool and Wesson emblem packed in a custom-fitted carrying case. Available in either bright blue or stainless steel.

Prices: $691.00 (32 Mag. w/blue finish, mounts only) to **$1145.00** (445 Supermag, stainless steel w/$1\frac{1}{2}$X-4X scope)

HUNTER PAC

WICHITA ARMS PISTOLS

SILHOUETTE PISTOL
$1207.00

SPECIFICATIONS
Calibers: 308 Win. F.L., 7mm IHMSA and 7mm×308
Barrel length: 14^{15}/$_{16}$″
Weight: 4^{1}/$_{2}$ lbs.
Action: Single-shot bolt action
Sights: Wichita Multi-Range Sight System
Grips: Right-hand center walnut grip or right-hand rear walnut grip
Features: Glass bedded; bolt ground to precision fit; adjustable Wichita trigger

SILHOUETTE PISTOL
(Right Hand Rear Grip)

Also available:
WICHITA CLASSIC PISTOL $2950.00
Engraved Model 4850.00

INTERNATIONAL PISTOL
$595.00 (10″ Barrel)
$645.00 (14″ Barrel)

SPECIFICATIONS
Calibers: 7-30 Waters, 7mm Super Mag., 7R (30-30 Win. necked to 7mm), 30-30 Win., 357 Mag., 357 Super Mag., 32 H&H Mag., 22 RFM, 22 LR
Barrel lengths: 10″ and 14″ (10^{1}/$_{2}$″ for centerfire calibers)
Weight: 3 lbs. 2 oz. (10″ barrel); 4 lbs. 7 oz. (14″ barrel)
Action: Top-break, single-shot, single action only
Sights: Patridge front sight; rear sight adjustable for windage and elevation
Grips and Forend: Walnut
Safety: Cross bolt

INTERNATIONAL PISTOL

WILDEY PISTOLS

These gas-operated pistols are designed to meet the needs of hunters who want to use handguns for big game. The Wildey pistol includes such features as: • Ventilated rib • Reduced recoil • Double-action trigger mechanism • Patented hammer and trigger blocks and rebounding fire pin • Sights adjustable for windage and elevation • Stainless construction • Fixed barred for increased accuracy • Increased action strength (with 3-lug and exposed face rotary bolt) • Selective single or autoloading capability • Ability to handle high-pressure loads

SPECIFICATIONS
Calibers: 45 Win. Mag., 475 Wildey Mag.
Capacity: 7 shots
Barrel lengths: 5″, 6″, 7″, 8″, 10″, 12″
Overall length: 11″ with 7″ barrel
Weight: 64 oz. with 5″ barrel
Height: 6″

SURVIVOR MODEL in 45 Win. Mag.	Prices
5″, 6″ or 7″ models	$1295.00
Same model w/8″ or 10″ barrels	1295.00
With square trigger guard, **add**	35.00
With new vent rib, **add**	30.00

SURVIVOR MODEL in 475 Wildey Mag.	
8″ or 10″ barrels	1316.00
With square trigger guard, **add**	35.00
With new vent rib, **add**	30.00

HUNTER MODEL in 45 Win. Mag.	
8″, 10″ or 12″ barrels	$1400.00
With square trigger guard, **add**	35.00

HUNTER MODEL in 475 Wildey Mag.	
8″ or 10″ barrels	1400.00
With 12″ barrel	1449.00
W/square trigger guard (8″, 10″, 12″ barrels)	
add	35.00

Also available:
Interchangeable barrel extension assemblies **$523.00** (5″ barrel) to **$648.95** (12″ barrel).

For addresses and phone numbers of manufacturers and distributors included in this section, turn to *DIRECTORY OF MANUFACTURERS AND SUPPLIERS* at the back of the book.

ACTION ARMS

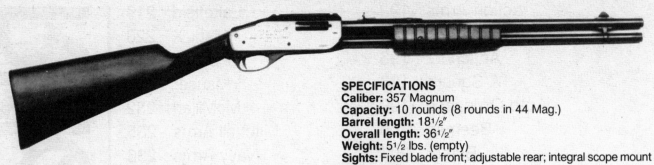

IMI TIMBER WOLF
$299.00 ($385.00 Chrome)

SPECIFICATIONS
Caliber: 357 Magnum
Capacity: 10 rounds (8 rounds in 44 Mag.)
Barrel length: 18½"
Overall length: 36½"
Weight: 5½ lbs. (empty)
Sights: Fixed blade front; adjustable rear; integral scope mount on receiver
Stock: Walnut
Operation: Locked breech
Safety system: Push button on trigger guard

AMT RIFLES

LIGHTNING (Stock Folded)
$295.99

This stainless steel rifle features a tapered or bull barrel, diamond finished and Pope crowned, grooved for scope mount. Fixed sights and recoil pad are standard.

SPECIFICATIONS:
Caliber: 22 LR Semiautomatic
Capacity: 30 rounds
Barrel length (stock folded): 17½"
Overall length: 26½" (37" w/stock extended)
Weight: 6¼ lbs. (tapered barrel); 6½ lbs. (bull barrel)
Features: Checkered handle and forearm are black matte fiberglass filled nylon

SPECIFICATIONS
Caliber: 22 LR Semiautomatic
Capacity: 10 rounds
Barrel length: 22"
Overall length: 40½"
Weight: 6 lbs.
Features: Uncle Mike's swivel studs for strap attachment; removable recoil pad provides storage for ammo, cleaning rod and survival knife; grooves for scope mount; synthetic stock is black matte fiberglass filled nylon, checkered at forearm and grip
Also available:
22 MAGNUM RIMFIRE (MATCH GRADE)
  w/free-floating barrel $449.99

SMALL GAME HUNTER II RIFLE
$299.99
(Scope not included)

ANSCHUTZ SPORTER RIFLES

SPORTER MODELS

MODEL 1700D CUSTOM
$1258.00 (22 LR)
$1416.00 (22 Hornet & 222 Rem.)
$1118.00 (22 LR Featherweight)
$1327.00 (22 LR Featherweight Deluxe)

BAVARIAN 1700
$1258.00 (22 LR)
$1416.00 (22 Hornet & 222 Rem.)

MODEL 1700D CLASSIC
$1228.00 (22 LR)
$1387.00 (22 Hornet & 222 Rem.)

MODEL 1700 GRAPHITE CUSTOM
$1183.00 (22 LR)

SPECIFICATIONS

	Custom	Bavarian	Classic	Mannlicher 1773D	Graphite Custom
	22 Long Rifle, 22 Hornet, 222 Remington, 22 Hornet				22 LR
Length—Overall	43″	43″	43″	39″	41″
Barrel	24″	24″	24″	19³/₄″	22″
Pull	14″	14″	14″	14″	14″
Drop at—Comb	1¹/₄″	1¹/₄″	1¹/₄″	1¹/₄″	1¹/₄″
Monte Carlo	1″	—	—	1³/₄″	1″
Heel	1¹/₂″	1¹/₂″	1¹/₂″	2³/₈″	1¹/₂″
Average Weight	7¹/₂ lbs.	7¹/₂ lbs.	6³/₄ lbs.	6¹/₄ lbs.	7¹/₄ lbs.
Trigger—Single Stage 5096 (.222 Rem., 5095)	•	•	•		•
Rate of Twist	Right Hand—one turn in 16.5″ for .22 LR; 1-16″ for .22 Hornet; 1-14″ for .222 Rem.				

ANSCHUTZ SPORTER RIFLES

MATCH 64 SPORTER MODELS

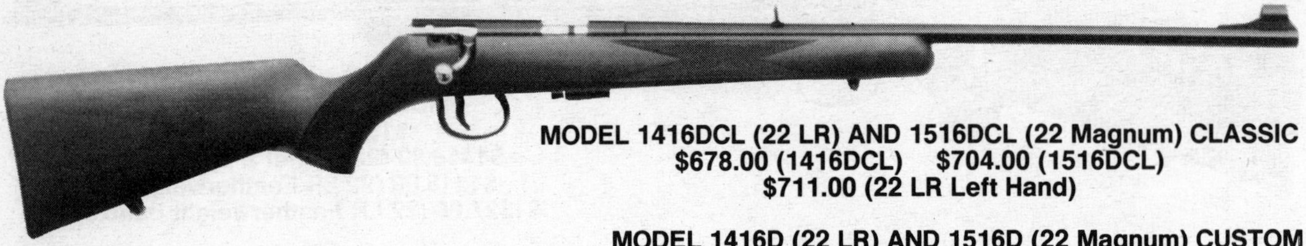

MODEL 1416DCL (22 LR) AND 1516DCL (22 Magnum) CLASSIC
$678.00 (1416DCL) $704.00 (1516DCL)
$711.00 (22 LR Left Hand)

MODEL 1416D (22 LR) AND 1516D (22 Magnum) CUSTOM
$690.00 (22 LR) $716.00 (22 Magnum)
(not shown)

1418D (22 LR) AND 1518D (22 Magnum) MANNLICHER
$1053.00 (22 LR) $1073.00 (22 Magnum)
$1537.00 (22 Hornet)

MODEL 525 SPORTER
$528.00

MANNLICHER 1733D
$1537.00

SPECIFICATIONS

	Classic 1416D** 1516D	Custom 1416D 1516D	Mannlicher* 1418D 1518D	Model 525 Sporter
Length—Overall	41″	41″	38″	43″
Barrel	22½″	22½″	19¾″	24″
Pull	14″	14″	14″	14″
Drop at—Comb	1¼″	1¼″	1¼″	1⅛″
Monte Carlo	1½″	1½″	1½″	1¾″
Heel	1½″	2½″	2½″	2⅝″
Average Weight	5½ lbs.	6 lbs.*	5½ lbs.	6½ lbs.
Rate of Twist Right Hand—one turn in 16.5″ for .22 LR; 1–16″ for .22 Mag				
Take Down Bolt Action With Removable Firing Pin	•	•	•	
¾″ Swivel			•	
Swivel Studs	•	•		•

** 5¼ lbs. in 1416D Fiberglass. * Specifications for **Mannlicher 1733D** on previous page.

ANSCHUTZ MATCH RIFLES

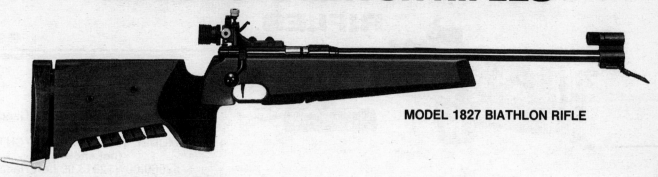

MODEL 1827 BIATHLON RIFLE

BIATHLON RIFLES SPECIFICATIONS

Model	1827B	1827BT	1450B
Barrel	21½" (³/₄" dia.)	21½" (³/₄" dia.)	19½" (¹¹/₁₆" dia.)
Action	Super Match 54	T. Bolt	Mark 2000
Trigger	1 lb. 3.5 oz. 2 stage #5020 adjustable* from 3½ oz. to 2 lbs.	1 lb. 3.5 oz., 2 stage #5020 adjustable* from 3½ oz. to 2 lbs.	2 lbs. 9 oz. 2 stage #5066
Safety	Slide safety	Slide safety	Slide safety
Stock	European Walnut, cheek piece, stippled pistol grip and front stock.	European Walnut, cheek piece, stippled pistol grip and front stock.	Blond finished European hardwood, stippled pistol grip.
Sights	6827 Sight Set with snow caps furnished with rifle and 10 click adjustment.	6827 Sight Set with snow caps furnished with rifle and 10 click adjustment.	6529 front sight. 6805/10 rear sight is extra.
Overall length	42½"	42½"	36"
Weight	8½ lbs. with sights	8½ lbs. with sights	5 lbs. without sights
Price	$2233.00	$3449.00 ($3794.00 L.H.)	$765.00

MODEL 64MS

MODEL 54.18MS-REP DELUXE

METALLIC SILHOUETTE RIFLES

Prices:

64MS	$ 912.00
Left Hand	957.00
54.18MS	1488.00
Left Hand	1594.00
54.18MS-REP	1766.00
54.18MS-REP DELUXE	2055.00
1700 FWT	1118.00
1700 FWT DELUXE	1327.00

SPECIFICATIONS AND FEATURES (22 LR)

Model	64MS	54.18MS	54.18MS-REP DELUXE*	1700 FWT*
Grooved for scope	•	•	•	•
Tapped for scope mount	•	•	•	•
Overall length	39.5"	41"	41–49"	41"
Barrel length	21½"	22"	22–30"	22"
Length of pull	13½"	13¾"	13¾"	14"
High cheekpiece with Monte Carlo effect	•		•	
Drop at Comb	1½"	1½"	1½"	1¼"
Average weight	8 lbs.	8 lbs. 6 oz.	7 lbs. 12 oz.	6¼ lbs.
Trigger: Stage Factory adjusted weight Adjustable weight	#5091 Two 5.3 oz. 4.9–7 oz.	#5018 Two 3.9 oz. 2.1–8.6 oz.	#5018 Two 3.9 oz. 2.1–8.6 oz.	#5096 Single 2.6 lbs. 2.6–4.4 lbs.
Safety	Slide	Slide	Slide	Wing
True Left-hand Model	•	•	•	

ANSCHUTZ INTERNATIONAL TARGET RIFLES

**MODEL 1913
SUPER MATCH**
$2980.00 ($3148.00 Left Hand)

**MODEL 1910 SUPER MATCH II
(not shown)**
$2660.00 ($2813.00 Left Hand)

**MODEL 1911
PRONE MATCH**
$2086.00 ($2209.00 Left Hand)

MODEL 1803D (not shown)
$1012.00

**MODEL 1808DRT (not shown)
SUPER RUNNING $1759.00**

MODEL 1903D (not shown)
$1070.00   ($1143.00 Left Hand)

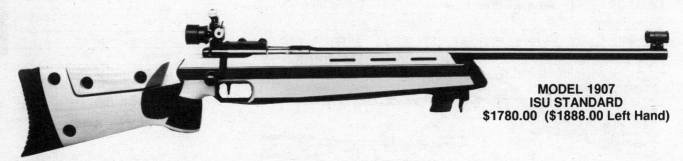

**MODEL 1907
ISU STANDARD**
$1780.00 ($1888.00 Left Hand)

INTERNATIONAL MATCH RIFLES: SPECIFICATIONS AND FEATURES

Model	1913	1911	1910	1907	DRT-Super
Barrel Length **O/D**	27 1/4" 7/8" (23.4 mm)	27 1/4" 7/8" (23.4 mm)	27 1/4" 7/8" (23.4 mm)	26" 7/8" (22 mm)	32 1/2" 7/8" (22 mm)
Stock	Int'l.- Thumb Hole Adj. Palm Rest Adj. Hand Rest	Prone	Int'l.- Thumb Hole	Standard	Thumb Hole
Cheek Piece **Butt Plate**	Adj. Adj. Hook 10 Way Hook	Adj. Adj. 4 Way	Adj. Adj. Hook 10 Way Hook	Removable Adj. 4 Way	Adj. Adj. 4 Way
Recommended **Sights**	6820, 6823 *6820 Left	6820, 6823 *6820 Left	6820, 6823 *6820 Left	6820, 6823 *6820 Left	Grooved for Scope Mounts
Overall Length	45"-46"	45"-46"	45"-46"	43 3/4"-44 1/2"	50 1/2"
Overall Length **to Hook**	49.6"-51.2"		49.6"-51.2"		
Weight (approx) **without sights**	15.2 lbs.	11.7 lbs.	13.7 lbs.	11.2 lbs.	9.4 lbs.
True Left- **Hand Version**	1913 Left	1911 Left	1910 Left	1907 Left	1808 Left

Trigger
   Stage
   Factory Set Wt.
   Adjust. Wt.
	#5018
	 Two
	 3.9 oz.
	 2.1-8.6 oz.
		#5018
		 Two
		 3.9 oz.
		 2.1-8.6 oz.
			#5018
			 Two
			 3.9 oz.
			 2.1-8.6 oz.
				#5018
				 Two
				 3.9 oz.
				 2.1-8.6 oz.
					5020D
					 Single
					 1.2 lbs.
					 14 oz.-2.4 lbs.

ANSCHUTZ TARGET RIFLES

THE ACHIEVER

THE ACHIEVER
$395.00

This rifle has been designed especially for young shooters and is equally at home on range or field. It meets all NRA recommendations as an ideal training rifle.

SPECIFICATIONS
Caliber: 22 LR
Capacity: 5- or 10-shot clips available

Action: Mark 2000-type repeating
Barrel length: 19$\frac{1}{2}$″
Overall length: 35$\frac{1}{2}$″–36$\frac{2}{3}$″
Weight: 5 lbs.
Trigger: #5066-two stage (2.6 lbs.)
Safety: Slide
Sights: Hooded ramp front; Lyman folding-leaf rear, adjustable for elevation
Stock pull: 12$\frac{1}{2}$″
Stock: European hardwood

MODEL 2013

MODEL 2013
$3700.00 ($3905.00 Left Hand)

SPECIFICATIONS
Caliber: 22 LR
Barrel length: 19$\frac{3}{4}$″
Overall length: 43″ to 45$\frac{1}{2}$″
Weight: 15.5 lbs. (without sights)
Trigger: #5018, two-stage, 3.9 oz. (factory set wt.)
Sights: #6820
Stock: International with adjustable palm rest and hand rest
Feature: Adjustable cheekpiece

MODEL 2007 ISU STANDARD
$2650.00 ($2736.00 Left Hand)
(not shown)

SPECIFICATIONS
Caliber: 22 LR
Barrel length: 19$\frac{3}{4}$″
Overall length: 43$\frac{1}{2}$″ to 44$\frac{1}{2}$″
Weight: 10.8 lbs. (without sights)
Trigger: #5018, two-stage, 3.9 oz. (factory set wt.)
Sights: #6820
Stock: Standard ISU
Feature: Adjustable cheekpiece

A-SQUARE RIFLES

CAESAR MODEL (Left Hand)
$2550.00

SPECIFICATIONS
Calibers: 7mm Rem. Mag., 7mm STW, 30-06, 300 H&H Mag., 300 Win. Mag., 300 Wby. Mag., 8mm Rem. Mag., 338 Win. Mag., 340 Wby. Mag., 338 A-Square Mag., 9.3×62mm, 9.3×64mm, 375 H&H, 375 Weatherby, 375 JRS, 375 A-Square Mag., 416 Taylor, 416 Hoffman, 416 Rem. Mag., 404 Jeffery, 425 Express, 458 Win. Mag., 458 Lott, 450 Ackley Mag., 460 Short A-Square, 470 Capstick and 495 A-Square Mag.

CAESAR MODEL (416 Hoffman)
w/2x7 Variable Scope and
3-Leaf Express Sights

Features: Selected Claro walnut stock with oil finish; three-position safety; three-way adjustable target trigger; flush detachable swivels; leather sling; dual recoil lugs; coil spring ejector; ventilated recoil pad; premium honed barrels; contoured ejection port

HANNIBAL MODEL (416 Rigby)
w/2xLER Scope and 3-Leaf
Express Sights

HANNIBAL MODEL
$2495.00

SPECIFICATIONS
Calibers: Same calibers as the Caesar Model (above), plus 378 Wby. Mag., 416 Rigby, 416 Wby. Mag., 460 Wby Mag. and 500 A-Square
Barrel lengths: 20″ to 26″
Length of pull: 12″ to 15¼″

Finish: Deluxe walnut stock; oil finish; matte blue
Features: Flush detachable swivels, leather sling, dual recoil lugs, coil spring ejector, ventilated recoil pad, premium honed barrels, contoured ejection port, three-way adjustable target-style trigger, Mauser-style claw extractor and controlled feed, positive safety

AUTO-ORDNANCE

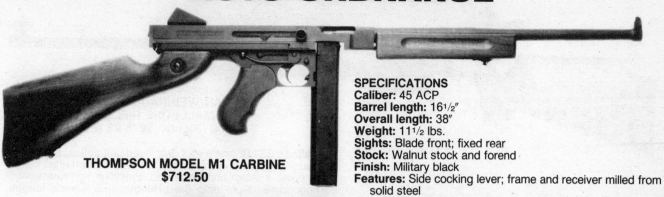

THOMPSON MODEL M1 CARBINE
$712.50

SPECIFICATIONS
Caliber: 45 ACP
Barrel length: 16½″
Overall length: 38″
Weight: 11½ lbs.
Sights: Blade front; fixed rear
Stock: Walnut stock and forend
Finish: Military black
Features: Side cocking lever; frame and receiver milled from solid steel

SPECIFICATIONS
Caliber: 45 ACP and 10mm
Barrel length: 16″
Overall length: 42″
Weight: 11½ lbs.
Sights: Blade front; open rear adjustable
Stock: Walnut stock; vertical forend

THOMPSON DELUXE MODEL 1927 A1
$735.00 (45 Cal.)
$745.00 (10mm)

Also available:
THOMPSON 1927A-1C LIGHTWEIGHT (45 cal.). Same as the 1927A1 model, but 20% lighter. **Price: $707.00**
THOMPSON MODEL 1927A3. Same as above, but in caliber 22 LR. **Weight:** 7 lbs. **Price: $487.50**

VIOLIN CARRYING CASE (for gun, drum & extra magazines) $105.00

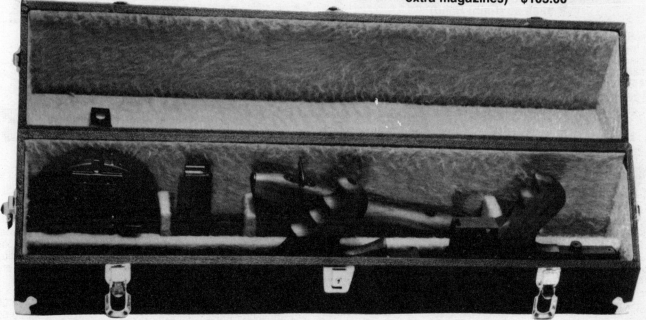

BEEMAN RIFLES

BEEMAN/WEIHRAUCH HW 60M
SMALLBORE RIFLE
$798.00 (Right) $878.95 (Left)

Caliber: 22 LR, single shot. Improved bolt action. Adjustable match trigger with push button safety. Precision rifled barrel. Stippled forearm and pistol grip. Precision aperture sights, hooded front sight ramp. **Barrel length:** 26.8". **Overall length:** 45.7". **Weight:** 10.8 lbs.

BEEMAN/WEIHRAUCH HW 60J-ST
BOLT-ACTION RIFLE
$889.50 (60J) $584.95 (60J-ST)

Calibers: 222 Rem. (60J); 22 LR (60J-ST). Features include: walnut stock with cheekpiece; cut-checkered pistol grip and forend; polished blue finish; oil-finished wood. **Sights:** Hooded blade on ramp front; open rear adjustable. **Barrel length:** 22.8". **Overall length:** 41.7". **Weight:** 6½ lbs. Imported from Germany.

BEEMAN/WEIHRAUCH HW 660 MATCH RIFLE
$889.50 (Right Hand)

Caliber: 22 LR. Match-type walnut stock with adjustable cheekpiece and buttplate. Adjustable match trigger; stippled pistol grip and forend; forend accessory rail. **Sights:** Globe front; match aperture rear. **Barrel length:** 26". **Overall length:** 45.3". **Weight:** 10.7 lbs. Imported from Germany.

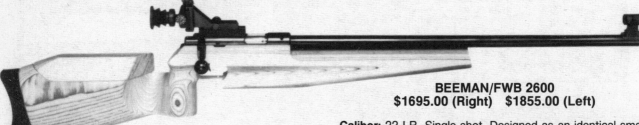

BEEMAN/FWB 2600
$1695.00 (Right) $1855.00 (Left)

Caliber: 22 LR. Single shot. Designed as an identical smallbore companion to the Beeman/FWB 600 Match air rifle. Free-floated 26.3" bull barrel. **Weight:** 10.8 lbs. Super rigid stock of laminated hardwood is cut low to permit complete ventilation around barrel. Match trigger has fingertip weight adjustment dial. With adjustable comb and match sights.
Also available:
FWB 2600 FREE RIFLE (26.1" barrel) **$2498.00**
Left Hand Model **2650.00**

BLASER RIFLES

MODEL R 84 BOLT ACTION

SPECIFICATIONS
Calibers: (interchangeable)
    Standard: 22-250, 243 Win., 6mm Rem., 25-06, 270 Win.,
        280 Rem., 30-06
    Magnum: 257 Weatherby Mag., 264 Win. Mag., 7mm Rem.
        Mag., 300 Win. Mag., 300 Weatherby Mag., 338
        Win. Mag., 375 H&H
Barrel lengths: 23″ (Standard) and 24″ (Magnum)

Overall length: 41″ (Standard) and 42″ (Magnum)
Weight: (w/scope mounts) 7 lbs. (Standard) and 7¼ lbs.
    (Magnum)
Safety: Locks firing pin and bolt handle
Stock: Two-piece Turkish walnut stock and forend; solid black
    recoil pad, handcut checkering (18 lines/inch, borderless)
Length of pull: 13¾″
Prices:
Std. & Mag. calibers w/scope mounts **$2300.00**
L.H. Std. and Mag. cal. w/scope mounts **2350.00**
Interchangeable barrels **600.00**
Deluxe Model Right Hand **2600.00**
    Left Hand **2650.00**
Super Deluxe Model Right Hand **2950.00**
    Left Hand **3000.00**

BRNO RIFLES

MODEL ZKK 600

MODEL ZKK 602

MODEL ZKK SPECIFICATIONS

| Model | Action Type | Caliber | Barrel Specifications | | | Overall Length | Weight | Magazine Capacity | Sighted In |
			Length	Rifling Twist	#Lands				
ZKK 600	bolt	7mm Mauser 270 Win. 30-06 Spring.	23.6 in	1 in 10″ 1 in 10″ 1 in 9″	4 4 4	43.7 in.	7.2 lbs.	5	110 yd.
ZKK 601	bolt	243 Win. 308 Win.	23.6 in.	1 in 12″ 1 in 10″	4 4	43.1 in.	8.2 lbs.	5	110 yd.
ZKK 602	bolt	300 Win. Mag. 375 H&H 458 Win. Mag.	25.2 in.	1 in 10″ 1 in 12″ 1 in 12″	4 4 4	45.3 in.	9.4 lbs.	5 4 4	110 yd.

Prices:
Model ZKK 600 Standard Walnut stock $609.00
Model ZKK 601 Monte Carlo Stock Walnut 609.00

Model ZKK 600 or 601 Synthetic stock $559.00
Model ZKK 602 Standard Walnut stock 835.00
                 Synthetic stock 745.00

BRNO RIFLES

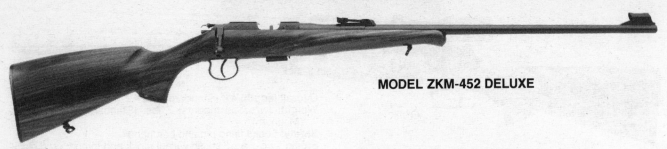

MODEL ZKM-452 DELUXE

MODEL ZKM-452

SPECIFICATIONS
Caliber: 22 LR
Capacity: 5 rounds
Barrel length: 23.6″
Overall length: 42.6″
Weight: 6.1 lbs. (unloaded)
Safety: Thumb safety

Sights: Hooded front; tangent adjustable rear
Stock: European hardwood or checkered walnut
Finish: Lacquer
Features: Firing-pin blocking safety; 5- and 10-round detachable magazines; receiver grooved for .22 scope mounts; hammer-forged barrel threaded to receiver
Prices:
w/Hardwood stock $305.00
w/Deluxe walnut stock 349.00

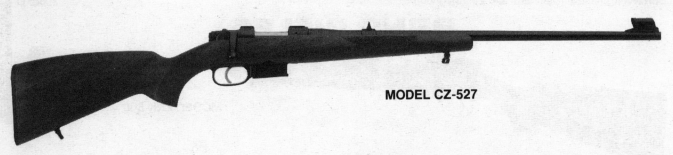

MODEL CZ-527

MODEL CZ-527

SPECIFICATIONS
Calibers: 22 Hornet, 222 Rem., 223 Rem.
Capacity: 5 rounds
Barrel length: 23.6″
Overall length: 42.4″
Weight: 6.2 lbs. (unloaded)
Safety: Thumb safety
Sights: Hooded front; drift adjustable rear

Stock: Checkered walnut or synthetic
Finish: Lacquer
Features: Mauser-type bolt and non-rotating claw extractor; hammer-forged barrel; integral dovetail scope bases w/recoil stop; detachable 5-round magazine
Prices:
w/Walnut stock $665.00
w/Synthetic stock 599.00

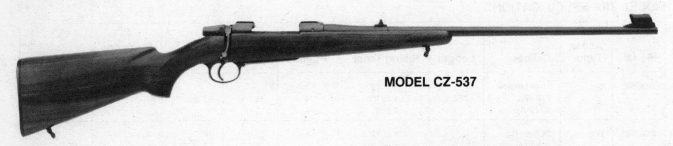

MODEL CZ-537

MODEL CZ-537

SPECIFICATIONS
Calibers: 270 Win., 308 Win., 30-06
Capacity: 5 rounds
Barrel length: 23.6″
Overall length: 44.7″
Weight: 7.9 lbs. (unloaded)
Safety: Thumb safety (locks trigger and bolt)

Sights: Hooded front; adjustable rear
Stock: Checkered walnut or synthetic
Finish: Lacquer
Features: Streamlined bolt shroud w/cocking indicator; integral dovetail scope bases w/recoil stop; controlled-feed claw extractor; forged, one-piece bolt
Prices:
w/Walnut stock $669.00
w/Synthetic stock 599.00

BROWNING LEVER ACTION RIFLES

MODEL 1886 LEVER ACTION CARBINE
$749.95

The Model 1886 rifle was John Browning's first lever-action repeater design to be manufactured. Winchester realized the opportunity to carry this unique, stronger action design and paid Browning ''more money than there is in Ogden'' (Utah, where Browning lived and worked) for the rights to produce the 1886 rifle. Virtually identical to the original, the new Model 1886 has the following specifications.

Caliber: 45-70 Government. **Capacity:** 8 rounds. **Action:** Lever action. **Barrel length:** 22″, round. **Overall length:** 40³/₄″. **Weight:** 8 lbs. 3 oz. **Sights:** Adjustable folding-leaf rear. Fea-

tures: Full-length magazine, classic-style forearm with barrel bands; saddle ring; metal crescent buttplate; select walnut with satin finish (all metal surfaces deeply blued).

Also available:
LIMITED EDITION HIGH GRADE. Features high-grade select walnut stock and forearm with finely cut checkering in a gloss finish. Receiver and lever are grayed steel embellished with scroll engraving depicting scenes of mule deer and grizzly bear. **Price: $1175.00**

MODEL 1885 SINGLE SHOT
$809.95

Calibers: 22-250; 223, 30-06, 270, 7mm Rem. Mag., 45-70 Govt. **Bolt system:** Falling block. **Barrel length:** 28″ (recessed muzzle). **Overall length:** 43¹/₂″. **Weight:** 8 lbs. 12 oz. **Action:** High wall type, single shot, lever action. **Sights:** Drilled and tapped for scope mounts; two-piece scope base available.

Open sights on 45-70 Govt. only. **Hammer:** Exposed, serrated, three-position with inertia sear. **Stock and Forearm:** Select Walnut, straight grip stock and Schnabel forearm with cut checkering. Recoil pad standard.

MODEL 81 BLR HIGH POWER
$509.95 (Short Action with Sights)
$539.95 (Long Action with Sights)

Short Action Calibers: 223 Rem., 22-250 Rem., 243 Win., 7mm-08 Rem., 284 Win. and 308 Win. **Action:** Lever action with rotating head, multiple lug breech bolt with recessed bolt face. Side ejection. **Barrel length:** 20″. Individually machined from forged, heat treated chrome-moly steel; crowned muzzle. **Rifling:** 243 Win., one turn in 10″; 308 and 358 Win., one turn in 12″. **Magazine:** Detachable, 4-round capacity. **Overall length:** 39³/₄″. **Approximate Weight:** 6 lbs. 15 oz. **Trigger:** Wide, grooved finger piece. Short crisp pull of 4¹/₂ pounds. Travels with lever. **Receiver:** Non-glare top. Drilled and tapped to accept most top scope mounts. Forged and milled steel. All parts are machine-finished and hand-fitted. Surface deeply polished. **Sights:** Low profile, square notch, screw adjustable

rear sight. Gold bead on a hooded raised ramp front sight. Sight radius: 17³/₄″. **Safety:** Exposed, 3-position hammer. Trigger disconnect system. Inertia firing pin. **Stock and forearm:** Select walnut with tough oil finish and sure-grip checkering, contoured for use with either open sights or scope. Straight grip stock. Deluxe recoil pad installed.

Also available:
MODEL 81 BLR LONG ACTION. Calibers: 30-06, 270, 7mm Magnum. **Barrel length:** 22″ (30-06, 270) and 24″ (7mm Mag.). **Overall length:** 42¹/₂″ (30-06, 270) and 44¹/₂″ (7mm Mag.). **Weight:** 8 lbs. 8 oz. (30-06, 270) and 8 lbs. 13 oz. (7mm Mag.).

BROWNING RIFLES

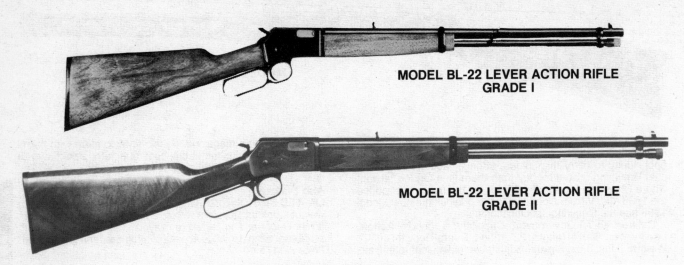

MODEL BL-22 LEVER ACTION RIFLE GRADE I

MODEL BL-22 LEVER ACTION RIFLE GRADE II

MODEL BL-22 SPECIFICATIONS

Action: Short throw lever action. Lever travels through an arc of only 33 degrees and carries the trigger with it, preventing finger pinch between lever and trigger on the upward swing. The lever cycle ejects the fired shell, cocks the hammer and feeds a fresh round into the chamber. **Magazine:** Rifle is designed to handle 22 caliber ammunition *in any combination* from tubular magazine. Magazine capacity is 15 Long Rifles, 17 Longs and 22 Shorts. The positive magazine latch opens and closes easily from any position. **Safety:** A unique disconnect system prevents firing until the lever and breech are fully closed and pressure is released from and reapplied to the trigger. An inertia firing pin and an exposed hammer with a half-cock position are other safety features. **Receiver:** Forged and milled steel. Grooved. All parts are machine-finished and hand-fitted. **Trigger:** Clean and crisp without creep. Average pull 5 pounds. Trigger gold-plated on Grade II model. **Stock and forearm:** Forearm and straight grip butt stock are shaped from select, polished walnut. Hand checkered on Grade II model. Stock dimensions:

Length of Pull	13 1/2″
Drop at Comb	1 5/8″
Drop at Heel	2 1/4″

Sights: Precision, adjustable folding leaf rear sight. Raised bead front sight. **Scopes:** Grooved receiver will accept the Browning 22 riflescope (Model 1217) and two-piece ring mount (Model 9417) as well as most other groove or tip-off type mounts or receiver sights. **Engraving:** Grade II receiver and trigger guard are engraved with tasteful scroll designs. **Barrel length:** 20″; recessed muzzle. **Overall length:** 36 3/4″. **Weight:** 5 pounds.

Price: Grade I	$301.50
Grade II	343.50

MODEL A-BOLT 22 BOLT ACTION
$374.95
$384.95 with Sights

Caliber: 22 LR. **Barrel length:** 22″. **Overall length:** 40 1/4″. **Average weight:** 5 lbs. 9 oz. **Action:** Short throw bolt. Bolt cycles a round with 60° of bolt rotation. Firing pin acts as secondary extractor and ejector, snapping out fired rounds at prescribed speed. **Magazine:** Five and 15-shot magazine standard. Magazine/clip ejects with a push on magazine latch button. **Trigger:** Gold colored, screw adjustable. Pre-set at approx. 4 lbs. **Stock:** Laminated walnut, classic style with pistol grip. **Length of pull:** 13 3/4″. **Drop at comb:** 3/4″. **Drop at heel:** 1 1/2″. **Sights:** Available with or without sights (add $10 for sights). Ramp front and adjustable folding leaf rear on open sight model. **Scopes:** Grooved receiver for 22 mount. Drilled and tapped for full-size scope mounts.

Also available:

In 22 Magnum with open sights	$439.95
In 22 Magnum without sights	429.95
Gold Medallion Model (no sights)	496.95

BROWNING RIFLES

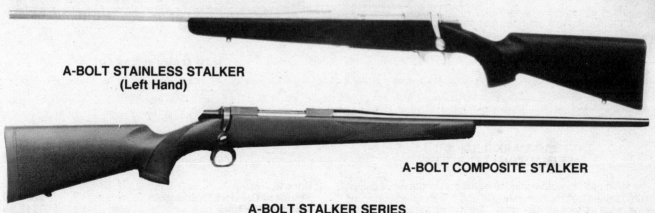

A-BOLT BOLT-ACTION RIFLE

A-BOLT BOLT-ACTION CENTERFIRE RIFLES

Calibers: Long Action 25-06 Rem., 270 Win., 280 Rem., 30-06 Sprg.; **Long Action Magnum** 375 H&H, 7mm Rem. Mag., 300 Win. Mag., 338 Win. Mag. **Action:** Short throw bolt of 60 degrees. Plunger-type ejector. **Magazine:** Detachable. Depress the magazine latch and the hinged floorplate swings down. The magazine can be removed from the floorplate for reloading or safety reasons. **Trigger:** Adjustable within the average range of 3 to 6 pounds. Also grooved to provide sure finger control. **Stock and forearm:** Stock is select grade American walnut cut to the lines of a classic sporter with a full pistol grip.

Scopes: Closed. Clean tapered barrel. Receiver is drilled and tapped for a scope mount; or select **Hunter** model has open sights. **Barrel lengths:** 20″ (Micro Medallion); 22″ (Short

and Long Action); 26″ (Long Action Magnum). Hammer-forged rifling where a precision machined mandrel is inserted into the bore. The mandrel is a reproduction of the rifling in reverse. As hammer forces are applied to the exterior of the barrel, the barrel is actually molded around the mandrel to produce flawless rifling and to guarantee a straight bore. Free-floated. **Overall length:** 44$\frac{1}{4}$″. **Weight:** 7 lbs. 8 oz. in Magnum; 6 lbs. 8 oz. in Short Action; 7 lbs. in Standard (Long Action).

Short Action A-Bolt available in 22-250 Rem., 223 Rem., 243 Win., 257 Roberts, 284 Win., 7mm-08 Rem. and 308 Win.

Prices:

Hunter	$509.95
Hunter w/Open sights	574.95
Medallion No sights	596.95
Medallion Left-Hand	621.95
Medallion 375 H&H w/Open sights	696.95
Medallion 375 H&H L.H., open sights	721.95
Micro Medallion No sights	596.95
Gold Medallion	809.95

A-BOLT STAINLESS STALKER
(Left Hand)

A-BOLT COMPOSITE STALKER

A-BOLT STALKER SERIES

Browning's A-Bolt Stalker series is available in a Stainless version or Composite stock version. The graphite-fiberglass composite stock resists the nicks and scrapes of hard hunting and is resistant to weather and humidity. Its recoil-absorbing properties also make shooting a more pleasant experience. The stock is checkered for a good grip and has a non-glare textured finish. The A-Bolt Composite or Stainless Stalker share the same features of Browning's A-Bolt Hunter rifle (above). All exposed metal surfaces of the Composite Stalker have a non-glare matte blued finish.

Prices:

Composite Stalker	$524.95
Stainless Stalker No sights	664.95
Stainless Stalker Left Hand	684.95
Stainless Stalker 375 H&H w/Open sights	764.95
Same as above in Left Hand	786.95

A-BOLT EURO-BOLT
$699.95 (No Sights)

This new A-Bolt rifle features a schnabel-style forearm and a rounded bolt shroud plus a continental-style cheekpiece that provides improved handling and shooting comfort. The finish is low-luster blueing and satin-finished walnut. See specifications above for A-Bolt models.

BROWNING RIFLES

22 SEMIAUTOMATIC RIMFIRE RIFLES
GRADES I AND VI

SPECIFICATIONS
Caliber: 22 LR. **Overall length:** 37″. **Barrel length:** 19¼″.
Weight: 4 lbs. 4 oz. **Safety:** Cross-bolt type. **Capacity:** 11
cartridges in magazine, 1 in chamber. **Trigger:** Grade I is blued;
Grade VI is gold colored. **Sights:** Gold bead front, adjustable
folding leaf rear; drilled and tapped for Browning scope mounts.
Length of pull: 13¾″. **Drop at comb:** 1³⁄₁₆″. **Drop at heel:**
2⁵⁄₈″. **Stock & Forearm:** Grade I, select walnut with checkering
(18 lines/inch); Grade VI, high-grade walnut with checkering
(22 lines/inch).
Grade I $344.95
Grade VI 708.95

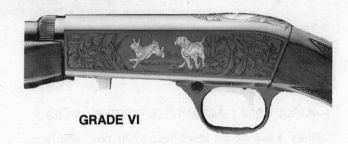

GRADE VI

BAR MARK II SAFARI

BAR MARK II SAFARI
SEMIAUTOMATIC RIFLES

The BAR has been upgraded to include an engraved receiver,
a redesigned bolt release, new gas and buffeting systems, and
a removable trigger assembly. Additional features include:
cross-bolt safety with enlarged head; hinged floorplate, 4-shot
capacity (1 in chamber); gold trigger; select walnut stock and
forearm with cut-checkering and swivel studs; 13¾″ length of
pull; 2″ drop at heel; 1⁵⁄₈″ drop at comb; and a recoil pad (magnum calibers only).

Prices:
Standard Calibers Open sights $664.95
Magnum Calibers 713.95
(Deduct **$17** without sights)

Model	Calibers	Barrel Length	Sight Radius*	Overall Length	Average Weight	Rate of Twist (Right Hand)
Magnum	270 Weatherby	24″	19½″	45″	8 lbs. 6 oz.	1 in 10″
Magnum	338 Win. Mag.	24″	19½″	45″	8 lbs. 6 oz.	1 in 12″
Magnum	300 Win. Mag.	24″	19½″	45″	8 lbs. oz.	1 in 10″
Magnum	7mm Rem. Mag.	24″	19½″	45″	8 lbs. 6 oz.	1 in 9½″
Standard	30-06 Sprg.	22″	17½″	43″	7 lbs. 6 oz.	1 in 10″
Standard	270 Win.	22″	17½″	43″	7 lbs. 9 oz.	1 in 10″
Standard	243 Win.	22″	17½″	43″	7 lbs. 10 oz.	1 in 10″

* All models are available with or without open sights. All models drilled and tapped for scope mounts.

CLIFTON ARMS

SCOUT RIFLE
$2600.00

Several years ago, in response to Colonel Jeff Cooper's concept of an all-purpose rifle, which he calls the "Scout Rifle," Clifton Arms developed the integral, retractable bipod and its accompanying state-of-the-art composite stock. Further development resulted in an integral butt magazine well for storage of cartridges inside the buttstock. These and other components make up the Clifton Scout Rifle. Built to the customer's choice of action, the rifle incorporates all the features specified by Col. Cooper.

SPECIFICATIONS
Calibers: 243, 7mm-08, 30-06, 308, 350 Rem. Mag.
Barrel length: 19″ to 19½″ (longer or shorter lengths available; made with Shilen stainless premium match-grade steel)
Weight: 7 to 8 lbs.
Sights: Forward-mounted Burris 2¾X Scout Scope attached to integral scope base pedestals machined in the barrel; Warner rings; reserve iron sight is square post dovetailed into a ramp integral to the barrel, plus a large aperture "ghost ring" mounted on the receiver bridge.
Features: Standard action is Ruger 77 MKII stainless; metal finish options include Polymax, NP3 and chrome sulphide; left-hand rifles available.

COLT RIFLES

COLT SPORTER LIGHTWEIGHTS

The Colt Sporter semiautomatic rifle fires from a closed bolt, is easy to load and unload, and has a buttstock and pistol grip made of tough nylon. A round, ribbed handguard is fiberglass-reinforced to ensure better grip control. **Calibers:** 223 Rem., 7.62×39mm and 9mm. **Barrel length:** 16″. **Weight:** 7 lbs. 2 oz. (7 lbs. 5 oz. in 7.62×39mm) **Capacity:** 5 rounds. **Price:** **$877.95 ($859.95 in 7.62×39mm)**

SPORTER RIFLES

The Colt sporter is range-selected for top accuracy. It has a 3-9X rubber armored variable power scope mount, carry handle with iron sight, Cordura nylon case and other accessories. **Caliber:** 223 Rem. **Barrel length:** 20″. **Weight:** 8 lbs. (8½ lbs. in Competition H-Bar). **Capacity:** 5 rounds.

Prices:

SPORTER	**$ 969.95**
MATCH H-BAR	938.95
TARGET GOV'T MODEL	897.95
COMPETITION H-BAR	989.95
W/Scope, accessories, range-selected	1489.95

DAKOTA ARMS

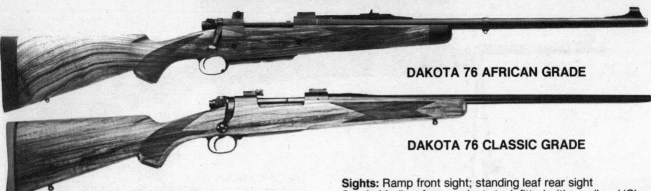

DAKOTA 76 AFRICAN GRADE

DAKOTA 76 CLASSIC GRADE

DAKOTA 76 RIFLES

SPECIFICATIONS
Calibers:
 Safari Grade: 338 Win. Mag., 300 Win. Mag., 375 H&H
 Mag., 458 Win. Mag.
 Classic Grade: 257 Roberts, 270 Win., 280 Rem., 30-06,
 7mm Rem. Mag., 338 Win. Mag., 300 Win.
 Mag., 375 H&H Mag., 458 Win. Mag.
Barrel lengths: 21″ or 23″ (Classic); 23″ only (Safari); 24″
(African)
Weight: 7½ lbs. (Classic); 8 lbs. (African); 8½ lbs. (Safari)
Safety: Three-position striker-blocking safety allows bolt op-
eration with safety on

Sights: Ramp front sight; standing leaf rear sight
Stock: Medium fancy walnut stock fitted with recoil pad (Classic); fancy walnut stock with ebony forend tip and recoil
pad (Safari)

Prices:
Safari Grade	**$3000.00**
Classic Grade	2300.00
African Grade	3500.00
Barreled actions:	
Safari Grade	1850.00
Classic Grade	1650.00
African Grade	2500.00
Actions:	
Safari Grade	1500.00
Classic Grade	1400.00

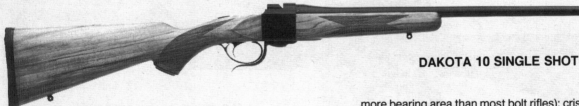

DAKOTA 10 SINGLE SHOT

DAKOTA 10 SINGLE SHOT

SPECIFICATIONS
Calibers: Most rimmed and rimless commercially loaded cal-
ibers
Barrel length: 23″
Overall length: 39½″
Weight: 5½ lbs.
Features: Receiver and rear of breech block are solid steel
without cuts or holes for maximum lug area (approx. 8 times

more bearing area than most bolt rifles); crisp, clean trigger
pull (trigger plate is removable, allowing action to adapt to
single set triggers); straight-line coil spring action and short
hammer fall combine for extremely fast lock time; unique
top tang safety is smooth and quiet (it blocks the striker
forward of the main spring); strong and positive extractor
and manual ejector equally adapted to rimmed or rimless
cases.

Price:	**$2300.00**
Barreled actions	1650.00
Action	1400.00

DAKOTA 22 LR SPORTER

DAKOTA 22 LR SPORTER

SPECIFICATIONS
Calibers: 22 LR
Capacity: 5-round clip

Barrel length: 22″ (chrome-moly, 1 turn in 16″)
Weight: 6½ lbs.
Stock: X Claro or English walnut with hand-cut checkering
Features: Plain bolt handle; swivels and single screw studs;
 ½-inch black pad; 13⅝″ length of pull

Price:	**$1500.00**
Barreled actions	1200.00

EAGLE ARMS RIFLES

MODEL EA-15 RIFLES

All EA-15 rifles include these standard features: upper and lower receivers precision machined from 7075 T6 aluminum forgings • receivers equipped with push-type pivot pin for easy disassembly • EZ-style forward assist mechanism that clears jammed shells from the chamber • trapdoor-style buttstock • full-size 30-round magazine

MODEL EA-15 MATCH RIFLE
(With Action Master or Match Grade Accessories)
$1075.00

SPECIFICATIONS
Caliber: 223
Barrel length: 20″ Douglas Premium fluted barrel
Weight: 8 lbs. 5 oz.; 8 lbs. 6 oz. w/Match Grade accessories
Stock: Fixed

Features: One-piece international-style upper receiver; solid aluminum handguard tube (allows for a free-floating barrel); compensator for reducing muzzle climb; NM Match Trigger Group & Bolt Carrier Group

MODEL EA-15 GOLDEN EAGLE MATCH RIFLE
$1075.00

SPECIFICATIONS
Caliber: 223
Barrel length: 20″ Douglas Premium extra heavy w/1:9″ twist
Weight: 12 lbs. 12 oz.
Sights: Elevation adjustable NM front sight w/set screw; E-2 style NM rear sight assembly with 1/2MOA adjustments for windage and elevation
Stock: Fixed

Also available:
EA-15 STANDARD (Wt. 7 lbs.)	$ 800.00
EA-15 w/E-2 Accessories (Wt. 8 lbs. 14 oz.)	895.00
Same as above with NM sights	890.00
EA-15 CARBINE w/E-2 Accessories 16″ barrel, Sliding buttstock (Wt. 6 lbs. 12 oz.)	895.00
EA-15 EAGLE EYE with National Match High Power accessories (Wt. 14 lbs.)	1495.00

EMF RIFLES

1875 "OUTLAW" REMINGTON-STYLE REVOLVING CARBINE
$880.00

Includes walnut stock, brass trim, blued finish and casehardened frame.
Calibers: 357, 44-40, 45 Colt
Barrel length: 20″
Overall length: 38″
Weight: 5 lbs.

EMF REPLICA RIFLES

1860 HENRY RIFLE
$1100.00

This lever-action rifle was patented by B. Tyler Henry and produced by the New Haven Arms Company, where Oliver Winchester was then president (he later gave his name to future models and the company itself). Production was developed between 1860 and 1865, with serial numbers 1 to 12000 (plus 2000 additional units in 1866, when the Winchester gun first appeared).

SPECIFICATIONS
Caliber: 44-40
Barrel length: 24¼″; upper half-octagonal w/magazine tube in one-piece steel
Overall length: 43¾″
Weight: 9¼ lbs.
Stock: Varnished American walnut wood
Features: Polished brass frame; brass buttplate

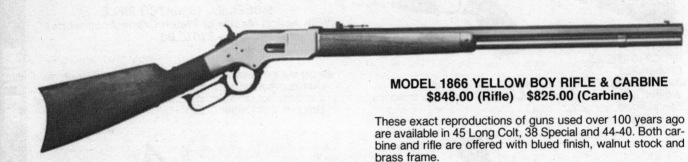

MODEL 1866 YELLOW BOY RIFLE & CARBINE
$848.00 (Rifle) $825.00 (Carbine)

These exact reproductions of guns used over 100 years ago are available in 45 Long Colt, 38 Special and 44-40. Both carbine and rifle are offered with blued finish, walnut stock and brass frame.

MODEL 1873 SPORTING RIFLE
$1050.00

SPECIFICATIONS
Caliber: 45 Long Colt
Barrel length: 24¼″ octagonal
Overall length: 43¼″
Weight: 8.16 lbs.
Features: Magazine tube in blued steel; frame is casehardened steel; stock and forend are walnut wood

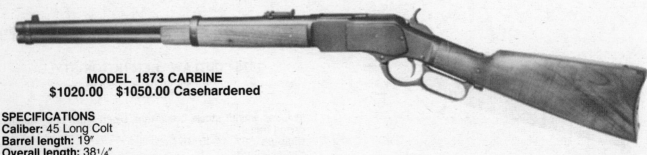

MODEL 1873 CARBINE
$1020.00 $1050.00 Casehardened

SPECIFICATIONS
Caliber: 45 Long Colt
Barrel length: 19″
Overall length: 38¼″
Weight: 7.38 lbs.
Features: Same as Sporting Rifle

EUROPEAN AMERICAN ARMORY

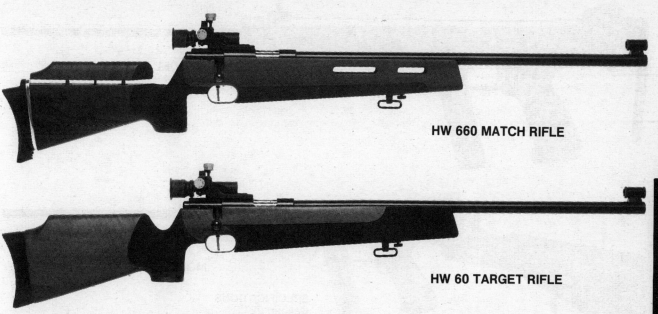

HW 660 MATCH RIFLE

HW 60 TARGET RIFLE

HW 660 MATCH RIFLE (SINGLE SHOT)
$757.50

SPECIFICATIONS
Caliber: 22 LR
Barrel length: 26.8"
Overall length: 45.7"
Weight: 10.8 lbs.
Sights: Match-type aperture rear; hooded ramp front
Finish: Blue

Stock: Stippled walnut
Features: Adjustable match trigger; push-button safety; walnut adjustable buttplate; left-hand model available
Also available:
HW 60 TARGET RIFLE. Same specifications as HW 660.
  $670.80

SABATTI ROVER 870 RIFLE

SABATTI ROVER 870 BOLT-ACTION RIFLE
$550.00

SPECIFICATIONS
Calibers: 22-250, 243 Win., 25-06 Rem., 270 Rem., 308 Win., 30-06, 7mm Rem. Mag., 300 Win. Mag., 338 Win. Mag.
Capacity: 5 rounds
Barrel length: 22"
Sights: Fully adjustable rear; drilled and tapped for scopes

Stock: One-piece European walnut, checkered and satin-finished, with rubber recoil pad
Features: Hammer-forged barrel with precision rifling; bolt has two locking lugs for precision lockup and strength; one-piece drop magazine and action housing w/hinged floorplate; safety system locks sear and trigger when engaged

FEATHER RIFLES

MODEL AT-22

MODEL F2 AT-22

MODEL AT-22

This 22 LR rifle breaks down to a compact, easy-to-stow and transportable 17″ package. It will accommodate any kind of 22 LR ammo and has set a new standard for autoloading rimfire rifles.

SPECIFICATIONS
Caliber: 22 LR
Capacity: 20 rounds
Type: Autoloader
Operation: Blowback
Barrel length: 17″
Overall length: 35″ (26″ w/stock folded)
Weight: 3.25 lbs.
Price: $249.95

Also available:
MODEL F2 AT-22. Same as Model AT-22, but with fixed buttstock made of high-impact polymer for a more traditional look. **Price:** $279.95

MODEL F9 AT-9

MODEL AT-9 (not shown)

Feather's AT-9 offers 3″ groups or less at 50 yards using standard, fully adjustable sights. Ideal for competitive use in rapid-fire events like pin-shooting, weekend plinking or personal security.

SPECIFICATIONS MODEL AT-9
Caliber: 9mm
Capacity: 25 rounds
Type: Autoloader
Operation: Blowback
Barrel length: 17″
Overall length: 35″ (26¹/₂″ w/stock folded)
Weight: 5 lbs.
Price: $390.00

Also available:
MODEL F9 AT-9. Same as Model AT-9, but with fixed buttstock made of high-impact polymer for a more traditional look. **Price:** $420.00

FRANCOTTE RIFLES

BOLT ACTION RIFLE

August Francotte rifles are available in all calibers for which barrels and chambers are made. All guns are custom made to the customer's specifications; there are no standard models. Most bolt-action rifles use commercial Mauser actions; however, the magnum action is produced by Francotte exclusively for its own production. Side-by-side and mountain rifles use either boxlock or sidelock action. Francotte system sidelocks are back-action type. Options include gold and silver inlay, special engraving and exhibition and museum grade wood. Francotte rifles are distributed in the U.S. by Armes de Chasse (see Directory of Manufacturers and Distributors for details).

BOLT ACTION RIFLE

SPECIFICATIONS
Calibers: 17 Bee, 7×64, 30-06, 270, 222R, 243W, 308W, 375 H&H, 416 Rigby, 460 Weatherby, 505 Gibbs
Barrel length: to customer's specifications
Weight: 8 to 12 lbs., or to customer's specifications
Stock: A wide selection of wood in all possible styles according to customer preferences
Engraving: Per customer specifications
Sights: All types of sights and scopes
Prices:
BOLT ACTION RIFLES
Standard bolt action (30-06, 270, 7×64, etc.)	$ 9,000
Short Bolt Action (222R, 243W, etc.)	10,000
Magnum action (416 Ribgy, 460 Wby., etc.)	15,000

BOXLOCK SIDE-BY-SIDE DOUBLE RIFLES
Std. boxlock double rifle (9.3×74R, 8×57JRS, 7×65R, etc.)	$20,000
Std. boxlock double (Magnum calibers)	25,000
Optional sideplates, **add**	1,700

SIDELOCK S/S DOUBLE RIFLES
Std. sidelock double rifle (9.3×74R, 8×57JRS, 7×65R, etc.)	$30,000
Std. sidelock double (Magnum calibers)	36,000
Special safari sidelock	**Price on request**

MOUNTAIN RIFLES
Standard boxlock	$15,000
Std. boxlock in magnum & rimless calibers	**Price on request**
Optional sideplates, **add**	1,700
Standard sidelock	27,000

CARL GUSTAF RIFLES

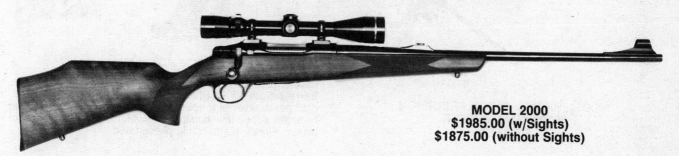

MODEL 2000
$1985.00 (w/Sights)
$1875.00 (without Sights)

The Carl Gustaf 2000 rifle, created by one of the oldest rifle-makers in the world, uses the latest Swedish hi-tech engineering, design and manufacturing methods to produce this fine hunting piece, while retaining the balance and sleek lines of its famous predecessor, the *Husqvarna*. Each rifle bears the "Crowned C" stamp, the exclusive Royal Swedish symbol of quality and durability.

SPECIFICATIONS
Calibers: 30-06, 308 Win., 6.5×55, 7×64, 9.3×63, 243, 270, 7mm Rem. Mag., 300 Win. Mag.
Capacity: 3-round clip (4-round clip optional)
Action: Bolt
Barrel length: 24″
Overall length: 44″
Weight: 7½ lbs.
Sights: Hooded ramp front; open rear (drilled and tapped for scope mounting)
Stock: Cheekpiece with Monte Carlo; Wundhammer palm swell on pistol grip (see also above)
Length of pull: 13¾″

HARRINGTON & RICHARDSON RIFLES

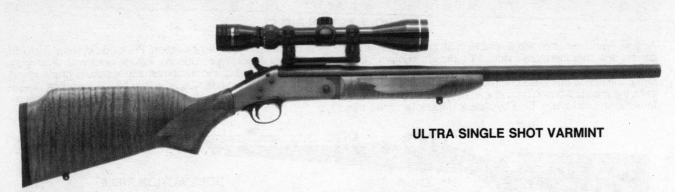

ULTRA SINGLE SHOT VARMINT

ULTRA SINGLE SHOT VARMINT RIFLE
$249.95

SPECIFICATIONS
Calibers: 223 Rem. and 22-250 Rem.
Action: Break-open; side lever release; positive ejection
Barrel length: 22″ heavy varmint profile
Weight: 7 to 8 lbs.
Sights: None (scope mount included)

Length of pull: 14¼″
Drop at comb: ¼″
Drop at heel: 1⅛″
Forend: Semi-beavertail
Stock: Monte Carlo; hand-checkered curly maple
Features: Sling swivels on stock and forend; patented transfer bar safety; automatic ejection; hammer extension; rebated muzzle; Uncle Mike recoil pad

HECKLER & KOCH RIFLES

MODEL HK PSG-1 HIGH PRECISION MARKSMAN'S RIFLE
$9325.00

SPECIFICATIONS
Caliber: 308 (7.62mm). **Capacity:** 5 rounds and 20 rounds. **Barrel length:** 25.6″. **Rifling:** 4 groove, polygonal. **Twist:** 12″, right hand. **Overall length:** 47.5″. **Weight:** 17.8 lbs. **Sights:** Hensoldt 6×42 telescopic. **Stock:** Matte black, high-impact plastic. **Finish;** Matte black, phosphated.

SPECIFICATIONS
Caliber: 308 Win. **Capacity:** 5 rounds. **Barrel length:** 19½″. **Overall length:** 42⅜″. **Weight:** 10½ lbs. **Sights:** Post front; aperture rear, adjustable for windage and elevation. **Stock:** Kevlar-reinforced fiberglass (wood grain) with thumbhole buttstock. **Features:** Bull barrel; PSG1 Marksman trigger group; clawlock scope mounts.

MODEL SR-9
$1369.00

HECKLER & KOCH

MODEL SR-9(T) TARGET RIFLE
$1799.00

SPECIFICATIONS
Same specifications as the Model SR-9 (above), but has adjustable MSG90 buttstock and PSG1 trigger group plus adjustable contoured grip.
Also available:
Model SR-9 (TC) Target Competition Rifle with adjustable PSG1 buttstock and contoured handgrip, trigger group and 5-round magazine. **$1946.00**

HEYM RIFLES

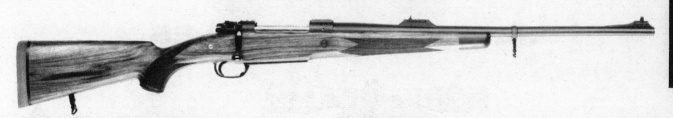

MODEL EXPRESS
$6550.00

SPECIFICATIONS
Calibers: 338 Lapua Magnum, 375 H&H, 416 Rigby, 378 Weatherby Magnum, 460 Weatherby Magnum, 450 Ackley, 500 A-Square, 500 Nitro Express

Also available:
MODEL EXPRESS 600 in 600 Nitro Express.
Price: $11,350.00
For Left-hand Model, **add** 595.00

MODEL 88B SIDE-BY-SIDE DOUBLE RIFLE

This German-built boxlock model has a modified Anson & Deeley action with standing sears, plus Purdey-type double underlocking lugs and Greener extension with crossbolt. Actions are furnished with sliding safeties and cocking indicators on the top tang, nonbreakable coil springs, front single set triggers and steel trigger guards.

SPECIFICATIONS
Calibers: 8×57 JRS, 9.3×74R and 30-06

Weight: 8 lbs.
Features: Ejectors, small action
Price: $12,500.00
In 375 H&H Mag. 14,450.00

Also available:
MODEL 88B/SS. Sidelock version of above **$16,600.00**
MODEL 88B "SAFARI". Same general specifications as above, except **calibers:** 375 H&H, 458 Win. Mag., 470 Nitro Express, 500 Nitro Express. **Weight:** 10 lbs., large frame.
Price: $16,400.00

IVER JOHNSON RIFLES

M-1 CARBINE

M-1 CARBINE

SPECIFICATIONS
Calibers: 30 Carbine and 9mm
Capacity: 15 and 30 rounds
Barrel length: 18"
Overall length: 35 1/2"
Weight: 5 1/2 lbs.
Sights: Military front; peep rear, adjustable for windage and elevation
Finish: Blue

Stock: Hardwood or walnut
Prices:
M-1 Carbine (30 caliber, hardwood stock)	$349.95
With walnut stock	384.95
M-1 Paratrooper w/telescoping stock	433.00
M-1 Carbine Full Auto	560.00
M-1 Carbine (9mm, hardwood stock)	365.75
With walnut stock	399.00
M-1 Paratrooper (9mm telescoping stock)	448.95

JAGERSPORTS RIFLES

**VOERE MODEL VEC 91
"LIGHTNING BOLT" RIFLE
$2500.00**

This first factory-made high-power caseless ammunition sporting and hunting rifle features two small batteries capable of delivering 5000 shots. The rifle will not fire unless the bolt is fully closed with the sliding safety in forward fire position. The trigger let-off is adjustable for 5 ounces to 7 pounds by an adjustment screw in the trigger guard. A free-floating barrel ensures a high level of accuracy. The rifle features a bolt action with twin forward locking lugs, a double protector from gas leaks, a two-stage fully adjustable electrical trigger, and electronic ignition.

SPECIFICATIONS
Caliber: 223 Rem.
Capacity: 5-shot detachable magazine
Barrel length: 20"
Overall length: 39"
Weight: 6 lbs.
Sights: Adjustable rear; ramp front
Stock: Select walnut, hand-checkered pistol-grip stock with schnabel forend
Finish: Hand-rubbed oil finish

Also available (not shown):
MODEL 2115 Semiauto. Gas-operated 22 LR, 22" barrel .... $ 550.00
MODEL 2150 Bolt Action. 24" barrel (26" optional) double-set trigger (single set or two-stage), 5-round capacity, side safety, Mauser action, claw extractor 1625.00
MODEL 2155 Bolt Action. 20" barrel, tang safety calibers 243, 270, 30-06 .... 900.00
MODEL 2155M Magnum. 7mm Rem. Mag. & 300 Win. Mag. 24" barrel, vent. recoil pad 925.00
MODEL 2165 Bolt Action. Same specifications as Model 2155 but w/adj. rear and ramp front sights, 22" barrel select walnut stock, rosewood forend/pistol-grip cap 1300.00
MODEL 2165M. Same as Model 2165, except with 24" barrel 3-shot magazine, calibers 7mm Rem. Mag. & 300 Win. Mag. 1400.00

JARRETT CUSTOM RIFLES

PRIVATE COLLECTION SERIES

All Jarrett Private Collection rifles include the following features: Metal finish • Top-mounted bolt release • Break-in and load development with 20 rounds • Setup for switch barrel • Serial number

MODELS 2 AND 3
$3495.00

MODEL 2 features: McMillan Mountain Rifle stock • Remington 700 Magnum receiver • Jarrett #4 tapered barrel (.308 bore w/1 in 12" twist) • Remington conversion trigger • Olive drab metal finish • Forest camo stock • 3.5x10x50 Leupold scope with A.O. matte finish • Pachmayr decelerator pad and Jarrett muzzle brake kit

MODEL 3 offers: Caliber 7mm STW • Jarrett .284 bore barrel w/1 in 10" twist (25 1/2" at crown) • Black textured stock • Leupold base w/30mm Redfield rings. Other specifications same as Model 1. Also available in 300 Win. Mag. with black metal and Old English Pachmayr 1" pad.

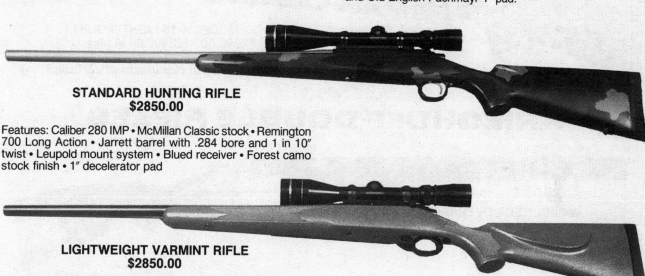

STANDARD HUNTING RIFLE
$2850.00

Features: Caliber 280 IMP • McMillan Classic stock • Remington 700 Long Action • Jarrett barrel with .284 bore and 1 in 10" twist • Leupold mount system • Blued receiver • Forest camo stock finish • 1" decelerator pad

LIGHTWEIGHT VARMINT RIFLE
$2850.00

Features: Caliber 223 • Remington XP-100 action • Jarrett barrel w/.224 bore and 1 in 14" twist (#4 tapered to 23" at crown) • Leupold mount system • Black Teflon metal finish • Gray textured-finish stock • 6.5x20 scope (optional) • Remington conversion trigger

SNIPER RIFLE
$3425.00 (w/o Scope)

Features McMillan stock • Remington 700 short action receiver • #6 taper Jarrett 308 barrel (1 in 12" twist) • Jewel trigger set at 15 oz. • Leupold mount system • Kahles 10X sniper scope • Black finish • Black texture paint on stock • Pachmayr decelerator (1" pad) • Jarrett muzzle brake

KDF RIFLES

MODEL K15
$1950.00 ($2000.00 in Magnum)

SPECIFICATIONS
Calibers: Standard—243, 6mm Rem., 25-06, 270 Win., 280 Rem., 308 Win., 30-06; **Magnum**—270 Wby., 7mm Rem., 300 Win., 300 Wby., 338 Win., 375 H&H, 411 KDF, 458 Win.
Capacity: 4 rounds (3 rounds in Magnum)
Barrel lengths: 24″ (26″ in Magnum)
Overall length: 44¹/₂″ (46¹/₂″ in Magnum)
Weight: 8 lbs. (approx.)
Receiver: Drilled and tapped for scope mounts (KDF bases available to take 1″ or 30mm rings)

Trigger: Competition-quality single stage; adjustable for travel, pull and sear engagement
Safety: Located on right-hand side
Stocks: Kevlar composite or laminate stock; Pachmayr decelerator pad; quick detachable swivels; AAA grade walnut stocks with 22-line hand-checkering; ebony forend; pistol grip cap and crossbolts (walnut stocks may be ordered in classic, schnabel or thumbhole style)
Features and options: Iron sights; recoil arrestor; choice of metal finishes; 3 locking lugs w/large contact area; 60-degree llft for fast loading; box-style magazine system; easily accessible bolt release catch; fully machined, hinged bottom metal

MODEL K-15 LIGHTWEIGHT
$1990.00   ($2400.00 in Magnum)
Note: For conversion of existing K-15 contact KDF
(see Directory of Manufacturers & Suppliers)

KRIEGHOFF DOUBLE RIFLES

MODEL TECK OVER/UNDER

MODEL ULM OVER/UNDER

SPECIFICATIONS
Calibers: 308, 30-06, 300 Win. Mag., 9.3×74R, 8×57JRS, 7×65R, 458 Win. Mag.
Barrel length: 25″
Action: Boxlock; double greener-type crossbolt and double barrel lug locking, steel receiver
Weight: 7¹/₂ lbs.
Triggers: Double triggers; single trigger optional
Safety: Located on top tang
Sights: Open sight with right angle front sight
Stock: German-styled with pistol grip and cheekpiece; oil-finished
Length of stock: 14³/₈″
Finish: Nickel-plated steel receiver with satin grey finish
Prices:
Model Teck (Boxlock) . . . . $ 8,300.00
  In 9.3×74R and 458 Win. Mag. 9,445.00
Teck-Handspanner (16 ga. receiver only;
  7×65R, 30-06, 308 Win.) 9,975.00
Also available:
TRUMPF SBS (Side-by-side boxlock) 13,900.00

SPECIFICATIONS
Calibers: 308 Win., 30-06, 300 Win. Mag., 375 H&H, 458 Win. Mag.
Barrel length: 25″
Weight: 7.8 lbs.
Triggers: Double triggers (front trigger=bottom; rear trigger=upper
Safety: Located on top tang
Sights: Open sight w/right angle front sight
Stock: German-styled with pistol grip and cheekpiece; oil-finished
Length of stock: 14³/₈″
Forearm: Semi-beavertail
Prices:
Model ULM (Sidelock) $13,900.00
Primus (Deluxe Sidelock) 17,750.00
Also available:
NEPTUN DRILLING 14,500.00

LAKEFIELD SPORTING RIFLES

MODEL 92S SILHOUETTE
$364.95 ($399.95 LH)

MODEL 90B BIATHLON
$534.95 ($589.95 LH)

SPECIFICATIONS

Model:	90B	92S
Caliber:	.22 Long Rifle Only	.22 Long Rifle
Capacity:	5-shot metal magazine	5-shot metal magazine
Action:	Self-cocking bolt action, thumb-operated rotary safety	Self-cocking bolt action, thumb-operated rotary safety
Stock:	One-piece target-type stock with natural finish hardwood; comes with clip holder, carrying & shooting rails, butt hook and hand stop	One-piece high comb, target-type with walnut finish hardwood
Barrel Length:	21″ w/snow cover	21″
Sights:	Receiver peep sights with 1/4 min. click micrometer adjustments; target front sight with inserts	None (receiver drilled and tapped for scope base)
Overall Length:	39⅝″	39⅝″
Approx. Weight:	8¼ lbs.	8 lbs.

MARK I
$119.95

MODEL 64B
$132.95
Also available:
MARK I "SMOOTH BORE" (20¾″ barrel) $119.95
MARK I YOUTH (19″ barrel) 119.95
MARK II & MARK II YOUTH (19″ barrel) 124.95
MARK II LEFT HAND (20½″ barrel) 139.95

SPECIFICATIONS

Model:	MARK I	MARK II	64B
Caliber:	.22 Short, Long or Long Rifle	.22 Long Rifle Only	.22 Long Rifle Only
Capacity:	Single Shot	10 Shot Clip Magazine	10 Shot Clip Magazine
Action:	Self Cocking Bolt Action. Thumb Operated Rotary Safety.	Self-Cocking Bolt Action. Thumb Operated Rotary Safety.	Semi-Automatic Side Ejection. Bolt Hold Open Device. Thumb Operated Rotary Safety.
Stock:	One Piece, Walnut Finish Hardwood, Monte Carlo Type with Full Pistol Grip. Checkering on Pistol Grip and Forend.		
Barrel Length:	20¾″	20¾″	20¼″
Sights:	Open Bead Front Sight, Adjustable Rear Sight, Receiver Grooved for Scope Mounting.		
Overall Length:	39½″	39½″	40″
Approx. Weight:	5½ lbs.	5½ lbs.	5½ lbs.

LAKEFIELD SPORTING RIFLES

MODEL 91T
$424.95

MODEL 91TR
$454.95 ($499.95 L.H.)

Model	91TR	91T
Caliber:	.22 Long Rifle	.22 Short, Long or Long Rifle
Capacity	5-shot clip magazine	Single shot
Action:	Self-cocking bolt action, thumb-operated rotary safety	Self-cocking bolt action thumb-operated rotary safety
Stock:	One-piece, target-type with walnut finish hardwood (also available in natural finish); comes with shooting rail and hand stop	One-piece, target-type walnut finish hardwood (also available in natural finish); comes with shootng rail and hand stop
Sights:	Receiver peep sights with ¼ min. click micrometer adjustments, target front sight with inserts	Receiver peep sights with ¼ min. click micrometer adjustments, target front sight with inserts
Overall Length:	43⅝″	43⅝″
Approx. Weight:	8 lbs.	8 lbs.

MARK X RIFLES
ACTIONS & BARRELED ACTIONS

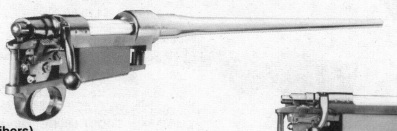

BARRELED ACTIONS
$352.00 (Standard Calibers)
$372.00 (7mm Rem. Mag., 300 Win. Mag.)
$435.00 (375 H&H, 458 Win. Mag.)
$352.00 (223, 7.62×39)

Hand-fitted with premium hammer-forged barrels created from corrosion resistant chrome vanadium steel. Each barreled action is carefully proofed and marked under close government control, ready to drop into the stock of your choice.

Calibers: 223, 22-250, 243, 25-06, 270, 7×57, 7mm Rem. Mag., 300 Win. Mag., 308, 30-06. **Barrel length:** 24″. **Weight:** 5½ lbs. (5¾ lbs. in 22-250, 243, and 25-06). **Rifling twist:** 10 (14 in 22-250 and 9.5 in 7×57).

Also available in 375 H&H Mag. and 458 Win. Mag. Same barrel length but different weights: 6 lbs. (375 H&H Mag.) and 5.75 lbs. (458 Win. Mag.). **Rifling twist:** 12 (375 H&H Mag.) and 14 (458 Win. Mag.).

MAUSER SYSTEM ACTIONS

Single Shot Action **$243.00**
Type A: 7×57mm to 30-06. Standard magazine
(3⅜″) and bolt face (.470″) **285.00**
Type B: 22-250 to 308. Short magazine (2⅞″);
standard bolt face **285.00**
Type C: 7mm Rem. Mag. to 458 Win. Mag. Standard
magazine and Magnum bolt face (.532″) **290.00**
Type D: 300 Win. Mag. to 375 H&H. Magnum
magazine (3¹¹⁄₁₆″) and Magnum bolt face **317.00**
Mini-Mark X (.17 to .223) **285.00**

MARK X RIFLES

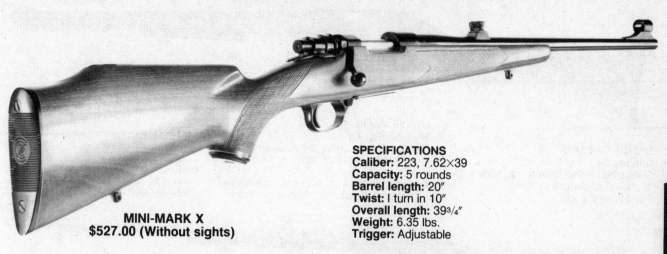

MINI-MARK X
$527.00 (Without sights)

SPECIFICATIONS
Caliber: 223, 7.62×39
Capacity: 5 rounds
Barrel length: 20″
Twist: I turn in 10″
Overall length: 39³/₄″
Weight: 6.35 lbs.
Trigger: Adjustable

SPECIFICATIONS
Calibers: 22-250, 243 Win., 25-06, 270 Win., 7×57, 308 Win., 30-06; 7mm Rem. Mag., 300 Win. Mag.
Capacity: 5 rounds; 3 in 7mm Rem. Mag., 300 Win. Mag.
Barrel length: 24″
Overall length: 45″
Twist: 1 turn in 10″
Weight: 7½ lbs.
Stock: Carbolite

MARK X VISCOUNT SPORTER
$568.00 ($590.00 Magnum calibers)

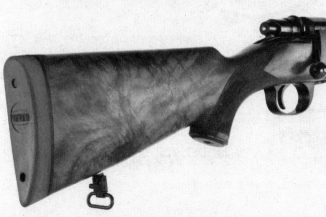

Features forged and machined Mauser System actions . . . Hammer-forged, chrome, vanadium steel barrels . . . Drilled and tapped for scope mounts and receiver sights . . . Hooded ramp front and fully adjustable rear sight . . . All-steel button release magazine floor plate . . . Detachable sling swivels . . . Silent sliding thumb safety . . . Prime European walnut stocks . . . Sculpted, low-profile cheekpiece . . . Rubber recoil butt plate . . . Steel grip cap.

Calibers: 22-250, 243 Win., 25-06, 270 Win., 7 × 57, 308 Win., 30-06, 7mm Rem. Mag., 300 Win. Mag. **Barrel length:** 24″. **Overall length:** 44″. **Weight:** 7 lbs. **Capacity:** 5 rounds.

Also available: **WHITWORTH EXPRESS RIFLE** with adjustable trigger, express sights, in 458 Win. Mag. and 375 H&H. **Price:** $870.00

MARK X WHITWORTH
$700.00 ($722.00 Magnum calibers)

RIFLES

MARLIN 22 RIFLES

MODEL 60
$148.75

SPECIFICATIONS
Caliber: 22 Long Rifle
Capacity: 14-shot tubular magazine with patented closure system
Barrel length: 22″

Overall length: 40½″
Weight: 5½ lbs.
Sights: Ramp front sight; adjustable open rear, receiver grooved for scope mount
Action: Self-loading; side ejection; manual and automatic "last-shot" hold-

open devices; receiver top has serrated, non-glare finish; cross-bolt safety
Stock: One-piece walnut-finished hardwood Monte Carlo stock with full pistol grip; Mar-Shield® finish

MODEL 60SS
$221.95

SPECIFICATIONS
Caliber: 22 LR
Capacity: 14 rounds
Barrel length: 22″
Overall length: 40½″

Weight: 5½ lbs.
Sights: Adjustable folding semi-buckhorn rear; ramp front sight with high-visibility post and removable Wide-Scan™ hood
Stock: Laminated two-tone Maine birch

with nickel-plated swivel studs and rubber rifle butt pad
Features: Micro-Groove® rifling; side ejection; manual bolt hold-open; automatic last-shot bolt hold-open; cross-bolt safety

MODEL 70HC
$168.90

SPECIFICATIONS
Caliber: 22 LR
Capacity: 7- and 15-shot clip magazine
Barrel length: 18″
Overall length: 36¾″

Weight: 5½ lbs.
Action: Self-loading; side ejection; manual bolt hold-open; receiver top has serrated, non-glare finish; cross-bolt safety

Sights: Adjustable open rear, ramp front; receiver grooved for scope mount
Stock: Monte Carlo walnut-finished hardwood with full pistol grip and Mar-Shield® finish

MODEL 70P "PAPOOSE"
$195.50

SPECIFICATIONS
Caliber: 22 LR
Capacity: 7-shot clip
Barrel length: 16¼″

Overall length: 35¼″
Weight: 3¼ lbs.
Action: Self-loading; side ejection; manual and "last-shot" bolt hold-open; receiver top has serrated non-glare finish; cross bolt safety

Sights: Adjustable open rear; ramp front; receiver grooved for scope mount
Stock: Walnut-finished hardwood with full pistol grip and Mar-Shield® finish
Features: Zippered carrying case included

MARLIN 22 RIFLES

MODEL 922 MAGNUM
$362.95

SPECIFICATIONS
Caliber: 22 Win. Mag. Rimfire
Capacity: 7-shot clip magazine
Barrel length: 20½"
Overall length: 39¾"

Weight: 6½ lbs.
Sights: Adjustable semi-buckhorn rear; ramp front sight with brass bead and removable Wide-Scan hood™
Stock: Monte Carlo American black wal-

nut with rubber rifle butt pad and swivel studs
Features: Side ejection; manual bolt hold-open; automatic last-shot bolt hold-open; magazine safety; Garand-type safety; Micro-Groove® rifling

MODEL 990L
$215.50

SPECIFICATIONS
Caliber: 22 LR (self-loading)
Capacity: 14 rounds
Barrel length: 22" Micro-Groove®
Overall length: 40½"

Weight: 5.75 lbs.
Sight: Folding semi-buckhorn rear
Stock: Laminated hardwood Monte Carlo
Features: Cross-bolt safety; manual and automatic last-shot bolt hold-open;

solid locking, spring-loaded magazine with patented closure system; swivel studs; rubber rifle butt pad; rustproof receiver grooved for scope mount; gold-plated steel trigger

MODEL 995
$198.80

SPECIFICATIONS
Caliber: 22 Long Rifle
Action: Self-loading
Capacity: 7-shot clip magazine
Barrel: 18" with Micro-Groove® rifling (16 grooves)

Overall length: 36¾"
Stock: Monte Carlo genuine American black walnut with full pistol grip; checkering on pistol grip and forend
Sights: Adjustable folding semi-buckhorn rear; ramp front sight with brass

bead, Wide-Scan™ hood
Weight: 5 lbs.
Features: Receiver grooved for tip-off scope mount; bolt hold-open device; cross-bolt safety

MARLIN BOLT ACTION RIFLES

MARLIN 15YN "LITTLE BUCKAROO™"
Single Shot 22 Beginner's Rifle
$152.15

SPECIFICATIONS
Caliber: 22 Short, Long or Long Rifle
Capacity: Single shot
Action: Bolt action; easy-load feed throat; thumb safety; red cocking indicator

Barrel length: 16¼" (16 grooves)
Overall length: 33¼"
Weight: 4¼ lbs.
Sights: Adjustable open rear; ramp front sight

Stock: One-piece walnut finish hardwood Monte Carlo with full pistol grip; tough Mar-Shield® finish

MODEL 25MN
$180.50

SPECIFICATIONS
Caliber: 22 Win. Mag Rimfire (not interchangeable with any other 22 cartridge)

Capacity: 7-shot clip magazine
Barrel length: 22" with Micro-Groove® rifling
Overall length: 41"
Weight: 6 lbs.

Sights: Adjustable open rear, ramp front sight; receiver grooved for scope mount
Stock: One-piece walnut-finished hardwood Monte Carlo with full pistol grip; Mar-Shield® finish

MODEL 25N
$158.00

Same specifications as Model 25MN, except **caliber** 22 LR and **weight** 5½ pounds.

MARLIN 880
$217.75

SPECIFICATIONS
Caliber: 22 Long Rifle
Capacity: 7-shot clip magazine
Action: Bolt action; positive thumb safety; red cocking indicator
Barrel: 22" with Micro-Groove® rifling (16 grooves)

Sights: Adjustable folding semi-buckhorn rear; ramp front with Wide-Scan™ with hood; receiver grooved for scope mount
Overall length: 41"
Weight: 5½ lbs.

Stock: Monte Carlo genuine American black walnut with full pistol grip; checkering on pistol grip and forend; tough Mar-Shield® finish; rubber butt pad; swivel studs

MARLIN BOLT ACTION RIFLES

MARLIN 881
$226.85

Specifications same as Marlin 880, except with tubular magazine that holds 17 Long Rifle cartridges. **Weight:** 6 lbs.

MODEL 882L
$254.55

SPECIFICATIONS
Caliber: 22 Win. Mag. Rimfire (not interchangeable with other 22 cartridges)
Capacity: 7-shot clip magazine

Barrel length: 22″ Micro-Groove®
Overall length: 41″
Weight: 6¹/₄ lbs.
Sights: Ramp front w/brass bead and removable Wide-Scan hood; adj. folding semi-buckhorn rear

Stock: Laminated hardwood Monte Carlo w/Mar-Shield® finish
Features: Swivel studs; rubber rifle butt pad; receiver grooved for scope mount; positive thumb safety; red cocking indicator

MARLIN 882 MAGNUM
$240.00

Specifications same as Model 883 Magnum, except with 7-shot clip magazine.

MARLIN 883 MAGNUM
$248.90

SPECIFICATIONS
Caliber: 22 Win. Mag. Rimfire (not interchangeable with any other 22 cartridge)
Capacity: 12-shot tubular magazine with patented closure system
Action: Bolt action; positive thumb

safety; red cocking indicator
Barrel: 22″ with Micro-Groove® rifling (20 grooves)
Sights: Adjustable folding semi-buckhorn rear; ramp front with Wide-Scan™ hood; receiver grooved for scope mount

Overall length: 41″
Weight: 6 lbs.
Stock: Monte Carlo genuine American black walnut with full pistol grip; checkering on pistol grip and underside of forend; rubber butt pad; swivel studs; tough Mar-Shield® finish

MODEL 883N
(Electroless Nickel-plated)
$274.70

RIFLES

MARLIN RIFLES

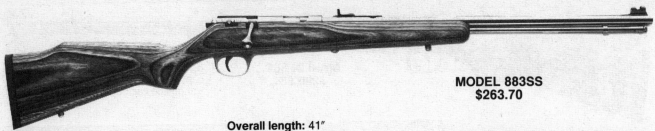

MODEL 883SS
$263.70

SPECIFICATIONS
Caliber: 22 Win. Mag. Rimfire
Capacity: 12-shot tubular magazine
Barrel length: 22"

Overall length: 41"
Weight: 6 lbs.
Sights: Adjustable folding semi-buckhorn rear; ramp front sight with high-visibility post and removable Wide-Scan™ hood

Stock: Laminated Monte Carlo two-tone brown Maine birch with nickel-plated swivel studs and rubber rifle butt pad
Features: Bolt action; red cocking indicator; positive thumb safety

MODEL 2000 TARGET
$559.50

SPECIFICATIONS
Caliber: 22 Long Rifle
Capacity: Single-shot; 5-shot adapter kit available

Action: Bolt action, 2-stage target trigger, red cocking indicator
Barrel length: 22" Micro-Groove with match chamber, recessed muzzle
Overall length: 41"
Weight: 8 lbs.

Sights: Hooded Lyman front sight with 7 aperture inserts; fully adjustable Lyman target rear peep sight
Stock: Fiberglass + Kevlar, textured blue paint

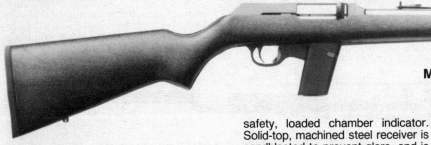

MODEL 9 CAMP CARBINE
$374.00

SPECIFICATIONS
Caliber: 9mm
Capacity: 4-shot clip (12-shot magazine available)
Action: Self-loading. Manual bolt hold-open. Garand-type safety, magazine

safety, loaded chamber indicator. Solid-top, machined steel receiver is sandblasted to prevent glare, and is drilled and tapped for scope mounting.
Barrel length: 16½" with Micro-Groove® rifling
Overall length: 35½"
Weight: 6¾ lbs.

Sights: Adjustable folding rear, ramp front sight with high visibility, orange front sight post; Wide-Scan™ hood. Receiver drilled and tapped for scope mount.
Stock: Walnut finished hardwood with pistol grip; tough Mar-Shield™ finish; rubber rifle butt pad; swivel studs
Also available: MODEL 9N (electroless nickel-plated): **$421.90**

MODEL 45
$374.00

SPECIFICATIONS
Caliber: 45 Auto
Capacity: 7-shot clip
Barrel length: 16½"

Overall length: 35½"
Weight: 6.75 lbs.
Sights: Adjustable folding rear; ramp front sight with high visibility, orange

front sight post; Wide-Scan™ hood
Stock: Walnut finished hardwood with pistol grip; rubber rifle butt pad; swivel studs

MARLIN LEVER ACTION CARBINES

MODEL 30AS
$344.25

SPECIFICATIONS
Caliber : 30-30
Capacity: 6-shot tubular magazine
Action: Lever action w/hammer block safety; solid top receiver w/side ejection
Barrel: 20" Micro-Groove® barrel
Overall length: 38 1/4"

Weight: 7 lbs.
Sights: Tapped for scope mount and receiver sight; also available in combination w/4x, 32mm, 1" scope
Stock: Walnut-finish hardwood stock w/ pistol grip; Mar-Shield® finish

MARLIN GOLDEN 39AS
$405.45

The Marlin lever-action 22 is the oldest (since 1891) shoulder gun still being manufactured.
Solid Receiver Top. You can easily mount a scope on your Marlin 39 by screwing on the machined scope adapter base provided. The screw-on base is a neater, more versatile method of mounting a scope on a 22 sporting rifle. The solid top receiver and scope adapter base provide a maximum in eye relief adjustment. If you prefer iron sights, you'll find the 39 receiver clean, flat and sandblasted to prevent glare. Exclusive brass magazine tube.

Micro-Groove® Barrel. Marlin's famous rifling system of multi-grooving has consistently produced fine accuracy because the system grips the bullet more securely, minimizes distortion, and provides a better gas seal.

And the Model 39 maximizes accuracy with the heaviest barrels available on any lever-action 22.

SPECIFICATIONS
Caliber: 22 Short, Long and Long Rifle
Capacity: Tubular magazine holds 26 Short, 21 Long and 19 Long Rifle Cartridges
Action: Lever action; solid top receiver; side ejection; one-step takedown; deeply blued metal surfaces; receiver top sandblasted to prevent glare;

hammer block safety; rebounding hammer
Barrel: 24" with Micro-Groove® rifling (16 grooves)
Overall length: 40"
Weight: 6 1/2 lbs.
Sights: Adjustable folding semi-buckhorn rear, ramp front sight with new Wide-Scan™ hood; solid top receiver tapped for scope mount or receiver sight; scope adapter base; offset hammer spur for scope use—works right or left
Stock: Two-piece genuine American black walnut with fluted comb; full pistol grip and forend; blued-steel forend cap; swivel studs; grip cap; white butt and pistol-grip spacers; tough Mar-Shield® finish; rubber rifle butt pad

MODEL 39 TAKE-DOWN
$418.95 (Incl. Carrying Case)

SPECIFICATIONS
Caliber: 22 Short, Long or Long Rifle
Capacity: Tubular magazine holds 16 Short, 12 Long, or 11 Long Rifle cartridges

Action: Lever action; solid top receiver; side ejection; rebounding hammer; one-step take-down; deep blued metal surfaces; gold-plated trigger
Barrel length: 16 1/2" lightweight barrel (16 grooves)
Overall length: 32 5/8"
Weight: 5 1/4 lbs.
Safety: Hammer block safety

Sights: Adjustable semi-buckhorn folding rear, ramp front with brass bead and Wide-Scan™ hood; top receiver tapped for scope mount and receiver sight; scope adapter base; offset hammer spur (right or left hand) for scope use
Stock: Two-piece straight-grip American black walnut with scaled-down forearm and blued steel forend cap; Mar-Shield® finish

MARLIN LEVER ACTION CARBINES

MODEL 1894 CLASSIC
$488.00

SPECIFICATIONS
Calibers: 218 Bee, 25-20 Win. and 32-20 Win.
Capacity: 6-shot tubular magazine
Barrel length: 22″ (6-groove rifling)
Overall length: 38¾″

Weight: 6¼ lbs.
Action: Lever action with squared finger lever; side ejection; solid receiver top sandblasted to prevent glare; hammer block safety
Sights: Adjustable semi-buckhorn folding rear, brass bead front; solid top receiver tapped for scope mount and receiver sight; offset hammer spur
Stock: Straight-grip American black walnut with Mar-Shield® finish; blued steel forend cap

MARLIN 1894S
$454.80

SPECIFICATIONS
Calibers: 44 Rem. Mag./44 Special, 45 Colt
Capacity: 10-shot tubular magazine
Action: Lever action w/square finger lever; hammer block safety

Barrel: 20″ Micro-Groove® barrel
Sights: Ramp front sight w/brass bead; adjustable semi-buckhorn folding rear and Wide-Scan® hood; solid top receiver tapped for scope mount or receiver sight

Overall length: 37½″
Weight: 6 lbs.
Stock: American black walnut stock w/ Mar-Shield™ finish; blued steel forend cap; swivel studs

MARLIN 1894CS 357 MAGNUM
$454.80

SPECIFICATIONS
Calibers: 357 Magnum, 38 Special
Capacity: 9-shot tubular magazine
Action: Lever action w/square finger lever; hammer block safety; side ejection; solid top receiver; deeply blued metal surfaces; receiver top sandblasted to prevent glare

Barrel: 18½″ long with Micro-Groove® rifling (12 grooves)
Sights: Adjustable semi-buckhorn folding rear, bead front; solid top receiver tapped for scope mount or receiver sight; offset hammer spur for scope use—adjustable for right- or left-hand use

Overall length: 36″
Weight: 6 lbs.
Stock: Straight-grip two-piece genuine American black walnut with white butt plate spacer; tough Mar-Shield® finish; swivel studs

MARLIN LEVER ACTION CARBINES

MARLIN 1895SS
$490.25

SPECIFICATIONS
Caliber: 45/70 Government
Capacity: 4-shot tubular magazine
Action: Lever action; hammer block safety; receiver top sandblasted to prevent glare

Barrel: 22" Micro-Groove® barrel
Sights: Ramp front sight w/brass bead; adjustable semi-buckhorn folding rear and Wide-Scan™ hood; receiver tapped for scope mount or receiver sight

Overall length: 40½"
Weight: 7½ lbs.
Stock: American black walnut pistol grip stock w/rubber rifle butt pad and Mar-Shield® finish; white pistol grip and butt spacers

MARLIN 336CS
$404.30 (Without Scope)

SPECIFICATIONS
Calibers: 30-30 Win., and 35 Rem.
Capacity: 6-shot tubular magazine
Action: Lever action w/hammer block safety; deeply blued metal surfaces; receiver top sandblasted to prevent glare

Barrel: 20" Micro-Groove® barrel
Sights: Adjustable folding semi-buckhorn rear; ramp front sight w/brass bead and Wide-Scan™ hood; tapped for receiver sight and scope mount; offset hammer spur for scope use (works right or left)

Overall length: 38½"
Weight: 7 lbs.
Stock: American black walnut pistol-grip stock w/fluted comb and Mar-Shield® finish; rubber rifle butt pad; swivel studs

MODEL 444SS
$490.25

SPECIFICATIONS
Caliber: 444 Marlin
Capacity: 5-shot tubular magazine
Barrel: 22" Micro-Groove®

Overall length: 40½"
Weight: 7½ lbs.
Stock: American black walnut pistol grip stock with rubber rifle butt pad; swivel studs

Sights: Ramp front sight with brass bead and Wide-Scan® hood; adjustable semi-buckhorn folding rear; receiver tipped for scope mount or receiver sight

MAUSER RIFLES

**MODEL 201 STANDARD
(22 WMR w/sights)**

MODEL 201 RIMFIRE

SPECIFICATIONS
Calibers: 22 LR or 22 WMR
Capacity: 5 shots (optional 8-shot available)
Barrel length: 21″
Overall length: 40″
Weight: 6½ lbs.
Sights: Metallic (optional)
Features: Receiver drilled and tapped for scope mounts; single-stage trigger (adj. from 1½ to 7 lbs.); positive silent tang safety locks bolt, sear and trigger; dual extractors for positive extraction of empty cases; hammer-forged steel barrels w/6 lands and grooves

Also available:
LUXUS MODELS with European walnut stocks, hand-checkered rosewood forends, rubber butt pad and 1″ quick disconnect sling swivels
Prices:
Standard 22 LR (without sights) $472.00
Standard 22 WMR (with sights) 534.00
Luxus 22 LR (without sights) 621.00
Luxus 22 WMR (with sights) 698.00

MODEL 107

MODEL 107

SPECIFICATIONS
Caliber: 22 LR
Capacity: 5 rounds (optional 8-shot available)
Barrel length: 21.6″
Overall Length: 40″
Weight: 5.1 lbs.
Length of pull: 13½″

Sights: Sliding rear sight adjustable to 200 meters
Features: 60° bolt throw locks into receiver groove; dual extractors for positive extraction of empty cases; all-steel floor plate and trigger guard; hammer-forged steel barrel with 6 lands and grooves; receiver accepts all rail scope mounts; two-stage trigger adjustable for weight and travel; positive silent tang safety locks bolt, sear and trigger
Price: $330.00

MODEL 86 PRECISION RIFLE (Not Shown)

SPECIFICATIONS
Caliber: 308 Win. (7.62×51)
Capacity: 9 shots (+ 1 in chamber)
Barrel length: 28.8″ (with muzzle break)
Overall length: 47.7″ (maximum)
Weight: 10.8 lbs.

Features: Match trigger adjustable for two-stage or single stage; trigger slack, pull and position adjustable externally; scope mount; detachable receiver sight; receiver of chrome/moly steel
Prices:
Model 86 w/Fiberglass stock $3921.00
Model 86 w/Match Thumbhole wood stock 4145.00

MAUSER RIFLES

MODEL 66 STUTZEN

MODEL 66

These bolt-action centerfire repeating rifles feature a telescopic short-stroke action that allows the receiver to be two inches shorter than in most standard bolt-action rifles. Model 66 also provides interchangeability of barrels.

SPECIFICATIONS
Calibers: Standard—243 Win., 270 Win., 30-06, 308 Win.
   Magnum—7mm Rem., 300 Win., 300 Wby.
   Safari—375 H&H, 458 Win.
Capacity: 3-shot internal magazine
Barrel lengths: 21″ (Stutzen); 24″ (Standard); 26″ (Magnum & Safari)
Overall lengths: 39″ (Stutzen); 42″ (Standard); 44″ (Magnum & Safari)

Weight: 7$\frac{1}{2}$ lbs. (Stutzen & Standard); 7.9 lbs. (Magnum); 9.3 lbs. (Safari)
Sights: Rectangular front blade and cover; open rear adjustable for windage and elevation
Features: Silent safety catch; barrel band front sling swivel; two large front bolt-locking lugs; mini-claw extractor for positive extraction of spent cases; single-stage adjustable trigger
Prices:
Standard calibers $1783.00
Magnum calibers 1873.00
Safari calibers 2079.00
Stutzen full stock models 1873.00

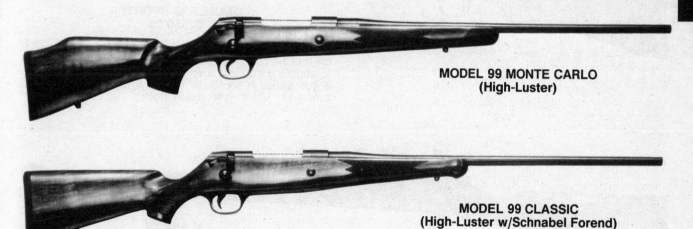

MODEL 99 MONTE CARLO
(High-Luster)

MODEL 99 CLASSIC
(High-Luster w/Schnabel Forend)

MODEL 99

SPECIFICATIONS
Calibers:
   Standard—243 Win., 25-06 Win., 270 Win., 30-06, 308 Win.
   Magnum—7mm Rem., 257 Wby., 270 Wby., 300 Wby., 300 Win., 338 Win., 375 H&H
Capacity: 4 shots (Standard); 3 shots (Magnum)
Barrel lengths: 24″ (Standard); 26″ (Magnum)
Overall lengths: 44″ (Standard); 46″ (Magnum)
Weight: 8 lbs.
Sights: None
Features: Chrome/Moly hammer-forged steel barrels; 60° bolt throw; 3 front bolt-locking lugs; stellite insert for strong lockup between receiver and barrel; jeweled bolt; dual cocking cam and patented two-stage floating firing pin for

fast lock time (1.6 milli-seconds); mini-claw extractor for positive extraction of spent cases; single-stage trigger (adj. from 1$\frac{1}{2}$ to 7 lbs.); steel floor plate and trigger guard
Prices:
MODEL 99 CLASSIC
Standard calibers (w/oil finish) $1130.00
   With High-Luster finish 1272.00
Magnum calibers (w/oil finish) 1180.00
   With High-Luster finish 1322.00
MODEL 99 MONTE CARLO STOCK
Standard calibers (w/oil finish) 1130.00
   With High-Luster finish 1272.00
Magnum calibers (w/oil finish) 1180.00
   With High-Luster finish 1322.00

McMILLAN SIGNATURE RIFLES

CLASSIC SPORTER
$2400.00

SPECIFICATIONS
Calibers:
Model SA: 22-250, 243, 6mm Rem., 6mm BR, 7mm BR, 7mm-08, 284, 308, 350 Rem. Mag.
Model LA: 25-06, 270, 280 Rem., 30-06
Model MA: 7mm STW, 7mm Rem. Mag., 300 Win. Mag., 300 Weatherby, 300 H&H, 338 Win. Mag., 340 Weatherby, 375 H&H, 416 Rem.

Capacity: 4 rounds; 3 rounds in magnum calibers
Weight: 7 lbs; 7 lbs. 9 oz. in long action
Barrel lengths: 22″, 24″, 26″
Options: Fibergrain; wooden stock, optics, 30mm rings, muzzle brakes, steel floor plates, iron sights

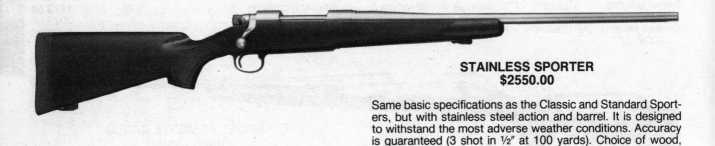

STAINLESS SPORTER
$2550.00

Same basic specifications as the Classic and Standard Sporters, but with stainless steel action and barrel. It is designed to withstand the most adverse weather conditions. Accuracy is guaranteed (3 shot in ½″ at 100 yards). Choice of wood, laminate or McMillan fiberglass stock.

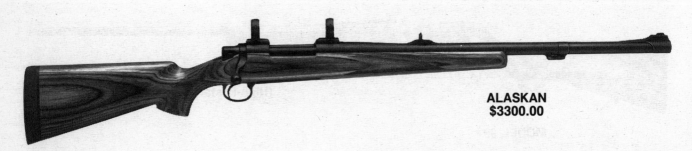

ALASKAN
$3300.00

SPECIFICATIONS
Calibers:
Model LA: 270, 280, 30-06
Model MA: 7mm Rem. Mag., 300 Win. Mag., 300 H&H, 300 Weatherby, 358 Win., 340 Weatherby, 375 H&H, 416 Rem.

Other specifications same as the Classic Sporter, except McMillan action is fitted to a match-grade barrel, complete with single-leaf rear sight, barrel band front sight, 1″ detachable rings and mounts, steel floorplate, electroless nickel finish. Monte Carlo stock features cheekpiece, palm swell and special recoil pad.
Also available: Stainless Steel Receiver, add **$150.00**

McMILLAN SIGNATURE RIFLES

TALON SPORTER
$2600.00

The all-new action of this model is designed and engineered specifically for the hunting of dangerous (African-type) game animals. Patterned after the renowned pre-64 Model 70, the Talon features a cone breech, controlled feed, claw extractor, positive ejection and three-position safety. Action is available in chromolybdenum and stainless steel. Drilled and tapped for scope mounting in long, short or magnum, left or right hand.

Same basic specifications as McMillan's Signature series, but offered in the following **calibers:**
Standard Action: 22-250, 243, 6mm Rem., 6mm BR, 7mm BR, 7mm-08, 284, 308, 350 Rem. Mag.
Long Action: 25-06, 270, 280 Rem., 30-06
Magnum Action: 7mm STW, 7mm Rem. Mag., 300 Win. Mag., 300 Weatherby, 300 H&H, 338 Win. Mag., 340 Weatherby, 375 H&H, 416 Rem.

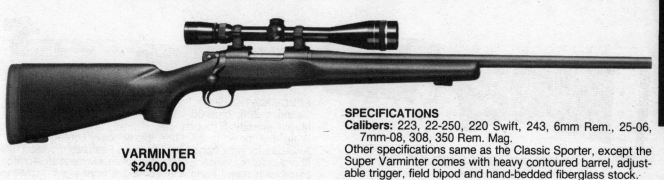

VARMINTER
$2400.00

SPECIFICATIONS
Calibers: 223, 22-250, 220 Swift, 243, 6mm Rem., 25-06, 7mm-08, 308, 350 Rem. Mag.
Other specifications same as the Classic Sporter, except the Super Varminter comes with heavy contoured barrel, adjustable trigger, field bipod and hand-bedded fiberglass stock.

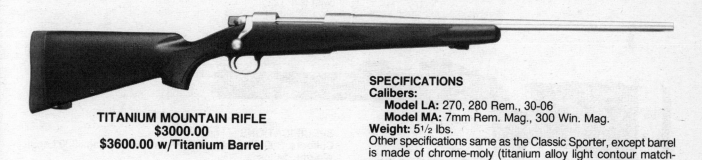

TITANIUM MOUNTAIN RIFLE
$3000.00
$3600.00 w/Titanium Barrel

SPECIFICATIONS
Calibers:
    Model LA: 270, 280 Rem., 30-06
    Model MA: 7mm Rem. Mag., 300 Win. Mag.
Weight: 5½ lbs.
Other specifications same as the Classic Sporter, except barrel is made of chrome-moly (titanium alloy light contour match-grade barrel is available at additional cost of **$500.00**).

.300 PHOENIX
$2995.00

SPECIFICATIONS
Caliber: 300 Phoenix
Barrel length: 27½"
Weight: 12½ lbs.
Stock: Fiberglass with adjustable cheekpiece
Feature: Available in left-hand action

McMILLAN SIGNATURE RIFLES

SAFARI
$3570.00 (Magnum)
TALON SAFARI $3600.00 (Super Magnum)

Super Magnum: 300 Phoenix, 338 Lapua, 378 Wby., 416 Rigby, 416 Wby., 460 Wby.
Other specifications same as the Classic Sporter, except for match-grade barrel, positive extraction McMillan Safari action, quick detachable 1″ scope mounts, positive locking steel floorplate, multi-leaf express sights, barrel band ramp front sight, barrel band swivels, and McMillan's Safari stock.

SPECIFICATIONS
Calibers:
Magnum: 300 Win. Mag., 300 Weatherby, 300 H&H, 338 Win. Mag., 340 Weatherby, 375 H&H, 404 Jeffrey, 416 Rem., 458 Win.

NATIONAL MATCH RIFLE
$2600.00

SPECIFICATIONS
Calibers: 308, 7mm-08
Mag. Capacity: 5 rounds
Weight: Approx. 11 lbs. (12½ lbs. w/heavy contour barrel)
Available for right-hand shooters only. Features modified ISU fiberglass stock with adjustable butt plate, stainless steel match barrel with barrel band and Tompkins front sight; McMillan repeating bolt action with clip shot and Canjar trigger. Barrel twist is 1:12″.

LONG RANGE RIFLE
$2600.00

SPECIFICATIONS
Calibers: 300 Win. Mag., 300 Phoenix, 7mm Mag., 338 Lapua
Weight: 14 lbs.
Barrel length: 26″
Available in right-hand only. Features a fiberglass stock with adjustable butt plate and cheekpiece. Stainless steel match barrel comes with barrel band and Tompkins front sight. McMillan solid bottom single-shot action and Canjar trigger. Barrel twist is 1:12″.

McMILLAN BENCHREST RIFLE
$2800.00 (not shown)

SPECIFICATIONS
Calibers: 6mm PPC, 243, 6mm BR, 6mm Rem., 308
Built to individual specifications to be competitive in hunter, light varmint and heavy varmint classes. Features solid bottom or repeating bolt action, Canjar trigger, fiberglass stock with recoil pad, stainless steel match-grade barrel and reloading dies. Right- or left-hand models.

MITCHELL ARMS

REPRODUCTIONS

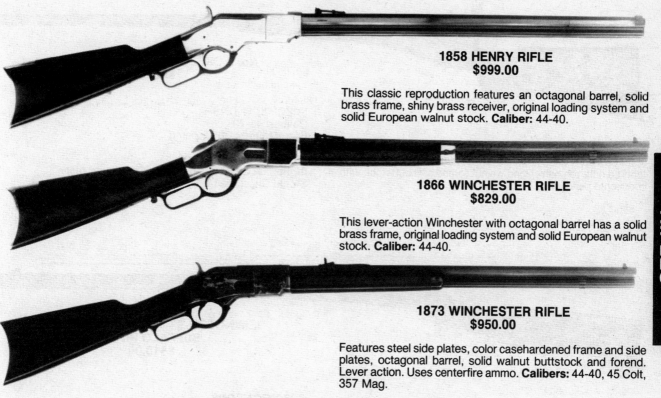

1858 HENRY RIFLE
$999.00

This classic reproduction features an octagonal barrel, solid brass frame, shiny brass receiver, original loading system and solid European walnut stock. **Caliber:** 44-40.

1866 WINCHESTER RIFLE
$829.00

This lever-action Winchester with octagonal barrel has a solid brass frame, original loading system and solid European walnut stock. **Caliber:** 44-40.

1873 WINCHESTER RIFLE
$950.00

Features steel side plates, color casehardened frame and side plates, octagonal barrel, solid walnut buttstock and forend. Lever action. Uses centerfire ammo. **Calibers:** 44-40, 45 Colt, 357 Mag.

22 CAL. MILITARY-STYLE RIFLES

MODEL M-16A1/22
$359.00

MODEL CAR-15/22
$359.95

These full-size, full-weight 22 caliber versions of the U.S. Army M-16 and CAR-15 models feature the new round hand guards and basket flash hiders. A 15-round magazine is concealed within each full-size magazine well.

NAVY ARMS RIFLES

No. 2 CREEDMOOR TARGET RIFLE
$695.00

This reproduction of the Remington No. 2 Creedmoor Rifle features a color casehardened receiver and steel trigger guard, tapered octagon barrel, and walnut forend and buttstock with checkered pistol grip.

SPECIFICATIONS
Caliber: 45-70
Barrel length: 30″, tapered
Overall length: 46″
Weight: 9 lbs.
Sights: Globe front, adjustable Creedmoor rear
Stock: Checkered walnut stock and forend

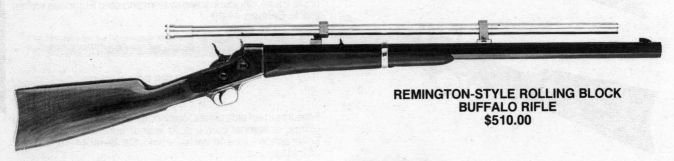

REMINGTON-STYLE ROLLING BLOCK BUFFALO RIFLE
$510.00

This replica of the rifle used by buffalo hunters and plainsmen of the 1800s features a casehardened receiver, solid brass trigger guard and walnut stock and forend. The tang is drilled and tapped to accept the optional Creedmoor sight.

SPECIFICATIONS
Caliber: 45-70
Barrel length: 26″ or 30″; full octagon or half-round
Sights: Blade front, open notch rear
Stock: Walnut stock and forend
Feature: Shown with optional 32½″ Model 1860 brass telescopic sight **$125.00**; Compact Model (18″) is **$130.00**

MODEL TU-KKW
$210.00

The TU-KKW is a replica of the ''Kleine Kaliber Wehrsport Gewehr'' 22-caliber training rifle used by the Germans in World War II. A full-size, full-weight 98K, it is complete with Mauser-style military sights, bayonet lug and cleaning rod. Unlike the original, this replica model features a 5-round detachable magazine.

SPECIFICATIONS
Caliber: 22 LR
Barrel length: 26″
Overall length: 44″
Weight: 8 lbs.
Sights: Open military style

Also available:
MODEL TU-33/40 w/20¾″ barrel **$200.00**
MODEL TU-KKW SNIPER TRAINER w/26″ barrel and
2.75 power Type 89 scope **275.00**

NAVY ARMS RIFLES

1873 WINCHESTER-STYLE RIFLE
$840.00

Known as "The Gun That Won the West," the "1873" was the most popular lever-action rifle of its time. This fine replica features a casehardened receiver.

SPECIFICATIONS
Caliber: 44-40 or 45 Long Colt
Barrel length: 24"
Overall length: 43"

Weight: 8¼ lbs.
Sights: Blade front; open ladder rear
Stock: Walnut

Also available:
1873 WINCHESTER-STYLE CARBINE
(19" barrel) $815.00
1873 WINCHESTER-STYLE SPORTING RIFLE
(30" full octagon bbl.) 895.00

RIFLES

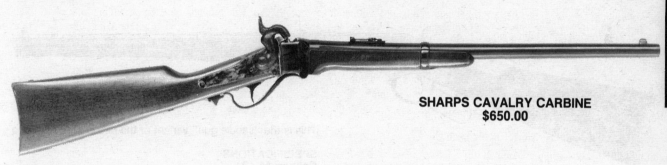

SHARPS CAVALRY CARBINE
$650.00

This Cavalry version of the Sharps rifle features a side bar and saddle ring.

SPECIFICATIONS
Caliber: 45-70

Barrel length: 22"
Overall length: 39"
Weight: 7¾ lbs.
Sights: Blade front; military ladder rear
Stock: Walnut

COWBOYS COMPANION
$160.00

The Cowboys Companion is a hard-hitting, economical semi-automatic sporting carbine. The 7.62×39 cartridge is fast becoming a popular deer cartridge, similar to the 30-30. The gun is one of the shortest, lightest 30 sporting carbines available to the American hunter.

SPECIFICATIONS
Caliber: 7.62×39
Capacity: 10 rounds (5-round hunting magazine available)

Barrel length: 16"
Overall length: 36"
Weight: 7½ lbs.
Sights: Post front; U-notch rear

Also available:
SKS "PARA" CARBINE. A military version of the Cowboys Companion, equipped with a folding bayonet. **Price: $170.00**

NAVY ARMS REPLICA RIFLES

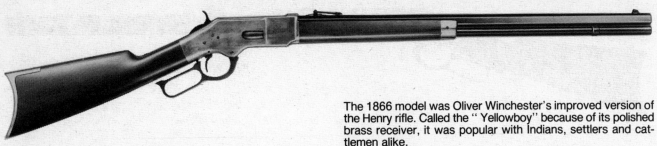

1866 "YELLOWBOY" RIFLE
$710.00

The 1866 model was Oliver Winchester's improved version of the Henry rifle. Called the "Yellowboy" because of its polished brass receiver, it was popular with Indians, settlers and cattlemen alike.

SPECIFICATIONS
Caliber: 44-40
Barrel length: 24″, full octagon
Overall length: 42½″
Weight: 8½ lbs.
Sights: Blade front; open ladder rear
Stock: Walnut

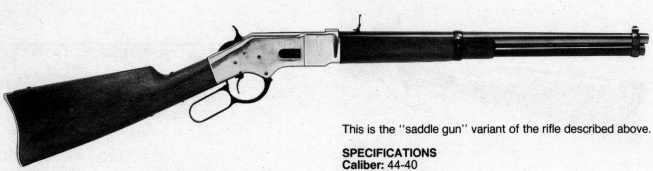

1866 "YELLOWBOY" CARBINE
$685.00

This is the "saddle gun" variant of the rifle described above.

SPECIFICATIONS
Caliber: 44-40
Barrel length: 19″, round
Overall length: 38¼″
Weight: 7¼ lbs.
Sights: Blade front; open ladder rear
Stock: Walnut

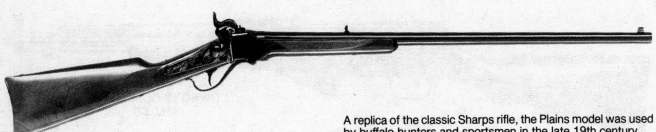

SHARPS PLAINS RIFLE
$715.00

A replica of the classic Sharps rifle, the Plains model was used by buffalo hunters and sportsmen in the late 19th century.

SPECIFICATIONS
Caliber: 45-70
Barrel length: 28½″
Overall length: 45¾″
Weight: 8 lbs. 10 oz.
Sights: Blade front; folding leaf rear
Stock: Walnut

NAVY ARMS REPLICA RIFLES

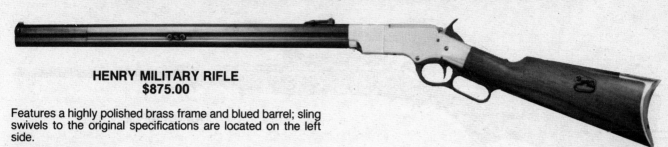

HENRY MILITARY RIFLE
$875.00

Features a highly polished brass frame and blued barrel; sling swivels to the original specifications are located on the left side.

SPECIFICATIONS
Calibers: 44-40 and 44 rimfire
Barrel length: 24″
Overall length: 43″
Weight: 9¼ lbs.
Stock: Walnut

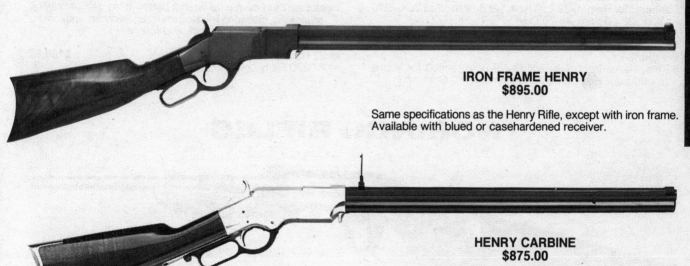

IRON FRAME HENRY
$895.00

Same specifications as the Henry Rifle, except with iron frame. Available with blued or casehardened receiver.

HENRY CARBINE
$875.00

The arm first utilized by the Kentucky Cavalry, with blued finish and brass frame.

SPECIFICATIONS
Caliber: 44-40
Barrel length: 23⅝″
Overall length: 45″
Weight: 8¾ lbs.

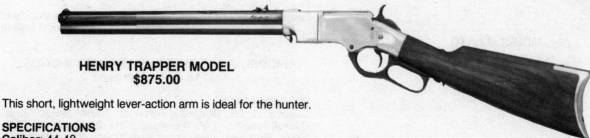

HENRY TRAPPER MODEL
$875.00

This short, lightweight lever-action arm is ideal for the hunter.

SPECIFICATIONS
Caliber: 44-40
Barrel length: 16½″
Overall length: 34½″
Weight: 7¼ lbs.

NEW ENGLAND FIREARMS RIFLES

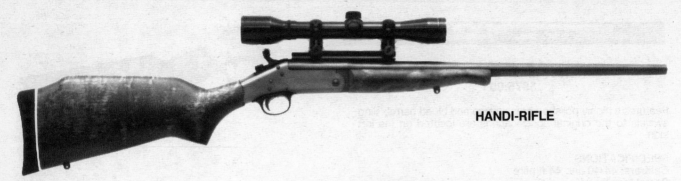

HANDI-RIFLE

HANDI-RIFLE

SPECIFICATIONS
Calibers: 22 Hornet, 22-250 Rem., 223 Rem., 243 Win., 270 Win., 30-30 Win., 45-70 Govt.
Action: Break-open; side lever release; positive ejection
Barrel length: 22″
Weight: 7 lbs.
Sights: Ramp front; fully adjustable rear; tapped for scope mounts (22 Hornet, 30-30 Win. and 45-70 Govt. only)

Length of pull: 14 1/4″
Drop at comb: 1 1/2″ (1 1/4″ in Monte Carlo)
Drop at heel: 2 1/8″ (1 1/8″ in Monte Carlo)
Stock: American hardwood, walnut finish; full pistol grip
Features: Semi-beavertail forend; patented transfer bar safety; automatic ejection; rebated muzzle; hammer extension; sling swivel studs on stock and forend
Prices:
In 22 Hornet, 223 Rem., 45-70 Govt. **$189.95**
In 22-250 Rem., 243 Win., 270 Win. and 30-30 Win. **199.95**

NORINCO RIFLES

MODEL 22 ATD SEMIAUTOMATIC
$168.00

SPECIFICATIONS
Caliber: 22 LR
Capacity: 11 rounds
Barrel length: 19.4″
Overall length: 36.6″
Weight: 4.6 lbs.
Sight radius: 16.3″
Finish: Blue
Features: All-steel receiver and barrel; checkered stock and forend; drilled and tapped for scope; easy takedown system

MODEL 22 ATD

MODEL JW-15 "BUCKHORN" BOLT ACTION
$118.00 (not shown)

SPECIFICATIONS
Caliber: 22 LR. **Capacity:** 5 rounds. **Barrel length:** 23.8″. **Overall length:** 41.5″. **Weight:** 5.5 lbs. **Sight radius:** 18.8″. **Finish:** Blue. **Features:** Mauser-style flat-top steel receiver with integral rib (fits all popular rimfire scope mounts); Model 70-style safety (locks both firing pin and bolt); detachable 5-shot magazine

PARKER-HALE RIFLES

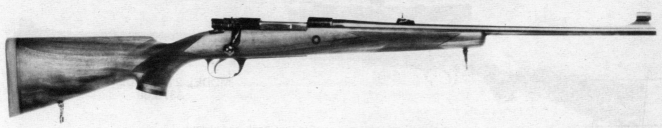

MODEL M81 CLASSIC
$900.00

SPECIFICATIONS
Calibers: 22-250, 243 Win., 6mm Rem., 270 Win., 6.5×55,
    7×57, 7×64, 308 Win., 30-06
Barrel length: 24″
Overall length: 44¹/₂″
Capacity: 4 rounds
Weight: 7.75 lbs.
Length of pull: 13¹/₂″
Stock: Checkered walnut
Features: All-steel trigger guard; adjustable trigger

MODEL M81 AFRICAN
$1050.00

SPECIFICATIONS
Calibers: 375 H&H, 9.3 × 62mm
Capacity: 3 rounds
Barrel length: 24″
Overall length: 44¹/₂″
Weight: 7.75 lbs.
Stock: Checkered walnut
Features: All-steel trigger guard, adjustable trigger, barrel band
    front swivel, African express rear sight, hand-engraved re-
    ceiver

MODEL 1100 LIGHTWEIGHT
$595.00

SPECIFICATIONS
Calibers: 22-250, 243 Win., 6mm Rem., 270 Win., 308 Win.,
    30-06
Barrel length: 22″
Overall length: 43″
Weight: 6¹/₂ lbs.
Capacity: 4 rounds
Length of pull: 13¹/₂″
Stock: Monte Carlo style, satin finished walnut with schnabel
    forend and wraparound checkering
Features: Slim profile barrel, alloy trigger guard and anodized
    bolt handle

PARKER HALE RIFLES ARE MANUFACTURED BY GIBBS RIFLE COMPANY

PARKER-HALE RIFLES

MODEL 2100 MIDLAND
$375.00

SPECIFICATIONS
Calibers: 22-250, 243 Win., 6mm Rem., 270 Win., 308 Win., 30-06
Capacity: 4 rounds
Barrel length: 22" (24" in cal. 22-250)
Overall length: 43"
Weight: 7 lbs.
Length of pull: 13½"

Stock: Checkered walnut
Sights: Hooded ramp front; adjustable flip-up rear

Also available:
MODEL 2600 MIDLAND SPECIAL in 22-250, 243 Win., 6mm Rem., 6.5×55, 7×57, 7×64, 30-06, 308 and 270. **Price: $360.00**
MODEL 2700 LIGHTWEIGHT in 22-250, 243 Win., 6mm Rem., 270 Win., 6.5×55, 7×57, 7×64, 308 Win. and 30-06. **Weight:** 6½ lbs. **Price: $415.00**

MODEL 1200 SUPER
$595.00

SPECIFICATIONS
Calibers: 22-250, 243 Win., 6mm Rem., 270 Win., 308 Win., 30-06
Capacity: 4 rounds
Barrel length: 24"
Overall length: 44½"

Weight: 7½ lbs.
Length of pull: 13½"
Also available:
MODEL 1200 SUPER CLIP in 22-250, 243 Win., 6mm Rem., 270 Win., 30-06 and 308 Win. Same specifications as Model 1200 Super, but weighs 7½ lbs. **Price: $640.00**

MODEL 1000 CLIP
$535.00

SPECIFICATIONS
Calibers: 22-250, 243 Win., 6mm Rem., 270 Win., 6.5×55, 7×57, 7×64, 308 Win. and 30-06
Capacity: 4 rounds
Barrel length: 22"
Overall length: 43"

Weight: 7¼ lbs.
Stock: Checkered walnut, Monte Carlo style
Features: Detachable magazine, Mauser-style 98 action
Also available:
MODEL 1000 STANDARD. Same specifications as the Model 1000 Clip, but with fixed 4-round magazine. **Price: $495.00**

PARKER HALE RIFLES ARE MANUFACTURED BY GIBBS RIFLE COMPANY

PARKER-HALE RIFLES

MODEL 1100M AFRICAN MAGNUM
$930.00

SPECIFICATIONS
Calibers: 357 H&H Magnum, 458 Win. Mag.
Capacity: 4 rounds
Barrel length: 24″

Overall length: 46″
Weight: 9½ lbs.
Stock: Checkered walnut, weighted, with two recoil lugs
Features: Vented recoil pad, shallow "V" rear sight, steel magazine with hinged floorplate

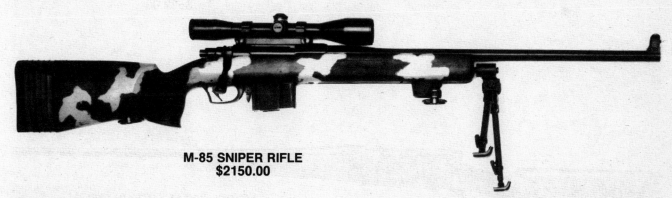

MODEL 1300C "SCOUT"
$595.00

SPECIFICATIONS
Calibers: 243 Win., 308 Win.
Capacity: 10 rounds
Barrel length: 20″

Overall length: 41″
Weight: 8½ lbs.
Stock: Checkered laminated birch wood
Features: Detachable magazine, muzzle brake

M-85 SNIPER RIFLE
$2150.00

SPECIFICATIONS
Caliber: 308 Win. (7.62 NATO)
Capacity: 10 or 20 rounds
Barrel length: 24¼″
Overall length: 45″
Weight: 12 lbs. 6 oz. (with scope)

Sights: Blade front (adjustable for windage); folding aperture rear (adjustable for elevation)
Stock: Fiberglass McMillan, adjustable for length of pull
Features: M-14 type detachable magazine; adjustable trigger; "quick-detach" bipod

PARKER HALE RIFLES ARE MANUFACTURED BY GIBBS RIFLE COMPANY

REMINGTON BOLT ACTION RIFLES

MODEL 700 ADL LS LAMINATED STOCK
$485.00   ($512.00 in 7mm Rem. Mag.)

The Model 700 ADL LS features a traditional wood stock made by laminating alternate strips of light and dark wood with waterproof adhesive and impregnating it with a phenolic resin for greater stability. Other features include low-gloss satin finish, cut checkering, sling swivel studs and open factory sights. **Calibers:** 243 Win., 270 Win., 30-06 and 7mm Rem. Mag. **Capacity:** 5 (4 in 7mm Rem. Mag.). **Barrel length:** 22″ (24″ in

7mm Rem. Mag.). **Weight:** 7¼ lbs. **Stock dimensions:** drop at heel 1⅜″; drop at comb ½″; length of pull 13⅜″.
Also available:
MODEL 700 ADL featuring Model 700 action, satin-finshed walnut stock with cheekpiece, cut-checkering and sling swivels studs. **Price: $439.00 ($465.00 in 7mm Rem. Mag.)**

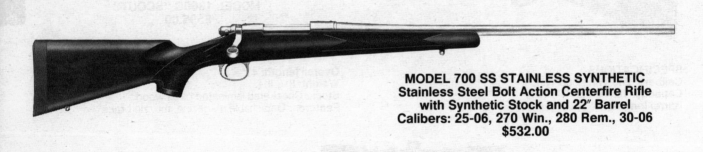

MODEL 700 SS STAINLESS SYNTHETIC
Stainless Steel Bolt Action Centerfire Rifle
with Synthetic Stock and 22″ Barrel
Calibers: 25-06, 270 Win., 280 Rem., 30-06
$532.00

MODEL 700 MOUNTAIN RIFLE
$524.00   ($532.00 Stainless Synthetic)

The lean barrel contour on this Model 700 enhances the accuracy of this light (6.75 lbs.) rifle. The pistol grip is pitched lower to position the wrist for better grip. The smooth cheekpiece positions the eye for accurate sighting. Features include

semi-finished walnut stock, 20-line deep-cut checkering, hinged magazine floorplate, sling swivel studs, and trim butt pad. Stainless synthetic model also available. For additional specifications, see Model 700 Specifications table.

REMINGTON BOLT ACTION RIFLES

MODEL 700 CLASSIC LIMITED EDITION
$524.00

Caliber: 222 Remington
Capacity: 5 shots (1 in chamber)
Barrel length: 24″
Overall length: 44¹/₂″
Weight: 7¹/₄ lbs.

Bolt: Jeweled with shrouded firing pin
Receiver: Drilled and tapped for scope mounts; fixed magazine with or without hinged floor plate
Stock: Cut-checkered select American walnut with quick detachable sling swivels installed; recoil pad standard equipment on Magnum rifles; installed at extra charge on others

MODEL 700 CS (Camo Synthetic)
$568.00
($595.00 in 7mm Rem. Mag. and 300 Wby. Mag.)

The Model 700™ is bedded to a synthetic stock fully camouflaged in Mossy Oak® Bottomland™. Stronger than wood and unaffected by weather, this stock will not warp or swell in rain, snow or heat. The Model 700 Camo Synthetic comes with a non-reflective matte finish on the bolt and is available in nine calibers. For additional specifications, see table on following page.

MODEL 700 BDL EUROPEAN
$524.00   ($551.00 in 7mm Rem. Mag.)

The Monte Carlo comb and raised cheekpiece of the stock on this new Model 700 BDL include finely cut skipline checkering on the pistol grip and forend. Offered in seven calibers from 243 Win. to the 7mm Rem. Mag. Features include hinged floorplate, sling swivel studs, hooded ramp front sight and adjustable rear sight. For additional specifications, see table on following page.

MODEL 700 BDL

This Model 700 features the Monte Carlo American walnut stock finished to a high gloss with finely cut skipline checkering. Also includes a hinged floorplate, sling swivels studs, hooded ramp front sight, and adjustable rear sight. Also available in stainless synthetic version (Model 700 BDL SS) with stainless steel barrel, receiver and bolt plus synthetic stock for maximum weather resistance.

MODEL 700 BDL
Magnum Calibers
$551.00   ($575.00 Left Hand)

Prices:
Model 700 BDL
In 17 Rem., 7mm Rem. Mag., 300 Win. Mag., 35 Whelen, 338 Win. Mag. **$551.00**
In 222 Rem., 22-250 Rem., 223 Rem., 6mm Rem., 243 Win., 25-06 Rem., 270 Win., 280 Rem., 7mm-08 Rem., 30-06, 308 Win. **524.00**
Left Hand in 22-250 Rem., 243 Win., 270 Win., 30-06, and 308 Win. **548.00**
Left Hand in 7mm Rem. Mag. and 338 Win. Mag. **575.00**
Model BDL SS (Stainless Synthetic) **585.00**
In Magnum calibers **612.00**

REMINGTON BOLT ACTION RIFLES

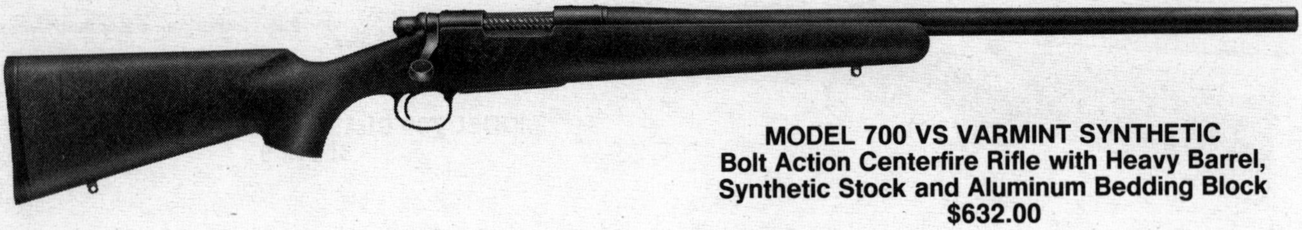

MODEL 700 VS VARMINT SYNTHETIC
Bolt Action Centerfire Rifle with Heavy Barrel, Synthetic Stock and Aluminum Bedding Block
$632.00

Also available:
MODEL 700 VS with wood stock in calibers 222 Rem., 22-250 Rem., 223 Rem., 6mm Rem., 243 Win., 7mm-08 Rem. and 308 Win. **Price: $557.00**

SPECIFICATIONS MODEL 700 (Continued on following page).

Calibers	Magazine Capacity	Barrel Length	Mtn. Rifle	Mtn Rifle SS	Limited Classic	Camo Synthetic	BDL Stainless Synthetic	ADL & BDL	BDL European	Varmint Special Wood	Varmint Special Synthetic	Twist R-H, 1 turn in
			Overall Length/Avg. Wt. (lbs.)									
17 Rem.	5	24″	—	—	—	—	—	43 5/8″/7 1/4	—	—	—	9″
220 Swift	5	24″	—	—	—	—	—	—	—	—	43 1/2″/8 1/2	14″
222 Rem.	5	24″	—	—	44 1/2″;7 1/4	—	—	43 5/8″/7 1/4	—	43 1/2″/9	—	14″
22-250 Rem.	4	24″	—	—	—	43 5/8″/6 3/4	—	43 5/8″/7 1/4	—	43 1/2″/9	43 1/2″/8 1/2	14″
	4	24″	—	—	—	—	—	43 5/8″/7 1/4	—	—	—	14″
223 Rem.	5	24″	—	—	—	—	43 5/8″/6 7/8	43 5/8″/7 1/4	—	43 1/2″/9	43 1/2″/8 1/2	12″
6mm Rem.	4	22″	—	—	—	—	—	41 5/8″/7 1/4	—	43 1/2″/9	—	9 1/8″
	4	24″	—	—	—	—	43 5/8″/6 7/8	—	—	—	—	9 1/8″
243 Win.	4	22″	41 5/8″/6 3/4	—	—	41 5/8″/6 3/4	—	41 5/8″/7 1/4	41 5/8″/7 1/4	43 1/2″/9	—	9 1/8″
	4	22″	—	—	—	—	—	41 5/8″/7 1/4	—	—	—	9 1/8″
	4	24″	—	—	—	—	43 5/8″/6 7/8	—	—	—	—	9 1/8″
25-06 Rem.	4	24″	—	—	—	—	44 1/2″/6 7/8	44 1/2″/7 1/4	—	—	—	10″
	4	22″	42 1/2″/6 3/4	42 1/2″/6 1/4	—	—	—	—	—	—	—	10″
257 Roberts	4	22″	41 5/8″/6 3/4	—	—	—	—	—	—	—	—	10″
270 Win.	4	22″	42 1/2″/6 3/4	42 1/2″/6 1/4	—	42 1/2″/6 3/4	—	42 1/2″/7 1/4	42 1/2″/7 1/4	—	—	10″
	4	22″	—	—	—	—	—	42 1/2″/7 1/4	—	—	—	10″
	4	24″	—	—	—	—	44 1/2″/6 7/8	—	—	—	—	10″
280 Rem.	4	22″	42 1/2″/6 3/4	42 1/2″/6 1/4	—	42 1/2″/6 3/4	—	42 1/2″/7 1/4	42 1/2″/7 1/4	—	—	9 1/4″
	4	24″	—	—	—	—	44 1/2″/6 7/8	—	—	—	—	9 1/4″
7mm-08 Rem.	4	22″	41 5/8″/6 3/4	—	—	42 1/2″/6 3/4	—	41 5/8″/7 1/4	41 5/8″/7 1/4	43 1/2″/9	—	9 1/4″
	4	24″	—	—	—	—	43 5/8″/6 7/8	—	—	—	—	9 1/4″
7mm Mauser (7 × 57)	4	22″	41 5/8″/6 3/4	—	—	—	—	—	—	—	—	9 1/4″
7mm Rem. Mag.[2]	3	24″	—	—	—	44 1/2″/7	44 1/2″/7	44 1/2/7 1/2	44 1/2″/7 1/2	—	—	9 1/4″
	3	24″	—	—	—	—	—	44 1/2″/7 1/2	—	—	—	9 1/4″
7mm Wby. Mag.	3	24″	—	—	—	—	44 1/2″/7	—	—	—	—	9″1/4
30-06	4	22″	42 1/2″/6 3/4	42 1/2″/6 1/4	—	42 1/2″/6 3/4	—	42 1/2″/7 1/4	42 1/2″/7 1/4	—	—	10″
	4	22″	—	—	—	—	—	42 1/2″/7 1/4	—	—	—	10″
	4	24″	—	—	—	—	44 1/2″/6 7/8	—	—	—	—	10″

[1] Varmint Special equipped with a 24″ barrel only. [2] Recoil pad included. LS = Laminated Stock. LH = Left Hand NOTE: Adjustable open sights are on Model 700™ ADL, Camo, BDL, BDL European, Safari, and Seven™. (Except Model Seven™ chambered for 17 Remington). The Mountain Rifle, Limited Classic, Stainless Synthetic and Varmint Specials do not have sights. All Model 700™ and Model Seven™ rifles come with sling swivel studs. The BDL, BDL European, Camo Snythetic, ADL, ADL LS, and Seven™ are furnished with sights. The BDL Stainless Synthetic, Mountain Rifle, Mountain Rifle Stainless Synthetic, Classic, and Varmint guns have clean barrels. All Remington centerfire rifles are drilled and tapped for scope mounts.

REMINGTON RIFLES

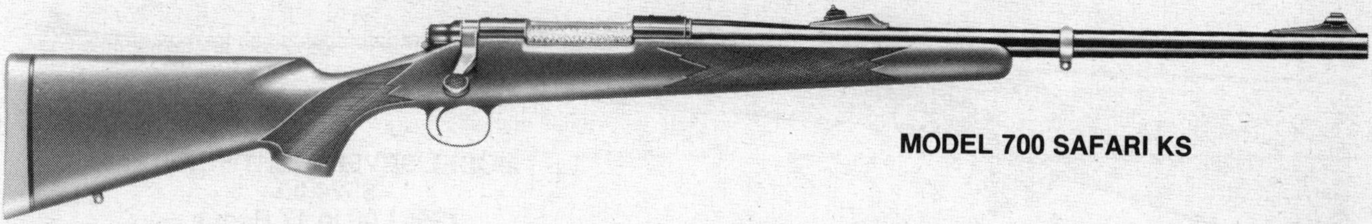

MODEL 700 SAFARI KS

Model 700 Safari Grade bolt-action rifles provide big game hunters with a choice of two stock materials. Model 700 Safari Monte Carlo (with Monte Carlo comb and cheekpiece) and Model 700 Safari Classic (with straight-line classic comb and no cheekpiece) are the wood-stocked models. Both Monte Carlo and Classic models are supplied with a satin wood finish decorated with hand-cut checkering 18 lines to the inch and fitted with two reinforcing cross bolts covered with rosewood plugs. The Monte Carlo model also has a rosewood pistol grip cap and forend tip. All models are fitted with sling swivel studs and 24″ barrels. Synthetic stock is available with simulated wood-grain finish and is reinforced with Kevlar® (KS). **Calibers:** 8mm Rem. Mag., 375 H&H Magnum, 416 Rem. Mag. and 458 Win. Mag. **Capacity:** 3 rounds. **Average weight:** 9 lbs. **Overall length:** 44 1/2″. **Rate of twist:** 10″ (8mm Rem. Mag.); 12″ (375 H&H Mag.); 14″ (416 Rem. Mag., 458 Win. Mag.).

Prices:

Classic Stock (Right Hand)	**$1001.00**
Left Hand	**1063.00**
Monte Carlo Stock (Right Hand)	**1001.00**
Kevlar®-reinforced Stock (Right Hand)	**1153.00**
Left Hand	**1215.00**
Kevlar®-reinforced Stock (22″ barreled action, R.H. only)	**1287.00**

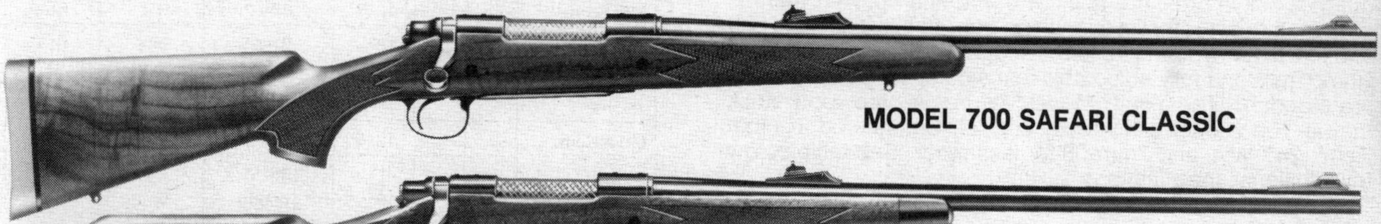

MODEL 700 SAFARI CLASSIC

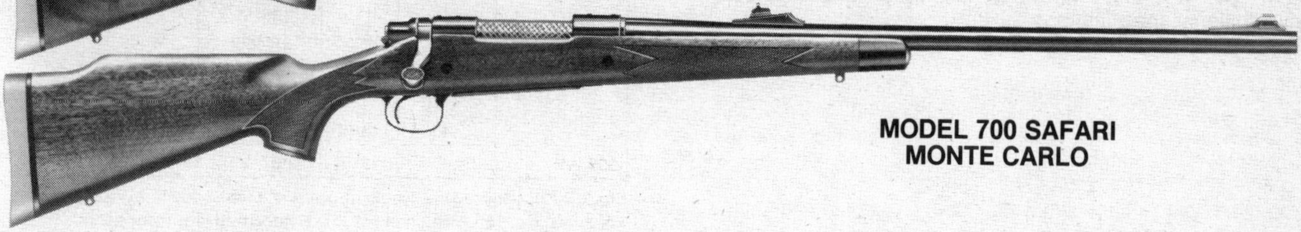

MODEL 700 SAFARI MONTE CARLO

SPECIFICATIONS MODEL 700 (Cont. from preceding page)

Calibers	Magazine Capacity	Barrel Length	Overall Length/Avg. Wt. (lbs.): Mtn. Rifle	Mtn Rifle SS	Limited Classic	Camo Synthetic	BDL Stainless Synthetic	ADL & BDL	BDL European	Varmint Special: Wood	Varmint Special: Synthetic	Twist R-H, 1 turn in
308 Win.	4	22″	41 5/8″/6 3/4	—	—	41 5/8″/6 3/4	—	41 5/8″/7 1/4	41 5/8″/7 1/4	—	—	10″
	4	24″	—	—	—	—	43 5/8″/6 7/8	—	—	43 1/2″/9	43 1/2″/8 1/2	12″
	4	22″	—	—	—	—	—	41 5/8″/7 1/4	—	—	—	10″
300 Win. Mag.[2]	3	24″	—	—	—	—	44 1/2″/7	44 1/2″/7	—	—	—	10″
300 Wby. Mag.[2]	3	24″	—	—	—	44 1/2″/7	44 1/2″/7	—	—	—	—	12″
35 Whelen[2]	4	22″	—	—	—	—	—	42 1/2″/7	—	—	—	16″
338 Win. Mag.[2]	3	24″	—	—	—	—	44 1/2″/7	44 1/2″/7 1/2	—	—	—	10″
	3	24″	—	—	—	—	—	44 1/2″/7 1/2	—	—	—	10″
Stock Dimensions	Length of Pull	13 3/8″	13 3/8″	13 3/8″	13 3/8″	13 3/8″	13 3/8″	13 3/8″	13 1/2″	13 3/8″		
	Drop at Comb (from centerline of bore)		3/8″	3/8″	3/8″	11/16″	1/2″	1/2″	1/2″	15/16″	5/8″	
	Drop at Heel (from centerline of bore)		3/8″	3/8″	3/4″	15/16″	3/8″	1 3/8″	1 3/8″	13/16″	5/8″	

REMINGTON BOLT ACTION RIFLES

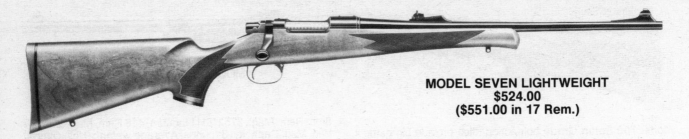

MODEL SEVEN LIGHTWEIGHT
$524.00
($551.00 in 17 Rem.)

MODEL SEVEN RIFLES

Every **Model Seven** is built to the accuracy standards of the famous Model 700 and is individually test fired to prove it. Its tapered 18 1/2″ Remington special steel barrel is free-floating out to a single pressure point at the forend tip. And there is ordnance-quality steel in everything from its fully enclosed bolt and extractor system to its steel trigger guard and floor plate. Ramp front and fully adjustable rear sights, sling swivel studs are standard. The Youth Model features a hardwood stock that is 1 inch shorter for easy control. Chambered in 6mm Rem., 243 Win. and 7mm-08 for less recoil. See table below for additional specifications.

SPECIFICATIONS MODEL SEVEN™

Calibers	Clip Mag. Capacity	Barrel Length	Overall Length	Twist R-H 1 turn in	Avg. Wt. (lbs.)
17 Rem.	5	18 1/2″	37 3/4″	9″	6
223 Rem.	5	18 1/2″	37 3/4″	12″	6 1/4
243 Win.	4	18 1/2″	37 3/4″	9 1/8″	6 1/4
	4	18 1/2″	36 3/4″ (Youth)	9 1/8″	6
6mm Rem.	4	18 1/2″	37 3/4″	9 1/8″	6 1/4
	4	18 1/2″	36 3/4″ (Youth)	9 1/8″	6
7mm-08 Rem.	4	18 1/2″	37 3/4″	9 1/4″	6 1/4
	4	18 1/2″	36 3/4″ (Youth)	9 1/4″	6
308 Win.	4	18 1/2″	37 3/4″	10″	6 1/4

Stock Dimensions: 13 3/16″ length of pull, 9/16″ drop at comb, 5/16″ drop at heel. Youth gun has 12 1/2″ length of pull. 17. Rem. provided without sights.

Note: New Model Seven Mannlicher and Model Seven KS versions are available from the Remington Custom Shop through your local dealer.

MODEL SEVEN YOUTH
$425.00

REMINGTON REPEATING RIFLES

MODEL 7400 (High Gloss Stock)
$503.00

Calibers: 243 Win., 270 Win., 280 Rem., 30-06, 308 Win., 35 Whelen and 30-06 Carbine (see below)
Capacity: 5 centerfire cartridges (4 in the magazine, 1 in the chamber); extra 4-shot magazine available
Action: Gas-operated; receiver drilled and tapped for scope mounts
Barrel length: 22″
Weight: 7¹/₂ lbs.
Overall length: 42″

Sights: Standard blade ramp front; sliding ramp rear
Stock: Satin or high-gloss (270 Win. and 30-06 only) walnut stock and forend; curved pistol grip; also available with Special Purpose non-reflective finish (270 Win. and 30-06 only)
Length of pull: 13³/₈″
Drop at heel: 2¹/₄″
Drop at comb: 1¹³/₁₆″

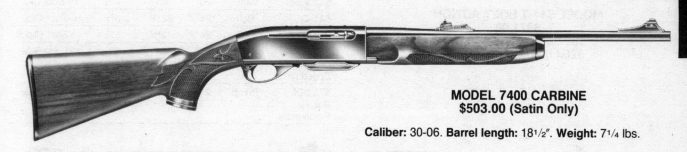

MODEL 7400 CARBINE
$503.00 (Satin Only)

Caliber: 30-06. **Barrel length:** 18¹/₂″. **Weight:** 7¹/₄ lbs.

MODEL 7600 (High Gloss Stock)
$480.00

Calibers: 243 Win., 270 Win., 280 Rem., 30-06, 308 Win., 35 Whelen, and 30-06 Carbine
Capacity: 5-shot capacity in all six calibers (4 in the removable magazine, 1 in the chamber)
Action: Pump action
Barrel length: 22″ (18¹/₂″ in 30-06 Carbine)
Overall length: 42″ (39¹/₈″ in 30-06 Carbine)
Weight: 7¹/₂ lbs. (7¹/₄ lbs. in 30-06 Carbine)
Sights: Standard blade ramp front sight; sliding ramp rear, both removable

Stock: Satin or high-gloss walnut; also available with Special Purpose non-reflective finish
Length of pull: 13³/₈″
Drop at heel: ¹⁵/₁₆″
Drop at comb: ⁹/₁₆″
Also available:
MODEL 7600 CARBINE with 18¹/₂″ barrel; chambered for 30-06 cartridge. **Price:** $480.00

REMINGTON RIMFIRE RIFLES

MODEL 522 VIPER (22 LR)
$159.00

Remington's new autoloading rimfire rifle utilizes a strong lightweight stock of PET resin that is impervious to changing temperatures and humidity. The receiver is made of a Du Pont high-tech synthetic. All exposed metal work, including barrel, breech bolt and trigger guard, have a non-glare, black matte finish. Stock shape is proportioned to fit the size and stature of younger or smaller shooters. The rifle's slim pistol grip accommodates all hands and the semi-beavertail forend provides a broad hand rest for youngsters. Other features include: factory-installed centerfire-type iron sights, detachable clip magazine, safety features, primary and secondary sears in trigger mechanism, and a protective ejection port shield.

MODEL 541-T BOLT ACTION
$371.00
$397.00 (Heavy Barrel)
$204.00 (Model 581-S)

RIMFIRE RIFLE SPECIFICATIONS

Model	Action	Barrel Length	Overall Length	Average Wt. (lbs.)	Magazine Capacity
522 Viper	Auto	20"	40"	4⅝	10-Shot Clip
541-T	Bolt	24"	42½"	5⅞	5-Shot Clip
581-S	Bolt	24"	42½"	5⅞	5-Shot Clip
552 BDL Deluxe Speedmaster	Auto	21"	40"	5¾	15 Long Rifle
572 BDL Deluxe Fieldmaster	Pump	21"	40"	5½	15 Long Rifle

MODEL 552 BDL DELUXE SPEEDMASTER
$256.00

A deluxe model with dependable mechanical features on the inside, plus special design and appearance extras on the outside. The 552 BDL rimfire semiautomatic rifle sports Remington custom-impressed checkering on both stock and forend. Tough Du Pont RK-W lifetime finish brings out the lustrous beauty of the walnut while protecting it. Sights are ramp-style in front and rugged big-game type fully adjustable in rear.

MODEL 572 BDL DELUXE FIELDMASTER
$269.00

Features of this rifle with big-game feel and appearance are: Du Pont's tough RK-W finish; centerfire-rifle-type rear sight fully adjustable for both vertical and horizontal sight alignment; big-game style ramp front sight; Remington impressed checkering on both stock and forend.

REMINGTON TARGET RIFLES

MODEL 40-XR KS
Rimfire Position Rifle
$1265.00 (w/Kevlar Stock)

Stock designed with deep forend for more comfortable shooting in all positions. Butt plate vertically adjustable. Exclusive loading platform provides straight line feeding with no shaved bullets. Crisp, wide, adjustable match trigger. Meets all International Shooting Union standard rifle specifications.

Action: Bolt action, single shot
Caliber: 22 Long Rifle rimfire
Capacity: Single loading
Sights: Optional at extra cost. Williams Receiver No. FPTK and Redfield Globe front match sight
Safety: Positive serrated thumb safety

Receiver: Drilled and tapped for receiver sight
Barrel: 24″ medium weight target barrel countersunk at muzzle. Drilled and tapped for target scope blocks. Fitted with front sight base
Bolt: Artillery style with lock-up at rear. 6 locking lugs, double extractors
Trigger: Adjustable from 2 to 4 lbs.
Overall length: 43½″
Average weight: 10½ lbs.
Stock: Position style with Monte Carlo, cheekpiece and thumb groove; five-way adjustable butt plate and full-length guide rail

MODEL 40-XC KS
National Match Course Rifle
$1345.00 (w/Kevlar Stock)

Chambered solely for the 7.62mm NATO cartridge, this match rifle was designed to meet the needs of competitive shooters firing the national match courses. Position-style stock, five-shot repeater with top-loading magazine, anti-bind bolt and receiver and in the bright stainless steel barrel. Meets all International Shooting Union Army Rifle specifications.

Action: Bolt action, single shot
Caliber: 7.62mm NATO
Capacity: Single loading
Barrel: 24″ heavy barrel
Overall length: 43½″

Average weight: 11 lbs.
Bolt: Heavy, oversized locking lugs and double extractors
Trigger: Adjustable from 1½ to 3 lbs.
Safety: Positive thumb safety
Sights: Optional at extra cost. Williams Receiver No. FPTK and Redfield Globe front match sight
Receiver: Drilled and tapped for receiver sight or target scope blocks
Stock: Position style with front swivel block on forend guide rail
Length of pull: 13½″

REMINGTON TARGET RIFLES

MODEL 40-XB "RANGEMASTER"
Centerfire Rifle
$1109.00   ($1171.00 Left Hand)

Barrels, in either standard or heavy weight, are unblued steel. Comb-grooved for easy bolt removal. Mershon White Line non-slip rubber butt plate supplied.

Action: Bolt—single shot in either standard or heavy barrel versions; repeater in heavy barrel only; receiver bedded to stock; barrel is free floating
Calibers: Single-shot, 220 Swift, 222 Rem., 223 Rem., 22-250 Rem., 6mm Rem., 222 Rem. Mag., 243 Win., 7.62mm NATO (308 Win.), 30-06, 30-338, 300 Win. Mag., 25-06 Rem., 6mm BR Rem., 7mm Rem. Mag., 7mm BR Rem.
Sights: No sights supplied; target scope blocks installed

Safety: Positive thumb operated
Receiver: Drilled and tapped for scope block and receiver sights
Barrel: Drilled and tapped for scope block and front target iron sight; muzzle diameter S2—approx. 3/4″, H2—approx. 7/8″; unblued stainless steel only, 27 1/4″ long
Trigger: Adjustable from 1 1/2 to 3 lbs. pull; special 2-oz. trigger available at extra cost; single shot models only
Stock: American walnut; adjustable front swivel block on rail; rubber non-slip butt plate
Overall length: Approx. 47″
Average weight: 10 1/2 to 11 1/4 lbs.

MODEL 40-XB KS (Kevlar® Stock)
$1265.00   ($1327.00 Left Hand)

Calibers: Same as above
Capacity: Single shot or 5-round repeater
Barrel length: 27 1/4″
Overall length: 47″
Weight: 10 1/4 lbs
Sights: Barrel drilled and tapped
Stock: Kevlar reinforced synthetic, matte black

MODEL 40-XBBR KS (Kevlar® stock)
BENCH REST CENTERFIRE RIFLE
$1345.00

Built with all the features of the extremely accurate Model 40-XB but modified to give the competitive bench rest shooter a standardized rifle that provides the inherent accuracy advantages of a short, heavy, extremely stiff barrel. Wider, squared off forend gives a more stable rest on sandbags or other supports and meets weight limitations for the sporter and light-varmint classes of National Bench Rest Shooters Association competition.

Action: Bolt, single shot only
Calibers: 222 Rem., 222 Rem. Mag., 22 Bench Rest Rem., 7.62 NATO (308 Win.), 6mm Bench Rest Rem., 223 Rem., 6×47
Barrel: 20″ and 24″; unblued stainless steel only
Overall length: 38″ to 42″
Average weight: 10 1/2 to 13 1/2 lbs.
Sights: Supplied with target scope blocks
Receiver: Drilled and tapped for target scope blocks
Safety: Positive thumb operated
Trigger: Adjustable from 1 1/2 to 3 1/2 lbs.; special 2-oz. trigger available at extra cost
Stock: Kevlar®; 12″ or 13″ length of pull

ROSSI RIFLES

PUMP-ACTION GALLERY GUNS

MODEL M62 SAC
$227.00   ($245.00 Nickel)

SPECIFICATIONS
Caliber: 22 LR
Capacity: 12 rounds
Barrel length: 16½"
Overall length: 32¾"
Weight: 4¼"
Finish: Blue

MODEL M62 SA
$227.00   ($245.00 Nickel)

SPECIFICATIONS
Caliber: 22 LR
Capacity: 13 rounds
Barrel length: 23"
Overall length: 39¼"
Weight: 5½" lbs.
Finish: Blue
Model M62 SA w/Octagonal barrel $253.00
Model 59 22 Magnum 280.00

PUMA LEVER-ACTION CARBINES

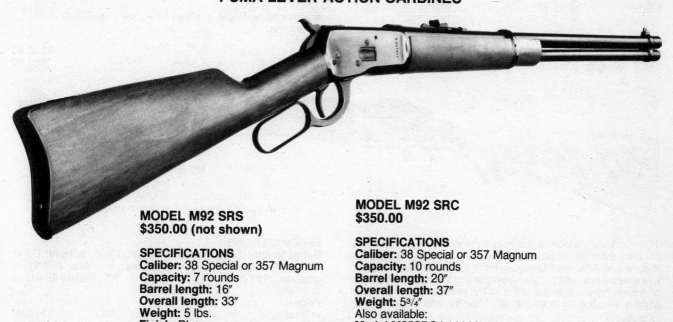

MODEL M92 SRS
$350.00 (not shown)

SPECIFICATIONS
Caliber: 38 Special or 357 Magnum
Capacity: 7 rounds
Barrel length: 16"
Overall length: 33"
Weight: 5 lbs.
Finish: Blue

MODEL M92 SRC
$350.00

SPECIFICATIONS
Caliber: 38 Special or 357 Magnum
Capacity: 10 rounds
Barrel length: 20"
Overall length: 37"
Weight: 5¾"
Also available:
Model M65SRC in 44 Magnum $367.00

RUGER CARBINES

RUGER MINI-14

Mechanism: Gas-operated, semiautomatic. **Materials:** Heat-treated chrome molybdenum and other alloy steels as well as music wire coil springs are used throughout the mechanism to ensure reliability under field-operating conditions. **Safety:** The safety blocks both the hammer and sear. The slide can be cycled when the safety is on. The safety is mounted in the front of the trigger guard so that it may be set to Fire position without removing finger from trigger guard. **Firing pin:** The firing pin is retracted mechanically during the first part of the unlocking of the bolt. The rifle can only be fired when the bolt is safely locked. **Stock:** One-piece American hardwood reinforced with steel liner at stressed areas. Sling swivels standard. Handguard and forearm separated by air space from barrel to promote cooling under rapid-fire conditions. **Field stripping:**

The Carbine can be field-stripped to its eight (8) basic sub-assemblies in a matter of seconds and without use of special tools.

MINI-14 SPECIFICATIONS
Caliber: 223 (5.56mm). **Barrel length:** 18½″. **Overall length:** 37¼″. **Weight:** 6 lbs. 8 oz. **Magazine:** 5-round, detachable box magazine. **Sights:** Rear adjustable for windage and elevation.

Prices:
Mini-14/5 Blued $491.50
K-Mini-14/5 Stainless Steel 542.00
(Scopes rings not included)

MINI-14 RANCH RIFLE

SPECIFICATIONS
Caliber: 223 (5.56mm). **Barrel length:** 18½″. **Overall length:** 37¼″. **Weight:** 6 lbs. 8 oz. **Magazine:** 5-round detachable

box magazine. Receiver milled for scope rings (included). Buffer in receiver.
Prices:
Mini-14/5R Blued $530.00
K-Mini-14/5R Stainless Steel 580.00

MINI THIRTY

This modified version of the Ruger Ranch rifle is chambered for the 7.62 × 39mm Soviet service cartridge (used in the SKS carbine and AKM rifle). Designed for use with telescopic sights, it features a low, compact scope mounting for greater accuracy and carrying ease, and a buffer in the receiver. A metal peep sight is installed for emergencies. Sling swivels are standard.

SPECIFICATIONS
Barrel length: 18½″. **Overall length:** 37⅛″. **Weight:** 6 lbs. 14 oz. (empty). **Magazine capacity:** 5 shots. **Rifling:** 6 grooves, right-hand twist, one turn in 10″. **Finish:** Blued or stainless.
Prices:
In Blue $530.00
In Stainless steel 580.00

RUGER CARBINES

STANDARD 10/22 CARBINE

DELUXE 10/22 SPORTER

MODEL K10/22 RB STAINLESS CARBINE

MODEL 10/22 CARBINE
22 LONG RIFLE CALIBER

Construction of the 10/22 Carbine is rugged and follows the Ruger design practice of building a firearm from integrated sub-assemblies. For example, the trigger housing assembly contains the entire ignition system, which employs a high-speed, swinging hammer to ensure the shortest possible lock time. The barrel is assembled to the receiver by a unique dual-screw dovetail system that provides unusual rigidity and strength—and accounts, in part, for the exceptional accuracy of the 10/22.

SPECIFICATIONS
Mechanism: Blow-back, semiautomatic. **Caliber:** 22 Long Rifle, high-speed or standard-velocity loads. **Barrel:** 18¹/₂″ long; barrel is assembled to the receiver by unique dual-screw dovetail mounting for added strength and rigidity. **Weight:** 5 lbs. **Overall length:** 37¹/₄″. **Sights:** ¹/₁₆″ brass bead front sight;

single folding leaf rear sight, adjustable for elevation; receiver drilled and tapped for scope blocks or tip-off mount adapter (included).
Magazine: 10-shot capacity, exclusive Ruger rotary design; fits flush into stock. **Trigger:** Curved finger surface, ³/₈″ wide. **Safety:** Sliding cross-button type; safety locks both sear and hammer and cannot be put in safe position unless gun is cocked. **Stocks:** 10/22 RB is birch; 10/22 SP Deluxe Sporter is American walnut. **Finish:** Polished all over and blued or anodized or brushed satin bright metal.

Model 10/22 RB Standard (Birch stock) **$201.50**
Model 10/22 DSP Deluxe (Hand-checkered
   American walnut) **254.50**
Model K10/22 RB Stainless **236.00**

RUGER SINGLE-SHOT RIFLES

The following illustrations show the variations currently offered in the Ruger No. 1 Single-Shot Rifle Series. Ruger No. 1 rifles have a Farquharson-type falling-block action and selected American walnut stocks. Pistol grip and forearm are hand-checkered to a borderless design. Price for any listed model is **$634.00** (except the No. 1 RSI International Model: **$656.00**). Barreled Actions (blued only): **$429.50**.

NO. 1A LIGHT SPORTER

Calibers: 243 Win., 270 Win., 30-06, 7×57mm. **Barrel length:** 22″. **Sights:** Adjustable folding-leaf rear sight mounted on quarter rib with ramp front sight base and dovetail-type gold bead front sight; open. **Weight:** 7¼ lbs.

NO. 1S MEDIUM SPORTER

Calibers: 218 Bee, 7mm Rem. Mag., 300 Win. Mag., 338 Win. Mag., 45-70. **Barrel length:** 26″ (22″ in 45-70). **Sights:** (same as above). **Weight:** 8 lbs. (7¼ lbs. in 45-70).

NO. 1B STANDARD RIFLE

Calibers: 218 Bee, 22 Hornet, 22-250, 220 Swift, 223, 243 Win., 6mm Rem., 25-06, 257 Roberts, 270 Win., 270 Wby. Mag., 7mm Rem. Mag., 280, 30-06, 300 Win. Mag., 300 Wby. Mag., 338 Win. Mag. **Barrel:** 26″. **Sights:** Ruger 1″ steel tip-off scope rings. **Weight:** 8 lbs.

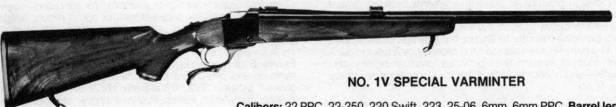

NO. 1V SPECIAL VARMINTER

Calibers: 22 PPC, 22-250, 220 Swift, 223, 25-06, 6mm, 6mm PPC. **Barrel length:** 24″ (26″ in 220 Swift). **Sights:** Ruger target scope blocks, heavy barrel and 1″ tip-off scope rings. **Weight:** 9 lbs.

See following page for additional Single-Shot models

RUGER RIFLES

NO. 1H TROPICAL RIFLE

Calibers: 375 H&H Mag., 404 Jeffery, 458 Win. Mag., 416 Rigby, 416 Rem. Mag. **Barrel length:** 24″ (heavy). **Sights:** Adjustable folding-leaf rear sight mounted on quarter rib with ramp front sight base and dovetail-type gold bead front sight; open. **Weight:** 8¼ lbs. for 375; 9 lbs. for 458. **Price:** **$634.00**

NO. 1RSI INTERNATIONAL
With Mannlicher Style Forearm

Calibers: 243 Win., 270 Win., 30-06 and 7×57mm. **Barrel length:** 20″ (lightweight). **Overall length:** 36½″. **Weight:** 7¼ lbs. **Sights:** Adjustable folding leaf rear sight mounted on quarter rib with ramp front sight base and dovetail-type gold bead front sight. **Price:** **$656.00**

BOLT ACTION RIFLES

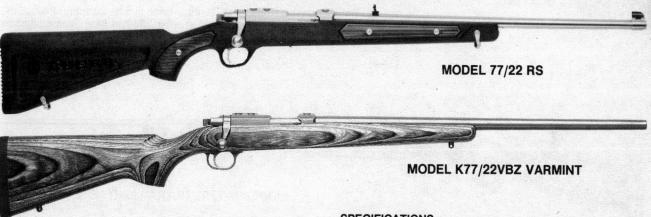

MODEL 77/22 RS

MODEL K77/22VBZ VARMINT

MODEL 77/22 RIMFIRE RIFLE

The Ruger 22-caliber rimfire 77/22 bolt-action rifle has been built especially to function with the patented Ruger 10-Shot Rotary Magazine concept. The magazine throat, retaining lips, and ramps that guide the cartridge into the chamber are solid alloy steel that resists bending or deforming.

The 77/22 weighs just under six pounds. Its heavy-duty receiver incorporates the integral scope bases of the patented Ruger Scope Mounting System, with 1-inch Ruger scope rings. With the 3-position safety in its "lock" position, a dead bolt is cammed forward, locking the bolt handle down. In this position the action is locked closed and the handle cannot be raised.

All metal surfaces are finished in non-glare deep blue or satin stainless. Stock is select straight-grain American walnut, hand checkered and finished with durable polyurethane.

An All-Weather, all-stainless steel **MODEL K77/22RS** features a stock made of glass-fiber reinforced Zytel. **Weight:** Approx. 6 lbs.

SPECIFICATIONS
Calibers: 22 LR and 22 Magnum. **Barrel length:** 20″. **Overall length:** 39¼″. **Weight:** 5 lbs. 14 oz. (w/o scope, magazine empty). **Feed:** Detachable 10-Shot Ruger Rotary Magazine.
Prices:

77/22R Blue, w/o sights, 1″ Ruger rings	**$402.00**
77/22RM Blue, walnut stock, plain barrel, no sights, 1″ Ruger rings, 22 Mag. ...	**402.00**
77/22RS Blue, sights included, 1″ Ruger rings	**424.00**
77/22RSM Blue, American walnut, iron sights	**424.00**
K77/22-RP Synthetic stock, stainless steel, plain barrel with 1″ Ruger rings	**397.00**
K77/22-RMP Synthetic stock, stainless steel, plain barrel, 1″ Ruger rings	**419.00**
K77/22-RSP Synthetic stock, stainless steel, gold bead front sight, folding-leaf rear, Ruger 1″ rings	**419.00**
K77/22RSMP Synthetic stock, metal sights, stainless	**445.20**
K77/22VBZ Varmint Laminated stock, scope rings, heavy barrel, stainless	**485.00**

RUGER BOLT ACTION RIFLES

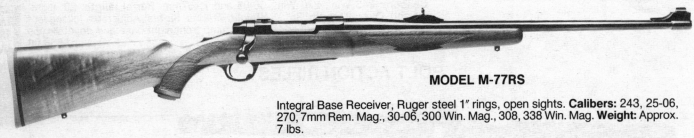

MODEL M-77R

Integral Base Receiver, 1" scope rings. No sights. **Calibers:** (Long action) 6mm Rem., 6.5×55mm, 7×57mm, 257 Roberts, 270, 280 Rem., 30-06 (all with 22" barrels); 25-06, 7mm Rem. Mag., 300 Win. Mag., 338 Win. Mag. (all with 24" barrels); and (Short Stroke action) 22-250, 223, 243, 308 (22" barrels). **Weight:** Approx. 7 lbs.

Price: **$558.00**
Also available:
M-77LRMKII LEFT HAND. Calibers 270, 30-06, 7mm Rem. Mag., 300 Mag. **558.00**

MODEL M-77RS

Integral Base Receiver, Ruger steel 1" rings, open sights. **Calibers:** 243, 25-06, 270, 7mm Rem. Mag., 30-06, 300 Win. Mag., 308, 338 Win. Mag. **Weight:** Approx. 7 lbs.

Price: **$617.00**

MODEL M-77RL ULTRA LIGHT

This big-game, bolt-action rifle encompasses the traditional features that have made the Ruger M-77 one of the most popular centerfire rifles in the world. It includes a sliding top tang safety, a one-piece bolt with Mauser-type extractor and diagonal front mounting system. American walnut stock is hand-checkered in a sharp diamond pattern. A rubber recoil pad, pistol-grip cap and studs for mounting quick detachable sling swivels are standard. Available in both long- and short-action versions, with Integral Base Receiver and 1" Ruger scope rings. **Calibers:** 223, 243, 257, 270, 30-06, 308. **Barrel length:** 20". **Weight:** Approx. 6 lbs.

Price: **$592.50**

RUGER BOLT ACTION RIFLES

MODEL M-77RSI INTERNATIONAL MANNLICHER

Mannlicher-type stock, Integral Base Receiver, open sights, Ruger 1″ steel rings.
Calibers: 243, 270, 30-06, 308. **Barrel length:** 18¹/₂″. **Weight:** Approx. 6 lbs.

Price **$623.50**

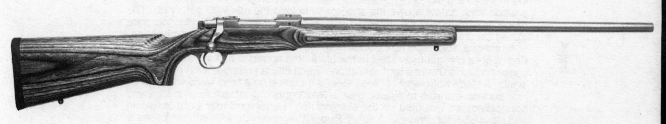

MODEL M-77 MARK II HEAVY BARREL TARGET

Features Mark II stainless steel bolt action, gray matte finish, two-stage adjustable
trigger. No sights. **Calibers:** 22-250, 220 Swift, 223, 243, 25-06 and 308. **Barrel
length:** 26″, hammer-forged, free-floating stainless steel. **Weight:** 9³/₄ lbs. **Stock:**
Laminated American hardwood with flat forend.

Price: KM77VTMKII **$665.00**

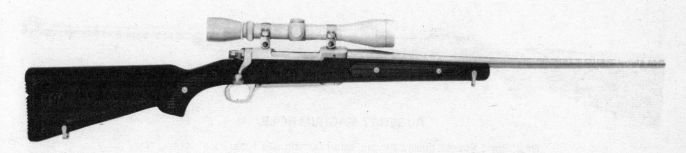

M-77 MARK II ALL-WEATHER

KM-77RPMKII ALL-WEATHER Receiver w/integral dovetails to
 accommodate Ruger 1″ rings, no sights, stainless steel, synthetic
 stock. **Calibers:** 223, 243, 270, 280, 30-06, 7mm Rem.
 Mag., 300 Win. Mag., 308, 338 Win. Mag. **$558.00**
KM-77RSPMKII ALL-WEATHER Receiver w/integral dovetails to
 accommodate Ruger 1″ rings, metal sights, stainless steel, synthetic
 stock. **Calibers:** 243, 270, 7mm Rem. Mag., 30-06,
 300 Win. Mag., 358 Win. Mag. **558.00**

RUGER BOLT ACTION RIFLES

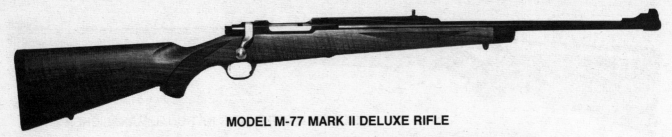

MODEL M-77 MARK II DELUXE RIFLE

For shooters who prefer a sporting rifle of premium quality and price, Ruger offers the M-77 Mark II Deluxe rifle. Its stock is precision machined from a single blank of medium quality walnut. Forend and pistol grip are hand-checkered in a diamond pattern with 18 lines per inch. Pistol grip cap, trigger guard and floorplate are blued steel. A black buttpad of live rubber, black forend cap and steel studs for quick detachable sling swivels are standard.

Action is standard short or long length in blued chrome-moly steel with stainless steel bolt. A fixed blade-type ejector working through a slot under the left locking lug replaces the plunger-type ejector used in the earlier M-77 models. A three-position wing safety allows the shooter to unload the rifle with safety on. The trigger guard houses the patented floorplate latch, which holds the floorplate closed securely to prevent accidental dumping of cartridges into the magazine.

An integral, solid sight rib extends from the front of the receiver ring. Machined from a solid chrome-moly steel barrel blank, the rib has cross serrations on the upper surface to reduce light reflections. Each rifle is equipped with open metal sights. A blade front sight of blued steel is mounted on a steel ramp with curved rear surface serrated to reduce glare. Rear sights (adjustable for windage and non-folding) are mounted on the sighting rib. The forward rear sight is folding and adjustable for windage. A set of Ruger 1″ scope rings with integral bases is standard.

Calibers: 270, 30-06, 7mm Rem. Mag., 300 Win. Mag., 338 Win. Mag. **Barrel lengths:** 22″ and 24″ (depending on caliber). **Capacity:** 4 rounds. **Overall length:** 42 1/8″ (approx.). **Weight:** 7 3/4 lbs. (avg., loaded); 7 1/2 lbs. (unloaded). **Length of pull:** 13 1/2″.

Price: $1550.00

RUGER 77 MAGNUM RIFLE

This "Bond Street" quality African safari hunting rifle features a sighting rib machined from a single bar of steel; Circassian walnut stock with black forend tip; steel floorplate and latch; a new Ruger Magnum trigger guard with floorplate latch designed flush with the contours of the trigger guard (to eliminate accidental dumping of cartridges); a three-position safety mechanism (see illustrations); Express rear sight; and front sight ramp with gold bead sight.

Calibers: 375 H&H, 404 Jeffery, 416 Rigby and 458 Win. Mag. **Capacity:** 4 rounds (375 H&H, 404 Jeffery) and 3 rounds (416 Rigby, 458 Win. Mag.). **Barrel thread diameter:** 1 1/8″. **Weight:** 9 1/4 lbs. (375 H&H, 404 Jeffery); 10 1/4 lbs. (416 Rigby and 458 Win. Mag.).

Price: $1550.00

RUKO-ARMSCOR RIFLES

MODEL M14P
$119.00

SPECIFICATIONS
Type: Bolt action
Caliber: 22 LR
Capacity: 10 rounds
Barrel length: 23″
Overall length: 41½″

Weight: 7 lbs.
Trigger pull: 14″
Stock: Mahogany
Finish: Blued
Also available:
MODEL M14D Bolt Action Deluxe **$129.00**

MODEL M1500
$189.00

SPECIFICATIONS
Type: Bolt action deluxe
Caliber: 22 Win. Mag.
Capacity: 5 rounds
Barrel length: 21½″

Overall length: 41¼″
Weight: 6.8 lbs.
Trigger pull: 14″
Stock: Mahogany
Finish: Blued

MODEL M20P
$119.00

SPECIFICATIONS
Type: Semiautomatic
Caliber: 22 LR
Capacity: 15 or 30 rounds
Barrel length: 21″
Overall length: 39¾″

Weight: 6½ lbs.
Trigger pull: 13″
Stock: Mahogany
Finish: Blued
Also available:
MODEL M2000 with deluxe stock **$129.00**
MODEL M20C (16½″ barrel; 5¼″ lbs.) **149.00**

SAKO RIFLES

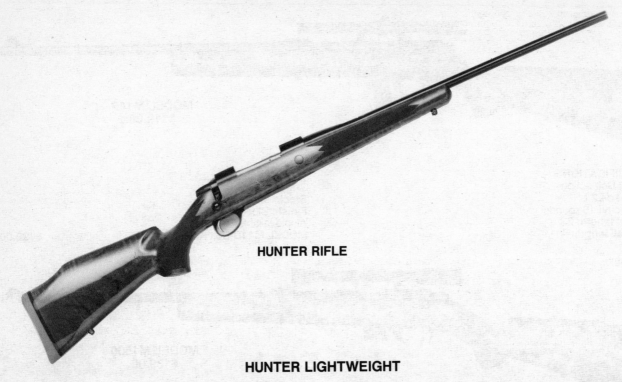

HUNTER RIFLE

HUNTER LIGHTWEIGHT

Here's one case of less being more. Sako has taken its famed bolt-action, centerfire rifle, redesigned the stock and trimmed the barrel contour. In fact, in any of the short action (A1) calibers—17 Rem., 222 or 223 Rem.—the Hunter weighs in at less than 7 pounds, making it one of the lightest wood stock production rifles in the world.

The same cosmetic upgrading and weight reduction have been applied to the entire Hunter line in all calibers and action lengths, standard and magnum. All the precision, quality and accuracy for which this Finnish rifle has been so justly famous are still here. Now it just weighs less.

The Sako trigger is a rifleman's delight—smooth, crisp and fully adjustable. If these were the only Sako features, it would still be the best rifle available. But the real quality that sets Sako apart from all others is its truly outstanding accuracy.

While many factors can affect a rifle's accuracy, 90 percent of any rifle's accuracy potential lies in its barrel. And the creation of superbly accurate barrels is where Sako excels.

The care that Sako takes in the cold-hammering processing of each barrel is unparalleled in the industry. As an example, after each barrel blank is drilled, it is diamond-lapped and then optically checked for microscopic flaws. This extra care affords the Sako owner lasting accuracy and a finish that will stay "new" season after season.

You can't buy an unfired Sako. Every gun is test fired using special overloaded proof cartridges. This ensures the Sako owner total safety and uncompromising ac-curacy. Every barrel must group within Sako specifications or it's scrapped. Not recycled. Not adjusted. Scrapped. Either a Sako barrel delivers Sako accuracy, or it never leaves the factory.

And hand-in-hand with Sako accuracy is Sako beauty. Genuine European walnut stocks, flawlessly finished and checkered by hand.

Available with a matte lacquer finish.

Prices:
Short Action (AI)
In 17 Rem., 222 Rem., 223 Rem. . . . . **$ 975.00**
Medium Action (AII)
In 22-250 Rem., 7mm-08, 243 Win. &
  308 Win. **975.00**
Long Action (AV)
In 25-06 Rem., 270 Win., 280 Rem., 30-06 . . . . . **1000.00**
In 7mm Rem. Mag., 300 Win. Mag.,
  338 Win. Mag. **1020.00**
In 300 Wby. Mag., 375 H&H Mag.,
  416 Rem. Mag. **1035.00**

LEFT-HANDED MODELS (Matte Lacquer Finish)
Medium Action (AII)
In 22-250 Rem., 7mm-08, 243 Win. &
  308 Win. **$1055.00**
Long Action (AV)
In 25-06 Rem., 270 Win., 280 Rem., 30-06 . . . . . **1085.00**
In 7mm Rem. Mag., 300 Win. Mag.,
  338 Win. Mag. **1100.00**
In 375 H&H Mag., 416 Rem. Mag. **1115.00**

SAKO RIFLES

DELUXE

All the fine-touch features you expect of the deluxe grade Sako are here—beautifully grained French walnut, superbly done high-gloss finish, hand-cut checkering, deep rich bluing and rosewood forend tip and grip cap. And of course the accuracy, reliability and superior field performance for which Sako is so justly famous are still here too. It's all here—it just weighs less than it used to. Think of it as more for less.

In addition, the scope mounting system on these Sakos is among the strongest in the world. Instead of using separate bases, a tapered dovetail is milled right into the receiver, to which the scope rings are mounted. A beautiful system that's been proven by over 20 years of use. Sako Original Scope Mounts and Sako scope rings are available in *low, medium,* and *high* in one-inch and 30mm.

Prices:
Short Action (AI)
In 17 Rem., 222 Rem. & 223 Rem. **$1325.00**
Medium Action (AII)
In 22-250 Rem., 243 Win., 7mm-08
   and 308 Win. 1325.00
Long Action (AV)
In 25-06 Rem., 270 Win., 280 Rem., 30-06 . . . . . 1365.00
In 7mm Rem. Mag., 300 Win. Mag. &
   338 Win. Mag. 1380.00
In 300 Wby. Mag., 375 H&H Mag.,
   416 Rem. Mag. 1395.00

SAKO SUPER DELUXE $2790.00

Sako offers the Super Deluxe to the most discriminating gun buyer. This one-of-a-kind beauty is available on special order.

SAKO RIFLES

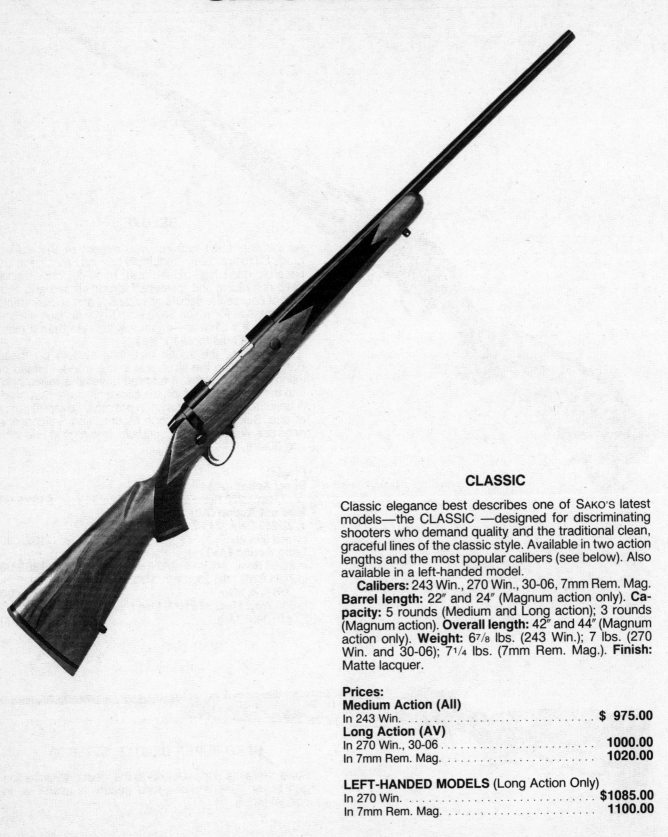

CLASSIC

Classic elegance best describes one of SAKO'S latest models—the CLASSIC —designed for discriminating shooters who demand quality and the traditional clean, graceful lines of the classic style. Available in two action lengths and the most popular calibers (see below). Also available in a left-handed model.

Calibers: 243 Win., 270 Win., 30-06, 7mm Rem. Mag. **Barrel length:** 22″ and 24″ (Magnum action only). **Capacity:** 5 rounds (Medium and Long action); 3 rounds (Magnum action). **Overall length:** 42″ and 44″ (Magnum action only). **Weight:** 6 7/8 lbs. (243 Win.); 7 lbs. (270 Win. and 30-06); 7 1/4 lbs. (7mm Rem. Mag.). **Finish:** Matte lacquer.

Prices:
Medium Action (All)
In 243 Win. . . . . $ 975.00
Long Action (AV)
In 270 Win., 30-06 . . . . 1000.00
In 7mm Rem. Mag. 1020.00

LEFT-HANDED MODELS (Long Action Only)
In 270 Win. $1085.00
In 7mm Rem. Mag. 1100.00

SAKO RIFLES

MODEL TRG-21
$3,850.00

SAKO, known for manufacturing the finest and most accurate production sporting rifles available today, presents the ultimate in sharpshooting systems: the **TRG-21 Target Rifle.** Designed for use when nothing less than total precision is demanded, this new SAKO rifle features a cold-hammer forged receiver, "resistance-free" bolt, stainless steel barrel and a fully adjustable polyurethane stock. Chambered in .308 Win. There is also a wide selection of optional accessories available. Designed, crafted and manufactured in Finland. For additional specifications, see the table on page 270.

• Cold-hammer forged receiver
• "Resistance-free" bolt
• Cold-hammer forged, stainless steel barrel
• Three massive locking lugs
• 60° bolt lift

• Free-floating barrel
• Detachable 10-round magazine
• Fully adjustable cheekpiece
• Infinitely adjustable buttplate
• Adjustable two-stage trigger pull
• Trigger adjustable for both length and pull
• Trigger also adjustable for horizontal or vertical pitch
• Safety lever inside the trigger guard
• Reinforced polyurethane stock

Optional features:
• Muzzle brake
• Quick-detachable one-piece scope mount base
• Available with 1" or 30mm rings
• Collapsible and removable bipod rest
• Quick-detachable sling swivels
• Wide military-type nylon sling

MODEL TRG-S
$730.00 ($765.00 in Magnum)

The new TRG-S has been crafted and designed around SAKO'S highly sophisticated and extremely accurate TRG-21 Target Rifle (above). The "resistance-free" bolt and precise balance of the TRG-S, plus its three massive locking lugs and short 60-degree bolt lift, are among the features that attract the shooter's attention. Also of critical importance is the cold-hammer forged receiver—

unparalleled for strength and durability. The detachable 5-round magazine fits securely into the polyurethane stock. The stock, in turn, is molded around a synthetic skeleton that provides additional support and maximum rigidity. For additional specifications, see the table on page 270.

SAKO CARBINE

SAKO MANNLICHER-STYLE CARBINE

Sako's Mannlicher-style Carbine combines the handiness and carrying qualities of the traditional, lever-action "deer rifle" with the power of modern, high-performance cartridges. An abbreviated 18¹/₂-inch barrel trims the overall length of the Carbine to just over 40 inches in the long (or AV) action calibers, and 38 inches in the medium (or AII) action calibers. Weight is a highly portable 7 and 6¹/₂ pounds, respectively (except in the 338 and 375 H&H calibers, which measures 7¹/₂ pounds).

As is appropriate for a rifle of this type, the Carbine is furnished with an excellent set of open sights; the rear is fully adjustable for windage, while the front is a nonglare serrated ramp with protective hood.

The Mannlicher Carbine is available in the traditional wood stock of European walnut done in a contemporary Monte Carlo style with hand-rubbed oil finish. Hand-finished checkering is standard. The Mannlicher-style full stock Carbine wears Sako's exclusive two-piece forearm, which joins beneath the barrel band and also features an oil finish. This independent forward section of the forearm eliminates the bedding problems normally associated with the full forestock. A blued steel muzzle cap puts the finishing touches on this European-styled Carbine.

Sako Mannlicher-Style Carbine Prices:
Medium Action
In 243 Win. and 308 Win. $1130.00
Long Action
In 270 Win. and 30-06 . . . . 1165.00
In 338 Win. Mag. 1180.00
In 375 H&H Mag. 1200.00

SAKO PPC BENCHREST/VARMINT RIFLE

Ever since Dr. Lou Palmisano and Farris Pindel introduced their custom-made PPC ammo in 1975, it has become widely recognized as the "world's most accurate cartridge," having broken well over 200 records since its debut. The impossible dream of making one-hole targets with five cartridges may never be realized, but PPC cartridges have come closer to that goal of perfection than anything in today's market.

Under an agreement with Dr. Palmisano, Sako has manufactured the PPC benchrest, heavy barrel, single-shot rifle in both 6 PPC and 22 PPC since late 1987; in 1988 they introduced factory-made ammo and brass.

SAKO PPC BENCHREST/VARMINT RIFLE
$1330.00

SPECIFICATIONS
Calibers: 22 PPC, 6 PPC
Action: A1-BR-PPC
Type: Single shot, bolt action
Barrel length: 23³/₄"
Weight: 8³/₄ lbs.
Finish: Oil-finished stock

SAKO RIFLES

**VARMINT
$1100.00**

The Sako Varmint is specifically designed with a prone-type stock for shooting from the ground or bench. The forend is extra wide to provide added steadiness when rested on sandbags or makeshift field rests.

Calibers: 17 Rem., 222 Rem. & 223 Rem. (Short Action); 22-250, 243 Win., 7mm-08 and 308 Win. (Medium Action). Also available in 6mm PPC and 22 PPC (single shot). **Price: $1330.00**

**SAFARI GRADE
$2625.00**

Crafted in the tradition of the classic British express rifles, Safari Grade is truly a professional's rifle. Every feature has been carefully thought out and executed with one goal in mind: performance. The magazine allows four belted magnums to be stored inside (instead of the usual three). The steel floorplate straddles the front of the trigger guard bow for added strength and security.

An express-style quarter rib provides a rigid, non-glare base for the rear sight, which consists of a fixed blade. The front swivel is carried by a contoured barrel band to keep the stud away from the off-hand under the recoil of big calibers. The front sight assembly is also a barrel-band type for maximum strength. The blade sits on a non-glare ramp and is protected by a steel hood.

The Safari's barreled action carries a subtle semi-matte blue, which lends an understated elegance to this eminently practical rifle. The functional, classic-style stock is of European walnut selected especially for its strength with respect to grain orientation as well as for color and figure. A rosewood forend tip, rosewood pistol grip cap with metal insert suitable for engraving, an elegant, beaded cheekpiece and presentation—style recoil pad complete the stock embellishments.

Calibers: 338 Win. Mag., 375 H&H Mag. and 416 Rem. Mag. See also **Specifications Table.**

SAKO RIFLES

LAMINATED STOCK MODELS

In response to the growing number of hunters and shooters who seek the strength and stability that a fiberglass stock provides, coupled with the warmth and feel of real wood, Sako features its Laminated Stock models.

Machined from blanks comprised of 36 individual layers of 1/16-inch hardwood veneers that are resin-bonded under extreme pressure, these stocks are virtually inert. Each layer of hardwood has been vacuum-impregnated with a permanent brown dye. The bisecting of various layers of veneers in the shaping of the stock results in a contour-line appearance similar to a piece of slab-sawed walnut. Because all Sako Laminated Stocks are of real wood, each one is unique, with its own shading, color and grain.

These stocks satisfy those whose sensibilities de-

mand a rifle of wood and steel, but who also want state-of-the-art performance and practicality. Sako's Laminated Stock provides both, further establishing it among the most progressive manufacturers of sporting rifles—and the *only* one to offer hunters and shooters their choice of walnut, fiberglass or laminated stocks in a wide range of calibers.

Laminated Stock Model Prices:
Medium Action
In 22-250, 243 Win., 308 Win. and 7mm-08 .... **$1110.00**
Long Action
In 25-06 Rem., 270 Win., 280 Rem. & 30-06 ... **1155.00**
In 7mm Rem. Mag., 300 Win. Mag. and
    338 Win. Mag. **1175.00**
In 375 H&H Mag., 416 Rem. Mag. **1185.00**

FIBERCLASS MODEL

In answer to the increased demand for Sako quality and accuracy in a true "all-weather" rifle, this fiberglass-stock version of the renowned Sako barreled action has been created. Long since proven on the bench rest circuit to be the most stable material for cradling a rifle, fiberglass is extremely strong, light in weight, and unaffected by changes in weather. Because fiberglass is inert, it does not absorb or expel moisture, hence it cannot swell, shrink or warp. It is impervious to the high humidity of equatorial jungles, the searing heat of arid deserts, or the rain and snow of the high mountains.

Not only is this rifle lighter than its wood counterpart, it appeals to the performance-oriented hunter who seeks results over appearance.

Prices:
Long Action (AV)
In 25-06 Rem., 270 Win., 280 Rem., 30-06 ..... **$1310.00**
In 7mm Rem. Mag., 300 Win. Mag. and
    338 Win. Mag. **1325.00**
In 375 H&H Mag., 416 Rem. Mag. **1340.00**

SAKO RIFLES

LEFT-HANDED MODELS

Sako's Left-Handed models are based on mirror images of the right-handed models enjoyed by Sako owners for many years; the handle, extractor and ejection port all are located on the port side. Naturally, the stock is also reversed, with the cheekpiece on the opposite side and the palm swell on the port side of the grip.

Otherwise, these guns are identical to the right-hand models. That means hammer-forged barrels, one-piece bolts with integral locking lugs and handles, integral scope mount rails, adjustable triggers and Mauser-type inertia ejectors.

Sako's Left-Handed rifles are available in all Long Action models, while the Hunter grade is available in both Medium and Long Action. The Hunter Grade carries a durable matte lacquer finish with generous-size panels of hand-cut checkering, a presentation-style recoil pad and sling swivel studs installed. The Deluxe model is distinguished by its rosewood forend tip and grip cap, its skip-line checkering and gloss lacquer finish atop a select-grade of highly figured European walnut. The metal work carries a deep, mirror-like blue that looks more like black chrome.

Prices:
Hunter Lightweight (Medium Action)
In 22-250 Rem. 243 Win., 308 Win., 7mm-08 . . . **$1055.00**
Hunter Lightweight (Long Action)
In 25-06, 270 Win., 280 Rem. & 30-06 . . . . **$1085.00**
In 7mm Rem. Mag., 300 Win. Mag. and
   338 Win. Mag. **1100.00**
In 375 H&H Mag., 416 Rem. Mag. **1115.00**

Deluxe (Long Action)
In 25-06, 270 Win. Mag., 280 Rem. & 30-06 . . . . **$1430.00**
In 7mm Rem. Mag., 300 Win. Mag. and
   338 Win. Mag. **1445.00**
In 375 H&H Mag., 416 Rem. Mag. **1460.00**

Classic Left-Handed (Long Action, Matte Lacquer Finish)
In 270 Win. **$1085.00**
In 7mm Rem. Mag. **1100.00**

SAKO RIFLES

Feature	SUPER DELUXE	TRG-21	SAFARI	CARBINE MANNLICHER STYLE	PPC BENCHREST/VARMINT	VARMINT	LAMINATED	FIBERCLASS	TRG-S MAGNUM	TRG-S	DELUXE	CLASSIC	HUNTER
Action	AV, AII, AV	*	AV	AII, AV	AI	AI, AII, AV	AII, AV	AV, AV	*	*	AV, AII, AV	AII, AV	AI, AII, AV
Left-handed											■ ■ ■	■	■ ■ ■ ■
Total length (inches)	41½, 42½, 44, 46, 46	46½	44	39½, 40½, 40½	43¾	43½, 43½	43½, 46, 46	44, 46, 46	47½	45½	41½, 42½, 44, 46, 46	42½, 44	41½, 42½, 44, 46
Barrel length (inches)	21¼, 21¾, 22, 24, 24	25¾	23½	18½, 18½, 18½	23¾	23, 23	21¾, 22, 24	22, 24, 24	24	22	21¼, 21¾, 22, 24, 24	21¾, 24	21¼, 21¾, 22, 24
Weight (lbs.)	6¼, 6½, 7¾, 7¾, 8¼	10½	8¼	6, 7¼, 7¾	8¾	8½, 8½	6½, 7¾, 7¾	7¼, 7¼, 8	7¾	7¾	6¼, 6½, 7¾, 7¾, 8¼	6, 7½	6¼, 6½, 7¾, 7¾, 8¼
17 Rem/10″	■					■					■		■
222 Rem/14″	■					■					■		■
223 Rem/12″	■					■					■		■
22 PPC/14″					■								
6 PPC/12″					■								
22-250 Rem/14″	■					■	■				■		■
243 Win/10″	■			■		■	■				■	■	■
308 Win/12″	■		■	■		■	■				■		■
7mm-08/9½″	■			■		■	■				■		■
25-06 Rem/10″	■						■				■		■
270 Win/10p	■			■							■		■
280 Rem/10″	■										■		■
30-06/10″	■			■							■		■
7mm Rem Mag/9½″	■						■	■	■		■	■	■
300 Win Mag/10″	■						■	■	■		■		■
300 Wby Mag/10″	■										■		■
338 Win Mag/10″	■		■	■			■	■			■		■
375 H&H Mag/12″	■		■	■			■	■			■		■
416 Rem Mag/14″	■							■			■		■
Lacquered	■ ■ ■ ■ ■										■ ■ ■ ■ ■		
Matte lacquered							■ ■ ■					■ ■	■ ■ ■ ■ ■
Oiled			■	■ ■ ■	■	■ ■							
Reinforced polyurethane		■							■	■			
Without sights	■ ■ ■ ■ ■			■	■ ■	■ ■ ■	■ ■ ■				■ ■ ■ ■ ■	■ ■	■ ■ ■ ■ ■
Open sights			■	■ ■ ■									■ ■
Scope mount rails	■ ■ ■ ■ ■	■	■	■ ■ ■	■	■ ■	■ ■ ■	■ ■ ■	■	■	■ ■ ■ ■ ■	■ ■	■ ■ ■ ■ ■
Magazine capacity	6, 5, 5, 4	10	4	5, 5, 3	0	6, 5	5, 5, 4	5, 4	**	5	5, 4, 4	6, 5	6, 5, 5, 4
Rubber recoil pad	■ ■ ■ ■ ■	■	■	■ ■ ■	■	■ ■	■ ■ ■	■	■	■	■ ■ ■ ■ ■	■ ■	■ ■ ■ ■ ■

Row groups (right-hand labels): Model / Dimensions / Caliber/Rate of Twist / Stock Finish / Sights / Mag. / Buttplate

* Cold-Hammer Forged Receiver

** 5 except for the .375 H&H which is 4

SAKO ACTIONS

Only by building a rifle around a Sako action do shooters enjoy the choice of three different lengths, each scaled to a specific family of cartridges. The AI (Short) action is miniaturized in every respect to match the 222 family, which includes everything from 17 Remington to 223 Remington. The AII (Medium) action is scaled down to the medium-length cartridges of standard bolt face—22-250, 243, 308, 7mm-08 or similar length cartridges.

The AV (Long) action is offered in either standard or Magnum bolt face and accommodates cartridges of up to 3.65 inches in overall length, including rounds like the 300 Weatherby and 375 H&H Magnum. **For left-handers, the Medium and Long actions are offered in either standard or Magnum bolt face.** All actions are furnished in-the-white only.

AI-1 (SHORT ACTION)
CALIBERS:
17 Rem., 222 Rem.
222 Rem. Mag.
223 Rem.
$495.00

AI PPC (Short Action)
Hunter 22 PPC and 6 PPC
$540.00

AI PPC (Short Action)
Single Shot 22 PPC and 6 PPC
$595.00

AII-1 (MEDIUM ACTION)
CALIBERS:
22-250 Rem. (AII-3)
243 Win.
308 Win.
7mm-08
$495.00

AV-4 (LONG ACTION)
CALIBERS:
25-06 Rem. (AV-1)
270 Win. (AV-1)
280 Rem. (AV-1)
30-06 (AV-1)
7mm Rem. Mag. (AV-4)
300 Win. Mag. (AV-4)
300 Wby. Mag. (AV-4)
338 Win. Mag. (AV-4)
375 H&H Mag. (AV-4)
416 Rem. Mag.
$495.00

Also available:
LEFT-HANDED ACTIONS
Medium and Long: $525.00

SAUER RIFLES

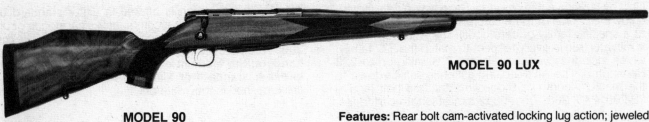

MODEL 90 LUX

MODEL 90

SPECIFICATIONS
Calibers: 25-06, 270, 30-06, 7mm Rem. Mag., 300 Win. Mag., 300 Wby. Mag., 338 Win., 375 H&H, 458 Win. Mag.
Barrel length: 24″ or 26″
Overall length: 44″ (standard calibers and 375 H&H, 458 Win. Mag.; 46¹/₈″ (for other calibers)
Weight: 7 lbs. 12 oz. to 10 lbs. 6 oz.
Sights: None furnished; drilled and tapped for scope mount
Stock: "Lux" Model has satin-gloss oil-finished European walnut stock; "Supreme" Model has high-gloss lacquer-finished American walnut stock. Both models feature Monte Carlo cut with sculptured cheekpiece, hand-checkered pistol grip and forend, rosewood pistol grip cap and forend tip, black rubber recoil pad, and fully inletted sling swivel studs.

Features: Rear bolt cam-activated locking lug action; jeweled bolt with an operating angle of 65°; fully adjustable gold-plated trigger; chamber loaded signal pin; cocking indicator; tang-mounted slide safety with button release; bolt release button (to operate bolt while slide safety is engaged); detachable 3 or 4-round box magazine; sling side scope mounts; leather sling (extra)
Engravings: Four distinctive hand-cut patterns on gray nitride receiver, trigger housing plate, magazine plate and bolt handle (extra)

Prices:
LUX or SUPREME MODEL 90	$1495.00
w/Engraving #1	2620.00
w/Engraving #2	3250.00
w/Engraving #3	3565.00
w/Engraving #4	4195.00

MODEL 90 ENGRAVING #2

MODEL 90 ENGRAVING #4

SAUER .458 SAFARI

The Sauer .458 Safari features a rear bolt cam-activated locking-lug action with a low operating angle of 65°. It has a gold plated trigger, jeweled bolt, oil finished bubinga stock and deep luster bluing. Safety features include a press bottom slide safety that engages the trigger sear, toggle joint and bolt. The bolt release feature allows the sportsman to unload the rifle while the safety remains engaged to the trigger sear and toggle joint. The Sauer Safari is equipped with a chamber loaded signal pin for positive identification. Specifications include:
Barrel Length: 24″ (heavy barrel contour). **Overall length:** 44″.
Weight: 10 lb. 6 oz. **Sights:** Williams open sights (sling swivels included). **Price:** $1995.95

SAVAGE CENTERFIRE RIFLES

MODEL 110GC

MODEL 110 BOLT ACTION CENTERFIRE RIFLES
Standard and Magnum Calibers

The Savage 100 Series features solid lockup, positive gas protection, precise head space, precision-rifled barrels, and select walnut-finished Monte Carlo stocks. See specifications table below for full details.

Prices:

Model 110CY	**$350.00**
Model 110F	**370.00**
Model 110FNS	**365.00**
Model 110FP	**380.00**
Model 110G	**355.00**
Model 110GC	**390.00**
Model 110GNS	**350.00**
Model 110GV	**365.00**

SPECIFICATIONS MODEL 110

Model	Calibers	Capacity (1) in Chamber	Barrel Length	Length	Pull	Avg. Wt. Lbs.	Twist R.H.	Stock	Sights†
	22–250 Rem.	5	22″	43½″	13½″	7½″	1 in 14″	Cut Checkered Walnut Finished Hardwood with Recoil Pad	110G Adjustable
	.223 Rem.	5	22″	43½″	13½″	7½	1 in 12″		
110G*	.243 Win.	5	22″	43½″	13½″	7½	1 in 10″		
	.250 Sav.	5	22″	43½″	13½″	7½	1 in 10″		
	.25-06 Rem.	5	22″	43½″	13½″	7½	1 in 10″		
110GN*	7mm-08 Rem.	5	24″	45½″	13½″	7¾	1 in 9½″		110GNS None
110F*	.270 Win.	5	22″	43½″	13½″	7¾	1 in 10″	Black Graphite Fiberglass Polymer with Recoil Pad	
	.300 Sav.	5	22″	43½″	13½″	7½	1 in 10″		110F Adjustable
	30-06 Spfld.	5	22″	43½″	13½″	7¾	1 in 10″		
110FNS*	.308 Win.	5	22″	43½″	13½″	7¾	1 in 10″		
	7mm Rem. Mag.	4	24″	45½″	13½″	7¾	1 in 9½″		110FNS None
	.300 Win. Mag.	4	24″	45½″	13½″	7¾	1 in 10″		
	.338 Win. Mag.	4	24″	45½″	13½″	7¾	1 in 10″		
110GC	.270 30-06 7mm Rem. Mag. .300 Win. Mag.	5 5 4 4	22″ 22″ 24″ 24″	43½″ 43½″ 45½″ 45½″	13½″ 13½″ 13½″ 13½″	6¾ 6¾ 7 7	1 in 10″ 1 in 10″ 1 in 9½″ 1 in 10″	Cut Checkered Walnut Finished Hardwood with Recoil Pad	Adj.
110GV	.22–250 .223	5 5	24″ 24″	45½″ 45½″	13½″ 13½″	7¾ 7¾	1 in 14″ 1 in 12″	Cut Checkered Walnut Finished Hardwood with Recoil Pad	None
110FP	.223 .308	5 5	24″ 24″	45½″ 45½″	13½″ 13½″	9 9	1 in 9″ 1 in 10″	Black Graphite Fiberglass Poly-mer	None
110CY	.223 Rem. .243 .300 Sav.	5	22″	42½″	12½″	6½″	1 in 12″ 1 in 10″ 1 in 10″	Cut Checkered Walnut Finished Hardwood with Recoil Pad	Adj.

* Left-hand models available in 270, 30-06, 7mm Rem. Mag.
All Model 110's are packed with a gunlock, ear puffs, and target.

† All receivers drilled and tapped for scope mounts.

RIFLES

SAVAGE CENTERFIRE RIFLES

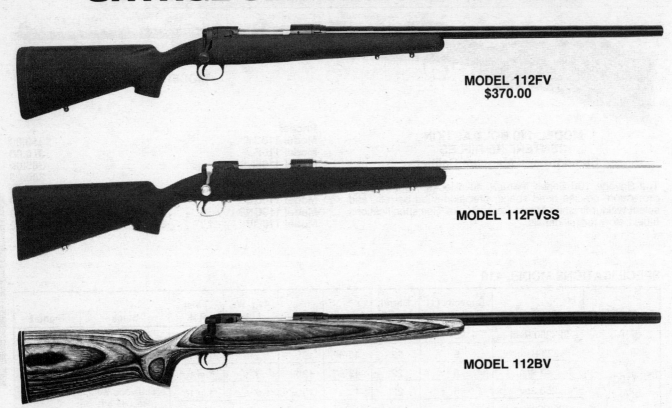

MODEL 112FV
$370.00

MODEL 112FVSS

MODEL 112BV

The Model 112FV was designed to meet the demand for a 26″ heavy barrel varmint rifle, incorporating the best features of the Savage Model 110—famous for its accuracy and dependability. Available with black Graphite Fiberglass Polymer stock and recoil pad, the Model 112FV is drilled and tapped for scope mounting. Shipped from the factory with gunlock, ear puffs, target and shooting glasses.

SPECIFICATIONS
Calibers: 22-250 and 223
Capacity: 5 rounds
Barrel length: 26″

Overall length: 47½″
Weight: 9 lbs.
Stock: Black Rynite®
Also available:

MODEL 112FVS. Same specifications and features as Model 112FV, except heavy-barrel varmint rifle with rigid solid bottom receiver. **$370.00**
MODEL FVSS. Same as Model 112FVS, except in stainless steel. **$460.00**
MODEL BV. Same as Model FVSS, but with ambidextrous laminated wood stock with Wundhammer swell. **$460.00**

MODEL 114CU
$480.00

Savage's Model 114CU is a high-grade sporting firearm designed with a straight classic American black walnut stock. Cut-checkering, fitted grip cap and recoil pad are complemented by a high-gloss luster metal polish finish. The staggered box-type magazine is removed with a push of a button, making loading and reloading quick and easy.

SPECIFICATIONS
Calibers: 270, 30-06, 7mm Rem Mag., 300 Win. Mag.
Capacity: 4 rounds (Magnum); 5 rounds (270 and 30-06)
Barrel length: 22″ (270 and 30-06) and 24″ (Magnum)
Overall length: 43½″ (270 and 30-06) and 45½″ (Magnum)
Weight: 7½ lbs. (270 and 30-06) and 7¾ lbs. (Magnum)
Sights: Deluxe adjustable; receivers drilled and tapped for scope mounts
Length of pull: 13½″

SAVAGE CENTERFIRE RIFLES

MODEL 116FSS

MODEL 116FSS
$470.00

Savage Arms has combined the strength of a black Graphite Fiberglass Polymer stock and the durability of a stainless-steel barrel and receiver to create this bolt-action rifle. The Model 116FSS weds rugged materials with the features of the highly accurate Savage Model 110 to make a rifle that satisfies the needs of demanding sportsmen. Major components are made from stainless steel, honed to a low reflective satin finish. Drilled and tapped for scope mounts, the 116FSS is offered in popular long-action calibers. Packed with gunlock, ear puffs and target.

SPECIFICATIONS
Calibers: 223, 243, 270, 30-06, 7mm Rem Mag., 300 Win. Mag., 338 Win. Mag.
Capacity: 4 (7mm Rem. Mag., 300 Win. Mag., 338 Win. Mag.); 5 (223, 243, 270, 30-06)
Barrel length: 22″ (223, 243, 270, 30-06); 24″ (7mm Rem. Mag., 300 Win. Mag., 338 Win. Mag.)
Overall length: 43½″–45½″
Weight: 7½–7¾ lbs.
Stock: Black Graphite Fiberglass Polymer

MODEL 116FCS

MODEL 116FCS
$510.00

This bolt-action rifle has the same quality features as the Model 116FSS plus a removable box magazine with recessed push-button release for ease in loading and unloading.

MODEL 116FSK "KODIAK"

MODEL 116FSK "KODIAK"
$510.00

The "Kodiak" features a compact 22″ barrel with a "shock suppressor" that reduces average linear recoil by more than 30% without loss of Magnum stopping power. Available in caliber .338 Win. Mag. For additional features, see the Model 116FSS.

SAVAGE CENTERFIRE RIFLES

MODEL 99C LEVER ACTION
$590.00

Clip magazine allows for the chambering of pointed, high-velocity big-bore cartridges. **Calibers:** 243 Win., 308 Win. **Action:** Hammerless, lever action, top tang safety. **Magazine:** Detachable clip; holds 4 rounds plus one in the chamber. **Stock:** Select walnut with high Monte Carlo and deep fluted comb.

Cut checkered stock and forend with swivel studs. Recoil pad and pistol grip cap. **Sights:** Detachable hooded ramp front sight, bead front sight on removable ramp adjustable rear sight. Tapped for top mount scopes. **Barrel length:** 22″. **Overall length:** 42³/₄″. **Weight:** 7³/₄ lbs.

SAVAGE MODEL 24F-12T TURKEY
with Camo Graphite Fiberglass Stock

SAVAGE MODEL 24F COMBINATION RIFLE/SHOTGUN

Match a 12- or 20-gauge shotgun with any of three popular centerfire calibers. Frame is color casehardened and barrel is a deep, lustrous blue and tapped, ready for scope mounting. Two-way top opening lever. All models are stocked with tough Graphite Fiberglass Polymer plus hammerblock safeties that limit hammer travel in the safe position. Other features include

interchangeable chokes (extra full tube supplied), and factory swivel studs.
Prices:
Model 24F-20 . . . . **$380.00**
Model 24F-12 . . . . 380.00
Model 24F-12T 400.00

SPECIFICATIONS MODEL 24F COMBINATION RIFLE/SHOTGUN

O/U Comb. Model	Gauge Caliber	Choke	Chamber	Barrel Length	O.A. Length	Twist R.H.	Stock
24F-20	20 ga./22 LR	Mod Barrel	3″	24″	40¹/₂″	1 in 14″	Black Graphite Fiberglass Polymer
	20 ga./22 Hor.					1 in 14″	
	20 ga./223					1 in 14″	
	20 ga./30/30					1 in 12″	
24F-12	12 ga./22 Hor.	Full Mod, IC Choke Tubes	3″	24″	40¹/₂″	1 in 14″	Black Graphite Fiberglass Polymer
	12 ga./223					1 in 14″	
	12 ga./30/30					1 in 12″	
24F-12T Turkey	12 ga./22 Hor.	Full Mod, IC Choke Tubes	3″	24″	40¹/₂″	1 in 14″	Camo Graphite Fiberglass Polymer
	12 ga./223					1 in 14″	

SPRINGFIELD RIFLES

SPRINGFIELD M1A STANDARD

SPRINGFIELD M1A STANDARD

SPECIFICATIONS
Caliber: 308 Win./7.62mm NATO (243 or 7mm-08 optional)
Capacity: 5, 10 or 20-round box magazine
Barrel length: 18¼"
Overall length: 40½"
Weight: 8¾ lbs.

Sights: Military square post front; military aperture rear, adjustable for windage and elevation
Sight radius: 22¾"
Rifling: 6 groove, RH twist, 1 turn in 11"
Finish: Walnut
Price: $1239.00
Also available:
BASIC M1A RIFLE w/painted black fiberglass stock, .308 caliber only. **Price:** $1065.00

M1A MATCH

SPECIFICATIONS
Caliber: 308 Win. (243 or 7mm-08 optional)
Barrel length: 22"
Over length: 44.375"
Trigger pull: 4½ lbs.
Weight: 10.06 lbs.

SPRINGFIELD M1A NATIONAL MATCH RIFLE

Features: Comes with National Match barrel, flash suppressor, gas cylinder, special glass-bedded walnut stock and match-tuned trigger assembly.
Price: $1539.00

Also available:
M1A SUPER MATCH. Features heavy match barrel and permanently attached figure-8-style operating rod guide, plus special heavy walnut match stock, longer pistol grip and contoured area behind rear sight for better grip.
Price: $1849.00

SPRINGFIELD M1A-A1 BUSH RIFLE

SPECIFICATIONS
Caliber: 308 Win./7.62mm (243 or 7mm-08 optional)
Barrel length: 18.25" (w/o flash suppressor)
Overall length: 40.5"
Weight: 8.75 lbs.

Sight radius: 22.75"
Features: Other specifications same as M1A Standard
Prices:
With walnut stock $1249.00
With folding stock 1399.00

STEYR-MANNLICHER RIFLES

SPORTER SERIES

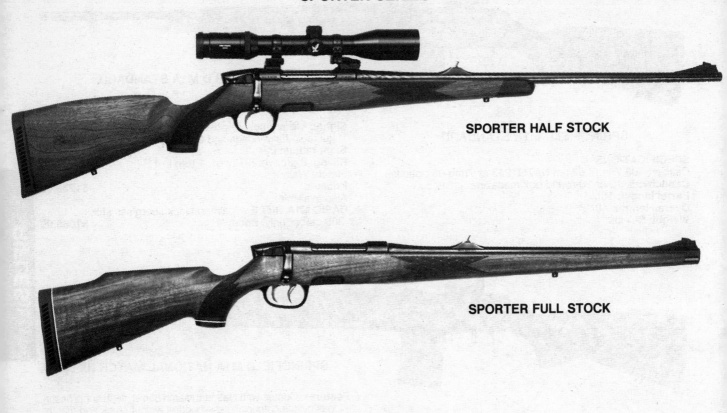

SPORTER HALF STOCK

SPORTER FULL STOCK

SPORTER SERIES

All Sporter models feature hand-checkered wood stocks, a five-round detachable rotary magazine, and a choice of single or double-set triggers. M actions are available in left-hand models. S (Magnum) action are available in half stock only.

SPECIFICATIONS
Calibers: See table on the following page
Barrel length: 20″ (Full Stock); 23.6″ (Half Stock)
Overall length: 39″ (Full)
Weight:
  Model SL—6.16 lbs. (Full) and 6.27 lbs. (Half Stock)
  Model L—6.27 lbs. (Full) and 6.38 lbs. (Half)
  Model M—6.82 lbs. (Full) and 7 lbs. (Half).
Features: SL and L Models have rifle-type rubber butt pad

Prices:
Models SL, L, M Full Stock	$2179.00
Models SL, L, M Half Stock	2023.00
Model M Left Hand Full Stock	2335.00
Model M Left Hand Half Stock	2179.00
Model M Professional (w/black synthetic half stock and iron sights)	1710.00
Varmint Rifle Half stock, 26″ heavy barrel	2179.00

MODEL M PROFESSIONAL

STEYR-MANNLICHER RIFLES

MANNLICHER LUXUS
(Half Stock)

MANNLICHER LUXUS

The Mannlicher Luxus is the premier rifle in the Steyr lineup. It features a hand-checkered walnut stock, smooth action, combination shotgun set trigger, steel in-line three-round magazine (detachable), rear tang slide safety, and European-designed receiver. **Calibers:** See table below. **Barrel length:** 20″ (Full Stock); 23.6″ (Half Stock).

Prices:
Luxus Models
Half Stock **$2648.00**
Full Stock **2804.00**
Luxus S (Magnum) Models (26″ barrel,
Half Stock only) **2804.00**

RIFLES

MODELS:	222 Rem.	222 Rem. Mag.	223 Rem.	5.6×50 Mag.	5.6×57	243 Win.	308 Win	6.5×57	270 Win.	7×64	30-06 Spr.	9.3×62	6.5×68	7mm Rem. Mag.	300 Win. Mag.	8×685	22-250 Rem.	6mm Rem.	6.5×55	7.5 Swiss	7×57	8×57 JS	375 H&H Mag.	458 Win. Mag.
Sporter (SL)	●	●	●	●																				
(L)					●	●	●										●	●						
(M)								●	●	●	●	●							●	●	●	●		
S and S/T													●	●	●	●							●	●
Professional (M)								●	●	●	●	●							●	●	●	●		
Luxus (L)					●	●	●																	
(M)								●	●	●	●	●							●	●				
(S)													●	●	●	●								
Varmint	●		●		●	●	●								●		●							
Match UIT					●																			
SSG					●	●																		

STEYR SSG

STEYR SSG

The Steyr SSG features a black synthetic Cycolac stock (walnut optional), heavy Parkerized barrel, five-round standard (and optional 10-round) staggered magazine, heavy-duty milled receiver. **Calibers:** 243 Win. and 308 Win. **Barrel length:** 26″. **Overall length:** 44.5″. **Weight:** 8.5 lbs. **Sights:** Iron sights; hooded ramp front with blade adjustable for elevation; rear standard V-notch adjustable for windage. **Features:** Sliding safety; 1″ swivels.

Prices:
Model SSG-PI Cycolac Half Stock **$2043.00**
Model SSG-PII **2229.00**
Model SSG Marksman Scope Mount **224.00**
Model SSG P-II Sniper (308 Win.) **1783.00**
With Walnut Stock **2231.00**
Model SSG P-III (26″ heavy barrel) **3162.00**
Model SSG P-IV Urban (16¾″ heavy barrel) **2603.00**

STEYR-MANNLICHER RIFLES

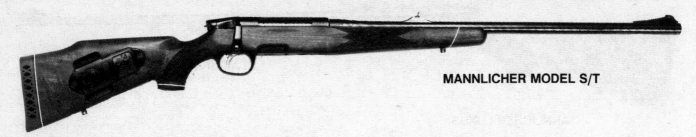

MANNLICHER MODEL S/T

MANNLICHER MODEL S-S/T MAGNUM

The Mannlicher S/T is a heavy-barreled version of the Sporter S Model designed specifically for big game hunting. It features a hand-checkered walnut stock, five-round rotary magazine, optional butt stock magazine, and double-set or single trigger. **Calibers:** 6.5×68, 7mm Rem. Mag., 300 Win. Mag., 8×685,

375 H&H Mag., 338 Win. **Barrel length:** 26″. **Weight:** 8.36 lbs. (Model S); 9 lbs. (Model S/T).

Prices:
Model S	**$2179.00**
Model S/T (w/optional butt magazine)	**2335.00**

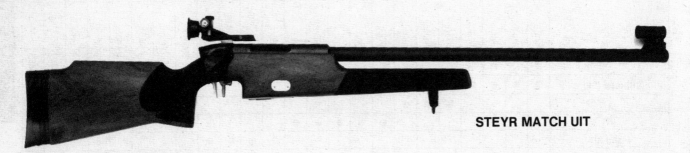

STEYR MATCH UIT

STEYR MATCH UIT

Designed especially for target competition, the Steyr Match UIT features a walnut competition stock, stipple-textured pistol grip, adjustable straight and wide trigger, adjustable first-stage trigger pull, enlarged bolt handle for rapid fire, cold hammer-forged barrel, and non-glare band for sighting. **Caliber:** 308 Win. **Overall length:** 44″. **Weight:** 10 lbs.

Prices:
Steyr Match SPG-UIT	**$3995.00**
10-shot magazine	143.00
Model SPG-CISM	4295.00
Model SPG-T	3695.00

AUG S.A. SEMIAUTO RIFLE

AUG S.A. SEMIAUTOMATIC RIFLE

SPECIFICATIONS
Caliber: 223
Capacity: 30-round magazine
Barrel lengths: 16″ or 20″
Price: $1375.00

THOMPSON/CENTER RIFLES

THE CONTENDER CARBINE
$460.00

Available in 9 **calibers:** 17 Rem., 22 LR, 22 LR Match, 22 Hornet, 223 Rem., 7×30 Waters, 30-30 Win., 35 Rem. and 375 Win. **Barrels** are 21 inches long and are interchangeable, with adjustable iron sights and tapped and drilled for scope mounts. **Weight:** Only 5 lbs. 3 oz.
Also available:
Contender Vent Rib Carbine
 With standard walnut stock **$480.00**
 With 21″ 17 Rem. barrel **490.00**

Contender Youth Model Carbine
 W/16¼″ bbl., walnut Youth stock **$425.00**
 With 16¼″ 45 Colt/.410 barrel **455.00**
Contender Carbine
 w/Match Grade barrel & Rynite stock **435.00**
 w/Match Grade 22LR barrel **470.00**
 w/Rynite Stock & 21″ barrel **425.00**
 In 17 Rem. **455.00**

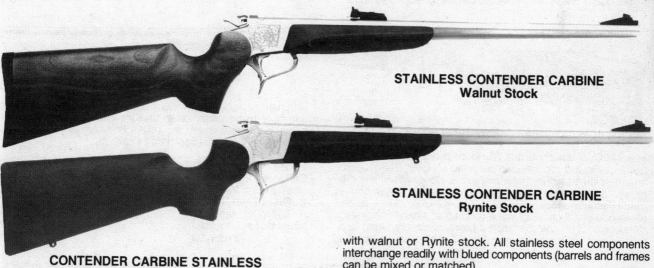

STAINLESS CONTENDER CARBINE
Walnut Stock

STAINLESS CONTENDER CARBINE
Rynite Stock

CONTENDER CARBINE STAINLESS

Available in 22LR, 22 Hornet, 223 Rem., 7-30 Waters, 30-30 Win. and .410 bore. Same specifications as standard model,

with walnut or Rynite stock. All stainless steel components interchange readily with blued components (barrels and frames can be mixed or matched).
Prices:
Stainless Carbine Standard **$216.00**
Stainless Carbine w/vent rib **240.00**

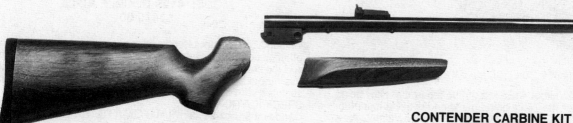

CONTENDER CONVERSION KIT

Available in 22LR, 22 Hornet, 223 Rem., 30-30 Win. and .410 smoothbore. Each kit contains a buttstock, blued 21″ barrel, forend and sights.

CONTENDER CARBINE KIT
Walnut Stock

Prices:
With Walnut stock **$270.00**
With Rynite stock **245.00**

TIKKA RIFLES

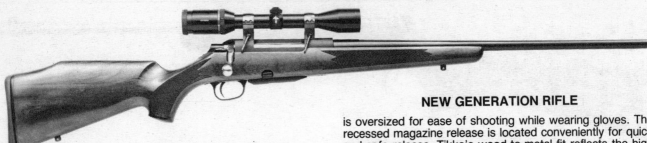

NEW GENERATION RIFLE

With the consolidation of three renowned Finnish firearms manufacturers—Tikka, Sako and Valmet—a "new generation" of Tikka rifles becomes a reality. These new rifles feature a "smooth as silk" bolt action made possible by a sleeve constructed of a space-age synthetic Polyarylamide material reinforced with fiberglass. The overall look of the rifle is enhanced by a walnut stock with matte lacquer finish and diamond point checkering. A short bolt throw allows for rapid firing, and a free-floating barrel increases accuracy. Barrel quality itself is ensured through Tikka's cold-hammered forging process. The trigger guard, made of synthetic materials for added strength,

is oversized for ease of shooting while wearing gloves. The recessed magazine release is located conveniently for quick and safe release. Tikka's wood-to-metal fit reflects the high standards of Finnish craftsmanship throughout. **Calibers:** 223 Rem., 22-250 Rem., 243 Win., 308 Win., 270 Win., 30-06, 7mm Rem. Mag., 300 Win. Mag., and 338 Win. Mag. **Barrel length:** 22" (24" in Magnum). **Weight:** 7 1/8 lbs.

Prices NEW GENERATION:

Calibers 223 Rem., 22-250 Rem., 243 Win., 308 Win., 270 Win. and 30-06	**$835.00**
Calibers 7mm Rem. Mag., 300 Win. Mag., 338 Win. Mag.	860.00
Magazines (5 rounds)	66.50
(3 rounds)	55.00

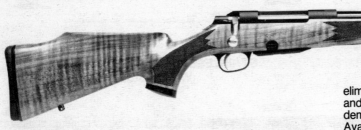

PREMIUM GRADE RIFLE

The TIKKA Premium Grade rifle is designed and crafted by Sako of Finland for the discriminating shooter. This superb firearm features a detachable magazine, along with a "smooth as silk" bolt that is encased in a polymer sleeve. The luxurious matte lacquer stock incorporates a roll-over cheek-piece, rosewood pistol grip cap and forend tip and hand-checkered throughout. The cold-hammered barrel is deeply blued and free floated for maximum accuracy. The two action lengths

eliminate unnecessary weight and each trigger is designed and built to be crisp, clean and travel-free. For those who demand the very finest, the TIKKA Premium is a must. Available in a wide assortment of calibers.

Prices PREMIUM GRADE:

Calibers 223 Rem., 22-250 Rem., 243 Win., 308 Win., 270 Win., 30-06	**$1030.00**
Calibers 7mm Rem. Mag., 300 Win. Mag., 338 Win. Mag.	1070.00
Magazines (5 rounds)	66.50
(3 rounds)	55.00

MODEL 412S DOUBLE RIFLE
$1470.00

The renowned Valmet 412S line of fine firearms is now being produced under the Tikka brand name and is being manufactured to the same specifications as the former Valmet. As a result of a joint venture entered into by Sako Ltd., the production facilities for these firearms are now located in Italy. The manufacture of the 412S series is controlled under the rigid quality standards of Sako Ltd., with complete interchangeability of parts between firearms produced in Italy and

Finland. Tikka's double rifle offers features and qualities no other action can match: rapid handling and pointing qualities and the silent, immediate availability of a second shot. As such, this model overcomes the two major drawbacks usually associated with this type of firearm: price and accuracy.
SPECIFICATIONS
Calibers: 9.3×74R
Barrel length: 24"
Overall length: 40"
Weight: 8 1/2 lbs.
Stock: European walnut
Other: Automatic ejectors

TIKKA RIFLES

TIKKA WHITETAIL/BATTUE

Originally designed by Tikka for wild boar shooting in the French marketplace, this unique rifle is now being introduced to the North American audience because of its proven success. The primary purpose of the rifle is for snap-shooting when quickness is a requirement in the field. The raised quarter-rib, coupled with the wide "V"-shaped rear sight, allow the shooter a wide field of view. This enables him to zero in on a moving target swiftly. Also features a hooded front sight. A 3-round detachable magazine is available as an option.

The 20½" barrel (overall length: 40½") is perfectly balanced and honed to ensure the accuracy for which Tikka is famous. The stock is finished in soft matte lacquer, enhancing its beauty and durability. Weight is 7 pounds.

Prices:
In 308 Win., 270 Win., 30-06 . . . . **$860.00**
In 7mm Mag., 300 Win. Mag., 338 Win. Mag. **895.00**

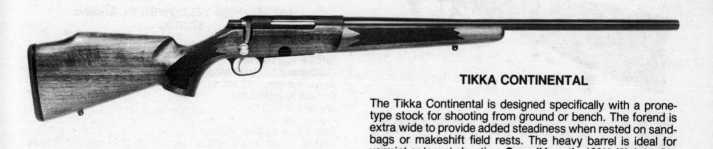

TIKKA CONTINENTAL

The Tikka Continental is designed specifically with a prone-type stock for shooting from ground or bench. The forend is extra wide to provide added steadiness when rested on sandbags or makeshift field rests. The heavy barrel is ideal for varmint or target shooting. **Overall length:** 43¾". **Weight:** 8½ lbs.

Price:
In 223 Rem., 22-250 Rem., 243 Win., 308 Win. . . **$1090.00**

A. UBERTI REPLICA RIFLES & CARBINES

ALL UBERTI FIREARMS AVAILABLE IN SUPER GRADE, PRESTIGE AND ENGRAVED FINISHES

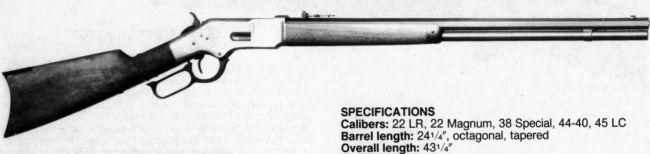

MODEL 1866 SPORTING RIFLE
$780.00

SPECIFICATIONS
Calibers: 22 LR, 22 Magnum, 38 Special, 44-40, 45 LC
Barrel length: 24¼″, octagonal, tapered
Overall length: 43¼″
Weight: 8.16 lbs.
Frame: Elevator and buttplate in brass
Stock: Walnut
Sights: Vertically adjustable rear; horizontally adjustable front

MODEL 1866 YELLOWBOY CARBINE
$720.00

SPECIFICATIONS
Calibers: 22 LR, 22 Magnum, 38 Special, 44-40, 45 LC
Barrel length: 19″, round, tapered
Overall length: 38¼″
Weight: 7.380 lbs.
Frame: Brass
Stock and forend: Walnut
Sights: Vertically adjustable rear; horizontally adjustable front

The first gun to carry the Winchester name, this model was born as the 44-caliber rimfire cartridge Henry and is now chambered for 22 LR and 44-40.

MODEL 1871 ROLLING BLOCK
BABY CARBINE
$460.00

SPECIFICATIONS
Calibers: 22 LR, 22 Hornet, 22 Magnum, 357 Magnum
Barrel length: 22″
Overall length: 35½″
Weight: 4.85 lbs.
Stock & forend: Walnut

Trigger guard: Brass
Sights: Fully adjustable rear; ramp front
Frame: Color-casehardened steel

A. UBERTI REPLICA RIFLES & CARBINES

SPECIFICATIONS
Calibers: 357 Magnum, 44-40 and 45. Hand-checkered. Other specifications same as Model 1866. Also available in 20″ octagon or 30″ barrel length with pistol-grip stock (extra).

MODEL 1873 SPORTING RIFLE
$900.00

SPECIFICATIONS
Calibers: 357 Mag., 44-40, 45 LC
Barrel length: 19″ round, tapered
Overall length: 38¼″
Weight: 7.38 lbs.
Sights: Fixed front; vertically adjustable rear

1873 CARBINE
$890.00

SPECIFICATIONS
Calibers: 44-40, 45 LC
Barrel length: 24¼″ (half-octagon, with tubular magazine)
Overall length: 43¾″
Weight: 9.26 lbs.
Frame: Brass
Stock: Varnished American walnut

HENRY RIFLE
$895.00 (44-40 Cal.)
$900.00 (45 LC & 44 Spec.)

HENRY CARBINE (not shown)
$900.00

SPECIFICATIONS
Caliber: 44-40
Capacity: 12 shots
Barrel length: 22¼″
Weight: 9.04 lbs.

Also available: **HENRY TRAPPER. Barrel length:** 16¼″ or 18″. **Overall length:** 35¾″ or 37¾″. **Weight:** 7.383 lbs. or 7.934 lbs. **Capacity:** 8 or 9 shots. **Price:** $900.00

RIFLES

ULTRA LIGHT ARMS

MODEL 28
(7mm Rem. Mag.)

MODEL 20 SERIES
$2400.00 ($2500.00 Left Hand)

SPECIFICATIONS
Calibers (Short Action): 6mm Rem., 17 Rem., 22 Hornet, 222 Rem., 222 Rem. Mag., 22-250 Rem., 223 Rem., 243 Win., 250-3000 Savage, 257 Roberts, 257 Ackley, 7mm Mauser, 7mm Ack., 7mm-08 Rem., 284 Win., 300 Savage, 308 Win., 358 Win.
Barrel length: 22″
Weight: 4.75 lbs.
Safety: Two-position safety allows bolt to open or lock with sear blocked
Stock: Kevlar/Graphite composite; choice of 7 or more colors

Also available:
MODEL 24 SERIES (Long Action) in 270 Win.,
30-06, 25-06, 7mm Express $2500.00
Same as above in Left-Hand Model 2600.00
MODEL 28 SERIES (Magnum Action) in 264 Win.,
7mm Rem., 300 Win., 338 . . . . 2900.00
Same as above in Left-Hand Model 3000.00

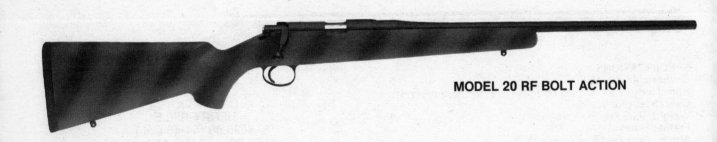

MODEL 20 RF BOLT ACTION

MODEL 20 RF
(Single Shot or Repeater)
$800.00

SPECIFICATIONS
Caliber: 22 LR
Barrel length: 22″ (Douglas Premium #1 Contour)
Weight: 5½ lbs.
Sights: None (drilled and tapped for scope)
Stock: Composite

UNIQUE RIFLES

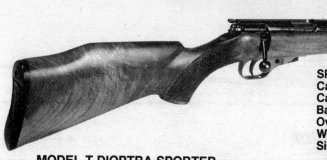

MODEL T DIOPTRA SPORTER
$700.00

SPECIFICATIONS
Caliber: 22 LR or 22 Magnum bolt action
Capacity: 5 or 10 shots (5 shots only in 22 Mag.)
Barrel length: 23.6″
Overall length: 41.1″
Weight: 6.4 lbs.
Sights: Adjustable rear; lateral and vertical correction; dovetailed grooves on receiver for scope or Micro-Match target sight
Features: French walnut Monte Carlo stock; firing adjustment safety (working in firing pin)

MODEL T UIT STANDARD RIFLE
$1250.00

SPECIFICATIONS
Caliber: 22 LR
Barrel length: 25.6″
Overall length: 44.1″
Weight: 10.4 lbs.
Sights: Micro-Match target sight
Stock: French walnut
Features: Adjustable buttplate and cheek rest; fully adjustable firing; left-hand stock and action available

MODEL T/SM SILHOUETTE
$825.00

SPECIFICATIONS
Caliber: 22 LR or 22 Magnum
Capacity: 5- or 10-shot magazine (5-shot only in 22 Mag.)
Barrel length: 20.5″
Overall length: 38.4″
Weight: 6.6 lbs.
Sights: Dovetailed grooves on receiver for scope or Micro-Match target sight
Stock: French walnut Monte Carlo stock (left-hand stock available)

MODEL TGC CENTERFIRE
$1190.00

SPECIFICATIONS
Calibers: 243 Win., 270 Win., 7mm-08, 7mm Rem. Mag., 308 Win., 30-06, 300 Win. Mag.
Capacity: 3- or 5-shot magazine
Barrel length: 24″ bolt action (interchangeable barrel)
Overall length: 44.8″
Weight: 8.4 lbs.
Sights: Dovetailed grooves on receiver for scope
Stock: French walnut Monte Carlo stock (left-hand stock available)

WEATHERBY MARK V RIFLES

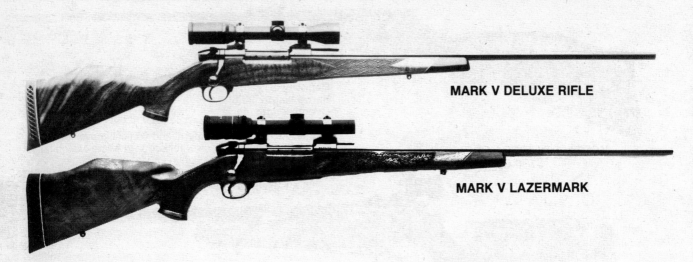

MARK V DELUXE RIFLE

MARK V LAZERMARK

MARK V DELUXE (24″ barrel)   **Prices**
240 , 257, 270, 7mm, 300 Wby. Mag., 30-06 . . . . **$1225.00**
375 H&H **1377.00**

MARK V DELUXE (26″ barrel)
224 Wby. Mag. and 22-250 Wby Mag. **$1196.00**

MARK V DELUXE (cont.)
240, 257, 7mm Wby. Mag., 30-06 . . . . **$1239.00**
300 Wby. Mag. and 340 Wby. Mag. **1270.00**
378 Wby. Mag. **1305.00**
416 Wby. Mag. **1346.00**
460 Wby. Mag. **1660.00**

SPECIFICATIONS MARK V RIFLES (see also following page)

Caliber	Model	Barrelled Action	Weight *	Overall Length	Magazine Capacity	Barrel Length/ Contour	Rifling	Length of Pull	Drop at Comb	Monte Carlo	Drop at Heel
.224 WBY Mag	Varmintmaster Mark V Deluxe	RH 26″	6 1/2 lbs.	45 3/8″	4 + 1 in chamber	26″ #2	1 - 14″ twist	13 1/2″	5/8″	1/4″	1 1/8″
22-.250	Varmintmaster Mark V Deluxe	RH 26″	6 1/2 lbs.	45 3/8″	3 + 1 in chamber	26″ #2	1 - 14″ twist	13 1/2″	5/8″	1/4″	1 1/8″
.240 WBY Mag.	Mark V Deluxe	RH 24″ or 26″	8 lbs.	44 5/8″ or 46 5/8″	4 + 1 in chamber	24″ #1 or 26″ #2	1 - 9 1/2″ twist	13 5/8″	5/8″	1/4″	1 1/8″
	Lazermark	RH 24″ or 26″	8 lbs.	44 5/8″ or 46 5/8″	4 + 1 in chamber	24″ #1 or 26″ #2	1 - 9 1/2″ twist	13 5/8″	5/8″	1/4″	1 1/8″
	Classicmark	RH 24″ or 26″	8 lbs.	44 5/8″ or 46 5/8″	4 + 1 in chamber	24″ #1 or 26″ #2	1 - 9 1/2″ twist	13 1/2″	7/8″	--	1 1/8″
.250 Savage	Whitetail Deluxe	RH 22″	6 lbs.	41 3/8″	3 + 1 in chamber	22″ #1	1 - 9 1/2″ twist	13 1/2″	5/8″	1/4″	1 1/8″
.257 WBY Mag.	Mark V Sporter	RH 24″	8 lbs.	44 5/8″	3 + 1 in chamber	24″ #1	1 - 9 1/2″ twist	13 5/8″	1″	5/8″	1 5/8″
	Mark V Deluxe	RH 24″ or 26″	8 lbs.	44 5/8″ or 46 5/8″	3 + 1 in chamber	24″ #1 or 26″ #2	1 - 9 1/2″ twist	13 5/8″	5/8″	1/4″	1 1/8″
	Lazermark	RH 24″ or 26″	8 lbs.	44 5/8″ or 46 5/8″	3 + 1 in chamber	24″ #1 or 26″ #2	1 - 9 1/2″ twist	13 5/8″	5/8″	1/4″	1 1/8″
	Classicmark	RH 24″ or 26″	8 lbs.	44 5/8″ or 46 5/8″	3 + 1 in chamber	24″ #1 or 26″ #2	1 - 9 1/2″ twist	13 1/2″	7/8″	--	1 1/8″
	Weathermark	RH 24″ or 26″	7 1/2 lbs.	44 5/8″ or 46 5/8″	3 + 1 in chamber	24″ #1 or 26″ #2	1 - 9 1/2″ twist	13 1/2″	7/8″	--	1 1/8″
	Alaskan	RH 24″ or 26″	7 1/2 lbs.	44 5/8″ or 46 5/8″	3 + 1 in chamber	24″ #1 or 26″ #2	1 - 9 1/2″ twist	13 1/2″	7/8″	--	1 1/8″
.270 WIN	Mark V Sporter	RH 22″	8 lbs.	42 5/8″	4 + 1 in chamber	22″ #1	1 - 10″ twist	13 5/8″	1″	5/8″	1 5/8″
	Classicmark	RH 22″	8 lbs.	42 5/8″	4 + 1 in chamber	22″ #1	1 - 10″ twist	13 1/2″	7/8″	--	1 1/8″
	Weathermark	RH 22″	7 1/2 lbs.	42 5/8″	4 + 1 in chamber	22″ #1	1 - 10″ twist	13 1/2″	7/8″	--	1 1/8″
	Alaskan	RH 22″	7 1/2 lbs.	42 5/8″	4 + 1 in chamber	22″ #1	1 - 10″ twist	13 1/2″	7/8″	--	1 1/8″
.270 WBY Mag.	Mark V Sporter	RH 24″	8 lbs.	44 5/8″	3 + 1 in chamber	24″ #1	1 - 9 1/2″ twist	13 5/8″	1″	5/8″	1 5/8″
	Mark V Deluxe	RH 24/26″, LH 24″	8 lbs.	44 5/8″ or 46 5/8″	3 + 1 in chamber	24″ #1 or 26″ #2	1 - 9 1/2″ twist	13 5/8″	5/8″	1/4″	1 1/8″
	Lazermark	RH 24″ or 26″	8 lbs.	44 5/8″ or 46 5/8″	3 + 1 in chamber	24″ #1 or 26″ #2	1 - 9 1/2″ twist	13 5/8″	5/8″	1/4″	1 1/8″
	Classicmark	RH 24/26″, LH 24″	8 lbs.	44 5/8″ or 46 5/8″	3 + 1 in chamber	24″ #1 or 26″ #2	1 - 9 1/2″ twist	13 1/2″	7/8″	--	1 1/8″
	Weathermark	RH 24″ or 26″	7 1/2 lbs.	44 5/8″ or 46 5/8″	3 + 1 in chamber	24″ #1 or 26″ #2	1 - 9 1/2″ twist	13 1/2″	7/8″	--	1 1/8″
	Alaskan	RH 24″ or 26″	7 1/2 lbs.	44 5/8″ or 46 5/8″	3 + 1 in chamber	24″ #1 or 26″ #2	1 - 9 1/2″ twist	13 1/2″	7/8″	--	1 1/8″
7mm Rem. Mag.	Mark V Sporter	RH 24″	8 lbs.	44 5/8″	3 + 1 in chamber	24″ #1	1 - 9 1/2″ twist	13 5/8″	1″	5/8″	1 5/8″
	Classicmark	RH 24″	8 lbs.	44 5/8″	3 + 1 in chamber	24″ #1	1 - 9 1/2″ twist	13 1/2″	7/8″	--	1 1/8″
	Weathermark	RH 24″	7 1/2 lbs.	44 5/8″	3 + 1 in chamber	24″ #1	1 - 9 1/2″ twist	13 1/2″	7/8″	--	1 1/8″
	Alaskan	RH 24″	7 1/2 lbs.	44 5/8″	3 + 1 in chamber	24″ #1	1 - 9 1/2″ twist	13 1/2″	7/8″	--	1 1/8″
7mm WBY Mag.	Mark V Sporter	RH 24″	8 lbs.	44 5/8″	3 + 1 in chamber	24″ #1	1 - 9 1/2″ twist	13 5/8″	1″	5/8″	1 5/8″
	Mark V Deluxe	RH 24/26″, LH 24″	8 lbs.	44 5/8″ or 46 5/8″	3 + 1 in chamber	24″ #1, 26″ #2	1 - 9 1/2″ twist	13 5/8″	5/8″	1/4″	1 1/8″
	Lazermark	RH 24/26″, LH 24″	8 lbs.	44 5/8″ or 46 5/8″	3 + 1 in chamber	24″ #1, 26″ #2	1 - 9 1/2″ twist	13 5/8″	5/8″	1/4″	1 1/8″
	Classicmark	RH 24/26″, LH 24″	8 lbs.	44 5/8″ or 46 5/8″	3 + 1 in chamber	24″ #1, 26″ #2	1 - 9 1/2″ twist	13 1/2″	7/8″	--	1 1/8″
	Weathermark	RH 24″ or 26″	7 1/2 lbs.	44 5/8″ or 46 5/8″	3 + 1 in chamber	24″ #1, 26″ #2	1 - 9 1/2″ twist	13 1/2″	7/8″	--	1 1/8″
	Alaskan	RH 24″ or 26″	7 1/2 lbs.	44 5/8″ or 46 5/8″	3 + 1 in chamber	24″ #1, 26″ #2	1 - 9 1/2″ twist	13 1/2″	7/8″	--	1 1/8″

WEATHERBY MARK V RIFLES

MARK V SPORTER

MARK V SPORTER (22″ barrel)　　　　　　　**Prices**
In cal. 270, 30-06 . . . . **$732.00**
MARK V SPORTER (24″ barrel)
In cal. 257, 270, 7mm, 300 Wby. Mag.,
　　7mm Rem. Mag., 300, 338 Win. **732.00**
In cal. 375 H&H **833.00**
MARK V SPORTER (26″ barrel)
In cal. 257, 270, 7mm Wby. Mag. . . . . **N/A**
In cal. 300, 340 Wby. Mag. **780.00**

LAZERMARK (24″ and 26″ barrels)　　　　　　**Prices**
In 240, 257, 270, 7mm, 300 Wby. Mag. **$1355.00**
In 460 Wby. Mag. **1844.00**
In 416 Wby. Mag. (24″ barrel only) **1573.00**
In 378 Wby. Mag. (26″ barrel only) **1356.00**

SPECIFICATIONS MARK V RIFLES (cont.)

Caliber	Model	Barrelled Action	Weight *	Overall Length	Magazine Capacity	Barrel Length/ Contour	Rifling	Length of Pull	Drop at Comb	Monte Carlo	Drop at Heel
30-06 Springfield	Mark V Sporter	RH 22″	8 lbs.	42 5/8″	4 + 1 in chamber	22″ #1	1-10″ twist	13 5/8″	1″	5/8″	1 5/8″
	Mark V Deluxe	RH 24/ 26″, LH 24″	8 lbs.	44 5/8″ or 46 5/8″	4 + 1 in chamber	24″ #1 or 26″ #2	1-10″ twist	13 5/8″	5/8″	1/4″	1 1/8″
	Lazermark	RH 24″ or 26″	8 lbs.	44 5/8″ or 46 5/8″	4 + 1 in chamber	24″ #1 or 26″ #2	1-10″ twist	13 5/8″	5/8″	1/4″	1 1/8″
	Classicmark	RH 22″, LH 22″	8 lbs.	42 5/8″	4 + 1 in chamber	22″ #1	1-10″ twist	13 1/2″	7/8″	--	1 1/8″
	Weathermark	RH 22″	7 1/2 lbs.	42 5/8″	4 + 1 in chamber	22″ #1	1-10″ twist	13 1/2″	7/8″	--	1 1/8″
	Alaskan	RH 22″	7 1/2 lbs.	42 5/8″	4 + 1 in chamber	22″ #1	1-10″ twist	13 1/2″	7/8″	--	1 1/8″
.300 Win. Mag.	Mark V Sporter	RH 24″	8 lbs.	44 1/2″	3 + 1 in chamber	24″ #1	1 - 10″ twist	13 5/8″	1″	5/8″	1 5/8″
	Weathermark	RH 24″	7 1/2 lbs.	44 1/2″	3 + 1 in chamber	24″ #1	1 - 10″ twist	13 1/2″	7/8″	--	1 1/8″
	Alaskan	RH 24″	7 1/2 lbs.	44 1/2″	3 + 1 in chamber	24″ #1	1 - 10″ twist	13 1/2″	7/8″	--	1 1/8″
.300 WBY Mag.	Mark V Sporter	RH 26″	8 lbs.	46 5/8″	3 + 1 in chamber	26″ #2	1 - 9 1/2″ twist	13 5/8″	1″	5/8″	1 5/8″
	Mark V Deluxe	RH 24/26″, LH 24/26″	8 lbs.	44 5/8″ or 46 5/8″	3 + 1 in chamber	24″ #1 or 26″ #2	1 - 9 1/2″ twist	13 5/8″	5/8″	1/4″	1 1/8″
	Lazermark	RH 24/26″, LH 24/26″	8 lbs.	44 5/8″ or 46 5/8″	3 + 1 in chamber	24″ #1 or 26″ #2	1 - 9 1/2″ twist	13 5/8″	5/8″	1/4″	1 1/8″
	Classicmark	RH 24″ or 26″, LH 26″	8 lbs.	44 5/8″ or 46 5/8″	3 + 1 in chamber	24″ #1 or 26″ #2	1 - 9 1/2″ twist	13 1/2″	7/8″	--	1 1/8″
	Weathermark	RH 24″ or 26″	7 1/2 lbs.	44 5/8″ or 46 5/8″	3 + 1 in chamber	24″ #1 or 26″ #2	1 - 9 1/2″ twist	13 1/2″	7/8″	--	1 1/8″
	Alaskan	RH 24″ or 26″	7 1/2 lbs.	44 5/8″ or 46 5/8″	3 + 1 in chamber	24″ #1 or 26″ #2	1 - 9 1/2″ twist	13 1/2″	7/8″	--	1 1/8″
.338 Win Mag.	Mark V Sporter	RH 24″	8 lbs.	44 1/2″	3 + 1 in chamber	24″ #2	1 - 9 1/2″ twist	13 5/8″	1″	5/8″	1 5/8″
	Weathermark	RH 24″	7 1/2 lbs.	44 1/2″	3 + 1 in chamber	24″ #2	1 - 9 1/2″ twist	13 1/2″	7/8″	--	1 1/8″
	Alaskan	RH 24″	7 1/2 lbs.	44 1/2″	3 + 1 in chamber	24″ #2	1 - 9 1/2″ twist	13 1/2″	7/8″	--	1 1/8″
.340 WBY Mag.	Mark V Sporter	RH 26″	8 1/2 lbs.	46 5/8″	3 + 1 in chamber	26″ #2	1 - 9 1/2″ twist	13 5/8″	1″	5/8″	1 5/8″
	Mark V Deluxe	RH 26″	8 1/2 lbs.	46 5/8″	3 + 1 in chamber	26″ #2	1 - 9 1/2″ twist	13 5/8″	5/8″	1/4″	1 1/8″
	Lazermark	RH 26″	8 1/2 lbs.	46 5/8″	3 + 1 in chamber	26″ #2	1 - 9 1/2″ twist	13 5/8″	5/8″	1/4″	1 1/8″
	Classicmark	RH 26″	8 1/2 lbs.	46 5/8″	3 + 1 in chamber	26″ #2	1 - 9 1/2″ twist	13 1/2″	7/8″	--	1 1/8″
	Weathermark	RH 26″	8 lbs.	46 5/8″	3 + 1 in chamber	26″ #2	1 - 9 1/2″ twist	13 1/2″	7/8″	--	1 1/8″
	Alaskan	RH 26″	8 lbs.	46 5/8″	3 + 1 in chamber	26″ #2	1 - 9 1/2″ twist	13 1/2″	7/8″	--	1 1/8″
.375 H&H Mag.	Mark V Sporter	RH 24″	8 1/2 lbs.	44 5/8″	3 + 1 in chamber	24″ #3	1 - 12″ twist	13 5/8″	1″	5/8″	1 5/8″
	Classicmark	RH 24″	8 1/2 lbs.	44 5/8″	3 + 1 in chamber	24″ #3	1 - 12″ twist	13 1/2″	7/8″	--	1 1/8″
	Weathermark	RH 24″	8 1/2 lbs.	44 5/8″	3 + 1 in chamber	24″ #3	1 - 12″ twist	13 1/2″	7/8″	--	1 1/8″
	Alaskan	RH 24″	8 1/2 lbs.	44 5/8″	3 + 1 in chamber	24″ #3	1 - 12″ twist	13 1/2″	7/8″	--	1 1/8″
.378 WBY Mag.	Mark V Deluxe	RH 26″	8 1/2 lbs.	46 5/8″	2 + 1 in chamber	26″ #3	1-12″ twist	13 5/8″	5/8″	1/4″	1 1/8″
	Lazermark	RH 26″	8 1/2 lbs.	46 5/8″	2 + 1 in chamber	26″ #3	1-12″ twist	13 5/8″	5/8″	1/4″	1 1/8″
	Classicmark	RH 26″	8 1/2 lbs.	46 5/8″	2 + 1 in chamber	26″ #3	1-12″ twist	13 1/2″	7/8″	--	1 1/8″
**.416 WBY Mag.	Mark V Deluxe	RH 24″ or 26″	9 1/2 lbs.	44 3/4″ or 46 3/4″	2 + 1 in chamber	24″ or 26″ #3.5	1-14″ twist	14″	5/8″	1/4″	1 1/8″
	Lazermark	RH 24″	9 1/2 lbs.	44 3/4″ or 46 3/4″	2 + 1 in chamber	24″	1-14″ twist	14″	5/8″	1/4″	1 1/8″
	Classicmark	RH 24″ or 26″	9 1/2 lbs.	44 3/4″ or 46 3/4″	2 + 1 in chamber	24″ or 26″ #3.5	1-14″ twist	14″	7/8″	--	1 1/8″
**.460 WBY Mag.	Mark V Deluxe	RH 24″ or 26″	10 1/2 lbs.	44 3/4″ or 46 3/4″	2 + 1 in chamber	24″ or 26″ #4	1-16″ twist	14″	5/8″	1/4″	1 1/8″
	Lazermark	RH 24″ or 26″	10 1/2 lbs.	44 3/4″ or 46 3/4″	2 + 1 in chamber	24″ or 26″ #4	1-16″ twist	14″	5/8″	1/4″	1 1/8″
	Classicmark	RH 26″	10 1/2 lbs.	46 3/4″	2 + 1 in chamber	26″ #4	1-16″ twist	14″	7/8″	--	1 1/8″

* Weight approximate due to stock density and bore diameter. ** Available with Weatherby Accubrake only. Safari Grade Custom, Safari Classic and Crown Custom rifles are also available. Consult your Weatherby dealer or the Weatherby Custom Shop for specifications.

WEATHERBY MARK V RIFLES

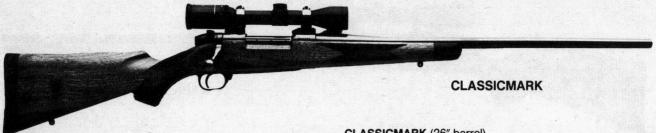

CLASSICMARK

CLASSICMARK (22″ barrel)   **Prices**
In 270 Win. and 30-06 . . . . **$1295.00**
CLASSICMARK (24″ barrel)
In 240, 257, 270, 7mm, 300 Wby. Mag.,
   7mm Mag. **1295.00**

CLASSICMARK (26″ barrel)
In 375 H&H **$1425.00**
In 240, 257, 270, 7mm Wby. Mag. **1310.00**
In 300 Wby. Mag. **1323.00**
In 378 Wby. Mag. **1356.00**
In 416 Wby. Mag. **1411.00**
In 460 Wby. Mag. **1573.00**

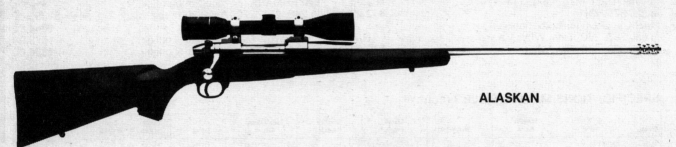

ALASKAN

The Alaskan model rifle with Mark V bolt action features Weatherby's Weathermark™ composite stock with special non-glare finish. The electroless nickel finish is stainless and impervious to rust. The stock, which features raised point checkering, is color impregnated for a durable, scratch-resistant finish and is teamed with satin-finished metalwork to reduce game-spooking glare. See table on previous page for specifications.

ALASKAN (22″ barrel)   **Prices**
In cal. 270, 30-06 . . . . **$799.00**
ALASKAN (24″ barrel)
In cal. 257, 270, 7mm, 300 Wby. Mag.,
   7mm Rem. Mag., 300, 338 Win. **799.00**
In cal. 375 H&H **949.00**
ALASKAN (26″ barrel)
In cal. 257, 270, 7mm Wby. Mag. **833.00**
In cal. 300, 340 Wby. Mag. **833.00**

WEATHERMARK

The Weathermark™ rifle features the Mark V bolt action and features a special composite stock that is guaranteed not to warp, preserving accuracy. The stock is the same as the Alaskan model (see above). For complete specifications, see the table on the previous page.

WEATHERMARK (22″ barrel)   **Prices**
In cal. 270, 30-06 . . . . **$599.00**
WEATHERMARK (24″ barrel)
In cal. 257, 270, 7mm, 300 Wby. Mag.,
   7mm Rem. Mag., 300, 338 Win. **599.00**
In cal. 375 H&H **711.00**

WEATHERMARK (26″ barrel)
In cal. 257, 270, 7mm Wby. Mag. **$625.00**
In cal. 300, 340 Wby. Mag. **625.00**

VARMINTMASTER (26″ barrel)   **Prices**
In 224 Wby. Mag. and 22-250 . . . . **$1196.00**
WHITETAIL LTD. EDITION (22″ barrel)
In 250 Savage **1366.00**

WEATHERBY RIFLES

VANGUARD VGX DELUXE
$699.00

VANGUARD CLASSIC
$549.00

VANGUARD WEATHERGUARD
$499.00

SPECIFICATIONS VANGUARD RIFLES

Caliber	Model	Barrelled Action	Weight *	Overall Length	Magazine Capacity	Barrel Length/ Contour	Rifling	Length of Pull	Drop at Comb	Monte Carlo	Drop at Heel
22-250	Vanguard VGX	RH 24"	8 1/2 lbs.	44"	4 + 1 in chamber	24" #3	1-14" twist	13 5/8"	7/8"	1/2"	1 1/2"
.223 Rem.	Vanguard Classic	RH 24"	7 3/4 lbs.	44"	4 + 1 in chamber	24" #1	1-14" twist	13 7/8"	7/8"	--	1 1/8"
	Weatherguard	RH 24"	7 1/2 lbs.	44"	4 + 1 in chamber	24" #1	1-14" twist	13 7/8"	5/8"	--	1"
.243 WIN	Vanguard VGX	RH 24"	8 lbs.	44"	4 + 1 in chamber	24" #2	1-10" twist	13 5/8"	7/8"	1/2"	1 1/2"
	Vanguard Classic	RH 24"	7 3/4 lbs.	44"	4 + 1 in chamber	24" #1	1-10" twist	13 7/8"	7/8"	--	1 1/8"
	Weatherguard	RH 24"	7 1/2 lbs.	44"	4 + 1 in chamber	24" #1	1-10" twist	13 7/8"	5/8"	--	1"
.270 WIN	Vanguard VGX	RH 24"	8 lbs.	44 "	4 + 1 in chamber	24" #2	1-10" twist	13 5/8"	7/8"	1/2"	1 1/2"
	Vanguard Classic	RH 24"	7 3/4 lbs.	44 1/2"	4 + 1 in chamber	24" #1	1-10" twist	13 7/8"	7/8"	--	1 1/8"
	Weatherguard	RH 24"	7 1/2 lbs.	44 1/2"	4 + 1 in chamber	24" #1	1-10" twist	13 7/8"	5/8"	--	1"
	Alaskan	RH 24"	7 1/2 lbs.	44 1/2"	4 + 1 in chamber	24" #1	1-10" twist	13 7/8"	5/8"	--	1"
.270 WBY Mag.	Vanguard VGX	RH 24"	8 lbs.	44 1/2"	3 + 1 in chamber	24" #2	1-10" twist	13 5/8"	7/8"	1/2"	1 1/2"
7mm Rem. Mag.	Vanguard VGX	RH 24"	8 lbs.	44 "	4 + 1 in chamber	24" #2	1-10" twist	13 5/8"	7/8"	1/2"	1 1/2"
	Vanguard Classic	RH 24"	7 3/4 lbs.	44 1/2"	3 + 1 in chamber	24" #1	1-10" twist	13 7/8"	7/8"	--	1 1/8"
	Weatherguard	RH 24"	7 lbs.	44 1/2"	3 + 1 in chamber	24" #1	1-10" twist	13 7/8"	7/8"	--	1"
	Alaskan	RH 24"	7 lbs.	44 1/2"	3 + 1 in chamber	24" #1	1-10" twist	13 7/8"	5/8"	--	1"
7mm-08 Rem.	Vanguard Classic	RH 24"	7 3/4 lbs.	44"	4 + 1 in chamber	24" #1	1-10" twist	13 7/8"	7/8"	--	1 1/8"
	Weatherguard	RH 24"	7 1/2 lbs.	44"	4 + 1 in chamber	24" #1	1-10" twist	13 7/8"	7/8"	--	1"
30-06 Springfield	Vanguard VGX	RH 24"	8 lbs.	44 "	4 + 1 in chamber	24" #2	1-10" twist	13 5/8"	7/8"	1/2"	1 1/2"
	Vanguard Classic	RH 24"	7 3/4 lbs.	44 1/2"	4 + 1 in chamber	24" #1	1-10" twist	13 7/8"	7/8"	--	1 1/8"
	Weatherguard	RH 24"	7 1/2 lbs.	44 1/2"	4 + 1 in chamber	24" #1	1-10" twist	13 7/8"	7/8"	--	1"
	Alaskan	RH 24"	7 1/2 lbs.	44 1/2"	4 + 1 in chamber	24" #1	1-10" twist	13 7/8"	5/8"	--	1"
.300 WIN Mag.	Vanguard VGX	RH 24"	8 lbs.	44 1/2"	3 + 1 in chamber	24" #2	1-10" twist	13 5/8"	7/8"	1/2"	1 1/2"
.300 WBY Mag.	Vanguard VGX	RH 24"	8 lbs.	44 1/2"	3 + 1 in chamber	24" #2	1-10" twist	13 5/8"	7/8"	1/2"	1 1/2"
.308 WIN	Vanguard Classic	RH 24"	7 3/4 lbs.	44"	4 + 1 in chamber	24" #1	1-10" twist	13 7/8"	7/8"	--	1 1/8"
	Weatherguard	RH 24"	7 1/2 lbs.	44"	4 + 1 in chamber	24" #1	1-10" twist	13 7/8"	5/8"	--	1 1/8"
.338 WIN Mag.	Vanguard VGX	RH 24"	8 lbs.	44 1/2"	3 + 1 in chamber	24" #2	1-10" twist	13 5/8"	7/8"	1/2"	1 1/2"

*Weight Approximate—varies due to stock density.

WINCHESTER BOLT ACTION RIFLES

MODEL 70 FEATHERWEIGHT WINTUFF
$572.00 $562.00 (Walnut)

MODEL 70 FEATHERWEIGHT CLASSIC
$749.00

SPECIFICATIONS MODEL 70 FEATHERWEIGHT

Model	Caliber	Magazine Capacity*	Barrel Length	Overall Length	Nominal Length Of Pull	Nominal Drop At Comb	Nominal Drop At Heel	Nominal Weight (Lbs.)	Rate of Twist 1 Turn In	Bases Rings or Sights
70 WALNUT FEATHERWEIGHT	22-250 Rem.	5	22"	42"	13 1/2"	9/16"	7/8"	7	14"	B + R
Standard Grade Walnut	223 Rem.	6	22	42	13 1/2	9/16	7/8	7	12	B + R
	243 Win.	5	22	42	13 1/2	9/16	7/8	7	10	B + R
	6.5×55mm Swedish	5	22	42 1/2	13 1/2	9/16	7/8	7	7.87	B + R
	270 Win.	5	22	42 1/2	13 1/2	9/16	7/8	7 1/4	10	B + R
	280 Rem.	5	22	42 1/2	13 1/2	9/16	7/8	7 1/4	10	B + R
	7mm-08 Rem.	3	22	42	13 1/2	9/16	7/8	7	9.5	B + R
	7mm Rem. Mag	5	24	44 1/2	13 1/2	9/16	7/8	7 1/2	9.5	B + R
	30-06 Spfld.	5	22	42 1/2	13 1/2	9/16	7/8	7 1/4	10	B + R
	308 Win.	3	22	42	13 1/2	9/16	7/8	7	12	B + R
	300 Win. Mag.	3	24	44 1/2	13 1/2	9/16	7/8	7 1/2	10	B + R
70 WINTUFF FEATHERWEIGHT	22-250 Rem.	5	22	42	13 1/2	9/16	7/8	6 3/4	14	B + R
Brown Laminate	223 Rem.	6	22	42	13 1/2	9/16	7/8	6 3/4	12	B + R
	243 Win.	5	22	42	13 1/2	9/16	7/8	6 3/4	10	B + R
	270 Win.	5	22	42 1/2	13 1/2	9/16	7/8	7	10	B + R
	308 Win.	5	22	42	13 1/2	9/16	7/8	6 3/4	12	B + R
	30-06 Spfld.	5	22	42 1/2	13 1/2	9/16	7/8	7	10	B + R
70 WALNUT FEATHERWEIGHT CLASSIC	270 Win.	5	22	43	14	9/16	7/8	7 1/4	10	B + R
Standard Grade Walnut	280 Rem.	5	22	43	14	9/16	7/8	7 1/4	10	B + R
Controlled Round Feeding	30-06 Spfld.	5	22	43	14	9/16	7/8	7 1/4	10	B + R

* For additional capacity, add one round in chamber when ready to fire. Drops are measured from center line of bore. Rate of twist is right-hand.

WINCHESTER BOLT ACTION RIFLES

MODEL 70 LIGHTWEIGHT RIFLE
$485.00

MODEL 70 LIGHTWEIGHT RIFLE

Model 70 Lightweight Walnut	$471.00
Model 70 Win-Tuff Lightweight	471.00
Model 70 Win-Cam Lightweight	471.00

SPECIFICATIONS: MODEL 70 LIGHTWEIGHT

Model	Caliber	Magazine Capacity (A)	Barrel Length	Overall Length	Nominal Length Of Pull	Nominal Drop At		Nominal Weight (Lbs.)	Rate of Twist 1 Turn In
						Comb	Heel		
70 WALNUT	223 Rem.	6	22	42	13¾	$^9/_{16}$	⅞	6¼	12
	243 Win.	5	22	42	13¾	$^9/_{16}$	⅞	6¼	10
Checkered,	270 Win.	5	22	42½	13¾	$^9/_{16}$	⅞	6½	10
No Sights	280 Rem.	5	22	42½	13¾	$^9/_{16}$	⅞	6½	10
	30-06 Spgfld.	5	22	42½	13¾	$^9/_{16}$	⅞	6½	10
	308 Win.	5	22	42	13¾	$^9/_{16}$	⅞	6¼	12

(A) For additional capacity, add one round in chamber when ready to fire. Drops are measured from center line of bore. Rate of twist is right-hand. No sights.

MODEL 70 SM
(Synthetic Composite Stock, Matte)
$576.00
$604.00 (375 H&H MAGNUM)

SPECIFICATIONS MODEL 70 SM (SYNTHETIC STOCK)

Caliber	Magazine Capacity	Barrel Length	Overall Length	Nominal Length Of Pull	Nominal Drop At		Nominal Weight (Lbs.)	Rate of Twist 1 Turn In	Bases Rings or Sights
					Comb	Heel			
223 Rem.	6	24″	44½″	14″	$^9/_{16}$″	⅞″	7	12″	B+R
22-250 Rem.	5	24	44½	14	$^9/_{16}$	⅞	7	14	B+R
243 Win.	5	24	44½	14	$^9/_{16}$	⅞	7	10	B+R
270 Win.	5	24	45	14	$^9/_{16}$	⅞	7⅜	10	B+R
308 Win.	5	24	44½	14	$^9/_{16}$	⅞	7	12	B+R
30-06 Spfld.	5	24	45	14	$^9/_{16}$	⅞	7⅜	10	B+R
7mm Rem. Mag.	3	24	45	14	$^9/_{16}$	⅞	7⅝	9½	B+R
300 Win. Mag.	3	24	45	14	$^9/_{16}$	⅞	7⅝	10	B+R
338 Win. Mag.	3	24	45	14	$^9/_{16}$	⅞	7⅝	10	B+R
375 H&H Mag.	3	24	45	14	$^9/_{16}$	⅞	8	12	Sights

RIFLES

WINCHESTER BOLT ACTION RIFLES

MODEL 70 SUPER GRADE
$997.00 (not shown)

The Winchester Model 70 Super Grade features a bolt with true claw-controlled feeding of belted magnums. The stainless steel claw extractor on the bolt grasps the round from the magazine and delivers it to the chamber and later extracts the spent cartridge. A gas block doubles as bolt stop and the bolt guard rail assures smooth action. Winchester's 3-position safety and field-strippable firing pin are standard equipment.

Other features include a satin finish select walnut stock with sculptured cheekpiece designed to direct recoil forces rearward and away from the shooter's cheek; an extra-thick honeycomb recoil; all-steel bottom metal; and chrome molybdenum barrel with cold hammer-forged rifling for optimum accuracy. Specifications are listed in the table below.

SPECIFICATIONS WINCHESTER MODEL 70 SUPER GRADE RIFLE

Caliber	Maga-zine Capacity*	Barrel Length	Over-all Length	Nominal Length of Pull	Nominal Drop at Comb	Heel	MC	Nominal Weight (Lbs.)	Rate of Twist 1 Turn in	Bases & Rings or Sights
270 Win.	5	24″	45″	14	$9/16″$	$7/8″$	—	$7 3/4$	10	B + R
30-06 Spfld.	5	24	45	14	$9/16$	$7/8$	—	$7 3/4$	10	B + R
7mm Rem. Mag.	3	24	45	14	$9/16$	$7/8$	—	$7 3/4$	$9 1/2$	B + R
300 Win. Mag.	3	24	45	14	$9/16$	$7/8$	—	$7 3/4$	10	B + R
338 Win. Mag.	3	24	45	14	$9/16$	$7/8$	—	$7 3/4$	10	B + R

* For additional capacity, add one round in chamber when ready to fire. Drops are measured from center line of bore. Rate of twist is right-hand.

SPECIFICATIONS MODEL 70 VARMINT (WALNUT STOCK)

Caliber	Magazine Capacity	Barrel Length	Overall Length	Nominal Length Of Pull	Nominal Drop At Comb	Heel	Nominal Weight (Lbs.)	Rate of Twist 1 Turn In	Bases & Rings or Sights
223 Rem.	6″	26″	46″	$13 1/2″$	$9/16″$	$7/8″$	9	12″	—
22-250 Rem.	5	26	46	$13 1/2$	$9/16$	$7/8$	9	14	—
243 Win.	5	26	46	$13 1/2$	$9/16$	$7/8$	9	10	—
308 Win.	5	26	46	$13 1/2$	$9/16$	$7/8$	9	12	—

* For additional capacity, add one round in chamber when ready to fire. Drops are measured from center line of bore. B+R = Bases and Rings included. Rate of twist is right-hand.

MODEL 70 HEAVY BARREL VARMINT RIFLE
$700.00

Winchester's Varmint Rifle features a Sporter stock with undercut cheekpiece and 26″ counter-bored barrel. Rubber butt pad, swivel studs and receiver drilled and tapped for scope are standard, as is Winchester's 3-position safety. Also available in composite stock and matte finished barrel and receiver.

MODEL 70 HEAVY BARREL VARMINT RIFLE SPECIFICATIONS

Model	Caliber	Magazine Capacity (A)	Barrel Length	Overall Length	Nominal Length Of Pull	Nominal Drop At Comb	Heel	MC	Nominal Weight (Lbs.)	Rate of Twist 1 Turn In	Sights
70 VARMINT	22-250 Rem.	5	26″	46″	$13 3/4″$	$9/16″$	$1 5/16″$	$3/4″$	9	14″	—
	223 Rem.	6	26	46	$13 3/4$	$9/16$	$1 5/16$	$3/4$	9	12	—
	243 Win.	5	26	46	$13 3/4$	$9/16$	$1 5/16$	$3/4$	9	10	—
	308 Win.	5	26	46	$13 3/4$	$9/16$	$1 5/16$	$3/4$	9	12	—

(A) For additional capacity, add one round in chamber when ready to fire. Drops are measured from center line of bore. Rate of twist is right-hand.

WINCHESTER BOLT ACTION RIFLES

MODEL 70 SPORTER & SUPER EXPRESS RIFLES
$556.00 ($816.00 SUPER EXPRESS)

MODEL 70 SPORTER WINTUFF
$572.00

SPECIFICATIONS MODEL 70 SPORTER

Model	Caliber	Magazine Capacity A	Barrel Length	Overall Length	Nominal Length Of Pull	Nominal Drop At Comb	Heel	Nominal Weight (Lbs.)	Rate of Twist 1 Turn In	Bases & Rings or Sights
70 SPORTER	223 Rem.	6	24″	44½″	14″	9/16″	7/8″	7¼	12″	B+R
	22-250 Rem.	5	24	44½	14	9/16	7/8	7¼	14	B+R
	243 Win.	5	24	44½	14	9/16	7/8	7¼	10	Sights
	243 Win.	5	24	44½	14	9/16	7/8	7¼	10	B+R
	25-06 Rem.	5	24	45	14	9/16	7/8	7½	10	Sights
	264-Win. Mag.	3	24	45	14	9/16	7/8	7½	9	Sights
	270 Win.	5	24	45	14	9/16	7/8	7½	10	Sights
	270 Win.	5	24	45	14	9/16	7/8	7½	10	B+R
	270 Weath. Mag.	3	24	45	14	9/16	7/8	7½	10	B+R
	30-06 Spfld.	5	24	45	14	9/16	7/8	7½	10	Sights
	30-06 Spfld.	5	24	45	14	9/16	7/8	7½	10	B+R
	7mm Rem. Mag.	3	24	45	14	9/16	7/8	7½	9½	Sights
	7mm Rem. Mag.	3	24	45	14	9/16	7/8	7½	9½	B+R
	300 Win. Mag.	3	24	45	14	9/16	7/8	7½	10	Sights
	300 Weath. Mag.	3	24	45	14	9/16	7/8	7½	10	B+R
	338 Win. Mag.	3	24	45	14	9/16	7/8	7½	10	Sights
	338 Win. Mag.	3	24	45	14	9/16	7/8	7½	10	B+R
70 SPORTER WINTUFF	270 Win.	5	24″	44½″	14	9/16″	7/8″	7⅝	10	B+R
	30-06 Spfld.	5	24	44½	14	9/16	7/8	7⅝	10	B+R
	7mm Rem. Mag.	3	24	44½	14	9/16	7/8	7⅞	9½	B+R
	300 Win.Mag.	3	24	44½	14	9/16	7/8	7⅞	10	B+R
	300 Weath. Mag.	3	24	44½	14	9/16	7/8	7⅞	10	B+R
	338 Win. Mag.	3	24	44½	14	9/16	7/8	7⅞	10	B+R

SPECIFICATIONS MODEL 70 DBM (DETACHABLE BOX MAGAZINE) (Photo and prices on next page)

Caliber	Magazine Capacity*	Barrel Length	Overall Length	Nominal Length Of Pull	Nominal Drop At Comb	Heel	Nominal Weight (Lbs.)	Rate of Twist 1 Turn In	Bases Rings or Sights
233 Rem.	4	24″	45″	14″	9/16″	7/8″	7	12″	B+R
22-250 Rem.	4	24	45	14	9/16	7/8	7	14	B+R
243 Win.	4	24	45	14	9/16	7/8	7	10	B+R
243 Win.	4	24	45	14	9/16	7/8	7	10	Sights
270 Win.	4	24	45	14	9/16	7/8	7⅜	10	B+R
270 Win.	4	24	45	14	9/16	7/8	7⅜	10	Sights
308 Win.	4	24	45	14	9/16	7/8	7	12	B+R
308 Win.	4	24	45	14	9/16	7/8	7	12	Sights
30-06 Spfld.	4	24	45	14	9/16	7/8	7⅜	10	B+R
30-06 Spfld.	4	24	45	14	9/16	7/8	7⅜	10	Sights
7mm Rem. Mag.	3	24	45	14	9/16	7/8	7⅜	9½	B+R
7mm Rem. Mag.	3	24	45	14	9/16	7/8	7⅜	9½	Sights
300 Win. Mag.	3	24	45	14	9/16	7/8	7⅜	10	B+R
300 Win. Mag.	3	24	45	14	9/16	7/8	7⅜	10	Sights

WINCHESTER BOLT ACTION RIFLES

MODEL 70 SPORTER DBM
$598.00
$618.00 (Synthetic Stock)

WINCHESTER RANGER®
BOLT ACTION CENTERFIRE RIFLE
$440.00

The Ranger Bolt Action Rifle comes with an American hardwood stock, a wear-resistant satin walnut finish, ramp bead-post front sight, steel barrel, hinged steel magazine floorplate, three-position safety and engine-turned, anti-bind bolt. The receiver is drilled and tapped for scope mounting; accuracy is enhanced by thermoplastic bedding of the receiver. Barrel and receiver are brushed and blued.

WINCHESTER RANGER®
YOUTH BOLT ACTION CARBINE
$465.00

This carbine offers dependable bolt action performance combined with a scaled-down design to fit the younger, smaller shooter. It features anti-bind bolt design, jeweled bolt, three-position safety, contoured recoil pad, ramped bead front sight, semi-buckhorn folding leaf rear sight, hinged steel magazine floorplate, and sling swivels. Receiver is drilled and tapped for scope mounting. Stock is of American hardwood with protective satin walnut finish. Pistol grip, length of pull, overall length, and comb are all tailored to youth dimensions (see table).

SPECIFICATIONS RANGER & YOUTH RIFLE

Model	Caliber	Magazine Capacity	Barrel Length	Overall Length	Nominal Length Of Pull	Nominal Drop At Comb	Nominal Drop At Heel	Nominal Weight (Lbs.)	Rate of Twist 1 Turn in	Bases & Rings Sights
70 RANGER	223 Rem.	6	22″	42″	13$\frac{1}{2}$″	$\frac{9}{16}$″	$\frac{7}{8}$″	6$\frac{3}{4}$	12″	Sights
	243 Win.	5	22	42	13$\frac{1}{2}$	$\frac{9}{16}$	$\frac{7}{8}$	6$\frac{3}{4}$	10	Sights
	270 Win.	5	22	42$\frac{1}{2}$	13$\frac{1}{2}$	$\frac{9}{16}$	$\frac{7}{8}$	6$\frac{3}{4}$	10	Sights
	30-06 Spfld.	5	22	41$\frac{1}{2}$	13$\frac{1}{2}$	$\frac{9}{16}$	$\frac{7}{8}$	6$\frac{3}{4}$	10	Sights
70 RANGER LADIES/ YOUTH	243 Win.	5	22	41	12$\frac{1}{2}$	$\frac{3}{4}$	1	6$\frac{1}{2}$	10	Sights
	308 Win.	5	22	41	12$\frac{1}{2}$	$\frac{3}{4}$	1	6$\frac{1}{2}$	12	Sights

For additional capacity, add one round in chamber when ready to fire. Drops are measured from center line of bore. Rate of twist is right-hand.

WINCHESTER LEVER ACTION
CARBINES & RIFLES

The top choice for lever-action styling and craftsmanship. Metal surfaces are highly polished and blued. American walnut stock

MODEL 94 STANDARD WALNUT RIFLE

and forearm have a protective stain finish with precise-cut wraparound checkering. It has a 20-inch barrel with hooded blade front sight and semi-buckhorn rear sight. **Calibers:** 30-30 Win., 32 Win. Special and 7-30 Waters.

Prices:
30-30 Win., checkered **$362.00**
30-30 Win., 7-30 Waters, 32 Win. Special **335.00**

With 16-inch short-barrel lever action and straight forward styling. Compact and fast-handling in dense cover, it has a magazine capacity of five shots (9 in 45 Colt or 44 Rem. Mag./

MODEL 94 WALNUT TRAPPER CARBINE

44 S&W Special). **Calibers:** 30-30 Winchester, 357 Mag., 45 Colt, and 44 Rem. Mag./44 S&W Special.

Prices:
30-30 Winchester **$335.00**
357 Mag., 45 Colt, 44 Rem. Mag./44 S&W
    Special **354.00**

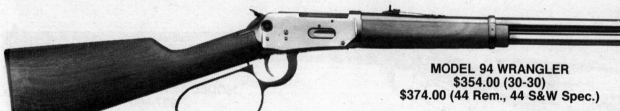

MODEL 94 WRANGLER
$354.00 (30-30)
$374.00 (44 Rem., 44 S&W Spec.)

MODEL 94 SPECIFICATIONS

Model	Caliber	Magazine Capacity (A)	Barrel Length	Overall Length	Nominal Length Of Pull	Nominal Drop At		Nominal Weight (Lbs.)	Rate of Twist 1 Turn in	Rings Sights
						Comb	Heel			
94 CHECKERED WALNUT	30-30 Win.	6	20"	37³/₄"	13"	1¹/₈"	1⁷/₈"	6¹/₂	12"	Rifle
94 STANDARD WALNUT	30-30 Win.	6	20	37³/₄	13	1¹/₈	1⁷/₈	6¹/₂	12	Rifle
	32 Win.	6	20	37³/₄	13	1¹/₈	1⁷/₈	6¹/₂	12	Rifle
	7-30 Waters	6	20	37³/₄	13	1¹/₈	1⁷/₈	6¹/₂	9.9	Rifle
94 TRAPPER CARBINE WALNUT	30-30 Win.	5	16	33³/₄	13¹/₂	1¹/₈	1⁷/₈	6¹/₈	12	Rifle
	44 Rem. Mag.	9	16	33³/₄	13¹/₂	1¹/₈	1⁷/₈	6	38	Rifle
	44 S&W Spec.	9	16	33³/₄	13¹/₂	1¹/₈	1⁷/₈	6	38	Rifle
	357 Mag.	9	16	33³/₄	13¹/₂	1¹/₈	1⁷/₈	6	16	Rifle
	45 Colt	9	16	33³/₄	13¹/₂	1¹/₈	1⁷/₈	6	38	Rifle
94 WRANGLER WALNUT	30-30 Win.	5	16	33³/₄	13¹/₂	1¹/₈	1⁷/₈	6¹/₈	12	Rifle
	44 Rem. Mag.	9	16	33³/₄	13¹/₂	1¹/₈	1⁷/₈	6	12	Rifle
	44 S&W Spec.	9	16	33³/₄	13¹/₂	1¹/₈	1⁷/₈	6	12	Rifle

(A) for additional capacity, add one round in chamber when ready to fire. Drops are measured from center line of bore. Rate of twist is right-hand.

WINCHESTER LEVER ACTION RIFLES

MODEL 94 RANGER
$296.00 ($348.00 with Scope)

Model 94 Ranger is an economical version of the Model 94. Lever action is smooth and reliable. In 30-30 Winchester, the rapid-firing six-shot magazine capacity provides two more shots than most centerfire hunting rifles.

MODEL 94 BIG BORE WALNUT
$374.00

Winchester's powerful 307 and 356 hunting calibers combined with maximum lever-action power and angled ejection provide hunters with improved performance and economy.

MODEL 94 WIN-TUFF RIFLE
$374.00

Includes all features and specifications of standard Model 94 plus tough laminated hardwood styled for the brush-gunning hunter who wants good concealment and a carbine that can stand up to all kinds of weather.

MODEL 94 SPECIFICATIONS

Model	Caliber	Magazine Capacity (A)	Barrel Length	Overall Length	Nominal Length Of Pull	Nominal Drop At Comb	Nominal Drop At Heel	Nominal Weight (Lbs.)	Rate of Twist 1 Turn in	Sights
94 WIN-TUFF	30-30 Win.	6	20"	37¾"	13½"	1⅛"	1⅞"	6½	12"	Rifle
94 BIG BORE WALNUT	307 Win.	6	20	37¼	13½	1⅛	1⅞	6½	12	Rifle
	356 Win.	6	20	37¾	13½	1⅛	1⅞	6½	12	Rifle
RANGER	30-30 Win.	6	20	37¾	13½	1⅛	1⅞	6½	12	Rifle
Scope 4X32 and see-through mounts	30-30 Win.	6	20	37¾	13½	1⅛	1⅞	6½	12	R/S

(A) For additional capacity, add one round in chamber when ready to fire. Drops are measured from center line of bore. R/S-Rifle sights and Bushnell® Sportview™ scope with mounts. Rate of twist is right-hand.

WINCHESTER RIFLES

MODEL 9422 LEVER-ACTION RIMFIRE RIFLES

These Model 9422 rimfire rifles combine classic 94 styling and handling in ultra-modern lever action 22s of superb craftsmanship. Handling and shooting characteristics are superior because of their carbine-like size.

Positive lever action and bolt design ensure feeding and chambering from any shooting position. The bolt face is T-slotted to guide the cartridge with complete control from magazine to chamber. A color-coded magazine follower shows when the brass magazine tube is empty. Receivers are grooved for scope mounting. Other functional features include exposed hammer with half-cock safety, hooded bead front sight, semi-buckhorn rear sight and side ejection of spent cartridges.

Stock and forearm are American walnut with checkering, high-luster finish, and straight-grip design. Internal parts are carefully finished for smoothness of action.

MODEL 9422 WALNUT

Considered one of the world's finest production sporting arms, this lever action rimfire (shown above) holds 21 Short, 17 Long or 15 Long Rifle cartridges.

Model 9422 Walnut Magnum gives exceptional accuracy at longer ranges than conventional 22 rifles. It is designed specifically for the 22 Winchester Magnum Rimfire cartridge and holds 11 cartridges.

Model 9422 Win-Cam Magnum features laminated non-glare, green-shaded stock and forearm. American hardwood stock is bonded to withstand all weather and climates. **Model 9422 Win-Tuff** is also availale to ensure resistance to changes in weather conditions, or exposure to water and hard knocks.

SPECIFICATIONS MODEL 9422

Model	Caliber	Magazine Capacity	Barrel Length	Overall Length	Nominal Length Of Pull	Nominal Drop At Comb	Nominal Drop At Heel	Nominal Weight (Lbs.)	Rate of Twist 1 Turn in	Sights	Prices
9422 WALNUT	22 S, L, LR	21S,17L,15LR	20½″	37⅛″	13½″	1⅛″	1⅞″	6¼	16″	Rifle	$376.00
	22WMR Mag.	11	20½	37⅛	13½	1⅛	1⅞	6¼	16	Rifle	393.00
9422 WIN-TUFF	22 S, L, LR	21S,17L,15LR	20½″	37⅛″	13½″	1⅛″	1⅞″	6¼	16″	Rifle	376.00
	22WMR Mag.	11	20½	37⅛	13½	1⅛	1⅞	6¼	16	Rifle	393.00
9422 WIN-CAM	22WMR Mag.	11	20½″	37⅛″	13½″	1⅛″	1⅞″	6¼	16″	Rifle	393.00

WMR-Winchester Magnum Rimfire. S-Short, L-Long, LR-Long Rifle. Drops are measured from center line of bore.

MODEL 52B RIMFIRE BOLT ACTION (Limited)
$576.00

SPECIFICATIONS
Caliber: 22 LR
Capacity: 5 rounds
Barrel length: 24″

Overall length: 42⅛″
Length of pull: 13⅝″
Drop at comb: 1⅜″
Drop at heel: 2 5/16″
Weight: 7 lbs.

RIFLES

WINSLOW RIFLES

SPECIFICATIONS

Stock: Choice of two stock models. **The Plainsmaster** offers pinpoint accuracy in open country with full curl pistol grip and flat forearm. **The Bushmaster** offers lighter weight for bush country; slender pistol with palm swell; beavertail forend for light hand comfort. Both styles are of hand-rubbed black walnut. Length of pull—13½ inches; plainsmaster ⅜ inch castoff; Bushmaster ³⁄₁₆ inch castoff; all rifles are drilled and tapped to incorporate the use of telescopic sights; rifles with receiver or open sights are available on special order; all rifles are equipped with quick detachable sling swivel studs and white-line recoil pad. All Winslow stocks incorporate a slight castoff to deflect recoil, minimizing flinch and muzzle jump. **Magazine:** Staggered box type, four shot. (Blind in the stock has no floorplate). **Action:** Mauser Mark X Action. **Overall length:** 43″ (Standard Model); 45″ (Magnum); all Winslow rifles have company name and serial number and grade engraved on the action and caliber engraved on barrel. **Barrel:** Douglas barrel premium grade, chrome moly-type steel; all barrels, 20 caliber through 35 caliber, have six lands and grooves; barrels larger than 35 caliber have eight lands and grooves. All barrels are finished to (.2 to .4) micro inches inside the lands and grooves. **Total weight** (without scope): 7 to 7½ lbs. with 24″ barrel in standard calibers 243, 308, 270, etc; 8 to 9 lbs. with 26″ barrel in Magnum calibers 264 Win., 300 Wby., 458 Win., etc. Winslow rifles are made in the following calibers:

Standard cartridges: 22-250, 243 Win., 244 Rem., 257 Roberts, 308 Win., 30-06, 280 Rem., 270 Win., 25-06, 284 Win., 358 Win., and 7mm (7×57).

Magnum cartridges: 300 Weatherby, 300 Win., 338 Win., 358 Norma, 375 H.H., 458 Win., 257 Weatherby, 264 Win., 270 Weatherby, 7mm Weatherby, 7mm Rem., 300 H.H., 308 Norma.

Left-handed models available in most calibers.

WINSLOW BASIC RIFLE

The Basic Rifle, available in the Bushmaster stock, features one ivory diamond inlay in a rose-wood grip cap and ivory trademark in bottom of forearm. Grade 'A' walnut jeweled bolt and follower. **Price: $1750.00 and up.** With **Plainsmaster stock: $100.00** extra. **Left-hand model: $1850.00 and up.**

WINSLOW VARMINT

This 17-caliber rifle is available with Bushmaster stock or Plainsmaster stock, which is a miniature of the original with high roll-over cheekpiece and a round leading edge on the forearm, modified spoon billed pistol grip. Available in 17/222, 17/222 Mag. 17/233, 222 Rem. and 223. Regent grade shown. With **Bushmaster stock: $1750.00 and up.** With **Plainsmaster stock: $100.00** extra. **Left-hand model: $1850.00 and up.**

Shotguns

For addresses and phone numbers of manufacturers and distributors included in this section, turn to *DIRECTORY OF MANUFACTURERS AND SUPPLIERS* at the back of the book.

AMERICAN ARMS

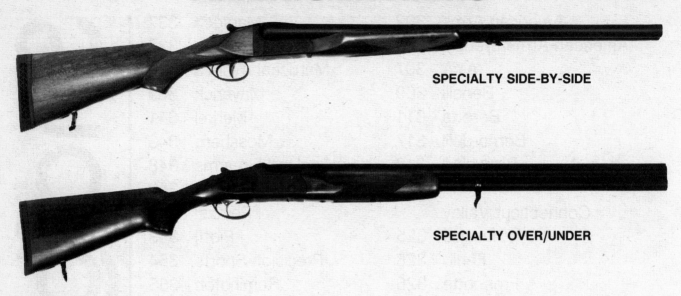

SPECIALTY SIDE-BY-SIDE

SPECIALTY OVER/UNDER

SPECIFICATIONS

Model	Gauge	Bbl Lgth.	Chamber	Chokes	Avg. Wgt.	Prices
WT/OU	10	26″	3 1/2″	CT-2	9 lbs. 10 oz.	$945.00
WS/OU	12	24″, 28″	3 1/2″	CT-3	7 lbs. 2 oz.	719.00
TS/SS	10	26″	3 1/2″	CT-2	10 lbs. 13 oz.	639.00
TS/SS	12	26″	3 1/2″	CT-3	7 lbs. 6 oz.	639.00
WS/SS	10	32″	3 1/2″	SF/SF	11 lbs. 3 oz.	639.00

CT-3 = Choke tubes IC/M/F. CT-2 = Choke tubes F/F.
SF = Steel Full Choke. SST = Single Selective Trigger.
ASE = Auto selective ejector. Drop at Comb = 1 1/8″. Drop at Heel = 2 3/8″.

BASQUE SERIES

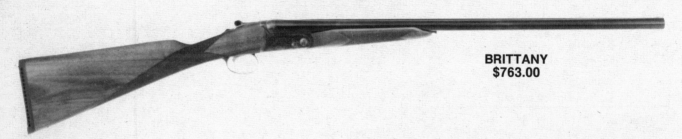

BRITTANY
$763.00

SPECIFICATIONS
Gauges: 12, 20
Chamber: 3″
Barrel length: 26″
Weight: 6 lbs. 7 ozs. (20 ga.); 6 lbs. 15 oz. (12 ga.)
Chokes: CT-3

Features: Engraved case-colored frame; single selective trigger with top tang selector; automatic selective ejectors; manual safety; hard chrome-lined barrels; walnut English-style straight stock and semi-beavertail forearm w/cut checkering and oil-rubbed finish; ventilated rubber recoil pad; and choke tubes with key

AMERICAN ARMS

SILVER I OVER AND UNDER
(W/Fixed Chokes & Extractors)

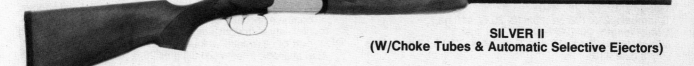

SILVER II
(W/Choke Tubes & Automatic Selective Ejectors)

SILVER SPORTING • TRAP • SKEET

SPECIFICATIONS

Model	Gauge	Bbl. Length	Chamber	Chokes	Avg. Weight	Prices
Silver I	12	26"–28"	3"	IC/M-M/F	6 lbs. 15 oz.	$ 549.00
	20	26"–28"	3"	IC/M-M/F	6 lbs. 12 oz.	
	28	26"	2 3/4"	IC/M	5 lbs. 14 oz.	609.00
	.410	26"	3"	IC/M	6 lbs. 6 oz.	
Silver II	12	26"–28"	3"	CT-3	6 lbs. 15 oz.	
	16	26"	2 3/4"	IC/M	6 lbs. 13 oz.	
	20	26"	3"	CT-3	6 lbs. 12 oz.	699.00
	28	26"	2 3/4"	IC/M	5 lbs. 14 oz.	
	.410	26"	3"	IC/M	6 lbs. 6 oz.	1129.00
	28/.410 Set	26"	2 3/4"–3"	IC/M	6 lbs. 6 oz.	
Sporting	12	28"	2 3/4"	CTS	7 lbs. 6 oz.	899.00
Trap	12	30"	2 3/4"	CT-4	7 lbs. 12 oz.	899.00
Skeet	12	28"	2 3/4"	CT-4	7 lbs. 6 oz.	899.00

CT-3 Choke Tubes IC/M/F   CT-4 Choke Tubes SK/IC/M/F   Cast Off = 3/8"   CTS = SK/SK/IC/M
Silver I and II: Pull = 14 1/8"; Drop at Comb = 1 3/8"; Drop at Heel = 2 3/8"
Silver Sporting: Pull = 14 3/8"; Drop at Comb = 1 1/2"; Drop at Heel = 2 3/8"
Silver Trap/Skeet: Pull 14 3/8"; Drop at Comb = 1 1/2"; Drop at Heel = 1 5/8"

AMERICAN ARMS

BASQUE SERIES

GRULLA #2
$2943.00

SPECIFICATIONS
Gauges: 12, 20, 28, .410
Chambers: 2³/₄″ (28 ga.); 3″ (12, 20 & .410 ga.)
Barrel length: 26″ (28″ also in 12 ga.)
Weight: 6 lbs. 4 oz. (12 ga.); 5 lbs. 11 oz. (20 & 28 ga.); 5 lbs. 13 oz. (.410)

Chokes: IC/M (M/F also in 12 ga.)
Features: Hand-fitted and finished high-grade classic double; double triggers; automatic selective ejectors; fixed chokes; concave rib; case-colored sidelock action w/engraving; English-style straight stock; splinter forearm and checkered butt of oil rubbed walnut
Also available in sets (20 & 28 or 28 & .410): **$4089.00**

GENTRY SIDE-BY-SIDE
$625.00 (12 or 20 Ga.)
$655.00 (28 or .410 Ga.)

Features boxlocks with engraved English-style scrollwork on side plates; one-piece, steel-forged receiver; chrome barrels; manual thumb safety; independent floating firing pin.

SPECIFICATIONS
Gauges: 12, 20, 28, .410
Chambers: 3″ (except 28 gauge, 2³/₄″)
Barrel lengths: 26″, choked IC/M (all gauges); 28″, choked M/F (12 and 20 gauges)

Weight: 6 lbs. 15 oz. (12 ga.); 6 lbs. 7 oz. (20 and .410 ga.); 6 lbs. 5 oz. (28 ga.)
Drop at comb: 1³/₈″
Drop at heel: 2³/₈″
Other features: Fitted recoil pad; flat matted rib; walnut pistol-grip stock and beavertail forend with hand-checkering; gold front sight bead

DERBY SIDE-BY-SIDE
$999.50

Features functioning side locks with English-style hand engraving on side plates; one-piece, steel-forged receiver; chrome barrels; automatic safety

SPECIFICATIONS
Gauges: 12 and 20
Chambers: 3″
Barrel lengths: 26″, choked IC/M; 28″, choked M/F (12 gauge)
Weight: 6 lbs. 12 oz. (12 ga.); 6 lbs. 6 oz. (20 ga.)
Sights: Gold bead front sight

Stock: Walnut and splinter forend with hand-checkering
Length of pull: 14¹/₈″
Drop at comb: 1³/₈″
Drop at heel: 2³/₈″
Features: Walnut straight stock and splinter forearm; auto selective ejectors; fixed chokes; single non-selective trigger; frame and sidelocks finished with antique silver and machine engraving.

AMERICAN ARMS/FRANCHI SHOTGUNS

MODEL 48AL (Recoil)
$609.00
$640.00 (Slug Barrel)

SPORTING 2000
$1619.00

FALCONET 2000
$1419.00

SHOTGUNS

SPECIFICATIONS

Model	Ga.	Action Type	Barrel Length	Chamber	Choke*	Length of Pull	Drop at Comb	Drop at Heel	Nominal weight (lbs.)
48 AL	12/20	SA	24," 26," 28"	2³/₄"	FC	14¹/₄"	1¹/₂"	2³/₈"	5¹/₂–6¹/₂
Sporting 2000	12	O/U	28"	2³/₄"	SK/FC	14¹/₄"	1¹/₂"	2³/₈"	7
Falconet 2000	12	O/U	26"	2³/₄"	FC	14¹/₄"	1¹/₂"	2³/₈"	6

*FC = Franchokes (IC-M-F)

AMERICAN ARMS/FRANCHI SHOTGUNS

FRANCHI SPAS-12
$713.00

This Franchi 12-gauge shotgun is designed for law enforcement and personal defense. It operates as a pump action and/or semiautomatic action (a manual action selector switch is located at the bottom of the forearm). The barrel features a muzzle protector and is made of chrome-moly steel with a hard-chromed bore and matte finish. A rifle-type aperture rear sight and blade front sight are standard, along with cylinder bore choking (modified and full choke tubes are available as accessories). The muzzle is threaded externally for mounting the SPAS-12 choke tubes (SPAS-12 and standard Franchi tubes are *not* interchangeable; 2¾″ only). The receiver/frame is lightweight alloy with non-reflective anodized finish. The fire control system is easily removable for maintenance with two push pins; a magazine cut-off button is located on the right side of the receiver, and the primary crossbolt safety button is in front of the trigger guard. A secondary "tactical" safety lever is located on the left side of the trigger guard, and the bolt/carrier latch release button is on the left side of the receiver.

The SPAS-12 operates as a recoil-operated semiautomatic and/or pump action. The operating mode is easily selected by pressing the selector button located on the underside of the forearm. The SPAS-12 is designed to shoot 2¾″ shells only. Two safety systems are standard.

SPECIFICATIONS
Gauge: 12; 2¾″ chamber
Capacity: 7 rounds
Choke: Cylinder bore
Barrel length: 21½″
Overall length: 41″
Weight: 8 lbs. 12 oz.
Stock: Nylon full-length stock with full pistol grip and serrated nylon forearm

LAW-12
$686.00

Same general specifications as the **SPAS-12,** except this high-power 12-gauge shotgun has gas-operated action, plus ambidextrous safety, decocking lever and adjustable sights.

AYA SHOTGUNS

SIDELOCK SHOTGUNS

AYA sidelock shotguns are fitted with London Holland & Holland system sidelocks, double triggers with articulated front trigger, automatic safety and ejectors, cocking indicators, bushed firing pins, replaceable hinge pins and chopper lump barrels. Stocks are of figured walnut with hand-cut checkering and oil finish, complete with a metal oval on the buttstock for engraving of initials.

Exhibition grade wood is available as are many special options, including a true left-hand version and Purdey-style self-opener.

Barrel lengths: 26″, 27″, 28″ and 29″. **Weight:** 5 to 7 pounds, depending on gauge.

Model	Prices
MODEL 1: Sidelock in 12 and 20 gauge with special engraving and exhibition quality wood	$7000.00
MODEL 2: Sidelock in 12, 16, 20, 28 gauge and .410 bore	3700.00
MODEL 53: Sidelock in 12, 16 and 20 gauge with 3 locking lugs and side clips	5300.00
MODEL 56: Sidelock in 12 gauge only with 3 locking lugs and side clips	8200.00
MODEL XXV/SL: Sidelock in 12 and 20 gauge only with Churchill-type rib	4300.00

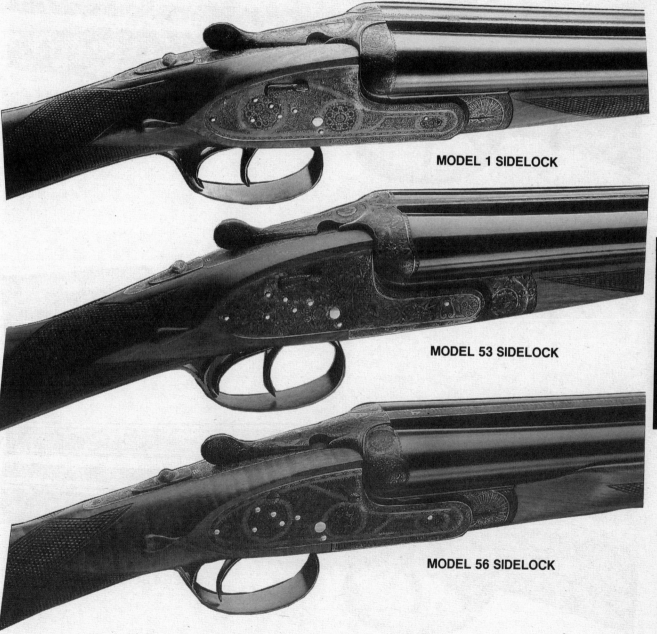

MODEL 1 SIDELOCK

MODEL 53 SIDELOCK

MODEL 56 SIDELOCK

SHOTGUNS

AYA SHOTGUNS

BOXLOCK SHOTGUNS

AYA boxlocks use the Anson & Deeley system with double locking lugs, incorporating detachable cross pin and separate plate to allow easy access to the firing mechanism. Barrels are chopper lump, firing pins are bushed, plus automatic safety and ejectors and metal oval for engraving of initials.

Barrel lengths: 26″, 27″ and 28″. **Weight:** 5 to 7 pounds, depending on gauge.

Model	Price
MODEL XXV BOXLOCK: 12 and 20 gauge only	**$3300.00**
MODEL 4 BOXLOCK: 12, 16, 20, 28, .410 ga.	2000.00
MODEL 4 DELUXE BOXLOCK: Same gauges as above	3500.00

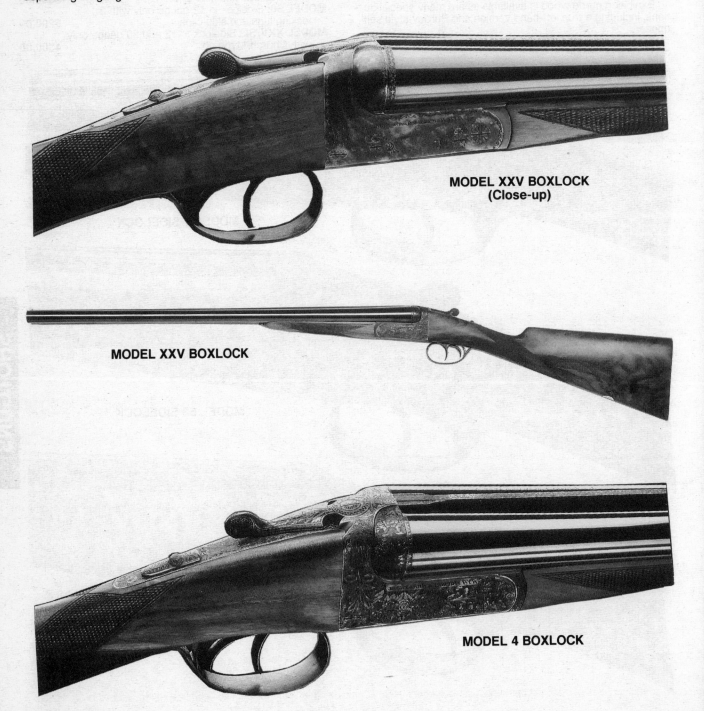

MODEL XXV BOXLOCK
(Close-up)

MODEL XXV BOXLOCK

MODEL 4 BOXLOCK

BENELLI SHOTGUNS

MODEL M1 SUPER 90 SERIES

See table on the following page for specifications.

MODEL M1 SUPER 90 DEFENSE
$764.00 (w/Pistol Grip)
$814.00 (w/Ghost-Ring Sighting System)

MODEL M1 SUPER 90 SLUG
$724.00 ($764.00 w/Ghost-Ring Sighting System)

MODEL M1 SUPER 90 FIELD
$799.00

Also available:
Model M1 Super 90 Sporting Special
   with 18¹/₂″ barrel $829.00
Model M1 Super 90 Tactical w/18¹/₂″ bbl. 829.00
Model M1 Super 90 Entry 814.00
   w/Ghost Ring Sight 859.00

Model M1 Super 90 Sporting Special $829.00
Model M3 Super 90 Pump/Auto Series
   Standard 919.00
   w/Ghost Ring Sight 949.00
   w/Folding Stock 1029.00

MONTEFELTRO SUPER 90
$824.00 (21″, 24″, 26″ or 28″ Barrel)
$844.00 (Left Hand w/26″ or 28″ Barrel)

BLACK EAGLE COMPETITION
$1099.00

Benelli's new Black Eagle Competition shotgun combines the best technical features of the Montefeltro Super 90 and the classic design of the old SL 80 Series. It comes standard with a specially designed two-piece receiver of steel and aluminum, adding to its reliability and resistance to wear. A premium high-

gloss walnut stock and gold-plated trigger are included, along with a Montefeltro rotating bolt. The Black Eagle Competition has no complex cylinders and pistons to maintain. Features include etched receiver, competition stock and mid-rib bead.

SHOTGUNS

BENELLI SHOTGUNS

SUPER BLACK EAGLE (26″ Barrel)

SUPER BLACK EAGLE
$1079.00

Benelli's new Super Black Eagle shotgun offers the advantage of owning one 12-gauge auto that fires every type of 12-gauge currently available. It has the same balance, sighting plane and fast-swinging characteristics whether practicing on the sporting clays course with light target loads or touching off a 3½″ magnum steel load at a high-flying goose.

The Super Black Eagle also features a specially strengthened steel upper receiver mated to the barrel so as to endure the toughest shotgunning. The alloy lower receiver keeps the overall weight low, making this model as well balanced and point-able as possible. Distinctive high-gloss or satin walnut stocks and a choice of dull finish or blued metal add up to a universal gun for all shotgun hunting and sports.

SPECIFICATIONS
Chamber: 3½″ (accepts 3″ and 2¾″)
Capacity: 2 shells (3½″) or 3 shells (2¾″ or 3″)
Barrel length: 26″ or 28″ (24″ slug barrel also available)
Overall length: 47⅝″ or 49⅝″
Weight: 7 lbs. 3 oz. (26″); 7 lbs. 5 oz. (28″)
Choke: Screw-in; Skeet, IC, Modified, Imp. Mod., Full
Stock: Satin walnut (28″) with drop adjustment kit; high-gloss walnut (26″) with drop adjustment kit; or synthetic stock
Finish: Matte black finish on receiver, barrel and bolt (28″); blued finish on receiver and barrel (26″) with bolt mirror polished
Features: Montefeltro rotating bolt with dual locking lugs

SPECIFICATIONS BENELLI SHOTGUNS

	Gauge (Chamber)	Operation	Magazine Capacity*	Barrel Length	Overall Length	Weight (in lbs.)	Choke	Metal Finish	Stock	Sights
Super Black Eagle (28)	12 (3½ in.)	semi-auto inertia recoil	3	28 in.	49⅝ in.	7.3	S, IC, M, IM, F**	matte	satin walnut or polymer	front & mid rib bead
Super Black Eagle (26)	12 (3½ in.)	semi-auto inertia recoil	3	26 in.	47⅝ in.	7.1	S, IC, M, IM, F**	matte or blued	polymer, satin or gloss walnut	front & mid rib bead
Super Black Eagle (24)	12 (3½ in.)	semi-auto inertia recoil	3	24 in.	45⅝ in.	7.0	S, IC, M, IM, F**	matte	polymer	front & mid rib bead
Super Black Eagle Custom Slug	12 (3 in.)	semi-auto inertia recoil	3	24 in.	45½ in.	7.6	rifled barrel	matte	satin walnut or polymer	scope mount base
Black Eagle Competition Gun	12 (3 in.)	semi-auto inertia recoil	4	28 or 26in.	49⅝ or 47⅝in.	7.3/7	S, IC, M, IM, F**	blued	satin walnut	front & mid rib bead
Montefeltro Super 90 (28/26)	12 (3 in.)	semi-auto inertia recoil	4	28 or 26in.	49½ or 47½in.	7.4/7	S, IC, M, IM, F**	blued	gloss walnut	bead
Montefeltro Super 90 (24/21)	12 (3 in.)	semi-auto inertia recoil	4	24 or 21 in.	45½ or 42½ in.	6.9/6.7	S, IC, M, IM, F**	blued	gloss walnut	bead
Montefeltro Left Hand	12 (3 in.)	semi-auto inertia recoil	4	28 or 26 in.	49½ or 47½ in.	7.4/7	S, IC, M, IM, F**	blued	gloss walnut	bead
Montefeltro 20 Gauge	20 (3 in.)	semi-auto inertia recoil	4	26 in.	47½ in.	5.75	S, IC, M, IM, F**	blued	gloss walnut	bead
M1 Super 90 Field (28)	12 (3 in.)	semi-auto inertia recoil	3	28 in.	49½ in.	7.4	S, IC, M, IM, F**	matte	polymer standard	bead
M1 Super 90 Field (26)	12 (3 in.)	semi-auto inertia recoil	3	26 in.	47½ in.	7.3	S, IC, M, IM, F**	matte	polymer standard	bead
M1 Super 90 Field (24)	12 (3 in.)	semi-auto inertia recoil	3	24 in.	45½ in.	7.2	S, IC, M, IM, F**	matte	polymer standard	bead
M1 Super 90 Field (21)	12 (3 in.)	semi-auto inertia recoil	3	21 in.	42½ in.	7	S, IC, M, IM, F**	matte	polymer standard	bead
M1 Super 90 Sporting Special (18½)	12 (3 in.)	semi-auto inertia recoil	3	18½ in.	39¾ in.	6.5	IC, M, F**	matte	polymer standard	ghost ring
M1 Super 90 Tactical (18½)	12 (3 in.)	semi-auto inertia recoil	7	18½ in.	39¾ in.	6.5	IC, M, F**	matte	polymer pistol grip or polymer standard	ghost ring
M1 Super 90 Slug	12 (3 in.)	semi-auto inertia recoil	7	19¾ in.	41in.	6.7	Cylinder	matte	polymer standard	rifle or ghost ring
M1 Super 90 Defense	12 (3 in.)	semi-auto inertia recoil	7	19¾ in.	41in.	7.1	Cylinder	matte	polymer pistol grip	rifle or ghost ring
M1 Super 90 Entry	12 (3 in.)	semi-auto inertia recoil	5	14 in.	35½ in.	6.7	Cylinder	matte	polymer pistol grip or polymer standard	rifle or ghost ring
M3 Super 90	12 (3 in.)	semi-auto/pump inertia recoil	7	19¾ in.	41in.	7.9	Cylinder	matte	polymer pistol grip	rifle or ghost ring
M3 Super 90 Folding Stock	12 (3 in.)	semi-auto/pump inertia recoil	7	19¾ in.	41in. 31in. (folded)	7.6	Cylinder	matte	folding tubular steel	rifle

*Magazine capacity given for 2¾ inch shells   **Skeet, Improved Cylinder, Modified, Improved Modified, Full

BERETTA SHOTGUNS

SERIES 682 COMPETITION TRAP O/U

Available in Competition Mono, Over/Under or Mono Trap Over/Under Combo Set, the 12-gauge 682X trap guns boast hand-checkered walnut stock and forend with International or Monte Carlo left- or right-hand stock.

Features: Adjustable gold-plated, single selective sliding trigger for precise length of pull fit; fluorescent competition front sight; step-up top rib; non-reflective black matte finish; low profile improved boxlock action; manual safety with barrel selector; 2³/₄″ chambers; auto ejector; competition recoil pad buttplate; stock with silver oval for initials; silver inscription inlaid on trigger guard; handsome fitted case. **Weight:** Approx. 8 lbs.

Barrel length/Choke	Prices
30″ Imp. Mod./Full (Silver)	$2495.00
30″ or 32″ Mobilchoke® (Black or Silver)	2570.00
Top Single 32″ or 34″ Mobilchoke®	2650.00
Pigeon (Silver)	2760.00
Unsingle	2650.00
Combo.: 30″ or 32″ Mobilchoke® (Top)	3400.00
30″ IM/F (Top)	3340.00
32″ Mobilchoke® (Mono)	3400.00

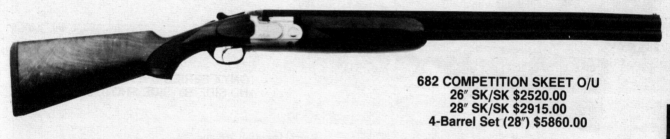

682 COMPETITION SKEET O/U
26″ SK/SK $2520.00
28″ SK/SK $2915.00
4-Barrel Set (28″) $5860.00

This skeet gun sports hand-checkered premium walnut stock, forged and hardened receiver, manual safety with trigger selector, auto ejector, stock with silver oval for initials, silver inlaid on trigger guard. Price includes fitted case.
Gauges: 12; 4-barrel sets in 12, 20, 28 and .410
Action: Low profile hard chrome-plated boxlock

Trigger: Single adjustable sliding trigger
Barrels: 26″ or 28″ rust blued barrels with 2³/₄″ chambers
Stock dimensions: Length of pull 14³/₈″; drop at comb 1 ¹/₂″; drop at heel 2¹/₃″
Sights: Fluorescent front and metal middle bead
Weight: Approx. 8 lbs.

MODEL 682 SUPER TRAP

MODEL 682 SUPER TRAP

Beretta's 12 gauge over/under shotgun features a revolutionary adjustable stock. Comb is adjustable with interchangeable comb height adjustments. Length of pull is also adjustable with interchangeable butt pad spacers. Also features ported barrels and tapered step rib, satin-finished receiver and adjustable trigger.
Barrel lengths: 30″, 32″, 34″; chamber 2³/₄″
Chokes: Choice of Mobilchoke®, IM/F, Full

Prices:
Model 682 Super Trap O/U (Mobilchoke®)	$2885.00
Same as above with IM/F choke	2820.00
Model 682 Top Single Super Trap	
32″ barrel and Mobilchoke	3060.00
Same as above with Full choke	2990.00
Model 682 Top Combo Super Trap	3790.00
Same as above w/o Mobilchoke®	3865.00

BERETTA SHOTGUNS

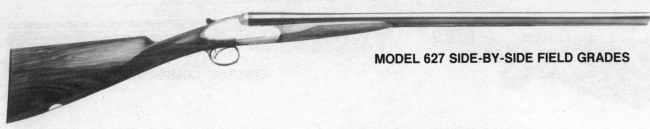

MODEL 627 SIDE-BY-SIDE FIELD GRADES

These good-looking field models feature low profile solid box-lock design, hand-fitted stocks and forends of handsome European walnut with deep diamond hand-checkering, tang-mounted safety/barrel selectors, single-selective trigger and metal bead sight. 12 gauge barrels are chambered 3". **Model 627EL** boasts scroll-engraved side plates. **Model 627EELL** features game-scene engraving.

Model 627EL Field $3270.00
12 ga., 26" Mobilchoke®
12 ga., 28" Mobilchoke®

Model 627EELL $5405.00
12 ga., 28" Mobilchoke®
12 ga., 26" Mobilchoke®
12 ga., English stock, 26" or 28" Mobilchoke®

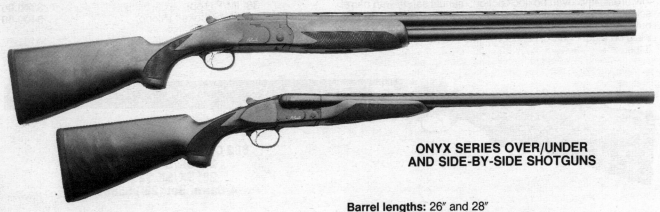

ONYX SERIES OVER/UNDER AND SIDE-BY-SIDE SHOTGUNS

The **Model 626 Onyx** has a full-figured American walnut stock, lustrous black semi-matte finish on the barrels and receiver, and metal front bead on vent rib.

SPECIFICATIONS
Gauges: 12, 20
Chamber: 3"

Barrel lengths: 26" and 28"
Chokes: Mobilchoke® screw-in system
Weight: 6 lbs. 10 oz. (12 ga.); 6 lbs. (20 ga.)
Stock: American walnut with recoil pad (English stock available)
Features: Automatic ejectors; matte black finish on barrels and receiver to reduce glare
Prices: . . . . **$1355.00 to $1870.00**
2-Barrel Set (20 & 28 ga.) 2085.00
Ultralight 1525.00

MODEL ASE 90

Features drop-out trigger group assembly for ease in cleaning, inspection, or in-the-field replacement. Also has wide ventilating top and side rib, hard-chromed bores, and a strong competition-style receiver in coin-silver finish and gold inlay with P. Beretta initials.

SPECIFICATIONS
Gauge: 12
Barrel lengths: 28" (Pigeon, Skeet, Sporting Clays); 30" (Trap and Sporting Clays); 30" and 32" Combo (Top Combo Trap); 30" and 34" Combo (Top Combo Trap)
Chokes: IM/F Trap or MCT (Trap); MC4 (Sporting Clays); SK/SK (Skeet); IM/F (Pigeon)
Prices:
Model ASE 90 (Pigeon, Trap, Skeet) **$8070.00**
Model ASE 90 (Sporting Clays) 8140.00
Model ASE 90 (Top Combo) . . . . N/A

BERETTA SHOTGUNS
SPORTING CLAY SHOTGUNS 12 AND 20 GAUGE

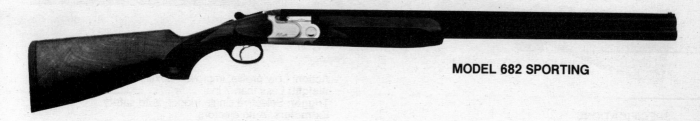

MODEL 682 SPORTING

MODELS 682/686/687 SPORTING CLAYS

This competition-style shotgun for sporting clays features 28″ or 30″ barrels with four flush-mounted screw-in choke tubes (Full, Modified, Improved Cylinder and Skeet), plus hand-checkered stock and forend of fine walnut, 2¾″ chambers and adjustable trigger. New **Model 682 Continental Course Sporting** has tapered rib and schnabel forend. **Model 682 Super Sporting** has ported barrels, adjustable comb height inserts and length of pull. **Model 686 Onyx Hunter Sport** has black matte receiver and **686 Hunter Sport** has coin silver receiver with scroll engraving. **Model 687EL Sporting** has sideplates with scroll engraving.

Prices:

682 Sporting	$2605.00
682 Continental Course Sporting	2715.00
682 Super Sport	2760.00
682 Super Sporting	2925
682 Sporting Combo	3470.00
686 Onyx Hunter Sport	1385.00
686 Hunter Sport	1425.00
686 Sporting Combo	2605.00
687 Sporting	2560.00
687 Sporting Combo	3410.00
687EL Sporting	3225.00
687EELL Sporting	4705.00

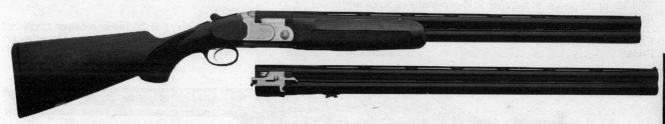

MODEL 686 SPORTING COMBO

MODELS 686/687 SPORTING COMBO

Beretta's 12 gauge over/under features interchangeable 28″ and 30″ barrels for versatility in competition at different courses with short and long passing shots. **Chamber:** 3″. **Mobilchoke®** screw-in tube system. Prices listed above.

VITTORIA

VITTORIA

This new 12-gauge semiautomatic shotgun with short recoil operation is available with 24″ or 26″ barrels and Mobilchoke®. A slug version is also available with rifled sights and choke tube. Finish is non-reflective matte on all exposed wood and metal surfaces. Checkered walnut stock and forend; sling swivels.

SPECIFICATIONS
Gauge: 12
Barrel lengths: 24″, 26″; 24″ Slug
Weight: 7 lbs.
Stock: Walnut
Sights: Bead front on vent rib
Price: $700.00

BERETTA SHOTGUNS

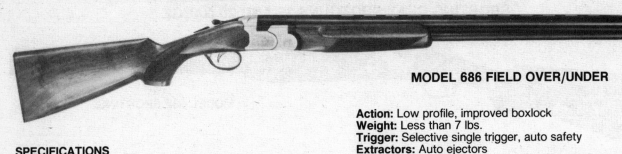

MODEL 686 FIELD OVER/UNDER

Action: Low profile, improved boxlock
Weight: Less than 7 lbs.
Trigger: Selective single trigger, auto safety
Extractors: Auto ejectors
Stock: Choice walnut, hand-checkered and hand-finished with a tough gloss finish

SPECIFICATIONS
Gauge: 28
Barrels/chokes: 26″ and 28″ with Mobilchoke® screw-in choke tubes

Price: **$1355.00**

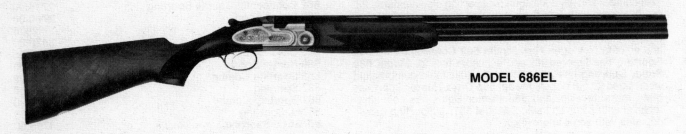

MODEL 686EL

This 12- or 20-gauge over/under field gun features scroll engraving on sideplates, European walnut stock and forend, hard-chromed bores, Mobilchoke® system of interchangeable choke tubes, and gun case.
Price: **$2200.00**

Also available:
Model 686 Silver with highly polished silver receiver, traditional blued finish barrels, and rubber recoil pad, plus Mobilchoke®
Price: **$1385.00**

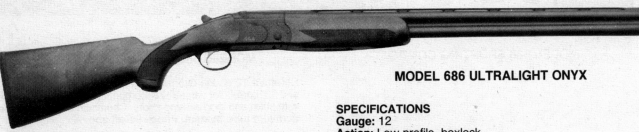

MODEL 686 ULTRALIGHT ONYX

SPECIFICATIONS
Gauge: 12
Action: Low profile, boxlock
Barrel length: 26″ or 28″
Trigger: Single, selective gold trigger
Safety: Automatic
Stock: Walnut, hand-checkered
Price: **$1525.00**

This new 12-gauge over/under field gun features the payload of a 12-gauge gun in a 20-gauge weight (approx. 5 lbs. 13 oz.). Chambered for 2¾″, the Ultralight has a matte black finish on its receiver with a gold inlay of the P. Beretta signature.

MODEL 687L FIELD GRADE O/U

The **687L** features Mobilchoke® in 12 and 20 gauge; strong boxlock action handsomely tooled with floral hand-engraved decorative side plates, finest quality walnut stock accented with silver monogram plate, selective auto ejectors and fitted case.
Price: **$1870.00**

BERETTA SHOTGUNS

MODEL 687EL FIELD GRADE (not shown)

Features game scene engraving on receiver with gold highlights. Available in 12, 20 gauge (28 ga. and .410 in small frame).

SPECIFICATIONS
Barrels/chokes: 26″ and 28″ with Mobilchoke®
Action: Low-profile improved boxlock
Weight: 7 lbs. 2 oz.
Trigger: Single selective with manual safety
Extractors: Auto ejectors

MODEL 687EELL (not shown)
$4625.00

In 12, 20 or 28 ga., this model features the Modilchoke® choke system, a special premium walnut, custom-fitted stock and exquisitely engraved sideplate with game-scene motifs.
Also available:

Model 687EELL Combo (20 and 28 ga.)	$5130.00
Model 687EL (12, 20, 28 ga.; 26″ or 28″ bbl.)	3180.00
Model 687EL Small Frame (.410)	3320.00

MODEL 1201F

This All-Weather semiautomatic shotgun features an adjustable space-age technopolymer stock and forend with recoil pad. Lightweight, it sports a unique weather-resistant matte black finish to reduce glare, resist corrosion and aid in heat dispersion; short recoil action for light and heavy loads. **Gauge:** 12. **Chamber:** 3″. **Barrel lengths:** 24″, 26″ and 28″. **Choke:** Mobilchoke® (Full, Modified). **Weight:** 7.4 lbs.
Price: $625.00

Also available:
Model 1201 Riot (Law Enforcement) with 20″ barrel (2³/₄″ or 3″ shells) and Improved Cylinder choke (7-round capacity). **$660.00**
Model 1201 Riot w/pistol grip **705.00**

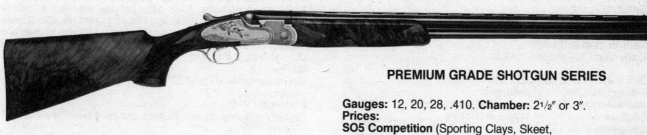

PREMIUM GRADE SHOTGUN SERIES

Gauges: 12, 20, 28, .410. **Chamber:** 2¹/₂″ or 3″.
Prices:

These hand-crafted over/under and side-by-side shotguns feature custom engraved or game scenes, casehardened, gold-inlay, scroll or floral patterns, all available on receivers. Sidelock action. Stocks are of select European walnut, hand-finished and hand-checkered. Also available in Competition Skeet, Trap, Sporting Clays and Custom Sidelock Side-by-Side models. Barrels are constructed of Boehler high-nickel antinit steel.

SO5 Competition (Sporting Clays, Skeet, Trap)	$12,300.00
SO6 O/U Competition (Sporting Clays, Skeet, Trap)	16,600.00
SO6 EELL Custom Sidelock (12 gauge only)	27,300.00
SO9 Custom Sidelock (12, 20, 28, .410 ga.)	28,500.00
452 Custom Sidelock Side/Side (12 ga.)	22,470.00
452 EELL Custom Sidelock Side/Side (12 ga.)	30,680.00
Extra barrels and leather cases available: each	4,000.00

BERETTA SHOTGUNS

MODEL 390 SUPER TRAP

This gas-operated semiautomatic has an innovative gas system that handles a variety of loads. A self-regulating valve automatically adjusts gas pressure to handle anything from 2¹/₂″ target loads to heavy 3″ magnums. Matte finish models for turkey/waterfowl and Deluxe models with gold-engraved receiver and deluxe wood are available. Also offered are **Model 390 Super Trap** and **390 Super Skeet** with ported barrels and adjustable comb height and length of pull.

SPECIFICATIONS
Gauge: 12
Barrel lengths: 24″, 26″, 28″, 30″

Weight: 7 lbs.
Sights: Ventilated rib with front bead
Action: Locked breech, gas-operated
Safety: Crossbolt (reversible)
Prices:

390 Field	$ 775.00
390 Matte Finish	775.00
390 Deluxe	935.00
390 Super Trap	1210.00
390 Super Skeet	1160.00

MODEL 303 YOUTH GUN

MODEL 303 SEMIAUTOMATIC

This gas-operated autoloader features Mobilchoke® screw-in choke tubes and a magazine cut-off that allows shooters to hand-feed a lighter or heavier load into the breech without emptying the magazine. Disassembly takes one minute.

MODEL 303 GENERAL SPECIFICATIONS

Gauge: 12 or 20
Barrel lengths: 24″, 26″, 28″, 30″, 32″
Weight: 7 lbs. (12 gauge) and 6 lbs. (20 gauge)
Safety: Crossbolt
Action: Locked breech, gas-operated
Sights: Vent rib with front metal bead
Length of pull: 14⁷/₈″
Capacity: Plugged to 2 rounds

303 YOUTH SPECIFICATIONS
Gauge: 20 (2³/₄″ or 3″ chamber)
Barrel length: 24″
Chokes: Mobilchoke® screw-in chokes
Length of pull: 13¹/₂″

MODEL 303 PRICES:

Upland	$735.00
Field (English)	735.00
Youth	735.00
Skeet	735.00
Trap	735.00
With Mobilchoke® F, IM, M	775.00
Sporting Clays	835.00

MODEL 303 COMPETITION TRAP & SKEET
(not shown)
$735.00   ($775.00 w/Mobilchoke®)

The Beretta A303 Competition guns are versions of the proven A303 semiautomatic. Their gas-operated systems lessen recoil; other features include wide floating vent rib with fluorescent front and mid-rib bead sights. The A303 also comes with hand-checkered stock and forend of select European walnut, plus gold-plated trigger.
Gauge: 12
Barrel lengths: 26″ and 28″ (Skeet); 30″ and 32″ (Trap);   28″ (Sporting)
Chamber: 2³/₄″
Sight: Ventilated rib with fluorescent front bead, metal middle bead
Action: Semiautomatic, locked breech, gas-operated
Safety: Crossbolt
Ejector: Auto
Trigger: Gold-plated
Stock: Select walnut
Weight: 8 lbs.
Buttplate: Special trap recoil pad

BERNARDELLI SHOTGUNS

Bernardelli shotguns are the creation of the Italian firm of Vincenzo Bernardelli, known for its fine quality firearms and commitment to excellence for more than a century. Most of the long arms featured below can be built with a variety of options, customized for the discriminating sportsman. With the exceptions indicated for each gun respectively, options include choice of barrel lengths and chokes; pistol or straight English grip stock; single selective or non-selective trigger; long tang trigger guard; checkered butt; beavertail forend; hand-cut rib; automatic safety; custom stock dimensions; standard or English recoil pad; extra set of barrels; choice of luggage gun case.

MODEL 112 EM
$1798.00 (Single Trigger)

Features ejectors, English stock and splinter forend. **Barrel length:** 26³⁄₄″ (3″ chamber). **Choke:** Improved Cylinder and Improved Modified. **Safety:** Manual. **Weight:** 6¹⁄₂ lbs.
Price (with ejector and multi-choke): **$1971.00**

BRESCIA SIDE-BY-SIDE
$2482.00

Available in 12, 16, or 20 gauge, the Brescia side-by-side features Greener or Purdey locks, small engravings, hardened marbled mounting, chrome-lined barrels, finely grained stock. Prices on request.

HOLLAND & HOLLAND TYPE SIDELOCK SIDE-BY-SIDE

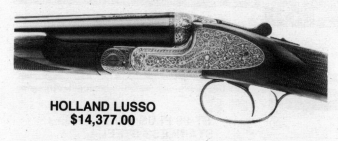

HOLLAND LUSSO
$14,377.00

These 12-gauge Holland & Holland style sidelock side-by-sides feature sidelocks with double safety levers, reinforced breech, three round Purdey locks, automatic ejectors, right trigger folding, striker retaining plates, best-quality walnut stock and finely chiselled high-grade engravings. The eight shotguns in this series differ only in the amount and intricacy of engravings. Prices range from **$10,757.00** to **$57,922.00** (with gold engravings).

HOLLAND V.B. LISCIO
$10,757.00

BROWNING AUTOMATIC SHOTGUNS

AUTO-5 STALKER

SPECIFICATIONS AUTO-5 SHOTGUNS

Model	Chamber	Barrel Length	Overall Length	Average Weight	Chokes Available
12 Gauge Light	2³/₄"	30"	49¹/₂"	8 lbs. 7 oz.	Invector-Plus
Light	2³/₄"	28"	47¹/₂"	8 lbs. 4 oz.	Invector-Plus
Light	2³/₄"	26"	45¹/₂"	8 lbs. 1 oz.	Invector-Plus
Lt. Buck Special	2³/₄"	24"	43¹/₂"	8 lbs.	Slug/buckshot
Light	2³/₄"	22"	41¹/₂"	7 lbs. 13 oz.	Invector-Plus
Magnum	3"	32"	51¹/₄"	9 lbs. 2 oz.	Invector-Plus
Magnum	3"	30"	49¹/₄"	8 lbs. 13 oz.	Invector-Plus
Magnum	3"	28"	47¹/₄"	8 lbs. 11 oz.	Invector-Plus
Magnum	3"	26"	45¹/₄"	8 lbs. 9 oz.	Invector-Plus
Mag. Buck Special	3"	24"	43¹/₄"	8 lbs. 8 oz.	Slug/buckshot
Light Stalker	2³/₄"	28"	47¹/₂"	8 lbs. 4 oz.	Invector-Plus
Light Stalker	2³/₄"	26"	45¹/₂"	8 lbs. 1 oz.	Invector-Plus
Magnum Stalker	3"	30"	49¹/₄"	8 lbs. 13 oz.	Invector-Plus
Magnum Stalker	3"	28"	47¹/₄"	8 lbs. 11 oz.	Invector-Plus
20 Gauge Light	2³/₄"	28"	47¹/₈"	6 lbs. 10 oz.	Invector
Light	2³/₄"	26"	45¹/₄"	6 lbs. 8 oz.	Invector
Magnum	3"	28"	47¹/₄"	7 lbs. 3 oz.	Invector
Magnum	3"	26"	45¹/₄"	7 lbs. 1 oz.	Invector

AUTO-5 MODELS

	Prices
Light 12, Hunting & Stalker, Invector Plus	$734.95
Light 20, Hunting, Std. Invector	719.95
3" Magnum 12, Hunting & Stalker, Invector Plus	756.95
3" Magnum 12, Hunting & Stalker	742.95
3" Magnum 20, Standard Invector	742.95
Light 12, Buck Special	724.95
3" Magnum 12 ga. Buck Special	746.95
Extra Barrels	194.95–269.95

BT-99 STANDARD SINGLE BARREL TRAP

SPECIFICATIONS
Gauge: 12 ga. w/2³/₄" chamber
Choke: Invector-Plus
Barrel lengths: 32" and 34"; ported barrel
Overall length: 48¹/₂" w/32" barrel; 50¹/₂" w/34" barrel
Weight: 8 lbs. 6 oz. to 8 lbs. 10 oz.
Stock: Conventional or Monte Carlo
Prices: (w/Conventional or Monte Carlo Stock)

Grade I Competition	$1225.00
Stainless	1650.00
Pigeon Grade	1430.00
Signature Painted	1260.00

SPECIFICATIONS BT-99 PLUS/BT-99 MICRO PLUS

Model	Barrel Length	Overall Length	Average Weight
Micro BT-99 Plus	34"	50¹/₂"	8 lbs. 10 oz.
Micro BT-99 Plus	32"	48¹/₂"	8 lbs. 8 oz.
Micro BT-99 Plus	30"	46¹/₂"	8 lbs. 6 oz.
Micro BT-99 Plus	28"	44¹/₂"	8 lbs. 4 oz.
BT-99 Plus	34"	51¹/₄"	8 lbs. 12 oz.
BT-99 Plus	32"	49¹/₄"	8 lbs. 10 oz.

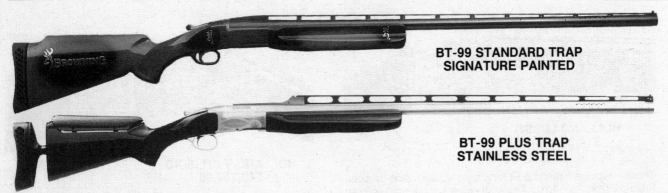

**BT-99 STANDARD TRAP
SIGNATURE PAINTED**

**BT-99 PLUS TRAP
STAINLESS STEEL**

BT-99 PLUS & BT 99 MICRO PLUS

These handsome 12-gauge trap guns come with 28", 30", 32" or 34" ported barrels (unless specified otherwise) and Invector-Plus choke (2³/₄" chamber). See specifications chart for additional information.

Prices:

Grade I	$1780.00
Grade I without ported barrels	1765.00
Stainless	2150.00
Pigeon Grade	1985.00
Signature Painted	1815.00

BROWNING CITORI O/U SHOTGUNS

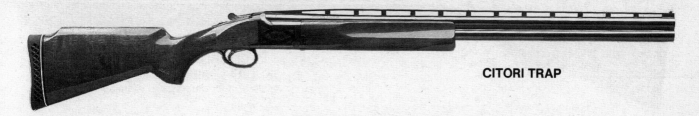

CITORI TRAP

Models	Prices
TRAP MODELS (High Post Target Rib)	
Std. 12 Ga., Monte Carlo or Conventional Stock	
Grade I Invector-Plus	$1380.00
Grade III Invector-Plus	1896.00
Grade VI Invector-Plus	2690.00
SKEET MODELS (High Post Target Rib)	
Standard 12 and 20 Gauge	
Grade I Invector-Plus	1380.00
Grade III Invector-Plus	1896.00
Grade VI Invector-Plus	2690.00
Standard 28 Gauge and .410 Bore	
Grade I	1315.00
Grade III	1860.00
Grade VI	2650.00

SPECIFICATIONS CITORI TRAP & SKEET

Gauge	Model	Chamber	Barrel Length	Overall Length	Average Weight	Chokes	Grades Available
CITORI TRAP							
12	Conventional	2¾"	32"	49"	8 lbs. 11 oz.	Invector Plus	I, III, VI
12	Monte Carlo	2¾"	32"	49"	8 lbs. 10 oz.	Invector Plus	I, III, VI
12	Conventional	2¾"	30"	47"	8 lbs. 7 oz.	Invector Plus	I, III, VI
12	Monte Carlo	2¾"	30"	47"	8 lbs. 6 oz.	Invector Plus	I, III, VI
CITORI SKEET							
12	Standard	2¾"	28"	45"	8 lbs.	Invector Plus	I, III, VI
12	Standard	2¾"	26"	43"	7 lbs.15 oz.	Invector Plus	I, III, VI
20	Standard	2¾"	28"	45"	7 lbs. 4 oz.	Invector	I, III, VI
20	Standard	2¾"	26"	43"	7 lbs. 1 oz.	Invector	I, III, VI
28	Standard	2¾"	28"	45"	6 lbs. 15 oz.	S-S	I, III, VI
28	Standard	2¾"	26"	43"	6 lbs. 10 oz.	S-S	I
.410	Standard	2¾"	28"	45"	7 lbs. 6 oz.	S-S	I, III, VI
.410	Standard	2¾"	26"	43"	7 lbs. 3 oz.	S-S	I
20,28,.410	3 Gauge Set	2¾"	28"	45"	7 lbs. 4 oz.	S-S	I, III, VI
12,20,28,.410	4 Gauge Set	2¾"	28"	45"	8 lbs. 5 oz.	S-S	I, III, VI
12,20,28,.410	4 Gauge Set	2¾"	26"	43"	8 lbs. 3 oz.	S-S	I, III, VI

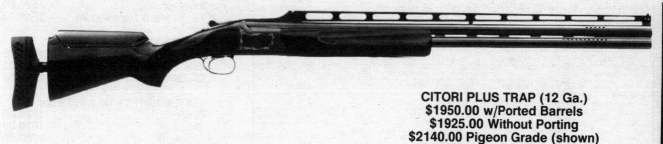

CITORI PLUS TRAP (12 Ga.)
$1950.00 w/Ported Barrels
$1925.00 Without Porting
$2140.00 Pigeon Grade (shown)
$1985.00 Signature Painted

CITORI PLUS COMBO TRAP O/U

Browning's Citori Plus Combo is two trap guns in one—a single barrel trap gun for singles and an over/under trap gun for doubles. It features Browning's recoil reducer system, fully adjustable stock dimension, back-bored barrels, optional barrel porting, ventilated side ribs, and the Invector-Plus choke tube system.

SPECIFICATIONS
Gauge: 12; 2¾" chamber
Barrel lengths: 30" and 32"
Chokes: Invector-Plus
Overall length: 47¼" (30" barrel); 49¼" (32" barrel)
Weight: 9 lbs. 5 oz. (30" barrel); 9 lbs. 7 oz. (32" barrel)

Stock: Monte Carlo style comb w/recoil reducer system, fully adjustable for drop, trap-style recoil pad, cast and length of pull; modified beavertail forearm; stock and forearm are select walnut with high-gloss finish and cut-checkering
Features: Back-bored barrel; blued steel receiver with engraved rosette scroll design; automatic ejectors; barrel selector in top tang safety; gold-colored trigger; manual top tang safety
Price:
Plus Combo Grade I Invector-Plus with ported barrels (furnished w/single barrel plus standard o/u barrel) and fitted luggage case **$3300.00**

BROWNING CITORI O/U SHOTGUNS

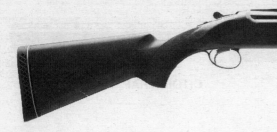

CITORI GRADE I HUNTING
12 Gauge, 3¹/₂" Magnum

SPECIFICATIONS CITORI OVER/UNDER SHOTGUNS

Gauge	Model	Chamber	Barrel Length	Overall Length	Average Weight	Chokes Available	Grades Available
12	Hunting	3½" Mag.	30"	47"	8 lbs. 10 oz.	Invector-Plus	I
12	Hunting	3½" Mag.	28"	45"	8 lbs. 9 oz.	Invector-Plus	I
12	Hunting	3"	30"	47"	8 lbs. 4 oz.	Invector-Plus	I
12	Hunting	3"	28"	45"	8 lbs. 1 oz.	Invector-Plus	I, III, VI
12	Hunting	3"	26"	43"	7 lbs. 15 oz.	Invector-Plus	I, III, VI
12	Lightning	3"	28"	45"	8 lbs. 1 oz.	Invector-Plus	I, GL, III, VI
12	Lightning	3"	26"	43"	7 lbs. 15 oz.	Invector-Plus	I, GL III, VI
12	Superlight	2¾"	28"	45"	6 lbs. 12 oz.	Invector-Plus	I, III, VI
12	Superlight	2¾"	26"	43"	6 lbs. 10 oz.	Invector-Plus	I, III, VI
12	Upland Special	2¾"	24"	41"	6 lbs. 11 oz.	Invector-Plus	I
20	Hunting	3"	28"	45"	6 lbs. 12 oz.	Invector	I, III, VI
20	Hunting	3"	26"	43"	6 lbs. 10 oz.	Invector	I, III, VI
20	Lightning	3"	28"	45"	6 lbs. 14 oz.	Invector	I, GL, III, VI
20	Lightning	3"	26"	43"	6 lbs. 9 oz.	Invector	I, GL, III, VI
20	Lightning	3"	24"	41"	6 lbs. 6 oz.	Invector	I
20	Micro Lightning	2¾"	24"	41"	6 lbs. 3 oz.	Invector	I, III, VI
20	Superlight	2¾"	26"	43"	6 lbs.	Invector	I, III, VI
20	Upland Special	2¾"	24"	41"	6 lbs.	Invector	I
28	Hunting	2¾"	28"	45"	6 lbs. 11 oz.	M-F	I
28	Hunting	2¾"	26"	43"	6 lbs. 10 oz.	IC-M	I
28	Lightning	2¾"	28"	45"	6 lbs. 11 oz.	M-F	I
28	Lightning	2¾"	26"	43"	6 lbs. 10 oz.	IC-M	I, III, VI
28	Superlight	2¾"	26"	43"	6 lbs. 10 oz.	IC-M	I, III, VI
.410	Hunting	3"	28"	45"	7 lbs.	M-F	I
.410	Hunting	3"	26"	43"	6 lbs. 14 oz.	IC-M	I
.410	Lightning	3"	28"	45"	7 lbs.	M-F	I
.410	Lightning	3"	26"	43"	6 lbs. 14 oz.	IC-M	I, III, VI
.410	Superlight	3"	28"	45"	6 lbs. 14 oz.	M-F	I
.410	Superlight	3"	26"	43"	6 lbs. 13 oz.	IC-M	I, III, VI

CITORI HUNTING, LIGHTNING & SUPERLIGHT MODELS

HUNTING & LIGHTNING 28 Gauge, .410 Bore	PRICES
Grade I Hunting	$1155.00
Grade I Lightning	1200.00
Grade III Lightning	1900.00
Grade VI Lightning	2695.00

HUNTING & LIGHTNING 12 & 20 Gauge	
Grade I Invector	1165.00
Grade I Lightning Invector	1198.00
Grade I Micro, 20 ga.	1228.00
Gran Lightning Invector	1630.00
Grade III Invector	1715.00
Grade III Lightning Invector	1745.00
Gr. III Micro Lightning Inv.	1775.00
Grade VI Invector	2485.00
Grade VI Lightning Invector	2530.00
Gr. VI Micro Lightning Inv.	2515.00

SUPERLIGHT 12 & 20 Ga.	
Grade I Invector	1215.00
Grade III Invector	1750.00
Grade VI Invector	2540.00

SUPERLIGHT 28 Ga./.410 Bore	
Grade I	1220.00
Grade III	1920.00
Grade VI	2700.00

SKEET SETS

4-BARREL SKEET SET
12 gauge with one removable forearm and four sets of barrels, 12, 20, 28 and .410 gauges, high post target rib.
(Furnished with fitted luggage case for gun and extra barrels)

Grade 1	$4250.00
Grade III	4860.00
Grade VI	5500.00

3-BARREL SKEET SET
20 gauge with one removable forearm and three sets of barrels, 20, 28 and .410 bore.

Grade 1	$2960.00
Grade III	3560.00
Grade VI	4200.00

* **$2520.00** with Standard Invectors

BROWNING CITORI O/U SHOTGUNS

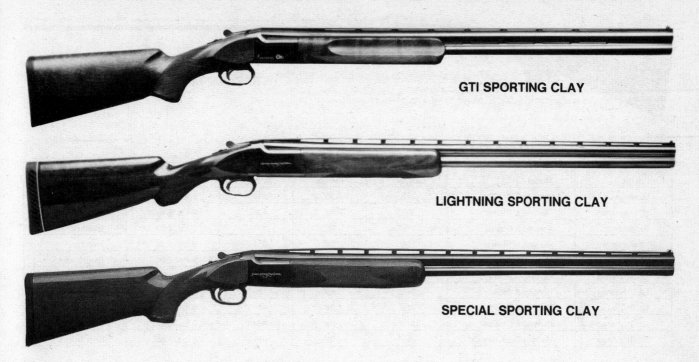

GTI SPORTING CLAY

LIGHTNING SPORTING CLAY

SPECIAL SPORTING CLAY

SPECIFICATIONS CITORI O/U SPORTING CLAYS

Model	Chamber	Barrel Length	Overall Length	Average Weight
Special Sporting	2¾"	32"	49"	8 lbs. 5 oz.
Special Sporting	2¾"	30"	47"	8 lbs. 3 oz.
Special Sporting	2¾"	28"	45"	8 lbs. 1 oz.
Lightning Sporting	3"	30"	47"	8 lbs. 8 oz.
Lightning Sporting	3"	28"	45"	8 lbs. 6 oz.
GTI	2¾"	30"	47"	8 lbs. 2 oz.
GTI	2¾"	28"	45"	8 lbs.

Prices: (w/Invector-Plus Chokes)
Special Sporting (Grade I)* $1360.00
Special Sporting, Signature Painted* 1390.00
Special Sporting, Pigeon Grade* 1550.00
Lightning Sporting, Gr. I, 3″ ch. 1360.00
Lightning Sporting, Signature Painted, 3″ ch. 1390.00
   Same as above with low rib 1330.00
Lightning Sporting, Pigeon Gr., 3″ ch. 1550.00
   Same as above with low rib 1488.00
GTI Invector-Plus* 1380.00
GTI, Signature Painted* 1410.00
* Includes ported barrels

RECOILLESS TRAP
$1670.00

SPECIFICATIONS
Gauge: 12, Standard or Micro
Chamber: 2³/₄″
Barrel length: 27″ or 30″
Overall length: 47⁵/₈″ (27″ barrel); 51⁵/₈″ (30″ barrel)
Weight: 8 lbs. 10 oz.

BROWNING PUMP SHOTGUNS

BPS 3¹/₂″ MAGNUM (12 Gauge)

SPECIFICATIONS BPS MAGNUMS

Gauge	Model	Chamber Length	Barrel Length	Overall Weight	Average Available	Chokes
10 Magnum	Hunting & Stalker	3¹/₂″	30″	51³/₄″	9 lbs. 8 oz.	Invector
10 Magnum	Hunting & Stalker	3¹/₂″	28″	49³/₄″	9 lbs. 6 oz.	Invector
10 Magnum	Hunting & Stalker	3¹/₂″	26″	47³/₄″	9 lbs. 4 oz.	Invector
10 Magnum	Hunting & Stalker	3¹/₂″	24″	45³/₄″	9 lbs. 4 oz.	Invector
10 Magnum	Hunting Buck Special	3¹/₂″	24″	45³/₄″	9 lbs. 2 oz.	Slug/Buckshot
12, 3¹/₂″ Mag	Hunting & Stalker	3¹/₂″	30″	51³/₄″	8 lbs. 12 oz.	Invector-Plus
12, 3¹/₂″ Mag	Hunting & Stalker	3¹/₂″	28″	49³/₄″	8 lbs. 9 oz.	Invector-Plus
12, 3¹/₂″ Mag	Hunting & Stalker	3¹/₂″	26″	47³/₄″	8 lbs. 6 oz.	Invector-Plus
12, 3¹/₂″ Mag	Hunting & Stalker	3¹/₂″	24″	45³/₄″	8 lbs. 3 oz.	Invector-Plus
12, 3¹/₂″ Mag	Hunting Buck Special	3¹/₂″	24″	45³/₄″	8 lbs. 7 oz.	Slug/Buckshot

BPS PIGEON GRADE

SPECIFICATIONS BPS 12 & 20 GAUGE PUMP

Model	Barrel Length	Overall Length	Average Weight	Chokes Available
12 Gauge Hunting & Pigeon	32″	52¹/₂″	7 lbs. 14 oz.	Invector-Plus
Hunting, Stalker & Pigeon	30″	50³/₄″	7 lbs. 12 oz.	Invector-Plus
Hunting, Stalker & Pigeon	28″	48³/₄″	7 lbs. 11 oz.	Invector-Plus
Hunting, Stalker & Pigeon	26″	46³/₄″	7 lbs. 10 oz.	Invector-Plus
Standard Buck Special	24″	44³/₄″	7 lbs. 10 oz.	Slug/Buckshot
Upland Special	22″	42¹/₂″	7 lbs. 8 oz.	Invector-Plus
Hunting, Stalker & Pigeon	22″	42¹/₂″	7 lbs. 7 oz.	Invector-Plus
Game Gun Turkey Special	20¹/₂″	40⁷/₈″	7 lbs. 7 oz.	Invector
Game Gun Deer Special	20¹/₂″	40⁷/₈″	7 lbs. 7 oz.	Special Inv./Rifled
20 Gauge Hunting	28″	48³/₄″	7 lbs. 1 oz.	Invector
Hunting	26″	46³/₄″	7 lbs.	Invector
Youth/Ladies	22″	41³/₄″	6 lbs. 11 oz.	Invector
Upland Special	22″	42¹/₂″	6 lbs. 12 oz.	Invector

Prices:

Invector Hunting & Stalker 10 ga.	**$584.95**
Invector Waterfowl 10 ga.	749.95
Invector-Plus Hunting & Stalker	584.95
Invector Hunting, Stalker & Upland Special 12 ga. only	**442.95**
Invector-Plus Hunting, Stalker & Upland Spec.	462.95
Buck Special 12 ga. only	448.95
Buck Special 10 ga. & 3¹/₂″ 12 ga.	589.95
BPS Youth & Ladies 20 ga. only	442.95
BPS 3¹/₂″ Magnum	584.95
Pigeon Grade 12 ga. only	619.95
Deer Special Game Gun	527.95
Turkey Special Game Gun	499.95

BROWNING SHOTGUNS

MODEL A-500R SEMIAUTOMATIC
$559.95
$592.95 Buck Special

Designed and built in Belgium, the 12-gauge A-500 employs a short recoil system with a strong four-lug bolt design. There is no gas system to collect powder residues or grime, and no pistons, ports or cylinders to clean. Only one extractor is needed to pull the shell from the chamber. The stock has no drilled holes to accommodate action springs, making it that much stronger (especially where it bolts against the receiver). See table below for additional specifications.

SPECIFICATIONS
Gauge: 12
Choke: Invector
Stock dimensions: Length of pull 14¼"; drop at comb 1½"; drop at heel 2½"
Safety: Cross bolt, right or left hand
Action: Short recoil-operated with four lug rotary bolt
Finish: Deep high-polished blued finish; receiver lightly engraved with scroll pattern

MODEL A-500G GAS-OPERATED SHOTGUN
$652.95
$672.95 Buck Special

Additional features:
Safety: Crossbolt, right or left hand
Capacity: 4 rounds (2¾") or 3 rounds (3") with plug removed (with plug installed, 2 round in magazine, one in chamber)
Recoil pad: Ventilated style, standard
Stock and forearm: Select walnut, full pistol grip stock with gloss finish and cut checkering
Barrel and receiver finish: Deep, high polish blued finish; gold accents on receiver
Trigger: gold colored
Stock dimensions: Length of pull 14⅜"; drop at comb 1½"; drop at heel 2"
Action: Gas operated with 4-lug rotary bolt

SPECIFICATIONS MODEL A-500G & A-500R

Model	Chamber	Barrel Length	Overall Length	Average Weight
A-500G Hunting	3"	30"	51½"	8 lbs. 1 oz.
A-500G Hunting	3"	28"	49½"	7 lbs. 15 oz.
A-500G Hunting	3"	26"	47½"	7 lbs. 13 oz.
A-500G Sporting Clays	3"	30"	51½"	8 lbs. 2 oz.
A-500G Sporting Clays	3"	28"	49½"	8 lbs.
A-500R Hunting	3"	30"	51½"	8 lbs. 1 oz.
A-500R Hunting	3"	28"	49½"	7 lbs. 15 oz.
A-500R Hunting	3"	26"	47½"	7 lbs. 13 oz.
A-500R Buck Special	3"	24"	45½"	7 lbs. 11 oz.

MODEL BSA 10 SEMIAUTOMATIC
$899.95

SPECIFICATIONS
Gauge: 10 w/3½" chamber
Choke: Standard Invector
Capacity: Four 3½" loads in magazine, 1 in chamber (plug removed)
Action: Gas-operated
Barrel lengths: 26", 28", 30"

Rib: High-post floating rib
Overall length: 48" (26" barrel); 50" (28" barrel); 52" (30" barrel)
Weight: 10 lbs. 7 oz. to 10 lbs. 13 oz.
Safety: Cross-bolt with enlarged head
Trigger pull: 4½ lbs.
Recoil pad: Standard
Extra barrels: $229.95

BROWNING SHOTGUNS

MODEL 42 LIMITED EDITION (GRADE V) PUMP SHOTGUN

MODEL 42 GRADE I AND V

After more than 75 years, the ageless Winchester Model 12, one of the most popular shotguns ever produced (over 2 million), is offered as part of Browning's Limited Edition Model 42 Program. It is available in .410 bore.

SPECIFICATIONS
Gauge: .410 bore
Capacity: 5 3-inch loads in magazine (w/plug removed), one in chamber; 2 loads in magazine (w/plug installed), one in chamber
Barrel length: 26″
Overall length: 46″
Chamber: 3″
Choke: Full
Weight: 6 lbs. 4 oz.
Trigger: Approx. 4½ lbs. trigger pull
Receiver: Grade I: deeply blued. Grade V: engraved with gold game scenes
Stock and forearm: Grade I: select walnut w/semi-gloss finish and cut checkering. Grade V: select high grade walnut with high gloss finish (both grades include steel grip cap)

Length of pull: 14″
Drop at heel: 2½″
Drop at comb: 1½″
Prices:
Grade I .410 bore . . . . $ 799.95
Grade V .410 bore 1360.00

MODEL 325 (not shown)
$1540.00 w/Ported Barrels
$1470.00 w/o Ported Barrels

SPECIFICATIONS
Gauges: 12 and 20
Chamber: 2¾″
Choke: Invector-Plus or conventional (28″ and 30″ barrels only)
Barrel lengths: 28″, 30″ and 32″
Overall length: 45½″ (28″ barrel)
Weight: 6 lbs. 12 oz. (28″ barrel)

CHURCHILL SHOTGUNS

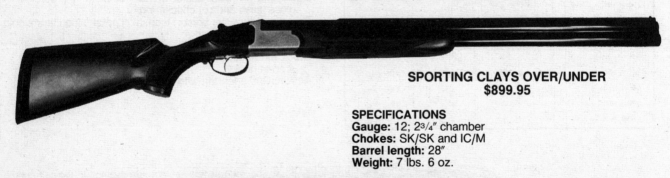

SPORTING CLAYS OVER/UNDER
$899.95

SPECIFICATIONS
Gauge: 12; 2¾″ chamber
Chokes: SK/SK and IC/M
Barrel length: 28″
Weight: 7 lbs. 6 oz.

TURKEY AUTOMATIC SHOTGUNS
$569.95

SPECIFICATIONS
Gauge: 12
Chokes: ICT choke system
Barrel lengths: 25″ (Standard & Turkey); 26″ and 28″ (Standard only)

Stock: Hand-checkered walnut w/satin finish
Features: Magazine cut-off (shoots all loads interchangeably w/o alterations); non-glare finish; vent rib w/mid-bead; gold trigger; receiver has engraved turkey scene

CONNECTICUT VALLEY CLASSICS

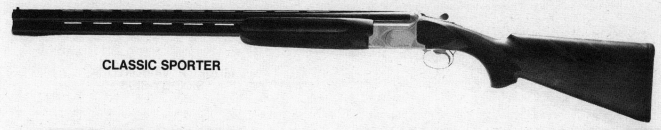

CLASSIC SPORTER

CVC CLASSIC 101 SPORTER

The designers of the new CVC "Classic Sporter" and "Classic Waterfowler" trace their lineage back to the well-known "Classic Doubles" and Winchester over/under shotguns. They have used the proven strength and durability of the old M-101 design and integrated these qualities with advanced engineering and manufacturing techniques. In addition to the basic specifications listed below, the CVC Classic models feature the following: Frame, monoblock and key integral parts are machined from solid steel bar stock. . . Tang spacer is an integral part of the frame to ensure rigid alignment for solid

lockup of buttstock to frame. . . Chrome molybdenum steel barrels; chrome-lined bores and chambers (suitable for steel shot use). . . Barrels have elongated forcing cones for reduced recoil; interchangeable screw-in chokes are included. . . Stock and forend are full, fancy-grade American black walnut, hand-checkered with a low-luster satin finish and fine-line engraving. . . Waterfowler model has non-reflective surface.

Prices:

Classic Sporter	**$2195.00**
Classic Sporter Stainless	2395.00
Waterfowler	1895.00

CONNECTICUT VALLEY CLASSICS SPECIFICATIONS

Model	Symbol	Gauge	Barrel Length	Overall Length	Length of Pull	Drop at Comb	Drop at Heel	Nominal Weight
Classic Sporter	CV-S28	12	28"	44 7/8"	14 1/2"	1 1/2"	2 1/8"	7 3/4"
	CV-S30	12	30"	46 7/8"	14 1/2"	1 1/2"	2 1/8"	7 3/4"
	CV-S32	12	32"	48 7/8"	14 1/2"	1 1/2"	2 1/8"	7 3/4"
Classic Sporter-Stainless	CV-SS28	12	28"	44 7/8"	14 1/2"	1 1/2"	2 1/8"	7 3/4"
	CV-SS30	12	30"	46 7/8"	14 1/2"	1 1/2"	2 1/8"	7 3/4"
	CV-SS32	12	32"	48 7/8"	14 1/2"	1 1/2"	2 1/8"	7 3/4"
Classic Field-Waterfowler	CV-W30	12	30"	46 7/8"	14 1/2"	1 1/2"	2 1/8"	7 3/4"

Chambers: All Connecticut Valley Classics have 3" chambers. **Interchangeable Chokes:** All Connecticut Valley Classics have the internal CV Choke System, and each gun includes the following four chokes: Full, Modified, Improved Cylinder and Skeet. CV Choke Systems are fully compatible with previously manufactured Classic Doubles In-Choke and Winchoke interchangeable choke tubes.

Interchangeable Choke System Options: Two options are available at additional cost to the standard CV Choke System: CV Plus Choke System, a 2 3/8" choke tube system for an extra 7/8" choke length using the standard CV choke tube barrel threading; and the Briley Competition Choke System, a factory-installed 2 3/4" flush-mounted system.

FERLIB SHOTGUNS

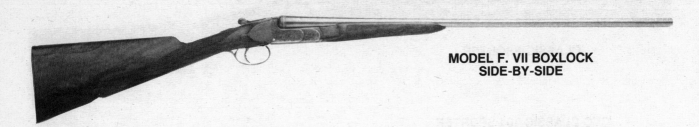

**MODEL F. VII BOXLOCK
SIDE-BY-SIDE**

Hand-crafted by the small European artisan firm of the same name, Ferlib shotguns are high-quality, hand-fitted side-by-sides. With Anson & Deeley boxlock design, all Ferlib doubles are available in 12, 16, 20 and 28 gauge and .410 bore, with automatic ejectors, double triggers with front trigger hinged (non-selective single trigger is optional), hand-rubbed oil-finished straight grip stock with classic forearm (beavertail optional). Dovetail lump barrels have soft-luster blued finish; top rib is concave with file-cut matting. **Barrel length:** 25″–28″. **Stock dimensions:** Length of pull, 14½″; drop at comb, 1½″; drop at heel, 2¼. **Weight:** 12 ga., 6 lbs. 8 oz.—6 lbs. 14 oz.; 16 ga., 6 lbs. 4 oz.—6 lbs. 10 oz.; 20 ga., 5 lbs. 14 oz.—6 lbs. 4 oz.; 28 ga. and .410, 5 lbs. 6 oz.—5 lbs. 11 oz.

Model F. VII w/scalloped frame, full-coverage English scroll engraving, coin finish, select walnut stock . . . . **$ 7500.00**
Model F. VII/SC w/scalloped frame, game scene with either bulino engraved or gold inlayed birds and scroll accents with coin finish, special walnut stock with extra figure and color **9000.00**
Model F. VII/Sideplate w/game scene engraving, gold inlayed birds and coin finish, special walnut stock, extra figure and color **13,000.00**

FRANCOTTE SHOTGUNS

BOXLOCK SIDE-BY-SIDE SHOTGUN

There are no standard Francotte models, since every shotgun is custom made in Belgium to the purchaser's individual specifications. Features and options include Anson & Deeley boxlocks or Auguste Francotte system sidelocks. All guns have custom-fitted stocks. Available are exhibition-grade stocks as well as extensive engraving and gold inlays. U.S. agent for Auguste Francotte of Belgium is Armes de Chasse (see Directory of Manufacturers and Distributors).

SPECIFICATIONS
Gauges: 12, 16, 20, 28, .410; also 24 and 32
Chambers: 2½″, 2¾″ and 3″
Barrel length: to customer's specifications
Forend: to customer's specifications
Stock: Deluxe to exhibition grade; pistol, English or half-pistol grip
Prices:
Basic Boxlock **$16,000**
Basic Boxlock (28 & .410 ga.) 20,000
Optional sideplates, add 1,700
Basic Sidelock 20,000
Basic Sidelock (28 & .410 ga.) 25,000

GARBI SIDELOCK SHOTGUNS

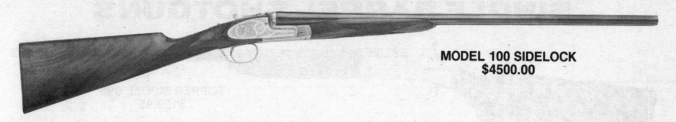

MODEL 100 SIDELOCK
$4500.00

Like this Model 100 shotgun, all Spanish-made Garbi models featured here are Holland & Holland pattern sidelock ejector guns with chopper lump (demibloc) barrels. They are built to English gun standards with regard to design, weight, balance and proportions, and all have the characteristic "feel" associated with the best London guns. All of the models offer fine 24-line hand-checkering, with outstanding quality wood-to-metal and metal-to-metal fit. The Model 100 is available in 12, 16, 20 and 28 gauge and sports Purdey-style fine scroll and rosette engraving, partly done by machine.

MODEL 200
$8500.00

MODELS 101, 103A and 103B (not shown)

Available in 12, 16, 20, and 28 gauge, the sidelocks are hand-crafted with hand-engraved receiver and select walnut straight grip stock.

SPECIFICATIONS
Barrels: 25″ to 30″ in 12 ga.; 25″ to 28″ in 16, 20 and 28 ga.; high-luster blued finish; smooth concave rib (optional Churchill or level, file-cut rib)
Action: Holland & Holland pattern sidelock; automatic ejectors; double triggers with front trigger hinged; case-hardened

Stock/forend: Straight grip stock with checkered butt (optional pistol grip); hand-rubbed oil finish; classic (splinter) forend (optional beavertail)
Weight: 12 ga. game, 6 lbs. 8 oz. to 6 lbs. 12 oz.; 12 ga. pigeon or wildfowl, 7 lbs.—7lbs. 8 oz.; 16 ga., 6 lbs. 4 oz. to 6 lbs. 10 oz.; 20 ga., 5 lbs. 15 oz.—6 lbs. 4 oz.; 28 ga., 5 lbs. 6 oz.—5 lbs. 10 oz.
Prices:
Model 101 . . . . $5750.00
Model 103A 7100.00
Model 103B 9900.00

Also available:
MODEL 200 in 12, 16, 20 or 28 gauge; features Holland pattern stock ejector double, heavy-duty locks, Continental-style floral and scroll engraving, walnut stock.

HARRINGTON & RICHARDSON SINGLE BARREL SHOTGUNS

TURKEY MAG
$169.95

SPECIFICATIONS
Gauge: 12 (3½″ chamber); Turkey Full screw-in choke
Barrel length: 24″
Overall length: 40″
Weight: 6 lbs.

Sights: Bead sights
Stock & forearm: American hardwood with recoil pad; swivel and studs
Finish: Mossy Oak camo coverage and sling

HARRINGTON & RICHARDSON
SINGLE BARREL SHOTGUNS

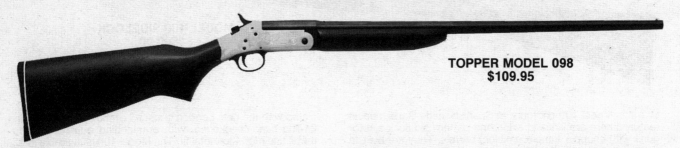

TOPPER MODEL 098
$109.95

SPECIFICATIONS
Gauges: 12, 20 and .410 (3″ chamber)
Chokes: Modified (12 and 20 ga.); Full (.410 ga.)
Barrel lengths: 26″ and 28″

Weight: 5 to 6 lbs.
Action: Break-open; side lever release; automatic ejection
Stock: Full pistol grip; American hardwood; black finish with white buttplate spacer
Length of pull: 14½″

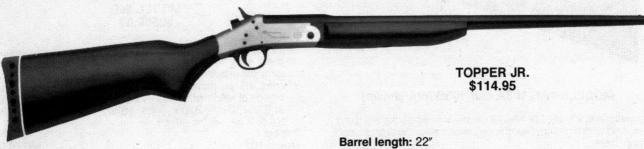

TOPPER JR.
$114.95

SPECIFICATIONS
Gauges: 20 and .410 (3″ chamber)
Chokes: Modified (20 ga.); Full (.410 ga.)

Barrel length: 22″
Weight: 5 to 6 lbs.
Stock: Full pistol grip; American hardwood; black finish; white line spacer; recoil pad
Finish: Satin nickel frame; blued barrel

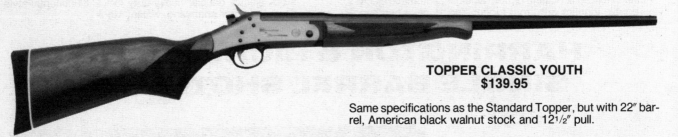

TOPPER CLASSIC YOUTH
$139.95

Same specifications as the Standard Topper, but with 22″ barrel, American black walnut stock and 12½″ pull.

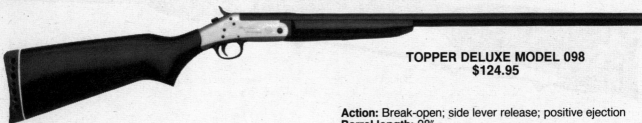

TOPPER DELUXE MODEL 098
$124.95

Action: Break-open; side lever release; positive ejection
Barrel length: 28″
Weight: 5 to 6 lbs.
Stock: American hardwood, black finish, full pistol grip stock with semi-beavertail forend; white line spacer; ventilated recoil pad
Finish: Satin nickel frame; blued barrel

SPECIFICATIONS
Gauge: 12 (3½″ chamber)
Chokes: Screw-in Modified (Full, Extra Full Turkey and Steel Shot also available)

IGA SHOTGUNS

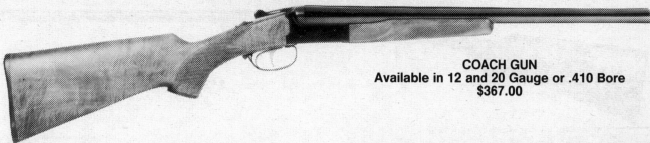

COACH GUN
Available in 12 and 20 Gauge or .410 Bore
$367.00

The **IGA CLASSIC SIDE-BY-SIDE COACH GUN** sports a 20-inch barrel. Lightning fast, it is the perfect shotgun for hunting upland game in dense brush or close quarters. This endurance-tested workhorse of a gun is designed from the ground up to give you years of trouble-free service. Two massive underlugs provide a super-safe, vise-tight locking system for lasting strength and durability. The mechanical extraction of spent shells and double-trigger mechanism assure reliability. The au-

tomatic safety is actuated whenever the action is opened, whether or not the gun has been fired. The polish and blue is deep and rich, and the solid sighting rib is matte-finished for glare-free sighting. Chrome-moly steel barrels with micro-polished bores give dense, consistent patterns. The classic stock and forend are of durable hardwood . . . oil finished, hand-rubbed and hand-checkered.

Improved Cylinder/Modified choking and its short barrel make the IGA coach gun the ideal choice for hunting in close quarters, security and police work. 3-inch chambers.

UPLANDER SIDE-BY-SIDE
Available in 12, 20, 28 Gauge or .410 Bore
$383.00
$425.00 (12 and 20 Gauge w/Choke Tubes)

The **IGA SIDE-BY-SIDE** is a rugged shotgun, endurance-tested and designed to give years of trouble-free service. A vise-tight, super-safe locking system is provided by two massive underlugs for lasting strength and durability. Two design features which make the IGA a standout for reliability are its positive mechanical extraction of spent shells and its traditional double-trigger mechanism. The safety is automatic in that every

time the action is opened, whether the gun has been fired or not, the safety is actuated. The polish and bluing are deep and rich. The solid sighting rib carries a machined-in matte finish for glare-free sighting. Barrels are of chrome-moly steel with micro-polished bores to give dense, consistent patterns. The stock and forend are available with either traditional stock or the legendary English-style stock. Both are of durable Brazilian hardwood, oil-finished, hand-rubbed and hand-checkered.

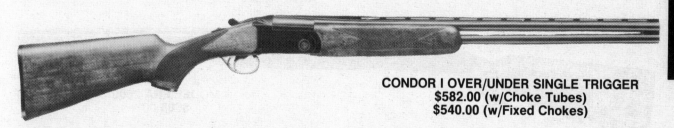

CONDOR I OVER/UNDER SINGLE TRIGGER
$582.00 (w/Choke Tubes)
$540.00 (w/Fixed Chokes)

The **IGA OVER/UNDER SINGLE TRIGGER** is a workhorse of a shotgun, designed for maximum dependability in heavy field use. The super-safe lock-up system makes use of a sliding underlug, the best system for over/under shotguns. A massive monobloc joins the barrel in a solid one-piece assembly at the breech end. Reliability is assured, thanks to the mechanical extraction system. Upon opening the breech, the spent shells are partially lifted from the chamber, allowing easy removal by hand. IGA barrels are of chrome-moly steel with micro-polished bores to give tight, consistent patterns. They are specifically formulated for use with steel shot where Federal migratory

bird regulations require. Atop the barrel is a sighting rib with an anti-glare surface. The buttstock and forend are of durable hardwood, hand-checkered and finished with an oil-based formula that takes dents and scratches in stride.

The IGA **Condor I** over/under shotgun is available in 12 and 20 gauge with 26- and 28-inch barrels with choke tubes and 3-inch chambers; 12 and 20 gauge with 26- and 28-inch barrels choked IC/M and Mod./Full, 3-inch chambers.

Also available: **Condor II O/U** in 12 gauge, double trigger, 26″ barrel IC/M or 28″ barrel M/F. **Price: $432.00**

IGA SHOTGUNS

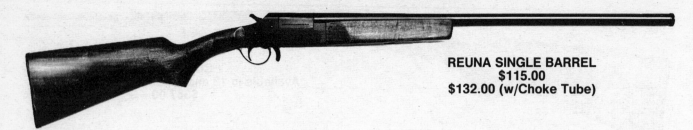

REUNA SINGLE BARREL
$115.00
$132.00 (w/Choke Tube)

IGA's entry-level single barrel shotgun features a feeling of heft and quality not found in other shotguns similarly priced. Single mechanical extraction makes for convenient removal of spent shells. For ease of operation and maximum safety, the Reuna is equipped with an exposed hammer, which must be cocked manually before firing.

The Reuna single barrel shotgun is available with a choke tube in 12 and 20 gauge and with fixed chokes in 12 and 20 gauge or .410 bore. Both the buttstock and semi-beavertail forearm are of durable Brazilian hardwood. The squared-off design of the firearm enhances stability and provides an additional gripping surface for greater comfort.

NEW

REUNA YOUTH MODEL SINGLE BARREL
$127.00

The Youth Model is designed especially for the young shooter. All the same features of the conventional-size model are included in the youth version, complemented by an easy-handling shorter barrel (22″), shortened stock and ventilated recoil pad. In 20 gauge and .410 (Full choke).

MODEL ERA 2000
$665.00

The **ERA 2000** was designed to provide maximum strength and safety in the lockup system. For additional rigidity, the system locks through the frame of the receiver, thus minimizing any barrel movement at the moment of discharge. The receiver has been styled to create a free-flowing look to the eye, while its lustrous deep bluing enhances the overall appearance.

The mechanical extraction system enables the spent shells to be partially lifted from the chamber for easy removal. The triggers operate mechanically and do not depend on inertia from recoil to activate for a second shot. The safety is manual.

Moly-chrome steel barrels, micro-polished to give tight, consistent patterns, are specifically formulated for use with steel shot. The ventilated rib has an anti-glare surface to minimize distortion.

The ERA 2000 stock and forend are constructed of oil-finished Brazilian hardwood. Hand-finished checkering provides for a sharp, sure gripping surface. Available in 12 gauge with 26″ or 28″ barrels (choke tubes). See table on following page for additional specifications.

IGA SHOTGUNS

IGA SHOTGUNS SPECIFICATIONS

	Gauge				Barrel Length					Chokes		Other Specifications				Dimensions			
	12	20	28	410	20"	22"	24"	26"	28"	Fixed	Choke tubes	Chamber	Weight (lbs.)	Extractors	Triggers	Length of pull	Drop at comb	Drop at heel	Overall length
Coach Gun Side by Side	■	■		■	■					IC&M		3"	6¾	■	D.T.	14½"	1½"	2½"	36½"
Uplander Side by Side	■	■						■		IC&M	IC&M	3"	7½	■	D.T.	14½"	1½"	2½"	42"
Uplander Side by Side	■	■							■	M&F	M&F	3"	7½	■	D.T.	14½"	1½"	2½"	44"
Uplander Side by Side			■					■		IC&M		2¾"	6¾	■	D.T.	14½"	1½"	2½"	42"
Uplander Side by Side				■				■		F&F		3"	6¾	■	D.T.	14½"	1½"	2½"	42"
English Stock Side by Side		■					■	■		IC&M		3"	6½	■	D.T.	14½"	1⅜"	2⅜"	40"/42"
ERA 2000 Over/Under	■							■	■	F, M&IC		3"	8	■	S.T.	14½"	1½"	2½"	43½"/45½"
Condor I Over/Under	■	■						■		IC&M	IC&M	3"	8	■	S.T.	14½"	1½"	2½"	43½"
Condor I Over/Under	■	■							■	M&F	M&F	3"	8	■	S.T.	14½"	1½"	2½"	45½"
Condor II Over/Under	■							■		IC&M		3"	8	■	D.T.	14½"	1½"	2½"	43½"
Condor II Over/Under	■								■	M&F		3"	8	■	D.T.	14½"	1½"	2½"	45½"
Reuna Single Barrel	■								■	F	F	3"	6¼	■		14½"	1½"	2½"	44½"
Reuna Single Barrel	■							■		M		3"	6¼	■		14½"	1½"	2½"	42½"
Reuna Single Barrel		■						■		F	F	3"	6¼	■		14½"	1½"	2½"	42½"
Reuna Single Barrel				■				■		F		3"	6	■		14½"	1½"	2½"	42½"
Reuna-Youth Model Single Barrel		■		■		■				F		3"	5	■		13	1½"	2½"	37

SHOTGUNS

ITHACA SHOTGUNS

FOR SPECIFICATIONS, SEE FOLLOWING PAGE

MODEL 87 FIELD GRADES

Made in much the same manner as 50 years ago, Ithaca's Model 37 pump (now designated as Model 87) features Roto-forged barrels hammered from 11″ round billets of steel, then triple-reamed, lapped and polished. The receivers are milled from a solid block of ordnance grade steel, and all internal parts—hammer, extractors, slides and carriers—are milled and individually fitted to each gun.

Prices:

Model 87 Supreme	**$667.50**
Model 87 Deluxe Vent	462.50
Model 87 Camo Field	457.50
Model 87 English	462.50
Model 87 Turkey Field w/Tube	393.75
Model 87 Turkey Field w/Fixed Choke	380.00
Model 87 Turkey Field Camo w/Tube	436.25
Model 87 Turkey Field Camo w/Fixed Choke . . .	422.50

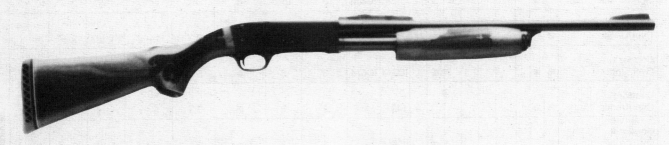

MODEL 87 DEERSLAYER

The first shotgun developed to handle rifled slugs successfully, Ithaca's Deerslayer shotgun remains first choice for many big-game hunters around the world. The Deerlayer's design results in an "undersized" cylinder bore—from the forcing cone all the way to the muzzle. This enables the slug to travel smoothly down the barrel with no gas leakage or slug rattle. The new Deerslayer II features the world's first production rifled barrel for shotguns; moreover, the Deerslayer's barrel is permanently screwed into the receiver for solid frame construction, which insures better accuracy to about 85 yards.

Prices:

Deerslayer SB Basic	**$363.75**
Deerslayer SB Deluxe	400.00
Deerslayer DSR Deluxe	430.00
Deerslayer II	488.75
Deerslayer II Brenneke	533.75

MODEL 87 FIELD TURKEY GUN
(Camo-seal Finish)

ITHACA SHOTGUNS

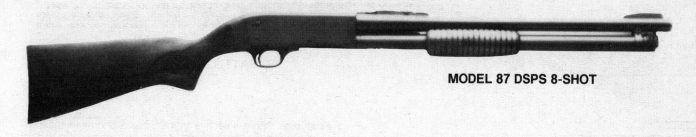

MODEL 87 DSPS 8-SHOT

SPECIFICATIONS ITHACA MODEL 87 SHOTGUNS

Type	Gauge	Bbl In.	Chokes	Chamb.	Cap.	Wt.	Type	Gauge	Bbl In.	Chokes	Chamb.	Cap.	Wt.
Supreme	12	30	CT	3″	5	7	Deerslayer II	12	25	DSR1	3″	5	7
	12	28	CT	3″	5	7		12	20	DSR1	3″	5	7
	12	26	CT	3″	5	7		20	25	DSR1	3″	5	6.8
	20	26	CT	3″	5	6.8		20	20	DSR1	3″	5	6.8
Deluxe Vent	12	30	CT	3″	5	7	Deerslayer II Brenneke	12	25	DSR2	3″	5	7
	12	28	CT	3″	5	7	Extra Barrel Vent Rib	12	30	CTt	3″	N/A	2.1
	12	26	CT	3″	5	7		12	28	CT	3″	N/A	2.1
	20	26	CT	3″	5	6.8		12	26	CT	3″	N/A	2.1
English	20	26	CT	3″	5	6.8		12	24	CT	3″	N/A	2.1
	20	24	CT	3″	5	6.8		20	28	CT	3″	N/A	2
Camo Field	12	28	CT	3″	5	7		20	26	CT	3″	N/A	2
	12	24	CT	3″	5	7		20	24	CT	3″	N/A	2
	12	28	CT	3″	5	7	Extra Barrel Deer SB	12	25	DS	3″	N/A	2.1
	12	24	CT	3″	5	7		12	20	DS	3″	N/A	2.1
Turkey Camo w/Tube	12	24	Full CT	3″	5	7		20	25	DS	3″	N/A	2
	12	22	Full CT	3″	5	7		20	20	DS	3″	N/A	2
Turkey Camo Fixed Choke	12	24	Full	3″	5	7	Extra Barrel Deer DSR	12	25	DSR	3″	N/A	2.1
	12	22	Full	3″	5	7		12	20	DSR	3″	N/A	2.1
Turkey Field w/Tube	12	24	Full CT	3″	5	7		20	25	DSR	3″	N/A	2
	12	22	Full CT	3″	5	7		20	20	DSR	3″	N/A	2
Turkey Field Fixed Choke	12	24	Full	3″	5	7	Hand Grip	12	19	CYL	3″	5	6.5
	12	22	Full	3″	5	7		20	19	CYL	3″	5	6
Deerslayer SB Deluxe	12	25	DS	3″	5	7		12	20	CYL	3″	8	5.5
	20	20	DS	3″	5	7	DSPS	12	20	DS	3″	5	7
	20	25	DS	3″	5	6.8		12	19	DS	3″	5	7
	20	20	DS	3″	5	6.8		12	19	DS	3″	8	7
Deerslayer SB Basic	12	25	DS	3″	5	7		12	20	DSR1	3″	5	7
	12	20	DS	3″	5	7		12	25	DSR1	3″	5	7
	20	25	DS	3″	5	6.8	M&P	12	20	CYL	3″	5	7
	20	20	DS	3″	5	6		20	20	CYL	3″	5	6.5
Deerslayer DSR Deluxe	12	25	DSR	3″	5	7		12	20	CYL	3″	8	7
	12	20	DSR	3″	5	7							
	20	25	DSR	3″	5	6.8							
	20	20	DSR	3″	5	6.8							

CT = Full Mod IC Tubes; DS = Smooth Bore Deer; DSR = Rifled Bore Deer; DSR1 = Fixed Rifled Bore Deer 1/34; DSR2 = Fixed Rifled Bore Deer 1/25

SHOTGUNS

KBI SHOTGUNS

SABATTI GRADE I OVER/UNDER
$499.00

SPECIFICATIONS
Gauges: 12, 20, 28, .410
Barrel lengths: 26″ (IC/M); 28″ (M/F, W/ICT)
Weight: 7½ lbs. (12 ga.); 6½ lbs. (20 ga.)
Stock: European walnut with checkered pistol grip and forend

Features: Single selective trigger; blued engraved receiver; ventilated rib; chrome-lined barrels; positive non-slip thumb-type safety (locks the trigger but allows bolt to be opened safely for unloading and inspection of chamber); available with or without deluxe sights; rear sight adjustable for windage and elevation; swivel posts; recoil pad

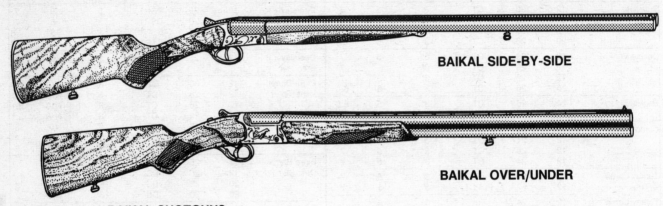

BAIKAL SIDE-BY-SIDE

BAIKAL OVER/UNDER

BAIKAL SHOTGUNS

Baikal shotguns are manufactured by Russian arms producers. The **Single Barrel** model has a chrome-lined barrel bore and chamber, non-auto safety and automatic ejector with external disengaging lever. Available in 12 or 20 gauge. Additional specifications are listed in the table below.
Price: . . . . **$ 89.00**

The **Side by Side** model also has chrome-lined barrels and chambers and comes with double triggers and extractors.
Price: **$379.00**
The **Over/Under** model features either double trigger and extractors or single selective trigger and auto ejectors.
Price: **$479.00**

BAIKAL SHOTGUN SPECIFICATIONS

Model	Article Number	Gauge	Barrel Length in.	Chamber in.	Chokes	Weight lb.
Single	GD1000	12	28	2¾″	F	6
Single	GD1019	12	28	2¾″	M	6
Single	GD1027	12	26	2¾″	IC	6
Single	GD1035	20	28	3″	F	5½
Single	GD1043	20	28	3″	M	5½
Single	GD1051	20	26	3″	IC	5½
Single	GD1078	410	26	3″	F	5½
Side/Side—DT	GE1006	12	28	2¾″	M/F	6¾
Side/Side—DT	GE1014	12	26	2¾″	IC/M	6¾
O/U—DT	GP1006	12	28	2¾″	M/F	7
O/U—DT	GP1014	12	26	2¾″	IC/M	7
O/U—SST	GP1065	12	28	2¾″	M/F	7
O/U—SST	GP1073	12	26	2¾″	IC/M	7

KRIEGHOFF SHOTGUNS

(See following page for additional Specifications and Prices)

MODEL K-80 SPORTING CLAY

MODEL K-80 TRAP, SKEET, SPORTING CLAY AND LIVE BIRD

Barrels: Made of Boehler steel; free-floating bottom barrel with adjustable point of impact; standard Trap and Live Pigeon ribs are tapered step; standard Skeet, Sporting Clay and International ribs are tapered or parallel flat.
Receivers: Hard satin-nickel finish; casehardened; blue finish available as special order
Triggers: Wide profile, single selective, position adjustable. Removable trigger option available (add'l **$1000.00**)
Weight: 8½ lbs. (Trap); 8 lbs. (Skeet)

Ejectors: Selective automatic
Sights: White pearl front bead and metal center bead
Stocks: Hand-checkered and epoxy-finished Select European walnut stock and forearm; quick-detachable palm swell stocks available in five different styles and dimensions
Safety: Push button safety located on top tang.
Also available:
SKEET SPECIAL (28″ and 30″ barrel; tapered flat or 8mm rib; 2 choke tubes). **Price: $6250.00** (Standard)

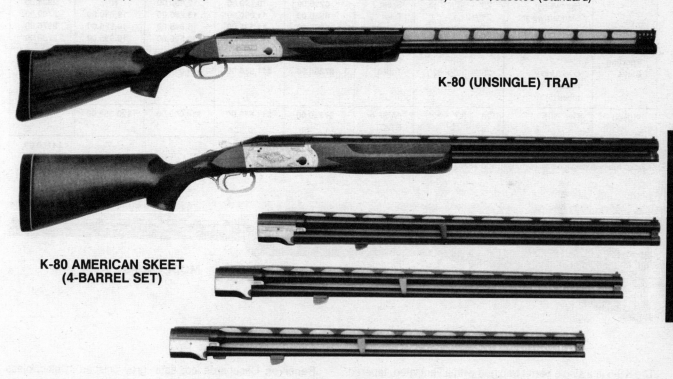

K-80 (UNSINGLE) TRAP

**K-80 AMERICAN SKEET
(4-BARREL SET)**

**MODEL ULM-P
O/U SIDELOCK LIVE BIRD GUN
$14,950.00**

SPECIFICATIONS
Gauge: 12
Chamber: 2¾″
Barrel: 28″ or 30″ long; tapered, ventilated rib
Choke: Top, Full; bottom, Imp. Mod.
Trigger action: Single trigger, non-selective bottom-top; hand-detachable sidelocks with coil springs; optional release trigger

Stock: Selected fancy English walnut, oil finish; length, 14⅜″; drop at comb, 1⅜″; optional custom-made stock
Forearm: Semi-beavertail
Engraving: Light scrollwork; optional engravings available
Weight: Approx. 8 lbs.
Also available in Skeet and Trap models

KRIEGHOFF SHOTGUNS

SPECIFICATIONS AND PRICES MODEL K-80 (see also preceding page)

Model	Description	Bbl Length	Choke	Standard	Bavaria	Danube	Gold Target	Extra Barrels
Trap	Over & Under	30″/32″	IM/F	$ 6695.00	$11,195.00	$13,395.00	$19,695.00	$2385.00
	Unsingle	32″/34″	Full	7300.00	11,800.00	14,000.00	20,300.00	3250.00
	Top Single	34″ only	Full	9380.00	13,880.00	16,000.00	22,380.00	3250.00
	Combo (unsingle)	⎧ 30″ + 32″ ⎨ 30″ + 34″	IM/F+F	9380.00	13,880.00	16,080.00	22,380.00	
		⎩ 32″ + 34″	CT/CT + CT	10,370.00	14,870.00	17,070.00	23,370.00	

Optional Features:*
Screw-in chokes (O/U, Top or Unsingle) **$400.00**
Single factory release **375.00**
Double factory release **625.00**

Model	Description	Bbl Length	Choke	Standard	Bavaria	Danube	Gold Target	Extra Barrels
Skeet	4-Barrel Set	28″/12 ga.	Tula					$2700.00
		28″/20 ga.	Skeet ⎫	$14,200.00	$18,700.00	$20,900.00	$27,200.00	2625.00
		28″/28 ga.	Skeet ⎬					2625.00
		28″/.410 ga.	Skeet ⎭					2625.00
	2-Barrel Set	28″/12 ga.	Tula	10,985.00	15,435.00	17,635.00	23,935.00	3990.00
	Lightweight	28″ + 30″/12 ga.	Skeet	6290.00	10,790.00	12,990.00	N/A	2385.00
	Standardweight	28″/12 ga.	Tula	6550.00	11,050.00	13,250.00	19,550.00	2700.00
		28″ + 30″/12 ga.	Skeet	6895.00	11,395.00	13,595.00	19,895.00	2975.00
	International	28″/12 ga.	Tula	6995.00	11,495.00	13,695.00	19,995.00	2700.00
Sporting Clays	Over/Under w/screw-in tubes (5)	28″ + 30″ + 32″/ 12 ga.	Tubes	$7350.00	$11,850.00	$14,050.00	$20,350.00	$2975.00
Pigeon	Live Bird	28″ + 30″ + 32″	IM/SF or CT/CT	$7350.00	$11,850.00	$14,050.00	$20,350.00	

Optional engravings: Super Scroll **$1150.00**

* Choke tubes in single barrel (w/tubes): add **$335.00**. In O/U barrel (5 tubes) add **$490.00**.

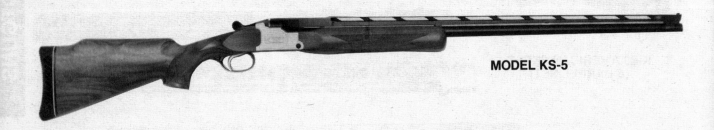

MODEL KS-5

The KS-5 is a single barrel trap gun with a ventilated, tapered and adjustable step rib, casehardened receiver in satin grey matte or blue, finished in electroless nickel. It features an adjustable point of impact by means of different optional fronthangers. Screw-in chokes and adjustable stock are optional. Trigger is adjustable externally for poundage.

SPECIFICATIONS
Gauge: 12
Chamber: 2³/₄″
Barrel length: 32″ or 34″
Choke: Full; optional screw-in chokes
Rib: Tapered step; ventilated
Trigger: Weight of pull adjustable; optional release

Receiver: Casehardened; satin grey finished in electroless nickel; now available in blue
Grade: Standard; engraved models on special order
Weight: Approximately 8.6-8.8 lbs.
Case: Aluminum
Prices:
With full choke and case **$3575.00**
With screw-in choke and case **4350.00**
Screw-in choke barrels **2525.00**
Regular barrels **1875.00**

Also available:
KS-5 SPECIAL. Same as **KS-5** except barrel has fully adjustable rib and stock. **Price: $4450.00**

MAGTECH SHOTGUNS

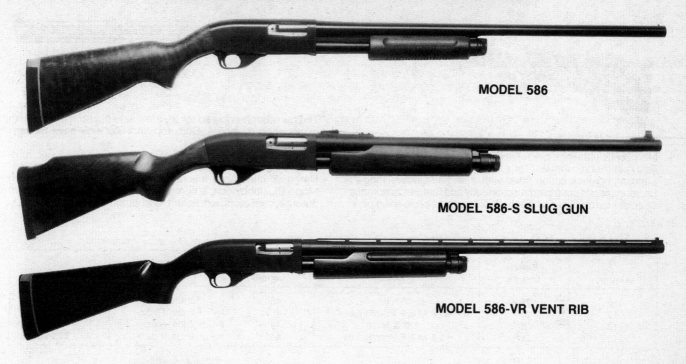

MODEL 586

MODEL 586-S SLUG GUN

MODEL 586-VR VENT RIB

MODEL 586
$225.00

SPECIFICATIONS
Gauge: 12 (2³/₄″ or 3″ chamber)
Barrel length: 28″
Chokes: Full, Mod. or Imp.
Overall length: 48¹/₂″
Weight: 8 lbs.

Also available:
MODEL 586-P Pump Action w/19″ hammer-forged
   Cylinder choke barrel, 7.75 lbs. **$219.00**
MODEL 586-S Slug Gun w/Monte Carlo stock,
   24″ Cyl. bore barrel, rifle sights **235.00**
MODEL 586-VR w/vent rib (26″ or 28″ bbl.) **255.00**

MARLIN SHOTGUNS

MARLIN MODEL 55
GOOSE GUN
$274.75

High-flying ducks and geese are the Goose Gun's specialty. The Marlin Goose Gun has an extra-long 36-inch full-choked barrel and Magnum capability, making it the perfect choice for tough shots at wary waterfowl. It also features a quick-loading 2-shot clip magazine, a convenient leather carrying strap and a quality ventilated recoil pad.

SPECIFICATIONS
Gauge: 12; 2³/₄″ Magnum, 3″ Magnum or 2³/₄″ regular shells
Choke: Full
Capacity: 2-shot clip magazine
Action: Bolt action; positive thumb safety; red cocking indicator
Stock: Walnut-finish hardwood with pistol grip and ventilated
   recoil pad; swivel studs; tough Mar-Shield® finish
Barrel length: 36″
Sights: Bead front sight and U-groove rear sight
Overall length: 56³/₄″
Weight: About 8 lbs.

MAROCCHI AVANZA SHOTGUNS

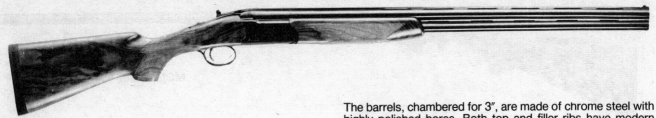

Marocchi's ultralight, quick handling over and under is an ideal field gun that moves fast for sporting clays as well. It houses a strong boxlock action fitted with a single selective trigger. Barrel cycling is controlled mechanically and features automatic selective extractors and ejectors, plus unbreakable firing pins.

The barrels, chambered for 3″, are made of chrome steel with highly polished bores. Both top and filler ribs have modern wide ventilated styling.

Features: Single selective trigger (5½ lb. pull); cut-checkered stock of select walnut; top and middle ribs are ventilated; 3″ chambers; mechanism is lightweight all steel with Mono-Block boxlock, automechanical barrel cycling, selective automatic ejectors/extractors, and automatic safety.

SPECIFICATIONS MAROCCHI AVANZA O/U

Gauge	Barrel Length	Chokes	Overall Length	Weight	Prices
12	28″	M & F	46½″	6 lbs. 9 oz.	**$769.00**
12	28″	IC & M & F Interchokes	46½″	6 lbs. 13 oz.	**829.00**
12	26″	IC & M	44½″	6 lbs. 6 oz.	**769.00**
12	26″	IC & M & F Interchokes	44½″	6 lbs. 9 oz.	**829.00**

AVANZA SPORTING CLAYS MODEL
$889.00

SPECIFICATIONS
Gauge: 12 (3″ chamber)
Barrel length: 28″
Choke: Interchangeable tubes in IC & Modified
Weight: 7 lbs.
Sights: Ventilated rib, front and mid beads
Trigger pull: 5½ lbs.

Stock: Checkered select walnut, beavertail forend
Features: Chrome steel double barrel over/under with highly polished bores; all steel mono block boxlock action; automatic safety; single selective trigger adjustable for length of pull without tools; automechanical barrel cycling; selective automatic ejectors/extractors; unbreakable firing pins

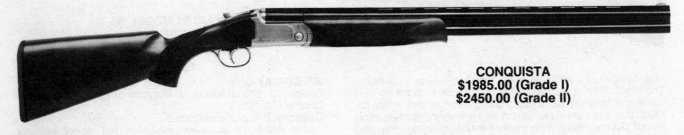

CONQUISTA
$1985.00 (Grade I)
$2450.00 (Grade II)

SPECIFICATIONS
Gauge: 12 (2¾″ chamber)
Barrel lengths: 28″, 30″, 32″
Overall length: 45″ (28″ barrel); 47″ (30″ barrel); 49″ (32″ barrel)
Weight: 8 lbs.

Length of pull: 14½″-14⅞″
Drop at heel: 2.2″
Drop at comb: 1.5″
Features: Deluxe sporting clays rubber buttpad; double vent rib (matted); lengthened forcing cones

MAVERICK PUMP ACTION SHOTGUNS

SECURITY ARMS AUTOLOADER
(18½″ Barrel)
$264.00

SECURITY ARMS PISTOL GRIP PUMP
(18½″ Barrel)
$199.00

BULLPUP MODEL 88
$291.00

SPECIFICATIONS
Gauge: 12; 2¾″ or 3″ chamber
Choke: Cylinder bore barrel
Barrel length: 18½″
Overall length: 26½″
Weight: 9½ lbs.
Sight: Open
Features: Same as Model 88

MODEL 91 PLAIN
$226.00
($234.00 w/Vent Rib)

SPECIFICATIONS
Gauge: 12; 2¾″, 3″ or 3½″ chamber
Choke: ACCU-Full
Barrel length: 28″
Overall length: 48″
Weight: 7.7 lbs.
Features: Synthetic stock and forend; thick rubber recoil pad;
   positive crossbolt safety design; Maverick Cablelock

MAVERICK PUMP ACTION SHOTGUNS

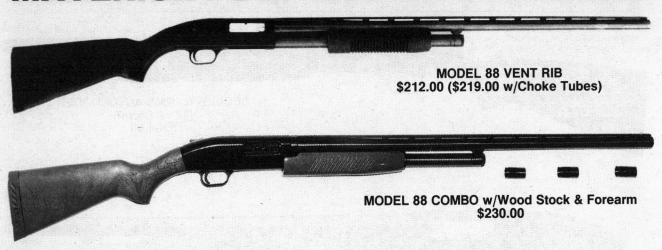

MODEL 88 VENT RIB
$212.00 ($219.00 w/Choke Tubes)

MODEL 88 COMBO w/Wood Stock & Forearm
$230.00

SPECIFICATIONS
Gauge: 12
Chamber: 2³/₄″ or 3″
Capacity: 6 shots (2³/₄″); 5 shots (3″)
Barrel length: 28″ Modified; 30″ Full
Overall length: 48″ (w/28″ barrel)
Weight: 7¹/₄ lbs. (w/28″ barrel)
Features: Rubber recoil pad; positive crossbolt safety; interchangeable barrels without tools; durable black synthetic stock and matching forend; high strength aluminum alloy receiver; steel-to-steel lockup between hardened barrel extension and bolt lock

Also available:
MODEL 88 PLAIN (Full or Mod. Choke) **$205.00**
MODEL 88 COMBO w/18¹/₂″ & 28″ bbl. 230.00
  w/Vent rib 238.00
  w/Choke tubes 246.00
MODEL 88 DEER COMBO (Plain) 243.00
  w/Vent rib 249.00
  w/Choke tubes 257.00

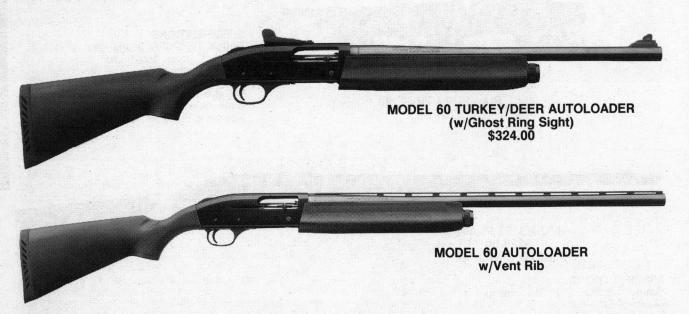

MODEL 60 TURKEY/DEER AUTOLOADER
(w/Ghost Ring Sight)
$324.00

MODEL 60 AUTOLOADER
w/Vent Rib

Maverick Model 60s have designated barrels for magnum and non-magnum loads. Magnum barrels fire both 2³/₄″ and 3″ magnum loads. Non-magnum barrels are designed to shoot standard 2³/₄″ field and target loads. All Model 60s have 5-round capacity and reduced recoil, plus interchangeable choke tubes. Barrels are 24″ (18¹/₂″ extra barrel for Combo, extra barrel non-magnum only).

Also available:
MODEL 60 AUTOLOADER Vent Rib (Tube-Mod.) . **$279.00**
MODEL 60 COMBO (w/extra barrel) 312.00

MERKEL OVER/UNDER SHOTGUNS

Merkel over-and-unders are the first hunting guns with barrels arranged one above the other, and they have since proved to be able competitors of the side-by-side gun. Merkel superiority lies in the following details:
- Available in 12, 16 and 20 gauge
- Lightweight (6.4 to 7.28 lbs.)
- The high, narrow forend protects the shooter's hand from the barrel in hot or cold climates.
- The forend is narrow and therefore lies snugly in the hand to permit easy and positive swinging.

- The slim barrel line provides an unobstructed field of view and thus permits rapid aiming and shooting.
- The over-and-under barrel arrangement reduces recoil error; the recoil merely pushes the muzzle up vertically.

All Merkel shotguns are manufactured by Jagd und Sportwaffen GmbH, Suhl, Thuringia, Germany; imported, distributed and retailed in the U.S. by GSI Inc. (see Directory of Manufacturers and Distributors).

MODEL 200E BOXLOCK

MODEL 201E BOXLOCK

MODEL 203E SIDELOCK

MERKEL OVER/UNDER SHOTGUN SPECIFICATIONS

Gauges: 12 and 20
Barrel lengths: 26¾" and 28"
Weight: 6.4 to 7.28 lbs.
Stock: English or pistol grip in European walnut
Features: Models 200E and 201E are boxlocks; Model 203E is a sidelock. All models include three-piece forearm, automatic ejectors, Kersten double crossbolt lock, Blitz action and single selective triggers. Model 203E has Holland & Holland ejectors.

Prices:
MODEL 200E Boxlock (w/scroll engraved
  casehardened receiver) . . . . $ 3395.00
MODEL 201E Boxlock (w/hunting scenes) 4195.00
MODEL 202E Sidelock (w/hunting scenes) 7995.00
MODEL 203E Sidelock (w/English-style
  engraving) 9695.00
MODEL 303E Sidelock (w/quick-detachable sidelock
  plates w/integral retracting hook 21,295.00

MERKEL SIDE-BY-SIDE SHOTGUNS

SPECIFICATIONS
Gauges: 12 and 20 (28 ga. and .410 in Models 47S and 147S)
Barrel lengths: 26″ and 28″ (25½″ in Models 47S and 147S)
Weight: 6 to 7 lbs.
Stock: English or pistol grip in European walnut
Features: Models 47E and 147E are boxlocks; Models 47S and 147S are sidelocks. All guns have cold hammer-forged barrels, double triggers, double lugs and Greener crossbolt locking systems and automatic ejectors.

Prices:
MODEL 8	$1295.00
MODEL 47E (Holland & Holland ejectors)	1595.00
MODEL 122 (H&H ejectors, engraved hunting scenes).	3195.00
MODEL 147 (H&H ejectors)	1795.00
MODEL 147E (engraved hunting scenes)	1995.00
MODEL 47S Sidelock (H&H ejectors)	4195.00
MODEL 147S Sidelock	5195.00
MODEL 247S (English-style engraving)	6895.00
MODEL 347S (H&H ejectors)	7895.00
MODEL 447S	8995.00

MODEL 47E BOXLOCK

MODEL 147E BOXLOCK

MODEL 47S SIDE-BY-SIDE

MODEL 147S SIDELOCK

MOSSBERG PUMP SHOTGUNS

MODEL 500 SPORTING

These slide-action Model 500's offer lightweight action and high tensile-strength alloys. They also feature the famous Mossberg "Safety on Top" and a full range of interchangeable barrels. Stocks are walnut-finished birch with rubber recoil pads with combs checkered pistol grip and forend. Cable locks are included with all Mossberg shotguns.

MODEL 500 GENERAL SPECIFICATIONS

Action: Positive slide-action
Gauge/Barrel: 12 or 20 gauge and .410 bore with free-floating vent. rib; ACCU-CHOKE interchangeable choke tubes; chambered for 2¾" standard and Magnum and 3" Magnum shells
Capacity: 6-shot (one less when using 3" Magnum shells); plug for 3-shot capacity included
Receiver: Aluminum alloy, deep blue/black finish; ordnance steel bolt locks in barrel extension for solid "steel-to-steel" lockup
Safety: Top tang, thumb-operated; disconnecting trigger
Sights: Mid-point and front bead
Stock/forend: Walnut-finished American hardwood with checkering; rubber recoil pad (new .410 Bantam model has plain barrel with synthetic stock)
Standard stock dimensions: 14" length of pull; 2½" drop at heel; 1½" drop at comb

MODEL 500
20" or 28" ACCU-Choke Barrel w/Vent Rib
$273.00

Also available:
TURKEY GUN (24" and 28" Barrel)
$253.00 w/Rifle Sights (24" bbl.)

MODEL 500 BANTAM
$253.00 (20 ga. w/ACCU-Choke & 22" Barrel)
$258.00 (.410 ga. w/Full Choke & 24" Barrel)

Also available:
BANTAM "JAKE"
(20 ga./22" Barrel)
$318.00

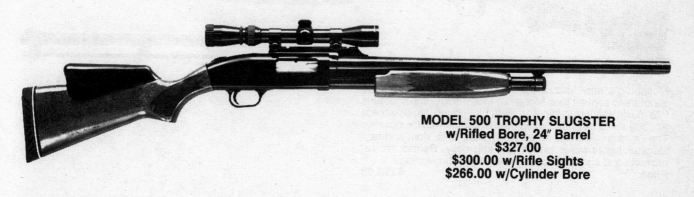

MODEL 500 TROPHY SLUGSTER
w/Rifled Bore, 24" Barrel
$327.00
$300.00 w/Rifle Sights
$266.00 w/Cylinder Bore

SHOTGUNS

MOSSBERG PUMP SHOTGUNS

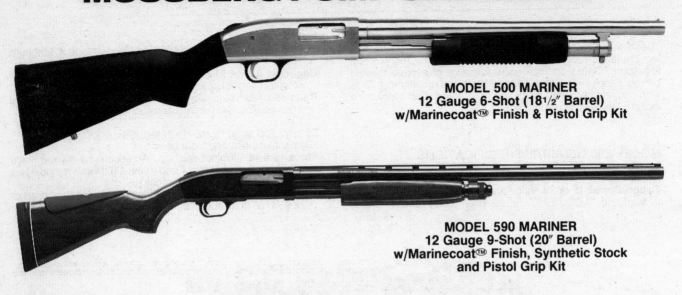

MODEL 500 MARINER
12 Gauge 6-Shot (18½" Barrel)
w/Marinecoat™ Finish & Pistol Grip Kit

MODEL 590 MARINER
12 Gauge 9-Shot (20" Barrel)
w/Marinecoat™ Finish, Synthetic Stock
and Pistol Grip Kit

MARINER MODELS 500 & 590

All carbon steel parts of these 12 gauge shotguns are treated with MARINECOAT™ protective finish, a unique Teflon and metal coating. This finish makes each Mariner 500 shotgun resistant to salt spray and water damage by actually penetrating into the steel pores. All stock and forearms are made of a high-strength synthetic material rather than wood to provide extra durability with minimum maintenance. Mariners are available in a variety of 6- or 9-shot versions. Pistol grip kit and QD swivel post included.

SPECIFICATIONS
Gauge: 12
Chambers: 2¾" and 3"
Capacity: 6-shot model—5-shot (3" chamber) and 6-shot (2¾" chamber)
9-shot model—8-shot (3" chamber) and 9-shot (2¾" chamber)
Barrel lengths: 18½" and 20"
Overall length: 40" w/20" barrel; 38½" w/18½" barrel
Weight: 6¾ lbs. w/18½" barrel
Stock dimensions: 14" pull; 1½" drop at comb; 2½" drop at heel
Features: Double slide bars; twin extractors; dual shell latches; ambidextrous safety
Price:
MODEL 500/590 MARINER 6- or 9-shot $353.00

MUZZLELOADING CONVERSION BARRELS

Mossberg's new Muzzleloading Conversion Barrels enable shooters to convert their Mossberg Model 500 pump shotguns into muzzleloaders in minutes. Both 3½-pound barrels accept No. 209 shotshell primer, which is in direct line with the powder. The 24-inch barrel has a fast 1:26" twist, while front and rear slugster sights make aiming fast and easy. Barrels are removable and can be submerged in water for cleaning.
Price: $172.00

MOSSBERG PUMP SHOTGUNS

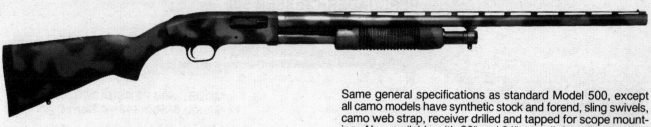

MODEL 500 CAMO
w/28″ ACCU-CHOKE Barrel

Same general specifications as standard Model 500, except all camo models have synthetic stock and forend, sling swivels, camo web strap, receiver drilled and tapped for scope mounting. Also available with 20″ and 24″ vent rib barrels.

Price: **$299.00**
w/Ghost Ring Sight **353.00**

MODEL 500 TURKEY/DEER CAMO COMBO

SPECIFICATIONS
Gauge: 12
Chamber: 3″
Barrel length: 20″ (ACCU-Choke w/one Extra Full choke tube) and 24″ Slugster barrel
Features: Synthetic forearm and buttstock; receiver drilled and tapped for scope mounting; quick disconnect posts and swivels, plus camo web sling, are supplied
Price: **$353.00**

MODEL HS410 HOME SECURITY

SPECIFICATIONS
Gauge: .410
Chambers: 2½″ and 3″
Barrel length: 18½″
Weight: 6¼ lbs.
Features: Synthetic stock, pistol grip forearm, spreader choke, rubber recoil pad, muzzle brake, cablelock, Home Security video tape, optional laser sight integral in forearm
Price: **$253.00**
w/Optional Laser Sight **451.00**

MOSSBERG PUMP SHOTGUNS

PERSUADER/CRUISER 500

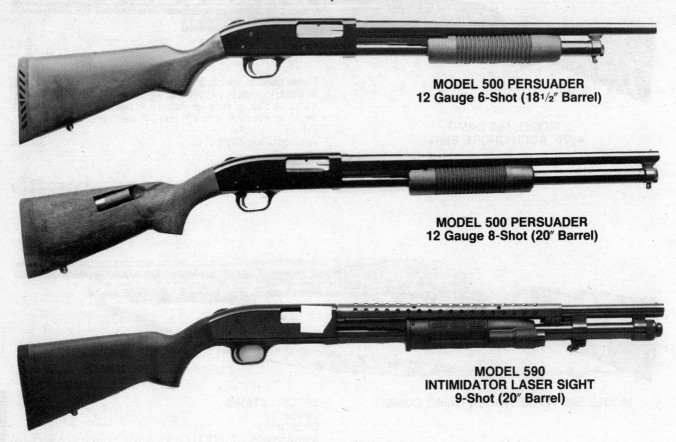

MODEL 500 PERSUADER
12 Gauge 6-Shot (18¹/₂″ Barrel)

MODEL 500 PERSUADER
12 Gauge 8-Shot (20″ Barrel)

MODEL 590
INTIMIDATOR LASER SIGHT
9-Shot (20″ Barrel)

MODEL 500/590 SPECIAL PURPOSE

These slide-action shotguns are available in 6-, 8- or 9-shot versions, chambered for both 2³/₄-inch and 3-inch shells.

Six-shot models have 18¹/₂-inch barrel, overall length of 37³/₄ inches and a weight of 6¹/₄ pounds with full buttstock. Eight-shot models have 20-inch barrels, overall length of 39³/₄ inches and weigh 6³/₄ pounds with full buttstock. Optional rifle sights available. Nine-shot 590 models have 20-inch barrels, overall length of 39³/₄ inches and weigh 7¹/₄ pounds with full buttstock. Speedfeed stock available.

All models are available in choice of blued or parkerized finish. Lightweight aluminum alloy receiver with steel locking bolt into barrel extension affords solid "steel-to-steel" lockup. Heavy-duty rubber recoil pads come on all full stock models; sling swivels on all models. Pistol grip kit included on all 6- and 8-shot bead sight models. Optional integral laser sight forearm available with 4.8 milliwatt patented water/shock re sistant battery powered laser on 6 or 9 shot models, blue or Parkerized finish.

Prices:
MODEL 500 PERSUADER/CRUISER 6-SHOT (12 ga., 18¹/₂″)
Wood or synthetic stock, blued, bead sight **$251.00**
Parkerized stock, blued, bead sight **274.00**
Ghost Ring Sight, blued (18¹/₂″) **300.00**
Ghost Ring Sight, Parkerized (18¹/₂″) **348.00**
Ghost Ring Sight, blued (20″) **359.00**
Ghost Ring Sight, Parkerized (20″) **406.00**
Cruise w/pistol grip **242.00**
MODEL 500 PERSUADER 8-SHOT
Synthetic stock, blued **251.00**
With rifle sight **272.00**
MODEL 590 9-SHOT (12 ga., 20″ barrel)
Synthetic stock, blued **305.00**
Speedfeed, blued **319.00**
Synthetic, Parkerized. **351.00**
Speedfeed, Parkerized **366.00**
Ghost Ring Sight, blued **359.00**
Ghost Ring Sight, Parkerized **406.00**
Intimidator Laser Sight Models
Synthetic stock, blued (18¹/₂″) **505.00**
Parkerized, (18¹/₂″) **527.00**
Synthetic stock, blued (20″) **556.00**
Parkerized, (20″) **601.00**

MOSSBERG SHOTGUNS

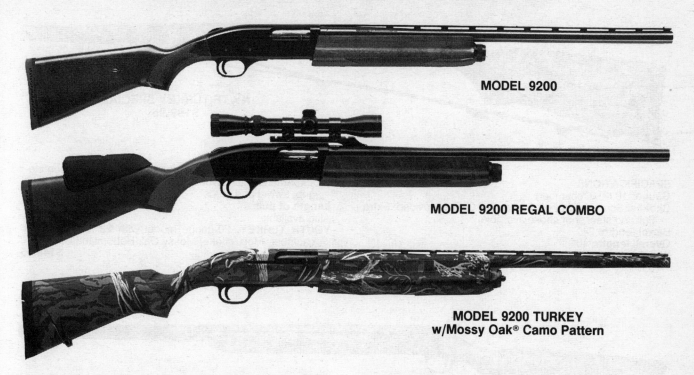

MODEL 9200

MODEL 9200 REGAL COMBO

MODEL 9200 TURKEY
w/Mossy Oak® Camo Pattern

This semiautomatic fires any sequence of 12-gauge loads from 2¼" field to 3" magnums. No barrels to change, no buttons to push, no adjustments to make. The 9200 has a gas regulating system that instantly compensates for varied pressures developed by a wide range of shotshell loads. For example, when firing light field loads, the system remains closed, with all available gases used to cycle the action.

SPECIFICATIONS
Gauge: 12
Capacity: 5 rounds (2¾" chamber)
Chokes: ACCU-Choke (Rifled bore in 24" Trophy Slugster model)

Barrel lengths: 24" and 28"
Overall length: 44" (24" barrel) and 48" (28" barrel)
Weight: 7.3 lbs. (24" barrel); 7.7 lbs. (28" barrel)
Stock: Walnut finish
Finish: Blued
Prices:
MODEL 9200 ACCU-Choke $373.00
MODEL 9200 Rifled Bore 393.00
MODEL 9200 Combo w/Trophy Scope Base 441.00
MODEL 9200 Combo w/Rifled Bore 432.00
MODEL 9200 Turkey Camo
   Mossy Oak Finish, Synthetic Stock 436.00
   Same as above w/OFM Camo Finish (28" bbl.) . 393.00
   Same as above w/Combo (24" Rifle Bore) 456.00

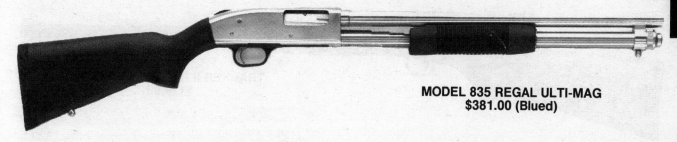

MODEL 835 REGAL ULTI-MAG
$381.00 (Blued)

The world's first shotgun chambered specifically for Federal Cartridge's 3½" 12 gauge Magnum shotshell, the **Ulti-Mag** fires all standard 12 gauge 2¾" and 3" field and target loads as well. Designed for waterfowlers who need a shotshell capable of delivering larger payloads of steel shot, the high-velocity (1300+ fps) load provides a 23 percent or more increase in steel shot capacity compared to conventional 12 gauge 3" Magnums.

The **Ulti-Mag** also features a "backbored" barrel that reduces recoil and improves patterns. With the ACCU-MAG choke tube system, stainless steel tubes fit flush with the muzzle to handle high-velocity steel shot loads with efficiency. Capacity is five shots with 3" or 3½" shells, and six shots with 2¾" shells. Other features include an ambidextrous safety, solid "steel-to-steel" lockup, high-strength aluminum alloy receivers with anodized finish, and walnut dual-comb stock.

NEW ENGLAND FIREARMS

NWTF TURKEY SPECIAL
$199.95

SPECIFICATIONS
Gauge: 10 (3½″ chamber)
Chokes: Screw-in chokes (Turkey Full Choke provided; Extra Full and steel shot choke available)
Barrel length: 24″
Overall length: 40″
Weight: 9¼ lbs.

Sights: Bead sights; drilled and tapped for scope mounting
Stock: American hardwood; Mossy Oak camo finish; full pistol grip; swivel and studs
Length of pull: 14½″
Also available:
YOUTH TURKEY. 20-gauge model with 22″ barrel and 3″ chamber, Mod. choke, Mossy Oak Bottomland Camo finish **$149.95**

TURKEY & GOOSE GUN
$149.95
($159.00 w/Camo Paint, Swivels & Sling)

SPECIFICATIONS
Gauge: 10 (3½″ chamber)
Choke: Full
Barrel length: 28″
Overall length: 44″

Weight: 9½ lbs.
Sights: Bead sights
Length of pull: 14½″
Stock: American hardwood; walnut or camo finish; full pistol grip; ventilated recoil pad

TRACKER II RIFLED SLUG GUN
$129.95

SPECIFICATIONS
Gauges: 12 and 20 (3″ chamber)
Choke: Rifled Bore
Barrel length: 24″
Overall length: 40″
Weight: 6 lbs.

Sights: Adjustable rifle sights
Length of pull: 14½″
Stock: American hardwood; walnut or camo finish; full pistol grip; recoil pad; sling swivel studs
Also available:
TRACKER SLUG GUN w/Cylinder Bore: **$124.95**

PARKER REPRODUCTIONS

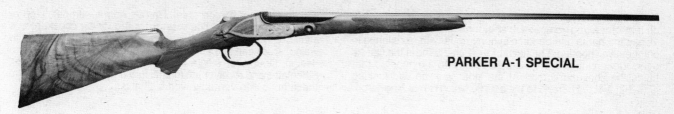

PARKER A-1 SPECIAL

Recognized by the shooting fraternity as the finest American shotgun ever produced, the Parker A-1 Special is again available. Exquisite engraving and rare presentation-grade French walnut distinguish the A-1 Special from any other shotguns in the world. Currently offered in 12 and 20 gauge, each gun is custom-fitted in its own oak and leather trunk case. Two models are offered: Hand Engraved and Custom Engraved. Also available in D Grade.

Standard features: Automatic safety, selective ejectors, skeleton steel butt plate, splinter forend, engraved snap caps, fitted leather trunk case, canvas and leather case cover, chrome barrel interiors, hand-checkering. The A-1 Special also features a 24k gold initial plate or pistol cap, 32 lines-per-inch checkering, selected wood and fine hand-engraving. Choose from single or double trigger, English or pistol grip stock (all models). Options include beavertail forend, additional barrels.

In addition to the A-1 Special, the D-Grade is available in 12, 20, 16/20 and 28 gauge. A 16-gauge, 28″ barrel can be ordered with a 20-gauge one or two-barrel set. The two-barrel sets come in a custom leather cased with a fitted over cover.

Prices:
D-GRADE
One Barrel—12, 20, 28 gauge	**$ 3370.00**
Two-barrel set	**4200.00**
16/20 Combo	**4870.00**
20/20/16 Combo	**5630.00**
A-1 SPECIAL Two-barrel set	**11,200.00**
A-1 SPECIAL 20/20/26 set	**13,200.00**
A-1 SPECIAL Custom engraved . . . . **from 11,000.00**

SPECIFICATIONS

Gauge	Barrel Length	Chokes	Chambers	Drop At Comb	Drop At Heel	Length of Pull	Nominal Weight	Overall Length
12	26	Skeet I & II or IC/M	$2^{3}/_{4}$	$1^{3}/_{8}$	$2^{3}/_{16}$	$14^{1}/_{2}$	$6^{3}/_{4}$	$42^{5}/_{8}$
12	28	IC/M or M/F	$2^{3}/_{4}$ & 3	$1^{3}/_{8}$	$2^{3}/_{16}$	$14^{1}/_{8}$	$6^{3}/_{4}$	$44^{5}/_{8}$
12	28	IC/M	3	$1^{3}/_{8}$	$2^{3}/_{16}$	$14^{1}/_{8}$	7+	$44^{5}/_{8}$
20	26	Skeet I & II or IC/M	$2^{3}/_{4}$	$1^{3}/_{8}$	$2^{3}/_{16}$	$14^{3}/_{8}$	$6^{1}/_{2}$	$42^{3}/_{8}$
20	28	M/F	3	$1^{3}/_{8}$	$2^{3}/_{16}$	$14^{3}/_{8}$	$6^{1}/_{2}$	$44^{5}/_{8}$
Combo 20 16	26 or 28 28	SI & IIC/M M/F SI & II IC/M M/F	$2^{3}/_{4}$ or 3 $2^{3}/_{4}$	$1^{3}/_{8}$	$2^{3}/_{16}$	$14^{3}/_{8}$	$6^{1}/_{2}$ *$6^{1}/_{4}$	$42^{5}/_{8}$- $44^{5}/_{8}$ $44^{5}/_{8}$
28	26	Skeet I & II or 1c/m	$2^{3}/_{4}$	$1^{3}/_{8}$	$2^{3}/_{16}$	$14^{3}/_{8}$	$5^{1}/_{3}$	$42^{5}/_{8}$
28	28	M/F	$2^{3}/_{4}$ & 3	$1^{3}/_{8}$	$2^{3}/_{16}$	$14^{3}/_{8}$	$5^{1}/_{3}$	$44^{5}/_{8}$

* *Note:* The 16-gauge barrels are lighter than the 20-gauge barrels.

PERAZZI SHOTGUNS

For the past 20 years or so, Perazzi has concentrated solely on manufacturing competition shotguns for the world market. Today the name has become synonymous with excellence in competitive shooting. The heart of the Perazzi line is the classic over/under, whose barrels are soldered into a monobloc that holds the shell extractors. At the sides are the two locking lugs that link the barrels to the action, which is machined from a solid block of forged steel. Barrels come with flat, step or raised ventilated rib. The walnut forend, finely checkered, is available with schnabel, beavertail or English styling, and the walnut stock can be of standard, Monte Carlo, Skeet or English design. Double or single non-selective or selective triggers. Sideplates and receiver are masterfully engraved and transform these guns into veritable works of art.

GAME MODELS

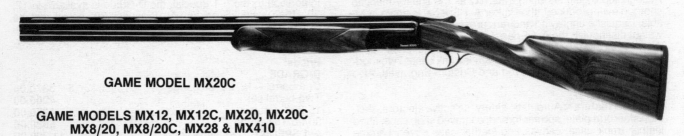

GAME MODEL MX20C

GAME MODELS MX12, MX12C, MX20, MX20C MX8/20, MX8/20C, MX28 & MX410

SPECIFICATIONS
Gauges: 12, 20, 28 & .410
Chambers: 2³/₄"; also available in 3"
Barrel lengths: 26" and 27¹/₂"
Weight: 6 lbs. 6 oz. to 7 lbs. 4 oz.
Trigger group: Non-detachable with coil springs and selective trigger

Stock: Interchangeable and custom made
Forend: Schnabel
Prices:
Standard Grade . . . . $ 7,650.00- 8,050.00
SC3 Grade 13,200.00-13,600.00
SCO Grade 21,750.00-22,150.00

AMERICAN TRAP COMBO MODELS

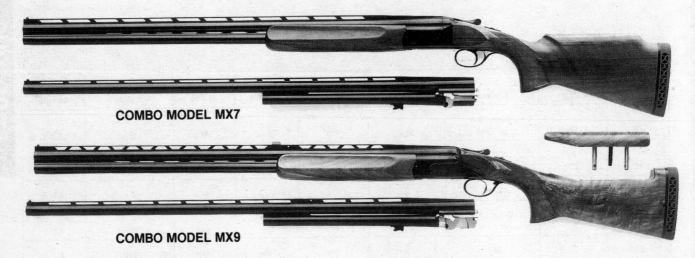

COMBO MODEL MX7

COMBO MODEL MX9

AMERICAN TRAP COMBO MODELS MX7, MX9, MX10, MX8 SPECIAL & DB81 SPECIAL

SPECIFICATIONS
Gauge: 12
Chamber: 2³/₄"
Barrel lengths: 29¹/₂" and 31¹/₂" (O/U); 32" and 34" (single barrel)
Chokes: Mod./Full (O/U); Full (single barrel)

Weight (avg.): 8 lbs. 6 oz.
Trigger group: Detachable and interchangeable with flat "V" springs
Stock: Interchangeable and custom made
Forend: Beavertail
Prices:
Standard Grade $10,250.00-10,870.00
SC3 Grade 16,150.00-16,800.00
SCO Grade 25,800.00-26,400.00
Gold Grade 28,650.00-29,300.00

PERAZZI SHOTGUNS

AMERICAN TRAP SINGLE BARREL
MODELS

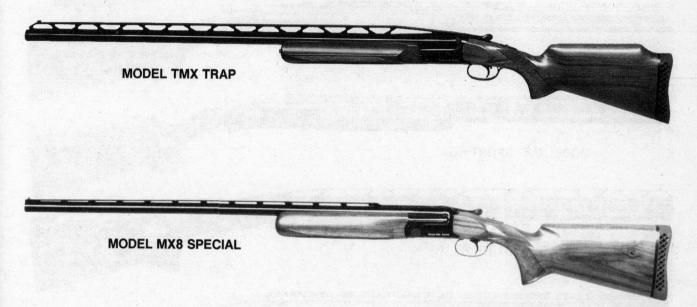

MODEL TMX TRAP

MODEL MX8 SPECIAL

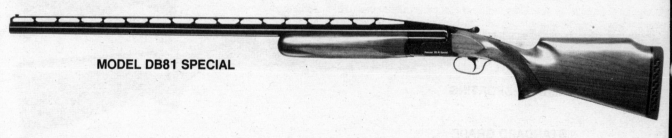

MODEL DB81 SPECIAL

AMERICAN TRAP SINGLE BARREL MODELS
MX9, MX10, TM1 SPECIAL, TMX SPECIAL
MX8 SPECIAL, DB81 SPECIAL

SPECIFICATIONS
Gauge: 12
Chamber: 2¾″
Barrel lengths: 32″ and 34″
Weight: 8 lbs. 6 oz.
Choke: Full
Trigger group: Detachable and interchangeable with coil springs

Stock: Interchangeable and custom made
Forend: Beavertail
Prices:
Standard Grade . . . . $ 5750.00-$ 9450.00
SC3 Grade 12,500.00-14,650.00
SCO Grade 16,850.00-23,200.00
Gold Grade 18,800.00-25,400.00

SHOTGUNS

PERAZZI SHOTGUNS

COMPETITION OVER/UNDER SHOTGUNS
TRAP, SKEET, PIGEON & SPORTING

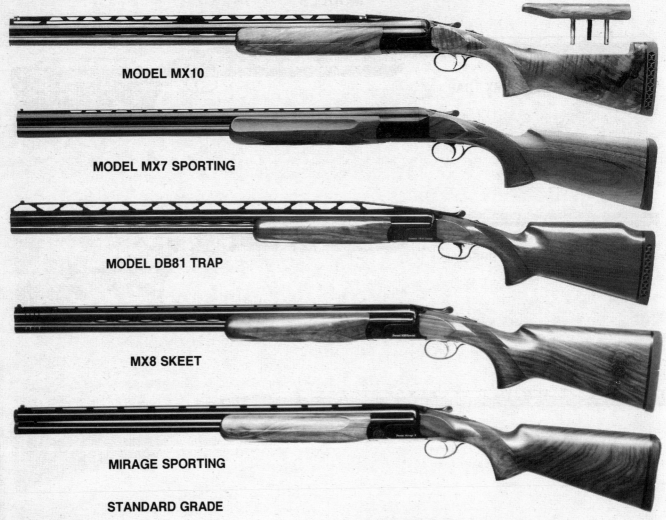

MODEL MX10

MODEL MX7 SPORTING

MODEL DB81 TRAP

MX8 SKEET

MIRAGE SPORTING

STANDARD GRADE

SPECIFICATIONS

Gauges: 12 and 20; 4 (Mirage Special only)
Barrel lengths: 27½″, 28⅜″, 29½″, 31½″
Prices:
MODEL MX7C 12 ga., non-removable trigger group
  27½″, 29½″ and 31½″ barrels . . . . $ 6100.00
MODEL MX9 12 ga.w/adj. stock and rib inserts
  29½″ and 31½″ barrels 9600.00
MODEL MX10 12 & 20 ga. w/adj. stock and rib
  29½″ and 31½″ bbl.; 20 ga. avail. w/29½″
  barrel only 10,000.00
MX8/20 20 ga. w/removable trigger group
  27½″, 28⅜″ and 29½″ barrels 7300.00
MIRAGE SPECIAL 12 ga. w/adj. trigger, all bbl.
  lengths 7700.00
MIRAGE SPECIAL SPORTING 12 ga. w/external
  selector and 5 chokes; 27½″, 28⅜″ &
  29½″ barrels 8100.00
MIRAGE SPECIAL SPORTING CLASSIC
  12 ga. 9150.00

MIRAGE MX8 12 ga. w/removable trigger group
  All barrel lengths 7300.00
MX8 SPECIAL 12 ga. w/adjustable trigger
  29½″ and 31½″ barrels 7700.00
DB81 SPECIAL w/adjustable trigger
  29½″ and 31½″ barrels 8800.00
MIRAGE SPECIAL 4 ga. w/adj. trigger,
  27½″ barrel 17,500.00

Also available:
SC3 Grade (Models MX9, MX10, MX8/20,
  SC3 and DB81 Special) . . . . . $12,450.00–$26,100.00
SCO Grade (same models as SC3
  Grade) 21,200.00– 23,900.00
GOLD Grade (same models
  as above) 23,920.00– 37,800.00
SCO Grade Sideplates (same
  models as above) 32,550.00– 51,200.00
GOLD Grade Sideplates (same
  models above) 37,800.00– 55,600.00

PIOTTI SHOTGUNS

One of Italy's top gunmakers, Piotti limits its production to a small number of hand-crafted, best-quality double-barreled shotguns whose shaping, checkering, stock, action and barrel work meets or exceeds the standards achieved in London prior to WWII. The Italian engravings are the finest ever and are becoming recognized as an art form in themselves.

All of the sidelock models exhibit the same overall design, materials and standards of workmanship; they differ only in the quality of the wood, shaping and sculpturing of the action, type of engraving and gold inlay work and other details. The Model Piuma differs from the other shotguns only in its Anson & Deeley boxlock design.

Also available: Bass-style sidelock over/under in 12 and 20 ga. **Price: $3400.00** (and up).

SPECIFICATIONS
Gauges: 10, 12, 16, 20, 28, .410
Chokes: As ordered
Barrels: 12 ga., 25″ to 30″; other gauges, 25″ to 28″; chopper lump (demi-bloc) barrels with soft-luster blued finish; level, file-cut rib or optional concave or ventilated rib
Action: Boxlock, Anson & Deeley; Sidelock, Holland & Holland pattern; both have automatic ejectors, double triggers with front trigger hinged (non-selective single trigger optional), coin finish or optional color case-hardening
Stock: Hand-rubbed oil finish (or optional satin luster) on straight grip stock with checkered butt (pistol grip optional)
Forend: Classic (splinter); optional beavertail
Weight: Ranges from 4 lbs. 15 oz. (.410 ga.) to 8 lbs. (12 ga.)

MODEL PIUMA BOXLOCK
$11,900.00

Anson & Deeley boxlock ejector double with chopper lump (demi-bloc) barrels, and scalloped frame. Very attractive scroll and rosette engraving is standard. A number of optional engraving patterns including game scene and gold inlays are available at additional cost.

MODEL KING NO. 1 SIDELOCK
$19,900.00

Best-quality Holland & Holland pattern sidelock ejector double with chopper lump barrels, level file-cut rib, very fine, full coverage scroll engraving with small floral bouquets, gold crown in top lever, name in gold, and gold crest in forearm, finely figured wood.

MODEL LUNIK SIDELOCK
$21,500.00

Best-quality Holland & Holland pattern sidelock ejector double with chopper lump (demi-bloc) barrels, level, filecut rib, Renaissance-style, large scroll engraving in relief, gold crown in top lever, gold name, and gold crest in forearm, finely figured wood.

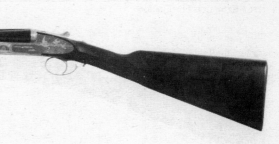

MODEL KING EXTRA (With Gold)
$30,000.00

Best-quality Holland & Holland pattern sidelock ejector double with chopper lump barrels, level filecut rib, choice of either bulino game scene engraving or game scene engraving with gold inlays, engraved and signed by a master engraver, exhibition grade wood.

PRECISION SPORTS SHOTGUNS

"600" SERIES DOUBLE BARREL SHOTGUNS

Superbly crafted by the Spanish gunmaking firm of Ignacio Ugartechea, the "600" Series doubles are offered in either extractor or ejector configurations. All models boast stocks of hand-checkered walnut, actions and parts machined from ordnance steel, standard auto safety, forged barrels, deep lustrous bluing and English scroll design engraving.
American (A) models: Single non-selective trigger, pistol grip, beavertail forend, butt plate, raised matted rib. **English** (E) models: Double triggers, straight grip, splinter forend, checkered butt, concave rib; XXV models have Churchill-type rib. **Chokes:** Imp. Cyl./Mod.; Mod./Full. **Weight:** 12 ga., 6¾-7 lbs.; 20 ga. 5¾ lbs.-6 lbs.; 28 and .410 ga., 5¼-5½ lbs. 3″ chambers on 20 and .410 ga.; 2¾ chambers on others. Bi-Gauge models have two sets of barrels, one set in each gauge.

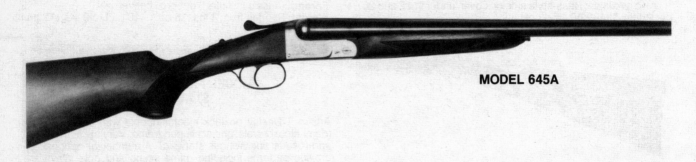

MODEL 645A

SIDE-BY-SIDE "600" SERIES SHOTGUNS

Model	Gauges	Action	Barrel Length	Price
640E (English)	12, 16, 20	Boxlock Ex.	26″, 28″	$ 849.95
640E (English)	28, .410	Boxlock Ex.	26″ (.410), 27″ (28 ga.)	939.95
640A (American)	12, 16, 20	Boxlock Ex.	26″, 28″	969.95
640A (American)	28, .410	Boxlock Ex.	26″ (.410), 27″ (28 ga.)	1079.95
640M "Big Ten", "Turkey Gun", "Goose Gun"	10 (3½″ Mag.)	Boxlock Ex.	26″, 30″, 32″	999.95
640 "Slug Gun"	12	Boxlock Ex.	25″	1119.95
645E (English)	12, 16, 20	Boxlock Ej.	26″, 28″	1089.95
645E (English)	28, .410	Boxlock Ej.	26″ (.410), 27″ (28 ga.)	1149.95
645A (American)	12, 16, 20	Boxlock Ej.	26″, 28″	1199.95
645A (American)	28, .410	Boxlock Ej.	26″ (.410), 27″ (28 ga.)	1309.95
645E-XXV (English)	12, 16, 20	Boxlock Ej.	25″	1099.95
645E-XXV (English)	28, .410	Boxlock Ej.	25″	1199.95
650E (English)**	12	Boxlock Ex.	28″	919.95
650A (American)	12	Boxlock Ex.	28″	1039.95
655E (English)	12	Boxlock Ej.	28″	1149.95
655A (American)	12	Boxlock Ej.	28″	1259.95

* Ex.=Extractor; Ej.=Ejector

BILL HANUS BIRDGUNS
$1269.95 ($1399.00 in 28 Ga.)

Gauges: 16, 20 and 28. **Barrel length:** 26″. **Choke:** Skeet 1/Skeet 2. **Features:** Straight stock; ejectors; boxlock; single non-selective trigger; case-colored receiver; Churchill rib.

REMINGTON PUMP SHOTGUNS

MODEL 870 EXPRESS (20 GA.)

MODEL 870 EXPRESS (12 & 20 GA.)
$277.00

Model 870 Express features the same action as the Wingmaster and is available with 3″ chamber and 26″ or 28″ vent-rib barrel. It has a hardwood stock with low-luster finish and solid butt pad. Choke is Modified REM Choke tube and wrench. **Overall length:** 48¹⁄₂″. **Weight:** 7¹⁄₄ lbs.

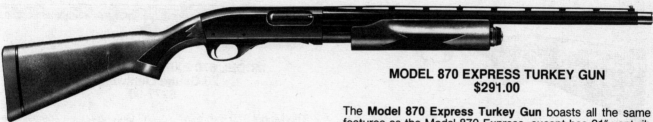

MODEL 870 EXPRESS TURKEY GUN
$291.00

The **Model 870 Express Turkey Gun** boasts all the same features as the Model 870 Express, except has 21″ vent rib barrel and Turkey Extra-Full REM Choke.

MODEL 870 EXPRESS DEER GUN
With Rifle Sights
$273.00   ($304.00 Fully Rifled)

This 12 gauge pump-action deer gun is for hunters who prefer open sights. Features a 20″ barrel, quick-reading iron sights, fixed Imp. Cyl. choke and Monte Carlo stock. Also available with fully rifled barrel.

MODEL 870 EXPRESS COMBO (not shown)
$376.00

The **Model 870 Express** in 12 and 20 gauge offers all the features of the standard Model 870, including twin-action bars, quick-changing barrels, REM Choke plus low-luster, checkered hardwood stock and no-shine finish on barrel and receiver. The Model 870 Combo is packaged with an extra 20″ deer barrel, fitted with rifle sights and fixed, Improved Cylinder choke (additional REM chokes can be added for special applications). The 3-inch chamber handles all 2³⁄₄″ and 3″ shells without adjustment.

REMINGTON PUMP SHOTGUNS

MODEL 870 EXPRESS DEER GUN
W/Cantilever Scope Mount & Rings
$348.00

The no-nonsense choice for whitetail hunting features a 20″ barrel for maneuverability and the sighting advantages of a Monte Carlo stock and barrel-mounted scope. Comes with Rifles and Imp. Cyl. REM Choke tubes designed for slugs or buckshot.

MODEL 870 EXPRESS "YOUTH" GUN
20 Gauge Lightweight
$277.00

The Model 870 Express "Youth" Gun has been specially designed for youths and smaller-sized adults. It's a 20-gauge lightweight with a 1-inch shorter stock and 21-inch barrel. Yet it is still all 870, complete with REM Choke and ventilated rib barrel. **Barrel length:** 21″. **Stock Dimensions:** Length of pull 12½″ (including recoil pad); drop at heel; 2½″ drop at comb 1⅝″. **Overall length:** 39″. **Average Weight:** 6½ lbs. **Choke:** REM Choke-Mod.

MODEL 870 EXPRESS SMALL GAUGE
$292.00

This shotgun is designed for shooters who want the light weight (6½ lbs.) and maneuverability of a .410 with the concealment advantages of the non-reflective metal and wood finish of Remington's Express line. The .410 comes with a 25″ Full Choke barrel (45½″ overall), with Modified REM Choke tube.

MODEL 870 EXPRESS SECURITY
(not shown)
$273.00

Intended for home defense, with an 18½″ Cylinder choke barrel and front bead sight. **Overall length:** 38½″. **Weight:** 7½ lbs.

REMINGTON PUMP SHOTGUNS

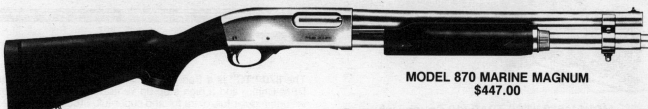

MODEL 870 MARINE MAGNUM
$447.00

Remington's **Model 870 Marine Magnum** is a versatile, multi-purpose security gun featuring a rugged synthetic stock and extensive, electroless nickel plating on all metal parts. This new shotgun utilizes a standard 12-gauge Model 870 receiver with a 7-round magazine extension tube and an 18″ cylinder barrel with bead front sight. The receiver, magazine extension and barrel are protected (inside and out) with heavy-duty, corrosion-resistant nickel plating. The synthetic stock and forend reduce the effects of moisture. The gun is supplied with a black rubber recoil pad, sling swivel studs, and positive checkering on both pistol grip and forend.

MODEL 870 SPS
$367.00

Remington's Special Purpose Synthetic All-Black model comes with a synthetic stock, 26″ or 28″ vent rib barrels and REM Choke tubes. Black sling furnished.

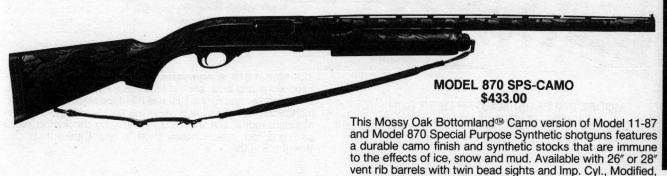

MODEL 870 SPS-CAMO
$433.00

This Mossy Oak Bottomland™ Camo version of Model 11-87 and Model 870 Special Purpose Synthetic shotguns features a durable camo finish and synthetic stocks that are immune to the effects of ice, snow and mud. Available with 26″ or 28″ vent rib barrels with twin bead sights and Imp. Cyl., Modified, and full REM Choke tubes.

MODEL 870 SPST TURKEY
$393.00

Same as the Model 870 SPS above, except with a 21″ vent rib turkey barrel and Extra-Full REM Choke tube. Also available with Mossy Oak Greenleaf Camo finish: **$447.00**

REMINGTON PUMP SHOTGUNS

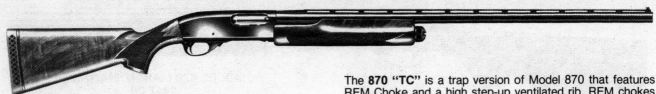

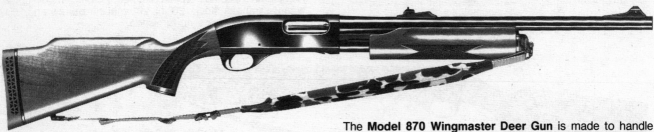

MODEL 870 "TC" TRAP (12 Gauge Only)
$613.00 ($628.00 w/Monte Carlo Stock)

The **870 "TC"** is a trap version of Model 870 that features REM Choke and a high step-up ventilated rib. REM chokes include regular full, extra full and super full. **Stock:** Redesigned stock and forend of select American walnut with cut-checkering and satin finish; length of pull 14³/₈"; drop at heel 1⁷/₈"; drop at comb 1³/₈". **Weight:** 8 lbs. (8¹/₂ lbs. w/Monte Carlo stock). **Barrel length:** 30". **Overall length:** 51".

MODEL 870 WINGMASTER
12 Gauge, Light Contour Barrel
$469.00 ($519.00 Left Hand)

This restyled **870 "Wingmaster"** pump has cut-checkering on its satin-finished American walnut stock and forend for confident handling, even in wet weather. Also available in Hi-Gloss finish. An ivory bead "Bradley"-type front sight is included. Rifle is available with 26", 28" and 30" barrel with REM Choke and handles 3" and 2³/₄" shells interchangeably. **Overall length:** 46¹/₂ (26" barrel), 48¹/₂" (28" barrel), 50¹/₂ (30" barrel). **Weight:** 7¹/₄ lbs. (w/26" barrel).

MODEL 870 BRUSHMASTER DEER GUN
$439.00 ($495.00 Left Hand)

The **Model 870 Wingmaster Deer Gun** is made to handle rifled slugs and buck shot. It features a 20-inch barrel with 3-inch chamber and fully adjustable rifle-type sights. Stock fitted with rubber recoil pad and white-line spacer. Also available in standard model, but with lacquer finish, no checkering, recoil pad, grip cap; special handy short forend. **Choke:** Imp. Cyl. **Weight:** 6¹/₄ lbs.

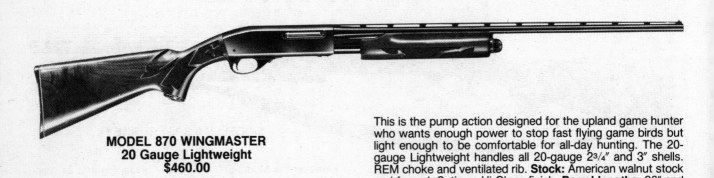

MODEL 870 WINGMASTER
20 Gauge Lightweight
$460.00

This is the pump action designed for the upland game hunter who wants enough power to stop fast flying game birds but light enough to be comfortable for all-day hunting. The 20-gauge Lightweight handles all 20-gauge 2³/₄" and 3" shells. REM choke and ventilated rib. **Stock:** American walnut stock and forend. Satin or Hi-Gloss finish. **Barrel lengths:** 26" and 28". **Average weight:** 6¹/₂ lbs.

REMINGTON PUMP SHOTGUNS

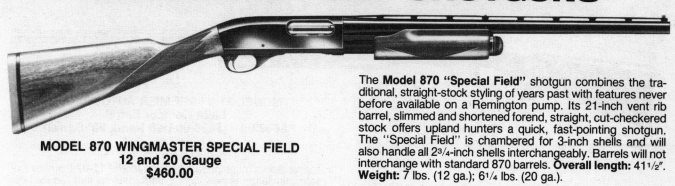

MODEL 870 WINGMASTER SPECIAL FIELD
12 and 20 Gauge
$460.00

The **Model 870 "Special Field"** shotgun combines the traditional, straight-stock styling of years past with features never before available on a Remington pump. Its 21-inch vent rib barrel, slimmed and shortened forend, straight, cut-checkered stock offers upland hunters a quick, fast-pointing shotgun. The "Special Field" is chambered for 3-inch shells and will also handle all 2¾-inch shells interchangeably. Barrels will not interchange with standard 870 barrels. **Overall length:** 41½". **Weight:** 7 lbs. (12 ga.); 6¼ lbs. (20 ga.).

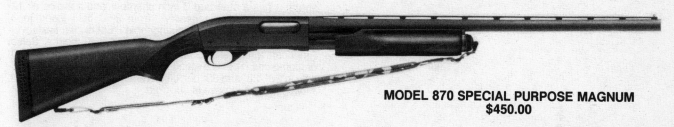

MODEL 870 SPECIAL PURPOSE MAGNUM
$450.00

Available in 12 gauge Magnum with 3-inch Mag. chamber, the **Model 870 SP (Special Purpose) Magnum** pump gun has been designed with waterfowlers and turkey hunters in mind. For concealment, all metal surfaces have been finished in non-glare, non-reflective Parkerized black. And all wood surfaces have been given a dull, non-reflective oil finish with a slightly rough feel for firmer grip. For ease of carrying, the SP Mag. Pump comes factory-equipped with a camo-patterned padded sling, attached at both ends by quick-detachable sling swivels. More than 2 inches wide at the shoulder, the sling is made of durable Du Pont nylon "Cordura." **Barrel:** 26" or 28" chrome-lined barrel bore; ventilated rib. **Choke:** Full. **Stock:** Supplied with dark-colored recoil pad and black line spacers. **Overall length:** 46½" with 26" barrel; 48½" with 28" barrel. **Weight:** Approx. 7¼ lbs.

MODEL 870 SP (SPECIAL PURPOSE) DEER GUN
$385.00

Gauge: 12. **Choke:** Imp. Cyl. Equipped with rifle sights, recoil pad. **Barrel length:** 20". **Overall length:** 40½." **Average weight:** 7 lbs.

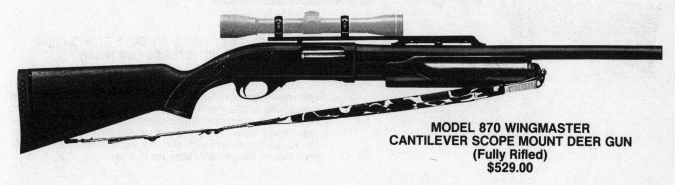

MODEL 870 WINGMASTER
CANTILEVER SCOPE MOUNT DEER GUN
(Fully Rifled)
$529.00

SHOTGUNS

REMINGTON SHOTGUNS

MODEL 11-87 PREMIER AUTOLOADER
Light Contour Barrel
$637.00   ($699.00 Left Hand, 28″ Barrel)

Remington's redesigned 12-gauge **Model 11-87 Premier Autoloader** features new, light-contour barrels that reduce both barrel weight and overall weight (more than 8 ounces). The shotgun has a standard 3-inch chamber and handles all 12-gauge shells interchangeably—from 2¾″ field loads to 3″ magnums. The gun's interchangeable REM choke system includes Improved Cylinder, Modified and Full chokes. Select American walnut stocks with fine-line, cut-checkering in satin or high-gloss finish are standard. Right-hand models are available in 26″, 28″ and 30″ barrels (left-hand models are 28″ only). A two-barrel gun case is supplied.

MODEL 11-87 PREMIER TRAP (12 Gauge)
$677.00 ($745.00 Left Hand)
$692.00 (w/Monte Carlo Stock; add $69 for L.H.)

A 30″ trap barrel offers trap shooters a REM Choke system with three interchangeable choke constrictions: trap full, trap extra full, and trap super full.

MODEL 11-87 PREMIER SKEET (12 Gauge)
$669.00 ($735.00 Left Hand)

This model features American walnut wood and distinctive cut checkering with satin finish, plus new two-piece butt plate. REM Choke system includes option of two skeet chokes—skeet and improved skeet. Trap and skeet guns are designed for 12-gauge target loads and are set to handle 2¾″ shells only. **Barrel length:** 26″. **Weight:** 8⅛ lbs.

REMINGTON SHOTGUNS

MODEL 11-87 SPS (Special Purpose Synthetic)
12 Gauge Autoloader, 3″ Chamber w/Wood or
Synthetic Stock and REM Chokes
26″ or 28″ Vent Rib Barrels
$619.00

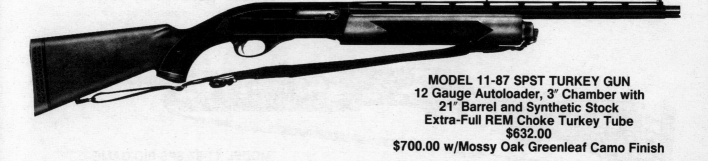

MODEL 11-87 SPST TURKEY GUN
12 Gauge Autoloader, 3″ Chamber with
21″ Barrel and Synthetic Stock
Extra-Full REM Choke Turkey Tube
$632.00
$700.00 w/Mossy Oak Greenleaf Camo Finish

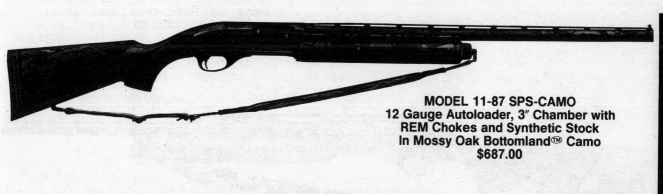

MODEL 11-87 SPS-CAMO
12 Gauge Autoloader, 3″ Chamber with
REM Chokes and Synthetic Stock
In Mossy Oak Bottomland™ Camo
$687.00

MODEL 11-87 SPORTING CLAYS
$725.00

Remington's new **Model 11-87 Premier Sporting Clays** features a target-grade, American walnut competition stock with a length of pull that is ³⁄₁₆″ longer and ¹⁄₄″ higher at the heel. The tops of the receiver, barrel and rib have a non-reflective matte finish. The rib is medium high with a stainless mid-bead and ivory front bead. The barrel (26″ or 28″) has a lengthened forcing cone to generate greater pattern uniformity; and there are 5 REM choke tubes—Skeet, Improved Skeet, Improved Cylinder, Modified and Full. All sporting clays choke tubes have a knurled end extending .45″ beyond the muzzle for fast field changes. Both the toe and heel of the butt pad are rounded. **Weight:** 7¹⁄₂ lbs. (26″); 7⁵⁄₈ lbs. (28″)

REMINGTON SHOTGUNS

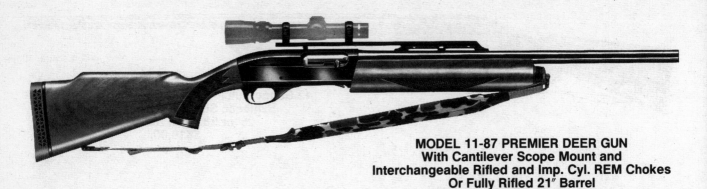

MODEL 11-87 PREMIER DEER GUN
With Cantilever Scope Mount and
Interchangeable Rifled and Imp. Cyl. REM Chokes
Or Fully Rifled 21″ Barrel
$647.00   ($679.00 Fully Rifled)

MODEL 11-87 SPS BIG GAME
12 Gauge w/I.C., Rifled & Turkey Super
Full Chokes, 21″ Rifle-Sighted Barrel and
Mossy Oak Bottomland Camo Pattern
$683.00

MODEL 11-87 SP DEER GUN
w/Cantilever Scope Mount

MODEL 11-87 SPECIAL PURPOSE DEER GUN
3″ Magnum
$599.00   ($625.00 Fully Rifled)

Features same finish as other SP models plus a padded, camo-style carrying sling of Cordura nylon with Q.D. sling swivels. Barrel is 21″ with rifle sights and rifled and IC choke (handles all 2³/₄″ and 3″ rifled slug and buckshot loads as well as high-velocity field and magnum loads; does not function with light 2³/₄″ field loads).

Also available with cantilever barrel and rings for scope mount. Includes interchangeable rifled and IC "REM" chokes.
Price: $653.00

REMINGTON AUTOLOADING SHOTGUNS

MODEL 1100 AUTOLOADING SHOTGUNS

The Remington Model 1100 is a 5-shot gas-operated auto-loading shotgun with a gas metering system designed to reduce recoil effect. This design enables the shooter to use all 2³/₄-inch standard velocity "Express" and 2³/₄-inch Magnum loads without any gun adjustments. Barrels, within gauge and versions, are interchangeable. The 1100 is made in gauges of 12, Lightweight 20, 28 and .410. All 12 and 20 gauge versions include REM Choke; interchangeable choke tubes in 26″ and 28″ (12 gauge only) barrels. The solid-steel receiver features decorative scroll work. Stocks come with fine-line checkering in a fleur-de-lis design combined with American walnut and a scratch-resistant finish. Features include white-diamond inlay in pistol-grip cap, white-line spacers, full beavertail forend, fluted-comb cuts, chrome-plated bolt and metal bead front sight. Made in U.S.A.

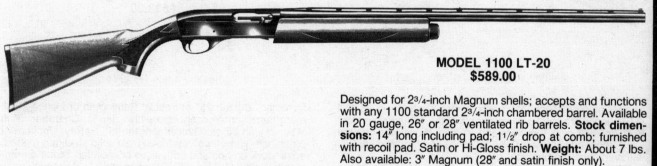

MODEL 1100 SPECIAL FIELD (12 & 20 GA.)
$589.00

The **Model 1100 "Special Field"** shotgun combines traditional, straight-stock styling with its 21-inch vent-rib barrel and slimmed and shortened forend, which offer upland hunters a quick, fast-pointing shotgun. Non-engraved receiver; non-Magnum extra barrels are interchangeable with standard Model 1100 barrels. **Overall length:** 41″. **Stock dimensions:** Length of pull 14¹/₈″; drop at comb 1¹/₂″; drop at heel 2¹/₂″. **Choke:** REM Choke system. **Weight:** 7¹/₄ lbs. (12 ga.); 6¹/₂ lbs. (20 ga.).

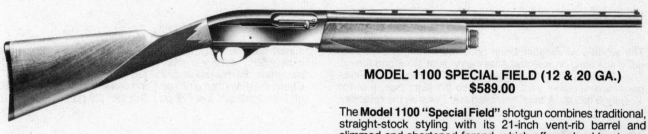

MODEL 1100 LT-20
$589.00

Designed for 2³/₄-inch Magnum shells; accepts and functions with any 1100 standard 2³/₄-inch chambered barrel. Available in 20 gauge, 26″ or 28″ ventilated rib barrels. **Stock dimensions:** 14″ long including pad; 1¹/₂″ drop at comb; furnished with recoil pad. Satin or Hi-Gloss finish. **Weight:** About 7 lbs. Also available: 3″ Magnum (28″ and satin finish only).

MODEL 1100 LT-20 DEER GUN
Lightweight 20 Gauge
$532.00

Features 20-inch (LT-20 gauge) barrels, Improved Cylinder choke. Rifle sights adjustable for windage and elevation. Recoil pad. Choked for both rifled slugs and buck shot. **Weight:** 6¹/₂ lbs. **Overall length:** 41″.

REMINGTON AUTOLOADING SHOTGUNS

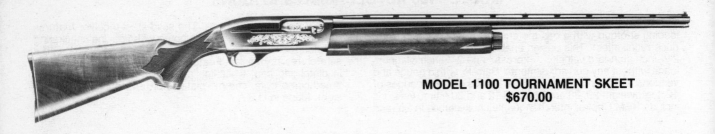

MODEL 1100 TOURNAMENT SKEET
$670.00

The world's winningest skeet gun, with high-grade positive cut-checkering on selected American walnut stock and forend. The LT-20, 28 and .410 gauge Model 1100 Tournament Skeet guns have a higher vent rib to match the sight picture of the 12-gauge model. A true "matched set," with all the reliability, superb balance, and low recoil sensation that make it the choice of over 50% of the entrants in the world skeet shooting championships. **Barrel lengths:** 25″ (28 ga. & .410 bore) and 26″. **Chokes:** REM Choke (20 ga.) and Skeet choke (28 and .410 ga.). **Weight:** 6¾ lbs. (20 ga.), 6½ lbs. (28 ga.), 7 lbs. (.410).

MODEL 1100 AUTOLOADER
28 and .410 Gauge
$633.00

The Remington Model 1100 Autoloading shotguns in 28 and .410 gauges are scaled-down models of the 12-gauge version. Built on their own receivers and frames, these small gauge shotguns are available in full (.410 only) and modified chokes with ventilated rib barrels.
   SPECIFICATIONS. Type: Gas-operated. **Capacity:** 5-shot with 28 ga. shells; 4-shot with 3″ .410 ga. shells; 3-shot plug furnished. **Barrel:** 25″ of special Remington ordnance steel; extra barrels interchangeable within gauge. **Chamber:** 3″ in .410, 2¾″ in 28 ga. **Overall length:** 45″. **Safety:** Convenient cross-bolt type. **Receiver:** Made from solid steel, top matted, scroll work on bolt and both sides of receiver. **Stock dimensions:** Walnut; 14″ long; 2½″ drop at heel; 1½″ drop at comb. **Average weight:** 6½ lbs. (28 ga.); 7 lbs. (.410).

MODEL 1100 LT-20 YOUTH GUN
Lightweight, 20 Gauge Only
$576.00

The Model 1100 LT-20 Youth Gun autoloading shotgun features a shorter barrel (21″) and stock. **Overall length:** 39½″. **Weight:** 6½ lbs.

REMINGTON SHOTGUNS

SP-10 MAGNUM SHOTGUN
$966.00

Remington's **SP-10 Magnum** is the only gas-operated semiautomatic 10 gauge shotgun made today. Engineered to shoot steel shot, the SP-10 delivers up to 34 percent more pellets to the target than standard 12 gauge shotgun and steel shot combinations. This autoloader features a non-corrosive, stainless steel gas system, in which the cylinder moves—not the piston. This reduces felt recoil energy by spreading the recoil over a longer period of time. The SP-10 has a ³/₈" vent rib with middle and front sights for a better sight plane. It is also designed to appear virtually invisible to the sharp eyes of waterfowl. The American walnut stock and forend have a protective, low-gloss satin finish that reduces glare, and positive

deep-cut checkering for a sure grip. The receiver and barrel have a matte finish, and the stainless steel breech bolt features a non-reflective finish. Remington's new autoloader also has a brown vented recoil pad and a padded camo sling of Cordura nylon for easy carrying. The receiver is machined from a solid billet of ordnance steel for total integral strength. The SP-10 vented gas system reduces powder residue buildup and makes cleaning easier.

Gauge: 10. **Barrel lengths & choke:** 26" REM Choke and 30" REM Choke. **Overall length:** 51¹/₂" (30" barrel) and 47¹/₂" (26" barrel). **Weight:** 11¹/₄ lbs. (30" barrel) and 11 lbs. (26" barrel).

MODEL SP-10 MAGNUM CAMO
10 Gauge Autoloader
with 23" Vent Rib Barrel
and Mossy Oak Bottomland Camo Pattern
$1050.00

MODEL SP-10 MAGNUM COMBO
10 Gauge Autoloader with REM Chokes
Extra 22" Barrel with Rifle Sights and
Extra-Full Turkey Choke Tube
$1104.00

PEERLESS OVER/UNDER
with Vent Rib and Engraved Side Plates

PEERLESS OVER/UNDER SHOTGUN
$1105.00

Practical, lightweight, well-balanced and affordable are the attributes of this new Remington shotgun. Features include an all-steel receiver, boxlock action and removable side plates (engraved with a pointer on one side and a setter on the other). The bottom of the receiver has the Remington logo, plus the words "Peerless, Field" and the serial number. Cut-checkering appears on both pistol grip and forend (shaped with finger grooves and tapered toward the front). The buttstock is fitted with a black, vented recoil pad. The stock is American walnut with an Imron finish. See also below for additional specifications and features.

SPECIFICATIONS
Gauge: 12 (3″ chamber)
Chokes: REM Choke System (1 Full, 1 Mod., 1 Imp. Cyl.)
Barrel lengths: 26″, 28″, 30″ with vent rib
Overall length: 43″ (26″ barrel); 45″ (28″ barrel); 47″ (30″ barrel)
Weight: 7 1/4 lbs. (26″); 7 3/8 lbs. (28″); 7 1/2 lbs. (30″)
Trigger: Single, selective, gold-plated
Safety: Automatic safety
Sights: Target gun style with mid-bead and Bradley-type front bead
Length of pull: 14 3/16″
Drop at comb: 1 1/2″
Drop at heel: 2 1/4″
Features: Solid, horseshoe-shaped locking bar with two rectangular lug extensions on either side of the barrel's mid-bore; fast lock time (3.28 milliseconds)

MODEL 90-T SINGLE BARREL TRAP GUN
$2995.00

Remington's **Model 90-T Single Barrel Trap** features a top-lever release and internal, full-width, horizontal bolt lockup. Barrels are overbored, with elongated forcing cones, and are available in 32″ and 34″ lengths. Shooters can choose barrels with either fixed chokes or Remington's interchangeable Trap Choke system. A medium-high, tapered, ventilated rib includes a white, Bradley-type front bead and stainless steel center bead. Choice of stocks includes Monte Carlo style with 1 3/8″, 1 1/2″ or 1 1/4″ drop at comb, or a conventional straight stock with 1 1/2″ drop. Standard length of pull is 14 3/8″. Stocks and modified beavertail forends are made from semi-fancy American walnut. Wood finish is low-lustre satin with positive, deep-cut checkering 20 lines to the inch. All stocks come with black, vented-rubber recoil pads. **Weight:** Approx. 8 3/4 lbs.

RIZZINI SHOTGUNS

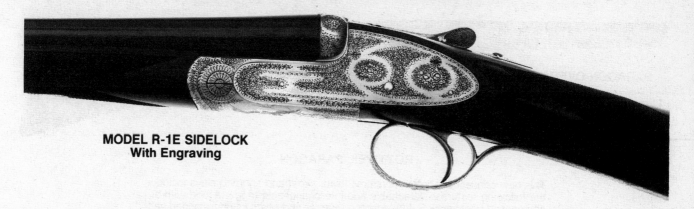

MODEL R-1E SIDELOCK
With Engraving

MODEL R-1 and R-2 SHOTGUNS

Rizzini offers two models: **R-1,** a sidelock ejector, and **R-2,** an Anson & Deeley boxlock with a removable inspection plate on the bottom of the action. The basic price of a Rizzini shotgun includes the choice of single or double triggers and a fitted leather trunk case (but not the cost of engraving). A wide variety of ornamental and game scene engravings are available.

Multi-gauge two-barrel sets (supplied with a single forearm) are available in .410/28 ga., 28/20 ga. or 20/16 ga. The actions and locks are carefully shaped and polished. The stock finish is hand-rubbed oil applied after the stock is filled and sealed. Options include stock ovals, hand-detachable locks, rib type, barrel length, weight of gun, and more.

SPECIFICATIONS
Gauges: 12, 16, 20, 28, .410
Barrel lengths: 25″ to 28″ (28 ga. and .410); 25″ to 30″ (12, 16 and 20 ga.)
Top ribs: Straight matted concave is standard; swamped smooth concave or level file cut rib are optional

Action: Anson & Deeley boxlock with inspection plate (Model R-2 only); Holland & Holland-type sidelock (Model R-1 only)
Weight: 4 lbs. 14 oz. to 6 lbs. (28 and .410); 5½ lbs. to 6 lbs. 12 oz. (20 ga.); 5 lbs. 12 oz. to 7 lbs. (16 ga.); 6 lbs. 4 oz. to 8 lbs. 4 oz. (12 ga.)
Stock & Forearm: High-luster hand-rubbed oil finish; straight-grip stock with checkered butt; classic forearm; pistol-grip stock and beavertail forearm optional
Trigger: Non-selective trigger (double trigger with front trigger hinged optional)
Prices:
MODEL R-1 in 12, 16 or 20 ga. (w/o engraving) **$40,000.00**
    In 28 ga. or .410 (w/o engraving) 46,000.00
MODEL R-2 in 12, 16 or 20 ga. (w/o engraving) 23,000.00
Engravings available:
Fine English scroll or ornamental with swans . .   8,700.00
Fracassi-style ornamental 21,700.00

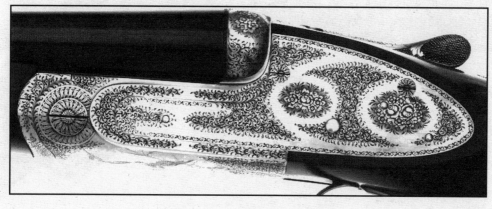

Close-up of engraved sideplate

ROTTWEIL SHOTGUNS

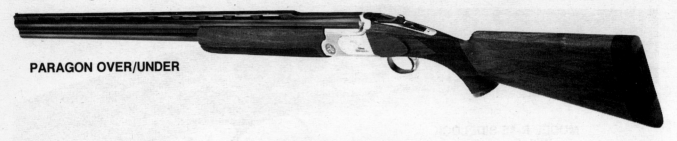

PARAGON OVER/UNDER

ROTTWEIL PARAGON

This new concept in shotgun systems, trap, skeet and sporting clays includes the following features: Detachable and interchangeable trigger action with superimposed hammers • Safety action on trigger and sears • Spring-loaded self-adjusting wedges • Ejector can be turned on and off at will • Top lever convertible for right- and left-handed shooters • Interchangeable firing pins (without disassembly) • Length and weight of barrels selected depending on application (see below) • Module system: Fully interchangeable receiver, barrels, stocks trigger action and forends • Select walnut stocks

Barrel lengths:

Field & Skeet	27½″	Sporting	28½″
American Skeet	28″	Trap	29″ & 30″
Parcours	28⅜″	American Trap Single	32″ & 34″

Price: .... **$5,200.00 to $7,200.00**

PARAGON
(Close-up Open)

RUGER SHOTGUNS

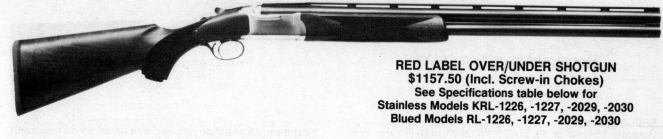

RED LABEL OVER/UNDER SHOTGUN
$1157.50 (Incl. Screw-in Chokes)
See Specifications table below for
Stainless Models KRL-1226, -1227, -2029, -2030
Blued Models RL-1226, -1227, -2029, -2030

These shotguns are made of hardened chrome molybdenum, other alloy steels and music wire coil springs. Features include boxlock action with single-selective mechanical trigger, selective automatic ejectors, automatic top safety, free-floating vent rib with serrated top surface to reduce glare, standard brass bead front sight, and stainless steel receiver. Stock and semi-beavertail forearm are shaped from American walnut with hand-cut checkering (20 lines per inch). Pistol-grip cap and rubber recoil pad are standard, and all wood surfaces are polished and beautifully finished. Available in 12 or 20 gauge with 3" chambers.

Screw-in choke inserts. Designed especially for the popular 12-gauge "Red Label" over/under shotgun. Easily installed with a key wrench packaged with each shotgun. Choke fits flush with the muzzle. Every shotgun is equipped with a Full, Modified, Improved Cylinder and two Skeet screw-in chokes. The muzzle edge of the chokes has been slotted for quick identification in or out of the barrels. Full choke has 3 slots; Modified, 2 slots; Improved Cylinder, 1 slot (Skeet has no slots).

ENGLISH FIELD OVER/UNDER
$1157.00 (w/Screw-in Chokes)
See Specifications table below for
Stainless Models KRLS-1226, -1227, -2029, -2030
Blued Models RLS-1226, -1227, -2029, -2030

SPORTING CLAYS OVER/UNDER
$1285.00 (w/Screw-in Chokes)
See Specifications table below for Model KRLS-1236

SPECIFICATIONS OVER & UNDER SHOTGUNS WITH SCREW-IN CHOKES

Catalog Number	Gauge	Chamber	Choke*	Barrel Length	Overall Length	**Sights	Approx. Wt. (lbs.)	Type Stock
KRL/RL-1226	12	3"	F,M,IC,S†	26"	43"	GBF	8	Pistol Grip
KRL/RL-1227	12	3"	F,M,IC,S†	28"	45"	GBF	8¼	Pistol Grip
KRLS/RLS-1226	12	3"	F,M,IC,S†	26"	43"	GBF	7½	Straight
KRLS/RLS-1227	12	3"	F,M,IC,S†	28"	45"	GBF	8	Straight
KRLS-1236	12	3"	M,IC,S†	30"	47"	GBF/GBM	7¾	Pistol Grip
KRL/RL-2029	20	3"	F,M,IC,S†	26"	43"	GBF	7¼	Pistol Grip
KRL/RL-2030	20	3"	F,M,IC,S†	28"	45"	GBF	7½	Pistol Grip
KRLS/RLS-2029	20	3"	F,M,IC,S†	26"	43"	GBF	7	Straight
KRLS/RLS-2030	20	3"	F,M,IC,S†	28"	45"	GBF	7¼	Straight

* F-Full, M-Modified, IC-Improved Cylinder; S-Skeet. ** GBF—Gold Bead Front Sight; GBM—Gold Bead Middle. Length of pull: 14⅛". Drop at comb: 1½". Drop at heel: 2½". † Two skeet chokes are standard with each shotgun. Sporting Clays shotgun has special chokes that are not interchangeable with other Red Label shotguns.

SHOTGUNS

SKB SHOTGUNS

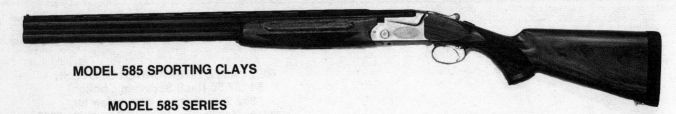

MODEL 585 SPORTING CLAYS

MODEL 585 SERIES

SPECIFICATIONS
Gauges: 12 (2³/₄" or 3"), 20 (3"), 28 (2³/₄"), .410 (3")
Barrel lengths:
  12 gauge—26", 28", 30", 32", 34" w/Inter-Choke tube
  20 or 28 gauge—26" and 28" w/Inter-Choke tube
  .410 gauge—26" and 28" w/Imp. Cyl., Mod./Mod. & Full
Overall length: 43 to 51³/₈"
Weight: 6.6 lbs. to 8¹/₂ lbs.
Sights: Metal front bead (Field Model); target sights on Trap, Skeet and Sporting Clay models
Stock: Hand-checkered walnut with high-gloss finish; target stocks available in standard or Monte Carlo

Features: Silver nitride receiver with game scene engraving; boxlock action; manual safety; automatic ejectors; single selective trigger; ventilated rib

Prices:
MODEL 585 Field	$1075.00
MODEL 585 Two-Barrel Field Set	1665.00
MODEL 585 Trap and Skeet	1105.00
MODEL 585 Two-Barrel Trap Combo	1664.00
MODEL 585 Sporting Clays	1162.00
MODEL 585 Skeet Set (20, 28, .410 ga.)	2648.00

MODEL 685 SPORTING CLAYS

MODEL 685 SERIES

Similar to Model 585 Deluxe, this model offers the following additional features: gold-plated trigger, semi-fancy American walnut stock, jeweled barrel block, and finely engraved scroll-work and game scenes on silver nitride receiver, top lever and trigger guard.

Prices:
MODEL 685 Field	$1504.00
MODEL 685 Two-Barrel Field Set	2170.00
MODEL 685 Trap and Skeet	1543.00
MODEL 685 Two-Barrel Trap Combo	2130.00
MODEL 685 Sporting Clays	1583.00
MODEL 685 Sporting Clays Sets	2263.00
MODEL 685 Skeet Set (20, 28, .410 ga.)	3101.00

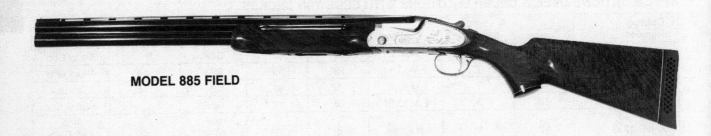

MODEL 885 FIELD

MODEL 885 SERIES

Similar to Model 685. Additional features include intricately engraved scrollwork and game scenes on silver nitride receiver, sideplates, top lever and trigger guard; select semi-fancy American walnut stock.

Prices:
MODEL 885 Field	$1864.00
MODEL 885 Two-Barrel Field Set	2730.00
MODEL 885 Trap and Skeet	1900.00
MODEL 885 Two-Barrel Trap Combo	2688.00
MODEL 885 Sporting Clays	1930.00
MODEL 885 Skeet Set (20, 28, .410 ga.)	3528.00

TIKKA SHOTGUNS
(Formerly Valmet)

TIKKA 412S OVER/UNDER FIELD GRADE
$1155.00

Designed for the experienced hunter, Tikka's 412S represents the pride and skill of "Old World" European craftsmanship. The barrels are polished to a mirror finish and deeply blued. Select American walnut stock and forearm highlight fine, deep-cut checkering. Other features include:

Time-proven action: Designed to handle large centerfire calibers for more durability and reliability.

Mechanical trigger: Fires two shots as fast as you can pull the trigger. Does not rely on the inertia from the recoil of the first shot to set the trigger for the second. In the event of a faulty primer or light hit, inertia trigger shotguns cannot function on the second round.

Single selective trigger: Selector button is located on the trigger for fast, easy selection.

Large trigger guard opening: Designed for cold weather shooting; permits easy finger movement when wearing gloves.

American walnut stock and forearm: Add greatly to overall appearance.

Superior stock design: A palm swell provides additional hand comfort. Length and angle (pitch) can be adjusted for a perfect fit with addition of factory spacers. Fine, deep-cut checkering.

Palm-filling forearm: Rounded and tapered for comfort and smooth, true swing, plus fine, deep-cut checkering.

Automatic ejectors: Select and eject fired rounds. Raise unfired shells for safe removal.

Chrome-lined barrels: For more consistent patterns. Eliminates pitting and corrosion, extends barrel life even with steel shot.

Stainless steel choke tubes: Added strength over regular carbon and alloy materials. Easily handles steel shot. Recessed so as not to detract from appearance. Tight tolerances enable truer patterns and enhance choke versatility.

Sliding locking bolt: Secure lockup between receiver and barrels. Wears in, not loose.

Matte nickel receiver: Non-glare and more resistant to wear and corrosion.

Wide vent rib: Cross-file pattern reduces glare. Fluorescent front and middle beads.

Automatic safety: Goes to safe position automatically when gun is opened.

Cocking indicators: Allow shooter to determine (through sight or feel) which barrel has been fired.

Steel receiver: Forged and machined for durability.

Chamber: 3-inch on all models

Two-piece firing pin: For more durability

Versatility: Change from over/under shotgun to shotgun/rifle, trap, skeet or double rifle. Precision tolerances require only minor initial fitting.

SPECIFICATIONS
Gauge: 12
Chambers: 3"
Weight: 7¼ lbs. w/26" barrels; 7½ lbs. w/28" barrels
Barrel lengths/chokes:
  26", 5 chokes (F, M, IM, IC & Skeet)
  28", 5 chokes (F, M, IM, IC & Skeet)

SPORTING CLAYS SHOTGUN (not shown)
$1270.00

Designed to accommodate the specific requirements of the shooter in this, the fastest growing shooting sport in America today. The Sporting Clays shotgun features a specially designed American walnut stock with a double palm swell finished with a soft satin lacquer for maximum protection with minimum maintenance. Available in 12 gauge with a selection of 5 recessed choke tubes. Other features include a 3" chamber, manual safety, customized sporting clay recoil pad, single selective trigger, blued receiver and 28" barrel with ventilated side and top rib with two iridescent beads. In addition, the shotgun is furnished with an attractive carrying case.

Manufactured in Italy, Tikka is designed and crafted by Sako of Finland, which has enjoyed international acclaim for the manufacture of precision sporting firearms since 1918.

TIKKA SHOTGUNS
(Formerly Valmet)

TIKKA 412S SHOTGUN/RIFLE
$1255.00

Tikka's unique 412S Shotgun/Rifle combination continues to be the most popular gun of its type in the U.S. Its features are identical to the 412S Field Grade over/under shotguns, including strong steel receiver, superior sliding locking mechanism with automatic safety, cocking indicators, mechanical triggers and two-piece firing pin. In addition, note the other features of this model—

Barrel regulation: Adjusts for windage simply by turning the screw on the muzzle. Elevation is adjustable by regulating the sliding wedge located between the barrels.

Compact: 24-inch barrels mounted on the low-profile receiver limit the overall length to 40 inches (about 5″ less than most bolt-action rifles with similar 24-inch barrels).

Single selective trigger: A barrel selector is located on the trigger for quick, easy selection. Double triggers are also available.

Choice of calibers: Choose from 222 or 308. Both are under the 12 gauge, 3″ chamber with Improved Modified choke.

Sighting options: The vent rib is cross-filed to reduce glare. The rear sight is flush-folding and permits rapid alignment with the large blade front sight. The rib is milled to accommodate Tikka's one-piece scope mount with 1″ rings. Scope mount is of "quick release" design and can be removed without altering zero.

European walnut stock: Stocks are available with palm swell for greater control and comfort. Quick detachable sling swivel. Length or pitch adjustable with factory spacers. Semi-Monte Carlo design.

Interchangeability: Receiver will accommodate Tikka's over/under shotgun barrels and double-rifle barrels with minor initial fitting.

SPECIFICATIONS
Gauge/Caliber: 12/222 or 12/308
Chamber: 3″ with Improved Modified choke
Barrel length: 24″
Overall length: 40″
Weight: 8 lbs.
Stock: European walnut with semi-Monte Carlo design

Extra Barrel Sets:
Over/Under **$635.00**
Shotgun/Rifle. **720.00**
Double Rifle **935.00**

WEATHERBY SHOTGUNS

ATHENA GRADE V CLASSIC FIELD

ATHENA GRADES IV & V OVER/UNDERS
$1950.00 to $2450.00

Receiver: The Athena receiver houses a strong, reliable box-lock action, yet it features side lock-type plates to carry through the fine floral engraving. The hinge pivots are made of a special high strength steel alloy. The locking system employs the time-tested Greener cross-bolt design. **Single selective trigger:** It is mechanically rather than recoil operated. This provides a fully automatic switchover, allowing the second barrel to be fired on a subsequent trigger pull, even in the event of a misfire. A flick of the trigger finger and the selector lever, located just in front of the trigger, is all the way to the left enabling you to fire the lower barrel first, or to the right for the upper barrel. The Athena trigger is selective as well. **Barrels:** The breech block is hand-fitted to the receiver, providing closest possible tolerances. Every Athena is equipped with a matted, ventilated rib and bead front sight. **Selective automatic ejectors:** The Athena contains ejectors that are fully automatic both in selection and action. **Slide safety:** The safety is the traditional slide type located conveniently on the upper tang on top of the pistol grip. **Stock:** Each stock is carved from specially selected Claro walnut, with fine line hand-checkering and high luster finish. Trap model has Monte Carlo stock only. *See Athena and Orion table for additional information and specifications.*

GRADE IV CHOKES
Fixed Choke
Field, .410 Gauge
Skeet, 12 or 20 Gauge
IMC Multi Choke
Field, 12, 20 or 28 Gauge
Trap, 12 Gauge
Trap, single barrel, 12 Gauge
Trap Combo, 12 Gauge

ORION GRADE II CLASSIC FIELD

ORION GRADES I, II & III OVER/UNDERS
$1050.00 (Grade I) to $1350.00 (Grade III)

For greater versatility, the Orion incorporates the integral multichoke (IMC) system. Available in Extra-full, Full, Modified, Improved Modified, Improved Cylinder and Skeet, the choke tubes fit flush with the muzzle without detracting from the beauty of the gun. Three tubes are furnished with each gun. The precision hand-fitted monobloc and receiver are machined from high-strength steel with a highly polished finish. The box-lock design uses the Greener cross-bolt locking system and special sears maintain hammer engagement. Pistol grip stock and forearm are carved of Claro walnut with hand-checkered diamond inlay pattern and high-gloss finish. Chrome moly steel barrels, and the receiver, are deeply blued. The Orion also features selective automatic ejectors, single selective trigger, front bead sight and ventilated rib. The trap model boasts a curved trap-style recoil pad and is available with Monte Carlo stock only. **Weight:** 12 ga. Field, 7½ lbs.; 20 ga. Field, 7½ lbs.; Trap, 8 lbs.

ORION CHOKES
Grade I
IMC Multi-Choke, Field, 12 or 20 Gauge
Grade II
Fixed Choke, Field, .410 Gauge
Fixed Choke, Skeet, 12 or 20 Gauge
IMC Multi Choke, Field, 12, 20 or 28 Gauge
IMC Multi Choke, Trap, 12 Gauge
Grade II Sporting Clays
12 Gauge only
Grade III
IMC Multi-choke, Field, 12 or 20 Gauge

WEATHERBY SHOTGUNS

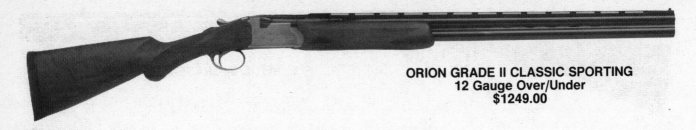

ORION GRADE II CLASSIC SPORTING
12 Gauge Over/Under
$1249.00

Additional Prices: **ORION GRADES I, II, III**

Orion I	$1050.00
Orion II Classic Field	1150.00
Orion II Trap	1207.00

Orion II Skeet	1193.00
Orion II Sporting Clays	1249.00
Orion III Field & Classic Field	1350.00

ATHENA & ORION OVER/UNDER SHOTGUN SPECIFICATIONS

Model	Gauge	Chamber	Barrel Length	Overall Length	Length of Pull	Drop at Heel	Drop at Comb	Bead Sight	Approx. Weight
Athena Grade V Classic Field	12 20	3″ 3″	30″, 28″ or 26″ 28″ or 26″	47″, 45″ or 43″ 45″ or 43″	14¼″ 14¼″	2.5 2.5	1.5 1.5	Brilliant front Brilliant front	6½–8 lbs. 6½–8 lbs.
Athena Grade IV Field	12 20 28 .410	3″ 3″ 2¾″ 3″	30″, 28″ or 26″ 28″ or 26″ 26″ 26″	47″, 45″ or 43″ 45″ or 43″ 43″ 43″	14¼″ 14¼″ 14¼″ 14¼″	2.5 2.5 2.5 2.5	1.5 1.5 1.5 1.5	Brilliant front Brilliant front Brilliant front Brilliant front	6½–8 lbs. 6½–8 lbs. 6½–8 lbs. 6½–8 lbs.
Orion Grade III Classic Field	12 20	3″ 3″	28″ 26″	45″ 43″	14¼″ 14¼″	2.5 2.5	1.5 1.5	Brilliant front Brilliant front	6½–8 lbs. 6½–8 lbs.
Orion Grade III Field	12 20	3″ 3″	30″, 28″ or 26″ 28″ or 26″	47″, 45″ or 43″ 45″ or 43″	14¼″ 14¼″	2.5 2.5	1.5 1.5	Brilliant front Brilliant front	6½–8 lbs. 6½–8 lbs.
Orion Grade II Classic Field	12 20 28	3″ 3″ 2¾″	30″, 28″ or 26″ 28″ or 26″ 26″	47″, 45″ or 43″ 45″ or 43″ 43″	14¼″ 14¼″ 14¼″	2.5 2.5 2.5	1.5 1.5 1.5	Brilliant front Brilliant front Brilliant front	6½–8 lbs. 6½–8 lbs. 6½–8 lbs.
Orion Grade I	12 20	3″ 3″	30″, 28″ or 26″ 28″ or 26″	47″, 45″ or 43″ 45″ or 43″	14¼″ 14¼″	2.5 2.5	1.5 1.5	Brilliant front Brilliant front	6½–8 lbs. 6½–8 lbs.
Orion Grade II Classic Sporting	12	2¾″	28″	45″	14¼″	2.25	1.5	Midpoint w/ white front	7½ lbs.
Orion Grade II Sporting	12	2¾″	30″ or 28″	47″ or 45″	14¼″	2.25	1.5	Midpoint w/ white front	7½–8 lbs.
Orion Grade II Skeet	12 20	2¾″ 2¾″	26″ 26″	45″ 45″	14¼″ 14¼″	2.5 2.5	1.5 1.5	Midpoint w/ white front Midpoint w/ white front	7½ lbs. 7¼ lbs.
Orion Grade II Single Trap	12	2¾″	32″	49½″	14⅜″	2⅛	1⅜	Midpoint w/ white front	8 lbs.
Orion Grade II Double Trap	12	2¾″	32″ or 30″	49½″ or 47½″	14⅜″	2⅛	1⅜	Midpoint w/ white front	8 lbs.

Weight varies due to wood density

WINCHESTER SECURITY SHOTGUNS

These tough 12-gauge shotguns provide backup strength for security and police work as well as all-around utility. The action is one of the fastest second-shot pumps made. It features a front-locking rotating bolt for strength and secure, single-unit lockup into the barrel. Twin-action slide bars prevent binding.

The shotguns are chambered for 3-inch shotshells. They handle 3-inch Magnum, 2¾-inch Magnum and standard 2¾-inch shotshells interchangeably. They have cross-bolt safety,

walnut-finished hardwood stock and forearm, black rubber butt pad and plain 18-inch barrel with Cylinder Bore choke. All are ultra-reliable and easy to handle.

Special chrome finishes on Police and Marine guns are actually triple-plated: first with copper for adherence, then with nickel for rust protection, and finally with chrome for a hard finish. This triple-plating assures durability and quality. Both guns have a forend cap with swivel to accommodate sling.

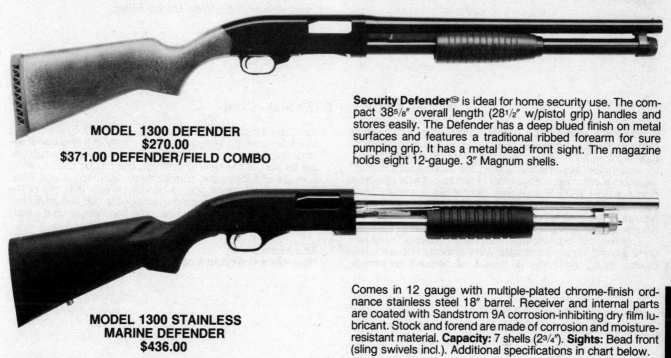

MODEL 1300 DEFENDER
$270.00
$371.00 DEFENDER/FIELD COMBO

Security Defender® is ideal for home security use. The compact 38⅝" overall length (28½" w/pistol grip) handles and stores easily. The Defender has a deep blued finish on metal surfaces and features a traditional ribbed forearm for sure pumping grip. It has a metal bead front sight. The magazine holds eight 12-gauge. 3" Magnum shells.

MODEL 1300 STAINLESS
MARINE DEFENDER
$436.00

Comes in 12 gauge with multiple-plated chrome-finish ordnance stainless steel 18" barrel. Receiver and internal parts are coated with Sandstrom 9A corrosion-inhibiting dry film lubricant. Stock and forend are made of corrosion and moisture-resistant material. **Capacity:** 7 shells (2¾"). **Sights:** Bead front (sling swivels incl.). Additional specifications in chart below.

SPECIFICATIONS MODEL 1300 DEFENDER

Model	Gauge	Barrel Length	Chamber	Capacity	Choke	Overall Length	Length of Pull	Drop At Comb/Heel		Weight (Lbs.)	Sights
Combo, Hardwood Stock and Pistol Grip	12	18"	3" Mag.	5	Cyl	38⅝"	14"	1½	2½"	6¼"	MBF
	12	28 VR	3" Mag.	5	W1M	48⅝	14"	1½	2½	7½	MBF
Hardwood Stock 5 Shot	12	18"	3" Mag.	5	Cyl.	38⅝"	14"	1⅜"	2¾"	6½	MBF
Hardwood Stock 8 Shot	12	18"	3" Mag.	8¹	Cyl.	38⅝"	14"	1⅜"	2¾"	6¾	MBF
Synthetic Pistol Grip	12	18"	3" Mag.	8¹	Cyl.	28½"	—	—	—	5¾	MBF
Synthetic Stock 12 Gauge	12	18"	3" Mag.	8¹	Cyl.	38⅝"	14"	1⅜"	2¾"	6¾	MBF
Synthetic Stock 20 Gauge	20	18"	3" Mag.	5	Cyl.	38⅝"	14"	1⅜"	2¾"	6	MBP
1300 Stainless Marine	12	18"	3" Mag.	7¹	Cyl.	38⅝	14"	1⅜"	2¾"	6¾	MBF
1300 Pistol Grip	12	18	3" Mag.	7¹	Cyl.	28⅝	14	—	—	5¾	MBF

* Includes one shotshell in chamber when ready to fire. ¹ Subtract one shell capacity for 3" shells. VR = Ventilated rib. Cyl. = Cylinder Bore. MBF = Metal bead front.

WINCHESTER SHOTGUNS

MODEL 1300 WALNUT SLUG HUNTER
(Smoothbore)
With Camo Sling

MODEL 1300 PUMP DEER SLUG GUNS

Winchester's Model 1300 Walnut Slug Hunter pump action shotgun features a rifled barrel with 8 lands and grooves, rifle-type sights, and a receiver that is factory-drilled and tapped for scope. Also available is a Model 1300 WinTuff Slug Hunter, featuring a Winchester Proof steel-rifled barrel with rifle-type sights. Model 1300 Walnut Slug Hunter has a smooth-bore barrel that comes with an extra long Sabot-rifled choke tube. Also included is an improved Cylinder Winchoke tube for traditional slug or buckshot shooting.

The Walnut models feature sculptured, cut-checkered forends, while the brown laminated WinTuff models have the traditional ribbed corn cob-style forend. All models have honey-

comb recoil pad and a crossbolt safety. The lockup is a chrome molybdenum high-speed, four-slug rotary bolt and barrel extension system (lockup does not require use of the receiver top as part of the locking system). The Model 1300 receiver is made of lightweight, corrosion-resistant, space age alloy. Because the rotary lockup is concentric with the bore of the barrel, recoil forces are used to unlock the bolt and drive both bolt and forend rearward to help the shooter set up the next shot. Additional specifications on the following page.

Also available:
Whitetail's Unlimited Model Beavertail forend . . . **$449.00**

MODEL 1300 WALNUT SLUG HUNTER (fully rifled)
Sights Drilled and Tapped
$445.00

SPECIFICATIONS MODEL 1300—12 GAUGE

Model	Symbol Number	Chamber	Shotshell Capacity*	Choke	Barrel Length & Type	Overall Length	Nominal Weight (Lbs.)	Rate of Twist 1 Turn in	Sights
1300 Walnut	6204	3″ Mag.	5	Cyl	22″ Rifled	42⅝″	7¼	35″	Rifle
1300 Whitetail's Unlimited	6287	3 Mag.	5	Cyl	22 Rifled	42⅝″	7¼	35	Rifle

* Includes one shotshell in chamber when ready to fire. W2-Improved Cylinder and rifled Sabot choke tubes. Cyl-Cylinder bore. Drilled and Tapped-Bases included.
Length of pull: 14″. Drop at comb: 1½″. Drop at heel: 2½″.

WINCHESTER SHOTGUNS

MODEL 1300 RANGER LADIES/YOUTH PUMP-ACTION SHOTGUN

Gauge: 20 gauge only; 3″ chamber; 5-shot magazine. **Barrel:** 22″ barrel w/vent. rib; Winchoke (Full, Modified, Improved Cylinder). **Weight:** 6 1/2 lbs. **Length:** 41 5/8″. **Stock:** Walnut or American hardwood with ribbed forend. **Sights:** Metal bead front. **Features:** Cross-bolt safety; black rubber butt pad; twin-action slide bars; front-locking rotating bolt; removable segmented magazine plug to limit shotshell capacity for training purposes.

MODEL 1300 RANGER 12 GAUGE DEER COMBO
22″ Rifled w/Sights & 28″ Vent Rib Barrels

SPECIFICATIONS MODEL 1300 RANGER, RANGER DEER & LADIES/YOUTH

Model	Gauge	Choke	Barrel Length & Type	Overall Length	Nominal Length of Pull	Nominal Weight (Lbs.)	Sights	Prices
1300 Ranger	12	W3	28″ VR	48 5/8″	14″	7 1/2	MBF	
	20	W3	28 VR	48 5/8	14	7 1/4	MBF	$294.00
	12	W3	26 VR	46 5/8	14	7 1/4	MBF	
	20	W3	26 VR	46 5/8	14	7 1/4	MBF	
1300 Ranger Deer Combo 12 ga. Extra Barrel	12 12	Cyl W3	22 28 VR	42 5/8	14	6 1/2	Rifle MBF	368.00*
1300 Ranger Deer Combo 20 ga. Extra Barrel	20 20	Cyl W3	22 Smooth 28 VR	42 5/8	14	6 1/2	Rifle MBF	368.00
1300 Ranger Deer Slug	12	Cyl	22 Smooth	42 5/8	14	6 3/4	Rifle	294.00
	12	Cyl	22 Rifled	48 5/8	14	6 3/4	MBF	333.00
	12	W2	22 Smooth	42 5/8	14	6 3/4	Rifle	345.00
1300 Ranger Ladies/Youth	20	W3	22 VR	41 5/8	13	6 1/2	MBF	312.00

All models have 3″ Mag. chambers and 5-shot shell capacity, including one shotshell in chamber when ready to fire. VR-Ventilated rib. Cyl.-Cylinder Bore, R-Rifled Barrel. MBF-Metal bead front. RT-Rifle type front and rear sights. Model 1300 and Ranger pump action shotguns have factory-installed plug which limits capacity to three shells. Ladies/Youth has factory-installed plug which limits capacity to one, two or three shells as desired. Extra barrels for Model 1300 and Ranger shotguns are available in 12 gauge, plain or ventilated rib, in a variety of barrel lengths and chokes; interchangeable with gauge. Winchoke sets with wrench come with gun as follows: W3W-Extra Full, Full, Modified tubes. W3-Full, Modified, Improved Cylinder tubes. W1M-Modified tube. W1F-Full tube. Nominal drop at comb: 1 1/2″; nominal drop at heel: 2 1/2″ (2 3/8″-Ladies' models). * **$390.00** with rifled barrel.

WINCHESTER SHOTGUNS

MODEL 1300 PUMP-ACTION WALNUT SHOTGUNS
$374.00

SPECIFICATIONS MODEL 1300 WALNUT

Model	Symbol Number	Gauge	Chamber	Shotshell Capacity*	Choke	Barrel Length & Type	Overall Length	Drop At Heel	Weight (Lbs.)
1300 Walnut	6014	12	3″ Mag.	5	W3	28″ VR	48⁵/₈″	2¹/₂″	7¹/₂
	6022	20	3″ Mag.	5	W3	28″ VR	48⁵/₈″	2¹/₂″	7¹/₄
	6071	12	3″ Mag.	5	W3	26″ VR	46⁵/₈″	1¹/₂″	7¹/₄
	6121	20	3″ Mag.	5	W3	26″ VR	46⁵/₈″	2¹/₂″	7¹/₄

* Includes one shotshell in chamber when ready to fire. VR-Ventilated rib. Winchoke sets with wrench come with gun as follows: W3-Full, Modified, Improved Cylinder tubes. All models have 14″ nominal length of pull; 1¹/₂″ drop at comb. Sights are metal bead front.

MODEL 1300 TURKEY SHOTGUN
$435.00 ($458.00 NWTF Model)

SPECIFICATIONS MODEL 1300 TURKEY

Model	Gauge	Barrel Length & Type	Chamber	Shotshell Capacity*†	Choke	Overall Length	Length of Pull	Drop At Comb/Heel		Weight (Lbs.)	Sights
NWTF Turkey Gun Wincam Series III	12	22″ VR	3″ Mag.	5	W3W	42⁵/₈″	14″	1¹/₂″	2¹/₂″	6³/₈	MBF
NWTF Series IV Gun of the Year	12	22″ VR	3″ Mag.	5	W3W	42⁵/₈″	14″	1¹/₂″	2¹/₂″	7	MBF
NWTF Series III	12	22″ Smooth	3″ Mag.	5	W3W	42⁵/₈″	14	1¹/₂″	2¹/₂″	7¹/₄	Rifle
Turkey	12	22″ VR	3″ Mag.	5	W3W	42⁵/₈″	14	1¹/₂″	2¹/₂″	7¹/₄	MBF

* Includes one shotshell in chamber when ready to fire. VR-Ventilated rib. MBF-Metal bead front. Winchoke sets with wrench come with gun as follows: W3W-Extra Full, Full, Modified tubes. W3-Full, Modified, Improved Cylinder tubes.

† Includes one shotshell in chamber when ready to fire. VR-Floating ventilated rib. MBF-Metal bead front. Winchoke sets with wrench come with gun as follows: W3-Full, Modified, Improved Cylinder tubes.

WINCHESTER SHOTGUNS

MODEL 1400 SEMIAUTO SHOTGUNS

MODEL 1400 SEMIAUTO WALNUT

SPECIFICATIONS MODEL 1400 SEMIAUTO

Model	Gauge	Barrel Length & Type	Chamber	Shotshell Capacity*	Choke	Overall Length	Length of Pull	Drop At Comb/Heel		Weight (lbs.)	Sights	Prices
1400	12	26″ VR	2³/₄″	3	W3″	46⅝″	14″	1¹/₂″	2¹/₂″	7¹/₂	MBF	
	20	26″ VR	2³/₄″	3	W3″	46¹/₈″	13¹/₂″	1¹/₂″	2¹/₂″	7¹/₄	MBF	
	12	28″ VR	2³/₄″	3	W3″	48⅝″	14″	1¹/₂″	2¹/₂″	7³/₄	MBF	$407.00
	20	28″ VR	2³/₄″	3	W3″	48¹/₈″	13¹/₂″	1¹/₂″	2¹/₂″	7¹/₂	MBF	
1400 Quail Unlimited	12	26″ VR	2³/₄″	3	W3″	46⅝″	14″	1¹/₂″	2¹/₂″	7¹/₄	MBF	$422.00
1400 Ranger	12	28″ VR	2³/₄″	3	W3″	48¹/₈″	13¹/₂″	1¹/₂″	2¹/₂″	7³/₄	MBF	
	12	26″ VR	2³/₄	3	W3″	48¹/₈″	13¹/₂″	1¹/₂″	2¹/₂″	7¹/₂	MBF	$367.00
	20	28″ VR	2³/₄″	3	W3″	48¹/₈″	13¹/₂″	1¹/₂″	2¹/₂″	7¹/₂	MBF	
	20	26″ VR	2³/₄″	3	W3″	46¹/₈	13¹/₂″	1¹/₂″	2¹/₂″	7¹/₄	MBF	
1400 Ranger Deer Combo (With Extra 28″ Barrel)	12	22″ Smooth	2³/₄″	3	Cyl	42⅝″	14″	1¹/₂″	2¹/₂″	7¹/₄	Rifle	$423.00
	12	28″ VR	2³/₄″	3	W3″						MBF	

* Includes one shotshell in chamber when ready to fire. VR-Ventilated rib. Cyl.-Cylinder Bore. MBF-Metal bead front. RT-Rifle type front and rear sights. Winchoke sets with wrench come with gun as follows: W1-Modified tube. W2 Improved Cylinder and rifled Sabot tubes. W3-Full, Modified, Improved Cylinder tubes. All models have 14″ nominal length of pull; 1¹/₂″ drop at comb; 2¹/₂″ drop at heel.

SHOTGUNS

WINCHESTER SHOTGUNS

MODEL 1001 O/U SHOTGUNS
$1099.00 Field Grade (shown)
$1253.00 Sporting Clays

SPECIFICATIONS MODEL 1001

Model	Gauge	Barrel Length & Type	Chamber	Choke*	Nominal Overall Length	Nominal Length of Pull	Nominal Drop at Comb	Heel	Weight (lbs.)	Sights
Field	12	28″	3″	IC, M, F	45″	14¼″	1½″	2″	7	MBF
Sporting Clays I	12	28″	2¾″	SK, IC, M, I-MOD	46″	14⅜″	1⅜″	2⅛″	7¾	MBM-WBF
Sporting Clays II	12	30″	2¾″	SK, IC, M, I-MOD	48″	14⅜″	1⅜″	2⅛″	7¾	MBM-WBF

* WinPlus choke tubes supplied with your 1001. Choke Code: IC = Improved Cylinder, M = Modified, I-MOD = Improved Modified, F = Full, SK = Skeet, MBF = Metal bead front. MBM = Metal bead middle. WBF = White bead front.

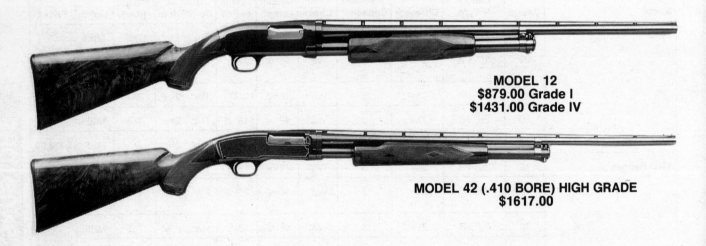

MODEL 12
$879.00 Grade I
$1431.00 Grade IV

MODEL 42 (.410 BORE) HIGH GRADE
$1617.00

SPECIFICATIONS CLASSIC TRADITION—LIMITED EDITIONS

Model	Gauge	Barrel Length	Chamber	Shotshell Capacity**	Choke	Overall Length*	Length of Pull*	Drop at Comb*/Heel		Weight (lbs.)	Sights
Model 12 (20 Gauge) Grade I	20 Gauge	26″	2¾″	6	IC	45″	14″	2½″	1½″	7	MBF
Grade IV	20 Gauge	26″	2¾″	6	IC	45″	14	2½″	1½″	7	WBF
Ducks Unlimited Model 12 (20 Gauge)	20 Gauge	26″	2¾″	6	IC	45″	14″	2½″	1½″	7	MBM-MBF
Model 42 (.410 Bore) High Grade	.410 Bore	26″	2¾″	6	F	45″	14″	2½″	1½″	7	MBF

* Nominal weight/measurement. **Includes one shotshell in chamber when ready to fire. IC = Improved Cylinder. F = Full Choke, MBF = Metal Bead Front, MBM = Metal Bead Middle, WBF = White Bead Front.

Black Powder

For addresses and phone numbers of manufacturers and distributors included in this section, turn to *DIRECTORY OF MANUFACTURERS AND SUPPLIERS* at the back of the book.

AMERICAN ARMS

MODEL HAWKEYE
$279.00 ($427.00 Stainless)

The new Hawkeye muzzleloader combines the traditional "cap-'n-ball" side hammer with the user-friendly features of the modern bolt-action rifle, including dual safety systems, striker fired in-line ignition system, and a contemporary designed stock fitted with a rubber recoil pad. Rifling is a fast 1 in 28".

SPECIFICATIONS
Calibers: 50 and 54
Barrel length: 22" round, tapered
Overall length: 41 1/2"
Weight: 6 3/4 lbs.
Receiver: Blued or stainless steel
Action: Adjustable trigger; side-mounted ambidextrous bolt handle
Sights: Ramp blade type with bead front; ramp-type rear, adjustable for windage and elevation; both sights removable; receiver drilled and tapped for Weaver No. 61 bases

REVOLVERS

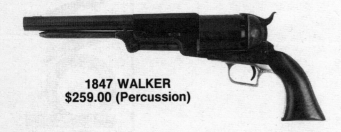

1847 WALKER
$259.00 (Percussion)

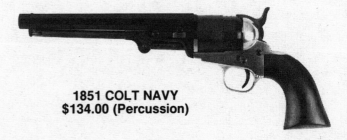

1851 COLT NAVY
$134.00 (Percussion)

This replica of the Texas Ranger's and Mexican War "Horse Pistol" was designed by Capt. Samuel Walker and built by Samuel Colt.

SPECIFICATIONS
Caliber: 44
Capacity: 6 shots
Barrel length: 9" round w/hinged loading lever
Overall length: 15 1/2"
Weight: 72 oz.
Features: Engraved blued steel cylinder; color casehardened steel frame and backstrap; solid brass trigger guard; one-piece walnut grip

This replica of the most famous revolver of the percussion era was used extensively during the Civil War and on the Western frontier.

SPECIFICATIONS
Caliber: 36
Capacity: 6 shots
Barrel length: 7 1/2" octagonal w/hinged loading lever
Overall length: 13"
Weight: 44 oz.
Features: Solid brass frame, trigger guard and backstrap; one-piece walnut grip; engraved blued steel cylinder

AMERICAN ARMS

REVOLVERS

1858 REMINGTON ARMY
$153.00 (Percussion)

This replica of the last of Remington's percussion revolvers saw extensive use in the Civil War.

SPECIFICATIONS
Caliber: 44
Capacity: 6 shots
Barrel length: 8″ octagonal w/creeping loading lever
Overall length: 13″
Weight: 38 oz.
Features: Two-piece walnut grips

1858 REMINGTON ARMY

1858 ARMY STAINLESS STEEL TARGET

1858 ARMY STAINLESS STEEL TARGET
$305.00

Same features and specifications as 1858 Remington Army, except fitted with adjustable rear target sight and ramp blade front sight. Stainless steel frame, barrel and cylinder.

1860 COLT ARMY
$137.00 (Percussion)

Union troops issued this sidearm during the Civil War and subsequent Indian Wars.

SPECIFICATIONS
Caliber: 44
Capacity: 6 shots
Barrel length: 8″ round w/creeping loading lever
Overall length: 13½″
Weight: 44 oz.
Features: Solid brass frame, trigger guard and backstrap; one-piece walnut grip; engraved blued steel cylinder

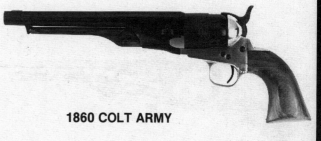

1860 COLT ARMY

BLACK POWDER

ARMSPORT

REPLICA REVOLVERS

MODEL 5145
COLT 1847 WALKER
$288.00

The largest of all Colt revolvers, this true copy of the original weighs 4½ lbs., making it also the most powerful (and only) revolver made at the time. **Caliber:** 44.

MODEL 5152
ENGRAVED REMINGTON 44 CALIBER
Gold & Nickel-Plated
$299.00

MODEL 5153
ENGRAVED COLT ARMY 44 CALIBER
$299.00

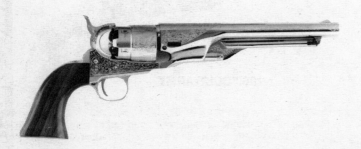

MODEL 5154
ENGRAVED COLT NAVY 36 CALIBER
$299.00

ARMSPORT

REPLICA REVOLVERS

MODEL 5133
COLT 1851 NAVY "REB"

A modern replica of a Confederate percussion revolver in 36 or 44 caliber, this has a polished brass frame, rifled blued barrel and polished walnut grips.
Price: **$149.00**

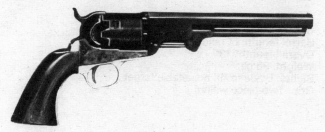

MODEL 5136
COLT 1851 NAVY STEEL

This authentic reproduction of the Colt Navy Revolver in 36 or 44 caliber, which helped shape the history of America, features a rifled barrel, casehardened steel frame, engraved cylinder, polished brass trigger guard and walnut grips.
Price: **$185.00**

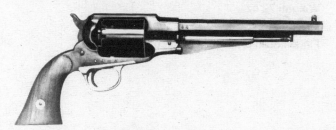

MODEL 5120
NEW REMINGTON ARMY
STEEL REVOLVER

One of the most accurate cap-and-ball revolvers of the 1860's. Its rugged steel frame and top strap made this 44 caliber the favorite of all percussion cap revolvers.
Price: **$210.00**
With brass frame: **160.00**
Also available:
Steel Target Model **240.00**

MODEL 5138
REMINGTON ARMY STAINLESS STEEL

This stainless-steel version of the 44-caliber Remington New Army Revolver is made for the shooter who seeks the best. Its stainless steel frame assures lasting good looks and durability.
Price: **$365.00**

MODEL 5139
COLT 1860 ARMY

This authentic 44-caliber reproduction offers the same balance and ease of handling for fast shooting as the original 1860 Army model.
Price: **$210.00**

MODEL 5140
COLT 1860 ARMY

Same as the Model 5139 Colt Army replica, but with brightly polished brass frame.
Price: **$149.00**

CVA REVOLVERS

1858 REMINGTON ARMY STEEL FRAME REVOLVER

1858 REMINGTON ARMY REVOLVER
Brass Frame:. **$169.95**
Steel Frame:. **229.95**
Kit—Brass only:. **145.95**

1858 REMINGTON TARGET MODEL
$239.95

Caliber: 44
Cylinder: 6-shot
Barrel length: 8″ octagonal
Overall length: 13″
Weight: 38 oz.
Sights: Blade front; adjustable target
Grip: Two-piece walnut

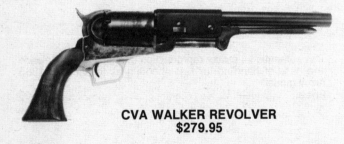

CVA WALKER REVOLVER
$279.95

Caliber: 44
Barrel: 9″ rounded with hinged-style loading lever
Cylinder: 6-shot engraved
Overall length: 15¹/₂″
Weight: 72 oz.
Grip: One-piece walnut
Front sight: Blade
Finish: Solid brass trigger guard

NEW MODEL POCKET REMINGTON
Finished $129.95

Caliber: 31 percussion
Barrel length: 4″ octagonal
Cylinder: 5 shots
Overall length: 7¹/₂″
Sights: Post in front; groove in frame in rear
Weight: 15 oz.
Finish: Solid brass frame

CVA REVOLVERS

Caliber: 36
Barrel length: 7¹/₂″ octagonal; hinged-style loading lever
Overall length: 13″
Weight: 44 oz.
Cylinder: 6-shot, engraved
Sights: Post front; hammer notch rear
Grip: One-piece walnut
Finish: Solid brass frame, trigger guard and backtrap; blued barrel and cylinder; color casehardened loading lever and hammer

1851 NAVY
BRASS-FRAMED REVOLVER
Finished $138.95
Kit $129.95

Calibers: 44
Barrel length: 7¹/₂″ rounded; creeping style
Overall length: 13″
Weight: 44 oz.
Cylinder: 6-shot, engraved
Sights: Blade front; hammer notch rear
Finish: Solid brass frame, trigger guard and backstrap; blued barrel and cylinder
Grip: One-piece walnut

1861 NAVY BRASS-FRAMED REVOLVER
Finished $139.95
Kit $129.95

Caliber: 36
Barrel length: 5¹/₂″ (octagonal w/creeping-style loading lever)
Overall length: 11¹/₂″
Weight: 40¹/₂ oz.
Cylinder: 6-shot semi-fluted
Grip: One-piece walnut
Sight: Hammer notch in rear
Finish: Solid brass frame, trigger guard and backstrap

Also available:
Engraved Nickel Plated Model with matching flask
Price: $219.95

SHERIFF'S MODEL REVOLVER
Brass Frame $157.95

Caliber: 44
Barrel length: 8″ rounded; creeping-style loading lever
Overall length: 13¹/₂″
Weight: 44 oz.
Cylinder: 6-shot, engraved and rebated
Sights: Blade front; hammer notch rear
Grip: One-piece walnut
Finish: Solid brass trigger guard; blued barrel and cylinder with color casehardened loading lever, hammer and frame

1860 ARMY REVOLVER
$231.95 (Steel Frame Only)

CVA REVOLVERS

WELLS FARGO MODEL
Brass Frame $129.95

Caliber: 31
Capacity: 5-shot cylinder (engraved)
Barrel length: 4″ octagonal
Overall length: 9″
Weight: 28 oz. (w/extra cylinder)
Sights: Post front; hammer notch rear
Grip: One-piece walnut

POCKET POLICE
Brass Frame $139.95

Caliber: 36
Capacity: 5-shot cylinder
Barrel length: 5¹/₂″ octagonal, with creeping-style loading lever
Overall length: 10¹/₂″
Weight: 26 oz.
Sights: Post front; hammer notch rear

THIRD MODEL DRAGOON
Steel Frame $239.95

Caliber: 44
Cylinder: 6-shot engraved
Barrel length: 7¹/₂″ rounded with hinged-style loading lever
Overall length: 14″
Weight: 66 oz.
Sights: Blade front; hammer notch rear
Grip: One-piece walnut

REMINGTON BISON
$247.95

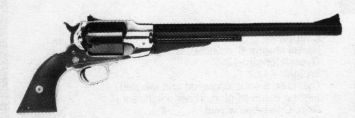

Caliber: 44
Cylinder: 6-shot
Barrel length: 10¹/₄″ octagonal
Overall length: 18″
Weight: 48 oz.
Sights: Fixed blade front; screw adjustable target rear
Grip: Two-piece walnut
Finish: Solid brass frame

CVA PISTOLS

KENTUCKY PISTOL
Finished $157.95
Percussion Kit $99.95

Caliber: 50 percussion
Barrel: 10¼", rifled, octagonal
Overall length: 15½"
Weight: 40 oz.
Finish: Blued barrel, brass hardware
Sights: Brass blade front; fixed open rear
Stock: Select hardwood
Ignition: Engraved, color casehardened percussion lock, screw adjustable sear engagement
Accessories: Brass-tipped, hardwood ramrod; stainless steel nipple or flash hole liner

PHILADELPHIA DERRINGER
$84.95 (Kit Only)

Caliber: 45 percussion
Barrel: 3¼" rifled, octagonal
Overall length: 7⅛"
Weight: 16 oz.
Finish: Brass hardware; blued barrel
Stock: Select hardwood
Ignition: Color casehardened and engraved, coil-spring back-action lock
Accessories: Stainless steel nipple

HAWKEN PISTOL
Finished $176.95
Kit $109.95

Caliber: 50 percussion
Barrel length: 9¾", octagonal
Overall length: 16½"
Weight: 50 oz.
Trigger: Early-style brass
Sights: Beaded steel blade front; fully adjustable rear (click adj. screw settings lock into position)
Stock: Select hardwood
Finish: Solid brass wedge plate, nose cap, ramrod thimbles, trigger guard and grip cap

VEST POCKET DERRINGER
Finished $69.95

Caliber: 31 Derringer
Barrel length: 2½" (single shot) brass
Overall length: 5"
Weight: 16 oz.
Grip: Two-piece walnut
Frame: Brass

SIBER PISTOL
$439.95

Caliber: 45 percussion
Barrel length: 10½", octagonal
Overall length: 12½"
Weight: 38 oz.
Sights: Blade front; rear adjustable for elevation
Stock: Fancy European walnut
Trigger: Adjustable single-set trigger with rear over-lateral limiting screw
Finish: Polished steel barrel, lock plate, hammer and trigger

BLACK POWDER

CVA RIFLES

VARMINT RIFLE
$234.95

Caliber: 32 percussion
Barrel length: 24″ octagonal; 7/8″ across flats
Rifling: 1 in 48″
Overall length: 40″
Weight: 6¾ lbs.
Lock: Color casehardened with 45° offset hammer

Trigger: Single trigger
Sights: Steel blade front; Patridge-style click-adjustable rear
Stock: Select hardwood
Features: Brass trigger guard, nose cap, wedge plate, thimble and buttplate

BUSHWACKER RIFLE
$159.95

Caliber: 50
Barrel length: 26″ blued octagonal
Overall length: 40″
Weight: 7½ lbs.
Sights: Brass blade front; fixed open semi-buckhorn rear

Stock: Walnut stained select hardwood with rounded nose
Trigger: Single trigger with oversized trigger guard
Features: Blued steel wedge plates; ramrod thimbles; blackened trigger guard and black plastic butt plate

ST. LOUIS HAWKEN RIFLE

Calibers: 50 and 54 percussion or flintlock (50 cal. only)
Barrel: 28″ octagonal 15/16″ across flats; hooked breech; rifling one turn in 66″, 8 lands and deep grooves
Overall length: 44″
Weight: 8 lbs.
Sights: Dovetail, beaded blade (front); adjustable open hunting-style dovetail (rear)
Stock: Select hardwood with beavertail cheekpiece

Triggers: Double set; fully adjustable trigger pull
Finish: Solid brass wedge plates, nose cap, ramrod thimbles, trigger guard and patch box
Prices:
50 Caliber Flintlock $259.95
50 Caliber Percussion 254.95
54 Caliber Percussion 214.95
Percussion Combo Kit 229.95

CVA RIFLES

APOLLO CARBELITE RIFLE
$349.95

Calibers: 50 and 54 percussion
Barrel length: 25" blued round, tapered w/octagonal one-piece receiver (drilled and tapped w/foul weather cover)
Rifling: 1 in 32"
Overall length: 43"
Weight: 7½ lbs.
Trigger: Box-type with hooking tumbler; auto safety system

Lock: In-line stainless steel percussion bolt with push lock safety
Sights: Front, ramp-mounted beaded blade; fully click adjustable rear
Stock: Bell & Carlson Carbelite composite w/Monte Carlo fluted comb, fully formed cheekpiece and pistol grip
Features: Solid rubber recoil pad; molded black oversized trigger guard; bottom screw attachment and blued thimble; sling swivels; coated fiberglass ramrod with blackened tip

APOLLO 90 SHADOW RIFLE
$314.95

Calibers: 50 and 54
Barrel length: 27" blued round taper with octagonal one-piece receiver
Overall length: 45"

Weight: 9½ lbs.
Trigger: Box-style with hooking tumbler; auto safety system
Sights: Ramp mounted brass bead with hood front; fully click adjustable rear; drilled and tapped
Stock: Black, textured epoxicoat hardwood with Monte Carlo fluted combo and fully formed cheekpiece and pistol grip
Features: Ventilated rubber recoil pad; molded black oversized trigger guard; bottom screw attachment and blued thimble

APOLLO SPORTER
$269.95

Caliber: 50
Barrel length: 25" blued round taper with octagonal one-piece receiver
Overall length: 43"
Weight: 8½ lbs.

Trigger: Box-style with hooking tumbler; auto safety system
Sights: Blued steel beaded blade front; adjustable hunting-style rear; drilled and tapped for scope mounts
Stock: Hardwood with pistol grip
Features: Buttplate and blued thimble; stainless percussion bolt; barrel and action formed from one piece of steel; in-line ignition

FRONTIER HUNTER CARBINE
$205.95

Calibers: 50 and 54 percussion
Barrel length: 24", blued, octagonal

Overall length: 40"
Weight: 7½ lbs.
Sights: Beaded steel blade front; hunting-style rear, fully click adjustable for windage and elevation
Stock: Select hardwood with straight grip; solid rubber recoil pad
Triggers: Single
Finish: Black trigger guard and wedge plate

BLACK POWDER

CVA RIFLES

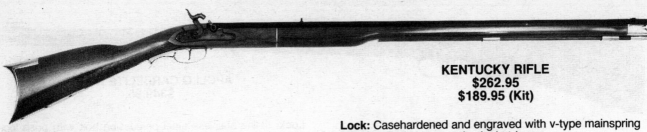

KENTUCKY RIFLE
$262.95
$189.95 (Kit)

Caliber: 50 percussion
Barrel length: 33¹/₂″ octagonal; ⁷/₈″ across flats
Rifling: 1 in 66″
Overall length: 48″
Weight: 7¹/₂ lbs.

Lock: Casehardened and engraved with v-type mainspring
Trigger: Early brass-style single trigger
Sights: Brass blade front; fixed open rear
Stock: Select hardwood
Features: Solid brass trigger guard, buttplate, toe plate, nose cap and thimble

TROPHY CARBINE
$254.95

Calibers: 50 and 54 percussion
Barrel length: 24″ half-round, half-octagonal; ¹⁵/₁₆″ across flats
Rifling: 1 in 32″
Overall length: 40″
Weight: 6³/₄ lbs.

Lock: Hawken-style with bridle and fly; engraved
Trigger: Single modern-style trigger integral with trigger guard
Sights: Ivory-colored beaded ramp mounted front; fully click adjustable rear
Stock: Walnut with Monte Carlo comb, pistol grip and formed cheekpiece
Features: Ventilated rubber recoil pad, molded black oversized trigger guard and blued thimble

FRONTIER CARBINE
$189.95 Percussion
$224.95 Flintlock
$137.95 Kit (Percussion Only)

Caliber: 50 percussion or flintlock
Barrel length: 24″ octagonal; ¹⁵/₁₆″ across flats
Rifling: 1 turn in 48″ (8 lands and deep grooves)
Overall length: 40″
Weight: 6 lbs. 9 oz.
Sights: Brass blade front; fully adjustable rear

Trigger: Early-style brass with tension spring
Stock: Select hardwood
Finish: Solid brass buttplate, trigger guard wedge plate, nose cap and thimble
Accessories: Stainless steel nipple, hardwood ramrod with brass tips and cleaning jag

EXPRESS DOUBLE BARREL RIFLE
Finished $525.95

Calibers: 50 and 54 percussion
Barrels: Two laser-aligned, tapered 28″ round; hooked breech
Rifling: 1 turn in 48″
Overall length: 44″
Weight: 10 lbs.
Locks: Plate is color hardened and engraved; includes bridle, fly, screw-adjustable sear engagement
Triggers: Double, color casehardened

Sights: Hunting-style rear, fully adjustable for windage and elevation; dovetailed, beaded blade front
Stock: Select hardwood
Finish: Polished steel wedge plates; color casehardened locks, hammers, triggers and trigger guard; engraved locks, hammers and tang

CVA RIFLES

TRACKER CARBINE
$254.95

Caliber: 50 percussion
Barrel length: 21″ blued, half-round, half-octagonal
Overall length: 37″
Weight: 6½ lbs.
Lock: Hawken-style with bridle and fly, color casehardened
Trigger: Single trigger integral with trigger guard

Sights: Steel beaded blued blade front; fully click adjustable rear
Stock: Matte finish with straight grip
Features: Ventilated rubber recoil pad; molded black oversized trigger guard and blued wedge plates and thimbles; drilled and tapped for scope mount

PLAINSMAN RIFLE
$143.95

Caliber: 50 percussion
Barrel length: 26″ octagonal (15/16″ across flats)
Overall length: 40″
Weight: 6½ lbs.
Trigger: Single trigger with large trigger guard

Sights: Brass blade front; fixed open rear
Stock: Select hardwood
Finish: Black trigger guard, wedge plate and thimble
Accessories: Color casehardened nipple, hardwood ramrod with brass tip and cleaning jag

STALKER RIFLE/CARBINE
$217.95
$239.95 (Left Hand)

Calibers: 50 and 54 percussion
Barrel length: 28″ octagonal (Rifle); 24″ (Carbine)
Overall length: 40″ (Carbine); 44″ (Rifle)
Weight: 7½ lbs.
Sights: Steel beaded blade front; hunting-style rear, fully click adjustable for windage and elevation (click adjustable screw settings lock into position); drilled and tapped for scope

Trigger: Single trigger with oversized trigger guard
Stock: Select hardwood with pistol grip and rubber recoil pad
Finish: Blackened trigger guard; blued thimble, wedge and wedge plate
Accessories: Color casehardened nipple, hardwood ramrod with brass tips and cleaning jag

CVA RIFLES/SHOTGUNS

SIERRA STALKER
$189.95

Caliber: 50 percussion
Barrel length: 28″ blued, octagonal; $^{15}/_{16}$″ across flats
Rifling: 1 in 32″
Overall length: 43$^1/_3$″
Weight: 7$^1/_4$ lbs.
Lock: Hawken-style with bridle and fly

Sights: Blued steel beaded blade front; fully click adjustable rear
Stock: Walnut-stained hardwood with Monte Carlo comb
Features: Ventilated rubber recoil pad, molded black oversized trigger guard and blued thimble

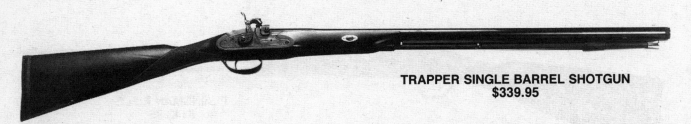

TRAPPER SINGLE BARREL SHOTGUN
$339.95

Gauge: 12 percussion
Barrel length: 28″ round, smoothbore; hooked breech; three interchangeable chokes (Imp., Mod. and Full)
Overall length: 46″
Weight: 6 lbs.
Trigger: Early-style steel

Lock: Color casehardened; engraved with v-type mainspring, bridle and fly
Sights: Brass bead front (no rear sight)
Stock: Select hardwood; English-style checkered straight grip
Features: German silver wedge plates; color casehardened engraved lock plate; hammer, trigger guard and tang

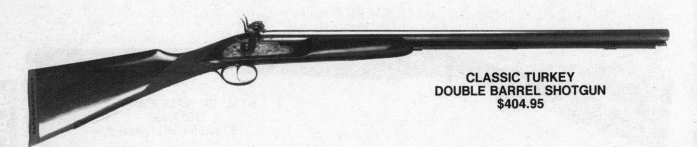

CLASSIC TURKEY
DOUBLE BARREL SHOTGUN
$404.95

Gauge: 12 percussion
Barrel length: 28″ round, smoothbore; double button-style breech, Modified choke
Overall length: 45″
Weight: 9 lbs.
Triggers: Hinged, gold-tone double triggers
Lock: Color casehardened; engraved with v-type mainspring, bridle and fly

Sights: Brass bead front (no rear sight)
Stock: Select hardwood; English-style checkered straight grip; wraparound forearm with bottom screw attachment
Features: Color casehardened engraved lock plates, trigger guard and tang

DIXIE

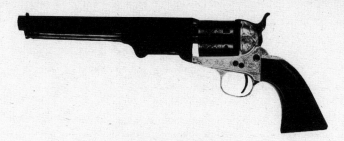

DIXIE NAVY REVOLVER
Plain Model $99.00
Engraved Model $139.95
Kit $84.95

This 36-caliber revolver was a favorite of the officers of the Civil War. Although called a Navy type, it is somewhat misnamed since many more of the Army personnel used it. Made in Italy; uses .376 mold or ball to fit and number 11 caps. Blued steel barrel and cylinder with brass frame.

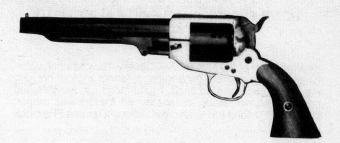

SPILLER & BURR 36 CALIBER
BRASS FRAME REVOLVER
$125.00   Kit $115.00

The 36-caliber octagonal barrel on this revolver is 7 inches long. The six-shot cylinder chambers mike .378, and the hammer engages a slot between the nipples on the cylinder as an added safety device. It has a solid brass trigger guard and frame with backstrap cast integral with the frame, two-piece walnut grips and Whitney-type casehardened loading lever.

REMINGTON 44 ARMY REVOLVER
$159.95

All steel external surfaces finished bright blue, including 8″ octagonal barrel (hammer is casehardened). Polished brass guard and two-piece walnut grips are standard.

DIXIE 1860 ARMY REVOLVER
$169.95

The Dixie 1860 Army has a half-fluted cylinder and its chamber diameter is .447. Use .451 round ball mold to fit this 8-inch barrel revolver. Cut for shoulder stock.

"WYATT EARP" REVOLVER
$130.00

This 44-caliber revolver has a 12-inch octagon rifled barrel and rebated cylinder. Highly polished brass frame, backstrap and trigger guard. The barrel and cylinder have a deep blue luster finish. Hammer, trigger, and loading lever are case-hardened. Walnut grips. Recommended ball size is .451.

RHO200 WALKER REVOLVER
$225.00   Kit $179.95

This 4½-pound, 44-caliber pistol is the largest ever made. Steel backstrap; guard is brass with Walker-type rounded-to-frame walnut grips; all other parts are blued. Chambers measure .445 and take a .450 ball slightly smaller than the originals.

DIXIE

FHO201 FRENCH CHARLEVILLE FLINT PISTOL
(Not shown)
$195.00

Reproduction of the Model 1777 Cavalry, Revolutionary War-era pistol. Has reversed frizzen spring; forend and lock housing are all in one; casehardened, round-faced, double-throated hammer; walnut stock; casehardened frizzen and trigger; shoots .680 round ball loaded with about 40 grains FFg black powder.

RHO301 THIRD MODEL DRAGOON
$199.95

This engraved-cylinder, 4½-pounder is a reproduction of the last model of Colt's 44 caliber "horse" revolvers. Barrel measures 7⅜ inches, ⅛ inch shorter than the original; color casehardened steel frame, one-piece walnut grips. Recommended ball size: .454.

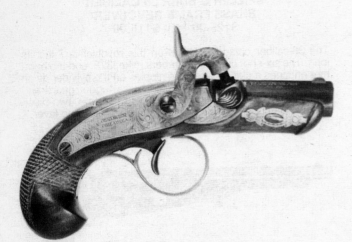

LINCOLN DERRINGER
$285.00   Kit $89.95

This 41-caliber, 2-inch browned barrel gun has 8 lands and 8 grooves and will shoot a .400 patch ball.

DSB-58 SCREW BARREL DERRINGER
(Not shown)
$89.00   Kit $74.95

Overall length: 6½". Unique loading system; sheath trigger, color case-hardened frame, trigger and center-mounted hammer; European walnut, one-piece, "bag"-type grip. Uses #11 percussion caps.

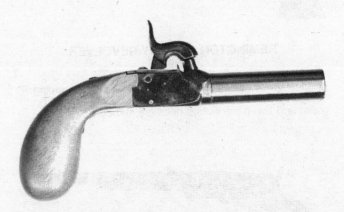

SCREW BARREL (FOLDING TRIGGER) PISTOL
$89.95 ($75.00 Kit)

This little gun, only 6½" overall, has a unique loading system that eliminates the need for a ramrod. The barrel is loosened with a barrel key, then unscrewed from the frame by hand. The recess is then filled with 10 grains of FFFg black powder, the .445 round ball is seated in the dished area, and the barrel is then screwed back into place. The .245×32 nipple uses #11 percussion caps. The pistol also features a sheath trigger that folds into the frame, then drops down for firing when the hammer is cocked. Comes with color casehardened frame, trigger and center-mounted hammer.

ABILENE DERRINGER (Not shown)
$81.50   Kit $51.95

An all-steel version of Dixie's brass-framed derringers. The 2½-inch, 41-caliber barrel is finished in a deep blue black; frame and hammer are case-hardened. Bore is rifled with 6 lands and grooves. Uses a tightly patched .395 round ball and 15 or 20 grains of FFFg powder. Walnut grips. Comes with wood presentation case.

DIXIE

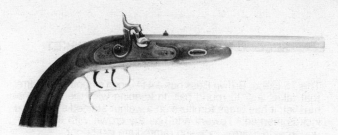

LePAGE PERCUSSION DUELING PISTOL
$259.95

This 45-caliber percussion pistol features a blued 10″ octagonal barrel with 12 lands and grooves; a brass-bladed front sight with open rear sight dovetailed into the barrel; polished silver-plated trigger guard and butt cap. Right side of barrel is stamped "LePage á Paris." Double-set triggers are single screw adjustable. **Overall length:** 16″. **Weight:** 2½ lbs.

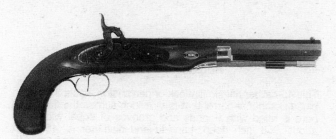

PEDERSOLI ENGLISH DUELING PISTOL
$265.00

This reproduction of an English percussion dueling pistol, created by Charles Moore of London, features a European walnut halfstock with oil finish and checkered grip. The 45-caliber octagonal barrel is 11″ with 12 grooves and a twist of 1 in 15″. Nose cap and thimble are silver. Barrel is blued; lock and trigger guard are color casehardened.

PEDERSOLI MANG TARGET PISTOL
$749.00

Designed specifically for the precision target shooter, this 38-caliber pistol has a 10⁷/₁₆″ octagonal barrel with 7 lands and grooves. Twist is 1 in 15″. Blade front sight is dovetailed into the barrel, and rear sight is mounted on the breech-plug tang, adjustable for windage. **Overall length:** 17¼″. **Weight:** 2½ lbs.

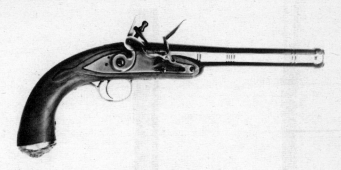

QUEEN ANNE PISTOL
$189.95
Kit $149.95

Named for the Queen of England (1702-1714), this flintlock pistol has a 7½″ barrel that tapers from rear to front with a cannon-shaped muzzle. The brass trigger guard is fluted and the brass butt on the walnut stock features a grotesque mask worked into it. **Overall length:** 13″. **Weight:** 2¼ lbs.

DIXIE PENNSYLVANIA PISTOL
Percussion $149.95   Kit $109.95
Flintlock $149.95   Kit $115.00

Available in 44-caliber percussion or flintlock. The bright luster blued barrel measures 10 inches long; rifled, ⁷/₈-inch octagonal and takes .430 ball; barrel is held in place with a steel wedge and tang screw; brass front and rear sights. The brass trigger guard, thimbles, nose cap, wedge plates and side plates are highly polished. Locks are fine quality with early styling. Plates measure 4³/₄ inches × ⁷/₈ inch. Percussion hammer is engraved and both plates are left in the white. The flint is an excellent style lock with the gooseneck hammer having an early wide thumb piece. The stock is walnut stained and has a wide bird's-head-type grip.

DIXIE

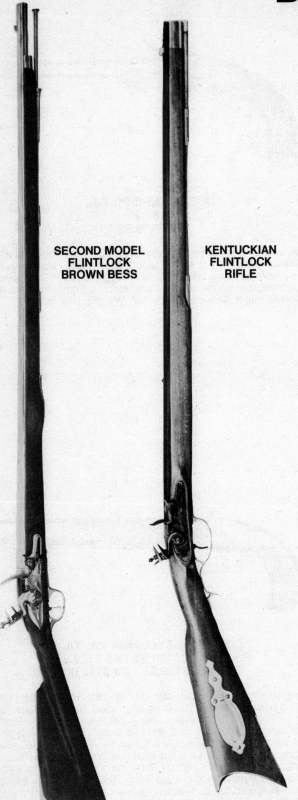

**SECOND MODEL
FLINTLOCK
BROWN BESS**

**KENTUCKIAN
FLINTLOCK
RIFLE**

SECOND MODEL BROWN BESS MUSKET
$530.00

This 75-caliber Brown Bess has a 41³/₄-inch smoothbore barrel that takes a .730 round ball. In keeping with the traditional musket, it has brass furniture on a walnut-stained stock. The lock is marked "Tower" and has the crown with the "GR" underneath. Barrel, lock and ramrod are left bright.
Kit: **$400.00**

THE KENTUCKIAN RIFLE
Flintlock $259.95
Percussion $249.95

This 45-caliber rifle, in flintlock or percussion, has a 33¹/₂-inch blued octagonal barrel that is ¹³/₁₆ inch across the flats. The bore is rifled with 6 lands and grooves of equal width and about .006 inch deep. Land-to-land diameter is .453 with groove-to-groove diameter of .465. Ball size ranges from .445 to .448. The rifle has a brass blade front sight and a steel open rear sight. The Kentuckian is furnished with brass butt plate, trigger guard, patch box, side plate, thimbles and nose cap plus case-hardened and engraved lock plate. Highly polished and finely finished stock in European walnut. **Overall length:** 48″. **Weight:** Approx. 6¹/₄ lbs.

DIXIE DOUBLE BARREL MAGNUM
MUZZLE LOADING SHOTGUN (Not shown)

A full 12-gauge, high-quality, double-barreled percussion shotgun with 30-inch browned barrels. Will take the plastic shot cups for better patterns. Bores are choked modified and full. Lock, barrel tang and trigger are case-hardened in a light gray color and are nicely engraved.
12 Gauge **$399.00**
12 Gauge Kit 350.00
10 Gauge Magnum (double barrel—right-hand = cyl. bore, left-hand = Mod.) 425.00
10 Gauge Magnum Kit 375.00

DIXIE

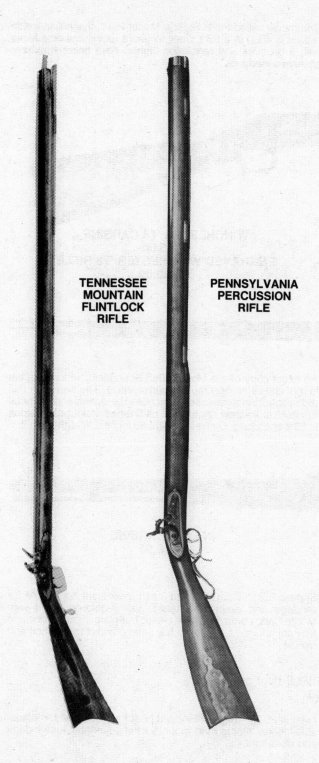

TENNESSEE MOUNTAIN FLINTLOCK RIFLE

PENNSYLVANIA PERCUSSION RIFLE

HAWKEN RIFLE (Not shown)
$250.00   Kit $220.00

Blued barrel is ¹⁵/₁₆″ across the flats and 30″ in length with a twist of 1 in 64″. Stock is of walnut with a steel crescent butt-plate, halfstock with brass nosecap. Double set triggers, front action lock and adjustable rear sight. Ramrod is equipped with jag. **Overall length:** 46½″. Average actual **weight:** about 8 lbs., depending on the caliber; shipping weight is 10 lbs. Available in either finished gun or kit. **Calibers:** 45, 50, and 54.

DIXIE TENNESSEE MOUNTAIN RIFLE
$495.00 Percussion or Flintlock

This 50-caliber rifle features double-set triggers with adjustable set screw, bore rifled with six lands and grooves, barrel of ¹⁵/₁₆ inch across the flats, brown finish and cherry stock. **Overall length:** 41½ inches. Right- and left-hand versions in flint or percussion. Kit: **$495.00**

DIXIE TENNESSEE SQUIRREL RIFLE
(Not shown)
$450.00

In 32-caliber flint or percussion, right hand only, cherry stock. Kit available: **$360.00**

PENNSYLVANIA RIFLE
Percussion or Flintlock $395.00
Kit (Flint or Perc.) $345.00

A lightweight at just 8 pounds, the 41½-inch blued rifle barrel is fitted with an open buckhorn rear sight and front blade. The walnut one-piece stock is stained a medium darkness that contrasts with the polished brass butt plate, toe plate, patchbox, side plate, trigger guard, thimbles and nose cap. Featuring double-set triggers, the rifle can be fired by pulling only the front trigger, which has a normal trigger pull of four to five pounds; or the rear trigger can first be pulled to set a springloaded mechanism that greatly reduces the amount of pull needed for the front trigger to kick off the sear in the lock. The land-to-land measurement of the bore is an exact .450 and the recommended ball size is .445. **Overall length:** 51½″.

PEDERSOLI WAADTLANDER RIFLE (Not shown)
$1295.00

This authentic re-creation of a Swiss muzzleloading target rifle features a heavy octagonal barrel (31″) that has 7 lands and grooves. **Caliber:** 45. Rate of twist is 1 turn in 48″. Double-set triggers are multi-lever type and are easily removable for adjustment. Sights are fitted post front and tang-mounted Swiss-type diopter rear. Walnut stock, color casehardened hardware, classic buttplate and curved trigger guard complete this reproduction. The original was made between 1839 and 1860 by Marc Bristlen, Morges, Switzerland.

DIXIE

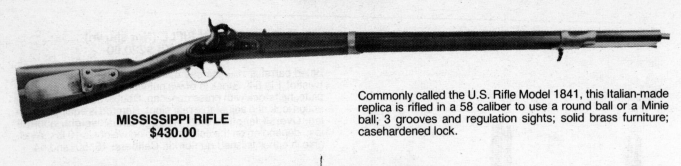

MISSISSIPPI RIFLE
$430.00

Commonly called the U.S. Rifle Model 1841, this Italian-made replica is rifled in a 58 caliber to use a round ball or a Minie ball; 3 grooves and regulation sights; solid brass furniture; casehardened lock.

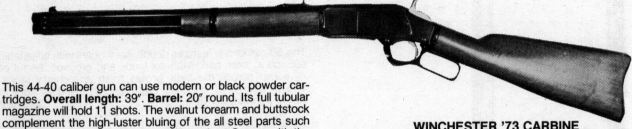

This 44-40 caliber gun can use modern or black powder cartridges. **Overall length:** 39″. **Barrel:** 20″ round. Its full tubular magazine will hold 11 shots. The walnut forearm and buttstock complement the high-luster bluing of the all steel parts such as the frame, barrel, magazine and buttplate. Comes with the trap door in the butt for the cleaning rod; leaf rear sight and blade front sight. This carbine is marked "Model 1873" on the tang and caliber "44-40" on the brass carrier block.

WINCHESTER '73 CARBINE
$895.00
ENGRAVED WINCHESTER '73 RIFLE
$1250.00

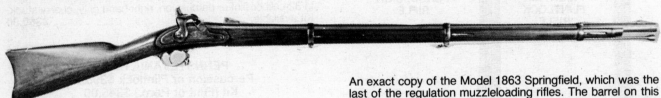

1863 SPRINGFIELD CIVIL WAR MUSKET
$475.00   Kit $330.00

An exact copy of the Model 1863 Springfield, which was the last of the regulation muzzleloading rifles. The barrel on this .58 caliber gun measures 40 inches. The action and all metal furniture is finished bright. The oil-finished walnut-stain stock is 53 inches long. **Overall length:** 56 inches. **Weight:** 9½ lbs.

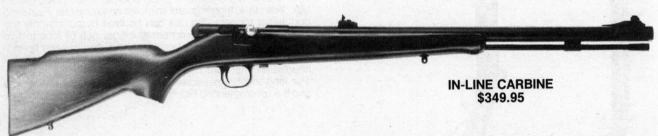

IN-LINE CARBINE
$349.95

Made in Italy by D. Pedersoli, this new rifle in 50 or 54 caliber features a sliding "bolt" that completely encloses cap and nipple, making it the most weather-proof muzzleloader available. **Barrel length:** 24″. **Overall length:** 41″. **Weight:** 6½ lbs.

Sights: Ramp front with red insert; rear sight adjustable for windage and elevation. **Stock:** Walnut-colored wood with Monte Carlo comb and black plastic buttplate. Features include fully adj. trigger, automatic slide safety, and chromed bolt and handle.

TRYON CREEDMOOR RIFLE (Not shown)
$595.00

This Tryon rifle features a high-quality back-action lock, double-set triggers, steel buttplate, patchbox, toe plate and curved trigger guard. **Caliber:** 45. **Barrel:** 32¾″, octagonal, with 1 twist in 20.87″. **Sights:** Hooded post front fitted with replaceable inserts; rear is tang-mounted and adjustable for windage and elevation.

DIXIE

U.S. MODEL 1861 SPRINGFIELD PERCUSSION RIFLE-MUSKET
$450.00   Kit $420.00

An exact re-creation of an original rifle produced by Springfield National Armory, Dixie's Model 1861 Springfield .58-caliber rifle features a 40″ round, tapered barrel with three barrel bands. Sling swivels are attached to the trigger guard bow and middle barrel band. The ramrod has a trumpet-shaped head with swell; sights are standard military rear and bayonet-attachment lug front. The percussion lock is marked "1861" on the rear of the lockplate with an eagle motif and "U.S. Springfield" in front of the hammer. "U.S." is stamped on top of buttplate. All furniture is "National Armory Bright." **Overall length:** 55¹³/₁₆″. **Weight:** 8 lbs.

1862 THREE-BAND ENFIELD RIFLED MUSKET
$485.00

One of the finest reproduction percussion guns available, the 1862 Enfield was widely used during the Civil War in its original version. This rifle follows the lines of the original almost exactly. The .58 caliber musket features a 39-inch barrel and walnut stock. Three steel barrel bands and the barrel itself are blued; the lock plate and hammer are case colored and the remainder of the furniture is highly polished brass. The lock is marked, "London Armory Co." **Weight:** 10½ lbs. **Overall length:** 55 inches.

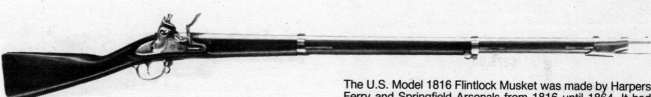

U.S. MODEL 1816 FLINTLOCK MUSKET
$725.00

The U.S. Model 1816 Flintlock Musket was made by Harpers Ferry and Springfield Arsenals from 1816 until 1864. It had the highest production of any U.S. flintlock musket and, after conversion to percussion, saw service in the Civil War. It has a .69 caliber, 42″ smoothbore barrel held by three barrel bands with springs. All metal parts are finished in "National Armory Bright." The lockplate has a brass pan and is marked "Harpers Ferry" vertically behind the hammer, with an American eagle placed in front of the hammer. The bayonet lug is on top of the barrel and the steel ramrod has a button-shaped head. Sling swivels are mounted on the trigger guard and middle barrel band. **Overall length:** 56½″. **Weight:** 9¾ lbs.

1858 TWO-BAND ENFIELD RIFLE
$425.00

This 33-inch barrel version of the British Enfield is an exact copy of similar rifles used during the Civil War. The .58 caliber rifle sports a European walnut stock, deep blue-black finish on the barrel, bands, breech-plug tang and bayonet mount. The percussion lock is color casehardened and the rest of the furniture is brightly polished brass.

EMF REVOLVERS

SHERIFF'S MODEL 1851

SHERIFF'S MODEL 1851 REVOLVER
$140.00 (Brass) $172.00 (Steel)

SPECIFICATIONS
Caliber: 36 Percussion
Ball diameter: .376 round or conical, pure lead
Barrel length: 5″
Overall length: 10½″
Weight: 39 oz.
Sights: V-notch groove in hammer (rear); truncated cone in front
Percussion cap size: #11

MODEL 1860 ARMY REVOLVER
$145.00 (Brass) $200.00 (Steel)

SPECIFICATIONS
Caliber: 44 Percussion
Barrel length: 8″
Overall length: 13⅝″
Weight: 41 oz.
Frame: Casehardened
Finish: High-luster blue with walnut grips
Also available as a **cased set** with steel frame, wood case, flask and mold: **$375.00**

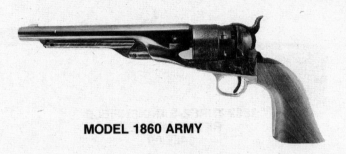

MODEL 1860 ARMY

SECOND MODEL 44 DRAGOON
$275.00

SPECIFICATIONS
Caliber: 44
Barrel length: 7½″ (round)
Overall length: 14″
Weight: 4 lbs.
Finish: Steel casehardened frame

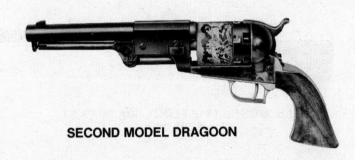

SECOND MODEL DRAGOON

MODEL 1862 POLICE REVOLVER
$200.00   ($150.00 Brass)

SPECIFICATIONS
Caliber: 36 Percussion
Capacity: 5-shot
Barrel length: 6½″
Also available as a steel **cased set: $294.00**

MODEL 1862 POLICE

EUROARMS OF AMERICA

COOK & BROTHER CONFEDERATE CARBINE
Model 2300: $378.00

Classic re-creation of the rare 1861, New Orleans-made Artillery Carbine. The lockplate is marked "Cook & Brother N.O. 1861" and is stamped with a Confederate flag at the rear of the hammer.

Caliber: 58 percussion
Barrel length: 24"
Overall length: 40 1/3"
Weight: 7 1/2 lbs.

Sights: Fixed blade front and adjustable dovetailed rear
Ramrod: Steel
Finish: Barrel is antique brown; buttplate, trigger guard, barrel bands, sling swivels and nose cap are polished brass; stock is walnut
Recommended ball sizes: .575 r.b., .577 Minie and .580 maxi; uses musket caps
Also available:
MODEL 2301 COOK & BROTHER FIELD with 33" barrel
Price: $549.60

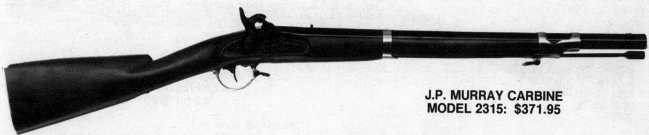

J.P. MURRAY CARBINE
MODEL 2315: $371.95

Replica of an extremely rare CSA Cavalry Carbine based on an 1841 design of parts and lock.

Caliber: 58 percussion
Barrel length: 23"
Features: Brass barrel bands and buttplate; oversized trigger guard; sling swivels

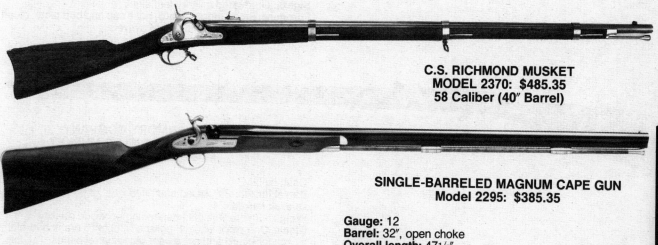

C.S. RICHMOND MUSKET
MODEL 2370: $485.35
58 Caliber (40" Barrel)

SINGLE-BARRELED MAGNUM CAPE GUN
Model 2295: $385.35

Euroarms of America offers a beautiful reproduction of a classic English-styled single-barreled shotgun. The lock is left in the white and displays a scroll engraving, as does the bow of the trigger guard. Uses #11 percussion caps and recommended wads are felt over powder and cardboard over shot.

Gauge: 12
Barrel: 32", open choke
Overall length: 47 1/2"
Weight: 7 1/2 lbs.
Stock: English style; European walnut with satin oil finish; moderate recoil, even with relatively heavy powder charges
Finish: Barrel, underrib, thimbles, nose cap, trigger guard and butt plate are deep, rich blue

BLACK POWDER

EUROARMS OF AMERICA

LONDON ARMORY COMPANY
2-BAND RIFLE MUSKET
Model 2270: $398.80

Caliber: 58 percussion
Barrel length: 33″, blued and rifled
Overall length: 49″
Weight: 8½ to 8¾ lbs., depending on wood density
Stock: One-piece walnut; polished "bright" brass butt plate, trigger guard and nose cap; blued barrel bands
Sights: Inverted 'V' front sight; Enfield folding ladder rear
Ramrod: Steel

LONDON ARMORY COMPANY
ENFIELD MUSKETOON
Model 2280: $371.95

Caliber: 58; Minie ball
Barrel length: 24″; round high-luster blued barrel
Overall length: 40½″
Weight: 7 to 7½ lbs., depending on density of wood
Stock: Seasoned walnut stock with sling swivels
Ramrod: Steel
Ignition: Heavy-duty percussion lock
Sights: Graduated military-leaf sight
Furniture: Brass trigger guard, nose cap and butt plate; blued barrel bands, lock plate, and swivels

LONDON ARMORY COMPANY
3-BAND ENFIELD RIFLED MUSKET
Model 2260: $424.40

Caliber: 58
Barrel length: 39″, blued and rifled
Overall length: 54″
Weight: 9½ to 9¾ lbs., depending on wood density
Stock: One-piece walnut; polished "bright" brass butt plate, trigger guard and nose cap; blued barrel bands
Ramrod: Steel; threaded end for accessories
Sights: Traditional Enfield folding ladder rear sight; inverted 'V' front sight
Also available:
MODEL 2261 with white barrel **$593.45**

EUROARMS OF AMERICA

1803 HARPERS FERRY FLINTLOCK RIFLE
Model 2305: $487.80

Caliber: 54 Flintlock
Barrel length: 33″, octagonal
Features: Walnut half stock with cheekpiece; browned barrel

1841 MISSISSIPPI RIFLE
Model 2310: $426.80

Caliber: 54 percussion
Barrel length: 33″, octagonal
Features: Walnut stock; brass barrel bands and buttplate;
sling swivels

1863 ZOUAVE RIFLE (2-Barrel Bands)
Model 2255: $436.60 (Range Grade)
Model 2250: $317.00 (Field Grade)

Caliber: 58 percussion
Barrel length: 33″, octagonal
Overall length: 48¹/₂″
Weight: 9¹/₂ to 9³/₄ lbs.
Sights: U.S. Military 3-leaf rear; blade front
Features: Two brass barrel bands; brass buttplate and nose
cap; sling swivels

1861 SPRINGFIELD RIFLE
Model 2360: $485.35

Caliber: 58 percussion
Barrel length: 40″
Features: 3 barrel bands

EUROARMS OF AMERICA

MODEL 1005

ROGERS & SPENCER REVOLVER
Model 1005: $207.30

Caliber: 44 Percussion; #11 percussion cap
Barrel length: 7¹/₂″
Sights: Integral rear sight notch groove in frame; brass truncated cone front sight
Overall length: 13³/₄″
Weight: 47 oz.
Finish: High gloss blue; flared walnut grip; solid frame design; precision-rifled barrel
Recommended ball diameter: .451 round or conical, pure lead

ROGERS & SPENCER ARMY REVOLVER
Model 1006 (Target): $218.30

Caliber: 44; takes .451 round or conical lead balls; #11 percussion cap
Weight: 47 oz.
Barrel length: 7¹/₂″
Overall length: 13³/₄″
Finish: High gloss blue; flared walnut grip; solid frame design; precision-rifled barrel
Sights: Rear fully adjustable for windage and elevation; ramp front sight

MODEL 1006

REMINGTON 1858
NEW MODEL ARMY ENGRAVED (Not shown)
Model 1040: $251.20

Classical 19th-century style scroll engraving on this 1858 Remington New Model revolver.

Caliber: 44 Percussion; #11 cap
Barrel length: 8″
Overall length: 14³/₄″
Weight: 41 oz.
Sights: Integral rear sight notch groove in frame; blade front sight
Recommended ball diameter: .451 round or conical, pure lead

ROGERS & SPENCER REVOLVER
LONDON GRAY (Not shown)
Model 1007: $224.40

Revolver is the same as Model 1005, except for London Gray finish, which is heat treated and buffed for rust resistance; same recommended ball size and percussion caps.

REMINGTON 1858
NEW MODEL ARMY REVOLVER
Model 1020: $195.10

This model is equipped with blued steel frame, brass trigger guard in 44 caliber.

Weight: 40 oz.
Barrel length: 8″
Overall length: 14³/₄″
Finish: Deep luster blue rifled barrel; polished walnut stock; brass trigger guard.
Also available:
MODEL 1010. Same as Model 1020, except with 6¹/₂″ barrel and in 36 caliber: **$195.10**

MODEL 1010
(36 Cal. w/6¹/₂″ barrel)

GONIC ARMS

MODEL GA-87 RIFLE
$493.38 Standard $526.06 Deluxe
$336.33 Kit

SPECIFICATIONS
Calibers: 30, 38, 44, 45, 50 Mag., 54 and 20 ga. smoothbore
Barrel length: 26″
Overall length: 43″
Weight: 6¹/₂ lbs.
Sights: Bead front; open rear (adjustable for windage and elevation); drilled and tapped for scope bases
Stock: American walnut (grey or brown laminated stock optional)

Length of pull: 14″
Trigger: Single stage (4-lb. pull)
Mechanism type: Closed-breech muzzleloader
Features: Ambidextrous safety; non-glare satin finish; newly designed loading system; all-weather performance guaranteed; faster lock time
Also available:
Brown or Grey Laminated Stock Models: $538.38 (Standard)

MODEL GA-90 PISTOL BARREL ASSEMBLY
Calibers 30, 38, 44, 45
$174.00 (16″ Barrel) $190.50 (24″ Barrel)
$209.00 Ignition System)

MODEL 93 MAGNUM RIFLE
$310.00

Gonic Arms' new blackpowder rifle has a unique loading system that produces better consistency and utilizes the full powder charge of the specially designed penetrator bullet (ballistics = 2650 foot-pounds at 1600 fps w/465-grain .500 bullet).

SPECIFICATIONS
Caliber: 50 Magnum
Barrel length: 26″

Overall length: 43″
Weight: 6 to 6¹/₂ lbs.
Sights: Open hunting sights (adjustable)
Features: Walnut stained hardwood stock; adjustable trigger; nipple wrench; drilled and tapped for scope bases; ballistics and instruction manual
Also available in stainless steel (price on request).

LYMAN

DEERSTALKER RIFLE
Percussion $339.95
Flintlock $359.95

Lyman's Deerstalker rifle incorporates many features most desired by muzzleloading hunters: higher comb for better sighting plane • non-glare hardware • 24″ octagonal barrel • casehardened side plate • Q.D. sling swivels • Lyman sight package (37MA beaded front; fully adjustable fold-down 16A rear) • walnut stock with 1/2″ black recoil pad • single trigger. Left-hand models available (same price). **Calibers:** 50 and 54, flintlock or percussion. **Weight:** 7 1/2 lbs.

DEERSTALKER CARBINE
Percussion $349.95
Flintlock $374.95

This carbine version of the famous Deerstalker Hunting Rifle is now available in 50 caliber percussion or flintlock and features a precision-rifled "stepped octagon" barrel with a 1 in 24″ twist for optimum performance with conical projectiles. The specially designed Lyman sight package features a fully adjustable Lyman 16A fold-down in the rear. The front sight is Lyman's 37MA white bead on an 18 ramp. Each rifle comes complete with a darkened nylon ramrod and modern sling and swivels set. Left-hand models available. **Weight:** 6 3/4 lbs.

GREAT PLAINS RIFLE
Percussion $409.95   (Kit $329.95)
Flintlock $439.95   (Kit $359.95)

The Great Plains Rifle has a 32-inch deep-grooved barrel and 1 in 66-inch twist to shoot patched round balls. Blued steel furniture including the thick steel wedge plates and steel toe plate; correct lock and hammer styling with coil spring dependability; and a walnut stock without a patch box. A Hawken-style trigger guard protects double-set triggers. Steel front sight and authentic buckhorn styling in an adjustable rear sight. Fixed primitive rear sight also included. Left-hand models available (same price). **Calibers:** 50 and 54.

LYMAN TRADE RIFLE
Percussion $309.95   (Kit $249.95)
Flintlock $339.95   (Kit $284.95)

The Lyman Trade Rifle features a 28-inch octagonal barrel, rifled one turn at 48 inches, designed to fire both patched round balls and the popular maxistyle conical bullets. Polished brass furniture with blued finish on steel parts; walnut stock; hook breech; single spring-loaded trigger; coil-spring percussion lock; fixed steel sights; adjustable rear sight for elevation also included. Steel barrel rib and ramrod ferrrule. **Caliber:** 50 or 54 percussion and flint. **Overall length:** 45″.

MITCHELL ARMS REVOLVERS

1851 COLT NAVY "WILD BILL HICKOK" MODEL

SPECIFICATIONS
Calibers: 36 and 44
Barrel length: 7½″ (brass or steel)
Frame: Polished solid brass or color case steel
Grips: Walnut
Price: **$225.00**

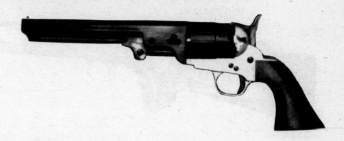

1860 COLT ARMY MODEL

SPECIFICATIONS
Caliber: 44
Barrel length: 7½″ (round rebated cylinder)
Weight: 2 lbs. 11 oz.
Frame: Steel
Grips: Walnut
Features: Detachable shoulder stock (optional)
Price: **$199.00**

Also available:
1861 COLT NAVY (36 or 44 cal.) **$225.00**
'51 NAVY SHERIFF'S MODEL (36 or 44 cal.) **225.00**

GENERAL CUSTER'S REMINGTON NEW MODEL ARMY

SPECIFICATIONS
Calibers: 36 and 44
Barrel length: 8″
Frame: Blued steel
Grips: Walnut
Features: Progressive rifling; brass trigger guard
Price: **$225.00**

REMINGTON "TEXAS" MODEL

SPECIFICATIONS
Calibers: 36 and 44
Barrel length: 8″ octagonal; blued steel
Frame: Bright brass
Grips: Walnut
Price: **$225.00**

MODERN MUZZLELOADING

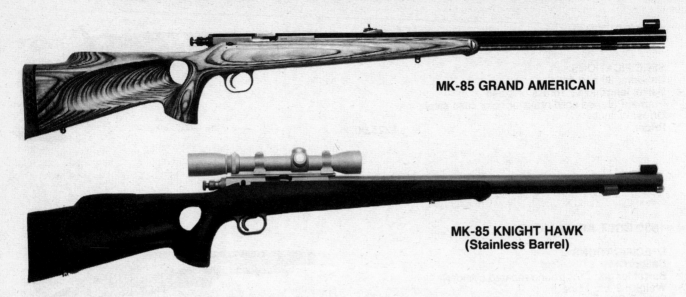

MK-85 GRAND AMERICAN

MK-85 KNIGHT HAWK
(Stainless Barrel)

MK-85 KNIGHT RIFLES

The MK-85 muzzleloading rifles (designed by William A. "Tony" Knight of Schuyler County, Missouri) are handcrafted, light-weight rifles capable of 1½-inch groups at 100 yards. They feature a one-piece, in-line bolt assembly, patented double safety system, Timney featherweight deluxe trigger system, recoil pad, and Lothar Walther barrels (1 in 32" twist in 50 and 54 caliber; 1 in 17" twist in 45 caliber).

SPECIFICATIONS
Calibers: 50 and 54
Barrel lengths: 20" and 24"
Overall length: 39" to 43"
Weight: 6 to 7¼ lbs.
Sights: Adjustable high-visibility open sights

Stock: Classic walnut, laminated, or composite
Features: Swivel studs installed; LS&B Perfect Memory nylon ramrod; combo tool; flush valve; hex keys, and more.
Prices:

MK-85 HUNTER (Walnut)	$ 529.95
MK-85 KNIGHT HAWK (24" Blued barrel)	619.95
Stainless barrel	729.95
MK-85 LIGHT KNIGHT (Walnut)	499.95
With Black Composite Stock	519.95
MK-85 PREDATOR (Stainless)	649.95
MK-85 STALKER (Laminated)	579.95
MK-85 GRAND AMERICAN (Blued barrel	
Shadow brown or black)	995.95
In Stainless Steel	1095.95

BK-92 BLACK KNIGHT

MODEL BK-92 BLACK KNIGHT
$349.95

SPECIFICATIONS
Calibers: 50 and 54
Barrel length: 24" (tapered non-glare w/open breech system)
Sights: Adjustable; tapped and drilled for scope mount
Stock: Black synthetic coated (see also below)

Features: Patented double safety system; in-line ignition system; 1 in 28" twist; stainless steel breech plug; adjustable trigger; ½" recoil pad; Knight precision loading ramrod; Monte Carlo stock
Also available:

With Hardwood stock	$379.95
With Composite stock	399.95

NAVY ARMS REVOLVERS

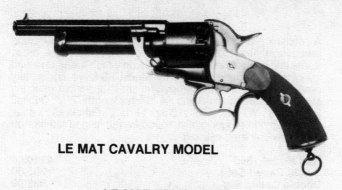

LE MAT CAVALRY MODEL

LE MAT NAVY MODEL

LE MAT REVOLVERS

Once the official sidearm of many Confederate cavalry officers, this 9 shot .44 caliber revolver with a central single shot barrel of approx. 65 caliber gave the cavalry man 10 shots to use against the enemy. **Barrel length:** 7⁵/₈″. **Overall length:** 14″. **Weight:** 3 lbs. 7 oz.

Cavalry Model	$595.00
Navy Model	595.00
Army Model	595.00

LE MAT ARMY MODEL

1862 POLICE MODEL

This is the last gun manufactured by the Colt Plant in the percussion era. It encompassed all the modifications of each gun starting from the early Paterson to the 1861 Navy. It was favored by the New York Poolice Dept. for many years. One-half fluted and rebated cylinder, 36 cal., 5 shot, .375 dia. ball, 18 grains of black powder, brass trigger guard and backstrap. Casehardened frame, loading lever and hammer—balance blue. **Barrel length:** 5¹/₂″.

1862 Police	$285.00
Law and Order Set	360.00

ROGERS & SPENCER REVOLVER

This revolver features a six-shot cylinder, octagonal barrel, hinged-type loading lever assembly, two-piece walnut grips, blued finish and case-hardened hammer and lever. **Caliber:** 44. **Barrel length:** 7¹/₂″. **Overall length:** 13³/₄″. **Weight:** 3 lbs.

Rogers & Spencer	$240.00
With satin finish	260.00

COLT WALKER 1847

The 1847 Walker replica comes in 44 caliber with a 9-inch barrel. **Weight:** 4 lbs. 8 oz. Well suited for the collector as well as the black powder shooter. Features include: rolled cylinder scene; blued and casehardened finish; and brass guard. Proof tested.

Colt Walker 1847	$260.00
Single Cased Set	385.00

ROGERS & SPENCER REVOLVER

NAVY ARMS REVOLVERS

REB MODEL 1860

A modern replica of the confederate Griswold & Gunnison percussion Army revolver. Rendered with a polished brass frame and a rifled steel barrel finished in a high-luster blue with genuine walnut grips. All Army Model 60's are completely proof-tested by the Italian government to the most exacting standards. **Calibers:** 36 and 44. **Barrel length:** 7¼". **Overall length:** 13". **Weight:** 2 lbs. 10 oz.-11 oz. **Finish:** Brass frame, backstrap and trigger guard, round barrel, hinged rammer on the 44 cal. rebated cylinder.

Reb Model 1860	$110.00
Single Cased Set	205.00
Double Cased Set	335.00
Kit	90.00

1851 NAVY "YANK"

Originally manufactured by Colt from 1850 through 1876, this model was the most popular of the Union revolvers, mostly because it was lighter and easier to handle than the Dragoon. **Barrel length:** 7½". **Overall length:** 14". **Weight:** 2 lbs. **Rec. ball diam.:** .375 R.B. (.451 in 44 cal) **Calibers:** 36 and 44. **Capacity:** 6 shot. **Features:** Steel frame, octagonal barrel, cylinder roll-engraved with Naval battle scene, backstrap and trigger guard are polished brass.

1851 Navy "Yank"	$145.00
Kit	120.00
Single Cased Set	245.00
Double Cased Set	405.00

These guns from the Colt line are 44 caliber and all six-shot. The cylinder was authentically roll engraved with a polished brass trigger guard and steel strap cut for shoulder stock. The frame, loading lever and hammer are finished in high-luster color case-hardening. Walnut grips. **Weight:** 2 lbs. 9 oz. **Barrel length:** 8". **Overall length:** 13⅝". **Caliber:** 44. **Finish:** Brass trigger guard, steel back strap, round barrel, creeping lever, rebated cylinder, engraved Navy scene. Frame cut for s/stock (4 screws).

1860 Army	$165.00
Single Cased Set	265.00
Double Cased Set	430.00
Kit	145.00

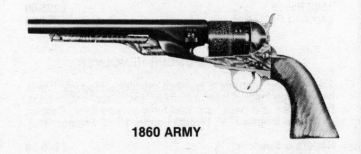

1860 ARMY

NAVY ARMS REVOLVERS

STAINLESS STEEL 1858 REMINGTON

Exactly like the standard 1858 Remington except that every part with the exception of the grips and trigger guard is manufactured from corrosion-resistant stainless steel. This gun has all the style and feel of its ancestor with all of the conveniences of stainless steel. **Caliber:** 44.

1858 Remington Stainless **$260.00**

TARGET MODEL REMINGTON REVOLVER

With its top strap solid frame, the Remington Percussion Revolver is considered the magnum of Civil War revolvers and is ideally suited to the heavy 44-caliber charges. Based on the Army Model, the target gun has target sights for controlled accuracy. Ruggedly built from modern steel and proof tested.

Remington Percussion Revolver **$200.00**

REMINGTON
NEW MODEL ARMY REVOLVER

REMINGTON NEW MODEL ARMY REVOLVER

This rugged, dependable, battle-proven Civil War veteran with its top strap and rugged frame was considered the magnum of C.W. revolvers, ideally suited for the heavy 44 charges. Blued finish. **Caliber:** 44. **Barrel length:** 8″. **Overall length:** 14¼″. **Weight:** 2 lbs. 8 oz.

Remington Army Revolver	**$160.00**
Single cased set	255.00
Double cased set	420.00
Kit	140.00

DELUXE 1858 REMINGTON-STYLE 44 CALIBER
(not shown)

Built to the exact dimensions and weight of the original Remington 44, this model features an 8″ barrel with progressive rifling, adjustable front sight for windage, all-steel construction with walnut stocks and silver-plated trigger guard. Steel is highly polished and finished in rich charcoal blue. **Barrel length:** 8″. **Overall length:** 14¼″. **Weight:** 2 lbs. 14 oz.

Deluxe 1858 Remington-Style 44 Cal. **$365.00**

ARMY 60 SHERIFF'S MODEL
(not shown)

A shortened version of the Army Model 60 Revolver. The Sheriff's model version became popular because the shortened barrel was fast out of the leather. This is actually the original snub nose, the predecessor of the detective specials or belly guns designed for quick-draw use. **Calibers:** 36 and 44.

Army 60 Sheriff's Model	**$110.00**
Kit	90.00

NAVY ARMS PISTOLS

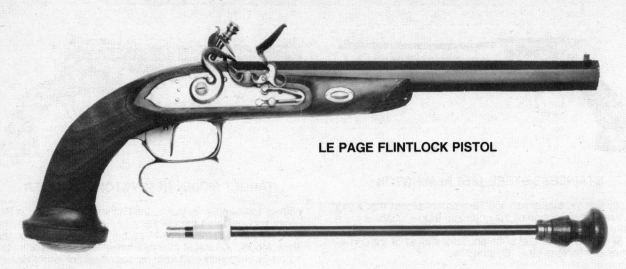

LE PAGE FLINTLOCK PISTOL

LE PAGE FLINTLOCK PISTOL
(44 Caliber)

The Le Page pistol is a beautifully hand-crafted reproduction featuring hand-checkered walnut stock with hinged buttcap and carved motif of a shell at the forward portion of the stock. Single-set trigger and highly polished steel lock and furniture together with a brown finished rifled barrel make this a highly desirable target pistol. **Barrel length:** 10½″. **Overall length:** 17″. **Weight:** 2 lbs. 2 oz.

Le Page Flintlock (rifled or smoothbore) **$550.00**

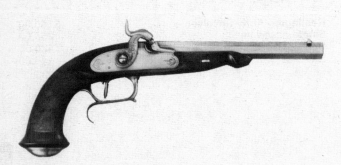

LE PAGE PERCUSSION PISTOL
(44 Caliber)

The tapered octagonal rifled barrel is in the traditional style with 7 lands and grooves. Fully adjustable single-set trigger. Engraved overall with traditional scrollwork. The European walnut stock is in the Boutet style. Spur-style trigger guard. Fully adjustable elevating rear sight. Dovetailed front sight adjustable for windage. **Barrel length:** 9″. **Overall length:** 15″. **Weight:** 2 lbs. 2 oz. **Rec. ball diameter:** 424 R.B.

Le Page Percussion **$475.00**

CASED LE PAGE PISTOL SETS

The case is French-fitted and the accessories are the finest quality to match.

Double Cased Flintlock Set **$1430.00**
French-fitted double-cased set comprising two Le Page pistols, turn screw, nipple key, oil bottle, cleaning brushes, leather covered flask and loading rod.

Double Cased Percussion Set **$1290.00**

Single Cased Flintlock Set **$760.00**
French-fitted single-cased set comprising one Le Page pistol, turn screw, nipple key, oil bottle, cleaning brushes, leather covered flask and loading rod.

Single Cased Percussion Set **$685.00**

NAVY ARMS PISTOLS

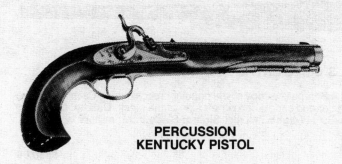

**PERCUSSION
KENTUCKY PISTOL**

**FLINTLOCK
KENTUCKY PISTOL**

KENTUCKY PISTOLS

The Kentucky Pistol is truly a historical American gun. It was carried during the Revolution by the Minutemen and was the sidearm of ''Andy'' Jackson in the Battle of New Orleans. Navy Arms Company has conducted extensive research to manufacture a pistol truly representative of its kind, with the balance and handle of the original for which it became famous.

Prices:

Flintlock	**$205.00**
Single Cased Flintlock Set	300.00
Double Cased Flintlock Set	515.00
Percussion	195.00
Single Cased Percussion Set	290.00
Double Cased Percussion Set	495.00

**HARPERS FERRY
FLINTLOCK PISTOL**

HARPERS FERRY PISTOLS

Of all the early American martial pistols, Harpers Ferry is one of the best known and was carried by both the Army and the Navy. Navy Arms Company has authentically reproduced the Harper's Ferry to the finest detail, providing a well-balanced and well-made pistol. **Weight:** 2 lbs. 9 oz. **Barrel length:** 10″. **Overall length:** 16″. **Caliber:** 58 smoothbore. **Finish:** Walnut stock; casehardened lock; brass-mounted browned barrel.

Harpers Ferry	**$265.00**

BLACK POWDER

NAVY ARMS RIFLES

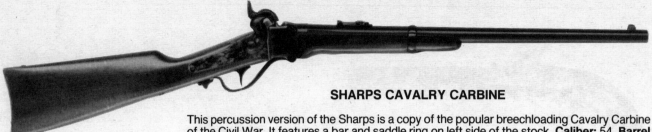

SHARPS CAVALRY CARBINE

This percussion version of the Sharps is a copy of the popular breechloading Cavalry Carbine of the Civil War. It features a bar and saddle ring on left side of the stock. **Caliber:** 54. **Barrel length:** 22″. **Overall length:** 39″. **Weight:** 7³/₄ lbs. **Sights:** Blade front; military ladder rear. **Stock:** Walnut.

Sharps Cavalry Carbine **$650.00**

1816 M.T. WICKHAM MUSKET

This version of the French 1777 Charleville musket was chosen by the U.S. Army in 1816 to replace the 1808 Springfield. Manufactured in Philadelphia by M.T. Wickham, it was one of the last contract models. **Caliber:** 69. **Barrel length:** 44¹/₂″. **Overall length:** 56¹/₄″. **Weight:** 10 lbs. **Sights:** Brass blade front. **Stock:** European walnut. **Feature:** Brass flashpan.

1816 M.T. Wickham Musket **$690.00**

MORTIMER FLINTLOCK RIFLE

This big-bore flintlock rifle, a former Gold Medal winner in the International Black Powder World Shoot, features a checkered stock (with cheekpiece), sling swivels, waterproof pan, roller frizzen and external safety. **Caliber:** 54. **Barrel length:** 36″. **Overall length:** 53″. **Weight:** 9 lbs. **Sights:** Blade front; notch rear. **Stock:** Walnut.

Mortimer Flintlock Rifle **$690.00**
   12 gauge drop-in barrel **285.00**

J.P. MURRAY CARBINE

Popular with the Confederate Cavalry, the J.P. Murray percussion carbine was originally manufactured in Columbus, Georgia, during the Civil War. **Caliber:** 58. **Barrel length:** 23¹/₂″. **Overall length:** 39¹/₄″. **Weight:** 8¹/₂ lbs. **Finish:** Walnut stock with polished brass.

J.P. Murray Carbine **$380.00**

NAVY ARMS RIFLES

1853 ENFIELD RIFLE MUSKET

The Enfield Rifle Musket marked the zenith in design and manufacture of the military percussion rifle and this perfection has been reproduced by Navy Arms Company. This and other Enfield muzzleloaders were the most coveted rifles of the Civil War, treasured by Union and Confederate troops alike for their fine quality and deadly accuracy. **Caliber:** 58. **Barrel length:** 39″. **Weight:** 10 lbs. 6 oz. **Overall length:** 55″. **Sights:** Fixed front; graduated rear. **Stock:** Seasoned walnut with solid brass furniture.

1853 Enfield Rifle Musket **$480.00**

1858 ENFIELD RIFLE

In the late 1850s the British Admiralty, after extensive experiments, settled on a pattern rifle with a 5-groove barrel of heavy construction, sighted to 1100 yards, designated the Naval rifle, Pattern 1858. **Caliber:** 58. **Barrel length:** 33″. **Weight:** 9 lbs. 10 oz. **Overall length:** 48.5″. **Sights:** Fixed front; graduated rear. **Stock:** Seasoned walnut with solid brass furniture.

1858 Enfield Rifle **$450.00**

1861 ENFIELD MUSKETOON

The 1861 Enfield Musketoon was the favorite long arm of the Confederate Cavalry. **Caliber:** 58. **Barrel length:** 24″. **Weight:** 7 lbs. 8 oz. **Overall length:** 40.25″. **Sights:** Fixed front; graduated rear. **Stock:** Seasoned walnut with solid brass furniture.

1861 Enfield Musketoon **$370.00**
Kit 345.00

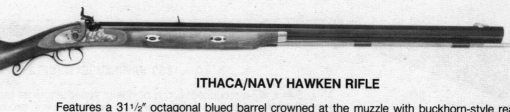

ITHACA/NAVY HAWKEN RIFLE

Features a 31½″ octagonal blued barrel crowned at the muzzle with buckhorn-style rear sight, blade front sight. Color casehardened percussion lock is fitted on walnut stock. Furniture is all steel and blued (except for nose cap and escutcheons). Available in 50 caliber only.

Ithaca/Navy Hawken Rifle **$400.00**
Kit 360.00

NAVY ARMS RIFLES

MISSISSIPPI RIFLE MODEL 1841

The historic percussion lock weapon that gained its name as a result of its performance in the hands of Jefferson Davis' Mississippi Regiment during the heroic stand at the Battle of Buena Vista. Also known as the "Yager" (a misspelling of the German Jaeger), this was one of the first percussion rifles adopted by Army Ordnance. The Mississippi is handsomely furnished in brass, including patch box for tools and spare parts. **Weight:** 9¹/₂ lbs. **Barrel length:** 32¹/₂". **Overall length:** 48¹/₂". **Calibers:** 54 and 58. **Finish:** Walnut finish stock, brass mounted.

Mississippi Rifle Model 1841 . . . . **$450.00**

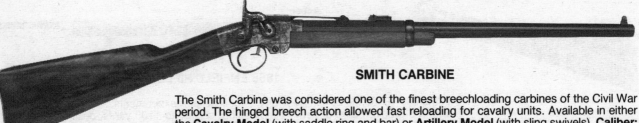

SMITH CARBINE

The Smith Carbine was considered one of the finest breechloading carbines of the Civil War period. The hinged breech action allowed fast reloading for cavalry units. Available in either the **Cavalry Model** (with saddle ring and bar) or **Artillery Model** (with sling swivels). **Caliber:** 50. **Barrel length:** 21¹/₂". **Overall length:** 39". **Weight:** 7³/₄ lbs. **Sights:** Brass blade front; folding ladder rear. **Stock:** American walnut.

Smith Carbine **$600.00**

1861 SPRINGFIELD RIFLE

One of the most popular Union rifles of the Civil War, the 1861 used the 1855-style hammer. The lockplate on this replica is marked "1861, U.S. Springfield." **Caliber:** 58. **Barrel length:** 40". **Overall length:** 56". **Weight:** 10 lbs. **Finish:** Walnut stock with polished metal lock and stock fitting.

1861 Springfield Rifle **$550.00**

1863 SPRINGFIELD RIFLE

An authentically reproduced replica of one of America's most historical firearms, the 1863 Springfield rifle features a full-size, three-band musket and precision-rifled barrel. **Caliber:** 58. **Barrel length:** 40". **Overall length:** 56". **Weight:** 9¹/₂ lbs. **Finish:** Walnut stock with polished metal lock and stock fittings. Casehardened lock available upon request.

1863 Springfield Rifle **$550.00**
Springfield Kit **450.00**

NAVY ARMS

JAPANESE MATCHLOCK

A favorite weapon of the Samurai warrior, the Matchlock was first introduced to Japan by the early traders from Portugal. It is now a recognized competition arm in the International Black Powder Championships. **Caliber:** 50. **Barrel length:** 41″. **Overall length:** 54¼″. **Weight:** 8½ lbs. **Sights:** Open.

Japanese Matchlock **$495.00**

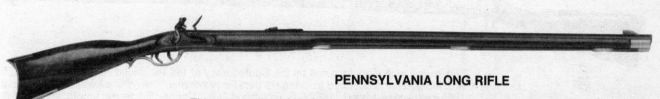

PENNSYLVANIA LONG RIFLE

This new version of the Pennsylvania Rifle is an authentic reproduction of the original model. Its classic lines are accented by the long, browned octagon barrel and polished lock plate. **Caliber:** 32 or 45 (flint or percussion. **Barrel length:** 40½″. **Overall length:** 56½″. **Weight:** 7½ lbs. **Sights:** Blade front; adjustable Buckhorn rear. **Stock:** Walnut.

Pennsylvania Long Rifle Flintlock **$410.00**
Percussion **395.00**

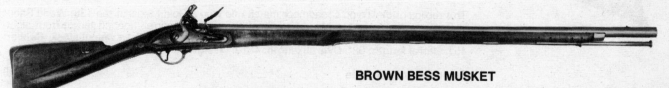

BROWN BESS MUSKET

Used extensively in the French and Indian War, the Brown Bess Musket proved itself in the American Revolution as well. This fine replica of the "Second Model" is marked "Grice" on the lock plate. **Caliber:** 75. **Barrel length:** 42″. **Overall length:** 59″. **Weight:** 9½ lbs. **Sights:** Lug front. **Stock:** Walnut.

Brown Bess Musket **$635.00**

BROWN BESS CARBINE (not shown)

Caliber: 75. **Barrel length:** 30″. **Overall length:** 47″. **Weight:** 7¾ lbs.
Brown Bess Carbine **$635.00**

Also available: **Economy Brown Bess** **490.00**

BLACK POWDER

NAVY ARMS RIFLES

1803 HARPERS FERRY RIFLE

This 1803 Harpers Ferry rifle was carried by Lewis and Clark on their expedition to explore the Northwest territory. This replica of the first rifled U.S. Martial flintlock features a browned barrel, casehardened lock and a brass patch box. **Caliber:** 54. **Barrel length:** 35″. **Overall length:** 50½″. **Weight:** 8½ lbs.

1803 Harpers Ferry Rifle **$555.00**

1862 C.S. RICHMOND RIFLE

This model was manufactured by the Confederacy at the Richmond Armory utilizing 1855 Rifle Musket parts captured from the Harpers Ferry Arsenal. This replica features the unusual 1855 lockplate, stamped "1862 C.S. Richmond, V.A." **Caliber:** 58. **Barrel length:** 40″. **Overall length:** 56″. **Weight:** 10 lbs. **Finish:** Walnut stock with polished metal lock and stock fittings.

1862 C.S. Richmond Rifle **$550.00**

TRYON CREEDMOOR RIFLE

This replica of the Tryon Creedmoor match rifle won a Gold Medal at the 13th World Shoot in Germany. It features a blued octagonal heavy match barrel, hooded target front sight, adjustable Vernier tang sight, double-set triggers, sling swivels and a walnut stock. **Caliber:** 451. **Barrel length:** 33″. **Overall length:** 48¼″. **Weight:** 9½ lbs.

Tryon Creedmoor Rifle **$680.00**

MODEL 1860 BRASS TELESCOPIC SIGHT

First used by snipers during the Civil War, this telescopic sight later became popular with hunters and target shooters in the late 19th century. It is available in the standard 32½″ length (shown mounted on a NO. 2 Creedmoor rifle) and a new compact 18″ version. Coated optics, 4 power. Mounts included.

Standard Model **$125.00**
Compact Model **130.00**

NAVY ARMS SHOTGUNS

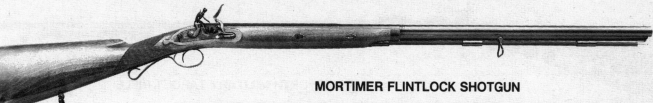

MORTIMER FLINTLOCK SHOTGUN

This replica of the Mortimer Shotgun features a browned barrel, casehardened furniture, sling swivels and checkered walnut stock. The lock contains waterproof pan, roller frizzen and external safety. **Gauge:** 12. **Barrel length:** 36″. **Overall length:** 53″. **Weight:** 7 lbs.

Mortimer Flintlock Shotgun **$670.00**

STEEL SHOT MAGNUM SHOTGUN

This shotgun, designed for the hunter who must use steel shot, features engraved polished lock plates, English-style checkered walnut stock (with cheekpiece) and chrome-lined barrels. **Gauge:** 10. **Barrel length:** 28″. **Overall length:** 45½″. **Weight:** 7 lbs. 9 oz. **Choke:** Cylinder/Cylinder.

Steel Shot Magnum Shotgun **$510.00**

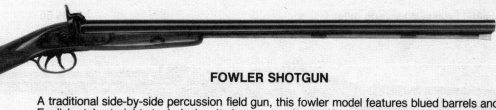

FOWLER SHOTGUN

A traditional side-by-side percussion field gun, this fowler model features blued barrels and English-style straight stock design. It also sports a hooked breech, engraved and color casehardened locks, double triggers and checkered walnut stock. **Gauge:** 12. **Chokes:** Cylinder/Cylinder. **Barrel length:** 28″. **Overall length:** 44½″. **Weight:** 7½ lbs.

Fowler Shotgun **$325.00**

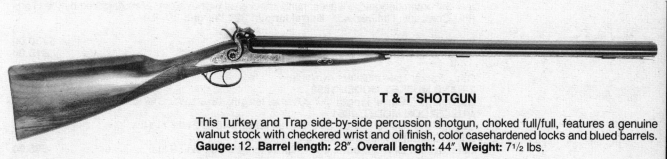

T & T SHOTGUN

This Turkey and Trap side-by-side percussion shotgun, choked full/full, features a genuine walnut stock with checkered wrist and oil finish, color casehardened locks and blued barrels. **Gauge:** 12. **Barrel length:** 28″. **Overall length:** 44″. **Weight:** 7½ lbs.

T & T Shotgun **$480.00**

BLACK POWDER

PARKER-HALE RIFLES

WHITWORTH MILITARY TARGET RIFLE

Recreation of Sir Joseph Whitworth's deadly and successful sniper and target weapon of the mid-1800s. Devised with a hexagonal bore with a pitch of 1 turn in 20 inches. Barrel is cold-forged from ordnance steel, reducing the build-up of black powder fouling. Globe front sight; open military target rifle rear sight has interchangeable blades of different heights. Walnut stock is hand-checkered. Manufactured by the Gibbs Rifle Company. **Caliber:** 451. **Barrel length:** 36″. **Weight:** 9¹/₂ lbs.

Whitworth Military Target Rifle **$815.00**

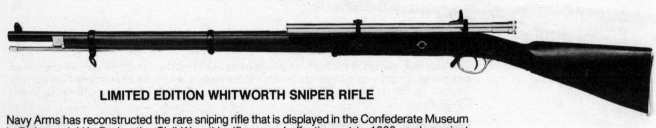

LIMITED EDITION WHITWORTH SNIPER RIFLE

Navy Arms has reconstructed the rare sniping rifle that is displayed in the Confederate Museum in Richmond, VA. During the Civil War, this rifle proved effective out to 1000 yards against Union troops. The scope mount has been altered slightly to permit offhand shooting, but it is virtually identical to the original. Manufactured by the Gibbs Rifle Company. **Caliber:** 451. **Barrel length:** 36″. **Overall length:** 52¹/₂″. **Weight:** 11 lbs.

Limited Edition Whitworth Rifle **$995.00**

VOLUNTEER RIFLE

Originally designed by Irish gunmaker William John Rigby, this relatively small-caliber rifle was issued to volunteer regiments during the 1860s. Today it is rifled by the cold-forged method, making one turn in 20 inches. Sights are adjustable: globe front and ladder-type rear with interchangeable leaves; hand-checkered walnut stock. Manufactured by the Gibbs Rifle Company. **Caliber:** 451. **Barrel length:** 32″. **Weight:** 9¹/₂ lbs.

Volunteer Rifle **$750.00**
    Same as above with 3-band barrel 815.00

Other Parker-Hale muskets available:
2-BAND MUSKET MODEL 1858
Caliber: 577. **Barrel length:** 33″. **Overall length:** 48¹/₂″. **Wt.:** 8¹/₂ lbs. **$550.00**
MUSKETOON MODEL 1861
Caliber: 577. **Barrel length:** 24″. **Overall length:** 40¹/₄″. **Wt.:** 7¹/₂ lbs. 450.00
3-BAND MUSKET MODEL 1853
Caliber: 577. **Barrel length:** 39″. **Overall length:** 55″. **Wt.:** 9 lbs. 585.00

PARKER-HALE RIFLES

1853 ENFIELD RIFLE

Commonly known as the 3-band Enfield, this is a high-quality replica of the 1853 Enfield rifle musket that was manufactured between 1853 and 1863 by various British contractors. Manufactured today by the Gibbs Rifle Company. **Caliber:** 577. **Barrel length:** 39″. **Overall length:** 55″. **Weight:** 9 lbs. **Rate of twist:** 1:48″; 3-groove barrel.

1853 Enfield Rifle **$585.00**

1858 ENFIELD RIFLE

One of the most accurate military rifles of the percussion era, the 1858 two-band Enfield was developed for the British Admiralty in the late 1850s. This replica of the Enfield Naval Pattern rifle has won many blackpowder national and world championships. Manufactured by the Gibbs Rifle Company. **Caliber:** 577. **Barrel length:** 33″. **Overall length:** 48¹/₂″. **Weight:** 8¹/₂ lbs. **Rate of twist:** 1:48″, 5-groove barrel.

1858 Enfield Rifle **$550.00**

1861 ENFIELD MUSKETOON

The British 1861 Musketoon was very popular with Confederate Cavalry and Artillery units. This reproduction, like all the Parker-Hale replicas, is constructed using the original 130-year-old gauges for authentic reference. Manufactured by the Gibbs Rifle Company. **Caliber:** 577. **Barrel length:** 24″. **Overall length:** 40¹/₄″. **Weight:** 7¹/₂ lbs. **Rate of twist:** 1:48″; 5-groove barrel.

1861 Enfield Musketoon **$450.00**

SHILOH SHARPS

MODEL 1874 BUSINESS RIFLE
$875.00

Calibers: 45-70, 45-90, 45-120, 50-70, 50-90 and 50-140. **Barrel:** 28-inch heavy-tapered round; dark blue. Double-set triggers adjustable set. **Sights:** Blade front, and sporting rear with leaf. Buttstock is straight grip rifle butt plate, forend sporting schnabel style. Receiver group and butt plate case-colored; wood is American walnut oil-finished. **Weight:** 9 lbs. 8 oz.

Also available:
MODEL 1874 SADDLE RIFLE w/26″ tapered octagonal barrel **$925.00**

MODEL 1874 MILITARY RIFLE
$995.00

Calibers: 45-70 and 50-70. **Barrel:** 30-inch round; dark blue. Blade front and Lawrence-style sights. Military-style forend with 3 barrel bands and 1¼-inch swivels. Receiver group, butt plate and barrel bands case-colored. Wood is oil finished. **Weight:** 8 lbs. 2 oz.

Also available:
1874 MILITARY CARBINE w/22″ round barrel. **Weight:** 7 lbs. 8 oz.   **$925.00**

SHILOH SHARPS RIFLE CARTRIDGE AVAILABILITY TABLE

MODEL	30–40	38–55	38–56	40–50 1¹¹⁄₁₆ B.N.	40–70 2¹⁄₁₀ B.N.	40–70 2¹⁄₄ B.N.	40–70 ST	40–90 ST	40–90 2⁵⁄₈ B.N.	44–77 B.N.	40–90 B.N.	45–70 2¹⁄₁₀ ST	45–90 2⁴⁄₁₀ ST	45–100 2⁶⁄₁₀ ST	45–110 2⁷⁄₈ ST	45–120 3¹⁄₄ ST	50–70 1³⁄₄ ST	50–100 2¹⁄₂ ST	40–65 WIN	40–60 Maynard ST
Long Range Express	X	X	X	X	X	X	X	X	X	X	X	X	X	X	X	X	X	X	X	X
No. 1 Sporting Rifle	X	X	X	X	X	X	X	X	X	X	X	X	X	X	X	X	X	X	X	X
No. 3 Sporting Rifle	X	X	X	X	X	X	X	X	X	X	X	X	X	X	X	X	X	X	X	X
Business Rifle	X	X	X	X	X	X	X	X	X	X	X	X	X	X	X	X	X	X	X	X
Carbine, Civ.	X	X	X	X	X	X						X	X				X	X		
1874 Military Rifle	X	X	X	X	X	X						X	X				X	X		X
1874 Saddle Rifle	X	X	X	X	X	X	X	X	X	X		X	X				X	X		X
1874 Military Carbine	X	X	X	X	X	X						X	X				X	X		X
Montana Roughrider	X	X	X	X	X	X	X	X	X	X	X	X	X	X	X	X	X	X	X	X
Hartford Model Rifle	X	X	X	X	X	X	X	X	X	X	X	X	X	X	X	X	X	X	X	X

B.N.-Bottleneck   ST-Straight

SHILOH SHARPS

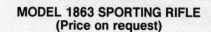

MODEL 1863 SPORTING RIFLE
(Price on request)

Caliber: 54. **Barrel:** 30″ tapered octagonal. Blade front sight, sporting rear with elevation leaf; double-set triggers with adjustable set; curved trigger plate, pistol grip buttstock with steel butt plate, schnabel-style forend; optional Tang sight. **Weight:** 9 lbs.
Also available:
MODEL 1863 PERCUSSION MILITARY RIFLE . . . . **Price on request**
MODEL 1863 PERCUSSION MILITARY CARBINE . . . . **Price on request**

MODEL 1874 SPORTING RIFLE NO. 1
$970.00

Calibers: 45-70, 45-90, 45-120, 50-70, 50-90 and 50-140. Features 28-inch or 30-inch tapered octagon barrel. Double-set triggers with adjustable set, blade front sight, sporting rear with elevation leaf and sporting tang sight adjustable for elevation and windage. Buttstock is pistol grip, shotgun butt, sporting forend style. Receiver group and butt plate case colored. Barrel is high finish blue-black; wood is American walnut oil finish. **Weight:** 10 lbs.

MODEL 1874 SPORTING RIFLE NO. 3
$870.00

Calibers: 45-70, 45-90, 45-120, 50-70, 50-90 and 50-140. **Barrel:** 30-inch tapered octagonal; with high finish blue-black. Double-set triggers with adjustable set, blade front sight, sporting rear with elevation leaf and sporting tang sight adjustable for elevation and windage. Buttstock is straight grip with rifle butt plate; trigger plate is curved and checkered to match pistol grip. Forend is sporting schnabel style. Receiver group and butt plate is case colored. Wood is American walnut oil-finished. **Weight:** 9 lbs. 8 oz.
Also available:
MODEL 1874 LONG RANGE EXPRESS . . . . $ 995.00
MODEL 1874 ROUGHRIDER 870.00
  With Semi-fancy Wood 950.00
HARTFORD MODEL 1033.00

MODEL 1874 CARBINE "CIVILIAN"
$895.00

Calibers: 45-70 and 45-90. **Barrel:** 24-inch round; dark blue. Single trigger, blade front and sporting rear sight, buttstock straight grip, steel rifle butt plate, forend sporting schnabel style. Case-colored receiver group and butt plate; wood has oil finish. **Weight:** 8 lbs. 4 oz.

BLACK POWDER

THOMPSON/CENTER

PENNSYLVANIA HUNTER

The 31" barrel on this model is cut rifled (.010" deep) with 1 turn in 66" twist. Its outer contour is stepped from octagon to round. Sights are fully adjustable for both windage and elevation. Stocked with select American black walnut; metal hardware is blued steel. Features a hooked breech system and coil spring lock. **Caliber:** 50. **Overall length:** 48". **Weight:** Approx. 7.6 lbs.

Pennsylvania Hunter Caplock $320.00
Pennsylvania Hunter Flintlock 335.00

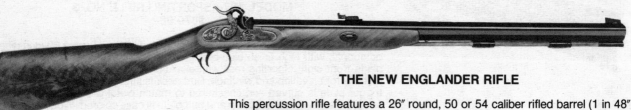

PENNSYLVANIA HUNTER CARBINE

Thompson/Center's new Pennsylvania Hunter Carbine is a 50-caliber carbine with 1:66" twist and cut-rifling. It was designed specifically for the hunter who uses patched round balls only and hunts in thick cover or brush. The 21" barrel is stepped from octagonal to round. **Overall length:** 38". **Weight:** 6½ lbs. **Sights:** Fully adjustable open hunting-style rear with bead front. **Stock:** Select American walnut. **Trigger:** Single hunting-style trigger. **Lock:** Color cased, coil spring, with floral design.

Pennsylvania Hunter Carbine Caplock $310.00
Pennsylvania Hunter Carbine Flintlock 325.00

THE NEW ENGLANDER RIFLE

This percussion rifle features a 26" round, 50 or 54 caliber rifled barrel (1 in 48" twist). **Weight:** 7 lbs. 15 oz.

New Englander Rifle $270.00
   With Rynite stock (24" barrel, right-hand only) 255.00
Left-Hand Model 290.00

THE NEW ENGLANDER SHOTGUN

This 12-gauge muzzleloading percussion shotgun weighs only 5 lbs. 2 oz. It features a 28-inch (screw-in full choke) round barrel and is stocked with selected American black walnut.

New Englander Shotgun $290.00
   With Rynite stock (26" barrel, right-hand only) 275.00
Left-Hand Model 310.00

THOMPSON/CENTER

THE HAWKEN
45, 50 and 54 caliber

Similar to the famous Rocky Mountain rifles made during the early 1800's, the Hawken is intended for serious shooting. Button-rifled for ultimate precision, the Hawken is available in 45, 50 or 54 caliber, flintlock or percussion. It features a hooked breech, double-set triggers, first-grade American walnut stock, adjustable hunting sights, solid brass trim and color casehardened lock. Beautifully decorated. **Weight:** Approx. 8½ lbs.

Hawken Caplock 45, 50 or 54 caliber	**$375.00**
Hawken Flintlock 50 caliber	**385.00**
Kit: Caplock	**275.00**
Kit: Flintlock	**295.00**

WHITE MOUNTAIN CAPLOCK CARBINE

WHITE MOUNTAIN CARBINE

This hunter's rifle with single trigger features a wide trigger guard bow that allows the shooter to fire the rifle in cold weather without removing his gloves. Its stock is of select American black walnut finished off with a rifle-type rubber recoil pad, and equipped with swivel studs and quick detachable sling swivels. A soft leather hunting-style sling is included. The barrel is stepped from octagonal to round. **Calibers:** 45, 50 and 54 (Hawken or Renegade loads). **Barrel length:** 21″. **Overall length:** 38″. **Weight:** 6½ lbs. **Sights:** Open hunting (Patridge) style, fully adjustable. **Lock:** Heavy-duty coil springs; decorated with floral design and color-cased. **Breech:** Hooked breech system.

White Mountain Carbine–Caplock (right-hand only)	**$335.00**
White Mountain Carbine–Flintlock (right-hand only)	**355.00**

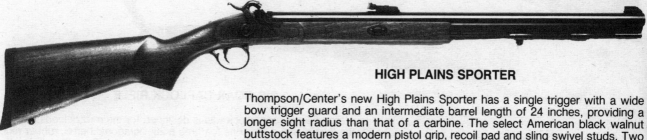

HIGH PLAINS SPORTER

Thompson/Center's new High Plains Sporter has a single trigger with a wide bow trigger guard and an intermediate barrel length of 24 inches, providing a longer sight radius than that of a carbine. The select American black walnut buttstock features a modern pistol grip, recoil pad and sling swivel studs. Two models are available: one with fully adjustable open hunting-style rear sight and the other with T/C's hunting-style tang peep sight. **Overall length:** 41″. **Weight:** 7 lbs. **Lock:** Heavy-duty coil springs; decorated with floral design and color cased.

High Plains Sporter (w/open hunting-style rear sight)	**$340.00**
High Plains Sporter (w/hunting-style tang peep sight)	**345.00**

BLACK POWDER

THOMPSON/CENTER

THE RENEGADE

Available in 50 or 54 caliber percussion, the Renegade was designed to provide maximum accuracy and maximum shocking power. It is constructed of superior modern steel with investment cast parts fitted to an American walnut stock, featuring a precision-rifled (26-inch carbine-type) octagonal barrel, hooked-breech system, coil spring lock, double-set triggers, adjustable hunting sights and steel trim. **Weight:** Approx. 8 lbs.

Renegade Caplock 50 and 54 caliber $335.00
Renegade Caplock Left Hand 345.00
Renegade Caplock Kit (right-hand) 245.00
Renegade Flintlock 50 caliber (R.H. only) 345.00

RENEGADE SINGLE TRIGGER HUNTER
50 and 54 Caliber

This single trigger hunter model, fashioned after the double triggered Renegade, features a large bow in the shotgun-style trigger guard. This allows shooters to fire the rifle in cold weather without removing their gloves. The octagon barrel measures 26″ and the stock is made of select American walnut. **Weight:** About 8 pounds.

Renegade Hunter $310.00

BIG BOAR CAPLOCK RIFLE

This new large 58 caliber caplock rifle is designed for the muzzleloading hunter who prefers larger game. The rifle features a 26″ octagonal barrel, rubber recoil pad, leather sling with QD sling swivels, and an adjustable open-style hunting rear sight with bead front sight. Stock is American black walnut.

Big Boar Caplock $340.00

THOMPSON/CENTER

SCOUT CARBINE with Rynite Stock

SCOUT CARBINE & PISTOL

Thompson/Center's new Scout Carbine & Pistol introduces a new "in-line ignition system" with a special vented breech plug that produces constant pressures from shot to shot, thereby improving accuracy. The patented trigger mechanism consists of only two moving parts—the trigger and the hammer—thus providing ease of operation and low maintenance. Both the carbine and pistol are available in 50 and 54 caliber. The carbine's 21″ barrel and the pistol's 12″ barrel are easily removable and readily interchangeable in either caliber. Their lines are reminiscent of the saddle guns and pistols of the "Old West," combining modern-day engineering with the flavor of the past. Both are suitable for left-hand shooters.

Scout Carbine	$395.00
Scout Carbine with Rynite Stock	295.00
Scout Pistol	315.00

THUNDER HAWK

THUNDER HAWK

Thompson/Center introduces a new in-line caplock rifle, the Thunder Hawk, which combines the features of an old-time caplock with the look and balance of a modern bolt-action rifle. The in-line ignition system ensures fast, positive ignition, plus an adjustable trigger for a crisp trigger pull. The 21″ barrel has an adjustable rear sight and bead-style front sight (barrel is drilled and tapped to accept T/C's Thunder Hawk scope rings or Quick Release Mounting System). The stock is American black walnut with rubber recoil pad and sling swivel studs. Rifling is 1 in 38″ twist, designed to fire patched round balls, conventional conical projectiles and sabot bullets. **Weight:** Approx. 6³/₄ lbs.

Thunder Hawk $275.00

GREY HAWK

GREY HAWK

T/C's new Grey Hawk is a stainless steel caplock rifle with a Rynite buttstock and a round 24″ barrel. It also features a stainless steel lock plate, hammer, thimble and trigger guard. Adjustable rear sight and bead-style front sight are blued. **Weight:** Approx. 7 lbs.

Grey Hawk $275.00

TRADITIONS

PIONEER PISTOL

PIONEER PISTOL
$169.00   ($119.00 Kit)

SPECIFICATIONS
Caliber: 45 percussion
Barrel length: 9⁵/₈″ octagonal with tenon; ¹³/₁₆″ across flats, rifled 1 in 16″; hooked breech
Overall length: 15″
Weight: 2³/₄ lbs.
Sights: Blade front; fixed rear
Trigger: Single
Stock: Beech
Lock: V-type mainspring
Features: German silver furniture; blackened hardware

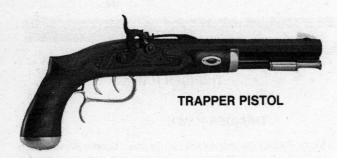

TRAPPER PISTOL

TRAPPER PISTOL
$170.00   ($130.00 Kit)

SPECIFICATIONS
Calibers: 45 and 50 percussion
Barrel length: 9³/₄″; octagonal (⁷/₈″ across flats) with tenon
Overall length: 16″
Weight: 2¹/₂ lbs.
Stock: Beech
Lock: Adjustable sear engagement with fly and bridle
Triggers: Double set, will fire set and unset
Sights: Primitive-style adjustable rear; brass blade front
Furniture: Solid brass; blued steel on assembled pistol

WILLIAM PARKER PISTOL
$252.00

SPECIFICATIONS
Calibers: 45 and 50 percussion
Barrel length: 10³/₈″ octagonal (¹⁵/₁₆″ across flats)
Overall length: 17¹/₂″
Weight: 2¹/₂ lbs.
Sights: Brass blade front; fixed rear
Stock: Walnut, checkered at wrist
Triggers: Double set; will fire set and unset
Lock: Adjustable sear engagement with fly and bridle; V-type mainspring
Features: Brass percussion cap guard; polished hardware, brass inlays and separate ramrod

WILLIAM PARKER PISTOL

TRADITIONS

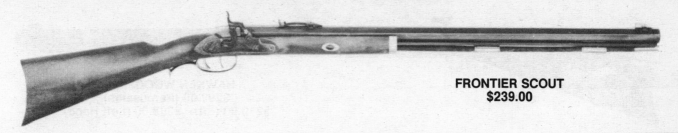

FRONTIER SCOUT
$239.00

SPECIFICATIONS
Calibers: 36, 45 and 50 percussion
Barrel length: 24″ (36 caliber); 26″ (45 and 50 caliber); octagonal (⁷⁄₈″ across flats) with tenon; rifled 1:48″ (36 cal.) and 1:66″ (45 and 50 cal.); hooked breech
Overall length: 39¹⁄₈″ (36 caliber); 41¹⁄₈″ (45 and 50 caliber)

Weight: 6 lbs.
Length of pull: 12¹⁄₄″
Sights: Primitive, adjustable rear, brass blade front
Stock: Beech
Lock: Adjustable sear engagement with fly and bridle
Furniture: Solid brass, blued steel

WHITETAIL RIFLE

WHITETAIL CARBINE

WHITETAIL RIFLE & CARBINE
$257.00 (Percussion)
$274.00 (Flintlock)

SPECIFICATIONS
Caliber: 50 flintlock or percussion
Barrel length: 26″ (rifle); 21″ (carbine); ¹⁵⁄₁₆″ octagonal tapering to round
Overall length: 39¹⁄₄″ (rifle); 36″ (carbine)

Weight: 5 lbs. 14 oz. (rifle); 5 lbs. 12 oz. (carbine)
Sights: Hunting-style rear, click adjustable for windage and elevation; beaded blade front with fluorescent dot
Trigger: Single
Stock: Select hardwood w/walnut stain, rubber recoil pad
Features: Sling swivels; oversized trigger guard; inletted wedge plates; engraved and color casehardened lock
Also available:
Synthetic Stock/Stainless Steel Barrel Model
Flintlock Rifle **$337.00**
Percussion Rifle **290.00**
Percussion Carbine **320.00**

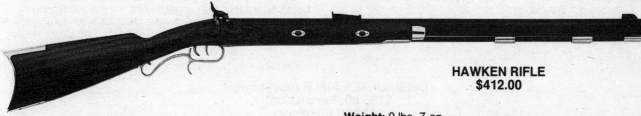

HAWKEN RIFLE
$412.00

SPECIFICATIONS
Calibers: 50 and 54 percussion
Barrel length: 32¹⁄₄″; octagonal (1″ across flats w/2 tenons); 1:66″ twist
Overall length: 50″

Weight: 9 lbs. 7 oz.
Lock: Adjustable sear engagement with fly and bridle
Stock: Walnut, beavertail cheekpiece
Triggers: Double set; will fire set and unset
Sights: Beaded blade front; hunting-style rear adjustable for windage and elevation
Furniture: Solid brass, blued steel; ornamentation on reverse side

BLACK POWDER

TRADITIONS

HAWKEN WOODSMAN
$292.00 (Percussion)
$210.00 (Kit) $309.00 (Left Hand)

SPECIFICATIONS
Calibers: 50 and 54 percussion
Barrel length: 28″ (octagonal); hooked breech; rifled 1 turn in 66″
Overall length: 45³/₄″
Weight: 7 lbs. 6 oz.

Triggers: Double set; will fire set or unset
Lock: Adjustable sear engagement with fly and bridle
Stock: Beech
Sights: Beaded blade front; hunting-style rear, fully screw adjustable for windage and elevation
Furniture: Solid brass, blued steel; unbreakable ramrod

PENNSYLVANIA RIFLE
$495.00 (Flintlock)
$467.00 (Percussion)

SPECIFICATIONS
Calibers: 45 and 50
Barrel length: 40¹/₄″; octagonal (⁷/₈″ across flats) with 3 tenons; rifled 1 turn in 66″
Overall length: 57¹/₂″

Weight: 9 lbs.
Lock: Adjustable sear engagement with fly and bridle
Stock: Walnut, beavertail style
Triggers: Double set; will fire set and unset
Sights: Primitive-style adjustable rear; brass blade front
Furniture: Solid brass, blued steel

PIONEER RIFLE & CARBINE
$227.00

SPECIFICATIONS
Calibers: 50 and 54 percussion (rifle only)
Barrel length: Carbine—24″ (1:32″); Rifle—27¹/₄″ (1:48″ or 1:66″), octagonal w/tenon
Overall length: 40³/₄″ (carbine); 44″ (rifle)
Weight: 6 lbs. 10 oz. (carbine); 7 lbs. (rifle)

Trigger: Sear adjustable
Stock: Beech
Sights: Buckhorn rear with elevation ramp, ajustable for windage and elevation; German silver blade front
Lock: Adjustable sear engagement; V-type mainspring
Features: Blackened hardware; German silver furniture; unbreakable ramrod

DEERHUNTER RIFLE (not shown)
$165.00 (Percussion)
$182.00 (Flintlock)
$149.00 (Percussion Kit)

SPECIFICATIONS
Caliber: 50
Barrel length: 26″ octagonal
Rifling twist: 1:48″ (percussion only); 1:66″ (flint or percussion)
Overall length: 39¹/₄″

Weight: 5 lbs. 14 oz.
Trigger: Single
Sights: Fixed rear; blade front
Features: Wooden ramrod; blackened furniture; inletted wedge plates

TRADITIONS

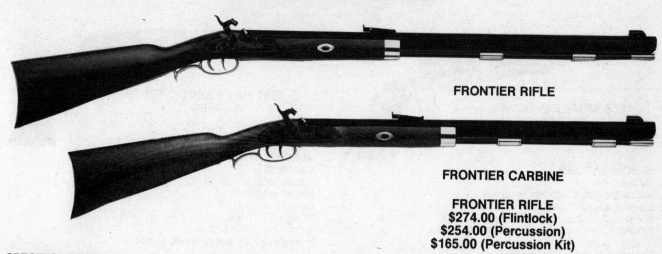

FRONTIER RIFLE

FRONTIER CARBINE

FRONTIER RIFLE
$274.00 (Flintlock)
$254.00 (Percussion)
$165.00 (Percussion Kit)

SPECIFICATIONS
Caliber: 50
Barrel length: 28″ octagonal (15/16″ across flats) with tenon; hooked breech, rifled 1 turn in 66″ (1 turn in 48″ optional)
Overall length: 44¾″
Weight: 7 lbs. 5 oz.
Lock: Adjustable sear engagement with fly and bridle
Triggers: Double set; will fire set and unset
Stock: Beech

Sights: Beaded blade front; hunting-style rear, adjustable for windage and elevation
Furniture: Solid brass, blued steel

Also available:
FRONTIER CARBINE with 24″ barrel (1:66″ or 1:32″ twist), 40½″ overall length; weight 6½ lbs.; percussion only in 50 caliber. **Price:** **$254.00**

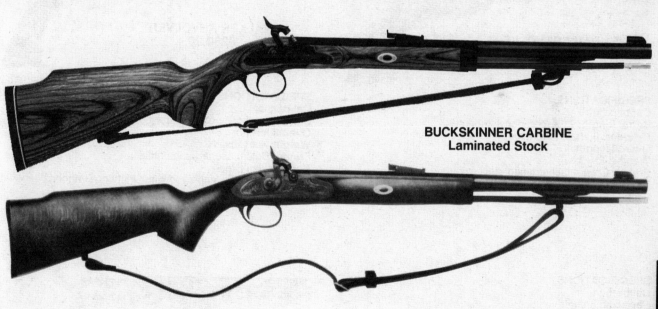

BUCKSKINNER CARBINE
Laminated Stock

BUCKSKINNER CARBINE
$290.00 (Flintlock and Left Hand)
$274.00 (Percussion)
$320.00 (Laminated Stock, Percussion)

SPECIFICATIONS
Caliber: 50
Barrel length: 21″ octagonal-to-round with tenon; 15/16″ across flats; 1:66″ twist
Overall length: 36¼″
Weight: 5 lbs. 15 oz.
Sights: Hunting-style, click adjustable rear; beaded blade front with white dot

Trigger: Single
Features: Blackened furniture; German silver ornamentation; belting leather sling and sling swivels; unbreakable ramrod

A. UBERTI

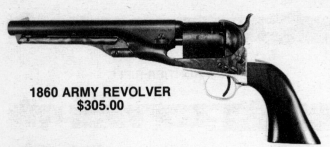

1860 ARMY REVOLVER
$305.00

SPECIFICATIONS
Caliber: 44
Barrel length: 8″ (round, tapered)
Overall length: 13¾″
Weight: 2.65 lbs.
Frame: One-piece, color casehardened steel
Trigger guard: Brass
Cylinder: 6 shots (engraved)
Grip: One-piece walnut

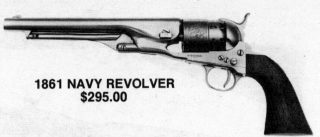

1861 NAVY REVOLVER
$295.00

SPECIFICATIONS
Caliber: 36
Capacity: 6 shots
Barrel length: 7½″
Overall length: 13″
Weight: 2.75 lbs.
Grip: One-piece walnut
Frame: Color casehardened steel

1851 NAVY REVOLVER
$280.00

SPECIFICATIONS
Caliber: 36
Barrel length: 7½″ (octagonal, tapered)
Cylinder: 6 shots (engraved)
Overall length: 13″
Weight: 2¾ lbs.
Frame: Color casehardened steel
Backstrap and trigger guard: Brass
Grip: One-piece walnut

WALKER REVOLVER
$360.00

SPECIFICATIONS
Caliber: 44
Barrel length: 9″ (round in front of lug)
Overall length: 15¾″
Weight: 4.41 lbs.
Frame: Color casehardened steel
Backsstrap: Steel
Cylinder: 6 shots (engraved with "Fighting Dragoons" scene)
Grip: One-piece walnut

SPECIFICATIONS
Caliber: 44
Capacity: 6 shots
Barrel length: 7½″ round forward of lug
Overall length: 13½″
Weight: 4 lbs.
Frame: Color casehardened steel
Grip: One-piece walnut
Also available:
2nd Model Dragoon w/square cylinder bolt shot .. $315.00
3rd Model Dragoon w/loading lever latch, steel
   backstrap, cut for shoulder stock 320.00

1st MODEL DRAGOON REVOLVER
$325.00

A. UBERTI

1858 Remington 44 Revolver
  7⁷/₈″ barrel, open sights $280.00
  With stainless steel and open sights **380.00**
  Target Model, black finish **330.00**
  Target Model, stainless steel **399.00**
Also available:
1858 New Navy (36 cal.) **280.00**
1858 New Army Revolving Carbine (18″ barrel) . . **425.00**

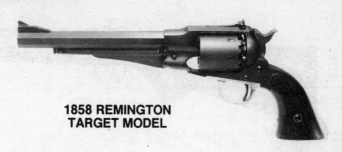

**1858 REMINGTON
TARGET MODEL**

Manufactured at Paterson, New Jersey, by the Patent Arms Manufacturing Company from 1836 to 1842, these were the first revolving pistols created by Samuel Colt. All early Patersons featured a 5-shot cylinder, roll-engraved with one or two scenes, octagon barrel and folding trigger that extends when the hammer is cocked.

SPECIFICATIONS
Caliber: 36
Capacity: 5 shots (engraved cylinder)
Barrel length: 7¹/₂″ octagonal
Overall length: 11¹/₂″
Weight: 2.552 lbs.
Frame: Color casehardened steel
Grip: One-piece walnut

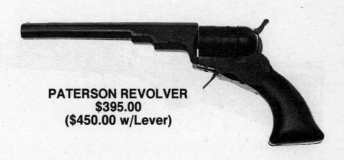

**PATERSON REVOLVER
$395.00
($450.00 w/Lever)**

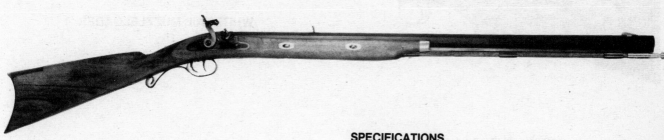

**SANTA FE HAWKEN RIFLE
$495.00
$449.00 Kit**

SPECIFICATIONS
Calibers: 50 and 54
Barrel length: 32″ octagonal
Overall length: 50″
Weight: 9¹/₂ lbs.
Stock: Walnut with beavertail cheekpiece
Features: Brown finish; double-set trigger; color casehardened lockplate; German silver wedge plates

BLACK POWDER

ULTRA LIGHT ARMS

MODEL 90
$950.00

This muzzleloader comes with a 28″ button-rifled barrel (1 in 48″ twist) and 13½″ length of pull. Fast ignition with in-line action and fully adjustable Timney trigger create consistent shots. Available in 45 or 50 caliber, each rifle has a Kevlar/ Graphite stock and Williams sights, plus integral side safety. Recoil pad, sling swivels and a hard case are all included. **Weight:** 6 lbs.

WHITE SYSTEMS

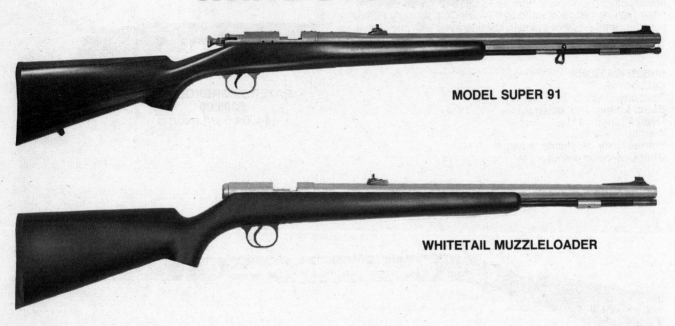

MODEL SUPER 91

WHITETAIL MUZZLELOADER

MODEL SUPER 91

This modern muzzleloading system features the following: Ordnance-grade stainless steel construction • Fast twist, shallow groove rifling • Stainless steel nipple and breech plug • Side swing safety (locks the striker, not just the trigger) • Classic stock configuration (fits right- or left-handed shooters • Fast second shot and easy access to nipple from either side for quick capping • Fully adjustable trigger

Calibers: 45 and 50
Barrel length: 24″
Rifling: 1 in 20″ (45 cal.); 1 in 24″ (50 cal.)
Weight: 7¾ lbs.
Sights: Fully adjustable Williams sights
Price: **$699.00**

WHITETAIL AND BISON MUZZLELOADING RIFLES

White's "G Series" rifles feature straight-line action with easy no-tool takedown in the field. A stainless-steel hammer system has an ambidextrous cocking handle that doubles as a sure-safe hammer-lock safety. Other features include the "Insta-Fire" one-piece nipple/breech plug system (with standard #11 percussion caps); fully adjustable open hunting sights; 22″ barrel with integrated ramrod guide and swivel studs.
Calibers: 45, 50 and 54.
Prices:
Bison (50 and 54 cal.) **$399.00**
Whitetail (45 and 50 cal.) 449.00
    Stainless steel 549.00

sights & scopes

For addresses and phone numbers of manufacturers and distributors included in this section, turn to *DIRECTORY OF MANUFACTURERS AND SUPPLIERS* at the back of the book.

AIMPOINT SIGHTS

AIMPOINT 5000 SIGHT
$319.95

The first sight with a true 30mm field of view, Aimpoint's 5000 allows the shooter to find the target quickly. With its patented lens system, this sight needs no parallax—the shooter does not have to center the red dot. The 5000 is available in two reticle patterns: regular 3-minute dot for precision shooting, or the Mag Dot (10 minutes) for speed shooting on pistols or on shotguns for turkey, deer and waterfowl. Each 5000 comes with 30mm rings, extension tube, lithium battery, polarizing filter and lens covers.

SPECIFICATIONS
System: Parallax free
Optical: Anti-reflex coated lenses
Adjustment: 1 click = 1/4-inch at 100 yards
Length: 5 1/2"
Weight: 5.8 oz.
Objective diameter: 36mm
Mounting system: 30mm rings
Magnification: 1X
Material: Anodized aluminum; blue or stainless finish
Diameter of dot: 3" at 100 yds. or Mag Dot reticle, 10" at 100 yards.

SERIES 3000 LONG/SHORT
$269.00 (Black or Stainless)

SERIES 3000 LONG SPECIFICATIONS
Weight: 5.15 oz.
Length: 6 7/8"
Magnification: 1X
Scope Attachment: 3X
Battery Choices: Lithium CR 1/3 N, 2L76, DL 1/3 N, Mercury (2) MP 675 or SP 675, Silver Oxide (2) D 375 H, Alkaline (2) LR 44
Material: Anodized Aluminum, Blue or Stainless Finish
Mounting: 1" Rings (Medium or High)

LASERDOT II
$319.00 (Black or Stainless)

SPECIFICATIONS
Length: 4"
Weight: 4.06 oz.
Diameter: 1"
Switch pad: 5.5" long cable and pressure switch (optional toggle switch available)
Material: 6061T aluminum
Finish: Black or stainless
Output beam: Wavelength 670 nm; Class IIIa limit; output aperture approx. 1/4" (6mm); beam divergence 0.5 Rad
Batteries: 1 X 3v Lithium
Battery life: Up to 15 hours continuous
Environmental: 0-30 C. operating 0-95% rh.; will withstand 2 meter drop; one meter immersion proof

AIMPOINT 5000 2-POWER
$400.00

Aimpoint has developed a fixed low-power electronic sight with a floating red dot; it is the only red-dot sight with built-in magnification. Shooters now have the speed and accuracy of a red-dot sight combined with the range of a low-power scope.

SPECIFICATIONS
System: Parallax free
Optical: Anti-reflex coated lens
Adjustment: clock = 1/4" at 100 yards
Length: 8 1/2"
Weight: 9 oz.
Objective diameter: 46mm
Diameter of dot: 1 1/2" at 100 yards
Mounting system: 30mm rings
Magnification: 2X
Material: Anodized aluminum; blue finish

LASERDOT AUTO LASER (Not Shown)
$351.00 (w/Mounts)

SPECIFICATIONS
Length: 4"
Weight: 4.5 oz.
Dot diameter: 1 1/2" at 100 yards
Switch pad: Toggle
Material: 6061T aluminum
Finish: Black or stainless
Batteries: 1x6v Lithium
Mounting: Laser Module w/choice of mount

BAUSCH & LOMB RIFLESCOPES

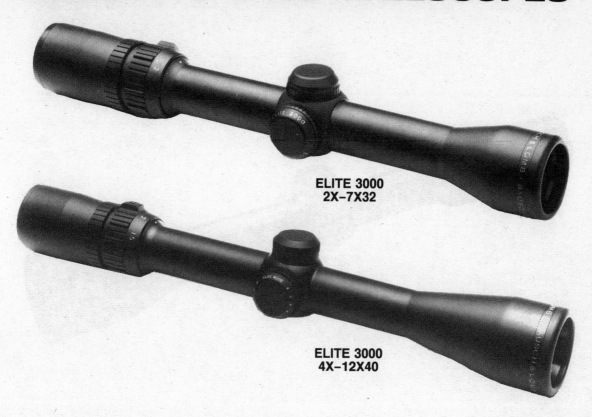

**ELITE 3000
2X–7X32**

**ELITE 3000
4X–12X40**

SPECIFICATIONS MODEL ELITE™ 3000 RIFLESCOPES

Model	Special Features	Actual Magnification	Obj. Lens Aperture (mm)	Field of View at 100 yds. (ft.)	Weight (oz.)	Length (in.)	Eye Relief (in.)	Exit Pupil (mm)	Click Value at 100 yds. (in.)	Adjust Range at 100 yds. (in.)	Selections	Price
30-4124A	Adjustable Objective	4X–12X	40	26.9@4X 9@12X	15.2	13.2	3	10@4X 3.33@12X	.25	±25	Medium to long-range variable makes superb choice for varmint or big game hunting.	$349.95
30-3940G		3X–9X	40	33.8@3X 11.5@9X	13.1	12.6	3	13.3@3X 4.44@9X	.25	±25	For the full range of hunting. From varmint to big game. Tops in versatility.	301.95
30-3940M	Matte Finish	3X–9X	40	33.8@3X 11.5@9X	13.1	12.6	3	13.3@3X 4.44@9X	.25	±25	For the full range of hunting. From varmint to big game. Tops in versatility.	319.95
30-3940S	Silver Finish	3X–9X	40	33.8@3X 11.5@9X	13.1	12.6	3	13.3@3X 4.44@9X	.25	±25	For the full range of hunting. From varmint to big game. Tops in versatility.	319.95
30-2732G		2X–7X	32	44.6@2X 12.7@7X	11.7	11.6	3	12.2@2X 4.6@7X	.25	±25	Compact variable for close-in brush or medium range shooting.	281.95
30-2732M	Matte Finish	2X–7X	32	44.6@2X 12.7@7X	11.7	11.6	3	12.2@2X 4.6@7X	.25	±25	Compact variable for close-in brush or medium range shooting.	297.95
30-3950G		3X–9X	50	31.5@3X 10.5@9X	19	15.7	3	12.5@3X 5.6@9X	.25	±25	All purpose variable with extra brightness.	359.95
30-3950M		3X–9X	50	31.5@3X 10.5@9X	19	15.7	3	12.5@3X 5.6@9X	.25	±25	All purpose variable with extra brightness.	369.95

BAUSCH & LOMB RIFLESCOPES

ELITE 4000
1.5X–6X36

SPECIFICATIONS MODEL ELITE™ 4000 RIFLESCOPES

Model	Special Features	Actual Magnification	Obj. Lens Aperture (mm)	Field of View at 100 yds. (ft.)	Weight (oz.)	Length (in.)	Eye Relief (in.)	Exit Pupil (mm)	Click Value at 100 yds. (in.)	Adjust Range at 100 yds. (in.)	Selections	Price
40-6244A	Adjustable Objective Sunshade	6X–24X	40	18@6X 4.5@24X	20.2	16.9	3	6.66@6X 1.66@24X	.125	±13	Varmint, target and silhouette long range shooting. Parallax focus adjustments for pinpoint accuracy.	$ 587.95
40-2104G		2.5X–10X	40	41.5@2.5X 10.8@10X	16	13.5	3	15.6@2.5 4@10X	.25	±25	All purpose hunting scope with 4 times zoom range for close-in brush and long range shooting.	513.95
40-2104M	Matte Finish	2.5X–10X	40	41.5@2.5X 10.8@10X	16	13.5	3	15.6@2.5X 4@10X	.25	±25	All purpose hunting scope with 4 times zoom range for close-in brush and long range shooting.	533.95
40-1636G		1.5X–6X	36	61.8@1.5X 16.1@6X	15.4	12.8	3	14.6@1.5X 6@6X	.25	±25	Compact wide angle for close-in and brush hunting. Maximum brightness. Excellent for shot guns.	479.95
40-1636M	Matte Finish	1.5X–6X	36	61.8@1.5X 16.1@6X	15.4	12.8	3	14.6@1.5X 6@6X	.25	±30	Compact wide angle for close-in and brush hunting. Maximum brightness. Excellent for shot guns.	499.95
40-1040	Ranging reticle, 30mm body tube	10X	40	10.5@10X	22.1	13.8	3.6	4@10X	.25	±60	The ultimate for precise pin-point accuracy with parallax focus and target adjustment.	1389.95

BEEMAN SCOPES

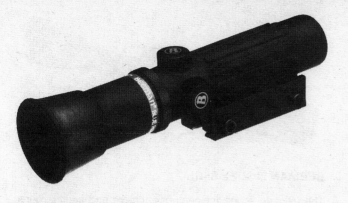

BEEMAN SS-2 W/FIREARM

SS-1 AND SS-2 SERIES

Beeman SS-1 and SS-2 short scopes are extra compact and rugged, due largely to breakthroughs in optical engineering and computer programming of lens formulas. Less than 7 inches long, both scopes pack 11 lenses that actually gather light for bigger, brighter targets than "projected spot" targets. Scope body and built-in mounts are milled as a single unit from a solid block of hi-tensile aircraft aluminum.

SS-1 Series	$198.50
SS-2 Series	from 289.95

BEEMAN SS-2

BEEMAN SS-2L "SKYLITE" RIFLESCOPE

BEEMAN SS-2L "SKYLITE" RIFLESCOPE

Features a brightly illuminated reticle powered by daylight and even moonlight (no batteries necessary). In addition to standard black reticle, supplementary color filters are available for different lighting and shooting situations. Filter options include:

white (for silhouette or target); red (for twilight and general purpose); yellow (for haze, fog and low light); green (for bright light and snow). A small electrical illuminator is also available for use in total darkness.

Beeman SS-2L w/color reticle, 3x	$298.50
Beeman SS-2L w/color reticle, 4x	359.95
Lamp	29.95
Filter Kit (green or yellow)	18.95

BEEMAN SS-3

SS-3 SERIES

Offers 1.5-4x zoom power for greater flexibility. Glare-free black matte finish is anodized into metal for deep sheen and extra toughness. Instant action dial around front of scope dials away parallax error and dials in perfect focus from 10 feet to infinity. Scope measures only 5¾ inches in length and weighs only 8.5 ounces. **SS-3 Series** **$299.95**

BEEMAN SCOPES

BEEMAN MODEL 66R

Every feature of the Model 66R has been carefully developed to make it the ultimate scope for centerfire, .22-caliber rimfire and adult air rifles. It can zoom instantly from 2 to 7X—an excellent range of magnification that provides sufficient high power for long-range shots requiring pinpoint accuracy, and very low power for times when speed and a broad field of view are needed. Speed Dials (with full saddle) with 1/2-minute adjustments per click and Range Focus are two of the 66R's star features. The 32mm objective lens up front provides a bright, wide field view, extends daily shooting time, and affords better viewing into shadows.

Model 66R 2-7X32 with Range Focus **$298.50**

BEEMAN MODEL 66RL

The ultimate scope for centerfire, rimfire and adult airguns. Zoom instantly from 2X to 7X—range that provides sufficient high power for long shots as well as very low power when a broad field of view is demanded. Features speed dials, Range Focus and 32mm objective lens.

Model 66RL w/Color Reticle Scope **$339.50**

BEEMAN MODEL 68R

The Model 68R with 4-12 zoom power meets the demand for a high-power scope suitable for airguns, rimfire and centerfire rifles. Higher magnifications are a necessity for metallic silhouette shooters. Field shooters who must make precise head shots on small game and vermin for a humane kill find the higher magnifications helpful. The big 40mm objective lens provides a brilliant sight picture, even at high power. Other features include Speed Dials with 1/4-minute clicks, Range Focus, full saddle, and the essential extra lens bracing required of airgun scopes.

Model 68R, Blue Ribbon 4-12X40 . . . . **$429.95**

BEEMAN MODEL 25
(Shown on Beeman P1 Air Pistol)

Beeman has improved upon the modified domestic pistol scope that was formerly recommended. Starting with the same dedication to quality, special Beeman Blue Ribbon® Scope features have been added to produce one of the finest scopes for air pistols (and a variety of other pistols). Features include Speed Dial elevation and windage knobs and the brightness and performance that only a 1" tube, top-quality lens system can offer. Full saddle. Especially recommended for Beeman P1/P2 air pistols.

Model 25 2X20 Blue Ribbon Pistol Scope **$154.95**

BURRIS SCOPES

SIGNATURE SERIES 3X-12X PLEX

The Signature Series features a computer-designed optical system, using the most advanced optical glass available. All models have **Hi-Lume** (multi-coated) lenses for maximum light transmission. Also features full-field wide angle field-of-view sight picture. The 6X-24X and 3X-12X models feature Burris' patented **Light Collector.** Also features new **Posi-Lock** to prevent recoil and protect against rough hunting use and temperature change. Allows shooter to lock internal optics of scope in position after rifle has been sighted in.

6X-24X SIGNATURE
w/Light Collector

Prices:

1.5X-6X Plex	$381.95
1.5X-6X Plex Safari	399.95
1.5X-6X Plex Silver Safari	408.95
1.5X-6X Heavy Plex	389.95
1.5X-6X Heavy Plex Safari	408.95
1.5X-6X Plex Posi-Lock	470.95
1.5X-6X Plex Posi-Lock Safari	488.95
2X-8X Plex	443.95
2X-8X Plex Safari	461.95
2X-8X Plex Silver Safari	469.95
2X-8X Plex Posi-Lock	532.95
2X-8X Plex Posi-Lock Safari	549.95
2X-8X Plex Posi-Lock Silver Safari	559.95
2.5X-10X Peep Plex	522.95
2.5X-10X Peep Plex Safari	540.95
2.5X-10X Plex	511.95
2.5X-10X Plex Safari	529.95
2.5X-10X Plex Silver Safari	538.95
2.5X-10X Plex Posi-Lock	600.95
2.5X-10X Plex Posi-Lock Safari	618.95
2.5X-10X Plex Posi-Lock Silver Safari	627.95
3X-9X Plex	455.95
3X-9X Plex Safari	472.95
3X-9X Plex Silver Safari	483.95
3X-9X Plex Posi-Lock	541.95
3X-9X Plex Posi-Lock Safari	559.95
3X-9X Plex Posi-Lock Silver Safari	568.95
3X-12X Plex	569.95
3X-12X Plex Safari	586.95
3X-12X Peep Plex	577.95
3X-12X Peep Plex Safari	595.95
3X-12X Plex Posi-Lock	657.95
3X-12X Plex Posi-Lock Safari	675.95
4X Plex	325.95
4X Plex Safari	341.95
6X Plex	340.95
6X Plex Safari	353.95
6X-24X Plex	600.95
6X-24X 2"-.5" Dot Silhouette	636.95
6X-24X Fine Flex Silhouette	622.95
6X-24X Plex Safari	611.95
6X-24X Fine Plex Silhouette Safari	632.95
6X-24X Peep Plex	602.95
6X-24X Peep Plex Safari	619.95
6X-24X Plex Posi-Lock	682.95
6X-24X Plex Posi-Lock Safari	699.95

GUNSITE SCOUT SCOPE (not shown)

Made for hunters who need a 7- to 14-inch eye relief to mount just in front of the ejection port opening, allowing hunters to shoot with both eyes open. The 15-foot field of view and 2¾X magnification are ideal for brush guns and handgunners who use the "two-handed hold."

1.5X Plex XER	$199.95
1.5X Plex XER Safari Finish	216.95
1.5X German 3 Post XER	219.95
1.5X Heavy Plex	209.95
1.5X Heavy Plex Safari	225.95
2.75X Heavy Plex	214.95
2.75X Heavy Plex Safari	232.95
2.75X German 3 Post XER	241.95
2.75X Plex XER	205.95
2.75X Plex XER Safari Finish	219.95

3X-9X RAC SCOPE
w/Automatic Rangefinder & Hi-Lume Lenses

When the crosshair is zeroed at 200 yards (or 1.8″ high at 100 yards), it will remain zeroed at 200 yards regardless of the power ring setting. The Range Reticle automatically moves to zero at ranges up to 500 yards as power is increased to fit the target between the stadia range wires. No need to adjust the elevation knob; bullet drop compensation is automatic.

3X-9X RAC CHP Safari Finish	$371.95
3X-9X RAC Crosshair Dot	356.95
3X-9X RAC Crosshair Plex	356.95

FULLFIELD SCOPES
Fixed Power with Hi-Lume Lenses
(not shown)

1½X Plex	$229.95
1½X Heavy Plex	237.95
2½X Plex	239.95
2½X Heavy Plex	248.95
4X Plex	255.95
4X Plex Safari Finish	273.95
4X Post Crosshair	264.95
6X Plex	274.95
6X Plex Safari Finish	292.95
6X 2.″ Dot	301.95
12X Plex	346.95
12X Fine Plex	346.95
12X ½″ Dot	372.95
12X Fine Plex Silhouette	370.95
12X ½″ Dot Silhouette	385.95

4X-12X FULLFIELD ARC SCOPE
w/Automatic Rangefinder Reticle

3X-9X Fullfield ARC Crosshair (Dot or Plex)	$356.95
3X-9X ARC Crosshair Plex	356.95

BURRIS SCOPES

FULLFIELD SCOPES
Variable Power w/Hi-Lume Lenses

Burris introduces its first 50mm objective scope, the 3.5X-10X-50mm (prices listed below).

1.75X-5X Plex	**$301.95**
1.75X-5X Plex Safari	319.95
1.75X-5X Post Crosshair	310.95
1.75X-5X Heavy Plex	310.95
1.75X-5X Heavy Plex Safari	328.95
2X-7X Plex	322.95
2X-7X Plex Silver Safari	341.95
2X-7X Plex Safari Finish	328.95
2X-7X Post Crosshair	331.95
2X-7X 3."-1." Dot	341.95

3X-9X Plex	**$331.95**
3X-9X Plex Silver Safari	356.95
3X-9X Plex Safari Finish	344.95
3X-9X Post Crosshair	344.95
3X-9X 3."-1." Dot	349.95
3.5X-10X-50mm Plex	408.95
3.5X-10X-50mm Plex Safari	426.95
3.5X-10X-50mm Plex Silver Safari	435.95
4X-12X Plex	406.95
4X-12X Fine Plex	406.95
4X-12X 2."-.7" Dot	422.95
4X-12X Peep Plex	413.95
6X-18X Plex	422.95
6X-18X Fine Plex	422.95
6X-18X Fine Plex Silhouette	445.95
6X-18X 2."-.7" Dot Silhouette	462.95
6X-18X Plex Safari	438.95
6X-18X Peep Plex	429.95
6X-18X Peep Plex Safari	447.95

MINI 3X-9X

MINI 2X-7X

MINI 6X

3X LER

MINI SCOPES

4X Plex	**$205.95**
4X Plex P.A. Airgun	237.95
4X Plex P.A.	237.95
4X Plex Silver Safari	230.95
6X Plex	219.95
6X Plex P.A. Airgun	251.95
6X Plex P.A.	251.95
6X HBR Fine Plex P.A.	283.95
6X HBR .375 Dot P.A.	296.95
6X HBR .375 Dot P.A. Silver Safari	326.95
6X HBR FCH P.A.	283.95
6X HBR FCH P.A. Silver Safari	314.95
2X-7X Plex	281.95
3X-9X Plex	289.95
3X-9X Plex Safari	299.95
3X-9X Plex Silver Safari	317.95
4X-12X Plex	383.95

LONG EYE RELIEF SCOPE
with Plex Reticle:

1X LER Plex	**$194.95**
1X LER 5" Dot	207.95
2X LER Plex	201.95
2X LER Plex Silver Safari	230.95
3X LER Plex	217.95
3X LER Plex P.A.	251.95
4X LER Plex	224.95
4X LER Plex P.A.	262.95
4X LER Plex P.A. Silver Safari	287.95
4X LER Plex Silver Safari	251.95
1.5X-4X LER Plex	315.95
1.5X-4X LER Plex Silver Safari	346.95
2X-7X LER Plex	308.95
2X-7X LER Plex Safari	326.95
2X-7X LER Plex Silver Safari	335.95
2X-7X LER Plex P.A.	347.95
3X-9X LER Plex	347.95
3X-9X LER Plex P.A.	378.95
3X-9X LER Plex Safari	363.95
3X-9X LER Plex Silver Safari	374.95

INTERMEDIATE EYE RELIEF
(IER) SCOPES

7X IER Plex	**$248.95**
7X IER Plex P.A.	283.95
7X IER Plex P.A. Silver Safari	308.95
10X IER Plex	308.95
10X IER Plex P.A.	335.95

BUSHNELL RIFLESCOPES

SPECIFICATIONS BUSHNELL TROPHY RIFLESCOPES

Model	Special Features	Actual Magnification	Obj. Lens Aperture (mm)	Field of View at 100 yds. (ft.)	Weight (oz.)	Length (in.)	Eye Relief (in.)	Exit Pupil (mm)	Click Value at 100 yds. (in.)	Adjust range at 100 yds. (in.)	Selection	Price
73-2545	Large objective	2.5X–10X	45	39@2.5X 10@10X	14	13.75	3	18@2.5X 4.5@10X	.25	±30	All purpose hunting with 4 times zoom for close-in and long range shooting.	$259.95
73-6184	Semi-turret target adjustments	6X–18X	40	17.3@6X 6@18X	17.9	14.8	3	6.6@6X 2.2@18X	.125	±20	Long range varmint centerfire or short range air rifle target precision accuracy.	277.95
73-4124	Wide angle	4X–12X	40	32@4X 11@12X	16.1	12.6	3	10@4X 3.3@12X	.25	±30	Medium to long range variable for varmint and big game. Range focus adjustment.	245.96
73-3940	Wide angle	3X–9X	40	42@3X 14@9X	13.2	11.7	3	13.3@3X 4.4@9X	.25	±30	All purpose variable, excellent for use from close to long range. Circular view provides a definite advantage over "TV screen" type scopes for running game—uphill or down.	169.95
73-3940S	Wide angle matte silver											179.95
73-3948	Wide angle matte black											179.95
73-2733	Wide angle	2X–7X	32	63@2X 18@7X	11.3	10	3	16@2X 4.6@7X	.25	±55	Low power variable for close in brush and medium range shooting.	177.95
73-1500	Wide angle	1.75X–5X	32	68@1.75X 23@5X	12.3	10.8	3.5	18.3@1.75X 6.4@5X	.25	±60	Shotgun, black powder or centerfire. Close-in brush hunting.	209.95
73-0440	Wide angle	4X	40	36	12.5	12.5	3	10	.25	±50	General purpose. Wide angle field of view.	129.95

TROPHY HANDGUN SCOPES

Model	Special Features	Actual Magnification	Obj. Lens Aperture (mm)	Field of View at 100 yds. (ft.)	Weight (oz.)	Length (in.)	Eye Relief (in.)	Exit Pupil (mm)	Click Value at 100 yds. (in.)	Adjust range at 100 yds. (in.)	Selection	Price
73-2632		2X–6X	32	21@2X 7@6X	9.6	9.1	9–26	16@2X 5.3@6X	.25	±25	Versatile, all-purpose, four times zoom range for close-in brush and long range shooting.	199.95
73-2632S	Silver											209.95
73-0232		2X	32	20	7.7	8.7	9–26	16	.25	±45	Designed for target and short to medium range hunting. Magnum recoil resistant.	163.95
73-0232S	Silver											175.95

SHOTGUN/HANDGUN SCOPE

Model	Special Features	Actual Magnification	Obj. Lens Aperture (mm)	Field of View at 100 yds. (ft.)	Weight (oz.)	Length (in.)	Eye Relief (in.)	Exit Pupil (mm)	Click Value at 100 yds. (in.)	Adjust range at 100 yds. (in.)	Selection	Price
73-0130	Illuminated dot reticle	1X	25	61	5.5	5.25	Untd	18	1.0	±40	30mm tube with rings, ext. tube polarization filter, amber coating. For black powder, shotgun and handgun shooting.	239.95

INTERAIMS ELECTRONIC RED DOT SIGHTS

The following features are incorporated into each model, including the MONO TUBE:

—5 YEAR WARRANTY—

- Sharp Red Dot
- Lightweight
- Compact
- Wide Field of View
- Parallaxfree
- True 1X for Unlimited Eye Relief
- Nitrogen Filled Tube
- Waterproof, Moisture Proof, Shockproof

- Rugged Aluminum Body
- Easy 1″ and 30mm Ring Mounting
- Manually Adjustable Light Intensity
- Windage and Elevation Adjustments
- Dielectrical Coated Lenses
- Battery—Polarized Filter—Extension Tube—Protective Rubber Eye Piece—All included

MONOTUBE CONSTRUCTIONS ONE V

Weight	Length	Battery	Finish
3.9 oz.	4¹/₂″	(1) 3 V Lithium	Black Satin Nickel

ONE V 1″ MODEL
$139.95

Also available:
1″ or 30mm rings in black or stainless steel **$11.95**

ONE V 30
$149.95

MONOTUBE CONSTRUCTIONS ONE V 30

Weight	Length	Battery	Finish
5.5 oz.	5.4″	(1) 3 V Lithium DL 2032	Black or Satin Chrome

LEUPOLD RIFLE SCOPES

VARI-X III LINE

The Vari-X III scopes feature a power-changing system that is similar to the sophisticated lens systems in today's finest cameras. Some of the improvements include an extremely accurate internal control system and a sharp, superb-contrast sight picture. All lenses are coated with **Multicoat 4**. Reticles are the same apparent size throughout power range, stay centered during elevation/windage adjustments. Eyepieces are adjustable and fog-free.

VARI-X III 1.5X5
Here's a fine selection of hunting powers for ranges varying from very short to those at which big game is normally taken. The exceptional field at 1.5X lets you get on a fast-moving animal quickly. With the generous magnification at 5X, you can hunt medium and big game around the world at all but the longest ranges. Duplex or Heavy Duplex **$487.50** In black matte finish: **$508.90**
Also available:
VARI-X III 1.75X32mm: $507.10. With matte finish: **$528.60**

VARI-X III 1.5X5

VARI-X III 2.5X8
This is an excellent range of powers for almost any kind of game, inlcuding varmints. In fact, it possibly is the best all-around variable going today. The top magnification provides plenty of resolution for practically any situation. **$525.00** In matte finish: **$564.40.** In silver finish (Duplex only) **$546.40**

VARI-X III 2.5X8

VARI-X III 3.5X10
The extra power range makes these scopes the optimum choice for year-around big game and varmint hunting. The adjustable objective model, with its precise focusing at any range beyond 50 yards, also is an excellent choice for some forms of target shooting. **$544.60.** With matte finish: **$566.10.** With adjustable objective: **$582.10.** With silver: **$566.10**

VARI-X III 3.5X10

VARI-X III 3.5X10–50mm
Leupold announces its first hunting scope designed specifically for low-light situations. The 3.5X10–50mm scope, featuring lenses coated with Multicoat 4, is ideal for twilight hunting (especially whitetail deer) because of its efficient light transmission. The new scope delivers maximum available light through its large 50mm objective lens, which translates into an exit pupil that transmits all the light the human eye can handle in typical low-light circumstances, even at the highest magnification: **$641.10.** With matte finish: **$662.50**

Also available:
VARI-X III 3.5X10-50mm Adj. Objective: $696.40. With matte finish: **$717.90.** Target Model: **$750.00**

VARI-X III 3.5X10–50mm

VARI-X III 4.5X14 (Adj. Objective)
This new model has enough range to double as a hunting scope and as a varmint scope. Duplex or Heavy Duplex: **$632.10**

VARI-X III 6.5X20
(With Adjustable Objective)

VARI-X III 6.5X20 (Adj. Objective)
This scope has the widest range of power settings in our variable line, with magnifications that are especially useful to hunters of all types of varmints. In addition, it can be used for any kind of big game hunting where higher magnifications are an aid: **$627.50.** With matte finish: **$658.90**

LEUPOLD RIFLE SCOPES

VARIABLE POWER SCOPES

VARI-X II 1X4

VARI-X II 3X9–50mm

VARI-X II 1X4 DUPLEX
This scope, the smallest of Leupold's VARI-X II line, is reintroduced in response to consumer demand for its large field of view: 70 feet at 100 yards. **$330.40**

VARI-X II 3X9–50mm
This LOV scope delivers a 5.5mm exit pupil, providing excellent low-light visibility. **$437.50**
With matte finish: 458.90

VARI-X II 2X7

VARI-X II 2X7
A compact scope, no larger than the Leupold M8-4X, offering a wide range of power. It can be set at 2X for close ranges in heavy cover or zoomed to maximum power for shooting or identifying game at longer ranges. **$373.20**
With matte finish: 394.60

VARI-X II 3X9 DUPLEX
A wide selection of powers lets you choose the right combination of field of view and magnification to fit the particular conditions you are hunting at the time. Many hunters use the 3X or 4X setting most of the time, cranking up to 9X for positive identification of game or for extremely long shots. The adjustable objective eliminates parallax and permits precise focusing on any object from less than 50 yards to infinity for extra-sharp definition. **$376.80**
Also available in matte or silver: 398.20

VARI-X II 4X12 MATTE FINISH

VARI-X II 4X12 (Adj. Objective)
The ideal answer for big game and varmint hunters alike. At 12.25 inches, the 4X12 is virtually the same length as Vari-X II 3X9. . . . . **$489.30**
With matte or silver finish: 510.70

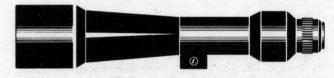

ARMORED SPOTTING SCOPE

SPOTTING SCOPES
Leupold's Golden Ring Armored Spotting Scopes feature extraordinary eye relief and crisp, bright roof prism optics housed in a lightweight, sealed, waterproof body. The Spotting Scopes come complete with a self-storing screw-on sunshade, lens caps, and a green canvas case. Now available in 12X40-60mm variable power with 30.8mm eye relief at 20X.
Prices:
20X50mm Compact Armored **$576.80**
25X50mm Compact Armored 616.10
    With reticle 633.90
30X60mm 633.90
12X40-60mm Variable Power 883.90

LEUPOLD SCOPES
THE COMPACT SCOPE LINE

The introduction of the Leupold Compacts has coincided with the increasing popularity of the new featherweight rifles. Leupold Compact scopes give a more balanced appearance atop these new scaled-down rifles and offer generous eye relief, magnification and field of view, yet are smaller inside and out. Fog-free.

2.5X COMPACT

2.5X COMPACT (Duplex or Heavy Duplex)
The 2.5X Compact is only 8½ inches long and weighs just 7.4 ounces. **$273.20**

4X COMPACT & 4X RF SPECIAL

4X COMPACT RF SPECIAL
The 4X RF Special is focused to 75 yards and has a Duplex reticle with finer crosshairs. **$292.90**

2X7 COMPACT

2X7 COMPACT
Two ounces lighter and a whole inch shorter than its full-size counterpart, this 2X7 is one of the world's most compact variable power scopes. It's the perfect hunting scope for today's trend toward smaller and lighter rifles. **$373.20**
Also available: **RF Special** (Fine Duplex) **$373.20**

3X9 COMPACT

3X9 COMPACT
The 3X9 Compact is a full-blown variable that's 3½ ounces lighter and 1.3 inches shorter than a standard 3X9. **$387.50**
Also available in black matte finish or silver **$408.90**

3X9 COMPACT SILVER

SHOTGUN SCOPES (not shown)

Leupold shotgun scopes are parallax-adjusted to deliver precise focusing at 75 yards (as opposed to 150 yards usually prescribed for rifle scopes). Each scope features a special Heavy Duplex reticle that is more effective against heavy, brushy backgrounds.

Prices:

2X Extended Eye Relief Model	$269.60
Vari-X II 1X4 Model	353.60
4X Model	314.30
Vari-X III 2X7 Model	398.20

LEUPOLD SCOPES

HANDGUN SCOPES

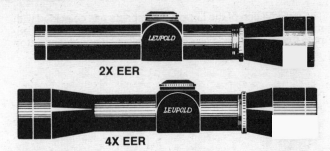

2X EER

4X EER

M8-2X EER
With an optimum eye relief of 12-24 inches, the 2X EER is an excellent choice for most handguns. It is equally favorable for carbines and other rifles with top ejection that calls for forward mounting of the scope. Available in black anodized or silver finish to match stainless steel and nickel-plated handguns. **$246.40**. In matte or silver finish: **$267.90**

M8-4X EER
Only 8.4 inches long and 7.6 ounces. Optimum eye relief 12-24 inches. Available in black anodized or silver finish to match stainless steel and nickel-plated handguns. In matte or silver finish: **$333.90**

Also available:
VARI-X 2.5X8 EER w/Multicoat 4: $480.40. In silver: **$501.80**

FIXED-POWER SCOPES

4X

M8-4X
The all-time favorite is the 4X, which delivers a widely used magnification and a generous field of view. **$292.90.** In black matte finish: **$314.30**

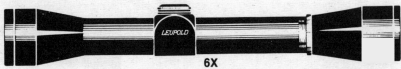

6X

M8-6X
Gaining popularity fast among fixed power scopes is the 6X, which can extend the range for big game hunting and double, in some cases, as a varmint scope. **$310.70**

6X42mm

M8-6X42mm W/Multicoat 4
Large 42mm objective lens features increased light gathering capability and a 7mm exit pupil. Great for varmint shooting at night. Duplex or Heavy Duplex: **$387.50**. In matte finish: **$408.90**

VARMINT SCOPES

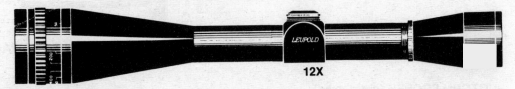

12X

8-12X STANDARD (Adj. Obj.)
Superlative optical qualities, outstanding resolution and magnification make the 12X a natural for the varmint shooter. Adjustable objective is standard for parallax-free focusing. **$508.90.** With Multicoat 4: **$428.60.** With CPC reticle or Dot: **$482.10**

Also available:
M8-12X VARMINT (Adj. Obj.) Target Dot Scopes w/Multicoat 4: **$453.60**
VARI-X III 6.5X20 VARMINT (Adj. Obj.) Target Dot w/Multicoat 4: **$717.90**

LYMAN SIGHTS

93 MATCH SIGHT

Designed with the serious shooter in mind, Lyman's globe front sight, the "93 Match," adapts to any rifle with a standard dovetail mounting block. The sight has a diameter of ⅞" and comes complete with 7 target inserts (it also accepts most of the popular line of Anschutz accessories). Because most target shooters prefer to travel with their sights disassembled from their rifles, the 93 Match has a special hooked locking bolt and nut to allow quick removal or installation. Bases are available in .860 (European) and .562 (American) hole spacing. The sight height is .550 from the top of the dovetail to the center of the aperture.

93 Match Sight **$45.00**

90 MJT UNIVERSAL TARGET RECEIVER SIGHT
(Not shown)

Designed to mount on a Marlin Model 2000 Target Rifle using standard Williams FP bases, this new Target Sight features target knobs scribed with audible click detents in minute and quarter-minute graduations, plus elevation and windage direction arrows. Adjustable zero scales allow adjustments to be made without disturbing pre-set zero; quick release slide allows slide to be removed with a press of the release button. Large ⅞" diameter non-glare .040 target aperture disk is standard. Adjustable from 1.060 to 1.560 above centerline of bore.

90 MJT Universal Target Receiver Sight **$79.95**

20 MJT ⅞" DIAMETER GLOBE FRONT SIGHT

Machined from one solid piece of steel designed for use with dovetail slot mounting in the barrel or with Lyman's 25A dovetail base. Height is .700" from bottom of dovetail to center of aperture. Supplied with 7 Anschutz-size steel apertures.

20 MJT Globe Front Sight **$36.00**

NO. 16 FOLDING LEAF SIGHT

Designed primarily as open rear sights with adjustable elevation, leaf sights make excellent auxiliary sights for scope-mounted rifles. They fold close to the barrel when not in use, and they can be installed and left on the rifle without interfering with scope or mount. Two lock screws hold the elevation blade adjustments firmly in place. A sight of this type could save the day if the scope becomes damaged through rough handling. (For installation on rifles without a dovetail slot, use Lyman No. 25 Base.) Leaf sights are available in the following heights:

16A—.400" high; elevates to .500"
16B—.345" high; elevates to .445"
16C—.500" high; elevates to .600"

No. 16 Folding Leaf Sight **$13.50**

BLACK POWDER SIGHTS

Lyman's front and rear hunting sight package for muzzleloading hunters features Lyman's #37 white bead front sight and #16 AML rear sight. Each has a special .360" dovetail designed specifically for European imports. The #37 front sight has a white bead that stands out in low light conditions, while the Lyman #16 fold-down rear sight is fully adjustable for elevation.

Black Powder Sight **$19.95**

SHOTGUN SIGHTS

Lyman shotgun sights are available for all shotguns. Equipped with oversized ivory beads that give perfect definition on either bright or dull days, they are easy to see under any light conditions. They quickly catch your eye on fast upland targets, and point out the lead on long passing shots. Lyman shotgun sights are available with white bead, and can be fitted to your gun in minutes.

No. 10 Front Sight (press fit) for use on double barrel, or ribbed single
-barrel guns **$5.00**
No. 10D Front Sight (screw fit) for use on non-ribbed single-barrel guns;
supplied with a wrench **6.50**
No. 11 Middle Sight (press fit). This small middle sight is intended for use on
double-barrel and ribbed single-barrel guns **5.00**

When you replace an open rear sight with a receiver sight, it is usually necessary to install a higher front sight to compensate for the higher plane of the new receiver sight.

MILLETT SIGHTS

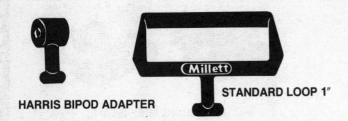

HARRIS BIPOD ADAPTER

STANDARD LOOP 1″

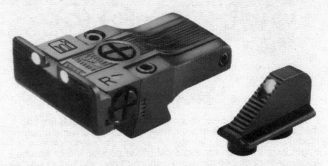

FLUSH-MOUNT HARRIS BIPOD ADAPTER

Millett's flush-mount sling swivels have a simple-to-use adapter for the Harris bipod, that detaches quickly so the loop can then be installed in the bipod loop receptacle. Will also fit Pachmayr flush-mount bases.

Harris Bipod Adapter	SS00004	**$8.70**

DUAL-CRIMP INSTALLATION TOOL KIT

The Dual-Crimp System is a new revolutionary way of installing front sights on autos. Now it is not necessary to heliarc or silver solder to get a good secure job. Dual-Crimp has a two-post, hollow rivet design that works very much like an aircraft rivet and withstands the heavy abuse of hardball ammo. Your choice of four styles and nine heights. Dual-Crimp is the quick and easy system for professionals. Requires a drill press.

Dual-Crimp Tool Set, Complete	**$142.95**
Application Tool	76.95
Reverse counterbore (solid carbide)	36.85
³/₁₆″ Drill (solid carbide)	17.05
Drill Jig	21.95
Complete Tool Kit (Stake-On)	87.95

FLUSH-MOUNT SLING SWIVELS

Millett's flush-mount redesigned Pachmayr sling swivels are quick detachable and beautifully styled in heat treated nickel steel. The sling swivel loop has been redesigned to guide the sling into the loop, eliminating twisitng and fraying on edges of sling. Millett flush-mount bases are much easier to install than the old Pachmayr design, with no threading and an easy to use step drill.

Flush-Mount Swivels (pair)	SS00001	**$15.65**
Loops Only	SS00002	8.70
Installation Drill	SS00003	16.75

3-DOT SYSTEM SIGHTS

Millett announces 3-Dot System sights for a wide variety of popular handguns.

**3-Dot System Front and Rear Sight
Selection Chart (partial listing only)**

DUAL-CRIMP™ FRONTS (White Dot) $15.25
DC 18500	.185 Height
DC 20004	.200 Height
DC 22512	.225 Height
DC31216	.312 Height
DC34020	.340 Height
DC36024	.360 Height

WIDE STAKE-ON FRONTS (White Dot) $15.25
(for Colt pistols only, after June 1988)
WS18504	.185 Height
WS20008	.200 Height
WS31220	.312 Height

SPECIAL-APPLICATION PISTOL FRONTS $15.25
GL00006	Glock 17, 17L & 19
RP85009	Ruger-P-85
RS22015	Ruger Std. Auto (Fixed Model)
SP22567	Sig Sauer P225/226, Dovetail
SW40513	S&W 3rd Generation, Dovetail
SW46913	S&W 3rd Generation, Dovetail
BE00010	Beretta Accurizer

AUTOPISTOL REAR SIGHTS $52.95
BE00003	Beretta
BA00008	Browning Hi-Power, Adjustable
BF00008	Browning Hi-Power, Fixed
CA00008	Colt-Hi-Profile
CC00008	Colt Custom Combat Lo-Profile
GC00008	Colt Gold Cup
RP85008	Ruger P-85
RS22003	Ruger Std. Auto
SP22005	Sig P220, 225, 226
SW40504	Smith & Wesson, _ALL_ Factory Adjustable (incl. 2nd & 3rd Generation)*
SW46904	Smith & Wesson, _ALL_ Factory Fixed (incl. 2nd & 3rd Generation)*

* 2nd Generation use DC Fronts; 3rd Generation use Dovetail Fronts

MILLETT REVOLVER SIGHTS

COLT REVOLVER

The Series 100 Adjustable Sight System offers today's discriminating Colt owner the finest quality replacement sight available. 12 crisp click stops for each turn of adjustment, delivers 5/8″ of adjustment per click at 100 yards with a 6″ barrel. For Colt Python, Trooper, Diamond Back, and new Frontier single action army.

Rear Only (White Outline)	CR00001	$46.95
Rear Only (Target Blade)	CR00002	46.95
Rear Only (Silhouette)	CR00003	46.95

Colt owners will really appreciate the high visibility feature of Colt front sights. Easy to install—just drill 2 holes in the new sight and pin on. All steel. Your choice of blaze orange or white bar. Fits 4″, 6″ & 8″ barrels only.

Colt Python & Anaconda (White or Orange Bar)	FB00007-8	$12.95
Diamond Back, King Cobra, Peacemaker	FB00015-16	12.95

SMITH & WESSON

The Series 100 Adjustable Sight System for Smith & Wesson revolvers provides the sight picture and crisp click adjustments desired by the discriminating shooter. 1/2″ of adjustment per click, at 100 yards on elevation, and 5/8″ on windage, with a 6″ barrel. Can be installed in a few minutes, using factory front sight.

Smith & Wesson N Frame:
N.312—Model 25-5, all bbl., 27-3½″ & 5″, 28-4″ & 6″
N.360—Model 25, 27, 29, 57, & 629-4, 6 & 6½″ bbl.
N.410—Model 27, 29, 57, 629 with 8⅜″ bbl.

Smith & Wesson K&L Frame:
K.312—Models 14, 15, 18, 48-4″, & 53
K&L360—Models 16, 17, 19, 48-6″, 8⅜″, 66, 686, 586

Smith & Wesson K&L-Frame		
Rear Only .312 (White Outline)	SK00001	$46.95
Rear Only .312 (Target Blade)	SK00002	46.95
Rear Only .360 (White Outline)	SK00003	46.95
Rear Only .360 (Target Blade)	SK00004	46.95
Rear Only .410 (White Outline)	SK00005	46.95
Rear Only .410 (Target Blade)	SK00006	46.95
Smith & Wesson K&N Old Style		
Rear Only .312 (White Outline)	KN00001	$46.95
Rear Only .312 (Target Blade)	KN00002	46.95
Rear Only .360 (White Outline)	KN00003	46.95
Rear Only .360 (Target Blade)	KN00004	46.95
Rear Only .410 (White Outline)	KN00005	46.95
Rear Only .410 (Target Blade)	KN00006	46.95
Smith & Wesson N-Frame		
Rear Only .312 (White Outline)	SN00001	$46.95
Rear Only .312 (Target Blade)	SN00002	46.95
Rear Only .360 (White Outline)	SN00003	46.95
Rear Only .360 (Target Blade)	SN00001	46.95
Rear Only .410 (White Outline)	SN00005	46.95
Rear Only .410 (Target Blade)	KN00006	46.95

RUGER

The high visibility white outline sight picture and precision click adjustments of the Series 100 Adjustable Sight System will greatly improve the accuracy and fast sighting capability of your Ruger. 3/4″ per click at 100 yard for elevation, 5/8″ per click for windage, with 6″ barrel. Can be easily installed, using factory front sight or all-steel replacement front sight which is a major improvement over the factory front. Visibility is greatly increased for fast sighting. Easy to install by drilling one hole in the new front sight.

The Red Hawk all-steel replacement front sight is highly visible and easy to pickup under all lighting conditions. Very easy to install. Fits the factory replacement system.

SERIES 100 Ruger Double Action Revolver Sights	
Rear Sight (fits all adjustable models)	$46.95
Front Sight (Security Six, Police Six, Speed Six)	12.95
Front Sight (Redhawk)	15.25

SERIES 100 Ruger Single Action Revolver Sights	
Rear Sight (Black Hawk Standard & Super; Bisley Large Frame, Single-Six	$46.95
Front Sight (Millett Replacement sights not available for Ruger single action revolvers).	

TAURUS	
Rear, .360 White Outline	$46.95
Rear, .360 Target Blade	46.95

DAN WESSON

This sight is exactly what every Dan Wesson owner has been looking for. The Series 100 Adjustable Sight System provides 12 crisp click stops for each turn of adjustment, with 5/8″ per click for windage, with a 6″ barrel. Can be easily installed, using the factory front or new Millett high visibility front sights.

Choice of white outline or target blade.

Rear Only (White Outline)	DW00001	$46.95
Rear Only (Target Blade)	DW00002	46.95
Rear Only (White Outline) 44 Mag.	DW00003	46.95
Rear Only (Target Blade) 44 Mag.	DW00004	46.95

If you want super-fast sighting capability for your Dan Wesson, the new Millett blaze orange or white bar front is the answer. Easy to install. Fits factory quick-change system. All steel, no plastic. Available in both heights.

Dan Wesson .44 Mag (White Bar) (high)	FB00009	$12.95
Dan Wesson .44 Mag (Orange Bar) (high)	FB00010	12.95
Dan Wesson 22 Caliber (White Bar) (low)	FB00011	12.95
Dan Wesson 22 Caliber (Orange Bar) (low)	FB00012	12.95

MILLETT AUTO PISTOL SIGHTS

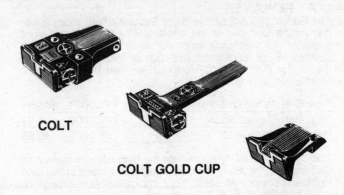

COLT

COLT GOLD CUP

MARK II HI-PROFILE

RUGER STANDARD AUTO

The Ruger Standard Auto Combo provides a highly visible sight picture even under low light conditions. The blaze orange or white bar front sight allows the shooter to get on target fast. Great for target use or plinking. Uses Factory Front Sight on adjustable model guns when using Millett target rear only. All other installations use Millett Front Sight. Easy to install.

Rear Only (White Outline)	$52.95
Rear Only (Silhouette Target Blade)	52.95
Rear Only (Target Blade)	52.95
Front Only (White), Fixed Model	15.25
Front Only (Orange), Fixed Model	15.25
Front Only (Serrated Ramp), Fixed Model	15.25
Front Only (Target-Adjustable Model/White Bar)	15.25
Front Only (Target-Adjustable Model/Orange Bar)	15.25
Front Only Bull Barrel (White or Orange Ramp)	16.75

RUGER P85

Rear (White Outline)	$52.95
Rear (Target Blade)	52.95
Front (White Ramp)	15.25
Front (Orange Ramp)	15.25
Front (Serrated Ramp)	15.25

TAURUS PT92

Rear (White Outline, use Beretta Front)	$52.95
Rear (Target Blade, use Beretta Front)	52.95
Front (White Bar)	23.95
Front (Orange Bar)	23.95
Front (Serrated Ramp)	23.95

AMT HARDBALLER

Rear (White Outline, use .185 DC Front)	$46.95
Rear (Target Blade, use .185 DC Front)	46.95

HECKLER & KOCH (P7 ONLY)

Rear (White Outline)	$32.95
Front (White Ramp)	15.25
Front (Blaze Orange Ramp)	15.25

COLT

Colt Gold Cup Marksman Speed Rear Only (Target .410 Blade)		$46.95
Custom Combat Low Profile Marksman Speed Rear Only (Target .410 Blade)		52.95
Colt Government & Commander (High Profile) Marksman Speed Rear Only (Target .410 Blade)	CA00018	52.95
Colt Gold Cup Rear (use DC or WS 200 Frt)		46.95
Colt Mark II Low-Profile Rear Only (DC 200 Front)		32.95

COLT WIDE STAKE FRONT SIGHTS (POST 6/88)

.185 WS White Bar	$15.25
.185 WS Orange Bar	$15.25
.185 WS Serrated Ramp	$15.25
.185 WS White Dot	$15.25
.200 WS White Bar	$15.25
.200 WS Orange Bare with Skirt	$15.25
.200 WS Serrated Ramp with Skirt	$15.25
.200 WS White Dot with Skirt	$15.25
.312 WS White Bar with Skirt	$15.25
.312 WS Orange Bar with Skirt	$15.25
.312 WS Serrated Ramp with Skirt	$15.25
.312 WS White Dot with Skirt	$15.25

SIG/SAUER P-220, P-225, P-226

Now Sig Pistol owners can obtain a Series-100 adjustable sight system for their guns. Precision click adjustment for windage and elevation makes it easy to zero when using different loads. The high visibility features assures fast sight acquisition when under the poorest light conditions. Made of high quality heat treated nickel steel and built to last. Extremely easy to install on P-225 and P-226. The P-220 and Browning BDA 45 require the Dual-Crimp front sight installation.

Sig P220-25-26 Rear Only (White)*	SP22003	52.95
Sig P220-25-26 Rear Only (Target)*	SP22004	52.95
Sig P225-6 (White) Dovetail Front*	SP22565	15.25
Sig P225-6 (Orange) Dovetail Front*	SP22566	15.25

* The Sig P220 Uses .360 Dual-Crimp Front Sight. The Sig P225-6 Uses a Dovetail Mount Front Sight

MILLETT AUTO PISTOL SIGHTS

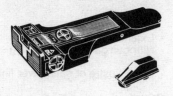

SMITH & WESSON 39/59

This sight system provides fast and accurate sighting capability even under low light conditions. The unique white outline rear blade teamed up with the blaze orange or white bar front sight creates a highly visible sight picture, ideal for match or duty use.

Rear Only (White outline)	SW39595	**$56.45**
Rear Only (Target Blade)	SW39596	56.45

Requires .340 Dual-Crimp Front

SMITH & WESSON 469, 669, 659, 459, 645 AUTOPISTOL SIGHTS

Rear Sight (white outline)	**$54.10**
Rear Sight (Target Blade)	54.10
Front Sight DC 312 white or orange	15.25

SMITH & WESSON 400/500/600 SERIES AUTOPISTOL SIGHTS

Rear Sight (white outline)	**$52.95**
Rear Sight (Target Blade)	52.95
Front Sight DC 312 white or orange	15.25

BROWNING HI-POWER

The Series 100 Adjustable Sight System for Browning Hi-Power will provide accurate high visibility sighting for both fixed and adjustable slides with no machine modifications required to the dovetail. Most adjustable slide model Hi-Powers can use the factory front sight as shown in the photo. The fixed slide model requires a new front sight installation. We highly recommend the Dual-Crimp front sight installation on this gun.

BROWNING HI-POWER (Adjustable Slide Model)

Rear Only (White Outline)	BA00009	**$52.95**
Rear Only (Target Blade)	BA00010	52.95

High-Power Requires .340 High Front Sight.

BROWNING HI-POWER (Fixed Slide Model)

Rear Only (White Outline)	BF00009	**$52.95**
Rear Only (Target Blade)	BF00010	52.95

High-Power Requires .340 High Front Sight.

MODELS CZ75/TZ75/TA90 AUTOPISTOL SIGHTS

Rear Sight (White Outline or Target Blade)	**$52.95**

COLT 45

This Series 100 High Profile Adjustable Sight is rugged, all steel, precision sight which fits the standard factory dovetail with no machine modifications required. This sight provides a highly visible sight picture even under low light conditions. Blaze orange or white bar front sight, precision click adjustments for windage and elevation makes the Colt .45 Auto Combo the handgunner's choice.

Rear Only (White Outline)	CA00009	**$52.95**
Rear Only (Target Blade)	CA00010	52.95
Rear (Marksman, .410 Blade)	CA00018	52.95

Colt Gov. and Com. Require .312 High Front Sight.

BERETTA ACCURIZER COMBO

This amazing new sight system not only provides a highly visible sight picture but also tunes the barrel lockup to improve your accuracy and reduce your group size by as much as 50%. The Beretta Accurizer sight system fits the 92S, 92SB, 84 and 85 models. Easy to install. Requires the drilling of one hole for installation. Your choice of rear blade styles. Front sight comes in white bar, serrated ramp or blaze orange.

Rear Only (White Outline)	BE00005	**$53.70**
Rear Only (Target Blade)	BE00006	53.70
Front Only (White Bar)	BE00007	23.95
Front Only (Orange Bar)	BE00008	23.95
Front Only (Serrated Ramp)	BE00009	23.95

Fits Models 92S, 92SB, 85, 84

NEW BAR-DOT-BAR™ TRITIUM NIGHT SIGHT COMBOS

Ruger P-85, 89, 90 Combo	**$135.00**
Sig Sauer P225/226/228 & New P220 Combo	135.00
Sig Sauer P220 (Prior to 10-90) Combo	135.00
Browning Hi-Power (Fixed Model) Combo	135.00
Browning Hi-Power (Fixed Model Dovetail Front)	135.00
Colt Auto Combo	135.00
Colt Custom Combat Low Profile Combo	135.00
CZ-75/TZ-75, TA-90 Combo	135.00
Glock 17, 19, 20, 21, 22, 23 Combo	135.00
S & W 3rd Generation Fixed Combo	135.00
S & W 2nd Generation Fixed Combo	135.00
Beretta 92SB, 85, 84 Combo	143.50
Taurus PT-92 Combo	143.50

NIKON SCOPES

PISTOL SCOPES

Key Features:
- Edge to edge sharpness for precise detection of camouflaged game
- Super multicoating and blackened internal metal parts provide extreme reduction of flare and image ghost-out
- Aluminum alloy one-piece 1″ tube provides lightweight but rugged construction (fully tested on Magnum calibers)
- ¼ MOA windage/elevation adjustment

- Extended eye relief
- Nitrogen gas filled and 0-ring sealed for water and fogproofing
- Black Lustre or satin silver finish

Prices:

2X20 EER	$234.00
1.5-4.5X24 EER	387.00

2X20 EER PISTOL SCOPE

1.5-4.5X24 EER PISTOL SCOPE

1.5-4.5X20 RIFLESCOPE

RIFLESCOPES

Key Features: Essentially the same as the **Pistol Scopes** (above). Available in black lustre and black matte finishes (3-9 available in silver).

Prices:

4X40	$295.00
1.5-4.5X20	387.00
2-7X32	426.00
3-9X40	443.00
4-12X40 AO	563.00
6.5-20X44 AO	653.00
3.5-10X50	653.00
4-12X50	712.00

4-12X40 AO RIFLESCOPE

6.5-20X44 AO RIFLESCOPE
⅛ MOA

4X40 RIFLESCOPE

3-9X40 RIFLESCOPE

3.5-10X50 RIFLESCOPE

4-12X50 AO RIFLESCOPE

PENTAX SCOPES

FIXED POWER

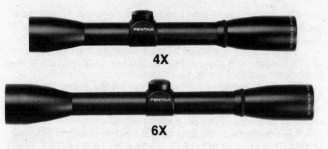

4X

6X

VARIABLE POWER

3X-9X

2X-7X

MINI 3X-9X

FIXED POWER RIFLESCOPES

Magnification: 4X
Field of view: 35′
Eye relief: 3.25″
Diameter: 1″
Weight: 12.2 oz.
Length: 11.6″
Prices: $280.00 (Glossy)
    300.00 (ProFinish)

Magnification: 6X
Field of view: 20′
Eye relief: 3.25″
Diameter: 1″
Weight: 13½ oz.
Length: 13.4″
Prices: $310.00 (Glossy)
    330.00 (ProFinish)

VARIABLE POWER RIFLESCOPES

Magnification: 1.5X-5X
Field of view: 66′-25′
Eye relief: 3″-3¼″
Diameter: 1″
Weight: 13 oz.
Length: 11″
Price: $330.00 (ProFinish)
    310.00 (Glossy)
    365.00 (Satin Chrome)

Magnification: 3X-9X
Field of view: 33′-13½′
Eye relief: 3″-3¼″
Diameter: 1″
Weight: 15 oz.
Length: 13″
Prices: $380.00 (Glossy)
    400.00 (ProFinish)
    420.00 (Satin Chrome)

Magnification: 2X-7X
Field of view: 42.5′-17′
Eye relief: 3″-3¼″
Diameter: 1″
Weight: 14 oz.
Length: 12″
Prices: $360.00 (Glossy)
    380.00 (ProFinish)
    400.00 (Satin Chrome)

Magnification: Mini 3X-9X
Field of view: 26½′-10½′
Eye relief: 3¼″
Diameter: 1″
Weight: 13 oz.
Length: 10.4″
Prices: $320.00 (Mini Glossy)
    340.00 (Mini ProFinish)

Also available:
4X-12X (Mini Glossy): **$410.00** (**$430.00** ProFinish)
6X-12X (Glossy): **$460.00** (**$500.00** ProFinish)
6X-12X Silhouette: $500.00

LIGHTSEEKER 3X-9X RIFLE SCOPE

Field of view: 36-14′
Eye relief: 3″
Diameter: 1″
Weight: 15 oz.
Length: 12.7″
Prices: $520.00 (Glossy)
    550.00 (ProFinish)
    550.00 (Satin)

Also available:
2X-8X (Glossy): **$450.00**
2X-8X (ProFinish): **$460.00**
2X-8X (Satin Chrome): **$480.00**
3X-10X (Glossy): **$540.00**
3X-10X (Pro Matte): **$560.00**
3X-10X (Chrome): **$580.00**
2.5X SG Plus (Glossy): **$280.00**
2.5X SG Plus (Pro Matte): **$290.00**

2X-8X LIGHTSEEKER

PISTOL SCOPES

Magnification: 2X
Field of view: 21′
Eye relief: 10″-24″
Diameter: 1″
Weight: 6.8 oz.
Length: 8¼″
Prices: $240.00 (Glossy)
    260.00 (Chrome-Matte)

Magnification: 1.5X-4X
Field of view: 16′-11′
Eye relief: 11″-25″/11″-18″
Diameter: 1″
Weight: 11 oz.
Length: 10″
Prices: $360.00 (Glossy)
    390.00 (Chrome-Matte)

Also available:
1.5X-4X (Glossy): **$360.00**
1.5X-4X (Satin Chrome): **$390.00**
2.5X-7X (Glossy): **$380.00**
2.5X-7X (Chrome-Matte): **$400.00**

1.5X-4X

REDFIELD SCOPES

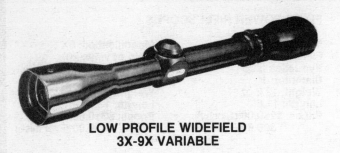

**LOW PROFILE WIDEFIELD
3X-9X VARIABLE**

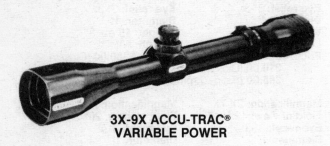

**3X-9X ACCU-TRAC®
VARIABLE POWER**

GOLDEN FIVE STAR SCOPES

This series of seven scopes incorporates the latest variable and fixed power scope features, including multi-coated and magnum recoil-resistant optical system, plus maximum light-gathering ability. Positive quarter-minute click adjustments for ease of sighting and optimum accuracy. Anodized finish provides scratch-resistant surface.

Golden Five Star Scopes:
4X Fixed Power	$236.95
6X Fixed Power	254.95
1X-4X Variable Power	289.95
2X-7X Variable Power	363.95
3X-9X Variable Power	325.95
3X-9X Nickel Plated Variable Power	345.95
3X-9X Black Matte Variable Power	333.95
3X-9X Nickel Matte Variable Power	342.95
3X-9X Accu-Trac Variable Power	372.95
4X-12X Variable Power (Adj. Objective)	416.95
4X-12X Accu-Trac (AO)	462.95
6X-18X Variable Power (Adj. Objective)	439.95
6X-18X Accu-Trac Variable Power (Adj. Obj.)	486.95

50mm Golden Five Star Scopes:
3X-9X 50mm Five Star Variable
116500 4 Plex	$395.95

3X-9X 50mm Five Star RealTree Camo
116505 4 Plex	412.95

3X-9X 50mm Five Star Matte Finish
116508 4 Plex	403.95

3X-9X 50mm Five Star Nickel Matte Finish
116900 4 Plex	395.95

LOW PROFILE WIDEFIELD

In heavy cover, game may jump out of the brush 10 feet away or appear in a clearing several hundred yards off, either standing or on the move.

The Widefield®, with 25% more field of view than conventional scopes, lets you spot game quicker, stay with it and see other animals that might be missed.

The patented Low Profile design means a low mounting on the receiver, allowing you to keep your cheek tight on the stock for a more natural and accurate shooting stance, especially when swinging on running game.

The one-piece, fog-proof tube is machined with high tensile strength aluminum alloy and is anodized to a lustrous finish that's rust-free and virtually scratch-proof. Available in 7 models.

WIDEFIELD LOW PROFILE SCOPES

1³/₄X-5X Low Profile Variable Power
113806 1³/₄X-5X 4 Plex	$357.95

2X-7X Low Profile Variable Power
111806 2X-7X 4 Plex	366.95

2X-7X Low Profile Nickel Matte Variable Power
111808 2X-7X 4 Plex	383.95

2X-7X Low Profile Accu-Trac Variable Power
111810 2X-7X 4 Plex AT	433.95

3X-9X Low Profile Variable Power
112806 3X-9X 4 Plex	407.95

3X-9X Low Profile Accu-Trac Variable Power
112810 3X-9X 4 Plex AT	452.95

2³/₄X Low Profile Fixed Power
141807 2³/₄X 4 Plex	260.95

4X Low Profile Fixed Power
143806 4X 4 Plex	290.95

6X Low Profile Fixed Power
146806 6X 4 Plex	315.95

3X-9X Low Profile RealTree Camo
112805 4 Plex	426.95

3X-9X Low Profile Nickel Matte Variable Power
112814 4 Plex	425.95

3X-9X Low Profile Black Matte Variable Power
112812 4 Plex	416.95

**3X-9X NICKEL-PLATED GOLDEN
FIVE STAR SCOPE**

50mm GOLDEN FIVE STAR SCOPE

REDFIELD SCOPES

THE ILLUMINATOR

Every sportsman knows that dawn and dusk are the most productive times to hunt. Game use the cover of darkness for security while feeding, blending in easily with the greens, grays and browns of the outdoors during dim light conditions.

With this new Illuminator series, you can add precious minutes to morning and evening hunting. These scopes actually compensate for the low light, letting you "see" contrasts between field and game.

Optimum resolution, contrast, color correction, flatness of field, edge-to-edge sharpness and absolute fidelity are improved by the unique air-spaced, triplet objective, and the advanced 5-element erector lens system.

The Illuminators also feature a zero tolerance nylon cam follower and thrust washers to provide absolute point of impact hold through all power ranges. The one-piece tube construction is virtually indestructible, tested at 1200g acceleration forces, and fog-free through the elimination of potential leak paths.

Offered in both the Traditional and Widefield® variable power configurations, the Illuminator is also available with the Accu-Trac® feature.

Also offered in a 30mm 3X-12X with a 56mm adjustable objective.

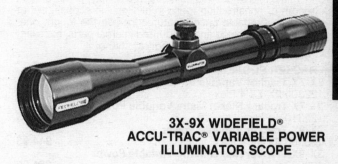

**3X-9X WIDEFIELD®
ACCU-TRAC® VARIABLE POWER
ILLUMINATOR SCOPE**

ILLUMINATOR SCOPES
4X Widefield Fixed Power
112906 4 Plex **$376.95**
2X-7X Widefield Variable Power
112910 4 Plex **498.95**
3X-9X Traditional Variable Power
123886 3X-9X 4 Plex **505.95**
3X-9X Widefield Variable Power
112886 3X-9X 4 Plex **536.95**
3X-9X Widefield Accu-Trac Variable Power
112880 3X-9X 4 Plex **615.95**
3X9 Widefield Var. Power Matte Finish
112888 . . . . **572.95**
3X-9X Widefield RealTree Camo Variable Power
112895 4 Plex **581.95**
3X-9X Widefield Nickel Matte Variable Power
112890 4 Plex AT **525.95**

**3X-9X WIDEFIELD® ILLUMINATOR
w/Nickel Matte Finish**

EXTENDED EYE RELIEF PISTOL SCOPES
(not shown)

Redfield mounts its own specially-designed internal lens assembly on a non-rotating ball pivot system that is integrated with the outer tube, adding strength to the scope at its greatest stress point. All pistol scopes feature ¼-minute click adjustments and 4-plex reticles. A nickel-plated finish is available to match stainless steel pistols and comes in three lengths.

Prices:
2½X Pistol Fixed Power **$224.95**
    Same as above in nickel plate **204.95**
4X Pistol Fixed Power **239.95**
    Same as above in nickel plate **253.95**
2X-6X Pistol Variable Power **283.95**
    Same as above in nickel plate **303.95**

THE ULTIMATE ILLUMINATOR
(not shown)

The first American-made scopes with a 30mm one-piece outer tube and a 56mm adjustable objective. Engineered with quarter-minute positive click adjustments, the Ultimate Illuminator features a European #4 reticle. Comes complete with a set of 30mm steel rings with exclusive Rotary Dovetail System and lens covers.

3X-9X Ultimate 30mm Var. Power **$652.95**
3X-12X Ultimate 30mm Variable Power
    (European #4 Adj. Obj.) **745.95**
3X-12X Ultimate 30mm Variable Power
    (4 Plex Adj. Obj.) **745.95**
3X-12X Ultimate 30mm Var. Matte Finish **754.95**

REDFIELD SCOPES

THE TRACKER

The Tracker series brings you a superior combination of price and value. It provides the same superb quality, precision and strength of construction found in all Redfield scopes, but at an easily affordable price. Features include the tough, one-piece tube, machined and hand-fitted internal parts, excellent optical quality and traditional Redfield styling.

TRACKER SCOPES:
2X-7X Tracker Variable Power
122300 2X-7X 4 Plex $216.95
2X-7X Tracker Nickel Matte Variable Power
122310 4 Plex 232.95
3X-9X Tracker Variable Power
123300 3X-9X 4 Plex 244.95
3X-9X Tracker Nickel Matte Variable Power
123320 4 Plex 251.95
3X-9X Tracker Nickel-Plated
123303 4 Plex 261.95
3X-9X Tracker RealTree Camo
123305 4 Plex 264.95
4X Tracker Fixed Power
135300 4X 4 Plex 169.95
4X 40mm Tracker Nickel Matte Fixed Power
135312 4 Plex 193.95
4X 40mm Tracker Black Matte Fixed Power
135320 4 Plex 184.95
4X 40mm Tracker RealTree Camo
135305 4 Plex 196.95
6X Tracker Fixed Power
135600 6X 4 Plex 190.95
Matte Finish
122308 2X-7X 4 Plex 232.95
123308 3X-9X 4 Plex 253.95
135608 6X 4 Plex 200.95
135308 4X 32mm 179.95

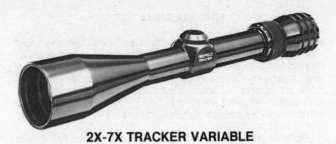

2X-7X TRACKER VARIABLE

6X TRACKER SCOPE FIXED

4X 40mm TRACKER SCOPES

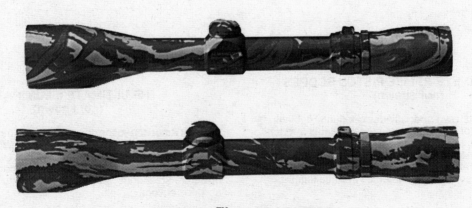

REALTREE™ CAMO SCOPES

These rifle scopes, featuring the popular RealTree™ camouflage pattern, are part of Redfield's Illuminator, Low-Profile Widefield and Tracker lines. Also available with 1X-4X shotgun scope **$314.95**

SAKO SCOPE MOUNTS

SCOPE MOUNTS

These new Sako scope mounts are lighter, yet stronger than ever. Tempered steel allows the paring of every last gram of unnecessary weight without sacrificing strength. Like the original mount, these rings clamp directly to the tapered dovetails on Sako rifles, thus eliminating the need for separate bases. Grooves inside the rings preclude scope slippage even under the recoil of the heaviest calibers. Nicely streamlined and finished in a rich blue-black to complement any Sako rifle.

Price: Low, medium, or high (1″) $67.00
Medium or high (30mm) 81.00

"ORIGINAL" SCOPE MOUNTS

Sako's "Original" scope mounts are designed and engineered to exacting specifications, which is traditional to all Sako products. The dovetail mounting system provides for a secure and stable system that is virtually immovable. Unique to this Sako mount is a synthetic insert that provides maximum protection against possible scope damage. It also affords additional rigidity by compressing itself around the scope. Manufactured in Finland.

Prices: 1″ Medium & High (Short, Medium
& Long Action) $125.00
30mm Medium & High (Short, Medium
& Long Action) 140.00

SCHMIDT & BENDER RIFLE SCOPES

2¹/₂-10X56 VARIABLE POWER SCOPE
$1080.00 ($1100.00 w/Glass Reticle)

4-12X42 VARIABLE POWER SCOPE
$989.00

Also available:
1.5-6X42 SNIPER $1387.00

SCHMIDT & BENDER SCOPES

1¼-4X20 VARIABLE POWER SCOPE
$830.00 ($849.00 w/Glass Reticle)

1½-6X42 VARIABLE POWER SCOPE
$898.00 ($918.00 w/Glass Reticle)

1½X15 FIXED POWER SCOPE
(Steel Tube w/o Mounting Rail)
$610.00

3-12X50 VARIABLE POWER SCOPE
$1013.00 ($1033.00 w/Glass Reticle)

4X36 FIXED POWER SCOPE
(Steel Tube w/o Mounting Rail)
$624.00

6X42 FIXED POWER SCOPE
(Steel Tube w/o Mounting Rail)
$680.00

10X42 FIXED POWER SCOPE
(Steel Tube w/o Mounting Rail)
$750.00

8X56 FIXED POWER SCOPE
(Steel Tube w/o Mounting Rail)
$765.00

SIMMONS SCOPES

44 MAG RIFLESCOPES

MODEL 1045

MODEL 1043
2-7X44mm

Field of view: 56'-16'
Eye relief: 3.3"
Length: 11.8"
Weight: 13 oz.
Price: $256.95

MODEL 1044
3-10X44mm

Field of view: 38'-12'
Eye relief: 3"
Length: 12.8"
Weight: 16.9 oz.
Price: $268.95

MODEL 1045
4-12X44mm

Field of view: 27'-9'
Eye relief: 3"
Length: 12.8"
Weight: 19.5 oz.
Price: $280.95

MODEL 3044
3-10X44mm

Field of view: 38'-11'
Eye relief: 3"
Length: 13.1"
Weight: 16.4 oz.
Price: $269.95

PROHUNTER RIFLESCOPES

MODEL 7710
3-9X40mm Wide Angle Riflescope

Field of view: 40'-15' at 100 yards
Eye relief: 3"
Length: 12.6"
Weight: 11.6 oz.
Features: Triplex reticle; silver finish
Price: **$169.95** (Same in black matte or black
    polish, Models 7711 and 7712)

MODEL 7710

MODELS 7711/7712

Also available:
2-7X32 Black Matte or Black Polish $159.95
4-12X40 Black Polish 179.95
6-18X40 (adj. obj. Black) 209.95
4.5X32 Silver 109.95
6X40 Black Matte 139.95

#1401

#1403

#1406

RIFLESCOPE ALLOY RINGS

Low 1" Set **Model 1401** $11.95
Medium 1" Set **Model 1403** 11.95
High 1" Set **Model 1404** 11.95
1" See-Thru Set **Model 1405** 13.95
1" Rings for 22 Grooved Receiver **Model 1406** 11.95
1" Rings extention for Compact Scopes
    Model 1409 . . . . 20.95

#1409

SIMMONS SCOPES

WHITETAIL CLASSIC RIFLESCOPES

Simmons' new Whitetail Classic Series features fully coated lenses and glare-proof BlackGranite finish. Its Mono-Tube construction means that front bell and tube and saddle and rear tube are all turned from one piece of aircraft aluminum.

This system eliminates 3 to 5 joints found in most other scopes in use today. The Whitetail Classic is therefore up to 400 times stronger than comparably priced scopes.

MODEL WTC10
4X32mm

Field of view: 35'
Eye relief: 4"
Length: 12"
Weight: 11.0 oz.
Price: $139.95

MODEL WTC10

MODEL WTC11
1.5-5X20mm

Field of view: 80'-23.5'
Eye relief: 3.5"
Length: 9½"
Weight: 9.9 oz.
Price: $174.95

MODEL WTC11

MODEL WTC12
2.5-8X36mm

Field of view: 48'-14.8'
Eye relief: 3"
Length: 12.8"
Weight: 12.9 oz.
Price: $189.95

MODEL WTC12

MODEL WTC13
3.5-10X40mm

Field of view: 35'-12'
Eye relief: 3"
Length: 12.8"
Weight: 16.9 oz.
Price: $209.95

MODEL WTC13

MODEL WTC14
2-10X44mm

Field of view: 50'-11'
Eye relief: 3"
Length: 12.8"
Weight: 16.9 oz.
Price: $256.95

MODEL WTC14

MODEL WT03

MODEL WTC15/35
3.5-10X50 Black
or Silver Granite

Field of view: 30.3'-11.3'
Eye relief: 3.2"
Length: 12.25"
Weight: 13.6 oz.
Price: $329.95

MODEL WTC16
4X40 Black Granite

Field of view: 36.8'
Eye relief: 4"
Length: 9.9"
Weight: 12 oz.
Price: $149.95

MODEL WTC23
3.5-10X40

Field of view: 34'-11.5'
Eye relief: 3.2"
Length: 12.4"
Weight: 12.8 oz.
Price: $209.95

MODEL WTC33
3.5-10X40 Silver

Same specifications as
Model WTC23
Price: $209.95

SIMMONS SCOPES

GOLD MEDAL SILHOUETTE SERIES

Simmons Gold Medal Silhouette Riflescopes are made of state-of-the-art drive train and erector tube design, a new windage and elevation indexing mechanism, camera-quality 100% multicoated lenses, and a super smooth objective focusing device.

High silhouette-type windage and elevation turrets house 1/8 minute click adjustments. The scopes have a black matte finish and crosshair reticle and are fogproof, waterproof and shockproof.

MODEL #23000
12X44mm

Field of view: 8.7'
Eye relief: 3.17"
Length: 14.5"
Weight: 18.3 oz.
Feature: Truplex Reticle, 100% Multi-Coat Lens system, black matte finish, obj. focus
Price: $449.95 (Crosshair)
      454.95 (Dot Reticle)

MODEL 23000/23001

MODEL 23002

MODEL #23001
24X44mm

Field of view: 4.3'
Eye relief: 3"
Length: 14.5"
Weight: 18.3 oz.
Feature: Truplex reticle, 100% Multi-Coat Lens System, black matte finish, obj. focus
Price: $455.95 (Crosshair)
      460.95 (Dot Reticle)

MODEL #23002
6-20X44mm

Field of view: 17.4'-5.4'
Eye relief: 3"
Length: 14.5"
Weight: 18.3 oz.
Feature: Truplex reticle, 100% Multi-Coat Lens System, black matte finish, obj. focus
Price: $499.95 (Crosshair)
      504.95 (Dot Reticle)

GOLD MEDAL HANDGUN SERIES

Simmons gold medal handgun scopes offer longer eye relief, no tunnel vision, light weight, high resolution, non-critical head alignment, compact size, and durability to withstand the heavy recoil of today's powerful handguns. Available in black and silver finishes, all have fully multicoated lenses and a Truplex reticle. Additional models on following page.

MODEL 22001

MODEL #22001
2.5-7X28mm

Field of view: 9.7'-4.0'
Eye relief: 8.9"-19.4"
Length: 9.2"
Weight: 9 oz.
Feature: Truplex reticle, 100% Multi-Coat Lens System, black polished finish.
Price: $319.95

MODEL #22002
2.5-7X28mm

Field of view: 9.7'-4.0'
Eye relief: 8.9"-19.4"
Length: 9.2"
Weight: 9 oz.
Feature: Truplex reticle, 100% Multi-Coat Lens System, black polished finish.
Price: $319.95

SWAROVSKI RIFLESCOPES

TRADITIONAL RIFLESCOPES

These fine Austrian-made sights feature brilliant optics with high-quality lens coating and optimal sighting under poor light and weather conditions. The Nova ocular system with telescope recoil damping reduces the danger of injury, especially with shots aimed in an upward direction. The main tube is selectable in steel or light metal construction. Because of Nova's centered reticle, the aiming mark remains in the center of the field of view regardless of corrections of the impact point. See **Specifications** table on the following page.

VARIABLE POWER

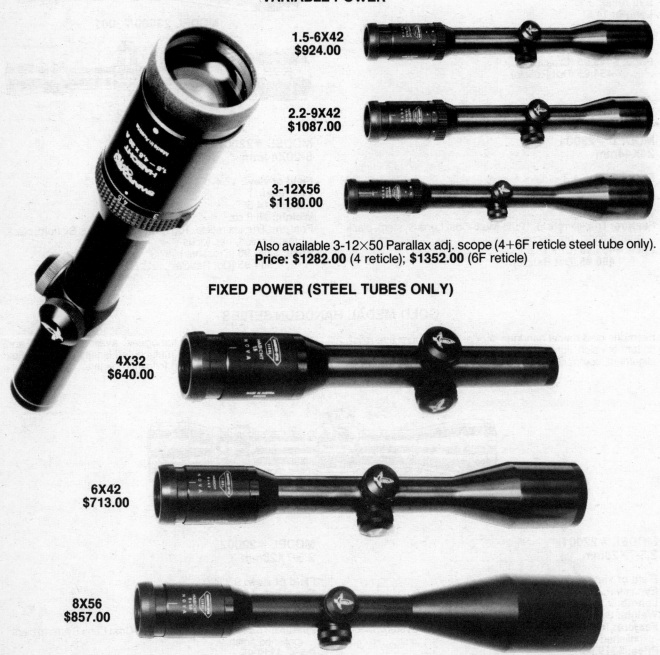

1.5-6X42
$924.00

2.2-9X42
$1087.00

3-12X56
$1180.00

Also available 3-12×50 Parallax adj. scope (4+6F reticle steel tube only).
Price: $1282.00 (4 reticle); **$1352.00** (6F reticle)

FIXED POWER (STEEL TUBES ONLY)

4X32
$640.00

6X42
$713.00

8X56
$857.00

SWAROVSKI RIFLESCOPES

SPECIFICATIONS TRADITIONAL RIFLESCOPES

Telescopic Sights	4X32	6X42	8X56	1.5-6X42	2.2-9X42	3-12X56
Magnification	4X	6X	8X	1.5-6X	2.2-9X	3-12X
Max. effective objective dia.	32mm	42mm	56mm	42mm	42mm	56mm
Exit pupil dia.	8mm	7mm	7mm	14.3-7mm	14.3-4.7mm	14.3-4.7mm
Field of view at 100m	10m	7m	5.2m	18.5-6.5m	12-4.5m	9-3.3m
Twilight effective factor (DIN 58388)	11.3	15.9	21.1	4.2-15.9	6.2-19.4	8.5-25.9
Intermediary tube dia. Steel-Standard	26mm	26mm	26mm	30mm	30mm	30mm
Objective tube dia.	38mm	48mm	62mm	48mm	48mm	62mm
Ocular tube dia.	40mm	40mm	40mm	40mm	40mm	40mm
Scope length	290mm	322mm	370mm	322mm	342mm	391mm
Weight (approx.) Steel	430g	500g	660g	570g	580g	710g
Light metal with rail	NA	NA	NA	480g	470g	540g
A change of the impact point per click in mm/100m	7	6	4	9	6	4

AMERICAN LIGHTWEIGHT RIFLESCOPE

This model features precision ground, coated and aligned optics sealed in a special aluminum alloy tube to withstand heavy recoil. Eye relief is 85mm and the recoiling eyepiece protects the eye. Positive click adjustments for elevation and windage change the impact point (approx. ¼″) per click at 100 yards, with parallax also set at 100 yards. Weight is only 13 ounces.

Prices:

1.5-4.5X20 with duplex reticle	**$595.00**
4X32 with duplex reticle	**495.00**
6X36 with duplex reticle	**538.00**
3-9X36 with duplex reticle	**640.00**

LOW MAGNIFICATION VARIABLE RIFLESCOPE
1.5-4.5X20

TASCO SCOPES

MODEL WA1.35×20

WORLD-CLASS WIDE-ANGLE® RIFLESCOPES

Features:
- 25% larger field of view
- Exceptional optics
- Fully coated for maximum light transmission
- Waterproof, shockproof, fogproof
- Non-removable eye bell
- Free haze filter lens caps
- TASCO's unique World Class Lifetime Warranty

This member of Tasco's World Class Wide Angle line offers a wide field of view—115 feet at 1X and 31 feet at 3.5X—and quick sighting without depending on a critical view. The scope is ideal for hunting deer and dangerous game, especially in close quarters or in heavily wooded and poorly lit areas. Other features include 1/2-minute positive click stops, fully coated lenses (including Supercon process), nonremovable eyebell and windage/elevation screws. Length is 9³/₄″, with 1″ diameter tube. Weight is 10.5 ounces.

WORLD-CLASS, WIDE-ANGLE VARIABLE ZOOM RIFLESCOPES

Model No.	Description	Reticle	Price
WA13.5X20	1X-3.5X Zoom (20mm)	Wide Angle 30/30	$229.00
WA2.58X40ST	2.5X-8X (40mm)	Wide Angle 30/30	206.00
WA2.58X40	2.5X-8X (40mm)	Wide Angle 30/30	199.00
WA39X40TV	3X-9X (40mm)	Wide Angle 30/30	199.00
WA4X32ST	4X (32mm)	Wide Angle 30/30	160.00
WA4X40	4X (40mm)	Wide Angle 30/30	160.00
WA6X40	6X (40mm)	Wide Angle 30/30	191.00
WA1.755X20	1.75X-5X Zoom (20mm)	Wide Angle 30/30	257.00
WA27X32	2X-7X Zoom (32mm)	Wide Angle 30/30	191.00
WA39X40	3X-9X Zoom (40mm)	Wide Angle 30/30	199.00
WA39X40ST	3X-9X (40mm)	Wide Angle 30/30	206.00
CW28X32 COMPACT	2X-8X (32mm)	Wide Angle 30/30	214.00
CW4X32 LE COMPACT	4X (32mm)	Wide Angle 30/30	183.00
ER39X40WA	3X-9X 40m Electronic Reticle	Electronic Red	458.00

WORLD-CLASS 1″ PISTOL SCOPES

Built to withstand the most punishing recoil, these scopes feature a 1″ tube that provides long eye relief to accommodate all shooting styles safely, along with fully coated optics for a bright, clear image and shot-after-shot durability. The 2X22 model is recommended for target shooting, while the 4X28 model and 1.25X-4X28 are used for hunting as well. All are fully waterproof, fogproof, shockproof and include haze filter caps.

SPECIFICATIONS

Model	Power	Objective Diameter	Finish	Reticle	Field of View @ 100 Yds	Eye Relief	Tube Diam.	Scope Length	Scope Weight	Prices
PWC2X22	2X	22mm	Blk Gloss	30/30	25′	11″–20″	1″	8.75″	7.3 oz.	$206.00
PWC2X22MA	2X	22mm	Matte Alum.	30/30	25′	11″–20″	1″	8.75″	7.3 oz.	206.00
PWC4X28	4X	28mm	Blk Gloss	30/30	8′	12″–19″	1″	9.45″	7.9 oz.	252.00
PWC4X28MA	4X	28mm	Matte Alum.	30/30	8′	12″–19″	1″	9.45″	7.9 oz.	252.00
P1.254X28	1.25X-4X	28mm	Blk Gloss	30/30	23′-9′	15″-23″	1″	9.25″	8.2 oz.	289.00
P1.254X28MA	1.25X-4X	28mm	Matte Alum.	30/30	23′-9′	15″-23″	1″	9.25″	8.2 oz.	289.00

TASCO SCOPES

PROPOINT MULTI-PURPOSE SCOPES

Tasco's ProPoint is a true 1X-30mm scope with electronic red dot reticle that features unlimited eye relief, enabling shooters to shoot with both eyes open. It is now available with a 3X booster, plus a special, open T-shaped electronic reticle with a dot in the center, making it ideal for fast-action pistol competition and bull's eye marksmanship. It also has application for rifle, shotgun, bow and black powder. The compact version (PDP2) houses a lithium battery pack, making it 1¼ inches narrower than previous models and lighter as well (5.5 oz.). A mercury battery converter is provided for those who prefer standard batteries.

Tasco's 3X booster with crosshair reticle weighs 6.1 oz. and is 5½ inches long. Model PB2 fits the new PDP2/PDP2MA, and because both units include separate windage and elevation systems the electronic red dot is movable within the crosshair. That means it can be set for two different distances, making it the ultimate rangefinder. Another 3X booster—the PB1—has no crosshairs and fits all other Pro-Point models. Specifications and prices are listed below.

3X BOOSTER

SPECIFICATIONS PROPOINT SCOPES*

Model	Power	Objective Diameter	Finish	Reticle	Field of View @ 100 Yds.	Eye Relief	Tube Diam.	Scope Length	Scope Weight	Prices
PDP2	1X	25mm	Matte Black	Illum. Red Dot	40'	Unltd.	30mm	5"	5.5 oz.	$267.00
PDP2ST	1X	25mm	Stainless Steel	Illum. Red Dot	40'	Unltd.	30mm	5"	5.5 oz.	267.00
PDP2BD	1X	25mm	Matte Black	Illum. Red Dot	40'	Unltd.	30mm	5"	5.5 oz.	267.00
PDP2BDST	1X	25mm	Stainless Steel	Illum. Red Dot	40'	Unltd.	30mm	5"	5.5 oz.	267.00
PDP3	1X	25mm	Black Matte	Illumn. Red Dot	52'	Unltd.	30mm	5"	5.5 oz.	367.00
PDP3ST	1X	25mm	Stainless Steel	Illum. Red Dot	52'	Unltd.	30mm	5"	5.5 oz.	367.00
PDP3BD	1X	25mm	Black Matte	Illum. Red Dot	52'	Unltd.	30mm	5"	5.5 oz.	367.00
PDP3BDST	1X	25mm	Stainless Steel	Illum. Red Dot	52'	Unltd.	30mm	5"	5.5 oz.	367.00
PB1	3X	14mm	Black Matte	NA	35'	3"	30mm	5.5"	6.3 oz.	183.00
PB2	3X	14mm	Black Matte	Crosshair	35'	3"	30mm	5.5"	6 oz.	183.00
PB3	2X	38mm	Black Matte	NA	30'	Unltd.	30mm	1.25"	2.6 oz.	214.00

* **Model PDP4-10** (1X40) available. Specifications to be announced. **$458.00**

TASCO RIFLE SCOPES

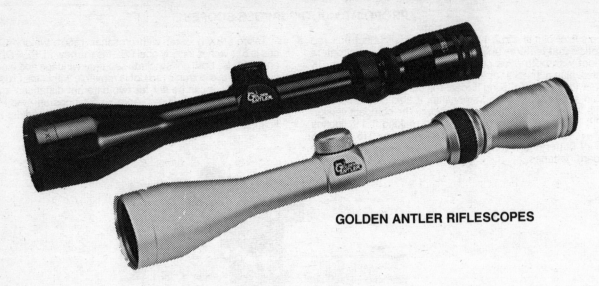

GOLDEN ANTLER RIFLESCOPES

GOLDEN ANTLER™ RIFLESCOPES

Model	Power	Objective Diameter	Finish	Reticle	Field of View @ 100 Yds.	Eye Relief	Tube Diam.	Scope Length	Scope Weight	Prices
GA4X32TV	4X	32mm	Blk. Gloss/ Matte Alum.	30/30TV	32'	3"	1"	13"	12.7 oz.	$ 79.00
GA4X40TV	4X	40mm	Black Gloss	30/30TV	32'	3"	1"	12"	12.5 oz.	99.00
GA2.510X44TV	2.5X-10X	44mm	Black Gloss	30/30TV	35'-9'	3.5"	1"	12.5"	14.4 oz.	214.00
GA39X32TV	3X-9X	32mm	Black Gloss	30/30TV	39'-13'	3"	1"	13.25"	12.2 oz.	102.00
GA39X32MA	3X-9X	32mm	Matte Aluminum	30/30TV	39'-13'	3"	1"	13.25"	12.2 oz.	102.00
GA39X40TV	3X-9X	40mm	Black Gloss	30/30TV	39'-13'	3"	1"	12.5"	13 oz.	135.00
GA39X40MA	3X-9X	40mm	Matte Aluminum	30/30TV	39'-13'	3"	1"	12.5"	13 oz.	135.00

SILVER ANTLER™ RIFLESCOPES

Model	Power	Objective Diameter	Finish	Reticle	Field of View @ 100 Yds.	Eye Relief	Tube Diam.	Scope Length	Scope Weight	Prices
SA2.5X32	2.5X	32mm	Black Gloss	30/30	42'	3.25"	1"	11"	10 oz.	$ 86.00
SA4X32	4X	32mm	Blk. Gloss/ Matte Alum.	30/30	32'	3"	1"	12"	12.5 oz.	79.00
SA4X40	4X	40mm	Black Gloss	30/30	32'	3"	1"	12"	12.5 oz.	99.00
SA39X32	3X-9X	32mm	Black Gloss	30/30	39'-13'	3"	1"	12"	11 oz.	102.00
SA39X32MA	3X-9X	32mm	Matte Aluminum	30/30	39'-13'	3"	1"	12"	11 oz.	102.00
SA39X40	3X-9X	40mm	Black Gloss	30/30	39'-13'	3"	1"	12.5"	13 oz.	135.00
SA39X40MA	3X-9X	40mm	Matte Aluminum	30/30	39'-13'	3"	1"	12.5"	13 oz.	135.00
SA2.51OX44	2.5X-10X	44mm	Black Gloss	30/30	35'-9'	3.5"	1"	12.5"	14.4 oz.	214.00

TASCO SCOPES

WORLD CLASS PLUS RIFLESCOPES

Large 44mm objective lenses—the same optics used in the Tasco Titan series—gather 21% more light than standard 40mm scopes, making them well suited for hunters who prefer the dusk and dawn hours. Fully coated optical glass with Super-Con® coating reduces internal reflections. All World Class Plus scopes are waterproof, fogproof and shockproof. **Length: 12.75″.**

SPECIFICATIONS

Model	Power	Objective Diameter	Finish	Reticle	Field of View @ 100 Yds.	Eye Relief	Tube Diam.	Scope Length	Scope Weight	Prices
WCP4X44	4X	44mm	Black Gloss	30/30	32′	3¼″	1″	12.75″	13.5 oz.	$310.00
WCP6X44	6X	44mm	Black Gloss	30/30	21′	3¼″	1″	12.75″	13.6 oz.	310.00
WCP39X44	3X-9X	4mm	Black Gloss*	30/30	39′-14′	3½″	1″	12.75″	15.8 oz.	370.00
DWCP39X44	3X-9X	44mm	Black Matte	30/30	39′-14′	3½″	1″	12.75″	15.8 oz.	370.00
WCP3.510X50	3.5X-10X	50mm	Black Gloss	30/30	30′-10.5′	3¾″	1″	13″	17.1 oz.	489.00
DWCP3.510X50	3.5X-10X	50mm	Black Matte	30/30	30′-10.5′	3¾″	1″	13″	17.1 oz.	489.00

* Also available in stainless **$370.00**

RUBBER ARMORED SCOPES

Extra padding helps these rugged scopes stand up to rough handling. Custom-fitting rings are included. Scopes feature:
• Fully coated optics
• Windage and elevation controls
• Waterproofing, fogproofing, shockproofing
• ¼-minute positive click stops
• Opti-centered 30/30 rangefinding reticle
• Haze filter caps

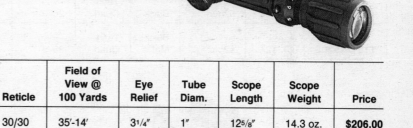

Model	Power	Objective Diameter	Finish	Reticle	Field of View @ 100 Yards	Eye Relief	Tube Diam.	Scope Length	Scope Weight	Price
RC39X40 A,B	3-9	40mm	Green Rubber	30/30	35′-14′	3¼″	1″	12⅝″	14.3 oz.	$206.00

"A" fits standard dove tail base.
"B" fits ⅜″ grooved receivers—most 22 cal. and airguns.

MAG IV RIFLESCOPES (not shown)

MAG IV scopes yield four times magnification range in a standard size riflescope and one-third more zooming range than most variable scopes. Features include: Fully coated optics and large objective lens to keep target in low light . . . Non-removable eye bell. . . ¼-minute positive click stops . . . Non-removable windage and elevation screws. . . Opticentered 30/30 rangefinding reticle . . . Waterproof, fogproof, shockproof.

SPECIFICATIONS

Model	Power	Objective Diameter	Finish	Reticle	Field of View @ 100 Yds.	Eye Relief	Tube Diam.	Scope Length	Scope Weight	Price
W312X40	3-12	40mm	Black	30/30	35′-9′	3⅛″	1″	12³⁄₁₆″	12 oz.	$183.00
W416X40†	4-16	40mm	Black	30/30	26′-6′	3⅛″	1″	14⅛″	15.6 oz.	229.00
W624X40†	6-24	40mm	Black	30/30	17′-4′	3″	1″	15⅜″	16.75 oz.	290.00

† Indicates focusing objective.

TASCO SCOPES

TITAN RIFLESCOPES

Tasco's Titan riflescope features image brightness and clarity, true multi-coating, strength and rigidity, lightweight aluminum with the strength of steel, and a 30mm tube diameter. It also includes fast focus, reticle center indicator, finger adjustable windage and elevation, titanium parts, special reticle design (located in the first image plane), and a 42mm objective lens. In addition, it offers one-piece body construction, individual serial number, special lubrication, extra wide field of view and maximum eye relief. Specifications and prices are listed below.

Model	Power	Objective Diameter	Finish	Reticle	Field of View @ 100 Yds.	Eye Relief	Tube Diam.	Scope Length	Scope Weight	Price
TT1.56X42	1.5X-6X	42mm	Black	Titan Quad	59'-20'	3.5"	30mm	12"	16.4 oz.	$764.00
TT156X42DS	1.5X-6X	42mm	Black Matte	Titan Quad	59'-20'	3.5"	30mm	12"	16.4 oz.	764.00
TT39X42DS	3X-9X	42mm	Black Matte	Titan Quad	37'-13'	5-4"	30mm	12.5"	16.8 oz.	733.00
TT39X42	3X-9X	42mm	Black	Titan Quad	37'-13'	5-4"	30mm	12.5"	16.8 oz.	733.00
TT312X52	3X-12X	52mm	Black	Titan Quad	28'-9'	3.5"	30mm	14"	19.9 oz.	911.00
TT312X52DS	3X-12X	52mm	Black Matte	Titan Quad	28'-9'	3.5"	30mm	14"	19.9 oz.	911.00

LASER POINT

Tasco's LaserPoint model is the first compact to have a multi-mode red dot (one second continuous followed by one second pulsating), making it the fastest and easiest dot to locate on the target. An index-guided diode designed with minimum astigmatism, maximum efficiency and battery life results in a much improved laser dot. Additional features include adjustable windage and elevation system, waterproofing and several optional mounts that require no gunsmithing.
Price: $458.00

WEATHERBY SUPREME SCOPES

WEATHERBY SUPREME SCOPES

As every hunter knows, one of the most difficult problems is keeping running game in the field of view of the scope. Once lost, precious seconds fade away trying to find the animal in the scope again. Too much time wasted means the ultimate frustration. No second shot. Or no shot at all. The Weatherby Wide Field helps you surmount the problem by increasing your field of view.

FEATURES

Optical excellence—now protected with multicoated anti-glare coating. • Fog-free and waterproof construction. • Constantly self-centered reticles. • Non-magnifying reticle. • 1/4″ adjustments. • Quick variable power change. • Unique luminous reticle. • Neoprene eyepiece. • Binocular-type speed focusing. • Rugged score tube construction. Autocom point-blank system.

4 POWER

These are fixed-power scopes for big game and varmint hunting. Bright, clear image. Multicoated lenses for maximum luminosity under adverse conditions. 32-foot field of view at 100 yards.

Prices:
Fixed Power
4X44 . . . . **$243.00**

Variable Power
1.75-5X20 . . . . **234.00**
2-7X34 . . . . **243.00**
3-9X44 . . . . **286.00**

3 TO 9 POWER

The most desirable variable for every kind of shooting from target to long-range big game. Outstanding light-gathering power. Fast, convenient focusing adjustment.

1³/₄ TO 5 POWER

A popular model for close-range hunting with large-bore rifles. Includes the Autocom system, which automatically compensates for trajectory and eliminates the need for range-finding without making elevation adjustments. Just aim and shoot!

SUPREME RIFLESCOPES SPECIFICATIONS

Item	1.75-5×20	2-7×34	4×44	3-9×44
Actual Magnification	1.7-5	2.1-6.83	3.9	3.15-8.98
Field of View @ 100 yards	66.6-21.4 ft.	59-16 ft.	32 ft.	36-13 ft.
Eye Relief (inches)	3.4	3.4	3.0	3.5
Exit Pupil dia. in mm	11.9-4	10-4.9	10	10-4.9
Clear Aperture of Objective	20mm	34mm	44mm	44mm
Twilight Factor	5.9-10	8.2-15.4	13.3	11.5-19.9
Tube Diameter	1″	1″	1″	1″
O.D. of Objective	1″	1.610″	2″	2″
O.D. of Ocular	1.635″	1.635″	1.635″	1.635″
Overall Length	10.7″	11.125″	12.5″	12.7″
Weight	11 oz.	10.4 oz.	11.6 oz.	11.6 oz.
Adjustment Graduations Major Divisions: Minor Divisions:	1 MOA 1/4 MOA	1 MOA 1/4 MOA	1 MOA 1/4 MOA	1 MOA 1/4 MOA
Maximum Adjustment (W&E)	60″	60″	60″	60″
Reticles Available	LUMIPLEX	LUMIPLEX	LUMIPLEX	LUMIPLEX

WIDEVIEW SCOPE MOUNTS

PREMIUM SEE-THRU SCOPE MOUNTS

Rifle	Model
Browning A Bolt	NN
Browning Semi-Auto	AA
Browning Lever Action	AA
Browning F.N. Bolt Action	CB
BSA, Medium & Long Action	DB
Glenfield 30 by Marlin	GG
H & R Bolt Action F.N. 300, 301, 317, 330, 370	CB
Husquvarna F.N. Action	CB
Interarms Mark X	CB
Ithaca BSA (Bolt Action)	DB
Marlin 336, 62, 36, 444	GG
Marlin 1893, 1894, 1895, 9, 45	GG
Marlin 465 F.N. Action	CB
Mauser F.N. 98, 2000, 3000	CB
Mossberg 800, 500	AA
Parker Hale 1000, 1000C, 1100, 1200, 1200C	CB
Parker Hale 2100	JB
Remington 7	SB
Remington 700, 721, 722, 725	DB
Remington 740, 742, 760	EB
Remington 788	FH
Remington 4, 6, 7400, 7600	EB8
Remington XP-100 Pistol 600, 660	HB
Revelation 200 Lever Action	GG
Ruger M-77 round receiver	DB
Ruger 44 rifle	QO
Ruger 10/22	OP
Savage 99	KM
Savage 110, 111, 112	IB
Savage 170	EB
Smith & Wesson 1500 Bolt	DB
Weatherby Mark V & Vanguard	DB
Western Field 740	GG
Winchester 88, 100	BB
Winchester 70, 70A, 670, 770 and Ser. #700, (except 375 H & H)	FB
Winchester 94AE Angle Eject	94 AE
Winchester 94 Side Mount	94

SHOTGUNS (Must Be Drilled and Tapped)

	Model
Ithaca, Remington, Winchester, Mossberg, etc. Note: Remington 1100 and Browning 5 Auto not recommended by Wideview for top mounts. Receivers should be .150 thousands or more in thickness.	BB

FOR WEAVER-STYLE BASES

	Model
Savage 24V	U-20
Straight Cut	U-10
20 Degree Angle Cut	U-20
Straight Cut 30 Millimeter	U-1030
20 Degree Angle Cut 30 Millimeter	U-2030

RING-STYLE MOUNTS

	Model
Dove Tail Solid Lock Ring Fits Any Redfield, Tasco, or Weaver Style Base	SR
Dove Tail Solid Lock 30 Millimeter	SR30
True-Fit Lo Ring	L-Ring

Rifle	Model
True-Fit Hi Ring	H-Ring
True-Fit Grooved Receiver	GR-Ring
Ruger High Rings M77R, M77RS, M77V	TU
Ruger High Rings No. 1-A, RSI, B, S, H, 3. 72/22	TU
Ruger Redhawk Hunter	UU
Ruger Mini-14/5R, K-Mini Thirty	TU
Ruger Redhawk, Hunter 30 millimeter	UU30

PREMIUM FLASHLIGHT MOUNT

	Model
Site Lite Mount	SL

22 RIMFIRE SEE-THRU MOUNT

	Model
For All 22 Caliber Rimfire Rifles With Grooved Receiver. Designed For 3/4 and 1" Diameter Scopes. Also Used On Air Rifles	22R

BLACK POWDER MOUNTS (See Thru)
Barrels Must Be Drilled and Tapped

	Model
CVA Frontier Carbine, Plainsman, Pennsylvania Long Rifle	GG
CVA Hawken, Hunter Hawken, Mountain Rifle, Blazer	GG
CVA Squirrel Rifle, Kentuckey, Kentuckey Hunter & Kit Rifles	GG
CVA St Louis Hawken (Except 12 Gage and 58 Caliber)	GG
Thompson Center, Renegade, Hawken, White Mountain, New Englander	GG
Traditions Frontier Carbine, Pioneer Rifle	GG
Traditions Pennsylvania Rifle, Hawken Woodsman, Frontier Rifle	GG
Traditions Trapper, Frontier Scout Kits for Hawken Woodsman, Frontier Rifle, Frontier Carbine	GG

BLACK POWDER SEE-THRU MOUNTS NO DRILLING OR TAPPING

	Model
Thompson Center Hawken (Ultra Precision See Thru Mounts Included)	TCH
Thompson Center Renegade (Ultra Precision See Thru Mounts Included)	TCR
CVA Stalker Rifle / Carbine	ii
CVA Apollo 90 Rifle/Carbine	ii
CVA Apollo Sporter	ii
CVA Shadow Rifle	ii
CVA Tracker Carbine	ii
CVA Hawken Deerslayer Rifle / Carbine	ii
CVA St. Louis Hawken Rifle	ii
CVA Trophy Carbine	ii
CVA Frontier Hunter Carbine	ii
Knight MK - 85, BK - 90	ii

COMPOUND BOW SCOPE MOUNT

	Model
Bow Scope Mount Right Hand	BSM-RH
Bow Scope Mount Left Hand	BSM-LH

WILLIAMS TWILIGHT SCOPES

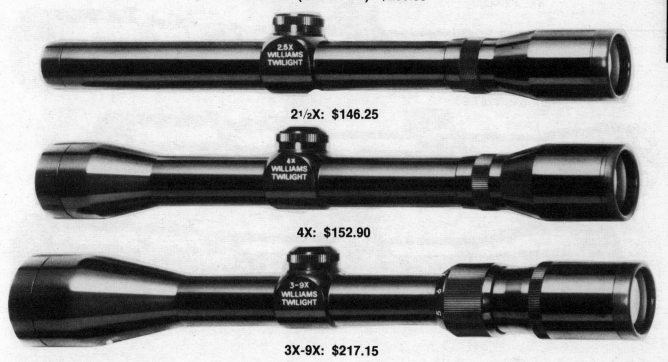

1.5X-5X (and 2X-6X): $206.65

2¹/₂X: $146.25

4X: $152.90

3X-9X: $217.15

The "Twilight" series of scopes was introduced to accommodate those shooters who want a high-quality scope in the medium-priced field. The "Twilight" scopes are waterproof and shockproof, have coated lenses and are nitrogen-filled. Resolution is sharp and clear. All "Twilight" scopes have a highly polished, rich, black, hard anodized finish.

There are five models available: the 2¹/₂x, the 4x, the 1.5x-5x, the 2x-6x, and the 3x-9x. They are available in T-N-T reticle only (which stands for "thick and thin").

OPTICAL SPECIFICATIONS	2.5X	4X	1.5X-5X At 1.5X	At 5X	2X-6X At 2X	At 6X	3X-9X At 3X	At 9X
Clear aperture of objective lens....	20mm	32mm	20mm	Same	32mm	Same	40mm	Same
Clear aperture of ocular lens......	32mm	32mm	32mm	Same	32mm	Same	32mm	Same
Exit Pupil......................	8mm	8mm	13.3mm	4mm	16mm	5.3mm	13.3mm	44.4mm
Relative Brightness..............	64	64	177	16	256	28	161.2	17.6
Field of view (degree of angle).....	6°10'	5°30'	11°	4°	8°30'	3°10'	7°	2°20'
Field of view at 100 yards........	32'	29'	57¾'	21'	45½'	16¾'	36½'	12¾'
Eye Relief......................	3.7"	3.6"	3.5"	3.5"	3"	3"	3.1"	2.9"
Parallax Correction (at).........	50 yds.	100 yds.	100 yds.	Same	100 yds.	Same	100 yds.	Same
Lens Construction...............	9	9	10	Same	11	Same	11	Same
MECHANICAL SPECIFICATIONS								
Outside diameter of objective end..	1.00"	1.525"	1.00"	Same	1.525"	Same	1.850"	1.850"
Outside diameter of ocular end....	1.455"	1.455"	1.455"	Same	1.455"	Same	1.455"	Same
Ouside diameter of tube.........	1"	1"	1"	Same	1"	Same	1"	Same
Internal adjustment graduation....	¼ min.	¼ min.	¼ min.	Same	¼ min.	Same	¼ min.	Same
Minimum internal adjustment......	75 min.	75 min.	75 min.	Same	75 min.	Same	60 min.	Same
Finish			Glossy Hard Black Anodized					
Length........................	10"	11¾"	10¾"	Same	11½"	11½"	12¾"	12¾"
Weight	8½ oz.	9½ oz.	10 oz.	Same	11½ oz.	Same	13½ oz.	Same

WILLIAMS

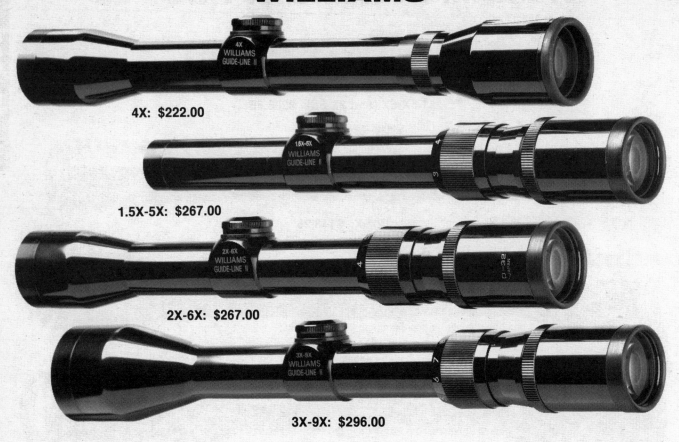

4X: $222.00

1.5X-5X: $267.00

2X-6X: $267.00

3X-9X: $296.00

GUIDELINE II SERIES

Patterned after the popular Twilight Series, Williams' new Guideline II Series features silent adjustment screws, streamlined adjustment caps and power adjustment rings. Fully multi-coated lenses ensure superior light gathering and brightness. Comes equipped with T-N-T reticle and a choice of matte or glossy black finish.

OPTICAL SPECIFICATIONS	4X	1.5X–5X		2X–6X		3X–9X	
		At 1.5X	At 5X	At 2X	At 6X	At 3X	At 9X
Clear aperture of objective lens	32mm	20mm	Same	32mm	Same	40mm	Same
Clear aperture of ocular lens	32mm	32mm	Same	32mm	Same	32mm	Same
Exit Pupil	8mm	13.3mm	4mm	16mm	5.3mm	13.3mm	44.4mm
Relative Brightness	64	177	16	256	28	161.2	17.6
Field of view (degree of angle)	5°30′	11°	4°	8°30′	3°10′	7°	2°20′
Field of view at 100 yards	29′	57¾′	21′	45½′	16¾′	36½′	12¾′
Eye Relief	3.6″	3.5″	3.5″	3″	3″	3.1″	2.9″
Parallax Correction (at)	100 yds.	100 yds.	Same	100 yds.	Same	100 yds.	Same
Lens Construction	9	10	Same	11	Same	11	Same
MECHANICAL SPECIFICATIONS							
Outside diameter of objective end . .	1.525″	1.00″	Same	1.525″	Same	1.850″	1.850″
Outside diameter of ocular end	1.455″	1.455″	Same	1.455″	Same	1.455″	Same
Outside diameter of tube	1″	1″	Same	1″	Same	1″	Same
Internal adjustment graduation	¼ min.	¼ min.	Same	¼ min.	Same	¼ min.	Same
Minimum internal adjustment	75 min.	75 min.	Same	75 min.	Same	60 min.	Same
Finish				Glossy Hard Black Anodized			
Length	11¾″	10¾″	Same	11½″	11½″	12¾″	12¾″
Weight	9½ oz.	10 oz.	Same	11½ oz.	Same	13½ oz.	Same

ZEISS RIFLESCOPES

THE C-SERIES

The C-Series was designed by Zeiss specifically for the American hunter. It is based on space-age alloy tubes with integral objective and ocular bells, and an integral adjustment turret. This strong, rigid one-piece construction allows perfect lens alignment, micro-precise adjustments and structural integrity. Other features include quick focusing, a generous 3½" of eye relief, rubber armoring, T-Star multi-layer coating, and parallax setting (free at 100 yards).

DIATAL-C 10×36T
$835.00

DIAVARI-C 3-9×36T
$975.00

DIATAL-C 6×32T
$715.00

DIATAL-C 4×32T
$680.00

DIAVARI-C 1.5-4.5×18T
$930.00

SPECIFICATIONS

	4×32	6×32	10×36	3-9×36		C1.5-4.5×18	
Magnification	4X	6X	10X	3X	9X	1.5X	4.5X
Objective Diameter (mm)/(inch)	1.26″	1.26″	1.42″	1.42″		15.0/0.6	18.0/0.7
Exit Pupil	0.32″	0.21″	0.14″	0.39″	0.16″	10.0	4.0
Twilight Performance	11.3	13.9	19.0	8.5	18.0	4.2	9.0
Field of View at 100 yds.	30′	20′	12′	36′	13′	72′	27′
Eye Relief	3.5″	3.5″	3.5″	3.5″	3.5″	3.5″	
Maximum Interval Adjustment (elevation and windage (MOA)	80	80	50	50		10.5′ @ 100 yds.	
Click-Stop Adjustment 1 click = 1 interval (MOA)	¼	¼	¼	¼		.36″ @ 100 yds.	
Length	10.6″	10.6″	12.7″	11.2″		11.8″	
Weight approx. (ounces)	11.3	11.3	14.1	15.2		13.4	
Tube Diameter	1″	1″	1″	1″		1″	
Objective Tube Diameter	1.65″	1.65″	1.89″	1.73″		1″	
Eyepiece O.D.	1.67″	1.67″	1.67″	1.67″		1.8″	

ZEISS RIFLESCOPES

THE "Z" SERIES

These new Zeiss riflescopes feature a surface that is harder and more resistant to abrasion and mechanical damage than the multiple coatings or bluings. The black, silken matte finish suppresses reflections and prevents finger prints. All optical elements are provided with the Zeiss T Star multi-coating. The size of the reticles in the Diavari Z-types changes with the power set; therefore, the ratio of the reticle size to the target size always remains the same.

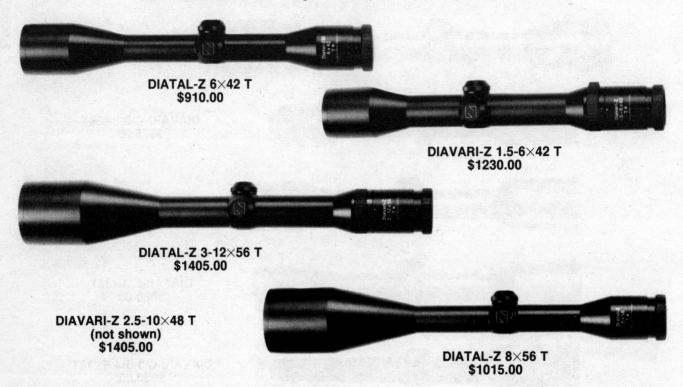

DIATAL-Z 6×42 T
$910.00

DIAVARI-Z 1.5-6×42 T
$1230.00

DIATAL-Z 3-12×56 T
$1405.00

DIAVARI-Z 2.5-10×48 T
(not shown)
$1405.00

DIATAL-Z 8×56 T
$1015.00

ZEISS RIFLESCOPES, ZM/Z-SERIES SPECIFICATIONS

Model	Diatal-ZM/Z 6×42 T*	Diavari-ZM/Z 1.5-6×42 T*	Diavari-ZM/Z 3-12×56 T*	Diatal-ZM/Z 8×56 T*	Diavari-ZM/Z 2.5-10×48 T
Magnification	6X	1.5X 6X	3X 12X	8X	2.5X-10X
Effective obj. diam. (mm, inch)	42/1.7	19.5/0.8 42/1.7	38/1.5 56/2.2	56/2.2	33/1.30 48/1.89
Diameter of exit pupil (mm)	7	13 7	12.7 4.7	7	13.2 4.8
Twilight factor	15.9	4.2 15.9	8.5 25.9	21.2	7.1 21.9
Field of view at 100 m (m)/ft. at 100 yds.	6.7/20.1	18/54.0 6.5/19.5	9.2/27.6 3.3/9.9	5/15.0	11.0/33.0 3.9/11.7
Approx. eye relief (cm, inch)	8/3.2	8/3.2	8/3.2	8/3.2	8/3.2
Click-stop adjustment 1 click = (cm at 100 m)/(inch at 100 yds.)	1/0.36	1/0.36	1/0.36	1/0.36	1/0.36
Max. adj. (elevation and windage) at 100 m (cm)/at 100 yds. (inch)	187	190	95	138	110/39.6
Center tube dia. (mm/inch)	25.4/1	30/1.18	30/1.18	25.4/1	30/1.18
Objective bell dia. (mm/inch)	48/1.9	48/1.9	62/2.44	62/2.44	54/2.13
Ocular bell dia. (mm/inch)	40/1.57	40/1.57	40/1.57	40/1.57	40/1.57
Length (mm/inch)	324/12.8	320/12.6	388/15.3	369/14.5	370/14.57
Approx. weight (ZM/Z) (g/ozs.)	35/400/15.3/14.1	586/562/20.7/19.8	765/731/27.0/25.8	550/520/19.4/18.3	715/680/25.2/24

Ammunition

For addresses and phone numbers of manufacturers and distributors included in this section, turn to *DIRECTORY OF MANUFACTURERS AND SUPPLIERS* at the back of the book.

FEDERAL AMMUNITION

The following pages include Federal's new or recent lines of cartridges and shotshells for 1993–94. For a complete listing of all Federal ammunition, call or write the Federal Cartridge Company (see Directory of Manufacturers in the Reference section for address and phone number).

PREMIUM CARTRIDGES

A Sierra 40-grain hollow-point bullet is featured in Federal's 223 Rem. Varmint load.

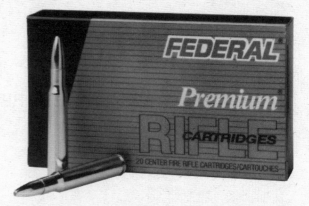

Federal's 30-06 Springfield cartridge (Premium Safari) is loaded with a Trophy Bonded 165-grain bullet.

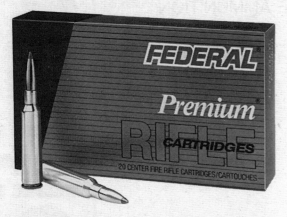

A 140-grain Nosler Partition bullet has been added to Federal's 6.5×55 Swedish cartridge.

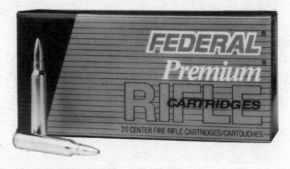

Federal's 300 Win. Mag. cartridge is loaded with the Trophy Bonded 200-grain bullet.

This varmint cartridge for the 22-250 Rem. delivers a muzzle velocity of 4000 fps.

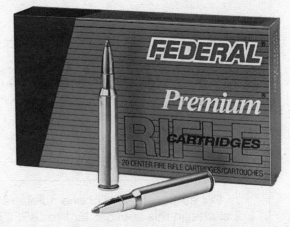

Federal's 7×64 Brenneke with a 160-grain Nosler Partition bullet has been added to the Premium line.

FEDERAL AMMUNITION

PREMIUM CARTRIDGES

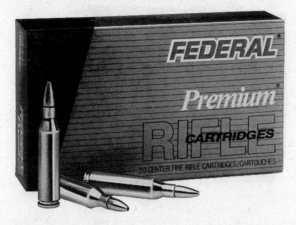

A Sierra 60-grain hollow-point bullet is now available to all 243 Win. shooters.

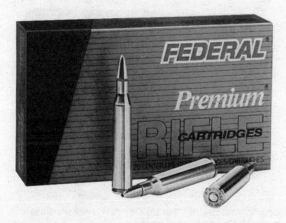

This 25-06 Rem. Varmint load features a Sierra 90-grain hollow-point bullet.

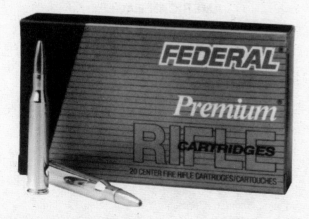

Federal's 270 Win. cartridge with its 140-grain Trophy Bonded bullet joins the Premium Safari line.

CLASSIC CARTRIDGES

Federal offers a 40 S&W cartridge with a 155-grain Hi-Shok jacketed hollow-point bullet.

A 230-grain Hi-Shok jacketed hollow-point bullet complements Federal's 45 Auto cartridge.

This 10mm auto cartridge uses a 155-grain Hi-Shok jacketed hollow-point bullet with a muzzle velocity of 1325 fps.

FEDERAL AMMUNITION

GOLD MEDAL LINE

Federal's Auto Match cartridge with its 185-grain Semi-Wadcutter bullet joins the Gold Medal line.

Federal's Gold Medal line now includes this 9mm Luger Match cartridge with a 124-grain Semi-Wadcutter bullet.

Two new paper trap loads—an Extra-Lite Skeet load and two new 24-gram International loads—have been added to the Gold Medal line.

PREMIUM SHOTSHELLS

This 20-gauge 3″ Premium shotshell contains 1¼ oz. of copper-plated No. 6 shot.

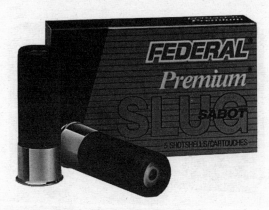

A copper-plated Sabot-style slug is offered with Federal's 12-gauge 3″ Premium slug load.

AMERICAN EAGLE

The American Eagle line includes this 22 LR cartridge with a 40-grain lead bullet.

HORNADY AMMUNITION

RIFLE CARTRIDGES

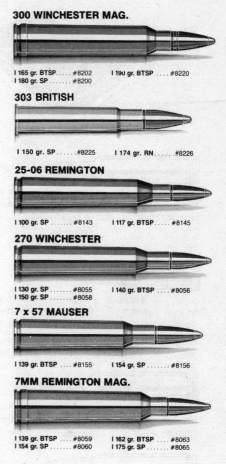

222 REMINGTON

50 gr. SX .... #8010   55 gr. SX .... #8015

223 REMINGTON

53 gr. HP .... #8023   55 gr. FMJ .... #8027
55 gr. SP .... #8025   60 gr. SP .... #8028

22-250 REMINGTON

53 gr. HP .... #8030   55 gr. FMJ .... #8037
55 gr. SP .... #8035   60 gr. SP .... #8039

220 SWIFT

NEW
50 gr. SP .... #8121   60 gr. HP .... #8122
                           55 gr. SP .... #8120

6MM REMINGTON

I 100 gr. BTSP .... #8166

243 WINCHESTER

75 gr. HP .... #8040   80 gr. FMJ .... #8043
I 100 gr. BTSP ...... #8046

257 ROBERTS

I 100 gr. SP ..... #8133   I 117 gr. BTSP ..... #8135

7MM WEATHERBY MAG   NEW

I 175 gr. SP .... #8067

30-30 WINCHESTER

I 150 gr. RN ...... #8080   I 170 gr. FP ...... #8085

308 WINCHESTER

I 150 gr. SP .... #8090   I 165 gr. SP ...... #8095
I 150 gr. BTSP .... #8091   I 165 gr. BTSP .... #8098
168 gr. BTHP (Match) .... #8097

30-06 SPRINGFIELD

I 150 gr. SP .... #8110   168 gr. BTHP
I 150 gr. BTSP .... #8111   (Match) .... #8117
I 165 gr. BTSP .... #8115   I 180 gr. SP .... #8118

300 WEATHERBY MAG   NEW

I 180 gr. SP .... #8222

300 WINCHESTER MAG.

I 165 gr. BTSP..... #8202   I 190 gr. BTSP .... #8220
I 180 gr. SP .... #8200

303 BRITISH

I 150 gr. SP ...... #8225   I 174 gr. RN ...... #8226

25-06 REMINGTON

I 100 gr. SP ..... #8143   I 117 gr. BTSP .... #8145

270 WINCHESTER

I 130 gr. SP ...... #8055   I 140 gr. BTSP .... #8056
I 150 gr. SP ...... #8058

7 x 57 MAUSER

I 139 gr. BTSP .... #8155   I 154 gr. SP ...... #8156

7MM REMINGTON MAG.

I 139 gr. BTSP .... #8059   I 162 gr. BTSP .... #8063
I 154 gr. SP ...... #8060   I 175 gr. SP ...... #8065

PISTOL CARTRIDGES

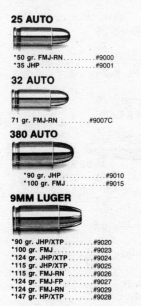

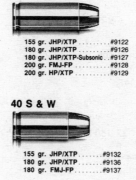
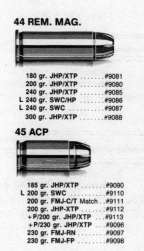

25 AUTO

*50 gr. FMJ-RN .... #9000
*35 JHP .... #9001

32 AUTO

71 gr. FMJ-RN .... #9007C

380 AUTO

*90 gr. JHP .... #9010
*100 gr. FMJ .... #9015

9MM LUGER

*90 gr. JHP/XTP .... #9020
*100 gr. FMJ .... #9023
*124 gr. JHP/XTP .... #9024
*115 gr. JHP/XTP .... #9025
*115 gr. FMJ-RN .... #9026
*124 gr. FMJ-FP .... #9027
*124 gr. FMJ-RN .... #9029
*147 gr. HP/XTP .... #9028

38 SPECIAL

*125 gr. JHP/XTP .... #9032
*140 gr. JHP/XTP .... #9035
L *148 gr. HBWC (Match)... #9043
*158 gr. JHP/XTP .... #9036
L *158 gr. LRN .... #9045
L *158 gr. SWC .... #9046
L *158 gr. SWC/HP .... #9047

357 MAG.

*125 gr. JHP/XTP .... #9050
*125 gr. JFP/XTP .... #9053
*140 gr. JHP/XTP .... #9055
*158 gr. JHP/XTP .... #9056
*158 gr. JFP/XTP .... #9058
L *158 gr. SWC .... #9065
L *158 gr. SWC/HP .... #9066

10MM AUTO

155 gr. JHP/XTP .... #9122
180 gr. JHP/XTP .... #9126
180 gr. JHP/XTP-Subsonic.. #9127
200 gr. FMJ-FP .... #9128
200 gr. HP/XTP .... #9129

40 S & W

155 gr. JHP/XTP .... #9132
180 gr. JHP/XTP .... #9136
180 gr. FMJ-FP .... #9137

44 REM. MAG.

180 gr. JHP/XTP .... #9081
200 gr. JHP/XTP .... #9080
240 gr. JHP/XTP .... #9085
L 240 gr. SWC/HP .... #9086
L 240 gr. SWC .... #9087
300 gr. JHP/XTP .... #9088

45 ACP

185 gr. JHP/XTP .... #9090
L 200 gr. SWC .... #9110
200 gr. FMJ-C/T Match .. #9111
200 gr. JHP-XTP .... #9112
+P/200 gr. JHP/XTP .... #9113
+P/230 gr. JHP/XTP .... #9096
230 gr. FMJ-RN .... #9097
230 gr. FMJ-FP .... #9098

REMINGTON CENTERFIRE RIFLE CARTRIDGES

223 REMINGTON (5.56MM)

No.	Bullet weight	Bullet style	Wt. case, lbs.
R223R1	55 gr.	Pointed Soft Point	15
R223R2	55 gr.	Hollow Point Power-Lokt®	15
R223R3	55 gr.	Metal Case	15
R223R4	60 gr.	Hollow Point	14

20 IN A BOX, 500 IN A CASE.

17 REMINGTON

No.	Bullet weight	Bullet style	Wt. case, lbs.
R17REM	25 gr.	Hollow Point Power-Lokt®	12

20 IN A BOX, 500 IN A CASE.

6MM REMINGTON

No.	Bullet weight	Bullet style	Wt. case, lbs.
R6MM1*	80 gr.	Pointed Soft Point	26
R6MM2*	80 gr.	Hollow Point Power-Lokt®	26
R6MM4	100 gr.	Pointed Soft Point Core-Lokt®	26
ER6MMRA	105 gr.	Extended Range	27

20 IN A BOX, 500 IN A CASE.

*May be used in rifles chambered for .244 Remington.

22 HORNET

No.	Bullet weight	Bullet style	Wt. case, lbs.
R22HN1	45 gr.	Pointed Soft Point	9
R22HN2	45 gr.	Hollow Point	9

20 IN A BOX, 500 IN A CASE.

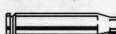

6MM BENCH REST REMINGTON

No.	Bullet weight	Bullet style	Wt. case, lbs.
R6MMBR	100 gr.	Pointed Soft Point	21

20 IN A BOX, 500 IN A CASE.

220 SWIFT

No.	Bullet weight	Bullet style	Wt. case, lbs.
R22051	50 gr.	Pointed Soft Point	10

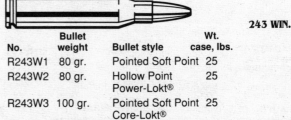

243 WIN.

No.	Bullet weight	Bullet style	Wt. case, lbs.
R243W1	80 gr.	Pointed Soft Point	25
R243W2	80 gr.	Hollow Point Power-Lokt®	25
R243W3	100 gr.	Pointed Soft Point Core-Lokt®	25
ERZ43WA	105 gr.	Extended Range	26

20 IN A BOX, 500 IN A CASE.

222 REMINGTON

No.	Bullet weight	Bullet style	Wt. case, lbs.
R222R1	50 gr.	Pointed Soft Point	14
R222R4	50 gr.	Hollow Point Power-Lokt®	14

20 IN A BOX, 500 IN A CASE.

222 REMINGTON MAGNUM

No.	Bullet weight	Bullet style	Wt. case, lbs.
R222M1	55 gr.	Pointed Soft Point	15

20 IN A BOX, 500 IN A CASE.

25-06 REMINGTON

No.	Bullet weight	Bullet style	Wt. case, lbs.
R25061	87 gr.	Hollow Point Power-Lokt®	27
R25062	100 gr.	Pointed Soft Point Core-Lokt®	27
R25063	120 gr.	Pointed Soft Point Core-Lokt®	27
ER2506A	122 gr.	Extended Range	

20 IN A BOX, 500 IN A CASE.

22-250 REMINGTON

No.	Bullet weight	Bullet style	Wt. case, lbs.
R22501	55 gr.	Pointed Soft Point	21
R22502	55 gr.	Hollow Point Power-Lokt®	21

20 IN A BOX, 500 IN A CASE.

REMINGTON CENTERFIRE RIFLE CARTRIDGES

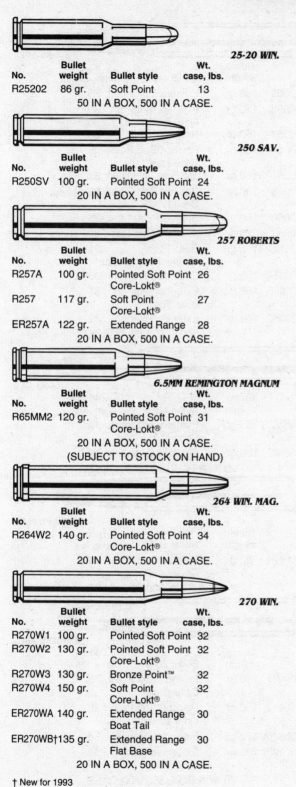

25-20 WIN.

No.	Bullet weight	Bullet style	Wt. case, lbs.
R25202	86 gr.	Soft Point	13

50 IN A BOX, 500 IN A CASE.

250 SAV.

No.	Bullet weight	Bullet style	Wt. case, lbs.
R250SV	100 gr.	Pointed Soft Point	24

20 IN A BOX, 500 IN A CASE.

257 ROBERTS

No.	Bullet weight	Bullet style	Wt. case, lbs.
R257A	100 gr.	Pointed Soft Point Core-Lokt®	26
R257	117 gr.	Soft Point Core-Lokt®	27
ER257A	122 gr.	Extended Range	28

20 IN A BOX, 500 IN A CASE.

6.5MM REMINGTON MAGNUM

No.	Bullet weight	Bullet style	Wt. case, lbs.
R65MM2	120 gr.	Pointed Soft Point Core-Lokt®	31

20 IN A BOX, 500 IN A CASE.
(SUBJECT TO STOCK ON HAND)

264 WIN. MAG.

No.	Bullet weight	Bullet style	Wt. case, lbs.
R264W2	140 gr.	Pointed Soft Point Core-Lokt®	34

20 IN A BOX, 500 IN A CASE.

270 WIN.

No.	Bullet weight	Bullet style	Wt. case, lbs.
R270W1	100 gr.	Pointed Soft Point	32
R270W2	130 gr.	Pointed Soft Point Core-Lokt®	32
R270W3	130 gr.	Bronze Point™	32
R270W4	150 gr.	Soft Point Core-Lokt®	32
ER270WA	140 gr.	Extended Range Boat Tail	30
ER270WB†	135 gr.	Extended Range Flat Base	30

20 IN A BOX, 500 IN A CASE.

† New for 1993

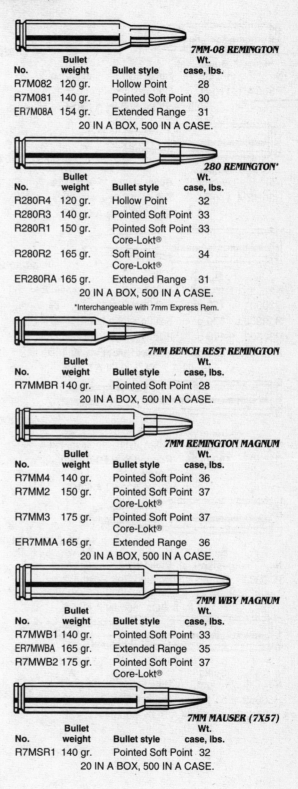

7MM-08 REMINGTON

No.	Bullet weight	Bullet style	Wt. case, lbs.
R7M082	120 gr.	Hollow Point	28
R7M081	140 gr.	Pointed Soft Point	30
ER7M08A	154 gr.	Extended Range	31

20 IN A BOX, 500 IN A CASE.

280 REMINGTON*

No.	Bullet weight	Bullet style	Wt. case, lbs.
R280R4	120 gr.	Hollow Point	32
R280R3	140 gr.	Pointed Soft Point	33
R280R1	150 gr.	Pointed Soft Point Core-Lokt®	33
R280R2	165 gr.	Soft Point Core-Lokt®	34
ER280RA	165 gr.	Extended Range	31

20 IN A BOX, 500 IN A CASE.

*Interchangeable with 7mm Express Rem.

7MM BENCH REST REMINGTON

No.	Bullet weight	Bullet style	Wt. case, lbs.
R7MMBR	140 gr.	Pointed Soft Point	28

20 IN A BOX, 500 IN A CASE.

7MM REMINGTON MAGNUM

No.	Bullet weight	Bullet style	Wt. case, lbs.
R7MM4	140 gr.	Pointed Soft Point	36
R7MM2	150 gr.	Pointed Soft Point Core-Lokt®	37
R7MM3	175 gr.	Pointed Soft Point Core-Lokt®	37
ER7MMA	165 gr.	Extended Range	36

20 IN A BOX, 500 IN A CASE.

7MM WBY MAGNUM

No.	Bullet weight	Bullet style	Wt. case, lbs.
R7MWB1	140 gr.	Pointed Soft Point	33
ER7MWBA	165 gr.	Extended Range	35
R7MWB2	175 gr.	Pointed Soft Point Core-Lokt®	37

7MM MAUSER (7X57)

No.	Bullet weight	Bullet style	Wt. case, lbs.
R7MSR1	140 gr.	Pointed Soft Point	32

20 IN A BOX, 500 IN A CASE.

REMINGTON CENTERFIRE RIFLE CARTRIDGES

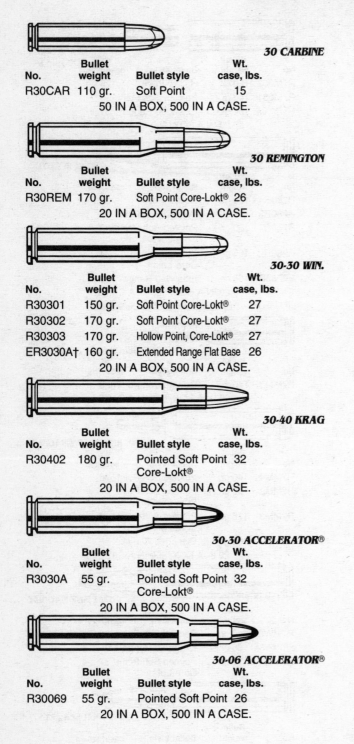

30 CARBINE

No.	Bullet weight	Bullet style	Wt. case, lbs.
R30CAR	110 gr.	Soft Point	15

50 IN A BOX, 500 IN A CASE.

30 REMINGTON

No.	Bullet weight	Bullet style	Wt. case, lbs.
R30REM	170 gr.	Soft Point Core-Lokt®	26

20 IN A BOX, 500 IN A CASE.

30-30 WIN.

No.	Bullet weight	Bullet style	Wt. case, lbs.
R30301	150 gr.	Soft Point Core-Lokt®	27
R30302	170 gr.	Soft Point Core-Lokt®	27
R30303	170 gr.	Hollow Point, Core-Lokt®	27
ER3030A†	160 gr.	Extended Range Flat Base	26

20 IN A BOX, 500 IN A CASE.

30-40 KRAG

No.	Bullet weight	Bullet style	Wt. case, lbs.
R30402	180 gr.	Pointed Soft Point Core-Lokt®	32

20 IN A BOX, 500 IN A CASE.

30-30 ACCELERATOR®

No.	Bullet weight	Bullet style	Wt. case, lbs.
R3030A	55 gr.	Pointed Soft Point Core-Lokt®	32

20 IN A BOX, 500 IN A CASE.

30-06 ACCELERATOR®

No.	Bullet weight	Bullet style	Wt. case, lbs.
R30069	55 gr.	Pointed Soft Point	26

20 IN A BOX, 500 IN A CASE.

30-06 SPFD.

No.	Bullet weight	Bullet style	Wt. case, lbs.
R30061	125 gr.	Pointed Soft Point	35
R30062	150 gr.	Pointed Soft Point Core-Lokt®	35
R30063	150 gr.	Bronze Point™	35
R3006B	165 gr.	Pointed Soft Point Core-Lokt®	35
R30064	180 gr.	Soft Point Core-Lokt®	35
R30065	180 gr.	Pointed Soft Point Core-Lokt®	35
R30066	180 gr.	Bronze Point™	35
R30067	220 gr.	Soft Point Core-Lokt®	35
R3006C	168 gr.	Boat Tail Hollow Point (Match)	31
ER3006A	152 gr.	Extended Range	30
ER3006B	165 gr.	Extended Range Boat Tail	31
ER3006C	178 gr.	Extended Range	32

20 IN A BOX, 500 IN A CASE.

300 SAV.

No.	Bullet weight	Bullet style	Wt. case, lbs.
R30SV2	150 gr.	Pointed Soft Point Core-Lokt®	29
R30SV3	180 gr.	Soft Point Core-Lokt®	29

20 IN A BOX, 500 IN A CASE.

300 H&H MAG.

No.	Bullet weight	Bullet style	Wt. case, lbs.
R300HH	180 gr.	Pointed Soft Point Core-Lokt®	39

20 IN A BOX, 500 IN A CASE.

300 WIN. MAG.

No.	Bullet weight	Bullet style	Wt. case, lbs.
R300W1	150 gr.	Pointed Soft Point Core-Lokt®	39
R300W2	180 gr.	Pointed Soft Point Core-Lokt®	39
ER300WA	178 gr.	Extended Range	38
ER300WB	190 gr.	Extended Range Boat Tail	39

20 IN A BOX, 500 IN A CASE.

† New for 1993

REMINGTON CENTERFIRE RIFLE CARTRIDGES

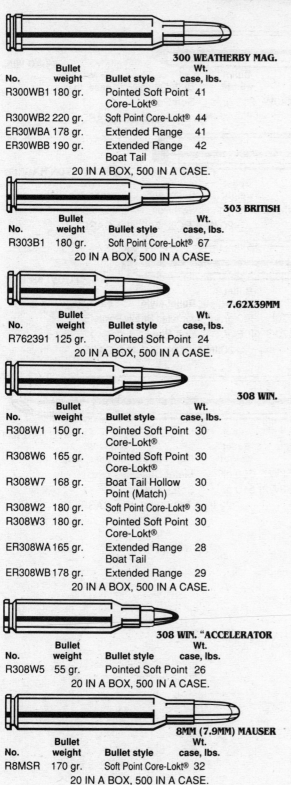

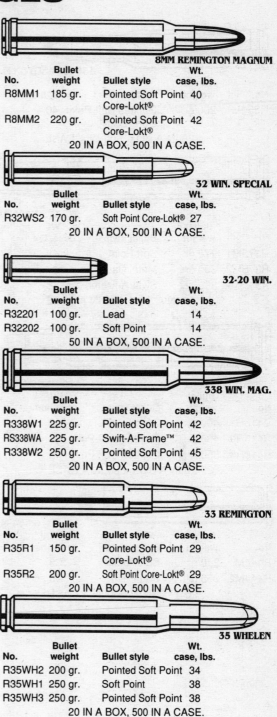

300 WEATHERBY MAG.

No.	Bullet weight	Bullet style	Wt. case, lbs.
R300WB1	180 gr.	Pointed Soft Point Core-Lokt®	41
R300WB2	220 gr.	Soft Point Core-Lokt®	44
ER30WBA	178 gr.	Extended Range	41
ER30WBB	190 gr.	Extended Range Boat Tail	42

20 IN A BOX, 500 IN A CASE.

303 BRITISH

No.	Bullet weight	Bullet style	Wt. case, lbs.
R303B1	180 gr.	Soft Point Core-Lokt®	67

20 IN A BOX, 500 IN A CASE.

7.62X39MM

No.	Bullet weight	Bullet style	Wt. case, lbs.
R762391	125 gr.	Pointed Soft Point	24

20 IN A BOX, 500 IN A CASE.

308 WIN.

No.	Bullet weight	Bullet style	Wt. case, lbs.
R308W1	150 gr.	Pointed Soft Point Core-Lokt®	30
R308W6	165 gr.	Pointed Soft Point Core-Lokt®	30
R308W7	168 gr.	Boat Tail Hollow Point (Match)	30
R308W2	180 gr.	Soft Point Core-Lokt®	30
R308W3	180 gr.	Pointed Soft Point Core-Lokt®	30
ER308WA	165 gr.	Extended Range Boat Tail	28
ER308WB	178 gr.	Extended Range	29

20 IN A BOX, 500 IN A CASE.

308 WIN. "ACCELERATOR

No.	Bullet weight	Bullet style	Wt. case, lbs.
R308W5	55 gr.	Pointed Soft Point	26

20 IN A BOX, 500 IN A CASE.

8MM (7.9MM) MAUSER

No.	Bullet weight	Bullet style	Wt. case, lbs.
R8MSR	170 gr.	Soft Point Core-Lokt®	32

20 IN A BOX, 500 IN A CASE.

8MM REMINGTON MAGNUM

No.	Bullet weight	Bullet style	Wt. case, lbs.
R8MM1	185 gr.	Pointed Soft Point Core-Lokt®	40
R8MM2	220 gr.	Pointed Soft Point Core-Lokt®	42

20 IN A BOX, 500 IN A CASE.

32 WIN. SPECIAL

No.	Bullet weight	Bullet style	Wt. case, lbs.
R32WS2	170 gr.	Soft Point Core-Lokt®	27

20 IN A BOX, 500 IN A CASE.

32-20 WIN.

No.	Bullet weight	Bullet style	Wt. case, lbs.
R32201	100 gr.	Lead	14
R32202	100 gr.	Soft Point	14

50 IN A BOX, 500 IN A CASE.

338 WIN. MAG.

No.	Bullet weight	Bullet style	Wt. case, lbs.
R338W1	225 gr.	Pointed Soft Point	42
RS338WA	225 gr.	Swift-A-Frame™	42
R338W2	250 gr.	Pointed Soft Point	45

20 IN A BOX, 500 IN A CASE.

33 REMINGTON

No.	Bullet weight	Bullet style	Wt. case, lbs.
R35R1	150 gr.	Pointed Soft Point Core-Lokt®	29
R35R2	200 gr.	Soft Point Core-Lokt®	29

20 IN A BOX, 500 IN A CASE.

35 WHELEN

No.	Bullet weight	Bullet style	Wt. case, lbs.
R35WH2	200 gr.	Pointed Soft Point	34
R35WH1	250 gr.	Soft Point	38
R35WH3	250 gr.	Pointed Soft Point	38

20 IN A BOX, 500 IN A CASE.

REMINGTON CENTERFIRE RIFLE CARTRIDGES

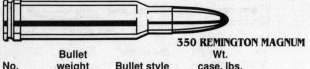

350 REMINGTON MAGNUM

No.	Bullet weight	Bullet style	Wt. case, lbs.
R350M1	200 gr.	Pointed Soft Point Core-Lokt®	40

20 IN A BOX, 500 IN A CASE.

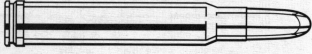

375 H&H MAGNUM

No.	Bullet weight	Bullet style	Wt. case, lbs.
R375M1	270 gr.	Soft Point	48
R375M2	300 gr.	Metal Case	48
RS375MA	300 gr.	Swift-A-Frame™	48

20 IN A BOX, 500 IN A CASE.

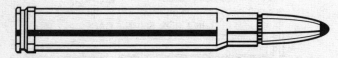

416 REMINGTON MAG.

No.	Bullet weight	Bullet style	Wt. case, lbs.
R416R1	400 gr.	Solid	56
R416R2	400 gr.	Pointed Soft Point	56
R416R3	350 gr.	Pointed Soft Point	52

20 IN A BOX, 500 IN A CASE.

444 MARLIN

No.	Bullet weight	Bullet style	Wt. case, lbs.
R444M	240 gr.	Soft Point	38
R444M2	265 gr.	Soft Point	40

20 IN A BOX, 500 IN A CASE.

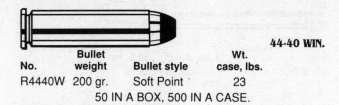

44-40 WIN.

No.	Bullet weight	Bullet style	Wt. case, lbs.
R4440W	200 gr.	Soft Point	23

50 IN A BOX, 500 IN A CASE.

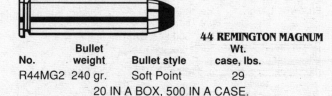

44 REMINGTON MAGNUM

No.	Bullet weight	Bullet style	Wt. case, lbs.
R44MG2	240 gr.	Soft Point	29

20 IN A BOX, 500 IN A CASE.

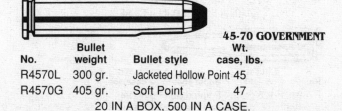

45-70 GOVERNMENT

No.	Bullet weight	Bullet style	Wt. case, lbs.
R4570L	300 gr.	Jacketed Hollow Point	45
R4570G	405 gr.	Soft Point	47

20 IN A BOX, 500 IN A CASE.

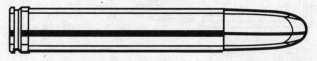

458 WIN. MAGNUM

No.	Bullet weight	Bullet style	Wt. case, lbs.
R458W1	500 gr.	Metal Case	61
R458W2	510 gr.	Soft Point	61

20 IN A BOX, 500 IN A CASE.

REMINGTON CENTERFIRE PISTOL AND REVOLVER CARTRIDGES

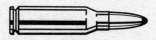

221 REMINGTON FIRE BALL®

No.	Bullet weight	Bullet style	Wt. case, lbs.
R221F	50 gr.	Pointed Soft Point	12

20 IN A BOX, 500 IN A CASE.

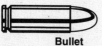

25 (6.35MM) AUTO. PISTOL

No.	Bullet weight	Bullet style	Wt. case, lbs.
R25AP	50 gr.	Metal Case	7

50 IN A BOX, 500 IN A CASE.

32 S&W

No.	Bullet weight	Bullet style	Wt. case, lbs.
R32SW	88 gr.	Lead	11

50 IN A BOX, 500 IN A CASE.

32 S&W LONG

No.	Bullet weight	Bullet style	Wt. case, lbs.
R32SWL	98 gr.	Lead	12

50 IN A BOX, 500 IN A CASE.

32 (7.65MM) AUTO. PISTOL

No.	Bullet weight	Bullet style	Wt. case, lbs.
R32AP	71 gr.	Metal Case	9

50 IN A BOX, 500 IN A CASE.

(+P) Ammunition with (+P) on the case headstamp is loaded to higher pressure. Use only in firearms designated for this cartridge and so recommended by the gun manufacturer.

357 MAGNUM

No.	Bullet weight	Bullet style	Wt. case, lbs.
R357M7	110 gr.	Semi-Jacketed Hollow Point	16
R357M1	125 gr.	Semi-Jacketed Hollow Point	17
R357M8	125 gr.	Semi-Jacketed Soft Point	17
R357M9	140 gr.	Semi-Jacketed Hollow Point	18
R357M2	158 gr.	Semi-Jacketed Hollow Point	19
R357M3	158 gr.	Soft Point	19
R357M5	158 gr.	Lead	19
R357M6	158 gr.	Lead (Brass Case)	20
R357M10	180 gr.	Semi-Jacketed Hollow Point	22
R357M11	140 gr.	Semi-Jacketed Hollow Point (Med. Vel.)	16
GS357MA†	125 gr.	Brass Jacketed Hollow Point	

50 IN A BOX, 500 IN A CASE.

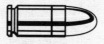

9MM LUGER AUTO. PISTOL

No.	Bullet weight	Bullet style	Wt. case, lbs.
R9MM5	88 gr.	Jacketed Hollow Point	20
R9MM1	115 gr.	Jacketed Hollow Point	22
R9MM3	115 gr.	Metal Case	22
R9MM2	124 gr.	Metal Case	22
R9MM6	115 gr.	Jacketed Hollow Point (+P)	13
R9MM7	140 gr.	JHP (Practice)	15
R9MM8	147 gr.	JHP	16
R9MM9†	147 gr.	MC	16
GS9MMC†	147 gr.	Brass Jacketed Hollow Point	

50 IN A BOX, 500 IN A CASE.

† New for 1993

REMINGTON CENTERFIRE PISTOL AND REVOLVER CARTRIDGES

380 AUTO. PISTOL

No.	Bullet weight	Bullet style	Wt. case, lbs.
R380A1	88 gr.	Jacketed Hollow Point	12
R380AP	95 gr.	Metal Case	12

50 IN A BOX, 500 IN A CASE.

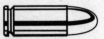

38 AUTO. COLT PISTOL

Adapted only for 38 Colt Sporting, Military and Pocket Model Automatic Pistols.

No.	Bullet weight	Bullet style	Wt. case, lbs.
R38ACP	130 gr.	Metal Case	16

50 IN A BOX, 500 IN A CASE.
(SUBJECT TO STOCK ON HAND)

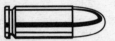

38 SUPER AUTO. COLT PISTOL

Adapted only for 38 Colt Super and Colt Commander Automatic Pistols.

No.	Bullet weight	Bullet style	Wt. case, lbs.
R38SU1	115 gr.	Jacketed Hollow Point (+P)	14

50 IN A BOX, 500 IN A CASE.

38 S&W

No.	Bullet weight	Bullet style	Wt. case, lbs.
R38SW	146 gr.	Lead	16

50 IN A BOX, 500 IN A CASE.

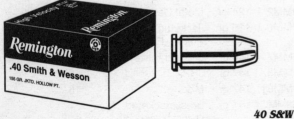

40 S&W

No.	Bullet weight	Bullet style	Wt. case, lbs.
R40SW1	155 gr.	Jacketed Hollow Point	18
R40SW2	180 gr.	Jacketed Hollow Point	20
GS40SWB†	180 gr.	Brass Jacketed Hollow Point	

38 SPECIAL

No.	weight	Bullet style	Bullet case, lbs.	Wt.
R38S1	95 gr.	Semi-Jacketed Hollow Point (+P)	13	
R38S10	110 gr.	Semi-Jacketed Hollow Point (+P)	13	
R38516	110 gr.	Semi-Jacketed Hollow Point	13	
R38S2	125 gr.	Semi-Jacketed Hollow Point (+P)	17	
R38S13	125 gr.	Semi-Jacket Soft Point (+P)	17	
R38S3	148 gr.	Targetmaster Lead Wadcutter, brass case	17	
R38S4	158 gr.	Targetmaster Lead Round Nose	18	
R38S5	158 gr.	Lead	18	
R38S6	158 gr.	Lead Semi-Wadcutter	18	
R38S14	158 gr.	Lead Semi-Wadcutter (+P)	18	
R38S7	158 gr.	Metal Point	18	
R38S12	158 gr.	Lead Hollow Point (+P)	18	
R38SMB	140 gr.	Multi-Ball	17	
GS38SB†	125 gr.	Brass Jacketed Hollow Point		

50 IN A BOX, 500 IN A CASE.

38 SHORT COLT

No.	Bullet weight	Bullet style	Wt. case, lbs.
R38SC	125 gr.	Lead	14

10MM AUTO.

No.	Bullet weight	Bullet style	Wt. case, lbs.
R10MM2	200 gr.	Metal Case	24
R10MM3	180 gr.	JHP (950 FPS)	22
R10MM4	180 gr.	JHP (HIGH VEL)	22

50 IN A BOX, 500 IN A CASE.

† New for 1993

> (+P) Ammunition with (+P) on the case headstamp is loaded to higher pressure. Use only in firearms designated for this cartridge and so recommended by the gun manufacturer.

REMINGTON CENTERFIRE PISTOL AND REVOLVER CARTRIDGES

41 REMINGTON MAGNUM

No.	Bullet weight	Bullet style	Wt. case, lbs.
R41MG3	170 gr.	Semi-Jacketed Hollow Point	24
R41mG1	210 gr.	Soft Point	26
R41mG2	210 gr.	Lead	26

50 IN A BOX, 500 IN A CASE.

44 S&W SPECIAL

No.	Bullet weight	Bullet style	Wt. case, lbs.
R44SW1	200 gr.	Lead Semi-Wadcutter	22
R44SW	246 gr.	Lead	25

50 IN A BOX, 500 IN A CASE.

44 REMINGTON MAGNUM

No.	Bullet weight	Bullet style	Wt. case, lbs.
R44MG5	180 gr.	Semi-Jacketed Hollow Point	29
R44MG1	310 gr.	Semi-Jacketed Hollow Point	27
R44MG1	240 gr.	Lead, Gas-Check	29
R44MG4	240 gr.	Lead	29
R44MG2	240 gr.	Soft Point	29
R44MG3	240 gr.	Semi-Jacketed Hollow Point	29

20 IN A BOX, 500 IN A CASE.

45 COLT

No.	Bullet weight	Bullet style	Wt. case, lbs.
R45C1	225 gr.	Lead Semi-Wadcutter	24
R45C	250 gr.	Lead	26

50 IN A BOX, 500 IN A CASE.

45 AUTO.

No.	Bullet weight	Bullet style	Wt. case, lbs.
R45AP1	185 gr.	Targetmaster Metal Case Wadcutter	11
R45AP2	185 gr.	Jacketed Hollow Point	11
R45AP4	230 gr.	Metal Case	13
R45AP6	185 gr.	Jacketed Hollow Point (+P)	21
GS45APB†	230 gr.	Brass Jacketed Hollow Point	

50 IN A BOX, 500 IN A CASE.

45 AUTO. SHOT CARTRIDGE

No.	Bullet style	Wt. case, lbs.
R45AP5	650 Pellets — No. 12 Shot	18

20 IN A BOX, 500 IN A CASE.

REMINGTON CENTERFIRE BLANK

No.	Caliber	No. in case	Wt. case, lbs.
R32BLNK	32 S&W	500	4
R38SWBL	38 S&W	500	7
R38BLNK	38 Special	500	7

50 IN A BOX.

† New for 1993

(+P) Ammunition with (+P) on the case headstamp is loaded to higher pressure. Use only in firearms designated for this cartridge and so recommended by the gun manufacturer.

REMINGTON RIMFIRE CARTRIDGES

22 LONG RIFLE

No.	Bullet weight and style	Wt. case, lbs.
6122	40 gr., Lead	40

50 IN A BOX, 5,000 IN A CASE.

100 PACK

No.	Bullet weight and style	Wt. case, lbs.
6100	40 gr., Lead	40

100 IN A BOX, 5,000 IN A CASE.

"HIGH VELOCITY" CARTRIDGES WITH GOLDEN™ BULLETS

YELLOW JACKET® CARTRIDGES HYPER-VELOCITY

22 SHORT

No.	Bullet weight and style	Wt. case, lbs.
1022	29 gr., Lead	29

50 IN A BOX, 5,000 IN A CASE.

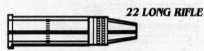

CBee® CARTRIDGES LOW NOISE LEVEL

Velocity of 720 f.p.s.; the quietness of an airgun, the impact of a .22 bullet.

22 LONG RIFLE

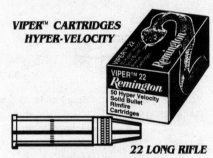

No.	Bullet weight and style	Wt. case, lbs.
1722	33 gr., Truncated Cone, Hollow Point	36

50 IN A BOX, 5,000 IN A CASE.

22 LONG

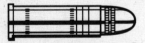

No.	Bullet weight and style	Wt. case, lbs.
1322	29 gr., Lead	31

50 IN A BOX, 5,000 IN A CASE.

CBee® 22 SHORT   CBee® 22 LONG

No.	Bullet weight and style	Wt. case, lbs.
CB-22S Short	30 gr., Lead	29
CB-22L Long	30 gr., Lead	30

50 IN A BOX, 5,000 IN A CASE.

VIPER™ CARTRIDGES HYPER-VELOCITY

22 LONG RIFLE

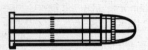

No.	Bullet weight and style	Wt. case, lbs.
1522	40 gr., Lead	40
1622	36 gr., Lead, Hollow Point	38

50 IN A BOX, 5,000 IN A CASE.

100 PACK

No.	Bullet weight and style	Wt. case, lbs.
1500	40gr., Lead	40
1600	36 gr., Lead, Hollow Point	38

100 IN A BOX, 5,000 IN A CASE.

22 LONG RIFLE

No.	Bullet weight and style	Wt. case, lbs.
1922	36 gr., Truncated Cone, Solid Point, Copper Plated	38

50 IN A BOX, 5,000 IN A CASE.

22 THUNDERBOLT™ CARTRIDGES

22 CYCLONE™
Hollow Point Long Rifle

No.	Bullet weight and style
CY22HP†	36 gr., Hollow Point

22 LONG RIFLE

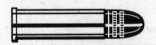

No.	Bullet weight and style	Wt. case, lbs.
TB22A	36 gr., Truncated Cone, Solid Point	40

50 IN A BOX, 5,000 IN A CASE.

† New for 1993

REMINGTON SHOTGUN SHELLS

PREMIER® TARGET LOADS

	No.	Gauge	Shell length, in.	Powder drams equiv.	Ounces of shot	Shot size	Case wt., lbs.	Per box
PREMIER® TARGET LOADS	RTL12L	12	2 3/4	2 3/4	1 1/8	7 1/2, 8, 8 1/2, 9	27	
	RTL12M•	12	2 3/4	3	1 1/8	7 1/2, 8, 9	27	
	RTL20	20	2 3/4	2 1/2	7/8	8, 9	41	
	RTL20M†	20	2 3/4	2 1/2	1	9	21	
REMLITE™ PREMIER® TARGET LOAD	LRTL12•	12	2 3/4	—	1 1/8	7 1/2, 8, 9	27	
DUPLEX® PREMIER® TARGET LOAD	MRTL12L•	12	2 3/4	2 3/4	1 1/8	7 1/2X8, 7 1/2X8 1/2†	27	
	MRTL12M•			3	1 1/8	7 1/2X8	27	
DUPLEX® SPORTING CLAYS	SC12L	12	2 3/4	2 3/4	1 1/8	7 1/2X8	27	
SKEET LOADS	SP28	28	2 3/4	2	3/4	9	37	
	SP410	410	2 1/2	Max.	1/2	9	22	
PREMIER® PIGEON LOADS	RTL12P•	12	2 3/4	3 1/4	1 1/4	7 1/2, 8	27	
PREMIER® INTERNATIONAL TARGET LOADS	RIT12L•	12	2 3/4	—	24 gm (1 oz.)	7 1/2, 9	54	

25 IN A BOX, 500 IN A CASE. • 25 IN A BOX, 250 PER CASE.

GAME LOADS

	No.	Gauge	Shell length, in.	Powder drams equiv.	Ounces of shot	Shot size	Case wt., lbs.	Per box
GAME LOAD	GL12	12	2 3/4	3 1/4	1	6, 7 1/2, 8	24	
	GL16	16	2 3/4	2 1/2	1	6, 7 1/2, 8	24	
	GL20	20	2 3/4	2 1/2	7/8	6, 7 1/2, 8	16	
HEAVY GAME LOAD	HGL12	12	2 3/4	3 3/4	1 1/4	4, 6, 7 1/2	30	
	HGL16	16	2 3/4	3 1/4	1 1/8	4, 6, 7 1/2	27	
	HGL20	20	2 3/4	2 3/4	1	4, 6, 7 1/2	24	
ALL PURPOSE SPORT LOADS	R 12SL	12	2 3/4	3 1/4	1	8		
	R 20SL	20	2 3/4	2 1/2	7/8	8		

25 IN A BOX, 250 IN A CASE

REMINGTON SHOTGUN SHELLS

PREMIER® MAGNUM BUCKSHOT
With Extra Hard Nickel-Plated Shot

Nickel-plated extra-hard buckshot and granulated poly-ethylene filler for reduced deformation and improved pattern

	No.	Gauge	Shell length, in.	Powder drams equiv.	Shot size	Pellets	Case wt., lbs.	Per box
PREMIER®	PR12SNBK	12	2 3/4	4	00	12	29	
MAGNUM	PR12SNBK	12	2 3/4	4	4	34	31	
EXTENDED	PR12HNBK	12	3	4	000	10	40	
RANGE	PR12HNBK	12	3	4	00	15	40	
BUCKSHOT	PR12HNBK	12	3	Max.	1	24	40	
WITH NICKEL	PR12HNBK	12	3	4	4	41	42	
PLATED SHOT								

10 IN A BOX, 250 RDS. PER CASE.

EXPRESS® BUCKSHOT LOADS AND "SLUGGER" RIFLED SLUGS

	No.	Gauge	Shell length, in.	Powder drams equiv.	Shot size	Pellets	Case wt., lbs.	Per box
"POWER PAKT"	SP12BK	12	2 3/4	3 3/4	000 Buck	8 Pellets	31	
EXPRESS®	SP12BK	12	2 3/4	3 3/4	00 Buck	9 Pellets	29	
BUCKSHOT	SP12BK	12	2 3/4	3 3/4	0 Buck	12 Pellets	32	
LOADS	SP12BK	12	2 3/4	3 3/4	1 Buck	16 Pellets	32	
	SP12BK	12	2 3/4	3 3/4	4 Buck	27 Pellets	31	
	SP16BK	16	2 3/4	3	1 Buck	12 Pellets	26	
	SP20BK	20	2 3/4	2 3/4	3 Buck	20 Shellets	24	
"POWER PAKT"	SP12SMAgBK	12	2 3/4	4	00 Buck	12 Pellets	34	
EXPRESS®	SP12SMAgBK	12	2 3/4	4	1 Buck	20 Pellets	34	
MAGNUM	SP12HMAgBK	12	3	4	000 Buck	10 Pellets	40	
BUCKSHOT	SP12HMAgBK	12	3	4	00 Buck	15 Pellets	40	
LOADS	SP12HMAgBK	12	3	4	1 Buck	24 Pellets	40	
	SP12HMAgBK	12	3	4	4 Buck	41 Pellets	42	

	No.	Gauge	Shell length, in.	Powder drams equiv.	Slug Weight, oz.	Slug Type	Case wt., lbs.	Per box
PREMIER® COPPER SOLID™ SABOT SLUGS	PR12RS†	12	2 3/4	Max.	1	Rifled Slug H.P.	–	
SLUGGER® MAGNUM	SP12SMAgRS	12	2 3/4	Max.	1	Rifled Slug	26	
RIFLED SLUG LOADS	SP12SMAgRS	12	3	Max.	1	Rifled Slug	26	
SLUGGER®	SP12RS	12	2 3/4	Max.	1	Rifled Slug H.P.	26	
RIFLED SLUG	SP16RS	16	2 3/4	3	4/5	Rifled Slug H.P.	24	
LOADS	SP20RS	20	2 3/4	2 3/4	5/8	Rifled Slug H.P.	19	
	SP410RS	.410 bore	2 1/2	Max.	1/5	Rifled Slug	8	

† New for 1993

REMINGTON SHOTGUN SHELLS

NITRO MAG®, EXPRESS® AND SHURSHOT® SHOTSHELLS

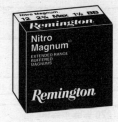   

	No.	Gauge	Shell length, in.	Powder drams equiv.	Ounces of shot	Shot size	Case wt., lbs.
NITRO	SP10HNM•	10	3 1/2	4 1/2	2 1/4	2, 4, 6	49
MAG®	SP12SNM•	12	2 3/4	Max.	1 1/2	2, 4, 6	34
EXTENDED	SP12NM•	12	3	4	1 5/8	2, 4, 6	35
RANGE	SP12HNM•	12	3	Max.	1 7/8	2, 4, 6	35
BUFFERED	SP20SNM•	20	2 3/4	Max.	1 1/8	4, 6	26
MAGNUMS	SP20HNM•	20	3	Max.	1 1/4	2, 4, 6, 7 1/2	30
EXPRESS®	SP12	12	2 3/4	3 3/4	1 1/4	BB, 2, 4, 5, 6, 7 1/2, 9	58
EXTRA LONG RANGE	SP16	16	2 3/4	3 1/4	1 1/8	4, 6, 7 1/2	52
LOADS	SP10MAG	16	2 3/4	Max.	1 1/4	BB, 2, 4	58
	SP20	20	2 3/4	2 3/4	1	4, 5, 6, 7 1/2, 9	47
	SP28	28	2 3/4	2 1/4	3/4	6, 7 1/2	36
	SP410	410	2 1/2	Max.	1/2	4, 6, 7 1/2	23
	SP4103	410	3	Max.	11/16	4, 5†, 6, 7 1/2, 9	31
SHURSHOT®	R12HD	12	2 3/4	3 1/4	1 1/8	6, 7 1/2, 8	29
HEAVY DOVE	R20HD	20	2 3/4	2 1/2	1	6, 7 1/2, 8	23
LOADS							
PREMIER®	PR12F	12	2 3/4	3 1/4	1 1/8	6, 7 1/2, 8	
FIELD	PR12HF	12	2 3/4	3 1/4	1 1/4	6, 7 1/2, 8	
LOADS	PR16F	16	2 3/4	2 3/4	1 1/8	6, 8	
	PR20F	20	2 3/4	2 1/2	1	6, 7 1/2, 8	

25 IN A BOX, 500 IN A CASE. • 25 IN A BOX, 250 PER CASE.

NEW STEEL WATERFOWL LOADS

	No.	Shell length, in.	Cham. Dr. EQ.	Powder drams equiv.	Ounces of shot	Shot size
NITRO-STEEL™	NSTL10MAG†	10	3 1/2§	Magnum	1 3/4	TT, T, BBB, BB, 2
	NSTL1235MAG†	12	3 1/2§	Magnum	1 9/16	TT, T, BBB, BB, 2
	NTL12HMAG†	12	3	Magnum	1 3/8	TT, T, BBB, BB, 1, 2, 3, 4
	NSTL12MAG†	12	3	Magnum	1 1/4	TT, T, BBB, BB, 1, 2, 3, 4
	NSTL12SMAG†	12	2 3/4	Magnum	1 1/4	T, BBB, BB, 1, 2, 3, 4
	NSTL20HMAG†	20	3	Magnum	1	2, 3, 4, 6
EXPRESS-STEEL™	STLSP12†	12	2 3/4	Max.	1 1/8	BB, 1, 2, 3, 4, 6
	STLSP12L†	12	2 3/4	Max.	1	2, 3, 4, 5, 6
	STLSP16†	16	2 3/4	Max.	15/16	2, 4, 6
	STLSP20†	20	2 3/4	Max.	3/4	2, 3, 4, 5, 6

† New for 1993

25 PER BOX, 250 ROUNDS PER CASE

WINCHESTER AMMUNITION
SUPER-X® CENTERFIRE RIFLE

WINCHESTER SYMBOL	CARTRIDGE
	218 Bee
X218B	46 gr. Hollow Point
	22 Hornet
X22H1	45 gr. Soft Point
X22H2	46 gr. Hollow Point
	22-250 Remington
X222501	55 gr. Pointed Soft Point
	222 Remington
X222R	50 gr. Pointed Soft Point
X222R1	55 gr. Full Metal Jacket
	***223 Remington**
X223RH	53 gr. Hollow Point
X223R	55 gr. Pointed Soft Point
X223R1	55 gr. Full Metal Jacket
X223R2	64 gr. Power Point
	225 Winchester
X2251	55 gr. Pointed Soft Point
	243 Winchester
X2431	80 gr. Pointed Soft Point
X2432	100 gr. Power Point
	6mm Remington
X6MMR1	80 gr. Pointed Soft Point
X6MMR2	100 gr. Power Point
	25-06 Remington
X25061	90 gr. Positive Expanding Point
X25062	120 gr. Positive Expanding Point
	25-20 Winchester
X25202	86 gr. Soft Point
	25-35 Winchester
X2535	117 gr. Soft Point
	250 Savage
X2503	100 gr. Silvertip

WINCHESTER SYMBOL	CARTRIDGE
	257 Roberts +P
X257P2	100 gr. Silvertip
X257P3	117 gr. Power Point
	264 Winchester Magnum
X2642	140 gr. Power Point
	270 Winchester
X2701	100 gr. Pointed Soft Point
X2705	130 gr. Power Point
X2703	130 gr. Silvertip
X2704	150 gr. Power Point
	280 Remington
X280R	140 gr. Power Point
	284 Winchester
X2842	150 gr. Power Point
	7mm Mauser (7x57)
X7MM1	145 gr. Power Point
	** ** 30-06 Springfield**
X30062	125 gr. Pointed Soft Point
X30061	150 gr. Power Point
X30063	150 gr. Silvertip
X30065	165 gr. Soft Point
X30064	180 gr. Power Point
X30066	180 gr. Silvertip
X30069	220 gr. Silvertip
	7mm Remington Magnum
X7MMR1	150 gr. Power Point
X7MMR2	175 gr. Power Point
	7.62 x 39mm Russian
X76239	123 gr. Pointed Soft Point
	30 Carbine
X30M1	110 gr. Hollow Soft Point
X30M2	110 gr. Full Metal Jacket

* NEW: 69 gr. Match Hollow Point Boattail

** NEW: 180 gr. Fail Safe Talon

WINCHESTER AMMUNITION

SUPER-X® CENTERFIRE RIFLE

WINCHESTER SYMBOL	CARTRIDGE
	30-30 Winchester
X30301	150 gr. Hollow Point
X30306	150 gr. Power Point
X30302	150 gr. Silvertip
X30303	170 gr. Power Point
X30304	170 gr. Silvertip
	30-40 Krag
X30401	180 gr. Power Point
	* 300 Winchester Magnum
X30WM1	150 gr. Power Point
X30WM2	180 gr. Power Point
X30WM3	220 gr. Silvertip
	300 H & H Magnum
X300H2	180 gr. Silvertip
	300 Savage
X3001	150 gr. Power Point
X3003	150 gr. Silvertip
X3004	180 gr. Power Point
	303 Savage
X3032	190 gr. Silvertip
	303 British
X303B1	180 gr. Power Point
	307 Winchester
+ X3075	150 gr. Power Point
X3076	180 gr. Power Point
	** 308 Winchester
X3085	150 gr. Power Point
X3082	150 gr. Silvertip
X3086	180 gr. Power Point
X3083	180 gr. Silvertip
	32 Winchester Special
X32WS2	170 gr. Power Point
X32WS3	170 gr. Silvertip
	32-20 Winchester
X32201	100 gr. Lead

* NEW: 180 gr. Fail Safe Talon
190 gr. Silvertip Boattail
** NEW: 168 gr. Match Hollow Point Boattail
180 gr. Fail Safe Talon

WINCHESTER SYMBOL	CARTRIDGE
	8mm Mauser (8x57)
X8MM	170 gr. Power Point
	*** 338 Winchester Magnum
X3381	200 gr. Power Point
X3383	225 gr. Soft Point
	35 Remington
X35R1	200 gr. Power Point
X35R3	200 gr. Silvertip
	356 Winchester
X3561	200 gr. Power Point
X3563	250 gr. Power Point
	357 Magnum
X3574P	158 gr. Jacketed Hollow Point
X3575P	158 gr. Jacketed Soft Point
	358 Winchester
X3581	200 gr. Silvertip
	375 Winchester
X375W	200 gr. Power Point
X375W1	250 gr. Power Point
	375 H & H Magnum
X375H1	270 gr. Power Point
X375H2	300 gr. Silvertip
X375H3	300 gr. Full Metal Jacket
	38-40 Winchester
X3840	180 gr. Soft Point
	38-55 Winchester
X3855	255 gr. Soft Point
	44 Remington Magnum
X44MSTHP2	210 gr. Silvertip Hollow Point
X44MHSP2	240 gr. Hollow Soft Point
	44-40 Winchester
X4440	200 gr. Soft Point
	45-70 Government
X4570H	300 gr. Jacketed Hollow Point
	458 Winchester Magnum
X4580	500 gr. Full Metal Jacket
X4581	510 gr. Soft Point

*** NEW: 250 gr. Fail Safe Talon

WINCHESTER AMMUNITION
RIFLE/PISTOL CARTRIDGES

SUPER-X RIMFIRE

WINCHESTER SYMBOL	CARTRIDGE	BULLET TYPE	WT. GRS.
Super-X High Velocity Cartridges - Copperplated Bullets			
X22S	22 Short	LRN	29
X22LR	22 Long Rifle	LRN	40
X22LR1	22 Long Rifle	LRN	40
X22LRH	22 Long Rifle	LHP	37
X22LRH1	22 Long Rifle	LHP	37
Super-X 22 Winchester Magnum Cartridge			
X22MH	22 Win. Mag.	JHP	40
X22MR1	22 Win. Mag.	FMC	40
Winchester Super Silhouette Cartridge			
XS22LR1	22 Long Rifle	LTC	42
Winchester Standard Velocity Cartridge			
XT22LR	22 Long Rifle Target	LRN	40
Other Winchester Rimfire Cartridges			
X22LRS	22 Long Rifle, Shot	#12 Shot	25
22BL	22 Short Blank	Black Powder	-
X22SCB	22 Short CB	LRN	29

PROMOTIONAL RIMFIRE

WINCHESTER SYMBOL	CARTRIDGE	BULLET TYPE	WT. GRS.
WW22LR	22 Long Rifle	LRN	40
WW22LRW	22 Long Rifle (Shrinkwrap)	LRN	40

SUPREME® CENTERFIRE RIFLE

WINCHESTER SYMBOL	CARTRIDGE
S22250R52	**Supreme 22-250 Remington** 52 gr. Hollow Point Boattail
S223M*	**Supreme 223 Remington** 69 gr. Match Hollow Point Boattail
S243W100	**Supreme 243 Winchester** 100 gr. Soft Point Boattail
S270W140	**Supreme 270 Winchester** 140 gr. Silvertip Boattail
S280R160	**Supreme 280 Remington** 160 gr. Silvertip Boattail
S7MAG S7MMRM160	**Supreme 7mm Remington Magnum** 139 gr. Soft Point Boattail 160 gr. Silvertip Boattail
S3030W150	**Supreme 30-30 Winchester** 150 gr. Silvertip
S308W150 S308W180 S308M* S308X*	**Supreme 308 Winchester** 150 gr. Silvertip Boattail 180 gr. Silvertip Boattail 168 gr. Match Hollow Point Boattail 180 gr. Fail Safe Talon
S3006S165 S3006S180 S3006X*	**Supreme 30-06 Springfield** 165 gr. Silvertip Boattail 180 gr. Silvertip Boattail 180 gr. Fail Safe Talon
S300WM190 S300WX*	**Supreme 300 Winchester Magnum** 190 gr. Silvertip Boattail 180 gr. Fail Safe Talon
S338X*	**Supreme 338 Winchester Magnum** 250 gr. Fail Safe Talon

*NEW

BLACK TALON™ CENTERFIRE PISTOL

WINCHESTER SYMBOL	CARTRIDGE
▷ S9MM **NEW**	**Supreme 9mm Luger** 147 gr. Supreme Expansion Talon
▷ S40SW **NEW**	**Supreme 40 Smith & Wesson** 180 gr. Supreme Expansion Talon
▷ S10MM **NEW**	**Supreme 10mm Auto** 200 gr. Supreme Expansion Talon
▷ S45A **NEW**	**Supreme 45 Automatic** 230 gr. Supreme Expansion Talon

WINCHESTER AMMUNITION
SUPER-X® CENTERFIRE PISTOL/REVOLVER CARTRIDGES

Subsonic™

WINCHESTER SYMBOL	CARTRIDGE
XSUB38S	**38 Special** 147 gr. Jacketed Hollow Point
XSUB9MM	**9mm** 147 gr. Jacketed Hollow Point
XSUB40SW	**40 Smith & Wesson** 180 gr. Jacketed Hollow Point
XSUB10MM	**10mm Automatic** 180 gr. Jacketed Hollow Point
XSUB45A	**45 Automatic** 230 gr. Jacketed Hollow Point

Silvertip®

WINCHESTER SYMBOL	CARTRIDGE
X32ASHP	**32 Automatic** 60 gr. Silvertip Hollow Point
X380ASHP	**380 Automatic** 85 gr. Silvertip Hollow Point
X38S9HP	**38 Special** 110 gr. Silvertip Hollow Point
X38SSHP X38S8HP	**38 Special +P** 95 gr. Silvertip Hollow Point 125 gr. Silvertip Hollow Point
X9MMSHP X9MMST147	**9mm Luger (Parabellum)** 115 gr. Silvertip Hollow Point 147 gr. Silvertip Hollow Point
X357SHP	**357 Magnum** 145 gr. Silvertip Hollow Point
X38ASHP	**38 Super Automatic +P** *(For use in 38 Super Automatic Pistols ONLY)* 125 gr. Silvertip Hollow Point
X40SWSTHP	**40 Smith & Wesson** 155 gr. Silvertip Hollow Point
X10MMSTHP	**10mm Automatic** 175 gr. Silvertip Hollow Point
X41MSTHP2	**41 Remington Magnum** 175 gr. Silvertip Hollow Point
X44STHPS2	**44 Smith & Wesson Special** 200 gr. Silvertip Hollow Point
X44MSTHP2	**44 Remington Magnum** 210 gr. Silvertip Hollow Point
X45ASHP2	**45 Automatic** 185 gr. Silvertip Hollow Point
X45CSHP2	**45 Colt** 225 gr. Silvertip Hollow Point

NEW: X10MMSTHP—**10mm Auto** 175 GR. Silvertip Hollow Point

Super Match™

WINCHESTER SYMBOL	CARTRIDGE
X38SMRP	**38 Special Match** 148 gr. Lead Mid-Range (clean cutting)
X9MMTCM	**9mm** 147 gr. Full Metal Jacket Truncated Cone
X40SWTCM	**40 Smith & Wesson** 155 gr. Full Metal Jacket Truncated Cone
X10MMTCM	**10mm Automatic** 155 gr. Full Metal Jacket Truncated Cone
X45AWCP	**45 Automatic** 185 gr. Full Metal Jacket Semi-Wad Cutter

Super-X

WINCHESTER SYMBOL	CARTRIDGE
X25AXP X25AP	**25 Automatic** 45 gr. Expanding Point 50 gr. Full Metal Jacket
X30LP	**30 Luger (7.65mm)** 93 gr. Full Metal Jacket
X30M1 X30M2	**30 Carbine** 110 gr. Hollow Soft Point 110 gr. Full Metal Jacket
X32SWP	**32 Smith & Wesson** 85 gr. Lead Round Nose
X32SWLP	**32 Smith & Wesson Long** 98 gr. Lead Round Nose
X32SCP	**32 Short Colt** 80 gr. Lead Round Nose
X32AP	***** **32 Automatic** 71 gr. Full Metal Jacket
X38SWP	**38 Smith & Wesson** 145 gr. Lead Round Nose
X380AP	****** **380 Automatic** 95 gr. Full Metal Jacket
X38S1P X38WCPSV	**38 Special** 158 gr. Lead Round Nose 158 gr. Lead Semi-Wad Cutter
X38S6PH X38S7PH X38SPD X38WCP	**38 Special +P** 110 gr. Jacketed Hollow Point 125 gr. Jacketed Hollow Point 158 gr. Lead Hollow Point Semi-Wad Cutter 158 gr. Lead Semi-Wad Cutter
X9LP	**9mm Luger (Parabellum)** 115 gr. Full Metal Jacket
X38A1P	**38 Super Automatic +P** *(For use in 38 Super Automatic Pistols ONLY)* 130 gr. Full Metal Jacket
X3573P X3576P X3571P X3574P X3575P	******* **357 Magnum** 110 gr. Jacketed Hollow Point 125 gr. Jacketed Hollow Point 158 gr. Lead Semi-Wad Cutter (Lubaloy) 158 gr. Jacketed Hollow Point 158 gr. Jacketed Soft Point
X41MP X41MJSP2 X41MHP2	**41 Remington Magnum** 210 gr. Lead Semi-Wad Cutter 210 gr. Jacketed Soft Point 210 gr. Jacketed Hollow Point
X44SP	**44 Smith & Wesson Special** 246 gr. Lead Round Nose
+ X44MWCP X44MHSP2	**44 Remington Magnum** 240 gr. Lead Semi-Wad Cutter (Med. Vel.) 240 gr. Hollow Soft Point
X45A1P2	**45 Automatic** 230 gr. Full Metal Jacket
X45CP2	**45 Colt** 255 gr. Lead Round Nose
X45WM2	**45 Winchester Magnum** *(Not for arms chambered for standard 45 Auto)* 230 gr. Full Metal Jacket

* NEW: 71 gr. Full Metal Jacket
** NEW: 95 gr. Full Metal Jacket
*** NEW: 180 gr. Supreme Expansion Talon

WINCHESTER AMMUNITION
SUPER-X® SHOTSHELLS

Game Loads

WINCHESTER SYMBOL	GAUGE	LENGTH INCHES	DRAM EQUIV.	Oz. SHOT	SHOT SIZES
Super-X Game Loads - High Brass					
X12	12	2¾	3¾	1¼	2,4,5,6,7½,8
X16H	16	2¾	3¼	1⅛	4,6,7½
X20	20	2¾	2¾	1	4,5,6,7½,8
X28	28	2¾	2¼	¾	6,7½
X28H	28	2¾	Max	1	6,7½,8
X41	410	2½	Max	½	4,6,7½
X413	410	3	Max	11/16	4,6,7½

WINCHESTER SYMBOL	GAUGE	LENGTH INCHES	DRAM EQUIV.	Oz. SHOT	SHOT SIZES
Super-X Game Loads - Low Brass					
XLH12	12	2¾	3¼	1¼	6,7½,8
XL12	12	2¾	3¼	1⅛	6,7½,8,9
XL16	16	2¾	2¾	1⅛	6,7½,8
XL20	20	2¾	2½	1	6,7½,8,9

WINCHESTER SYMBOL	GAUGE	LENGTH INCHES	DRAM EQUIV.	Oz. SHOT	SHOT SIZES
Double X Magnum Game Loads - Copperplated, Buffered Shot					
X103XC	10	3½	4½	2¼	BB,2,4
X123XC	12	3	4	1⅞	BB,2,4,6
X12MXC	12	3	4	1⅝	2,4,5,6
X12XC	12	2¾	3¾	1½	BB,2,4,5,6
X16XC	16	2¾	3¼	1¼	4,6
X203XC	20	3	3	1¼	2,4,6
X20XC	20	2¾	2¾	1⅛	4,6,7½

WINCHESTER SYMBOL	GAUGE	LENGTH INCHES	DRAM EQUIV.	Oz. SHOT	SHOT SIZES
Double X Magnum Turkey Loads - Copperplated, Buffered Shot					
X103XCT	10	3½	4½	2¼	6
XXT12L	12	3½	Max	2¼	4,6
X123MXCT	12	3	Max	2	4,5,6
X12HXCT	12	2¾	Max	1⅝	4,5,6

Slug Loads

WINCHESTER SYMBOL	GAUGE	LENGTH INCHES	DRAM EQUIV.	OZ.	TYPE
Super-X Slug Loads*					
XRS12	12	2¾	Max	1	Sabot Slug
XRS123	12	3	Max	1	Sabot Slug
X12RS15	12	2¾	Max	1	Rifled Slug
X16RS5	16	2¾	Max	⅘	Rifled Slug
XRS20	20	2¾	Max	⅝	Sabot Slug
X20RSM5	20	2¾	Max	¾	Rifled Slug
X41RS5	410	2½	Max	⅕	Rifled Slug

* NEW: X123RS15, 12 gauge, 3", FPS 1760

Super Steel® Drylok™ Non-Toxic Loads

WINCHESTER SYMBOL	GAUGE	LENGTH INCHES	DRAM EQUIV.	Oz. SHOT	SHOT SIZES
XSD12 NEW	12	2¾	Max	1	2,4,6
XS12 NEW	12	2¾	Max	1⅛	2,4,6
XS16	16	2¾	Max	⅞	2,4
XS20 NEW	20	2¾	Max	¾	4,6

Super Steel® Drylok™ Non-Toxic Magnum Loads

WINCHESTER SYMBOL	GAUGE	LENGTH INCHES	DRAM EQUIV.	Oz. SHOT	SHOT SIZES
XSM10 NEW	10	3½	Mag	1¾	BB,1,2
XSM12L NEW	12	3½	Mag	19/16	1,2
XSM123 NEW	12	3	Mag	1⅜	BB,1,2,3,4
XSV123 NEW	12	3	Mag	1¼	BB,1,2,3,4,5
XSM12 NEW	12	2¾	Mag	1¼	BB,1,2,3,4,6
XSM203 NEW	20	3	Mag	1	2,3,4

Super Steel® Drylok™ Non-Toxic Copper-plated Magnum Loads

WINCHESTER SYMBOL	GAUGE	LENGTH INCHES	DRAM EQUIV.	Oz. SHOT	SHOT SIZES
XSC10 NEW	10	3½	Mag	1⅝	T,BBB
XSC12L NEW	12	3½	Mag	19/16	T,BBB
XSCC123 NEW	12	3	Mag	1¼	T,BBB
XSC12 NEW	12	2¾	Mag	1⅛	T,BBB

Buckshot Loads

WINCHESTER SYMBOL	GAUGE	LENGTH INCHES	# PELLETS	SHOT SIZES
Super-X Buckshot Loads with Buffered Shot				
XB12L00	12	3½	18 Pellets	00 Buck
XB1231	12	3	24 Pellets	1 Buck
XB12300	12	3	15 Pellets	00 Buck
X12000B5	12	2¾	8 Pellets	000 Buck
X12RB	12	2¾	9 Pellets	00 Buck
X12RB5	12	2¾	9 Pellets	00 Buck
X120B5	12	2¾	12 Pellets	0 Buck
X121B5	12	2¾	16 Pellets	1 Buck
X124B5	12	2¾	27 Pellets	4 Buck
X16B5	16	2¾	12 Pellets	1 Buck
X20B5	20	2¾	20 Pellets	3 Buck
Double X Buckshot Loads - Copperplated, Buffered Shot				
+ X10C4B	10	3½	54 Pellets	4 Buck
X10C00B	10	3½	18 Pellets	00 Buck
X123C000B	12	3	10 Pellets	000 Buck
X12XC3B5	12	3	15 Pellets	00 Buck
X12XC0B5	12	2¾	12 Pellets	00 Buck
X12C1B	12	2¾	20 Pellets	1 Buck
X12XCMB5	12	3	41 Pellets	4 Buck
X12XC4B5	12	2¾	34 Pellets	4 Buck
X203C3B	20	3	24 Pellets	3 Buck

Ballistics

FEDERAL BALLISTICS

CLASSIC® CENTERFIRE RIFLE BALLISTICS (Approximate)

USAGE	FEDERAL LOAD NO.	CALIBER	GRAINS	GRAMS	BULLET STYLE**	FACTORY PRIMER NO.	VELOCITY MUZZLE	100 YDS.	200 YDS.	300 YDS.	400 YDS.	500 YDS.	ENERGY MUZZLE	100 YDS.	200 YDS.	300 YDS.	400 YDS.	500 YDS.
1	222A	222 Rem. (5.56x43mm)	50	3.24	Hi-Shok Soft Point	205	3140	2600	2120	1700	1350	1110	1095	750	500	320	200	135
5	222B		55	3.56	Hi-Shok FMJ Boat-tail	205	3020	2740	2480	2230	1990	1780	1115	915	750	610	485	385
1	223A	223 Rem. (5.56x45mm)	55	3.56	Hi-Shok Soft Point	205	3240	2750	2300	1910	1550	1270	1280	920	650	445	295	195
5	223B		55	3.56	Hi-Shok FMJ Boat-tail	205	3240	2950	2670	2410	2170	1940	1280	1060	875	710	575	460
1	22250A	22-250 Rem.	55	3.56		210	3680	3140	2660	2220	1830	1490	1655	1200	860	605	410	270
1	243A	243 Win. (6.16x51mm)	80	5.18	Hi-Shok Soft Point	210	3350	2960	2590	2260	1950	1670	1995	1550	1195	905	675	495
2	243B		100	6.48	Hi-Shok Soft Point	210	2960	2700	2450	2220	1990	1790	1945	1615	1330	1090	880	710
1	6A	6mm Rem.	80	5.18	Hi-Shok Soft Point	210	3470	3060	2690	2350	2040	1750	2140	1665	1290	980	735	540
2	6B		100	6.48	Hi-Shok Soft Point	210	3100	2830	2570	2330	2100	1890	2135	1775	1470	1205	985	790
2	2506B	25-06 Rem.	117	7.58	Hi-Shok Soft Point	210	2990	2730	2480	2250	2030	1830	2320	1985	1645	1350	1100	885
2	270A	270 Win.	130	8.42	Hi-Shok Soft Point	210	3060	2800	2560	2330	2110	1900	2700	2265	1890	1565	1285	1045
2	270B		150	9.72	Hi-Shok Soft Point RN	210	2850	2500	2180	1890	1620	1390	2705	2085	1585	1185	870	640
2	7A	7mm Mauser (7x57mm Mauser)	175	11.34	Hi-Shok Soft Point RN	210	2440	2140	1860	1600	1380	1200	2315	1775	1340	1000	740	565
2	7B		140	9.07	Hi-Shok Soft Point	210	2660	2450	2260	2070	1890	1730	2200	1865	1585	1330	1110	930
2	280B	280 Rem.	150	9.72	Hi-Shok Soft Point	210	2890	2670	2460	2260	2060	1880	2780	2370	2015	1695	1420	1180
2	7RA	7mm Rem. Magnum	150	9.72	Hi-Shok Soft Point	215	3110	2830	2570	2320	2090	1870	3220	2670	2200	1790	1450	1160
3	7RB		175	11.34	Hi-Shok Soft Point	215	2860	2650	2440	2240	2060	1880	3180	2720	2310	1960	1640	1370
1	30CA	30 Carbine (7.62x33mm)	110	7.13	Hi-Shok Soft Point RN	205	1990	1570	1240	1040	920	840	965	600	375	260	210	175
2	76239B	7.62x39mm Soviet	123	7.97	Hi-Shok Soft Point	210	2300	2030	1780	1550	1350	1200	1445	1125	860	655	500	395
2	3030A	30-30 Win.	150	9.72	Hi-Shok Soft Point FN	210	2390	2020	1680	1400	1180	1040	1900	1355	945	650	460	355
2	3030B		170	11.01	Hi-Shok Soft Point RN	210	2200	1900	1620	1380	1190	1060	1830	1355	990	720	535	425
1	3030C		125	8.10	Hi-Shok Hollow Point	210	2570	2090	1660	1320	1080	960	1830	1210	770	480	320	260
2	300A	300 Savage	150	9.72	Hi-Shok Soft Point	210	2630	2350	2100	1850	1630	1430	2305	1845	1460	1145	885	685
2	300B		180	11.66	Hi-Shok Soft Point	210	2350	2140	1940	1750	1570	1410	2205	1825	1495	1215	985	800
2	308A	308 Win. (7.62x51mm)	150	9.72	Hi-Shok Soft Point	210	2820	2530	2260	2010	1770	1560	2650	2140	1705	1345	1050	810
2	308B		180	11.66	Hi-Shok Soft Point	210	2620	2390	2180	1970	1780	1600	2745	2290	1895	1555	1270	1030
2	3006A	30-06 Springfield (7.62x63mm)	150	9.72	Hi-Shok Soft Point	210	2910	2620	2340	2080	1840	1620	2820	2280	1825	1445	1130	875
3	3006B		180	11.66	Hi-Shok Soft Point	210	2700	2470	2250	2040	1850	1660	2915	2435	2025	1665	1360	1105
1	3006C		125	8.10	Hi-Shok Soft Point	210	3140	2780	2450	2140	1850	1600	2735	2145	1660	1270	955	705
3	3006H		220	14.25	Hi-Shok Soft Point RN	210	2410	2130	1870	1630	1420	1250	2835	2215	1705	1300	985	760
3	3006J		180	11.66	Hi-Shok Soft Point RN	210	2700	2350	2020	1730	1470	1250	2915	2200	1630	1190	860	620
3	300WB	300 Win. Magnum	180	11.66	Hi-Shok Soft Point	215	2960	2750	2540	2340	2160	1980	3500	3010	2580	2195	1860	1565
2	303A	303 British	180	11.66	Hi-Shok Soft Point	210	2460	2230	2020	1820	1630	1460	2420	1995	1625	1315	1060	850
2	303B		150	9.72	Hi-Shok Soft Point	210	2690	2440	2210	1980	1780	1590	2400	1980	1620	1310	1055	840
2	32A	32 Win. Special	170	11.01	Hi-Shok Soft Point	210	2250	1920	1630	1370	1180	1040	1910	1395	1000	710	520	410
2	*8A	8mm Mauser (8x57mm JS Mauser)	170	11.01	Hi-Shok Soft Point	210	2360	1970	1620	1330	1120	1000	2100	1465	995	670	475	375
3	338C	338 Win. Magnum	225	14.58	Hi-Shok Soft Point	215	2780	2570	2370	2180	2000	1830	3860	3305	2815	2380	2000	1670
2	357G	357 Magnum	180	11.66	Hi-Shok Hollow Point	100	1550	1160	980	860	770	680	960	535	385	295	235	185
2	35A	35 Rem.	200	12.96	Hi-Shok Soft Point	210	2080	1700	1380	1140	1000	910	1920	1280	840	575	445	370
3	375A	375 H&H Magnum	270	17.50	Hi-Shok Soft Point	215	2690	2420	2170	1920	1700	1500	4340	3510	2810	2220	1740	1355
4	375B		300	19.44	Hi-Shok Soft Point	215	2530	2270	2020	1790	1580	1400	4265	3425	2720	2135	1665	1295
2	44A	44 Rem. Magnum	240	15.55	Hi-Shok Hollow Point	150	1760	1380	1090	950	860	790	1650	1015	640	485	395	330
2	4570A	45-70 Government	300	19.44	Hi-Shok Hollow Point	210	1880	1650	1430	1240	1110	1010	2355	1815	1355	1015	810	680

*Only for use in barrels intended for .323 inch diameter bullets. Do not use in 8x57mm J Commission Rifles (M1888) or in sporting or other military arms of .318 inch bore diameter.
**RN = Round Nose   FN = Flat Nose   FMJ = Full Metal Jacket   HP = Hollow Point

Usage Key: 1 = Varmints, predators, small game   2 = Medium game   3 = Large, heavy game   4 = Dangerous game   5 = Target shooting, training, practice

| WIND DRIFT IN INCHES 10 MPH CROSSWIND | | | | | HEIGHT OF BULLET TRAJECTORY IN INCHES ABOVE OR BELOW LINE OF SIGHT IF ZEROED AT ⊕ YARDS. SIGHTS 1.5 INCHES ABOVE BORE LINE. | | | | | | | | | | TEST BARREL LENGTH INCHES | FEDERAL LOAD NO. |
| | | | | | AVERAGE RANGE | | | | LONG RANGE | | | | | | | |
100 YDS.	200 YDS.	300 YDS.	400 YDS.	500 YDS.	50 YDS.	100 YDS.	200 YDS.	300 YDS.	50 YDS.	100 YDS.	200 YDS.	300 YDS.	400 YDS.	500 YDS.		
1.7	7.3	18.3	36.4	63.1	−0.2	⊕	−3.7	−15.3	+0.7	+1.9	⊕	−9.7	−31.6	−71.3	24	222A
0.9	3.4	8.5	16.8	26.3	−0.2	⊕	−3.1	−12.0	+0.6	+1.6	⊕	−7.3	−21.5	−44.6	24	222B
1.4	6.1	15.0	29.4	50.8	−0.3	⊕	−3.2	−12.9	+0.5	+1.6	⊕	−8.2	−26.1	−58.3	24	223A
0.8	3.3	7.8	14.5	24.0	−0.3	⊕	−2.5	−9.9	+0.3	+1.3	⊕	−6.1	−18.3	−37.8	24	223B
1.2	5.2	12.5	24.4	42.0	−0.4	⊕	−2.1	−9.1	+0.1	+1.0	⊕	−6.0	−19.1	−42.6	24	22250A
1.0	4.3	10.4	19.8	33.3	−0.3	⊕	−2.5	−10.2	+0.3	+1.3	⊕	−6.4	−19.7	−42.2	24	243A
0.9	3.6	8.4	15.7	25.8	−0.2	⊕	−3.3	−12.4	+0.6	+1.6	⊕	−7.5	−22.0	−45.4	24	243B
1.0	4.1	9.9	18.8	31.6	−0.3	⊕	−2.2	−9.3	+0.2	+1.1	⊕	−5.9	−18.2	−39.0	24	6A
0.8	3.3	7.9	14.7	24.1	−0.3	⊕	−2.9	−11.0	+0.5	+1.4	⊕	−6.7	−19.8	−40.6	24	6B
0.8	3.4	8.1	15.1	24.9	−0.2	⊕	−3.2	−12.0	+0.6	+1.6	⊕	−7.2	−21.4	−44.0	24	2506B
0.8	3.2	7.6	14.2	23.3	−0.2	⊕	−2.9	−11.2	+0.5	+1.5	⊕	−6.8	−20.0	−41.1	24	270A
1.2	5.3	12.8	24.5	41.3	−0.1	⊕	−4.1	−15.5	+0.9	+2.0	⊕	−9.4	−28.6	−61.0	24	270B
1.5	6.2	15.0	28.7	47.8	−0.1	⊕	−6.2	−22.6	+1.6	+3.1	⊕	−13.3	−40.1	−84.6	24	7A
1.3	3.2	8.2	15.4	23.4	−0.1	⊕	−4.3	−15.4	+1.0	+2.1	⊕	−9.0	−26.1	−52.9	24	7B
0.7	3.1	7.2	13.4	21.9	−0.2	⊕	−3.4	−12.6	+0.7	+1.7	⊕	−7.5	−21.8	−44.3	24	280B
0.8	3.4	8.1	15.1	24.9	−0.3	⊕	−2.9	−11.0	+0.5	+1.4	⊕	−6.7	−19.9	−41.0	24	7RA
0.7	3.1	7.2	13.3	21.7	−0.2	⊕	−3.5	−12.8	+0.7	+1.7	⊕	−7.6	−22.1	−44.9	24	7RB
3.4	15.0	35.5	63.2	96.7	+0.6	⊕	−12.8	−46.9	+3.9	+6.4	⊕	−27.7	−81.8	−167.8	18	30CA
1.5	6.4	15.2	28.7	47.3	+0.2	⊕	−7.0	−25.1	+1.9	+3.5	⊕	−14.5	−43.4	−90.6	20	76239B
2.0	8.5	20.9	40.1	66.1	+0.2	⊕	−7.2	−26.7	+1.9	+3.6	⊕	−15.9	−49.1	−104.5	24	3030A
1.9	8.0	19.4	36.7	59.8	+0.3	⊕	−8.3	−29.8	+2.4	+4.1	⊕	−17.4	−52.4	−109.4	24	3030B
2.2	10.1	25.4	49.4	81.6	+0.1	⊕	−6.6	−26.0	+1.7	+3.3	⊕	−16.0	−50.9	−109.5	24	3030C
1.1	4.8	11.6	21.9	36.3	0	⊕	−4.8	−17.6	+1.2	+2.4	⊕	−10.4	−30.9	−64.4	24	300A
1.1	4.6	10.9	20.3	33.3	+0.1	⊕	−6.1	−21.6	+1.7	+3.1	⊕	−12.4	−36.1	−73.8	24	300B
1.0	4.4	10.4	19.7	32.7	−0.1	⊕	−3.9	−14.7	+0.8	+2.0	⊕	−8.8	−26.3	−54.8	24	308A
0.9	3.9	9.2	17.2	28.3	−0.1	⊕	−4.6	−16.5	+1.1	+2.3	⊕	−9.7	−28.3	−57.8	24	308B
1.0	4.2	9.9	18.7	31.2	−0.2	⊕	−3.6	−13.6	+0.7	+1.8	⊕	−8.2	−24.4	−50.9	24	3006A
0.9	3.7	8.8	16.5	27.1	−0.1	⊕	−4.2	−15.3	+1.0	+2.1	⊕	−9.0	−26.4	−54.0	24	3006B
1.1	4.5	10.8	20.5	34.4	−0.3	⊕	−3.0	−11.9	+0.5	+1.5	⊕	−7.3	−22.3	−47.5	24	3006C
1.4	6.0	14.3	27.2	45.0	−0.1	⊕	−6.2	−22.4	+1.7	+3.1	⊕	−13.1	−39.3	−82.2	24	3006H
1.5	6.4	15.7	30.4	51.2	−0.1	⊕	−4.9	−18.3	+1.1	+2.4	⊕	−11.0	−33.6	−71.9	24	3006J
0.7	2.8	6.6	12.3	20.0	−0.2	⊕	−3.1	−11.7	+0.6	+1.6	⊕	−7.0	−20.3	−41.1	24	300WB
1.1	4.5	10.6	19.9	32.7	0	⊕	−5.5	−19.6	+1.4	+2.8	⊕	−11.3	−33.2	−68.1	24	303A
1.0	4.1	9.6	18.1	29.9	−0.1	⊕	−4.4	−15.9	+1.0	+2.2	⊕	−9.4	−27.6	−56.8	24	303B
1.9	8.4	20.3	38.6	63.0	+0.3	⊕	−8.0	−29.2	+2.3	+4.0	⊕	−17.2	−52.3	−109.8	24	32A
2.1	9.3	22.9	43.9	71.7	+0.2	⊕	−7.6	−28.5	+2.1	+3.8	⊕	−17.1	−52.9	−111.9	24	8A
0.8	3.1	7.3	13.6	22.2	−0.1	⊕	−3.8	−13.7	+0.8	+1.9	⊕	−8.1	−23.5	−47.5	24	338C
5.8	21.7	45.2	76.1	NA	⊕	−3.4	−29.7	−88.2	+1.7	⊕	−22.8	−77.9	−173.8	−321.4	18	357G
2.7	12.0	29.0	53.3	83.3	+0.5	⊕	−10.7	−39.3	+3.2	+5.4	⊕	−23.3	−70.0	−144.0	24	35A
1.1	4.5	10.8	20.3	33.7	−0.4	⊕	−5.5	−18.4	+1.0	+2.4	⊕	−10.9	−33.3	−71.2	24	375A
1.2	5.0	11.9	22.4	37.1	+0.5	⊕	−6.3	−21.2	+1.3	+2.6	⊕	−11.2	−33.3	−69.1	24	375B
4.2	17.8	39.8	68.3	102.5	⊕	−2.2	−21.7	−67.2	+1.1	⊕	−17.4	−60.7	−136.0	−250.2	20	44A
1.7	7.6	18.6	35.7	NA	⊕	−1.3	−14.1	−43.7	+0.7	⊕	−11.5	−39.7	−89.1	−163.1	24	4570A

These trajectory tables were calculated by computer using the best available data for each load. Trajectories are representative of the nominal behavior of each load at standard conditions (59°F temperature; barometric pressure of 29.53 inches; altitude at sea level). Shooters are cautioned that actual trajectories may differ due to variations in altitude, atmospheric conditions, guns, sights, and ammunition.

FEDERAL BALLISTICS

PREMIUM® HUNTING RIFLE BALLISTICS (Approximate)

USAGE	FEDERAL LOAD NO.	CALIBER	BULLET WGT. IN GRAINS	GRAMS	BULLET STYLE*	FACTORY PRIMER NO.	VELOCITY IN FEET PER SECOND (TO NEAREST 10 FEET) MUZZLE	100 YDS.	200 YDS.	300 YDS.	400 YDS.	500 YDS.	ENERGY IN FOOT/POUNDS (TO NEAREST 5 FOOT/POUNDS) MUZZLE	100 YDS.	200 YDS.	300 YDS.	400 YDS.	500 YDS.
1	P223E	223 Rem. (5.56x45mm)	55	3.56	Boat-tail HP	205	3240	2770	2340	1950	1610	1330	1280	935	670	465	315	215
1	P22250B	22-250 Rem.	55	3.56	Boat-tail HP	210	3680	3280	2920	2590	2280	1990	1655	1315	1040	815	630	480
1	P243C	243 Win. (6.16x51mm)	100	6.48	Boat-tail SP	210	2960	2760	2570	2380	2210	2040	1950	1690	1460	1260	1080	925
1	P243D	243 Win. (6.16x51mm)	85	5.50	Boat-tail HP	210	3320	3070	2830	2600	2380	2180	2080	1770	1510	1280	1070	890
2	P243E	243 Win. (6.16x51mm)	100	6.48	Nosler Partition**	210	2960	2730	2510	2300	2100	1910	1945	1650	1395	1170	975	805
2	P6C	6mm Rem.	100	6.48	Nosler Partition	210	3100	2830	2570	2330	2100	1890	2135	1775	1470	1205	985	790
2	P257B	257 Roberts (High Velocity +P)	120	7.77	Nosler Partition	210	2780	2560	2360	2160	1970	1790	2060	1750	1480	1240	1030	855
2	P2506C	25-06 Rem.	117	7.58	Boat-tail SP	210	2990	2770	2570	2370	2190	2000	2320	2000	1715	1465	1240	1045
2	P6555A	6.5x55 Swedish	140	9.07	Nosler Partition	210	2550	2350	2170	1990	1820	1660	2020	1725	1460	1230	1030	860
2	P270C	270 Win.	150	9.72	Boat-tail SP	210	2850	2660	2480	2300	2130	1970	2705	2355	2040	1760	1510	1290
2	P270D	270 Win.	130	8.42	Boat-tail SP	210	3060	2830	2620	2410	2220	2030	2700	2320	1980	1680	1420	1190
2	P270E	270 Win.	150	9.72	Nosler Partition	210	2850	2590	2340	2100	1880	1670	2705	2225	1815	1470	1175	930
2 NEW	P270T1	270 Win.	140	9.07	Trophy Bonded	210	2940	2700	2480	2260	2060	1860	2685	2270	1905	1590	1315	1080
2	P730A	7-30 Waters	120	7.77	Boat-tail SP	210	2700	2300	1930	1600	1330	1140	1940	1405	990	685	470	345
2	P7C	7mm Mauser (7x57mm Mauser)	140	9.07	Nosler Partition	210	2660	2450	2260	2070	1890	1730	2200	1865	1585	1330	1110	930
2	P764A	7x64 Brenneke	160	10.37	Nosler Partition	210	2650	2480	2310	2150	2000	1850	2495	2180	1895	1640	1415	1215
2	P280A	280 Rem.	150	9.72	Nosler Partition	210	2890	2620	2370	2140	1910	1710	2780	2295	1875	1520	1215	970
2 NEW	P708A	7mm-08	140	9.07	Nosler Partition	210	2800	2590	2390	2200	2020	1840	2435	2085	1775	1500	1265	1060
2	P7RD	7mm Rem. Magnum	150	9.72	Boat-tail SP	215	3110	2920	2750	2580	2410	2250	3220	2850	2510	2210	1930	1690
3	P7RE	7mm Rem. Magnum	165	10.69	Boat-tail SP	215	2950	2800	2650	2510	2370	2230	3190	2865	2570	2300	2050	1825
3	P7RF	7mm Rem. Magnum	160	10.37	Nosler Partition	215	2950	2770	2590	2420	2250	2090	3090	2715	2375	2075	1800	1555
2	P7RG	7mm Rem. Magnum	140	9.07	Nosler Partition	215	3150	2930	2710	2510	2320	2130	3085	2660	2290	1960	1670	1415
2	P3030D	30-30 Win.	170	11.01	Nosler Partition	210	2200	1900	1620	1380	1190	1060	1830	1355	990	720	535	425
2	P308C	308 Win. (7.62x51mm)	165	10.69	Boat-tail SP	210	2700	2520	2330	2160	1990	1830	2670	2310	1990	1700	1450	1230
3	P308E	308 Win. (7.62x51mm)	180	11.66	Nosler Partition	210	2620	2430	2240	2060	1890	1730	2745	2355	2005	1700	1430	1200
2	P3006D	30-06 Spring. (7.62x63mm)	165	10.69	Boat-tail SP	210	2800	2610	2420	2240	2070	1910	2870	2490	2150	1840	1580	1340
3	P3006F	30-06 Spring. (7.62x63mm)	180	11.66	Nosler Partition	210	2700	2500	2320	2140	1970	1810	2910	2510	2150	1830	1550	1350
2	P3006G	30-06 Spring. (7.62x63mm)	150	9.72	Boat-tail SP	210	2910	2690	2480	2270	2070	1880	2820	2420	2040	1710	1430	1180
3	P3006L	30-06 Spring. (7.62x63mm)	180	11.66	Boat-tail SP	210	2700	2540	2380	2220	2080	1930	2915	2570	2260	1975	1720	1495
2 NEW	P3006T1	30-06 Spring. (7.62x63mm)	165	10.69	Trophy Bonded	210	2800	2540	2290	2050	1830	1630	2870	2360	1915	1545	1230	975
3	P300WC	300 Win. Magnum	200	12.96	Boat-tail SP	215	2830	2680	2530	2380	2240	2110	3560	3180	2830	2520	2230	1970

PREMIUM® SAFARI RIFLE BALLISTICS (Approximate)

USAGE	FEDERAL LOAD NO.	CALIBER	BULLET WGT. IN GRAINS	GRAMS	BULLET STYLE*	FACTORY PRIMER NO.	VELOCITY IN FEET PER SECOND (TO NEAREST 10 FEET) MUZZLE	100 YDS.	200 YDS.	300 YDS.	400 YDS.	500 YDS.	ENERGY IN FOOT/POUNDS (TO NEAREST 5 FOOT/POUNDS) MUZZLE	100 YDS.	200 YDS.	300 YDS.	400 YDS.	500 YDS.
3	P300HA	300 H&H Magnum	180	11.66	Nosler Partition	215	2880	2620	2380	2150	1930	1730	3315	2750	2260	1840	1480	1190
3	P300WD2	300 Win. Magnum	180	11.66	Nosler Partition	215	2960	2700	2450	2210	1990	1780	3500	2905	2395	1955	1585	1270
3 NEW	P300WT1	300 Win. Magnum	200	12.96	Trophy Bonded	215	2800	2570	2350	2150	1950	1770	3480	2935	2460	2050	1690	1385
3	P338A2	338 Win. Magnum	210	13.60	Nosler Partition	215	2830	2590	2370	2160	1960	1770	3735	3140	2620	2170	1785	1455
3	P338B2	338 Win. Magnum	250	16.20	Nosler Partition	215	2660	2400	2150	1910	1690	1500	3925	3185	2555	2055	1590	1245
3 NEW	P338T1	338 Win. Magnum	225	14.58	Trophy Bonded	215	2800	2560	2330	2110	1900	1710	3915	3265	2700	2220	1800	1455
4	P375D	375 H&H Magnum	300	19.44	Solid	215	2530	2170	1840	1550	1310	1140	4265	3140	2260	1605	1140	860
4	P375F	375 H&H Magnum	300	19.44	Nosler Partition	215	2530	2320	2120	1930	1750	1590	4265	3585	2995	2475	2040	1675
4 NEW	P375T1	375 H&H Magnum	300	19.44	Trophy Bonded	215	2530	2280	2040	1810	1610	1425	4265	3450	2765	2190	1725	1350
4	P458A	458 Win. Magnum	350	22.68	Soft Point	215	2470	1990	1570	1250	1060	950	4740	3065	1915	1205	870	705
4	P458B	458 Win. Magnum	510	33.04	Soft Point	215	2090	1820	1570	1360	1190	1080	4945	3730	2790	2080	1605	1320
4	P458C	458 Win. Magnum	500	32.40	Solid	215	2090	1870	1670	1480	1320	1190	4850	3880	3085	2440	1945	1585
4	P416A	416 Rigby	410	26.57	Weldcore SP	215	2370	2110	1870	1640	1440	1280	5115	4050	3165	2455	1895	1485
4	P416B	416 Rigby	410	26.57	Solid	215	2370	2110	1870	1640	1440	1280	5115	4050	3165	2455	1895	1485
4	P470A	470 Nitro Express	500	32.40	Weldcore SP	215	2150	1890	1650	1440	1270	1140	5130	3965	3040	2310	1790	1435
4	P470B	470 Nitro Express	500	32.40	Woodleigh Solid	215	2150	1890	1650	1440	1270	1140	5130	3965	3040	2310	1790	1435

*HP = Hollow Point SP = Soft Point
**"Nosler" and "Partition" are registered trademarks of Nosler Bullets, Inc.
+P ammunition is loaded to a higher pressure. Use only in firearms so recommended by the gun manufacturer.

Usage Key: 1=Varmints, predators, small game 2=Medium game 3=Large, heavy game 4=Dangerous game 5=Target shooting, training, practice

PREMIUM® VARMINT RIFLE BALLISTICS (Approximate)

USAGE	FEDERAL LOAD NO.	CALIBER	BULLET WGT. IN GRAINS	GRAMS	BULLET STYLE	FACTORY PRIMER NO.	VELOCITY IN FEET PER SECOND (TO NEAREST 10 FEET) MUZZLE	100 YDS.	200 YDS.	300 YDS.	400 YDS.	500 YDS.	ENERGY IN FOOT/POUNDS (TO NEAREST 5 FOOT/POUNDS) MUZZLE	100 YDS.	200 YDS.	300 YDS.	400 YDS.	500 YDS.
1	P223V	223 Rem. (5.56x45mm)	40	2.59	Hollow Point Varmint	205	3650	3010	2450	1950	1530	1210	1185	805	535	340	205	130
1	P22250V	22-250 Rem.	40	2.59	Hollow Point Varmint	210	4000	3320	2720	2200	1740	1360	1420	980	660	430	265	165
1	P243V	243 Win. (6.16x51mm)	60	3.89	Hollow Point Varmint	210	3600	3110	2660	2260	1890	1560	1725	1285	945	680	475	325
1	P2506V	25-06 Rem.	90	5.83	Hollow Point Varmint	210	3440	3040	2680	2340	2030	1750	2365	1850	1435	1100	825	610

FEDERAL BALLISTICS

| WIND DRIFT IN INCHES 10 MPH CROSSWIND | | | | | HEIGHT OF BULLET TRAJECTORY IN INCHES ABOVE OR BELOW LINE OF SIGHT IF ZEROED AT ⊕ YARDS. SIGHTS 1.5 INCHES ABOVE BORE LINE. | | | | | | | | | | TEST BARREL LENGTH INCHES | FEDERAL LOAD NO. |
| | | | | | AVERAGE RANGE | | | | LONG RANGE | | | | | | | |
100 YDS.	200 YDS.	300 YDS.	400 YDS.	500 YDS.	50 YDS.	100 YDS.	200 YDS.	300 YDS.	50 YDS.	100 YDS.	200 YDS.	300 YDS.	400 YDS.	500 YDS.		
1.3	5.8	14.2	27.7	47.6	−0.3	⊕	−2.7	−10.8	+0.4	+1.4	⊕	−6.7	−20.5	−43.4	24	P223E
0.8	3.6	8.4	15.8	26.3	−0.4	⊕	−1.7	−7.6	0	+0.9	⊕	−5.0	−15.1	−32.0	24	P22250B
0.6	2.6	6.1	11.3	18.4	−0.2	⊕	−3.1	−11.4	+0.6	+1.5	⊕	−6.8	−19.8	−39.9	24	P243C
0.7	2.7	6.3	11.6	18.8	−0.3	⊕	−2.2	−8.8	+0.2	+1.1	⊕	−5.5	−16.1	−32.8	24	P243D
0.7	3.1	7.3	13.5	22.1	−0.2	⊕	−3.2	−11.9	+0.6	+1.6	⊕	−7.1	−20.9	−42.5	24	P243E
0.8	3.3	7.9	14.7	24.1	−0.3	⊕	−2.9	−11.0	+0.5	+1.4	⊕	−6.7	−19.8	−39.0	24	P6C
0.8	3.3	7.7	14.3	23.5	−0.1	⊕	−3.8	−14.0	+0.5	+1.9	⊕	−8.2	−24.0	−48.9	24	P257B
0.7	2.8	6.5	12.0	19.6	−0.2	⊕	−3.0	−11.4	+0.5	+1.5	⊕	−6.8	−19.9	−40.4	24	P2506C
0.8	3.5	8.3	15.1	25.1	0	⊕	−4.8	−17.1	+1.2	+2.4	⊕	−9.8	−28.2	−57.7	24	P6555A
0.7	2.7	6.3	11.6	18.9	−0.2	⊕	−3.4	−12.5	+0.7	+1.7	⊕	−7.4	−21.4	−43.0	24	P270C
0.7	2.8	6.6	12.1	19.7	−0.2	⊕	−2.8	−10.7	+0.5	+1.4	⊕	−6.5	−19.0	−38.5	24	P270D
0.9	3.9	9.2	17.3	28.5	−0.2	⊕	−3.7	−13.8	+0.8	+1.9	⊕	−8.3	−24.4	−50.5	24	P270E
0.8	3.2	7.6	14.2	23.0	−0.2	⊕	−3.3	−12.2	+0.6	+1.6	⊕	−7.3	−21.5	−43.7	24	P270T1
1.6	7.2	17.7	34.5	58.1	0	⊕	−5.2	−19.8	+1.2	+2.6	⊕	−12.0	−37.6	−81.7	24	P730A
1.3	3.2	8.2	15.4	23.4	−0.1	⊕	−4.3	−15.4	+1.0	+2.1	⊕	−9.0	−26.1	−52.9	24	P7C
0.7	2.8	6.6	12.3	19.5	−0.1	⊕	−4.2	−14.9	+0.9	+2.1		−8.7	−24.9	−49.4	24	P764A
0.9	3.8	9.0	16.8	27.8	−0.2	⊕	−3.6	−13.4	+0.7	+1.8		−8.0	−23.8	−49.2	24	P280A
0.8	3.1	7.3	13.5	21.8	−0.2	⊕	−3.7	−13.5	+0.8	+1.8		−8.0	−23.1	−46.6	24	P708A
0.5	2.2	5.1	9.3	15.0	−0.3	⊕	−2.6	−9.8	+0.4	+1.3	⊕	−5.9	−17.0	−34.2	24	P7RD
0.5	2.0	4.6	8.4	13.5	−0.2	⊕	−3.0	−10.9	+0.5	+1.5	⊕	−6.4	−18.4	−36.6	24	P7RE
0.6	2.5	5.6	10.4	16.9	−0.2	⊕	−3.1	−11.3	+0.6	+1.5	⊕	−6.7	−19.4	−39.0	24	P7RF
0.6	2.6	6.0	11.1	18.2	−0.3	⊕	−2.6	−9.9	+0.4	+1.3	⊕	−6.0	−17.5	−35.6	24	P7RG
0.9	8.0	19.4	36.7	59.8	−0.3	⊕	−8.3	−29.8	+2.4	+4.1	⊕	−17.4	−52.4	−109.4	24	P3030D
0.7	3.0	7.0	13.0	21.1	−0.1	⊕	−4.0	−14.4	+0.9	+2.0	⊕	−8.4	−24.3	−49.0	24	P308C
0.8	3.3	7.7	14.3	23.3	−0.1	⊕	−4.4	−15.8	+1.0	+2.2	⊕	−9.2	−26.5	−53.6	24	P308E
0.7	2.8	6.6	12.3	19.9	−0.2	⊕	−3.6	−13.2	+0.8	+1.8	⊕	−7.8	−22.4	−45.2	24	P3006D
0.7	3.0	7.3	13.4	27.7	−0.1	⊕	−4.0	−14.6	+0.9	+2.0	⊕	−8.6	−24.6	−49.6	24	P3006F
0.7	3.0	7.1	13.4	22.0	−0.2	⊕	−3.3	−12.4	+0.6	+1.7	⊕	−7.4	−21.5	−43.7	24	P3006G
0.6	2.6	6.0	11.0	17.8	−0.1	⊕	−3.9	−13.9	+0.9	+1.9	⊕	−8.1	−23.1	−46.1	24	P3006L
1.0	4.0	9.6	17.8	29.7	−0.1	⊕	−3.9	−14.5	+0.8	+2.0	⊕	−8.7	−25.4	−53.1	24	P3006T1
0.5	2.2	5.0	9.2	14.9	−0.2	⊕	−3.4	−12.2	+0.7	+1.7	⊕	−7.1	−20.4	−40.5	24	P300WC

| WIND DRIFT IN INCHES 10 MPH CROSSWIND | | | | | HEIGHT OF BULLET TRAJECTORY IN INCHES ABOVE OR BELOW LINE OF SIGHT IF ZEROED AT ⊕ YARDS. SIGHTS 1.5 INCHES ABOVE BORE LINE. | | | | | | | | | | TEST BARREL LENGTH INCHES | FEDERAL LOAD NO. |
| | | | | | AVERAGE RANGE | | | | LONG RANGE | | | | | | | |
100 YDS.	200 YDS.	300 YDS.	400 YDS.	500 YDS.	50 YDS.	100 YDS.	200 YDS.	300 YDS.	50 YDS.	100 YDS.	200 YDS.	300 YDS.	400 YDS.	500 YDS.		
0.9	3.7	8.8	16.3	27.1	−0.3	⊕	−3.5	−13.3	+0.7	+1.8	⊕	−8.0	−23.4	−48.6	24	P300HA
0.9	3.5	8.4	15.8	25.9	−0.2	⊕	−3.3	−12.4	+0.6	+1.6	⊕	−7.5	−22.1	−45.4	24	P300WD2
0.9	3.4	8.1	14.9	24.5	−0.1	⊕	−3.7	−13.8	+0.8	+1.9	⊕	−8.2	−23.9	−48.8	24	P300WT1
0.9	3.4	8.2	15.2	24.9	−0.2	⊕	−3.6	−13.6	+0.8	+1.8	⊕	−8.1	−23.6	−48.3	24	P338A2
1.1	4.5	10.8	20.3	33.6	−0.1	⊕	−4.6	−16.7	+1.1	+2.3	⊕	−9.8	−29.1	−60.2	24	P338B2
0.9	3.7	8.7	16.1	26.7	−0.2	⊕	−3.8	−14.1	+0.9	+1.9	⊕	−8.4	−24.5	−50.6	24	P338T1
1.7	7.2	17.6	33.9	56.5	⊕	−1.1	−9.1	−27.5	+0.5	⊕	−7.0	−24.2	−55.8	−106.5	24	P375D
0.9	3.9	9.1	17.0	27.8	0	⊕	−5.0	−17.7	+1.2	+2.5	⊕	−10.3	−29.9	−60.8	24	P375F
1.1	4.8	11.3	21.5	35.4	−0.1	⊕	−5.3	−18.8	+1.3	+2.6	⊕	−10.9	−32.8	−67.8	24	P375T1
2.5	11.0	27.6	52.6	83.9	⊕	−1.5	−11.0	−34.9	+0.1	⊕	−7.5	−29.1	−71.1	−138.0	24	P458A
1.9	7.9	18.9	35.3	56.8	⊕	−1.8	−13.7	−39.7	+0.4	⊕	−9.1	−32.3	−73.9	−138.0	24	P458B
1.5	6.1	14.5	26.9	43.7	⊕	−1.7	−12.9	−36.7	+0.4	⊕	−8.5	−29.5	−66.2	−122.0	24	P458C
1.3	5.7	13.6	25.6	42.3	⊕	−1.2	−9.8	−28.5	+0.6	⊕	−7.4	−24.8	−55.0	−101.6	24	P416A
1.3	5.7	13.6	25.6	42.3	⊕	−1.2	−9.8	−28.5	+0.6	⊕	−7.4	−24.8	−55.0	−101.6	24	P416B
1.6	7.0	16.6	31.1	50.6	⊕	−1.6	−12.6	−36.2	+0.8	⊕	−9.3	−31.3	−69.7	−128.6	24	P470A
1.6	7.0	16.6	31.1	50.6	⊕	−1.6	−12.6	−36.2	+0.8	⊕	−9.3	−31.3	−69.7	−128.6	24	P470B

These trajectory tables were calculated by computer using the best available data for each load. Trajectories are representative of the nominal behavior of each load at standard conditions (59°F temperature; barometric pressure of 29.53 inches; altitude at sea level). Shooters are cautioned that actual trajectories may differ due to variations in altitude, atmospheric conditions, guns, sights, and ammunition.

| WIND DRIFT IN INCHES 10 MPH CROSSWIND | | | | | HEIGHT OF BULLET TRAJECTORY IN INCHES ABOVE OR BELOW LINE OF SIGHT IF ZEROED AT ⊕ YARDS. SIGHTS 1.5 INCHES ABOVE BORE LINE. | | | | | | | | | | TEST BARREL LENGTH INCHES | FEDERAL LOAD NO. |
| | | | | | AVERAGE RANGE | | | | LONG RANGE | | | | | | | |
100 YDS.	200 YDS.	300 YDS.	400 YDS.	500 YDS.	50 YDS.	100 YDS.	200 YDS.	300 YDS.	50 YDS.	100 YDS.	200 YDS.	300 YDS.	400 YDS.	500 YDS.		
1.5	6.5	16.1	32.3	56.9	−0.4	⊕	−2.4	−10.7	+0.2	+1.2	⊕	−7.1	−23.4	−54.2	24	P223V
1.3	5.7	14.0	27.9	49.2	−0.4	⊕	−1.7	−8.1	0	+0.8	⊕	−5.6	−18.4	−42.8	24	P22250V
1.1	4.8	11.7	22.6	38.7	−0.4	⊕	−2.1	−9.2	+0.2	+1.1	⊕	−6.0	−18.9	−41.6	24	P243V
1.0	4.1	9.8	18.7	31.3	−0.3	⊕	−2.3	−9.4	+0.2	+1.1	⊕	−6.0	−18.3	−39.2	24	P2506V

FEDERAL BALLISTICS

CLASSIC® AUTOMATIC PISTOL BALLISTICS (Approximate)

USAGE	FEDERAL LOAD NO.	CALIBER	BULLET WGT. IN GRAINS	GRAMS	BULLET STYLE**	FACTORY PRIMER NO.	MUZZLE	25 YDS.	50 YDS.	75 YDS.	100 YDS.	MUZZLE	25 YDS.	50 YDS.	75 YDS.	100 YDS.	25 YDS.	50 YDS.	75 YDS.	100 YDS.	TEST BARREL LENGTH INCHES
3, 4	25AP	25 Auto (6.35mm Browning)	50	3.24	Full Metal Jacket	100	760	750	730	720	700	65	60	59	55	55	0.5	1.9	4.5	8.1	2
3, 4	32AP	32 Auto (7.65mm Browning)	71	4.60	Full Metal Jacket	100	905	880	855	830	810	129	20	115	110	105	0.3	1.4	3.2	5.9	4
3, 4	380AP	380 Auto (9x17mm Short)	95	6.15	Full Metal Jacket	100	955	910	865	830	790	190	175	160	145	130	0.3	1.3	3.1	5.8	3¾
3	380BP	380 Auto (9x17mm Short)	90	5.83	Hi-Shok JHP	100	1000	940	890	840	800	200	175	160	140	130	0.3	1.2	2.9	5.5	3¾
3, 4	9AP	9mm Luger (9x19mm Parabellum)	124	8.03	Full Metal Jacket	100	1120	1070	1030	990	960	345	315	290	270	255	0.2	0.9	2.2	4.1	4
3	9BP	9mm Luger (9x19mm Parabellum)	115	7.45	Hi-Shok JHP	100	1160	1100	1060	1020	990	345	310	285	270	250	0.2	0.9	2.1	3.8	4
NEW	9MS	9mm Luger (9x19mm Parabellum)	147	9.52	Hi-Shok JHP	100	975	950	930	900	880	310	295	285	265	255	0.3	1.2	2.8	5.1	4
3	40SWA	40 S&W	180	11.06	Hi-Shok JHP	100	985	955	930	905	885	390	365	345	330	315	0.3	1.2	2.8	5.0	4
3	40SWB	40 S&W	155	10.04	Hi-Shok JHP	100	1140	1080	1030	990	950	445	400	365	335	315	0.2	0.9	2.2	4.1	4
3	10C	10mm Auto	180	11.06	Hi-Shok JHP	150	1030	995	970	945	920	425	400	375	355	340	0.3	1.1	2.5	4.7	5
3	10E	10mm Auto	155	10.04	Hi-Shok JHP	150	1325	1225	1140	1075	1025	605	515	450	400	360	0.2	0.7	1.8	3.3	5
3	45A	45 Auto	230	14.90	Full Metal Jacket	150	850	830	810	790	770	370	350	335	320	305	0.4	1.6	3.6	6.6	5
4	45C	45 Auto	185	11.99	Hi-Shok JHP	150	950	920	900	880	860	370	350	335	315	300	0.3	1.3	2.9	5.3	5
3	45D	45 Auto	230	14.90	Hi-Shok JHP	150	850	830	810	790	770	370	350	335	320	300	0.4	1.6	3.7	6.7	5

Usage Key: 1 = Varmints, predators, small game   2 = Medium game   3 = Self defense   4 = Target shooting, training, practice

CLASSIC® REVOLVER BALLISTICS (Approximate)

USAGE	FEDERAL LOAD NO.	CALIBER	BULLET WGT. IN GRAINS	GRAMS	BULLET STYLE**	FACTORY PRIMER NO.	MUZZLE	25 YDS.	50 YDS.	75 YDS.	100 YDS.	MUZZLE	25 YDS.	50 YDS.	75 YDS.	100 YDS.	25 YDS.	50 YDS.	75 YDS.	100 YDS.	TEST BARREL LENGTH INCHES
4	32LA	32 S&W Long	98	6.35	Lead Wadcutter	100	780	700	630	560	500	130	105	85	70	55	0.5	2.2	5.6	11.1	4
4	32LB	32 S&W Long	98	6.35	Lead Round Nose	100	705	690	670	650	640	115	105	98	95	90	0.6	2.3	5.3	9.6	4
3	32HRA	32 H&R Magnum	95	6.15	Lead Semi-Wadcutter	100	1030	1000	940	930	900	225	210	190	185	170	0.3	1.1	2.5	4.7	4½
3	32HRB	32 H&R Magnum	85	5.50	Hi-Shok JHP	100	1100	1050	1020	970	930	230	210	195	175	165	0.2	1.0	2.3	4.3	4½
4	38B	38 Special	158	10.23	Lead Round Nose	100	755	740	723	710	690	200	190	183	175	170	0.5	2.0	4.6	8.3	4-V
3, 4	38C	38 Special	158	10.23	Lead Semi-Wadcutter	100	755	740	723	710	690	200	190	183	175	170	0.5	2.0	4.6	8.3	4-V
1, 3	38E	38 Special (High Velocity +P)	125	8.10	Hi-Shok JHP	100	945	920	898	880	860	248	235	224	215	205	0.3	1.3	2.9	5.4	4-V
1, 3	38F	38 Special (High Velocity +P)	110	7.13	Hi-Shok JHP	100	995	960	926	900	870	242	225	210	195	185	0.3	1.2	2.7	5.0	4-V
1, 3	38G	38 Special (High Velocity +P)	158	10.23	Semi-Wadcutter HP	100	890	870	855	840	820	278	265	257	245	235	0.3	1.4	3.3	5.9	4-V
3, 4	38H	38 Special (High Velocity +P)	158	10.23	Lead Semi-Wadcutter	100	890	870	855	840	820	270	265	257	245	235	0.3	1.4	3.3	5.9	4-V
1, 3	38J	38 Special (High Velocity +P)	125	8.10	Hi-Shok JSP	100	945	920	898	880	860	248	235	224	215	205	0.3	1.3	2.9	5.4	4-V
2, 3	357A	357 Magnum	158	10.23	Hi-Shok JSP	100	1235	1160	1104	1060	1020	535	475	428	395	365	0.2	0.8	1.9	3.5	4-V
1, 3	357B	357 Magnum	125	8.10	Hi-Shok JHP	100	1450	1350	1240	1160	1100	583	495	427	370	335	0.1	0.6	1.5	2.8	4-V
4	357C	357 Magnum	158	10.23	Lead Semi-Wadcutter	100	1235	1160	1104	1060	1020	535	475	428	395	365	0.2	0.8	1.9	3.5	4-V
1, 3	357D	357 Magnum	110	7.13	Hi-Shok JHP	100	1295	1180	1094	1040	990	410	340	292	260	235	0.2	0.8	1.9	3.5	4-V
2, 3	357E	357 Magnum	158	10.23	Hi-Shok JHP	100	1235	1160	1104	1060	1020	535	475	428	395	365	0.2	0.8	1.9	3.5	4-V
2	357G	357 Magnum	180	11.66	Hi-Shok JHP	100	1090	1030	980	930	890	475	425	385	350	320	0.2	1.0	2.4	4.5	4-V
NEW	357H	357 Magnum	140	9.07	Hi-Shok JHP	100	1360	1270	1200	1130	1080	575	500	445	395	360	0.2	0.7	1.6	3.0	4-V
1, 3	41A	41 Rem. Magnum	210	13.60	Hi-Shok JHP	150	1300	1210	1130	1070	1030	790	680	595	540	495	0.2	0.7	1.8	3.3	4-V
1, 3	44SA	44 S&W Special	200	12.96	Semi-Wadcutter HP	150	900	860	830	800	770	360	330	305	285	260	0.3	1.4	3.4	6.3	6½-V
2, 3	44A	44 Rem. Magnum	240	15.55	Hi-Shok JHP	150	1180	1130	1081	1050	1010	741	675	623	580	550	0.2	0.9	2.0	3.7	6½-V
1, 2	44B*	44 Rem. Magnum	180	11.66	Hi-Shok JHP	150	1610	1480	1365	1270	1180	1035	875	750	640	555	0.1	0.5	1.2	2.3	6½-V
1, 3	45LCA	45 Colt	225	14.58	Semi-Wadcutter HP	150	900	880	860	840	820	405	385	369	355	340	0.3	1.4	3.2	5.8	5½

+P ammunition is loaded to a higher pressure. Use only in firearms so recommended by the gun manufacturer.   "V" indicates vented barrel to simulate service conditions.
*Also available in 20-round box (A44B20).
**JHP=Jacketed Hollow Point   HP=Hollow Point   JSP=Jacketed Soft Point   FMJ=Full Metal Jacket   SWC=Semi-Wadcutter

GOLD MEDAL® MATCH PISTOL AND REVOLVER BALLISTICS (Approximate)

USAGE	FEDERAL LOAD NO.	CALIBER	BULLET WGT. IN GRAINS	GRAMS	BULLET STYLE**	FACTORY PRIMER NO.	MUZZLE	25 YDS.	50 YDS.	75 YDS.	100 YDS.	MUZZLE	25 YDS.	50 YDS.	75 YDS.	100 YDS.	25 YDS.	50 YDS.	75 YDS.	100 YDS.	TEST BARREL LENGTH INCHES
4 NEW	GM9MP	9mm Luger (9x19mm Parabellum)	124	8.03	FMJ-SWC Match	100	1120	1070	1030	990	960	345	315	290	270	255	0.2	0.9	2.2	4.1	4
4 NEW	GM38A	38 Special	148	9.59	Lead Wadcutter Match	100	710	670	634	600	560	166	150	132	115	105	0.6	2.4	5.7	10.8	4-V
4 NEW	GM44D	44 Rem. Magnum	250	16.20	MC Profile Match*	150	1180	1140	1100	1070	1040	775	715	670	630	600	0.2	0.8	1.9	3.6	6½-V
4 NEW	GM45B	45 Auto	185	11.99	FMJ-SWC Match	150	775	730	695	660	620	247	220	200	175	160	0.5	2.0	4.8	9.0	5

*MC Profile Match = Metal Case Profile Match   **FMJ = Full Metal Jacket   SWC = Semi-Wadcutter

FEDERAL BALLISTICS

GOLD MEDAL® .22 MATCH BALLISTICS (Approximate)

	TYPE	FEDERAL LOAD NO.	CART-RIDGE PER BOX	CALIBER	BULLET WGT. IN GRAINS	BULLET STYLE	VELOCITY IN FEET PER SECOND					ENERGY IN FOOT/POUNDS					WIND DRIFT IN INCHES 10 MPH CROSSWIND				HEIGHT OF BULLET TRAJECTORY IN INCHES ABOVE OR BELOW LINE OF SIGHT IF ZEROED AT ⊕ YARDS. SIGHTS 1.5 INCHES ABOVE BORE LINE.			
							MUZZLE	25 YDS.	50 YDS.	75 YDS.	100 YDS.	MUZZLE	25 YDS.	50 YDS.	75 YDS.	100 YDS.	25 YDS.	50 YDS.	75 YDS.	100 YDS.	25 YDS.	50 YDS.	75 YDS.	100 YDS.
NEW	Ultra-Match	UM1	50	22 Long Rifle	40	Solid	1140	1085	1035	995	965	115	104	95	88	82	0.3	1.2	2.6	4.5	0.2	⊕	−2.2	−6.6
NEW	Match	900	50	22 Long Rifle	40	Solid	1140	1085	1035	995	965	115	104	95	88	82	0.3	1.2	2.6	4.5	0.2	⊕	−2.2	−6.6
NEW	Target	711	50	22 Long Rifle	40	Solid	1150	1090	1045	1005	970	117	106	97	89	83	0.3	1.2	2.6	4.5	0.2	⊕	−2.2	−6.4

These ballistic specifications were derived from test barrels 24 inches in length.

GOLD MEDAL® MATCH RIFLE BALLISTICS (Approximate)

USAGE	FEDERAL LOAD NO.	CALIBER	BULLET WGT. IN GRAINS	BULLET WGT. IN GRAMS	BULLET STYLE*	FACTORY PRIMER NO.	VELOCITY IN FEET PER SECOND (TO NEAREST 10 FEET)										
							MUZZLE	100 YDS.	200 YDS.	300 YDS.	400 YDS.	500 YDS.	600 YDS.	700 YDS.	800 YDS.	900 YDS.	1000 YDS.
⑤NEW	GM223M	223 Rem. (5.56 x 45mm)	69	4.47	Boat-tail HP Match	205M	3000	2720	2460	2210	1980	1760	1560	1390	1240	1130	1060
⑤NEW	GM308M	308 Win. (7.62 x 51mm)	168	10.88	Boat-tail HP Match	210M	2600	2420	2240	2070	1910	1760	1610	1480	1360	1260	1170
⑤NEW	GM3006M	30-06 Springfield (7.62 x 63mm)	168	10.88	Boat-tail HP Match	210M	2700	2510	2330	2150	1990	1830	1680	1540	1410	1300	1210

FEDERAL LOAD NUMBER	ENERGY IN FOOT/POUNDS (TO NEAREST 5 FOOT/POUNDS)											WIND DRIFT IN INCHES 10 MPH CROSSWIND										HEIGHT OF BULLET TRAJECTORY IN INCHES ABOVE OR BELOW LINE OF SIGHT IF ZEROED AT ⊕ YARDS. SIGHTS 1.5 INCHES ABOVE BORE LINE.									
	MUZZLE	100 YDS.	200 YDS.	300 YDS.	400 YDS.	500 YDS.	600 YDS.	700 YDS.	800 YDS.	900 YDS.	1000 YDS.	100 YDS.	200 YDS.	300 YDS.	400 YDS.	500 YDS.	600 YDS.	700 YDS.	800 YDS.	900 YDS.	1000 YDS.	100 YDS.	200 YDS.	300 YDS.	400 YDS.	500 YDS.	600 YDS.	700 YDS.	800 YDS.	900 YDS.	1000 YDS.
GM223M	1380	1135	925	750	600	475	375	295	235	195	170	0.9	3.7	8.7	16.3	27.0	41.3	59.5	82.2	109.2	140.0	+1.6	⊕	−7.4	−21.9	−45.3	−79.8	−128.7	−194.1	−280.2	−388.7
GM308M	2520	2180	1870	1600	1355	1150	970	815	690	590	510	0.8	3.1	7.4	13.6	22.2	33.3	47.1	64.1	84.2	107.5	+17.5	+30.5	+36.6	+34.5	+22.9	⊕	−36.1	−87.8	−157.5	−247.4
GM3006M	2720	2350	2025	1730	1470	1245	1050	880	740	630	540	0.7	3.0	7.0	13.0	21.2	31.8	45.1	61.5	81.0	103.6	+16.1	+28.1	+33.8	+31.9	+21.1	⊕	−33.4	−81.3	−146.0	−230.1

*HP = Hollow Point

NYCLAD® PISTOL AND REVOLVER BALLISTICS (Approximate)

USAGE	FEDERAL LOAD NO.	CALIBER	BULLET WGT. IN GRAINS	BULLET WGT. IN GRAMS	BULLET STYLE*	FACTORY PRIMER NO.	VELOCITY IN FEET PER SECOND					ENERGY IN FOOT/POUNDS					MID-RANGE TRAJECTORY				TEST BARREL LENGTH INCHES
							MUZZLE	25 YDS.	50 YDS.	75 YDS.	100 YDS.	MUZZLE	25 YDS.	50 YDS.	75 YDS.	100 YDS.	25 YDS.	50 YDS.	75 YDS.	100 YDS.	
③	P9BP	9mm Luger (9x19mm Parabellum)	124	8.03	Nyclad Hollow Point	100	1120	1070	1030	990	960	345	315	290	270	255	0.2	0.9	2.2	4.1	4
④	P38B	38 Special	158	10.23	Nyclad Round Nose	100	755	740	723	710	690	200	190	183	175	170	0.5	2.0	4.6	8.3	4-V
①, ③	P38G	38 Special (High Velocity +P)	158	10.23	Nyclad SWC-HP	100	890	870	855	840	820	270	265	257	245	235	0.3	1.4	3.3	5.9	4-V
③	P38M	38 Special	125	8.10	Nyclad Hollow Point	100	825	780	730	690	650	190	170	150	130	115	0.4	1.8	4.3	8.1	2-V
①, ③	P38N	38 Special (High Velocity +P)	125	8.10	Nyclad Hollow Point	100	945	920	898	880	860	248	235	224	215	205	0.3	1.3	2.9	5.4	4-V
②, ③	P357E	357 Magnum	158	10.23	Nyclad SWC-HP	100	1235	1160	1104	1060	1020	535	475	428	395	365	0.2	0.8	1.9	3.5	4-V

Usage Key: ①=Varmints, predators, small game ②=Medium game ③=Self defense ④=Target shooting, training, practice

HYDRA-SHOK® PISTOL AND REVOLVER BALLISTICS (Approximate)

USAGE	FEDERAL LOAD NO.	CALIBER	BULLET WGT. IN GRAINS	BULLET WGT. IN GRAMS	BULLET STYLE*	FACTORY PRIMER NO.	VELOCITY IN FEET PER SECOND					ENERGY IN FOOT/POUNDS					MID-RANGE TRAJECTORY				TEST BARREL LENGTH INCHES
							MUZZLE	25 YDS.	50 YDS.	75 YDS.	100 YDS.	MUZZLE	25 YDS.	50 YDS.	75 YDS.	100 YDS.	25 YDS.	50 YDS.	75 YDS.	100 YDS.	
③	P380HS1	380 Auto (9x17mm Short)	90	5.83	Hydra-Shok HP	100	1000	940	890	840	800	200	175	160	140	130	0.3	1.2	2.9	5.5	3¾
③	P9HS1	9mm Luger (9x19mm Parabellum)	124	8.03	Hydra-Shok HP	100	1120	1070	1030	990	960	345	315	290	270	255	0.2	0.9	2.2	4.1	4
③	P9HS2	9mm Luger (9x19mm Parabellum)	147	9.52	Hydra-Shok HP	100	1000	960	920	890	860	325	300	275	260	240	0.3	1.2	2.8	5.1	4
③	P40HS1	40 S&W	180	11.06	Hydra-Shok HP	100	985	955	930	910	890	390	365	345	330	315	0.3	1.2	2.8	5.0	4
③ NEW	P40HS2	40 S&W	155	10.04	Hydra-Shok HP	100	1140	1080	1030	990	950	445	400	365	335	315	0.2	0.9	2.2	4.1	4
③	P10HS1	10mm Auto	180	11.06	Hydra-Shok HP	150	1030	995	970	945	920	425	400	375	355	340	0.3	1.1	2.5	4.7	5
③	P45HS1	45 Auto	230	14.90	Hydra-Shok HP	150	850	830	810	790	770	370	350	335	320	305	0.4	1.6	3.6	6.6	5
③	P38HS1	38 Special (High Velocity +P)	129	8.36	Hydra-Shok HP	100	945	930	910	890	870	255	245	235	225	215	0.3	1.3	2.9	5.3	4-V
③	P357HS1	357 Magnum	158	10.23	Hydra-Shok HP	100	1235	1160	1104	1060	1020	535	475	428	395	365	0.2	0.8	1.9	3.5	4-V
③	P44HS1	44 Rem. Magnum	240	15.55	Hydra-Shok HP	150	1180	1130	1081	1050	1010	741	675	623	580	550	0.2	0.9	2.0	3.7	6½-V

+P ammunition is loaded to a higher pressure. Use only in firearms so recommended by the gun manufacturer. "V" indicates vented barrel to simulate service conditions.
*HP = Hollow Point SWC = Semi-Wadcutter

REMINGTON BALLISTICS
CENTERFIRE RIFLE

CALIBER	REMINGTON Order No.	Wt.-Grs.	BULLET Style	Primer No.	Muzzle	VELOCITY – Feet Per Second 100 Yds.	200 Yds.	300 Yds.	400 Yds.	500 Yds.	ENERGY – Foot-Pounds Muzzle	100 Yds.
17 REM.	R17REM	25	Hollow Point Power-Lokt®	71/2	4040	3284	2644	2086	1606	1235	906	599
22 HORNET	R22HN1	45	Pointed Soft Point	61/2	2690	2042	1502	1128	948	840	723	417
	R22HN2	45	Hollow Point	61/2	2690	2042	1502	1128	948	840	723	417
220 SWIFT	R220S1	50	Pointed Soft Point	91/2	3780	3158	2617	2135	1710	1357	1586	1107
222 REM.	R222R1	50	Pointed Soft Point	71/2	3140	2602	2123	1700	1350	1107	1094	752
	R222R3	50	Hollow Point Power-Lokt®	71/2	3140	2635	2182	1777	1432	1172	1094	771
222 REM. MAG.	R222M1	55	Pointed Soft Point	71/2	3240	2748	2305	1906	1556	1272	1282	922
223 REM.	R223R1	55	Pointed Soft Point	71/2	3240	2747	2304	1905	1554	1270	1282	921
	R223R2	55	Hollow Point Power-Lokt®	71/2	3240	2773	2352	1969	1627	1341	1282	939
	R223R3	55	Metal Case	71/2	3240	2759	2326	1933	1587	1301	1282	929
	R223R4	60	Hollow Point Match	71/2	3100	2712	2355	2026	1726	1463	1280	979
22-250 REM.	R22501	55	Pointed Soft Point	91/2	3680	3137	2656	2222	1832	1493	1654	1201
	R22502	55	Hollow Point Power-Lokt®	91/2	3680	3209	2785	2400	2046	1725	1654	1257
243 WIN.	R243W1	80	Pointed Soft Point	91/2	3350	2955	2593	2259	1951	1670	1993	1551
	R243W2	80	Hollow Point Power-Lokt®	91/2	3350	2955	2593	2259	1951	1670	1993	1551
	R243W3	100	Pointed Soft Point Core-Lokt®	91/2	2960	2697	2449	2215	1993	1786	1945	1615
	ER243WA	105	Extended Range	91/2	2920	2689	2470	2261	2062	1874	1988	1686
6MM REM.	R6MM1	80	Pointed Soft Point	91/2	3470	3064	2694	2352	2036	1747	2139	1667
	R6MM4	100	Pointed Soft Point Core-Lokt®	91/2	3100	2829	2573	2332	2104	1889	2133	1777
	ER6MMRA	105	Extended Range	91/2	3060	2822	2596	2381	2177	1982	2183	1856
6MM BR REM.	R6MMBR	100	Pointed Soft Point	71/2	2550	2310	2083	1870	1671	1491	1444	1185
25-20 WIN.	R25202	86	Soft Point	61/2	1460	1194	1030	931	858	797	407	272
250 SAV.	R250SV	100	Pointed Soft Point	91/2	2820	2504	2210	1936	1684	1461	1765	1392
257 ROBERTS	R257	117	Soft Point Core-Lokt®	91/2	2650	2291	1961	1663	1404	1199	1824	1363
	ER257A	122	Extended Range	91/2	2600	2331	2078	1842	1625	1431	1831	1472
25-06 REM.	R25062	100	Pointed Soft Point Core-Lokt®	91/2	3230	2893	2580	2287	2014	1762	2316	1858
	R25063	120	Pointed Soft Point Core-Lokt®	91/2	2990	2730	2484	2252	2032	1825	2382	1985
	ER2506A	122	Extended Range	91/2	2930	2706	2492	2289	2095	1911	2325	1983
264 WIN. MAG.	R264W2	140	Pointed Soft Point Core-Lokt®	91/2M	3030	2782	2548	2326	2114	1914	2854	2406
270 WIN.	R270W1	100	Pointed Soft Point	91/2	3320	2924	2561	2225	1916	1636	2448	1898
	R270W2	130	Pointed Soft Point Core-Lokt®	91/2	3060	2776	2510	2259	2022	1801	2702	2225
	R270W3	130	Bronze Point	91/2	3060	2802	2559	2329	2110	1904	2702	2267
	R270W4	150	Soft Point Core-Lokt®	91/2	2850	2504	2183	1886	1618	1385	2705	2087
	ER270WB	135	ExtendedRange	9 1/2	3000	2780	2570	2369	2178	1995	2697	2315
	ER270WA	140	Extended Range Boat Tail	91/2	2960	2749	2548	2355	2171	1995	2723	2349
7MM BR REM.	R7MMBR	140	Pointed Soft Point	71/2	2215	2012	1821	1643	1481	1336	1525	1259
7MM MAUSER (7x57)	R7MSR1	140	Pointed Soft Point	91/2	2660	2435	2221	2018	1827	1648	2199	1843
7MM-08 REM.	R7M081	140	Pointed Soft Point	91/2	2860	2625	2402	2189	1988	1798	2542	2142
	R7M083	120	Hollow Point	91/2	3000	2725	2467	2223	1992	1778	2398	1979
	ER7M08A	154	Extended Range	91/2	2715	2510	2315	2128	1950	1781	2520	2155
280 REM.	R280R3	140	Pointed Soft Point	91/2	3000	2758	2528	2309	2102	1905	2797	2363
	R280R1	150	Pointed Soft Point Core-Lokt®	91/2	2890	2624	2373	2135	1912	1705	2781	2293
	R280R2	165	Soft Point Core-Lokt®	91/2	2820	2510	2220	1950	1701	1479	2913	2308
	R280R4§	120	Hollow Point	91/2	3150	2866	2599	2348	2110	1887	2643	2188
	ER280RA	165	Extended Range	91/2	2820	2623	2434	2253	2080	1915	2913	2520
7MM REM. MAG.	R7MM2	150	Pointed Soft Point Core-Lokt®	91/2M	3110	2830	2568	2320	2085	1866	3221	2667
	R7MM3	175	Pointed Soft Point Core-Lokt®	91/2M	2860	2645	2440	2244	2057	1879	3178	2718
	R7MM4	140	Pointed Soft Point	91/2M	3175	2923	2684	2458	2243	2039	3133	2655
	ER7MMA	165	Extended Range	91/2M	2900	2699	2507	2324	2147	1979	3081	2669
7MM WBY MAG.	R7MWB1	140	Pointed Soft Point	91/2M	3225	2970	2729	2501	2283	2077	3233	2741
	R7MWB2	175	Pointed Soft Point Core-Lokt®	91/2M	2910	2693	2486	2288	2098	1918	3293	2818
	ER7MWB4	165	Extended Range	91/2M	2950	2747	2553	2367	2189	2019	3188	2765
30 CARBINE	R30CAR	110	Soft Point	61/2	1990	1567	1236	1035	923	842	967	600
30 REM.	R30REM	170	Soft Point Core-Lokt®	91/2	2120	1822	1555	1328	1153	1036	1696	1253
30-30 WIN. ACCELERATOR®	R3030A	55	Soft Point	91/2	3400	2693	2085	1570	1187	986	1412	886
30-30 WIN.	R30301	150	Soft Point Core-Lokt®	91/2	2390	1973	1605	1303	1095	974	1902	1296
	R30302	170	Soft Point Core-Lokt®	91/2	2200	1895	1619	1381	1191	1061	1827	1355
	R30303	170	Hollow Point Core-Lokt®	91/2	2200	1895	1619	1381	1191	1061	1827	1355
	ER3030A	160	Extended Range	9 1/2	2300	1997	1719	1473	1268	1116	1879	1416
300 SAVAGE	R30SV3	180	Soft Point Core-Lokt®	91/2	2350	2025	1728	1467	1252	1098	2207	1639
	R30SV2	150	Pointed Soft Point Core-Lokt	91/2	2630	2354	2095	1853	1631	1432	2303	1845

Specifications are nominal. Ballistics figures established in test barrels. Individual rifles may vary from test-barrel specifications. *Illustrated (not shown actual size). ** Inches above or below line of sight. Hold low for positive numbers, high for negative numbers. †280 Rem. and 7mm Express™ Rem. are interchangeable. ‡Interchangeable in 244 Rem. §Subject to Stock on hand. [1]Bullet does not rise more than one inch above line of sight from muzzle to sighting on range. [2]Bullet does not rise more than three inches above line of sight from muzzle to sighting in range. NOTE: 0.0 indicates yardage at which rifle was sighted in.

REMINGTON BALLISTICS
CENTERFIRE RIFLE

ENERGY – Foot-Pounds				SHORT RANGE TRAJECTORY[1]						LONG RANGE TRAJECTORY[2]							
200 Yds.	300 Yds.	400 Yds.	500 Yds.	50 Yds.	100 Yds.	150 Yds.	200 Yds.	250 Yds.	300 Yds.	100 Yds.	150 Yds.	200 Yds.	250 Yds.	300 Yds.	400 Yds.	500 Yds	Barrel Length
388	242	143	85	0.1	0.5	0.0	-1.5	-4.2	-8.5	2.1	2.5	1.9	0.0	-3.4	-17.0	-44.3	24"
225	127	90	70	0.3	0.0	-2.4	-7.7	-16.9	-31.3	1.6	0.0	-4.5	-12.8	-26.4	-75.6	-163.4	24"
225	127	90	70	0.3	0.0	-2.4	-7.7	-16.9	-31.3	1.6	0.0	-4.5	-12.8	-26.4	-75.6	-163.4	
760	506	325	204	0.2	0.5	0.0	-1.6	-4.4	-8.8	1.3	1.2	0.0	-2.5	-6.5	-20.7	-47.0	24"
500	321	202	136	0.5	0.9	0.0	-2.5	-6.9	-13.7	2.2	1.9	0.0	-3.8	-10.0	-32.3	-73.8	24"
529	351	228	152	0.5	0.9	0.0	-2.4	-6.6	-13.1	2.1	1.8	0.0	-3.6	-9.5	-30.2	-68.1	
649	444	296	198	0.4	0.8	0.0	-2.2	-6.0	-11.8	1.9	1.6	0.0	-3.3	-8.5	-26.7	-59.5	24"
648	443	295	197	0.4	0.8	0.0	-2.2	-6.0	-11.8	1.9	1.6	0.0	-3.3	-8.5	-26.7	-59.6	
675	473	323	220	0.4	0.8	0.0	-2.1	-5.8	-11.4	1.8	1.6	0.0	-3.2	-8.2	-25.5	-56.0	24"
660	456	307	207	0.4	0.8	0.0	-2.1	-5.9	-11.6	1.9	1.6	0.0	-3.2	-8.4	-26.2	-57.9	
739	547	397	285	0.5	0.8	0.0	-2.2	-6.0	-11.5	1.9	1.6	0.0	-3.2	-8.3	-25.1	-53.6	
861	603	410	272	0.2	0.5	0.0	-1.6	-4.4	-8.7	2.3	2.6	1.9	0.0	-3.4	-15.9	-38.9	24"
947	703	511	363	0.2	0.5	0.0	-1.5	-4.1	-8.0	2.1	2.5	1.8	0.0	-3.1	-14.1	-33.4	
1194	906	676	495	0.3	0.7	0.0	-1.8	-4.9	-9.4	2.6	2.9	2.1	0.0	-3.6	-16.2	-37.9	
1194	906	676	495	0.3	0.7	0.0	-1.8	-4.9	-9.4	2.6	2.9	2.1	0.0	-3.6	-16.2	-37.9	24"
1332	1089	882	708	0.5	0.9	0.0	-2.2	-5.8	-11.0	1.9	1.6	0.0	-3.1	-7.8	-22.6	-46.3	
1422	1192	992	819	0.5	0.9	0.0	-2.2	-5.8	-11.0	2.0	1.6	0.0	-3.1	-7.7	-22.2	-44.8	
1289	982	736	542	0.3	0.6	0.0	-1.6	-4.5	-8.7	2.4	2.7	1.9	0.0	-3.3	-14.9	-35.0	
1470	1207	983	792	0.4	0.8	0.0	-1.9	-5.2	-9.9	1.7	1.5	0.0	-2.8	-7.0	-20.4	-41.7	
1571	1322	1105	916	0.4	0.8	0.0	-2.0	-5.2	-9.8	1.7	1.5	0.0	-2.7	-6.9	-20.0	-40.4	
963	776	620	494	0.3	0.0	-1.9	-5.6	-11.4	-19.3	2.8	2.3	0.0	-4.3	-10.9	-31.7	-65.1	15"
203	165	141	121	0.0	-4.1	-14.4	-31.8	-57.3	-92.0	0.0	-8.2	-23.5	-47.0	-79.6	-175.9	-319.4	24"
1084	832	630	474	0.2	0.0	-1.6	-4.7	-9.6	-16.5	2.3	2.0	0.0	-3.7	-9.5	-28.3	-59.5	24"
999	718	512	373	0.3	0.0	-1.9	-5.8	-11.9	-20.7	2.9	2.4	0.0	-4.7	-12.0	-36.7	-79.2	24"
1170	919	715	555	0.3	0.0	-1.9	-5.5	-11.2	-19.1	2.8	2.3	0.0	-4.3	-10.9	-32.0	-66.4	
1478	1161	901	689	0.4	0.7	0.0	-1.9	-5.0	-9.7	1.6	1.4	0.0	-2.7	-6.9	-20.5	-42.7	
1644	1351	1100	887	0.5	0.8	0.0	-2.1	-5.6	-10.7	1.9	1.6	0.0	-3.0	-7.5	-22.0	-44.8	24"
1683	1419	1189	989	0.5	0.9	0.0	-2.2	-5.7	-10.8	1.9	1.6	0.0	-3.0	-7.5	-21.7	-43.9	
2018	1682	1389	1139	0.5	0.8	0.0	-2.0	-5.4	-10.2	1.8	1.5	0.0	-2.9	-7.2	-20.8	-42.2	24"
1456	1099	815	594	0.3	0.7	0.0	-1.8	-5.0	-9.7	2.7	3.0	2.2	0.0	-3.7	-16.6	-39.1	
1818	1472	1180	936	0.5	0.8	0.0	-2.0	-5.5	-10.4	1.8	1.5	0.0	-2.9	-7.4	-21.6	-44.3	
1890	1565	1285	1046	0.4	0.8	0.0	-2.0	-5.3	-10.1	1.8	1.5	0.0	-2.8	-7.1	-20.6	-42.0	24"
1587	1185	872	639	0.7	1.0	0.0	-2.6	-7.1	-13.6	2.3	2.0	0.0	-3.8	-9.7	-29.2	-62.2	
1979	1682	1421	1193	0.5	0.8	0.0	-2.0	-5.3	-10.1	1.8	1.5	0.0	-2.8	-7.1	-20.4	-41.0	
2018	1724	1465	1237	0.5	0.8	0.0	-2.1	-5.5	-10.3	1.9	1.5	0.0	-2.9	-7.2	-20.7	-41.6	
1031	839	681	555	0.5	0.0	-2.7	-7.7	-15.4	-25.9	1.8	0.0	-4.1	-10.9	-20.6	-50.0	-95.2	15"
1533	1266	1037	844	0.2	0.0	-1.7	-5.0	-10.0	-17.0	2.5	2.0	0.0	-3.8	-9.6	-27.7	-56.3	24"
1793	1490	1228	1005	0.6	0.9	0.0	-2.3	-6.1	-11.6	2.1	1.7	0.0	-3.2	-8.1	-23.5	-47.7	
1621	1316	1058	842	0.5	0.8	0.0	-2.1	-5.7	-10.8	1.9	1.6	0.0	-3.0	-7.6	-22.3	-45.8	24"
1832	1548	1300	1085	0.7	1.0	0.0	-2.5	-6.7	-12.6	2.3	1.9	0.0	-3.5	-8.8	-25.3	-51.0	
1986	1657	1373	1128	0.5	0.8	0.0	-2.1	-5.5	-10.4	1.8	1.5	0.0	-2.9	-7.3	-21.1	-42.9	
1875	1518	1217	968	0.6	0.9	0.0	-2.3	-6.2	-11.8	2.1	1.7	0.0	-3.3	-8.3	-24.2	-49.7	
1805	1393	1060	801	0.2	0.0	-1.5	-4.6	-9.5	-16.4	2.3	1.9	0.0	-3.7	-9.4	-28.1	-58.8	24"
1800	1468	1186	949	0.4	0.7	0.0	-1.9	-5.1	-9.7	2.8	3.0	2.2	0.0	-3.6	-15.7	-35.6	
2171	1860	1585	1343	0.6	0.9	0.0	-2.3	-6.1	-11.4	2.1	1.7	0.0	-3.2	-8.0	-22.8	-45.6	
2196	1792	1448	1160	0.4	0.8	0.0	-1.9	-5.2	-9.9	1.7	1.5	0.0	-2.8	-7.0	-20.5	-42.1	
2313	1956	1644	1372	0.6	0.9	0.0	-2.3	-6.0	-11.3	2.0	1.7	0.0	-3.2	-7.9	-22.7	-45.8	24"
2240	1878	1564	1292	0.4	0.7	0.0	-1.8	-4.8	-9.1	2.6	2.9	2.0	0.0	-3.4	-14.5	-32.6	
2303	1978	1689	1434	0.5	0.9	0.0	-2.1	-5.7	-10.7	1.9	1.6	0.0	-3.0	-7.5	-21.4	-42.9	
2315	1943	1621	1341	0.3	0.7	0.0	-1.7	-4.6	-8.8	2.5	2.8	2.0	0.0	-3.2	-14.0	-31.5	
2401	2033	1711	1430	0.5	0.9	0.0	-2.2	-5.7	-10.8	1.9	1.6	0.0	-3.0	-7.6	-21.8	-44.0	24"
2388	2053	1756	1493	0.5	0.8	0.0	-2.1	-5.5	-10.3	1.9	1.6	0.0	-2.9	-7.2	-20.6	-41.3	
373	262	208	173	0.9	0.0	-4.5	-13.5	-28.3	-49.9	0.0	-4.5	-13.5	-28.3	-49.9	-118.6	-228.2	20"
913	666	502	405	0.7	0.0	-3.3	-9.7	-19.6	-33.8	2.2	0.0	-5.3	-14.1	-27.2	-69.0	-136.9	24"
521	301	172	119	0.4	0.8	0.0	-2.4	-6.7	-13.8	2.0	1.8	0.0	-3.8	-10.2	-35.0	-84.4	24"
858	565	399	316	0.5	0.0	-2.7	-8.2	-17.0	-30.0	1.8	0.0	-4.6	-12.5	-24.6	-65.3	-134.9	
989	720	535	425	0.6	0.0	-3.0	-8.9	-18.0	-31.1	2.0	0.0	-4.8	-13.0	-25.1	-63.6	-126.7	
989	720	535	425	0.6	0.0	-3.0	-8.9	-18.0	-31.1	2.0	0.0	-4.8	-13.0	-25.1	-63.6	-126.7	
1050	771	571	442	0.5	0.0	-2.7	-7.9	-16.1	-27.6	1.8	0.0	-4.3	-11.6	-22.3	-56.3	-111.9	
1193	860	626	482	0.5	0.0	-2.6	-7.7	-15.6	-27.1	1.7	0.0	-4.2	-11.3	-21.9	-55.8	-112.0	24"
1462	1143	806	685	0.3	0.0	-1.8	-5.4	11.0	18.8	2.7	2.2	0.0	-4.2	-10.7	-31.5	-65.6	

REMINGTON BALLISTICS
CENTERFIRE RIFLE

CALIBER	REMINGTON Order No.	Wt.-Grs.	BULLET Style	Primer No.	Muzzle	VELOCITY – Feet Per Second 100 Yds.	200 Yds.	300 Yds.	400 Yds.	500 Yds.	ENERGY – Foot-Pounds Muzzle	100 Yds.
30-40 Krag	R30402	180°	Pointed Soft Point Core-Lokt®	91/2	2430	2213	2007	1813	1632	1468	2360	1957
308 Win. Accelerator®	R308W5	55	Pointed Soft Point	91/2	3770	3215	2726	2286	1888	1541	1735	1262
308 Win.	R308W1	150	Pointed Soft Point Core-Lokt®	91/2	2820	2533	2263	2009	1774	1560	2648	2137
	R308W2	180	Soft Point Core-Lokt®	91/2	2620	2274	1955	1666	1414	1212	2743	2066
	R308W3	180	Pointed Soft Point Core-Lokt®	91/2	2620	2393	2178	1974	1782	1604	2743	2288
	R308W7	168	Boat Tail H.P. Match	91/2	2680	2493	2314	2143	1979	1823	2678	2318
	ER308WA	165	Extended Range Boat Tail	91/2	2700	2497	2303	2117	1941	1773	2670	2284
	ER308WB	178	Extended Range	91/2	2620	2415	2220	2034	1857	1691	2713	2306
30-06 Accelerator®	R30069	55	Pointed Soft Point	91/2	4080	3485	2965	2502	2083	1709	2033	1483
30-06 Springfield	R30061	125	Pointed Soft Point	91/2	3140	2780	2447	2138	1853	1595	2736	2145
	R30062	150	Pointed Soft Point Core-Lokt®	91/2	2910	2617	2342	2083	1843	1622	2820	2281
	R30063	150	Bronze Point	91/2	2910	2656	2416	2189	1974	1773	2820	2349
	R3006B	165	Pointed Soft Point Core-Lokt®	91/2	2800	2534	2283	2047	1825	1621	2872	2352
	R30064	180	Soft Point Core-Lokt®	91/2	2700	2348	2023	1727	1466	1251	2913	2203
	R30065	180	Pointed Soft Point Core-Lokt®	91/2	2700	2469	2250	2042	1846	1663	2913	2436
	R30066	180	Bronze Point	91/2	2700	2485	2280	2084	1899	1725	2913	2468
	R30067	220	Soft Point Core-Lokt®	91/2	2410	2130	1870	1632	1422	1246	2837	2216
	R3006C	168	Boat Tail H.P. Match	91/2	2710	2522	2346	2169	2003	1845	2739	2372
	ER3006A	152	Extended Range	91/2	2910	2654	2413	2184	1968	1765	2858	2378
	ER3006B	165	Extended Range Boat Tail	91/2	2800	2592	2394	2204	2023	1852	2872	2462
	ER3006C	178	Extended Range	91/2	2720	2511	2311	2121	1939	1768	2924	2491
300 H&H Mag.	R300HH	180	Pointed Soft Point Core-Lokt®	91/2M	2880	2640	2412	2196	1990	1798	3315	2785
300 Win. Mag.	R300W1	150	Pointed Soft Point Core-Lokt®	91/2M	3290	2951	2636	2342	2068	1813	3605	2900
	R300W2	180	Pointed Soft Point Core-Lokt®	91/2M	2960	2745	2540	2344	2157	1979	3501	3011
	RS300WA	200	Swift A-Frame™ PSP	9 1/2 M	2825	2595	2376	2167	1970	1783	3544	2989
	ER300WA	178	Extended Range	91/2M	2980	2769	2568	2375	2191	2015	3509	3030
	ER300WB	190	Extended Range Boat Tail	91/2M	2885	2691	2506	2327	2156	1993	3511	3055
300 Wby Mag.	R300WB1	180	Pointed Soft Point Core-Lokt®	91/2M	3120	2866	2627	2400	2184	1979	3890	3284
	R300WB2	220	Soft Point Core-Lokt®	91/2M	2850	2541	2283	1984	1736	1512	3967	3155
	ER30WBA	178	Extended Range	91/2M	3120	2902	2695	2497	2308	2126	3847	3329
	ER30WBB	190	Extended Range Boat Tail	91/2M	3030	2830	2638	2455	2279	2110	3873	3378
303 British	R303B1	180	Soft Point Core-Lokt®	91/2	2460	2124	1817	1542	1311	1137	2418	1803
7.62x39MM	R762391	125	Pointed Soft Point	71/2	2365	2062	1783	1533	1320	1154	1552	1180
32-20 Win.	R32201	100	Lead	61/2	1210	1021	913	834	769	712	325	231
	R32202	100	Soft Point	61/2	1210	1021	913	834	769	712	325	231
32 Win. Special	R32WS2	170	Soft Point Core-Lokt®	91/2	2250	1921	1626	1372	1175	1044	1911	1393
8MM Mauser	R8MSR	170	Soft Point Core-Lokt®	91/2	2360	1969	1622	1333	1123	997	2102	1463
8MM Rem. Mag.	R8MM1	185	Pointed Soft Point Core-Lokt®	91/2M	3080	2761	2464	2186	1927	1688	3896	3131
338 Win. Mag.	R338W1	225	Pointed Soft Point	91/2M	2780	2572	2374	2184	2003	1832	3860	3305
	R338W2	250	Pointed Soft Point	91/2M	2660	2456	2261	2075	1898	1731	3927	3348
	RS338WA	225	Swift A-Frame PSP	91/2M	2785	2517	2266	2029	1808	1605	3871	3165
35 Rem.	R35R1	150	Pointed Soft Point Core-Lokt®	91/2	2300	1874	1506	1218	1039	934	1762	1169
	R35R2	200	Soft Point Core-Lokt®	91/2	2080	1698	1376	1140	1001	911	1921	1280
350 Rem. Mag.	R350M1	200	Pointed Soft Point Core-Lokt®	91/2M	2710	2410	2130	1870	1631	1421	3261	2579
35 Whelen	R35WH1	200	Pointed Soft Point	91/2M	2675	2378	2100	1842	1606	1399	3177	2510
	R35WH2	250	Soft Point	91/2M	2400	2066	1761	1492	1269	1107	3197	2369
	R35WH3	250	Pointed Soft Point	91/2M	2400	2197	2005	1823	1652	1496	3197	2680
375 H&H Mag.	R375M1	270	Soft Point	91/2M	2690	2420	2166	1928	1707	1507	4337	3510
	RS375MA	300	Swift A-Frame PSP	91/2M	2530	2245	1979	1733	1512	1321	4262	3357
416 Rem. Mag.	R416R1	400	Solid	91/2M	2400	2042	1718	1436	1212	1062	5115	3702
	R416R2	400	Swift A-Frame PSP	91/2M	2400	2175	1962	1763	1579	1414	5115	4201
	R416R3	350	Swift A-Frame PSP	91/2M	2520	2270	2034	1814	1611	1429	4935	4004
44-40 Win.	R4440W	200	Soft Point	21/2	1190	1006	900	822	756	699	629	449
44 Rem. Mag.	R44MG2	240	Soft Point	21/2	1760	1380	1114	970	878	806	1650	1015
	R44MG3	240	Semi-Jacketed Hollow Point	21/2	1760	1380	1114	970	878	806	1650	1015
	R44MG6	210	Semi-Jacketed Hollow Point	21/2	1920	1477	1155	982	880	802	1719	1017
444 Mar.	R444M	240	Soft Point	91/2	2350	1815	1377	1087	941	846	2942	1755
45-70 Government	R4570G	405	Soft Point	91/2	1330	1168	1055	977	918	869	1590	1227
	R4570L	300	Jacketed Hollow Point	91/2	1810	1497	1244	1073	969	895	2182	1492
458 Win. Mag.	R458W1	500	Metal Case	91/2M	2040	1823	1623	1442	1237	1161	4620	3689
	R458W2	510	Soft Point	91/2M	2040	1770	1527	1319	1157	1046	4712	3547

Specifications are nominal. Ballistics figures established in test barrels. Individual rifles may vary from test-barrel specifications. *Illustrated (not shown actual size). ** Inches above or below line of sight. Hold low for positive numbers, high for negative numbers. †280 Rem. and 7mm Express™ Rem. are interchangeable. ‡Interchangeable in 244 Rem. §Subject to Stock on hand. [1]Bullet does not rise more than one inch above line of sight from muzzle to sighting on range. [2]Bullet does not rise more than three inches above line of sight from muzzle to sighting in range. NOTE: 0.0 indicates yardage at which rifle was sighted in.

REMINGTON BALLISTICS
CENTERFIRE RIFLE

ENERGY – Foot-Pounds				SHORT RANGE TRAJECTORY[1]						LONG RANGE TRAJECTORY[2]							
200 Yds.	300 Yds.	400 Yds.	500 Yds.	50 Yds.	100 Yds.	150 Yds.	200 Yds.	250 Yds.	300 Yds.	100 Yds.	150 Yds.	200 Yds.	250 Yds.	300 Yds.	400 Yds.	500 Yds	Barrel Length
1610	1314	1064	861	0.4	0.0	-2.1	-6.2	-12.5	-21.1	1.4	0.0	-3.4	-8.9	-16.8	-40.9	-78.1	24"
907	638	435	290	0.2	0.5	0.0	-1.5	-4.2	-8.2	2.2	2.5	1.8	0.0	-3.2	-15.0	-36.7	24"
1705	1344	1048	810	0.2	0.0	-1.5	-4.5	-9.3	-15.9	2.3	1.9	0.0	-3.6	-9.1	-26.9	-55.7	
1527	1109	799	587	0.3	0.0	-2.0	-5.9	-12.1	-20.9	2.9	2.4	0.0	-4.7	-12.1	-36.9	-79.1	
1896	1557	1269	1028	0.2	0.0	-1.8	-5.2	-10.4	-17.7	2.6	2.1	0.0	-4.0	-9.9	-28.9	-58.8	24"
1998	1713	1460	1239	0.2	0.0	-1.6	-4.7	-9.4	-15.9	2.4	1.9	0.0	-3.5	-8.9	-25.3	-50.6	
1942	1642	1379	1152	0.2	0.0	-1.6	-4.7	-9.4	-16.0	2.3	1.9	0.0	-3.5	-8.9	-25.6	-51.5	
1948	1635	1363	1130	0.2	0.0	-1.7	-5.1	-10.2	-17.2	2.5	2.1	0.0	-3.8	-9.6	-27.6	-55.8	
1074	764	530	356	0.4	1.0	0.9	0.0	-1.9	-5.0	1.8	2.1	1.5	0.0	-2.7	-12.5	-30.5	24"
1662	1269	953	706	0.4	0.8	0.0	-2.1	-5.6	-10.7	1.8	1.5	0.0	-3.0	-7.7	-23.0	-48.5	
1827	1445	1131	876	0.6	0.9	0.0	-2.3	-6.3	-12.0	2.1	1.8	0.0	-3.3	-8.5	-25.0	-51.8	
1944	1596	1298	1047	0.6	0.9	0.0	-2.2	-6.0	-11.4	2.0	1.7	0.0	-3.2	-8.0	-23.3	-47.5	
1909	1534	1220	963	0.7	1.0	0.0	-2.5	-6.7	-12.7	2.3	1.9	0.0	-3.6	-9.0	-26.3	-54.1	
1635	1192	859	625	0.2	0.0	-1.8	-5.5	-11.2	-19.5	2.7	2.3	0.0	-4.4	-11.3	-34.4	-73.7	
2023	1666	1362	1105	0.2	0.0	-1.6	-4.8	-9.7	-16.5	2.4	2.0	0.0	-3.7	-9.3	-27.0	-54.9	24"
2077	1736	1441	1189	0.2	0.0	-1.6	-4.7	-9.6	-16.2	2.4	2.0	0.0	-3.6	-9.1	-26.2	-53.0	
1708	1301	988	758	0.4	0.0	-2.3	-6.8	-13.8	-23.6	1.5	0.0	-3.7	-9.9	-19.0	-47.4	-93.1	
2045	1754	1497	1270	0.7	1.0	-0.0	-2.5	-6.6	-12.4	2.3	1.9	-0.0	-3.5	-8.6	-24.7	-49.4	
1965	1610	1307	1052	0.6	0.9	0.0	-2.3	-6.0	-11.4	2.0	1.7	0.0	-3.2	-8.0	-23.3	-47.7	
2100	1780	1500	1256	0.6	1.0	0.0	-2.4	-6.2	-11.8	2.1	1.8	0.0	-3.3	-8.2	-23.6	-47.5	
2111	1777	1486	1235	0.7	1.0	0.0	-2.6	-6.7	-12.7	2.3	1.9	0.0	-3.5	-8.8	-25.4	-51.2	
2325	1927	1583	1292	0.6	0.9	0.0	-2.3	-6.0	-11.5	2.1	1.7	0.0	-3.2	-8.0	-23.3	-47.4	24"
2314	1827	1424	1095	0.3	0.7	0.0	-1.8	-4.8	-9.3	2.6	2.9	2.1	0.0	-3.5	-15.4	-35.5	
2578	2196	1859	1565	0.5	0.8	0.0	-2.1	-5.5	-10.4	1.9	1.6	0.0	-2.9	-7.3	-20.9	-41.9	24"
2506	2086	1722	1412	0.6	1.0	0.0	-2.4	-6.3	-11.9	2.1	1.8	0.0	-3.3	-8.3	-24.0	-48.8	
2606	2230	1897	1605	0.5	0.8	0.0	-2.0	-5.4	-10.2	1.8	1.5	0.0	-2.9	-7.1	-20.4	-40.9	
2648	2285	1961	1675	0.5	0.9	0.0	-2.2	-5.7	-10.7	1.9	1.6	0.0	-3.0	-7.5	-21.4	-42.9	
2758	2301	1905	1565	0.4	0.7	0.0	-1.9	-5.0	-9.5	2.7	3.0	2.1	0.0	-3.5	-15.2	-34.2	
2480	1922	1471	1117	0.6	1.0	0.0	-2.5	-6.7	-12.9	2.3	1.9	0.0	-3.6	-9.1	-27.2	-56.8	24"
2870	2464	2104	1787	0.4	0.7	0.0	-1.8	-4.8	-9.1	2.6	2.9	2.0	0.0	-3.3	-14.3	-31.8	
2936	2542	2190	1878	0.4	0.8	0.0	-1.9	-5.1	-9.6	1.7	1.4	0.0	-2.7	-6.7	-19.2	-38.4	
1319	950	687	517	0.4	0.0	-2.3	-6.9	-14.1	-24.4	1.5	0.0	-3.8	-10.2	-19.8	-50.5	-101.5	24"
882	652	483	370	0.4	0.0	-2.5	-7.3	-14.3	-25.7	1.7	0.0	-4.8	-10.8	-20.7	-52.3	-104.0	24"
185	154	131	113	0.0	-6.3	-20.9	-44.9	-79.3	-125.1	0.0	-11.5	-32.3	-63.8	-106.3	-230.1	-413.3	24"
185	154	131	113	0.0	-6.3	-20.9	-44.9	-79.3	-125.1	0.0	-11.5	-32.3	-63.6	-106.3	-230.3	-413.3	
998	710	521	411	0.6	0.0	-2.9	-8.6	-17.6	-30.5	1.9	0.0	-4.7	-12.7	-24.7	-63.2	-126.9	24"
993	671	476	375	0.5	0.0	-2.7	-8.2	-17.0	-29.8	1.8	0.0	-4.5	-12.4	-24.3	-63.8	-130.7	24"
2494	1963	1525	1170	0.5	0.8	0.0	-2.1	-5.6	-10.7	1.8	1.6	0.0	-3.0	-7.6	-22.5	-46.8	24"
2815	2383	2004	1676	0.6	1.0	0.0	-2.4	-6.3	-12.0	2.2	1.8	0.0	-3.3	-8.4	-24.0	-48.4	
2837	2389	1999	1663	0.2	0.0	-1.7	-4.9	-9.8	-16.6	2.4	2.0	0.0	-3.7	-9.3	-26.6	-53.6	24"
2565	2057	1633	1286	0.2	0.0	-1.5	-4.6	-9.4	-16.0	2.3	1.9	0.0	-3.6	-9.1	-26.7	-54.9	
755	494	359	291	0.6	0.0	-3.0	-9.2	-19.1	-33.9	2.0	0.0	-5.1	-14.1	-27.8	-74.0	-152.3	24"
841	577	445	369		0.0	-3.8	-11.3	-23.5	-41.2	2.5	0.0	-6.3	-17.1	-33.6	-87.7	-176.4	
2014	1553	1181	897	0.2	0.0	-1.7	-5.1	-10.4	-17.9	2.6	2.1	0.0	-4.0	-10.3	-30.5	-64.0	20"
1958	1506	1145	869	0.2	0.0	-1.8	-5.3	-10.8	-18.5	2.6	2.2	0.0	-4.2	-10.6	-31.5	-65.9	
1722	1235	893	680	0.4	0.0	-2.5	-7.3	-15.0	-26.0	1.6	0.0	-4.0	-10.9	-21.0	-53.8	-108.2	24"
2230	1844	1515	1242	0.4	0.0	-2.2	-6.6	-12.6	-21.3	1.4	0.0	-3.4	-9.0	-17.0	-41.0	-77.8	
2812	2228	1747	1361	0.2	0.0	-1.7	-5.1	-10.3	-17.6	2.5	2.1	0.0	-3.9	-10.0	-29.4	-60.7	24"
2608	2001	1523	1163	0.3	0.0	-2.0	-6.0	-12.3	-21.0	3.0	2.5	0.0	-4.7		-35.6	-74.5	
2620	1832	1305	1001	0.4	0.0	-2.5	-7.5	-15.5	-27.0	1.7	0.0	-4.2	-11.3	-21.9	-56.7	-115.1	
3419	2760	2214	1775	0.4	0.0	-2.2	-6.5	-13.0	-22.0	1.5	0.0	-3.5	-9.3	-17.6	-42.9	-82.2	24"
3216	2557	2017	1587	0.3	0.0	-2.0	-5.9	-11.9	-20.2	2.9	2.4	0.0	-4.5	-11.4	-33.4	-68.7	
360	300	254	217	0.0	-6.5	-21.6	-46.3	-81.8	-129.1	0.0	-11.8	-33.3	-65.5	-109.5	-237.4	-426.2	24"
661	501	411	346	0.0	-2.7	-10.0	-23.0	-43.0	-71.2	0.0	-5.9	-17.6	-36.3	-63.1	-145.5	-273.0	
661	501	411	346	0.0	-2.7	-10.0	-23.0	-43.0	-71.2	0.0	-5.9	-17.6	-36.3	-63.1	-145.5	-273.0	20"
622	450	361	300	0.0	-2.2	-8.3	-19.7	-37.6	-63.2	0.0	-5.1	-15.4	-32.1	-56.7	-134.0	-256.2	
1010	630	472	381	0.6	0.0	-3.2	-9.9	-21.3	-38.5	2.1	0.0	-5.6	-15.9	-32.1	-87.8	-182.7	24"
1001	858	758	679	0.0	-4.7	-15.8	-34.0	-60.0	-94.5	0.0	-8.7	-24.6	-48.2	-80.3	-172.4	-305.9	24"
1031	767	625	533	0.0	-2.3	-8.5	-19.4	-35.9	-59.0	0.0	-5.0	-14.8	-30.1	-52.1	-119.5		
2924	2308	1839	1469	0.7	0.0	-3.3	-9.6	-19.2	-32.5	2.2	0.0	-5.2	-13.6	-25.8	-63.2	-121.7	24"
2640	1970	1516	1239	0.8	0.0	-3.5	-10.3	-20.8	-35.6	2.4	0.0	-5.6	-14.9	-28.5	-71.5	-140.4	

REMINGTON PISTOL/REVOLVER BALLISTICS

CALIBER	Order No.	Primer No.	Wt. Grs.	BULLET Style	VELOCITY (FPS) Muzzle	50 Yds.	100 Yds.	ENERGY (FT-LB) Muzzle	50 Yds.	100 Yds.	MID-RANGE TRAJECTORY 50 Yds.	100 Yds.	B.L.
(1) 221 REM. FIREBALL	R221F	7¹/₂	50°	Pointed Soft Point	2650	2380	2130	780	630	505	0.2"	0.8"	10"
(2) 25 (6.35MM) AUTO. PISTOL	R25AP	1¹/₂	50°	Metal Case	760	707	659	64	56	48	2.0"	8.7"	2"
(3) 6MM BR REM.	R6MMBR	7¹/₂	100°	Pointed Soft Point	Refer to page 30 for ballistics.								
(4) 7MM BR REM.	R7MMBR	7¹/₂	140°	Pointed Soft Point	Refer to page 30 for ballistics.								
(5) 32 S. & W.	R32SW	1¹/₂	88°	Lead	680	645	610	90	81	73	2.5"	0.5"	3"
(6) 32 S. & W. LONG	R32SWL	1¹/₂	98°	Lead	705	670	635	115	98	88	2.3"	10.5"	4"
(7) 32 (7.65MM) AUTO. PISTOL	R32AP	1¹/₂	71°	Metal Case	905	855	810	129	115	97	1.4"	5.8"	4"
(8) 357 MAG.	R357M7	5¹/₂	110	Semi-Jacketed H.P.	1295	1094	975	410	292	232	0.8"	3.5"	4"
Vented Barrel Ballistics	R357M1	5¹/₂	125	Semi-Jacketed H.P.	1450	1240	1090	583	427	330	0.6"	2.8"	4"
	GS357MA	5¹/₂	125	Brass-Jacketed Hollow Point	1220	1077	984	413	322	269	0.8"	3.7"	4"
(Refer to page 90 for test details)	R357M2	5¹/₂	158	Semi-Jacketed H.P.	1235	1104	1015	535	428	361	0.8"	3.5"	4"
	R357M3	5¹/₂	158	Soft Point	1235	1104	1015	535	428	361	0.8"	3.5"	4"
	R357M5	5¹/₂	158	Semi-Wadcutter	1235	1104	1015	535	428	361	0.8"	3.5"	4"
	R357M9	5¹/₂	140	Semi-Jacketed H.P.	1360	1195	1076	575	444	360	0.7"	3.0"	4"
	R357M10	5¹/₂	180	Semi-Jacketed H.P.	1145	1053	985	524	443	388	0.9"	3.9"	8"
	R357M11	5¹/₂	125°	Semi-Jacketed H.P. (Med. Vel.)	1220	1077	984	413	322	269	0.8"	3.7"	4"
	R357MB	5¹/₂	140	"Multi-Ball"	1155	829	663	418	214	136	1.2"	6.4"	4"
(9) 357 REM. MAXIMUM°°	357MX1	7¹/₂	158°	Semi-Jacketed H.P.	1825	1588	1381	1168	885	669	0.4"	1.7"	10"
(10) 9MM LUGER	R9MM1	1¹/₂	115	Jacketed H.P.	1155	1047	971	341	280	241	0.9"	3.9"	4"
AUTO. PISTOL	R9MM2	1¹/₂	124	Metal Case	1110	1030	971	339	292	259	1.0"	4.1"	4"
	R9MM3	1¹/₂	115°	Metal Case	1135	1041	973	329	277	242	0.9"	4.0"	4"
	R9MM5	1¹/₂	88	Jacketed H.P.	1500	1191	1012	440	277	200	0.6"	3.1"	4"
	R9MM6	1¹/₂	115	Jacketed H.P. (+P)‡	1250	1113	1019	399	316	265	0.8"	3.5"	4"
	R9MM7	1¹/₂	140°	Semi-Jacketed H.P. (Practice)	935	889	849	272	246	224	1.3"	5.5"	4"
	R9MM8	1¹/₂	147	Jacketed H.P. (Subsonic)	990	941	900	320	289	264	1.1"	4.9"	4"
	R9MM9	1¹/₂	147	Metal Case (Match)	990	920	868	191	165	146	1.2"	5.1"	4"
	GS9MMC	1¹/₂	147	Brass-Jacketed Hollow Point	990	942	900	320	289	265	1.3"	5.0"	4"
(11) 380 AUTO. PISTOL	R380AP	1¹/₂	95°	Metal Case	955	865	785	190	160	130	1.4"	5.9"	4"
	R380A1	1¹/₂	88	Jacketed H.P.	990	920	868	191	165	146	1.2"	5.1"	4"
(12) 38 SUPER AUTO. COLT PISTOL (B)	R38SU1	1¹/₂	115	Jacketed H.P. (+P)‡	1300	1147	1041	431	336	277	0.7"	3.3"	5"
(13) 38 S. & W.	R38SW	1¹/₂	146°	Lead	685	650	620	150	135	125	2.4"	10.0"	4"
(14) 38 SPECIAL	R38S1	1¹/₂	95	Semi-Jacketed H.P. (+P)‡	1175	1044	959	291	230	194	0.9"	3.9"	4"
Vented Barrel Ballistics	R38S10	1¹/₂	110	Semi-Jacketed H.P. (+P)‡	995	926	871	242	210	185	1.2"	5.1"	4"
	R38S16	1¹/₂	110	Semi-Jacketed H.P. (+P)‡	950	890	840	220	194	172	1.4"	5.4"	4"
	R38S2	1¹/₂	125°	Semi-Jacketed H.P. (+P)‡	945	898	858	248	224	204	1.3"	5.4"	4"
	GS38SB	1¹/₂	125	Brass-Jacketed Hollow Point	975	924	881	264	237	215	1.4"	5.2"	4"
	R38S3	1¹/₂	148	Targetmaster Lead W.C. Match	710	634	566	166	132	105	2.4"	10.8"	4"
	R38S4	1¹/₂	158	Targetmaster Lead	755	723	692	200	183	168	2.0"	8.3"	4"

REMINGTON PISTOL/REVOLVER BALLISTICS

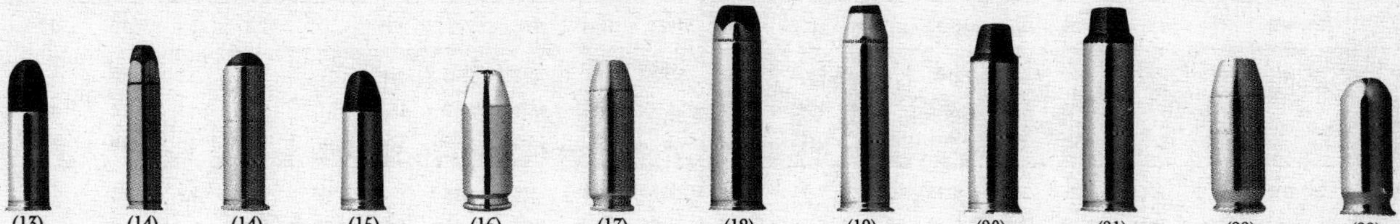

(13) (14) (14) (15) (16) (17) (18) (19) (20) (21) (22) (22)

CALIBER	OrderNo.	Primer No.	Wt. Grs.	Style	VELOCITY (FPS) Muzzle	50 Yds.	100 Yds.	ENERGY (FT-LB) Muzzle	50 Yds.	100 Yds.	MID-RANGE TRAJECTORY 50 Yds.	100 Yds.	B.L.
(14) 38 SPECIAL (continued)	R38S5	1½	158	Lead (Round Nose)	755	723	692	200	183	168	2.0"	8.3"	4"
	R38S14	1½	158	Semi-Wadcutter (+P)‡	890	855	823	278	257	238	1.4"	6.0"	4"
	R38S6	1½	158	Semi-Wadcutter	755	723	692	200	183	168	2.0"	8.3"	4"
	R38S12	1½	158	Lead H.P. (+P)‡	890	855	823	278	257	238	1.4"	6.0"	4"
	R38SMB	1½	140°	"Multi-Ball"	830	731	506	216	130	80	2.0"	10.6"	4"
(15) 38 SHORT COLT	R38SC	1½	125°	Lead	730	685	645	150	130	115	2.2"	9.4"	6"
(16) 40 S. & W.	R40SW1	5½	155°	Jacketed H.P.	1140	1026	948	447	362	309	0.9"	4.1"	4"
	R40SW2	5½	180	Jacketed H.P.	985	936	893	388	350	319	1.4"	5.0"	4"
	GS40SWB	5½	180	Brass-Jacketed Hollow Point	1015	960	914	412	368	334	1.3"	4.5"	4"
(17) 10MM AUTO.	R10MM2	2½	200	Metal Case	1160	1072	1007	597	510	450	0.9"	3.8"	5"
	R10MM3	2½	180°	Jacketed H. P. (Subsonic)	1055	997	951	445	397	361	1.0"	4.6"	5"
	R10MM4	2½	180	Jacketed H. P. (High Vel.)	1240	1124	1037	618	504	430	0.8"	3.4"	5"
(18) 41 REM. MAG.	R41MG1	2½	210	Soft Point	1300	1162	1062	788	630	526	0.7"	3.2"	4"
Vented Barrel Ballistics	R41MG2	2½	210	Lead	965	898	842	434	376	331	1.3"	5.4"	4"
	R41MG3	2½	170°	Semi-Jacketed H.P.	1420	1166	1014	761	513	388	0.7"	3.2"	4"
(19) 44 REM. MAG.	R44MG5	2½	180	Semi-Jacketed H.P.	1610	1365	1175	1036	745	551	0.5"	2.3"	4"
Vented Barrel Ballistics	R44MG1	2½	240	Lead Gas Check	1350	1186	1069	971	749	608	0.7"	3.1"	4"
	R44MG2	2½	240°	Soft Point	1180	1081	1010	741	623	543	0.9"	3.7"	4"
	R44MG3	2½	240	Semi-Jacketed H.P.	1180	1081	1010	741	623	543	0.9"	3.7"	4"
	R44MG4	2½	240	Lead (Med. Vel.)	1000	947	902	533	477	433	1.1"	4.8"	6"
	R44MG6	2½	210	Semi-Jacketed H.P.	1495	1312	1167	1042	803	634	0.6"	2.5"	6"
(20) 44 S. & W. SPECIAL	R44SW	2½	246	Lead	755	725	695	310	285	265	2.0"	8.3"	6"
	R44SW1	2½	200°	Semi-Wadcutter	1035	938	866	476	391	333	1.1"	4.9"	6"
(21) 45 COLT	R45C	2½	250	Lead	860	820	780	410	375	340	1.6"	6.6"	5"
	R45C1	2½	225	Semi-Wadcutter (Keith)	960	890	832	460	395	346	1.3"	5.5"	5"
(22) 45 AUTO.	R45AP1	2½	185	Targetmaster Lead W.C. Match	770	707	650	244	205	174	2.0"	8.7"	5"
	R45AP2	2½	185°	Jacketed H.P.	1000	939	889	411	362	324	1.1"	4.9"	5"
	R45AP4	2½	230	Metal Case	835	800	767	356	326	300	1.6"	6.8"	5"
	R45AP5	2½	Shot°	Shot	Number 12 shot.								
	R45AP6	2½	185	Jacketed H.P. (+P)‡	1140	1040	971	534	445	387	0.9"	4.0"	5"
	GS45APB	2½	230	Brass-Jacketed Hollow Point	875	836	801	391	357	327	1.4"	6.6"	5"
BLANK CARTRIDGES													
38 S. & W.	R38SWBL§	1½	-	Blank	-	-	-	-	-	-	-	-	-
32 S. & W.	R32BLNK	5½	-	Blank	-	-	-	-	-	-	-	-	-
38 SPECIAL	R38BLNK	1½	-	Blank	-	-	-	-	-	-	-	-	-

°Illustrated (not shown in actual size). °°Will not chamber in 357 Mag. or 38 Special handguns. ‡Ammunition with (+P) on the case headstamp is loaded to higher pressure. Use only in firearms designated for this cartridge and so recommended by the gun manufacturer. §Subject to stock on hand. (A)Adapted only for 38 Colt sporting, military and pocket model automatic pistols. These pistols were discontinued after 1928. (B)Adapted only for 38 Colt Super and Colt Commander automatic pistols. Not for use in sporting, military and pocket models.

WEATHERBY BALLISTICS

SUGGESTED USAGE	CARTRIDGE	BULLET Weight Grains	Bullet Type	VELOCITY in Feet per Second Muzzle	100 Yards	200 Yards	300 Yards	400 Yards	500 Yards	ENERGY in Foot-Pounds Muzzle	100 Yards	200 Yards	300 Yards	400 Yards	500 Yards	PATH OF BULLET Above or below line-of-sight of riflescopes mounted 1.5" above bore 100 Yards	200 Yards	300 Yards	400 Yards	500 Yards
V	.224 WM	55	Pt-Ex	3650	3192	2780	2403	2057	1742	1627	1244	944	705	516	370	2.8	3.7	0.0	-9.7	-27.7
V M	.240 WM	87	Pt-Ex	3523	3233	2943	2680	2432	2197	2398	2007	1673	1388	1143	933	2.5	3.3	0.0	-8.0	-22.0
		100	Pt-Ex	3406	3116	2844	2588	2346	2117	2577	2156	1796	1488	1222	996	2.8	3.5	0.0	-8.6	-23.6
		100	Partition	3406	3136	2881	2641	2413	2196	2577	2184	1843	1549	1293	1071	2.7	3.5	0.0	-8.3	-22.7
V M	.257 WM	87	Pt-Ex	3825	3456	3118	2803	2511	2236	2827	2308	1878	1518	1218	966	2.1	2.8	0.0	-7.2	-20.0
		100	Pt-Ex	3602	3280	2980	2701	2438	2190	2882	2389	1973	1620	1320	1065	2.4	3.2	0.0	-7.8	-21.6
		100	*Partition®	3555	3270	3004	2753	2516	2290	2806	2374	2053	1683	1405	1165	2.5	3.2	0.0	-7.8	-21.0
		120	Partition	3305	3045	2800	2568	2348	2139	2911	2472	2090	1758	1469	1219	3.0	3.7	0.0	-8.8	-24.0
V M	.270 WM	100	Pt-Ex	3760	3380	3033	2712	2412	2133	3139	2537	2042	1633	1292	1010	2.3	3.0	0.0	-7.8	-21.6
		130	Pt-Ex	3375	3100	2842	2598	2367	2147	3287	2773	2330	1948	1616	1331	2.9	3.6	0.0	-8.7	-23.7
		130	Partition	3375	3127	2893	2670	2458	2257	3287	2822	2415	2058	1714	1470	2.8	3.5	0.0	-8.3	-22.4
		150	Pt-Ex	3245	3019	2803	2598	2402	2215	3507	3034	2617	2248	1922	1634	3.0	3.7	0.0	-8.9	-23.8
		150	Partition	3245	3029	2823	2627	2439	2259	3507	3055	2655	2298	1981	1699	3.0	3.7	0.0	-8.7	-23.3
M	7MM WM	139	Pt-Ex	3340	3082	2838	2608	2389	2180	3443	2931	2486	2099	1761	1467	2.9	3.6	0.0	-8.7	-23.6
		140	Partition	3303	3069	2847	2636	2434	2241	3391	2927	2519	2159	1842	1562	2.9	3.6	0.0	-8.6	-23.1
		154	Pt-Ex	3260	3022	2797	2583	2379	2184	3633	3123	2675	2281	1934	1630	3.0	3.7	0.0	-9.0	-24.1
		160	Partition	3200	2991	2791	2600	2417	2241	3637	3177	2767	2401	2075	1784	3.1	3.8	0.0	-8.9	-23.8
B		175	Pt-Ex	3070	2879	2696	2520	2351	2188	3662	3220	2824	2467	2147	1861	3.4	4.1	0.0	-9.6	-25.4
M	.300 WM	150	Pt-Ex	3600	3297	3016	2751	2502	2266	4316	3621	3028	2520	2084	1709	2.4	3.1	0.0	-7.7	-21.0
		150	Partition	3600	3319	3057	2809	2575	2353	4316	3669	3111	2628	2208	1843	2.4	3.0	0.0	-7.5	-20.1
		165	Boat Tail	3450	3220	3003	2796	2598	2409	4360	3799	3303	2863	2473	2146	2.5	3.2	0.0	-7.6	-20.4
B		180	Pt-Ex	3300	3064	2841	2629	2426	2233	4352	3753	3226	2762	2352	1992	2.9	3.6	0.0	-8.6	-23.2
		180	Partition	3300	3085	2881	2686	2499	2319	4352	3804	3317	2882	2495	2150	2.8	3.5	0.0	-8.3	-22.3
		220	Rn-Ex	2905	2498	2125	1787	1491	1250	4122	3047	2206	1560	1085	763	5.3	6.6	0.0	-17.6	-51.3
B	.340 WM	200	Pt-Ex	3260	3011	2775	2552	2339	2137	4719	4025	3420	2892	2430	2027	3.1	3.8	0.0	-9.1	-24.7
		210	Partition	3250	3000	2763	2539	2325	2122	4924	4195	3559	3004	2520	2098	3.1	3.8	0.0	-9.2	-24.9
		250	Rn-Ex	3002	2672	2365	2079	1814	1574	5002	3963	3105	2399	1827	1375	1.7	0.0	-7.9	-24.0	-50.7
		250	Partition	2980	2780	2588	2404	2228	2059	4931	4290	3719	3209	2756	2354	3.7	4.4	0.0	-10.3	-27.5
B	.378 WM	270	Pt-Ex	3180	2976	2781	2594	2415	2243	6062	5308	4635	4034	3496	3015	1.2	0.0	-5.7	-16.6	-33.5
																3.1	3.8	0.0	-9.0	-23.9
		300	Rn-Ex	2925	2603	2303	2024	1764	1531	5701	4516	3535	2729	2074	1563	1.8	0.0	-8.3	-25.2	-53.5
A		300	FMJ	2925	2580	2262	1972	1710	1482	5701	4434	3408	2592	1949	1463	1.84	0.0	-8.6	-26.1	-55.9
A	.416 WM	400	Swift P	2650	2411	2185	1971	1770	1585	6239	5165	4242	3450	2783	2233	5.4	6.3	0.0	-15.1	-41.7
																2.2	0.0	-9.5	-27.7	-57.5
		400	Rn-Ex	2700	2390	2101	1834	1591	1379	6474	5073	3921	2986	2247	1688	5.7	6.8	0.0	-17.2	-48.4
																2.3	0.0	-10.2	-30.9	-65.4
		400	**Mono Solid®	2700	2397	2115	1852	1613	1402	6474	5104	3971	3047	2310	1747	5.7	6.7	0.0	-17.0	-47.4
																2.3	0.0	-10.1	-30.4	-64.3
A	.460 WM	500	RNSP	2600	2310	2039	1787	1559	1359	7507	5926	4618	3545	2701	2050	2.5	0.0	-10.8	-32.7	-69.2
		500	FMJ	2600	2330	2077	1839	1623	1426	7507	6030	4791	3755	2924	2258					

LEGEND: Pt-Ex = Pointed-Expanding   Rn-Ex = Round nose-Expanding   FMJ = Full Metal Jacket   P = Divided Lead Cavity or "H" Type

Note: These tables were calculated by computer using a standard modern scientific technique to predict trajectories and recoil energies from the best available cartridge data. Figures shown are expected to be reasonably accurate; however, the shooter is cautioned that performance will vary because of variations in rifles, ammunition, atmospheric conditions and altitude. Velocities were determined using 26-inch barrels; shorter barrels will reduce velocity by 30 to 65 fps per inch of barrel removed. Trajectories were computed with the line-of-sight 1.5 inches above the bore centerline. *B.C.:* Ballistic Coefficients supplied by the bullet manufacturers. * Partition is a registered trademark of Nosler, Inc. ** Monolithic Solid is a registered trademark of A-Square, Inc.

WINCHESTER BALLISTICS

CENTERFIRE PISTOL/REVOLVER CARTRIDGES

Cartridge	Symbol	Bullet Wt. Grs.	Type	Velocity (fps) Muzzle	50 Yds.	100 Yds.	Energy (ft-lbs.) Muzzle	50 Yds.	100 Yds.	Mid Range Traj. (In.) 50 Yds.	100 Yds.	Barrel Length Inches
25 Automatic	X25AXP	45	Expanding Point**	815	729	655	66	53	42	1.8	7.7	2
25 Automatic	X25AP	50	Full Metal Jacket	760	707	659	64	56	48	2.0	8.7	2
30 Luger (7.65mm)	X30LP	93	Full Metal Jacket	1220	1110	1040	305	255	225	0.9	3.5	4-1/2
30 Carbine #	X30M1	110	Hollow Soft Point	1790	1601	1430	783	626	500	0.4	1.7	10
30 Carbine #	X30M2	110	Full Metal Jacket	1740	1552	1384	740	588	468	0.4	1.8	10
32 Smith & Wesson	X32SWP	85	Lead-Round Nose	680	645	610	90	81	73	2.5	10.5	3
32 Smith & Wesson Long	X32SWLP	98	Lead-Round Nose	705	670	635	115	98	88	2.3	10.5	4
32 Short Colt	X32SCP	80	Lead-Round Nose	745	665	590	100	79	62	2.2	9.9	4
32 Automatic	X32ASHP	60	Silvertip Hollow Point	970	895	835	125	107	93	1.3	5.4	4
32 Automatic	X32AP	71	Full Metal Jacket	905	855	810	129	115	97	1.4	5.8	4
38 Smith & Wesson	X38SWP	145	Lead-Round Nose	685	650	620	150	135	125	2.4	10.0	4
380 Automatic	X380ASHP	85	Silvertip Hollow Point	1000	921	860	189	160	140	1.2	5.1	3-3/4
380 Automatic	X380AP	95	Full Metal Jacket	955	865	785	190	160	130	1.4	5.9	3-3/4
38 Special	X38S9HP	110	Silvertip Hollow Point	945	894	850	218	195	176	1.3	5.4	4V
38 Special Match	X38SMRP	148	Lead-Wad Cutter	710	634	566	166	132	105	2.4	10.8	4V
38 Special	X38S1P	158	Lead-Round Nose	755	723	693	200	183	168	2.0	8.3	4V
38 Special	X38WCPSV	158	Lead-Semi Wad Cutter	755	721	689	200	182	167	2.0	8.4	4V
38 Special + P#	X38SSHP	95	Silvertip Hollow Point	1100	1002	932	255	212	183	1.0	4.3	4V
38 Special + P#	X38S6PH	110	Jacketed Hollow Point	995	926	871	242	210	185	1.2	5.1	4V
38 Special + P#	X38S7PH	125	Jacketed Hollow Point	945	898	858	248	224	204	1.3	5.4	4V
38 Special + P#	X38S8PH	125	Silvertip Hollow Point	945	898	858	248	224	204	1.3	5.4	4V
38 Special Subsonic + P	XSUB38S	147	Jacketed Hollow Point	860	830	802	241	225	210	1.5	6.3	4
38 Special + P	X38SPD	158	Lead-Semi Wad Cutter Hollow Point	890	855	823	278	257	238	1.4	6.0	4V
38 Special + P	X38WCP	158	Lead-Semi Wad Cutter	890	855	823	278	257	238	1.4	6.0	4V
9mm Luger	X9LP	115	Full Metal Jacket	1155	1047	971	341	280	241	0.9	3.9	4
9mm Luger	X9MMSHP	115	Silvertip Hollow Point	1225	1095	1007	383	306	259	0.8	3.6	4
9mm Luger Black Talon	**S9MM**	**147**	**Supreme Expansion Talon**	**990**	**945**	**907**	**320**	**292**	**268**	**1.2**	**4.8**	**4**
9mm Luger Subsonic	XSUB9MM	147	Jacketed Hollow Point	990	945	907	320	292	268	1.2	4.8	4
9mm Luger	X9MMST147	147	Silvertip Hollow Point	1010	962	921	333	302	277	1.1	4.7	4
9mm Luger Match	X9MMTCM	147	Full Metal Jacket- Truncated Cone-Match	990	945	907	320	292	268	1.2	4.8	4
38 Super Automatic + P*	X38ASHP	125	Silvertip Hollow Point	1240	1130	1050	427	354	306	0.8	3.4	5
38 Super Automatic + P*	X38A1P	130	Full Metal Jacket	1215	1099	1017	426	348	298	0.8	3.6	5
357 Magnum #	X3573P	110	Jacketed Hollow Point	1295	1095	975	410	292	232	0.8	3.5	4V
357 Magnum #	X3576P	125	Jacketed Hollow Point	1450	1240	1090	583	427	330	0.6	2.8	4V
357 Magnum #	X357SHP	145	Silvertip Hollow Point	1290	1155	1060	535	428	361	0.8	3.5	4V
357 Magnum	X3571P	158	Lead-Semi Wad Cutter**	1235	1104	1015	535	428	361	0.8	3.5	4V
357 Magnum #	X3574P	158	Jacketed Hollow Point	1235	1104	1015	535	428	361	0.8	3.5	4V
357 Magnum #	X3575P	158	Jacketed Soft Point	1235	1104	1015	535	428	361	0.8	3.5	4V
New 357 Magnum Black Talon	**S357M**	**180**	**Supreme Expansion Talon**	**1180**	**1088**	**1020**	**557**	**473**	**416**	**0.8**	**3.6**	**8V**
40 Smith & Wesson	X40SWSTHP	155	Silvertip Hollow Point	1205	1096	1018	500	414	357	0.8	3.6	4
40 Smith & Wesson Match	X40SWTCM	155	Full Metal Jacket- Truncated Cone-Match	1125	1046	986	436	377	335	0.9	3.9	4
40 Smith & Wesson Black Talon	**S40SW**	**180**	**Supreme Expansion Talon**	**990**	**938**	**895**	**392**	**352**	**320**	**1.2**	**4.9**	**4**
40 Smith & Wesson Subsonic	XSUB40SW	180	Jacketed Hollow Point	990	936	891	390	350	317	1.2	4.9	4
10mm Automatic Match	X10MMTCM	155	Full Metal Jacket- Truncated Cone-Match	1125	1046	986	436	377	335	0.9	3.9	5
10mm Automatic	X10MMSTHP	175	Silvertip Hollow Point	1290	1141	1037	649	506	418	0.7	3.3	5-1/2
10mm Automatic Subsonic	XSUB10MM	180	Jacketed Hollow Point	990	936	891	390	350	317	1.2	4.9	5
10mm Automatic Black Talon	**S10MM**	**200**	**Supreme Expansion Talon**	**990**	**941**	**900**	**435**	**394**	**360**	**1.2**	**4.9**	**5**
41 Remington Magnum #	X41MSTHP2	175	Silvertip Hollow Point	1250	1120	1029	607	488	412	0.8	3.4	4V
41 Remington Magnum #	X41MHP2	210	Jacketed Hollow Point	1300	1162	1062	788	630	526	0.7	3.2	4V
44 Smith & Wesson Special #	X44STHPS2	200	Silvertip Hollow Point	900	860	822	360	328	300	1.4	5.9	6-1/2
44 Smith & Wesson Special	X44SP	246	Lead-Round Nose	755	725	695	310	285	265	2.0	8.3	6-1/2
44 Remington Magnum	X44MSTHP2	210	Silvertip Hollow Point	1250	1106	1010	729	570	475	0.8	3.5	4V
44 Remington Magnum	X44MHSP2	240	Hollow Soft Point	1180	1081	1010	741	623	543	0.9	3.7	4V
New 44 Remington Magnum Black Talon	**S44M**	**250**	**Supreme Expansion Talon**	**1330**	**1213**	**1119**	**982**	**817**	**695**	**0.7**	**2.9**	**6-1/2V**
45 Automatic	X45ASHP2	185	Silvertip Hollow Point	1000	938	888	411	362	324	1.2	4.9	5
45 Automatic Super-Match	X45AWCP	185	Full Metal Jacket- Semi Wad Cutter	770	707	650	244	205	174	2.0	8.7	5
45 Automatic	X45A1P2	230	Full Metal Jacket	835	800	767	356	326	300	1.6	6.8	5
45 Automatic Black Talon	**S45A**	**230**	**Supreme Expansion Talon**	**850**	**814**	**780**	**369**	**338**	**311**	**1.6**	**6.6**	**5**
45 Automatic Subsonic	XSUB45A	230	Jacketed Hollow Point	850	814	780	369	338	311	1.6	6.6	5
45 Colt Silvertip #	X45CSHP2	225	Silvertip Hollow Point	920	877	839	423	384	352	1.4	5.6	5-1/2
45 Colt	X45CP2	255	Lead-Round Nose	860	820	780	420	380	345	1.5	6.1	5-1/2
45 Winchester Magnum #	X45WM2	230	Full Metal Jacket	1400	1232	1107	1001	775	636	0.6	2.8	5

(Not for Arms Chambered for Standard 45 Automatic)

WINCHESTER BALLISTICS

SUPER-X CENTERFIRE RIFLE CARTRIDGES

Cartridge	Symbol	Game Selector Guide	CXP Guide Number	Bullet Wt. Grs.	Bullet Type	Barrel Length (In.)	Muzzle	100	200	300	400	500
							Velocity in Feet Per Second (fps)					
218 Bee	X218B	V	1	46	Hollow Point	24	2760	2102	1550	1155	961	850
22 Hornet	X22H1	V	1	45	Soft Point	24	2690	2042	1502	1128	948	840
22 Hornet	X22H2	V	1	46	Hollow Point	24	2690	2042	1502	1128	948	841
22-250 Remington	**S22250R52**	**V**	**1**	**52**	**Hollow Point Boattail**	**24**	**3750**	**3268**	**2835**	**2442**	**2082**	**1755**
22-250 Remington	X222501	V	1	55	Pointed Soft Point	24	3680	3137	2656	2222	1832	1493
222 Remington	X222R	V	1	50	Pointed Soft Point	24	3140	2602	2123	1700	1350	1107
222 Remington	X222R1	V	1	55	Full Metal Jacket	24	3020	2675	2355	2057	1783	1537
223 Remington	X223RH	V	1	53	Hollow Point	24	3330	2882	2477	2106	1770	1475
223 Remington	X223R	V	1	55	Pointed Soft Point	24	3240	2747	2304	1905	1554	1270
223 Remington	X223R1	V	1	55	Full Metal Jacket	24	3240	2877	2543	2232	1943	1679
223 Remington	X223R2	D	2	64	Power Point	24	3020	2621	2256	1920	1619	1362
New 223 Remington Match	**S223M***	**—**	**M**	**69**	**Hollow Point Boattail**	**24**	**3060**	**2740**	**2442**	**2164**	**1904**	**1665**
225 Winchester	X2251	V	1	55	Pointed Soft Point	24	3570	3066	2616	2208	1838	1514
243 Winchester	X2431	V	1	80	Pointed Soft Point	24	3350	2955	2593	2259	1951	1670
243 Winchester	X2432	D,O/P	2	100	Power Point	24	2960	2697	2449	2215	1993	1786
243 Winchester	**S243W100**	**D,O/P**	**2**	**100**	**Soft Point Boattail**	**24**	**2960**	**2712**	**2477**	**2254**	**2042**	**1843**
6mm Remington	X6MMR1	V	1	80	Pointed Soft Point	24	3470	3064	2694	2352	2036	1747
6mm Remington	X6MMR2	D,O/P	2	100	Power Point	24	3100	2829	2573	2332	2104	1889
25-06 Remington	X25061	V	1	90	Positive Expanding Point	24	3440	3043	2680	2344	2034	1749
25-06 Remington	X25062	D,O/P	2	120	Positive Expanding Point	24	2990	2730	2484	2252	2032	1825
25-20 Winchester #	X25202	V	1	86	Soft Point	24	1460	1194	1030	931	858	798
25-35 Winchester	X2535	D	2	117	Soft Point	24	2230	1866	1545	1282	1097	984
250 Savage	X2503	D,O/P	2	100	Silvertip	24	2820	2467	2140	1839	1569	1339
257 Roberts + P	X257P2	D,O/P	2	100	Silvertip	24	3000	2633	2295	1982	1697	1447
257 Roberts + P	X257P3	D,O/P	2	117	Power Point	24	2780	2411	2071	1761	1488	1263
264 Winchester Mag.	X2642	D,O/P	2	140	Power Point	24	3030	2782	2548	2326	2114	1914
270 Winchester	X2701	V	1	100	Pointed Soft Point	24	3430	3021	2649	2305	1988	1699
270 Winchester	X2705	D,O/P	2	130	Power Point	24	3060	2802	2559	2329	2110	1904
270 Winchester	X2703	D,O/P	2	130	Silvertip	24	3060	2776	2510	2259	2022	1801
270 Winchester	**S270**	**D,O/P**	**2**	**140**	**Silvertip Boattail**	**24**	**2960**	**2753**	**2554**	**2365**	**2183**	**2009**
270 Winchester	X2704	D,M	3	150	Power Point	24	2850	2585	2336	2100	1879	1673
280 Remington	X280R	D,O/P	2	140	Power Point	24	3050	2705	2428	2167	1924	1698
280 Remington	**S280R160**	**D,O/P**	**3**	**160**	**Silvertip Boattail**	**24**	**2840**	**2637**	**2442**	**2256**	**2078**	**1909**
284 Winchester	X2842	D,O/P,M	3	150	Power Point	24	2860	2595	2344	2108	1886	1680
7mm Mauser (7x57)	X7MM1	D	2	145	Power Point	24	2660	2413	2180	1959	1754	1564
7mm Remington Mag.	**S7MAG**	**D,O/P**	**2**	**139**	**Soft Point Boattail**	**24**	**3165**	**2935**	**2717**	**2509**	**2311**	**2121**
7mm Remington Mag.	X7MMR1	D,O/P,M	2	150	Power Point	24	3110	2830	2568	2320	2085	1866
7mm Remington Mag.	**S7MMRM160**	**D,O/P,M,L**	**3**	**160**	**Silvertip Boattail**	**24**	**2950**	**2745**	**2550**	**2363**	**2184**	**2012**
7mm Remington Mag.	X7MMR2	D,O/P,M	3	175	Power Point	24	2860	2645	2440	2244	2057	1879
7.62 x 39mm Russian	X76239	D,V	2	123	Soft Point	20	2365	2033	1731	1465	1248	1093
30 Carbine #	X30M1	V	1	110	Hollow Soft Point	20	1990	1567	1236	1035	923	842
30 Carbine #	X30M2	V	1	110	Full Metal Jacket	20	1990	1596	1278	1070	952	870
30-30 Winchester	X30301	D	2	150	Hollow Point	24	2390	2018	1684	1398	1177	1036
30-30 Winchester	X30306	D	2	150	Power Point	24	2390	2018	1684	1398	1177	1036
30-30 Winchester	X30302	D	2	150	Silvertip	24	2390	2018	1684	1398	1177	1036
30-30 Winchester	**S3030W150**	**D**	**2**	**150**	**Silvertip**	**24**	**2390**	**2018**	**1684**	**1398**	**1177**	**1036**
30-30 Winchester	X30303	D	2	170	Power Point	24	2200	1895	1619	1381	1191	1061
30-30 Winchester	X30304	D	2	170	Silvertip	24	2200	1895	1619	1381	1191	1061

Game Selector	CXP Class	Examples
V-Varmint	1	Prairie dog, coyote, woodchuck
D-Deer	2	Antelope, deer, black bear
O/P-Open or Plains	3	Elk, moose
M-Medium Game	3D	All game in category 3 plus large dangerous game (i.e. Kodiak bear)

Energy in Foot Pounds (ft-lbs.)						Trajectory, Short Range Yards						Trajectory, Long Range Yards						
Muzzle	100	200	300	400	500	50	100	150	200	250	300	100	150	200	250	300	400	500
778	451	245	136	94	74	0.3	0	-2.3	-7.2	-15.8	-29.4	1.5	0	-4.2	-12.0	-24.8	-71.4	-155.6
723	417	225	127	90	70	0.3	0	-2.4	-7.7	-16.9	-31.3	1.6	0	-4.5	-12.8	-26.4	-75.6	-163.4
739	426	230	130	92	72	0.3	0	-2.4	-7.7	-16.9	-31.3	1.6	0	-4.5	-12.8	-26.4	-75.5	-163.3
1624	**1233**	**928**	**689**	**501**	**356**	**0.1**	**0**	**-7**	**-2.4**	**-5.1**	**-9.1**	**1.2**	**1.1**	**0**	**-2.1**	**-5.5**	**-16.9**	**-36.3**
1654	1201	861	603	410	272	0.2	0.5	0	-1.6	-4.4	-8.7	2.3	2.6	1.9	0	-3.4	-15.9	-38.9
1094	752	500	321	202	136	0.5	0.9	0	-2.5	-6.9	-13.7	2.2	1.9	0	-3.8	-10.0	-32.3	-73.8
1114	874	677	517	388	288	0.5	0.9	0	-2.2	-6.1	-11.7	2.0	1.7	0	-3.3	-8.3	-24.9	-52.5
1305	978	722	522	369	256	0.3	0.7	0	-1.9	-5.3	-10.3	1.7	1.4	0	-2.9	-7.4	-22.7	-49.1
1282	921	648	443	295	197	0.4	0.8	0	-2.2	-6.0	-11.8	1.9	1.6	0	-3.3	-8.5	-26.7	-59.6
1282	1011	790	608	461	344	0.4	0.7	0	-1.9	-5.1	-9.9	1.7	1.4	0	-2.8	-7.1	-21.2	-44.6
1296	977	723	524	373	264	0.6	0.9	0	-2.4	-6.5	-12.5	2.1	1.8	0	-3.5	-9.0	-27.4	-59.6
1435	**1151**	**914**	**717**	**555**	**425**	**-0.2**	**0**	**-9**	**-3.1**	**-6.8**	**-12.1**	**1.6**	**1.4**	**0**	**-2.9**	**-7.4**	**-22.3**	**-46.7**
1556	1148	836	595	412	280	0.2	0.6	0	-1.7	-4.6	-9.0	2.4	2.8	2.0	0	-3.5	-16.3	-39.5
1993	1551	1194	906	676	495	0.3	0.7	0	-1.8	-4.9	-9.4	2.6	2.9	2.1	0	-3.6	-16.2	-37.9
1945	1615	1332	1089	882	708	0.5	0.9	0	-2.2	-5.8	-11.0	1.9	1.6	0	-3.1	-7.8	-22.6	-46.3
1946	**1633**	**1363**	**1128**	**926**	**754**	**0.1**	**0**	**-1.3**	**-3.8**	**-7.8**	**-13.3**	**1.9**	**1.6**	**0**	**-3.0**	**-7.6**	**-22.0**	**-44.8**
2139	1667	1289	982	736	542	0.3	0.6	0	-1.6	-4.5	-8.7	2.4	2.7	1.9	0	-3.3	-14.9	-35.0
2133	1777	1470	1207	983	792	0.4	0.8	0	-1.9	-5.2	-9.9	1.7	1.5	0	-2.8	-7.0	-20.4	-41.7
2364	1850	1435	1098	827	611	0.3	0.6	0	-1.7	-4.5	-8.8	2.4	2.7	2.0	0	-3.4	-15.0	-35.2
2382	1985	1644	1351	1100	887	0.5	0.8	0	-2.1	-5.6	-10.7	1.9	1.6	0	-3.0	-7.5	-22.0	-44.8
407	272	203	165	141	122	0	-4.1	-14.4	-31.8	-57.3	-92.0	0	-8.2	-23.5	-47.0	-79.6	-175.9	-319.4
1292	904	620	427	313	252	0.6	0	-3.1	-9.2	-19.0	-33.1	2.1	0	-5.1	-13.8	-27.0	-70.1	-142.0
1765	1351	1017	751	547	398	0.2	0	-1.6	-4.9	-10.0	-17.4	2.4	2.0	0	-3.9	-10.1	-30.5	-65.2
1998	1539	1169	872	639	465	0.5	0.9	0	-2.4	-4.9	-12.3	2.9	3.0	1.6	0	-6.4	-23.2	-51.2
2009	1511	1115	806	576	415	0.8	1.1	0	-2.9	-7.8	-15.1	2.6	2.2	0	-4.2	-10.8	-33.0	-70.0
2854	2406	2018	1682	1389	1139	0.5	0.8	0	-2.0	-5.4	-10.2	1.8	1.5	0	-2.9	-7.2	-20.8	-42.2
2612	2027	1557	1179	877	641	0.3	0.6	0	-1.7	-4.6	-9.0	2.5	2.8	2.0	0	-3.4	-15.5	-36.4
2702	2267	1890	1565	1285	1046	0.4	0.8	0	-2.0	-5.3	-10.1	1.8	1.5	0	-2.8	-7.1	-20.6	-42.0
2702	2225	1818	1472	1180	936	0.5	0.8	0	-2.0	-5.5	-10.4	1.8	1.5	0	-2.9	-7.4	-21.6	-44.3
2724	**2356**	**2029**	**1739**	**1482**	**1256**	**0.1**	**0**	**-1.2**	**-3.7**	**-7.5**	**-12.7**	**1.8**	**1.5**	**0**	**-2.9**	**-7.2**	**-20.6**	**-41.3**
2705	2226	1817	1468	1175	932	0.6	1.0	0	-2.4	-6.4	-12.2	2.2	1.8	0	-3.4	-8.6	-25.0	-51.4
2799	2274	1833	1461	1151	897	0.5	0.8	0	-2.2	-5.8	-11.1	1.9	1.6	0	-3.1	-7.8	-23.1	-47.8
2866	**2471**	**2120**	**1809**	**1535**	**1295**	**0.1**	**0**	**-1.4**	**-4.1**	**-8.3**	**-14.0**	**2.1**	**1.7**	**0**	**-3.2**	**-7.9**	**-22.6**	**-45.4**
2724	2243	1830	1480	1185	940	0.6	1.0	0	-2.4	-6.3	-12.1	2.1	1.8	0	-3.4	-8.5	-24.8	-51.0
2279	1875	1530	1236	990	788	0.2	0	-1.7	-5.1	-10.3	-17.5	1.1	0	-2.8	-7.4	-14.1	-34.4	-66.1
3093	**2660**	**2279**	**1944**	**1648**	**1389**	**0.1**	**0**	**-1.0**	**-3.2**	**-6.5**	**-11.1**	**1.6**	**1.3**	**0**	**-2.5**	**-6.3**	**-18.3**	**-36.6**
3221	2667	2196	1792	1448	1160	0.4	0.8	0	-1.9	-5.2	-9.9	1.7	1.5	0	-2.8	-7.0	-20.5	-42.1
3093	**2679**	**2311**	**1984**	**1694**	**1439**	**0.1**	**0**	**-1.2**	**-3.7**	**-7.5**	**-12.8**	**1.9**	**1.5**	**0**	**-2.9**	**-7.2**	**-20.6**	**-41.4**
3178	2718	2313	1956	1644	1372	0.6	0.9	0	-2.3	-6.0	-11.3	2.0	1.7	0	-3.2	-7.9	-22.7	-45.8
1527	1129	818	586	425	327	0.5	0	-2.6	-7.6	-15.4	-26.7	3.8	3.1	0	-6.0	-15.4	-46.3	-98.4
967	600	373	262	208	173	0.9	0	-4.5	-13.5	-28.3	-49.9	0	-4.5	-13.5	-28.3	-49.9	-118.6	-228.2
967	622	399	280	221	185	0.9	0	-4.3	-13.0	-26.9	-47.4	2.9	0	-7.2	-19.7	-38.7	-100.4	-200.5
1902	1356	944	651	461	357	0.5	0	-2.6	-7.7	-16.0	-27.9	1.7	0	-4.3	-11.6	-22.7	-59.1	-120.5
1902	1356	944	651	461	357	0.5	0	-2.6	-7.7	-16.0	-27.9	1.7	0	-4.3	-11.6	-22.7	-59.1	-120.5
1902	1356	944	651	461	357	0.5	0	-2.6	-7.7	-16.0	-27.9	1.7	0	-4.3	-11.6	-22.7	-59.1	-120.5
1902	**1356**	**944**	**651**	**461**	**357**	**0.5**	**0**	**-2.6**	**-7.7**	**-16.0**	**-27.9**	**3.9**	**3.2**	**0**	**-6.2**	**-16.1**	**-49.4**	**-105.2**
1827	1355	989	720	535	425	0.6	0	-3.0	-8.9	-18.0	-31.1	2.0	0	-4.8	-13.0	-25.1	-63.6	-126.7
1827	1355	989	720	535	425	0.6	0	-3.0	-8.9	-18.0	-31.1	2.0	0	-4.8	-13.0	-25.1	-63.6	-126.7

L-Large Game
XL-Extra Large Game

4 Cape Buffalo, elephant
M Match

\# Acceptable for use in pistols and revolvers also.
Bold type indicates Supreme product line

* Intended for use in fast twist barrels (e.g., 1 in 7 to 1 in 9).
Slower twist barrels may not sufficiently stabilize bullet.

WINCHESTER BALLISTICS

SUPER-X CENTERFIRE RIFLE CARTRIDGES

Cartridge	Symbol	Game Selector Guide	CXP Guide Number	Bullet Wt. Grs.	Bullet Type	Barrel Length (In.)	Muzzle	100	200	300	400	500
30-06 Springfield	X30062	V	1	125	Pointed Soft Point	24	3140	2780	2447	2138	1853	1595
30-06 Springfield	X30061	D,O/P	2	150	Power Point	24	2920	2580	2265	1972	1704	1466
30-06 Springfield	X30063	D,O/P	2	150	Silvertip	24	2910	2617	2342	2083	1843	1622
30-06 Springfield	X30065	D,O/P,M	2	165	Soft Point	24	2800	2573	2357	2151	1956	1772
30-06 Springfield	X30064	D,O/P,M	2	180	Power Point	24	2700	2348	2023	1727	1466	1251
30-06 Springfield	X30066	D,O/P,M,L	3	180	Silvertip	24	2700	2469	2250	2042	1846	1663
30-06 Springfield	X30069	M,L	3	220	Silvertip	24	2410	2192	1985	1791	1611	1448
30-06 Springfield	**S3006S165**	**D,O/P,M**	**2**	**165**	**Silvertip Boattail**	24	**2800**	**2597**	**2402**	**2216**	**2038**	**1869**
30-06 Springfield	**S3006S180**	**D,O/P,M,L**	**3**	**180**	**Silvertip Boattail**	24	**2700**	**2503**	**2314**	**2133**	**1960**	**1797**
New 30-06 Springfield Black Talon	**S3006X**	**D,O/P,M,L**	**3**	**180**	**Fail Safe Talon**	24	**2700**	**2486**	**2283**	**2089**	**1904**	**1731**
30-40 Krag	X30401	D	2	180	Power Point	24	2430	2099	1795	1525	1298	1128
300 Winchester Mag.	X30WM1	D,O/P	2	150	Power Point	24	3290	2951	2636	2342	2068	1813
300 Winchester Mag.	X30WM2	O/P,M,L	3	180	Power Point	24	2960	2745	2540	2344	2157	1979
300 Winchester Mag.	X30WM3	M,L,XL	3D	220	Silvertip	24	2680	2448	2228	2020	1823	1640
300 Winchester Mag.	**S300W**	**O/P,M,L**	**3D**	**190**	**Silvertip Boattail**	24	**2885**	**2698**	**2519**	**2347**	**2181**	**2023**
New 300 Winchester Mag. Black Talon	**S300WX**	**M,L**	**3D**	**180**	**Fail Safe Talon**	24	**2960**	**2732**	**2514**	**2307**	**2110**	**1923**
300 H. & H. Magnum	X300H2	O/P,M,L	3	180	Silvertip	24	2880	2640	2412	2196	1991	1798
300 Savage	X3001	D,O/P	2	150	Power Point	24	2630	2311	2015	1743	1500	1295
300 Savage	X3003	D,O/P	2	150	Silvertip	24	2630	2354	2095	1853	1631	1434
300 Savage	X3004	D	2	180	Power Point	24	2350	2025	1728	1467	1252	1098
303 Savage	X3032	D	2	190	Silvertip	24	1890	1612	1372	1183	1055	970
303 British	X303B1	D	2	180	Power Point	24	2460	2233	2018	1816	1629	1459
307 Winchester	X3076	D,M	2	180	Power Point	24	2510	2179	1874	1599	1362	1177
308 Winchester	X3085	D,O/P	2	150	Power Point	24	2820	2488	2179	1893	1633	1405
308 Winchester	X3082	D,O/P	2	150	Silvertip	24	2820	2533	2263	2009	1774	1560
308 Winchester	X3086	D,O/P,M	2	180	Power Point	24	2620	2274	1955	1666	1414	1212
308 Winchester	X3083	M,L	3	180	Silvertip	24	2620	2393	2178	1974	1782	1604
308 Winchester	**S308W150**	**D,O/P**	**2**	**150**	**Silvertip Boattail**	24	**2820**	**2559**	**2312**	**2080**	**1861**	**1659**
308 Winchester	**S308W180**	**D,O/P,M**	**3**	**180**	**Silvertip Boattail**	24	**2610**	**2424**	**2245**	**2074**	**1911**	**1756**
New 308 Winchester Black Talon	**S308X**	**D,O/P,M,L**	**3**	**180**	**Fail Safe Talon**	24	**2620**	**2409**	**2207**	**2015**	**1834**	**1664**
New 308 Winchester Match	**S308M**	**—**	**M**	**168**	**Hollow Point Boattail**	24	**2680**	**2485**	**2297**	**2118**	**1948**	**1786**
32 Win Special	X32WS2	D	2	170	Power Point	24	2250	1870	1537	1267	1082	971
32 Win Special	X32WS3	D	2	170	Silvertip	24	2250	1870	1537	1267	1082	971
32-20 Winchester #	X32201	V	1	100	Lead	24	1210	1021	913	834	769	712
8mm Mauser (8 x 57)	X8MM	D	2	170	Power Point	24	2360	1969	1622	1333	1123	997
338 Winchester Mag.	X3381	D,O/P,M	3	200	Power Point	24	2960	2658	2375	2110	1862	1635
338 Winchester Mag.	X3383	M,L,XL	3D	225	Soft Point	24	2780	2572	2374	2184	2003	1832
New 338 Winchester Mag. Black Talon	**S338X**	**M,L,XL**	**3D**	**250**	**Fail Safe Talon**	24	**2660**	**2461**	**2271**	**2089**	**1915**	**1752**
348 Winchester	Q3167	D,M	3	200	Silvertip	24	2520	2215	1931	1672	1443	1253
35 Remington	X35R1	D	2	200	Power Point	24	2020	1646	1335	1114	985	901
356 Winchester	X3561	D,M	2	200	Power Point	24	2460	2114	1797	1517	1284	1113
356 Winchester	X3563	M,L	3	250	Power Point	24	2160	1911	1682	1476	1299	1158
357 Magnum #	X3575P	V,D	2	158	Jacketed Soft Point	20	1830	1427	1138	980	883	809
358 Winchester	X3581	D,M	3	200	Silvertip	24	2490	2171	1876	1610	1379	1194
375 Winchester	X375W	D,M	2	200	Power Point	24	2200	1841	1526	1268	1089	980
375 Winchester	X375W1	D,M	2	250	Power Point	24	1900	1647	1424	1239	1103	1011
375 H. & H. Magnum	X375H1	M,L,XL	3D	270	Power Point	24	2690	2420	2166	1928	1707	1507
375 H. & H. Magnum	X375H2	M,L,XL	3D	300	Silvertip	24	2530	2268	2022	1793	1583	1397
375 H. & H. Magnum	X375H3	XL	4	300	Full Metal Jacket	24	2530	2171	1843	1551	1307	1126
38-40 Winchester #	X3840	D	2	180	Soft Point	24	1160	999	901	827	764	710
38-55 Winchester	X3855	D	2	255	Soft Point	24	1320	1190	1091	1018	963	917
44 Remington Magnum #	X44MSTHP2	V,D	2	210	Silvertip Hollow Point	20	1580	1198	993	879	795	725
44 Remington Magnum #	X44MHSP2	D	2	240	Hollow Soft Point	20	1760	1362	1094	953	861	789
44-40 Winchester #	X4440	D	2	200	Soft Point	24	1190	1006	900	822	756	699
45-70 Government	X4570H	D,M	2	300	Jacketed Hollow Point	24	1880	1650	1425	1235	1105	1010
458 Winchester Magnum	X4580	XL	4	500	Full Metal Jacket	24	2040	1823	1623	1442	1287	1161
458 Winchester Magnum	X4581	L,XL	3D	510	Soft Point	24	2040	1770	1527	1319	1157	1046

Energy in Foot Pounds (ft-lbs.)						Trajectory, Short Range Yards						Trajectory, Long Range Yards						
Muzzle	100	200	300	400	500	50	100	150	200	250	300	100	150	200	250	300	400	500
2736	2145	1662	1269	953	706	0.4	0.8	0	-2.1	-5.6	-10.7	1.8	1.5	0	-3.0	-7.7	-23.0	-48.5
2839	2217	1708	1295	967	716	0.6	1.0	0	-2.4	-6.6	-12.7	2.2	1.8	0	-3.5	-9.0	-27.0	-57.1
2820	2281	1827	1445	1131	876	0.6	0.9	0	-2.3	-6.3	-12.0	2.1	1.8	0	-3.3	-8.5	-25.0	-51.8
2873	2426	2036	1696	1402	1151	0.7	1.0	0	-2.5	-6.5	-12.2	2.2	1.9	0	-3.6	-8.4	-24.4	-49.6
2913	2203	1635	1192	859	625	0.2	0	-1.8	-5.5	-11.2	-19.5	2.7	2.3	0	-4.4	-11.3	-34.4	-73.7
2913	2436	2023	1666	1362	1105	0.2	0	-1.6	-4.8	-9.7	-16.5	2.4	2.0	0	-3.7	-9.3	-27.0	-54.9
2837	2347	1924	1567	1268	1024	0.4	0	-2.2	-6.4	-12.7	-21.6	1.5	0	-3.5	-9.1	-17.2	-41.8	-79.9
2873	2421	2114	1799	1522	1280	0.1	0	-1.4	-4.3	-8.6	-14.6	2.1	1.8	0	-3.3	-8.2	-23.4	-47.0
2914	2504	2140	1819	1536	1290	0.2	0	-1.6	-4.7	-9.4	-15.8	2.3	1.9	0	-3.5	-8.8	-25.3	-50.8
2914	2472	2083	1744	1450	1198	-0.1	0	-1.3	-4.1	-8.6	-14.9	2.1	1.8	0	-3.5	-8.7	-25.5	-51.8
2360	1761	1288	929	673	508	0.4	0	-2.4	-7.1	-14.5	-25.0	1.6	0	-3.9	-10.5	-20.3	-51.7	-103.9
3605	2900	2314	1827	1424	1095	0.3	0.7	0	-1.8	-4.8	-9.3	2.6	2.9	2.1	0	-3.5	-15.4	-35.5
3501	3011	2578	2196	1859	1565	0.5	0.8	0	-2.1	-5.5	-10.4	1.9	1.6	0	-2.9	-7.3	-20.9	-41.9
3508	2927	2424	1993	1623	1314	0.2	0	-1.7	-4.9	-9.9	-16.9	2.5	2.0	0	-3.8	-9.5	-27.5	-56.1
3512	3073	2679	2325	2009	1728	0.1	0	-1.3	-3.9	-7.8	-13.2	1.9	1.6	0	-3.0	-7.4	-21.1	-42.2
3503	2983	2528	2129	1780	1478	-0.2	0	-1	-3.2	-6.8	-11.8	1.6	1.4	0	-2.8	-7.1	-20.7	-42.1
3315	2785	2325	1927	1584	1292	0.6	0.9	0	-2.3	-6.0	-11.5	2.1	1.7	0	-3.2	-8.0	-23.3	-47.4
2303	1779	1352	1012	749	558	0.3	0	-1.9	-5.7	-11.6	-19.9	2.8	2.3	0	-4.5	-11.5	-34.4	-73.0
2303	1845	1462	1143	886	685	0.3	0	-1.8	-5.4	-11.0	-18.8	2.7	2.2	0	-4.2	-10.7	-31.5	-65.5
2207	1639	1193	860	626	482	0.5	0	-2.6	-7.7	-15.6	-27.1	1.7	0	-4.2	-11.3	-21.9	-55.8	-112.0
1507	1096	794	591	469	397	1.0	0	-4.3	-12.6	-25.5	-43.7		0	-6.8	-18.3	-35.1	-88.2	-172.5
2418	1993	1627	1318	1060	851	0.3	0	-2.1	-6.1	-12.2	-20.8	1.4	0	-3.3	-8.8	-16.6	-40.4	77.4
2519	1898	1404	1022	742	554	0.3	0	-2.2	-6.5	-13.3	-22.9	1.5	0	-3.6	-9.6	-18.6	-47.1	-93.7
2648	2061	1581	1193	888	657	0.2	0	-1.6	-4.8	-9.8	-16.9	2.4	2.0	0	-3.8	-9.8	-29.3	-62.0
2648	2137	1705	1344	1048	810	0.2	0	-1.5	-4.5	-9.3	-15.9	2.3	1.9	0	-3.6	-9.1	-26.9	-55.7
2743	2066	1527	1109	799	587	0.3	0	-2.0	-5.9	-12.1	-20.9	2.9	2.4	0	-4.7	-12.1	-36.9	-79.1
2743	2288	1896	1557	1269	1028	0.2	0	-1.8	-5.2	-10.4	-17.7	2.6	2.1	0	-4.0	-9.9	-28.9	-58.8
2649	2182	1782	1441	1154	917	0.2	0	-1.5	-4.4	-9.0	-15.4	2.2	1.8	0	-3.5	-8.7	-25.5	-52.3
2723	2348	2015	1719	1459	1232	0.2	0	-1.7	-5.0	-10.1	-17.0	2.5	2.1	0	-3.8	-9.4	-26.9	-54.0
2744	2319	1947	1624	1344	1107	-0.1	0	-1.4	-4.5	-9.4	-16.2	2.3	1.9	0	-3.7	-9.4	-27.4	-55.7
2680	2303	1970	1674	1415	1190	-0.1	0	-1.3	-4.1	-8.6	-14.9	2.1	1.8	0	-3.4	-8.7	-25.1	-50.7
1911	1320	892	606	442	356	0.6	0	-3.1	-9.2	-19.0	-33.2	2.0	0	-5.1	-13.8	-27.1	-70.9	-144.3
1911	1320	892	606	442	356	0.6	0	-3.1	-9.2	-19.0	-33.2	2.0	0	-5.1	-13.8	-27.1	-70.9	-144.3
325	231	185	154	131	113	0	-6.3	-20.9	-44.9	-79.3	-125.1	0	-11.5	-32.3	-63.6	-106.3	-230.3	-413.3
2102	1463	993	671	476	375	0.5	0	-2.7	-8.2	-17.0	-29.8	1.8	0	-4.5	-12.4	-24.3	-63.8	-130.7
3890	3137	2505	1977	1539	1187	0.5	0.9	0	-2.3	-6.1	-11.6	2.0	1.7	0	-3.2	-8.2	-24.3	-50.4
3862	3306	2816	2384	2005	1677	1.2	1.3	0	-2.7	-7.1	-12.9	2.7	2.1	0	-3.6	-9.4	-25.0	-49.9
3929	3363	2863	2422	2037	1703	-0.1	0	-1.3	-4.2	-8.8	-15.3	2.1	1.8	0	-3.5	-8.9	-25.7	-52.1
2820	2178	1656	1241	925	697	0.3	0	-2.1	-6.2	-12.7	-21.9	1.4	0	-3.4	-9.2	-17.7	-44.4	-87.9
1812	1203	791	551	431	360	0.9	0	-4.1	-12.1	-25.1	-43.9	2.7	0	-6.7	-18.3	-35.8	-92.8	-185.5
2688	1985	1434	1022	732	550	0.4	0	-2.3	-7.0	-14.3	-24.7	1.6	0	-3.8	-10.4	-20.1	-51.2	-102.3
2591	2028	1571	1210	937	745	0.6	0	-3.0	-8.7	-17.4	-30.0	2.0	0	-4.7	-12.4	-23.7	-58.4	-112.9
1175	715	454	337	274	229	0	-2.4	-9.1	-21.0	-39.2	-64.3	0	-5.5	-16.2	-33.1	-57.0	-128.3	-235.8
2753	2093	1563	1151	844	633	0.4	0	-2.2	-6.5	-13.3	-23.0	1.5	0	-3.6	-9.7	-18.6	-47.2	-94.1
2150	1506	1034	714	527	427	0.6	0	-3.2	-9.5	-19.5	-33.8	2.1	0	-5.2	-14.1	-27.4	-70.1	-138.1
2005	1506	1126	852	676	568	0.9	0	-4.1	-12.0	-24.0	-40.9	2.7	0	-6.5	-17.2	-32.7	-80.6	-154.1
4337	3510	2812	2228	1747	1361	0.2	0	-1.7	-5.1	-10.3	-17.6	2.5	2.1	0	-3.9	-10.0	-29.4	-60.7
4263	3426	2723	2141	1669	1300	0.3	0	-2.0	-5.9	-11.9	-20.3	2.9	2.4	0	-4.5	-11.5	-33.8	-70.1
4263	3139	2262	1602	1138	844	0.3	0	-2.2	-6.5	-13.5	-23.4	1.5	0	-3.6	-9.8	-19.1	-49.1	-99.5
538	399	324	273	233	201	0	-6.7	-22.2	-47.3	-83.2	-130.8	0	-12.1	-33.9	-66.4	-110.6	-238.3	-425.6
987	802	674	587	525	476	0	-4.7	-15.4	-32.7	-57.2	-89.3	0	-8.4	-23.4	-45.6	-75.2	-158.8	-277.4
1164	670	460	361	295	245	0	-3.7	-13.3	-29.8	-54.2	-87.3	0	-7.7	-22.4	-44.9	-76.1	-168.0	-305.8
1650	988	638	484	395	332	0	-2.7	-10.2	-23.6	-44.2	-73.3	0	-6.1	-18.1	-37.4	-65.1	-150.3	-282.5
629	449	360	300	254	217	0	-6.5	-21.6	-46.3	-81.8	-129.1	0	-11.8	-33.3	-65.5	-109.5	-237.4	-426.2
2355	1815	1355	1015	810	680	0	-2.4	-8.2	-17.6	-31.4	-51.5	0	-4.6	-12.8	-25.4	-44.3	-95.5	–
4620	3689	2924	2308	1839	1496	0.7	0	-3.3	-9.6	-19.2	-32.5	2.2	0	-5.2	-13.6	-25.8	-63.2	-121.7
4712	3547	2640	1970	1516	1239	0.8	0	-3.5	-10.3	-20.8	-35.6	2.4	0	-5.6	-14.9	-28.5	-71.5	-140.4

Reloading

For addresses and phone numbers of manufacturers and distributors included in this section, turn to *DIRECTORY OF MANUFACTURERS AND SUPPLIERS* at the back of the book.

HORNADY BULLETS

RIFLE BULLETS

17 CALIBER (.172)

25 gr. HP
#1710

22 CALIBER (.222)

40 gr. Jet
#2210

22 CALIBER (.223)

45 gr. Hornet
#2220

22 CALIBER (.224)

45 gr. BEE
#2229

45 gr. Hornet
#2230

50 gr. SXSP
#2240

50 gr. SP
#2245

22 CALIBER MATCH

52 gr. BTHP
#2249

22 CALIBER MATCH

53 gr. HP
#2250

55 gr. SXSP
#2260

55 gr. SP
#2265

55 gr. SP w c
#2266

55 gr. FMJ-BT w/c
#2267

60 gr. SP
#2270

60 gr. HP
#2275

22 CALIBER MATCH

68 gr. BTHP
#2278

22 CALIBER (.227)

70 gr. SP
#2280

6MM CALIBER (.243)

70 gr. SP
#2410

70 gr. SXSP
#2415

75 gr. HP
#2420

---

80 gr. FMJ
#2430

80 gr. SP Single Shot
Pistol   #2435

87 gr. SP
#2440

87 gr. BTHP
#2442

100 gr. SP
#2450
InterLock

100 gr. BTSP
#2453
InterLock

100 gr. RN
#2455
InterLock

25 CALIBER (.257)

60 gr. FP
#2510

75 gr. HP
#2520

87 gr. SP
#2530

100 gr. SP
#2540
InterLock

117 gr. RN
#2550
InterLock

117 gr. BTSP
#2552
InterLock

120 gr. HP
#2560
InterLock

6.5MM CALIBER (.264)

100 gr. SP
#2610

129 gr. SP
#2620
InterLock

140 gr. SP
#2630
InterLock

6.5MM CALIBER MATCH

140 gr. BTHP
#2633

160 gr. RN
#2640
InterLock

270 CALIBER (.277)

100 gr. SP
#2710

---

110 gr. HP
#2720

130 gr. SP
#2730
InterLock

140 gr. BTSP
#2735
InterLock

150 gr. SP
#2740
InterLock

150 gr. RN
#2745
InterLock

7MM CALIBER (.284)

100 gr. HP
#2800

120 gr. SP
#2810

120 gr. SP
Single Shot Pistol
#2811

120 gr. HP
#2815

139 gr. SP
#2820
InterLock

139 gr. FP
#2822
InterLock

139 gr. BTSP
#2825
InterLock

154 gr. SP
#2830
InterLock

154 gr. RN
#2835
InterLock

7MM MATCH

162 gr. BTHP
#2840

162 gr. BTSP
#2845
InterLock

175 gr. SP
#2850
InterLock

175 gr. RN
#2855
InterLock

HORNADY BULLETS

RIFLE BULLETS

30 CALIBER (.308)

100 gr. SJ
#3005

110 gr. SP
#3010

110 gr. RN
#3015

110 gr. FMJ
#3017

130 gr. SP
#3020

130 gr. SP
Single Shot Pistol
#3021

150 gr. SP
#3031
InterLock

150 gr. BTSP
#3033
InterLock

150 gr. RN (30-30)
#3035
InterLock

150 gr. FMJ-BT
#3037

165 gr. SP
#3040
InterLock

165 gr. BTSP
#3045
InterLock

30 CALIBER NATIONAL MATCH

168 gr. BTHP
#3050

170 gr. FP (30-30)
#3060
InterLock

180 gr. SP
#3070
InterLock

180 gr. BTSP
#3072
InterLock

180 gr. RN
#3075
InterLock

30 CALIBER MATCH

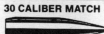
190 gr. BTHP
#3080

190 gr. BTSP
#3085
InterLock

220 gr. RN
#3090
InterLock

7.62 x 39 (.311)

123 gr. SP
#3140

123 gr. FMJ
#3147

303 CAL. and 7.7 JAP (.312)

150 gr. SP
#3120
InterLock

174 gr. RN
#3130
InterLock

32 SPECIAL (.321)

170 gr. FP
#3210
InterLock

8MM CALIBER (.323)

125 gr. SP
#3230

150 gr. SP
#3232
InterLock

170 gr. RN
#3235
InterLock

220 gr. SP
#3238
InterLock

338 CALIBER (.338)

200 gr. SP
#3310
InterLock

200 gr. FP
(33 Win.)
#3315
InterLock

225 gr. SP
#3320
InterLock

250 gr. RN
#3330
InterLock

250 gr. SP
#3335
Interlock

348 CALIBER (.348)

200 gr. FP
#3410
InterLock

35 CALIBER (.358)

180 gr. SP
Single Shot Pistol
#3505

200 gr. SP
#3510
InterLock

200 gr. RN
#3515
InterLock

250 gr. SP
#3520
Interlock

250 gr. RN
#3525
InterLock

375 CALIBER (.375)

220 gr. FP
(375 Win.)
#3705
InterLock

*270 gr. SP
#3710
InterLock

*270 gr. RN
#3715
InterLock

*300 gr. RN
#3720
InterLock

300 gr. BTSP
#3725
Interlock

*300 gr. FMJ-RN
#3727

416 CALIBER (.416)

NEW
340 gr. BTSP
#4163

400 gr. FMJ
#4167

400 gr. RN
#4165
Interlock

44 CALIBER (.430)

*265 gr. FP
#4300
InterLock

HORNADY BULLETS

RIFLE/PISTOL BULLETS

45 CALIBER (.458)

*300 gr. HP
#4500

*350 gr. RN
#4502
InterLock

*500 gr. RN
#4504
InterLock

*500 gr. FMJ-RN
#4507

750 gr. BTHP
#5165

PISTOL BULLETS

25 CALIBER (.251)

35 gr. HPXTP
#35450

50 gr. FMJ-RN
#3545

32 CALIBER (.311)

71 gr. FMJ-RN
#3200

32 CALIBER (.312)

85 gr. HP/XTP
#32050

100 gr. HP/XTP
#32070

9MM CALIBER (.355)

90 gr. HP/XTP
#35500

100 gr. FMJ
#3552

115 gr. HP/XTP
#35540

115 gr. FMJ-RN
#3555

124 gr. FMJ-FP
#3556

124 gr. FMJ-RN
#3557

124 gr. HP XTP
#35571

---

147 gr. HP/XTP
#35580

147 gr. FMJ
#3559

38 CALIBER (.357)

110 gr. HP/XTP
#35700

125 gr. HP/XTP
#35710

125 gr. FP/XTP
#35730

140 gr. HP/XTP
#35740

158 gr. HP/XTP
#35750

158 gr. FP/XTP
#35780

NEW
160 gr. CL-SIL
#3572

NEW
180 gr. CL-SIL
#3577

180 gr. JHP/XTP
#35771

10MM CALIBER (.400)

155 gr. HP/XTP
#40000

180 gr. HP/XTP
#40040

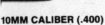
180 gr. FMJ-FP
#40041

200 gr. FMJ-FP
#4007

200 gr. HP/XTP
#40060

41 CALIBER (.410)

210 gr. HP/XTP
#41000

---

210 gr. CL-SIL
#4105

44 CALIBER (.430)

180 gr. HP/XTP
#44050

200 gr. HP/XTP
#44100

240 gr. HP/XTP
#44200

NEW
240 gr. CL-SIL
#4425

300 gr. HP/XTP
#44280

45 CALIBER (.451)

185 gr. HP/XTP
#45100

45 CALIBER MATCH
185 gr. SWC
#4513

200 gr. HP/XTP
#45140

45 CALIBER MATCH
200 gr. FMJ-C/T
#4515

230 gr. JHP/XTP
#45160

230 gr. FMJ-RN
#4517

230 gr. FMJ-FP
#4518

45 CALIBER (.452)

250 gr. Long
Colt HP/XTP
#45200

---

300 gr. HP/XTP
#45230

LEAD PISTOL BULLETS

32 CALIBER (.314)

90 gr. HBWC
#3252
*#1002

90 gr. SWC
#3250
*#1000

9MM CALIBER (.355)

124 gr. LRN
#3567
*#1005

38 CALIBER (.358)

148 gr. BBWC
#3580
*#1010

148 gr. HBWC
#3582
*#1020

148 gr. DEWC
*#1030

158 gr. RN
#3586
*#1050

158 gr. SWC
#3588
*#1040

158 gr. SWC/HP
#3589
*#1042

10MM CALIBER (.400)

180 gr. SWC
#1080

44 CALIBER (.430)

240 gr. SWC
#4430
*#1110

240 gr. SWC/HP
#4431
*#1111

45 CALIBER (.452)

200 gr. SWC
#4526
*#1210

200 gr. L-C/T
#4528
*#1220

230 gr. LRN
#4530
*#1230

NOSLER BULLETS

HANDGUN

Caliber/Diameter		Bullet Weight and Style	Sectional Density	Ballistic Coefficient	Part Number
9mm/.355"		90 Gr. Hollow Point	.102	.086	42050
		115 Gr. Full Metal Jacket	.130	.103	42059
		115 Gr. Hollow Point 250 Quantity Bulk Pack	.130	.110	43009 44848
38/.357"		125 Gr. Hollow Point 250 Quantity Bulk Pack	.140	.143	42055 44840
		150 Gr. Soft Point	.168	.153	42056
		150 Gr. IPSC 250 Quantity Bulk Pack	.168	.157	44839
		158 Gr. Hollow Point 250 Quantity Bulk Pack	.177	.182	42057 44841
		180 Gr. Silhouette NEW 250 Quantity Bulk Pack	.202	.210	42058 44851
10mm/.400"		135 Gr. Hollow Point NEW 250 Quantity Bulk Pack	.121	.093	44838 44852
		150 Gr. Hollow Point	.134	.106	44849
		170 Gr. Hollow Point	.152	.137	44844
		180 Gr. Hollow Point	.161	.147	44837
41/.410"		210 Gr. Hollow Point	.178	.170	43012
44/.429"		200 Gr. Hollow Point 250 Quantity Bulk Pack	.155	.151	42060 44846
		240 Gr. Soft Point	.186	.177	42068
		240 Gr. Hollow Point 250 Quantity Bulk Pack	.186	.173	42061 44842
		300 Gr. Hollow Point	.233	.206	42069
45/.451"		185 Gr. Hollow Point 250 Quantity Bulk Pack	.130	.142	42062 44847
		230 Gr. Full Metal Jacket	.162	.183	42064

HANDGUN

Caliber/Diameter		Bullet Weight and Style	Sectional Density	Ballistic Coefficient	Part Number
45 Colt/.451"		250 Gr. Hollow Point	.176	.177	43013

BALLISTIC TIP®

Caliber/Diameter		Bullet Weight and Style	Sectional Density	Ballistic Coefficient	Part Number
22/.224"		50 Gr. Spitzer (Orange Tip)	.142	.238	39522
		55 Gr. Spitzer (Orange Tip)	.157	.267	39526
6mm/.243"		70 Gr. Spitzer (Purple Tip)	.169	.310	39532
		95 Gr. Spitzer (Purple Tip)	.230	.379	39534
25/.257"		85 Gr. Spitzer (Blue Tip)	.183	.331	43004
		100 Gr. Spitzer (Blue Tip)	.216	.393	43005
6.5mm/.264"		100 Gr. Spitzer (Brown Tip)	.205	.350	43008
		120 Gr. Spitzer (Brown Tip)	.246	.458	43007
270/.277"		130 Gr. Spitzer (Yellow Tip)	.242	.433	39589
		140 Gr. Spitzer (Yellow Tip)	.261	.456	43983
		150 Gr. Spitzer (Yellow Tip)	.279	.496	39588
7mm/.284"		120 Gr. Spitzer (Red Tip)	.213	.417	39550
		140 Gr. Spitzer (Red Tip)	.248	.485	39587
		150 Gr. Spitzer (Red Tip)	.266	.493	39586
30/.308"		125 Gr. Spitzer (Green Tip)	.188	.366	43980
		150 Gr. Spitzer (Green Tip)	.226	.435	39585
		165 Gr. Spitzer (Green Tip)	.248	.475	39584
		180 Gr. Spitzer (Green Tip)	.271	.507	39583
338/.338"		200 Gr. Spitzer (Maroon Tip)	.250	.414	39595

NOSLER BULLETS

SOLID BASE® BOATTAIL

Caliber/Diameter	Bullet Weight and Style	Sectional Density	Ballistic Coefficient	Part Number
22/.224"	45 Gr. Hornet	.128	.144	35487
22/.224"	52 Gr. Hollow Point Match	.148	.224	25857
22/.224"	55 Gr. Spitzer w/cannelure	.157	.261	16339
22/.224"	60 Gr. Spitzer	.171	.266	30323
6mm/.243"	100 Gr. Spitzer	.242	.388	30390
25/.257"	120 Gr. Spitzer	.260	.446	30404
270/.277"	130 Gr. Spitzer	.242	.420	30394
7mm/.284"	NEW 120 Gr. Flat Point	.213	.195	41722
7mm/.284"	140 Gr. Spitzer	.248	.461	29599
30/.308"	150 Gr. Spitzer	.226	.393	27583
30/.308"	165 Gr. Spitzer	.248	.428	27585
30/.308"	180 Gr. Spitzer	.271	.491	27587

PARTITION®

Caliber/Diameter	Bullet Weight and Style	Sectional Density	Ballistic Coefficient	Part Number
6mm/.243"	85 Gr. Spitzer	.206	.315	16314
6mm/.243"	95 Gr. Spitzer	.230	.365	16315
6mm/.243"	100 Gr. Spitzer	.242	.384	35642
25/.257"	100 Gr. Spitzer	.216	.377	16317
25/.257"	115 Gr. Spitzer	.249	.389	16318
25/.257"	120 Gr. Spitzer	.260	.391	35643
6.5mm/.264"	125 Gr. Spitzer	.256	.449	16320
6.5mm/.264"	140 Gr. Spitzer	.287	.490	16321

PARTITION®

Caliber/Diameter	Bullet Weight and Style	Sectional Density	Ballistic Coefficient	Part Number
270/.277"	130 Gr. Spitzer	.242	.416	16322
270/.277"	150 Gr. Spitzer	.279	.465	16323
270/.277"	160 Gr. Semi Spitzer	.298	.434	16324
7mm/.284"	140 Gr. Spitzer	.248	.434	16325
7mm/.284"	150 Gr. Spitzer	.266	.456	16326
7mm/.284"	160 Gr. Spitzer	.283	.475	16327
7mm/.284"	175 Gr. Spitzer	.310	.519	35645
30/.308"	150 Gr. Spitzer	.226	.387	16329
30/.308"	165 Gr. Spitzer	.248	.410	16330
30/.308"	170 Gr. Round Nose	.256	.252	16333
30/.308"	180 Gr. Spitzer	.271	.474	16331
30/.308"	180 Gr. Protected Point	.271	.361	25396
30/.308"	200 Gr. Spitzer	.301	.481	35626
30/.308"	220 Gr. Semi Spitzer	.331	.351	16332
8mm/.323"	200 Gr. Spitzer	.274	.426	35277
338/.338"	210 Gr. Spitzer	.263	.400	16337
338/.338"	225 Gr. Spitzer	.281	.454	16336
338/.338"	250 Gr. Spitzer	.313	.473	35644
35/.358"	225 Gr. Spitzer	.251	.430	44800
35/.358"	250 Gr. Spitzer	.279	.446	44801
375/.375"	260 Gr. Spitzer	.264	.314	44850
375/.375"	300 Gr. Spitzer	.305	.398	44845

SIERRA BULLETS

RIFLE BULLETS

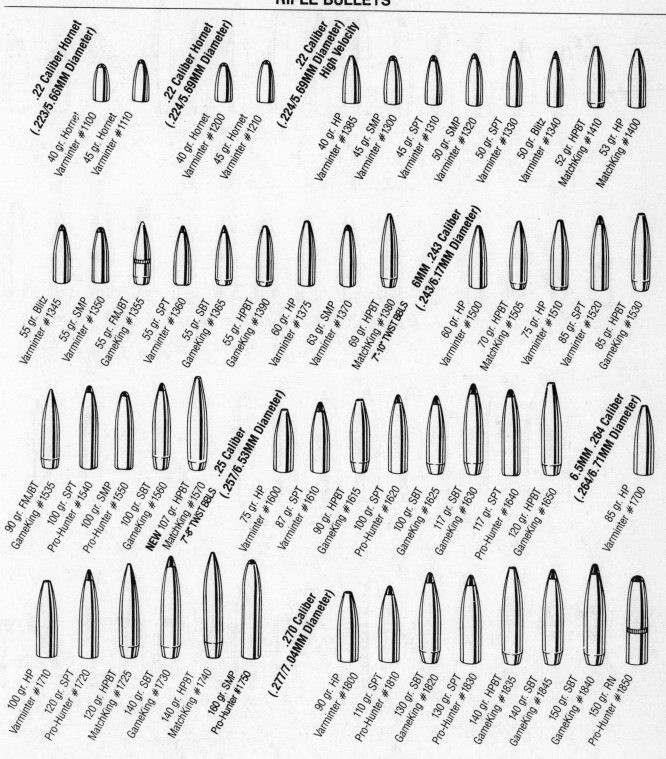

.22 Caliber Hornet (.223/5.66MM Diameter)
- 40 gr. Hornet Varminter #1100
- 45 gr. Hornet Varminter #1110

.22 Caliber Hornet (.224/5.69MM Diameter)
- 40 gr. Hornet Varminter #1200
- 45 gr. Hornet Varminter #1210

.22 Caliber (.224/5.69MM Diameter) High Velocity
- 40 gr. HP Varminter #1385
- 45 gr. SMP Varminter #1300
- 45 gr. SPT Varminter #1310
- 45 gr. SMP Varminter #1320
- 50 gr. SPT Varminter #1330
- 50 gr. Blitz Varminter #1340
- 52 gr. HPBT MatchKing #1410
- 53 gr. HP MatchKing #1400

- 55 gr. Blitz Varminter #1345
- 55 gr. SMP Varminter #1350
- 55 gr. FMJBT GameKing #1355
- 55 gr. SPT Varminter #1360
- 55 gr. SBT GameKing #1365
- 55 gr. HPBT GameKing #1390
- 60 gr. HP Varminter #1375
- 63 gr. SMP Varminter #1370
- 69 gr. HPBT MatchKing #1380 **7-10 TWST BBLS**

6MM .243 Caliber (.243/6.17MM Diameter)
- 60 gr. HP Varminter #1500
- 70 gr. HPBT MatchKing #1505
- 75 gr. HP Varminter #1510
- 85 gr. SPT Varminter #1520
- 85 gr. HPBT GameKing #1530

- 90 gr. FMJBT GameKing #1535
- 100 gr. SPT Pro-Hunter #1540
- 100 gr. SMP Pro-Hunter #1550
- 100 gr. SBT GameKing #1560
- **NEW** 107 gr. HPBT MatchKing #1570 **7-8 TWST BBLS**

.25 Caliber (.257/6.53MM Diameter)
- 75 gr. HP Varminter #1600
- 87 gr. SPT Varminter #1610
- 90 gr. HPBT GameKing #1615
- 100 gr. SPT Pro-Hunter #1620
- 100 gr. SBT GameKing #1625
- 117 gr. SBT GameKing #1630
- 117 gr. SPT Pro-Hunter #1640
- 120 gr. HPBT GameKing #1650

6.5MM .264 Caliber (.264/6.71MM Diameter)
- 85 gr. HP Varminter #1700

- 100 gr. HP Varminter #1710
- 120 gr. SPT Pro-Hunter #1720
- 120 gr. HPBT MatchKing #1725
- 140 gr. SBT GameKing #1730
- 140 gr. HPBT MatchKing #1740
- 160 gr. SMP Pro-Hunter #1750

.270 Caliber (.277/7.04MM Diameter)
- 90 gr. HP Varminter #1800
- 110 gr. SPT Pro-Hunter #1810
- 130 gr. SBT GameKing #1820
- 130 gr. SPT Pro-Hunter #1830
- 140 gr. HPBT GameKing #1835
- 140 gr. SBT GameKing #1845
- 150 gr. SBT GameKing #1840
- 150 gr. RN Pro-Hunter #1850

SIERRA BULLETS

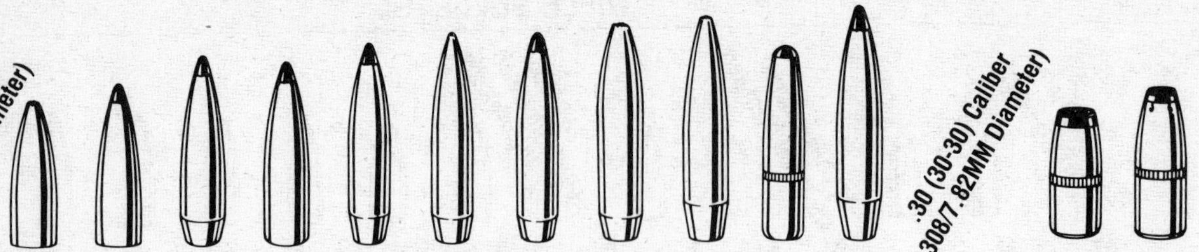

7MM .284 Caliber (.284/7.21MM Diameter)

100 gr. HP Varminter #1895
120 gr. SPT Pro-Hunter #1900
140 gr. SBT GameKing #1905
140 gr. SPT Pro-Hunter #1910
150 gr. SBT GameKing #1913
150 gr. HPBT MatchKing #1915
160 gr. SBT GameKing #1920
160 gr. HPBT GameKing #1925
168 gr. HPBT MatchKing #1930
170 gr. RN Pro-Hunter #1950
175 gr. SBT GameKing #1940

.30 (30-30) Caliber (.308/7.82MM Diameter)

125 gr. HP Pro-Hunter #2020
150 gr. FN Pro-Hunter #2000 POWER JACKET

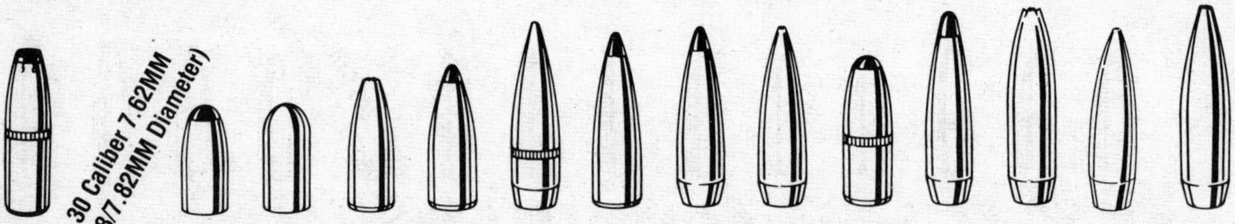

170 gr. FN Pro-Hunter #2010 POWER JACKET

.30 Caliber 7.62MM (.308/7.82MM Diameter)

110 gr. RN Pro-Hunter #200
110 gr. FMJ Pro-Hunter #2105
110 gr. HP Varminter #2110
125 gr. SPT Pro-Hunter #2120
150 gr. FMJBT GameKing #2115
150 gr. SPT Pro-Hunter #2130
150 gr. SBT GameKing #2125
150 gr. HPBT MatchKing #2190
150 gr. RN Pro-Hunter #2135
165 gr. SBT GameKing #2145
165 gr. HPBT GameKing #2140
155 gr. HPBT 1992 PALMA MatchKing #2155
168 gr. HPBT MatchKing #2200

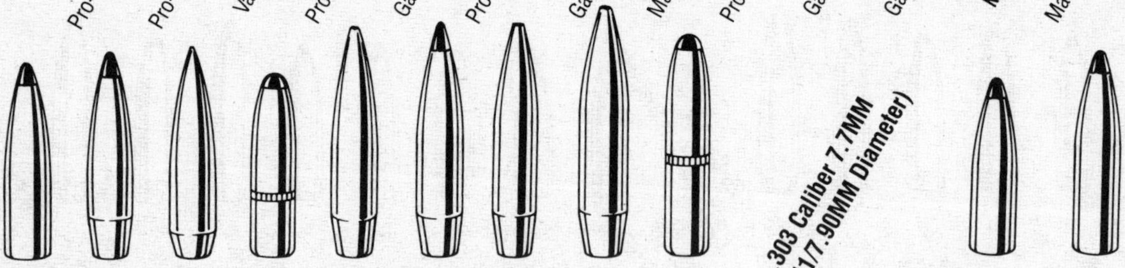

180 gr. SPT Pro-Hunter #2150
180 gr. SBT GameKing #2160
180 gr. HPBT MatchKing #2220
180 gr. RN Pro-Hunter #2170
190 gr. HPBT MatchKing #2210
200 gr. SBT GameKing #2165
200 gr. HPBT MatchKing #2230
220 gr. HPBT MatchKing #2240
220 gr. RN Pro-Hunter #2180

.303 Caliber 7.7MM (.311/7.90MM Diameter)

150 gr. SPT Pro-Hunter #2300
180 gr. SPT Pro-Hunter #2310

8MM (.323/8.20MM Diameter)

150 gr. SPT Pro-Hunter #2400
175 gr. SPT Pro-Hunter #2410
220 gr. SBT GameKing #2420

.338 Caliber (.338/8.59MM Diameter)

250 gr. SBT GameKing #2600

.35 Caliber (.358/9.09MM Diameter)

200 gr. RN Pro-Hunter #2800
225 gr. SBT GameKing #2850

.375 Caliber (.375/9.53MM Diameter)

200 gr. FN Pro-Hunter #2900 POWER JACKET
NEW 250 gr. SBT GameKing #2950
300 gr. SBT GameKing #3000

.45 Caliber (45.70) (.458/11.63MM Diameter)

300 gr. HP Pro-Hunter #8900

SIERRA BULLETS

HANDGUN BULLETS

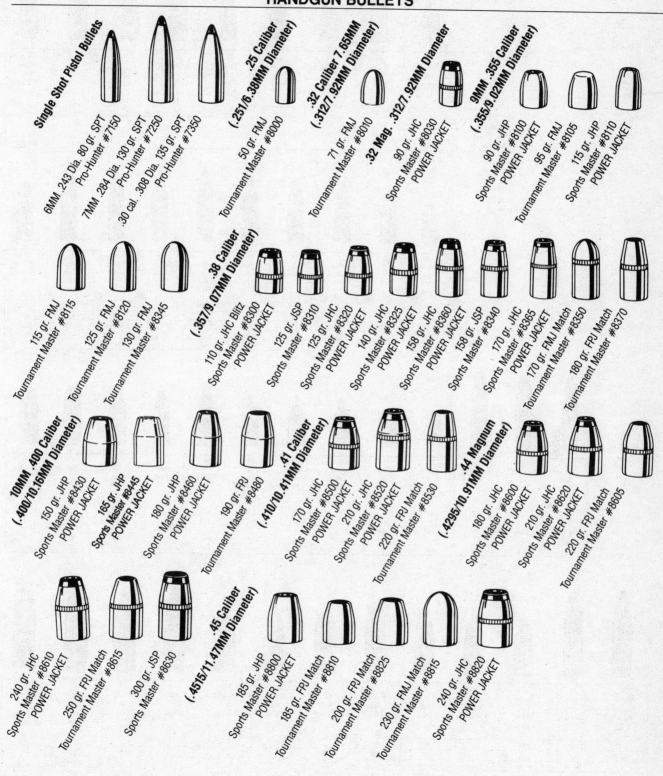

Single Shot Pistol Bullets

6MM .243 Dia. 80 gr. SPT Pro-Hunter #7150
7MM .284 Dia. 130 gr. SPT Pro-Hunter #7250
.30 cal. .308 Dia. 135 gr. SPT Pro-Hunter #7350

.25 Caliber (.251/6.38MM Diameter)

50 gr. FMJ Tournament Master #8000

.32 Caliber 7.65MM (.312/7.92MM Diameter)

71 gr. FMJ Tournament Master #8010

.32 Mag. .312/7.92MM Diameter

90 gr. JHC Sports Master #8030 POWER JACKET

9MM .355 Caliber (.355/9.02MM Diameter)

90 gr. JHP Sports Master #8100 POWER JACKET
95 gr. FMJ Tournament Master #8105
115 gr. JHP Sports Master #8110 POWER JACKET

115 gr. FMJ Tournament Master #8115
125 gr. FMJ Tournament Master #8120
130 gr. FMJ Tournament Master #8345

.38 Caliber (.357/9.07MM Diameter)

110 gr. JHC Blitz Sports Master #8300 POWER JACKET
125 gr. JSP Sports Master #8310
125 gr. JHC Sports Master #8320 POWER JACKET
140 gr. JHC Sports Master #8325 POWER JACKET
158 gr. JHC Sports Master #8360 POWER JACKET
158 gr. JSP Sports Master #8340
170 gr. JHC Sports Master #8365 POWER JACKET
170 gr. FMJ Match Tournament Master #8350
180 gr. FPJ Match Tournament Master #8370

10MM .400 Caliber (.400/10.16MM Diameter)

150 gr. JHP Sports Master #8430 POWER JACKET
165 gr. JHP Sports Master #8445 POWER JACKET
180 gr. JHP Sports Master #8460 POWER JACKET
190 gr. FPJ Tournament Master #8480

.41 Caliber (.410/10.41MM Diameter)

170 gr. JHC Sports Master #8500 POWER JACKET
210 gr. JHC Sports Master #8520 POWER JACKET
220 gr. FPJ Match Tournament Master #8530

.44 Magnum (.4295/10.91MM Diameter)

180 gr. JHC Sports Master #8600 POWER JACKET
210 gr. JHC Sports Master #8620 POWER JACKET
220 gr. FPJ Match Tournament Master #8605

240 gr. JHC Sports Master #8610 POWER JACKET
250 gr. FPJ Match Tournament Master #8615
300 gr. JSP Sports Master #8630

.45 Caliber (.4515/11.47MM Diameter)

185 gr. JHP Sports Master #8800 POWER JACKET
185 gr. FPJ Match Tournament Master #8810
200 gr. FPJ Match Tournament Master #8825
230 gr. FMJ Match Tournament Master #8815
240 gr. JHC Sports Master #8820 POWER JACKET

SPEER RIFLE BULLETS

Bullet Caliber & Type	22 Spire Soft Point	22 Spitzer Soft Point	22 Spire Soft Point	22 Spitzer Soft Point	22 218 Bee Flat Soft Point w/Cann.	22 Spitzer Soft Point	22 "TNT" Hollow Point	22 Hollow Point	22 Hollow Point B.T. Match
Diameter	.223"	.223"	.224"	.224"	.224"	.224"	.224"	.224"	.224"
Weight (grs.)	40	45	40	45	46	50	50	52	52
Ballist. Coef.	0.145	0.166	0.144	0.167	0.094	0.231	0.223	0.225	0.253
Part Number	1005	1011	1017	1023	1024	1029	1030	1035	1036

	25-20 Win. Flat Soft Point w/Cann.	25 Spitzer Soft Point	25 Spitzer Soft Point	25 Hollow Point	25 Spitzer Soft Point B.T.	25 Spitzer Soft Point B.T.	25 Spitzer Soft Point	6.5mm Spitzer Soft Point	6.5mm Spitzer Soft Point	270 Hollow Point
	.257"	.257"	.257"	.257"	.257"	.257"	.257"	.263"	.263"	.277"
	75	87	100	100	100	120	120	120	140	100
	0.133	0.300	0.369	0.255	0.393	0.435	0.410	0.433	0.496	0.225
	1237	1241	1405	1407	1408	1410	1411	1435	1441	1447
	100	100	100	100	100	100	100	100	100	100

	7mm Spitzer Soft Point	7mm Mag-Tip™ Soft Point	7mm Mag-Tip™ Soft Point	30 Round Soft Point Plinker™	30 Hollow Point	30 Round Soft Point	30 Carbine Round FMJ	30 Spire Soft Point	30 "TNT" Hollow Point	30 Hollow Point	30 Flat Soft Point	30 Flat Soft Point	30 Round Soft Point
	.284"	.284"	.284"	.308"	.308"	.308"	.308"	.308"	.308"	.308"	.308"	.308"	.308"
	160	160	175	100	110	110	110	110	125	130	130	150	150
	0.502	0.354	0.385	0.124	0.136	0.144	0.179	0.273	0.326	0.263	0.248	0.268	0.266
	1635	1637	1641	1805	1835	1845	1846	1855	1986	2005	2007	2011	2017
	100	100	100	100	100	100	100	100	**NEW!**	100	100	100	100

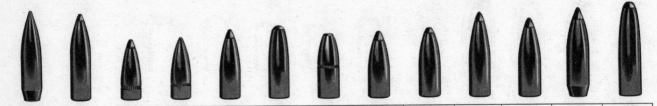

	30 Match Hollow Point B.T.	30 Spitzer Soft Point	303 Spitzer Soft Point w/Cann.	303 (7.62x39) FMJ w/Cann.	303 Spitzer Soft Point	303 Round Soft Point	32 Flat Soft Point	8mm Spitzer Soft Point	8mm Semi-Spitzer Soft Point	8mm Spitzer Soft Point	338 Spitzer Soft Point	338 Spitzer Soft Point B.T.	338 Semi-Spitzer Soft Point
	.308"	.308"	.311"	.311"	.311"	.311"	.321"	.323"	.323"	.323"	.338"	.338"	.338"
	190	200	125	123	150	180	170	150	170	200	200	225	275
	0.540	0.556	0.292	0.256	0.411	0.328	0.297	0.369	0.354	0.411	0.448	0.484	0.456
	2080	2211	2213	2214	2217	2223	2259	2277	2283	2285	2405	2406	2411

SPEER RIFLE BULLETS

22 FMJ B.T. w/Cann.	22 Spitzer Soft Point	22 Spitzer S.P. w/Cann.	22 FMJ B.T. w/Cann.	22 Semi-Spitzer Soft Point	6mm "TNT" Hollow Point	6mm Hollow Point	6mm Spitzer Soft Point	6mm Spitzer Soft Point B.T.	6mm Spitzer Soft Point	6mm Spitzer Soft Point B.T.	6mm Round Soft Point	6mm Spitzer Soft Point
.224"	.224"	.224"	.224"	.224"	.243"	.243"	.243"	.243"	.243"	.243"	.243"	.243"
55	55	55	62	70	70	75	80	85	90	100	105	105
0.269	0.255	0.241	0.307	0.214	0.282	0.234	0.365	0.404	0.385	0.430	0.207	0.443
1044	1047	1049	1050	1053	1206	1205	1211	1213	1217	1220	1223	1229
100	100	100	100	100	100	100	100	100	100	100	100	100

NEW!

270 Spitzer Soft Point	270 Spitzer Soft Point B.T.	270 Spitzer Soft Point	270 Spitzer Soft Point B.T.	270 Spitzer Soft Point	7mm Hollow Point	7mm Spitzer Soft Point	7mm Spitzer Soft Point	7mm Spitzer Soft Point B.T.	7mm Spitzer Soft Point B.T.	7mm Spitzer Soft Point	7mm Match Hollow Point B.T.	7mm Spitzer Soft Point B.T.
.277"	.277"	.277"	.277"	.277"	.284"	.284"	.284"	.284"	.284"	.284"	.284"	.284"
100	130	130	150	150	115	120	130	130	145	145	145	160
0.319	0.449	0.408	0.496	0.481	0.257	0.386	0.394	0.411	0.502	0.457	0.465	0.556
1453	1458	1459	1604	1605	1617	1620	1623	1624	1628	1629	1631	1634
100	100	100	100	100	100	100	100	100	100	100	100	100

30 FMJ B.T. w/Cann.	30 Spitzer Soft Point B.T.	30 Spitzer Soft Point	30 Mag-Tip™ Soft Point	30 Round Soft Point	30 Spitzer Soft Point B.T.	30 Spitzer Soft Point	30 Match Hollow Point B.T.	30 Flat Soft Point	30 Round Soft Point	30 Spitzer Soft Point B.T.	30 Spitzer Soft Point	30 Mag-Tip™ Soft Point
.308"	.308"	.308"	.308"	.308"	.308"	.308"	.308"	.308"	.308"	.308"	.308"	.308"
150	150	150	150	165	165	165	168	170	180	180	180	180
0.425	0.423	0.389	0.301	0.274	0.477	0.433	0.480	0.304	0.304	0.540	0.483	0.352
2018	2022	2023	2025	2029	2034	2035	2040	2041	2047	2052	2053	2059
100	100	100	100	100	100	100	100	100	100	100	100	100

35 Flat Soft Point	35 Flat Soft Point	35 Spitzer Soft Point	9.3mm Semi-Spitzer Soft Point	375 Semi-Spitzer Soft Point	375 Spitzer Soft Point B.T.	45 Flat Soft Point	45 Flat Soft Point	50 BMG FMJ
.358"	.358"	.358"	.366"	.375"	.375"	.458"	.458"	.510"
180	220	250	270	235	270	350	400	647
0.245	0.316	0.446	0.361	0.317	0.429	0.232	0.214	0.701
2435	2439	2453	2459	2471	2472	2478***	2479	2491
100	50	50	50	50	50	50	50	20

SPEER HANDGUN BULLETS

GOLD DOT HOLLOW POINT BULLETS

Caliber & Type	9mm Gold Dot Hollow Point	9mm Gold Dot Hollow Point	9mm Gold Dot Hollow Point	40/10mm Gold Dot Hollow Point	40/10mm Gold Dot Hollow Point	45 Gold Dot Hollow Point	45 Gold Dot Hollow Point
Diameter	.355"	.355"	.355"	.400"	.400"	.451"	.451"
Weight (grs.)	115	124	147	155	180	185	230
Ballist. Coef.	0.125	0.134	0.164	0.123	0.143	0.109	0.143
Part Number	3994	3998	4002	4400	4406	4470	4483
Box Count	100	100	100	100	100	100	100
	NEW!	NEW!	NEW!	NEW!	NEW!	NEW!	NEW!

HANDGUN BULLETS—JACKETED

Caliber & Type	25 TMJ	32 JHP	9mm JHP	38 JHP	38 JHP-SWC	38 TMJ	38 JHP	38 JSP	38 JSP-SWC	38 TMJ-Sil.	38 TMJ-Sil.
Diameter	.251"	.312"	.355"	.357"	.357"	.357"	.357"	.357"	.357"	.357"	.357"
Weight (grs.)	50	100	88	140	146	158	158	158	160	180	200
Ballist. Coef.	0.110	0.167	0.095	0.152	0.159	0.173	0.158	0.150	0.170	0.230	0.236
Part Number	3982	3981	4000	4203	4205	4207	4211	4217	4223	4229	4231
Box Count	100	100	100	100	100	100	100	100	100	100	100

Caliber & Type	40/10mm HP	40/10mm TMJ	40/10mm TMJ	41 AE HP	41 JHP-SWC	45 TMJ	45 Mag. JHP	45 SP	50 AE HP
Diameter	.400"	.400"	.400"	.410"	.410"	.451"	.451"	.451"	.500"
Weight (grs.)	180	180	200	180	200	230	260	300	325
Ballist. Coef.	0.188	0.143	0.208	0.138	0.113	0.153	0.183	0.199	0.149
Part Number	4401	4402	4403	4404	4405	4480	4481	4485	4495
Box Count	100	100	100	100	100	100	100	50	50

HANDGUN BULLETS—LEAD

Caliber	32 HB-WC	9mm RN	38 BB-WC	38 HB-WC	38 SWC	38 HP-SWC	38 RN	44 SWC
Diameter	.314"	.356"	.358"	.358"	.358"	.358"	.358"	.430"
Weight (grs.)	98	125	148	148	158	158	158	240
Part Number	4600*	4601*	4605*	4617*	4623*	4627*	4647	4660*

SPEER BULLETS

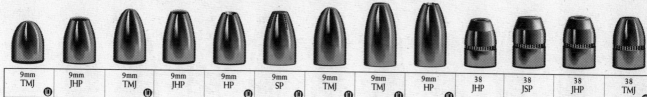

9mm TMJ	9mm JHP	9mm TMJ	9mm JHP	9mm HP	9mm SP	9mm TMJ	9mm TMJ	9mm HP	38 JHP	38 JSP	38 JHP	38 TMJ
.355"	.355"	.355"	.355"	.355"	.355"	.355"	.355"	.355"	.357"	.357"	.357"	.357"
95	100	115	115	115	124	124	147	147	110	125	125	125
0.131	0.111	0.177	0.118	0.099	0.115	0.114	0.208	0.190	0.122	0.140	0.135	0.146
4001	3983	3995*	3996	4003	3997	4004	4006	3990	4007	4011	4013	4015
100	100	100	100	100	100	100	100	100	100	100	100	100

41 JSP-SWC	41 TMJ-Sil.	44 Mag. JHP	44 JHP-SWC	44 JSP-SWC	44 Mag. JHP	44 Mag. JSP	44 TMJ-Sil.	44 Mag. SP	45 TMJ-Match	45 TMJ-Match	45 JHP	45 Mag. JHP
.410"	.410"	.429"	.429"	.429"	.429"	.429"	.429"	.429"	.451"	.451"	.451"	.451"
220	210	200	225	240	240	240	240	300	185	200	200	225
0.137	0.216	0.122	0.146	0.157	0.165	0.164	0.206	0.213	0.090	0.129	0.138	0.169
4417	4420	4425	4435	4447	4453	4457	4459	4463	4473	4475	4477	4479
100	100	100	100	100	100	100	100	50	100	100	100	100

45 SWC	45 RN	45 SWC
.452"	.452"	.452"
200	230	250
4677*	4690*	4683*

PLASTIC INDOOR AMMO

		Bullets	Cases
No. Per Box		50	50
Part No.	38 Cal.	8510	8515
	44 Cal.	8520	8525
	45 Cal.	8530	See Note

Note: Shown are 38 bullet and 38 case. 45 bullet is used with regular brass case.

SHOT SHELL CAPSULES

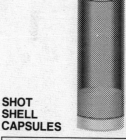

Empty Capsules with Base Plugs		
No. Per Box		50
Part No.	38/357	8780
	44	8782

SPEER BIG GAME BULLETS

GRAND SLAM

Bullet Caliber & Type	6mm GS Soft Point	25 GS Soft Point	270 GS Soft Point	270 GS Soft Point	7mm GS Soft Point	7mm GS Soft Point	7mm GS Soft Point	30 GS Soft Point	30 GS Soft Point
Diameter	.243"	.257"	.277"	.277"	.284"	.284"	.284"	.308"	.308"
Weight (grs.)	100	120	130	150	145	160	175	150	165
Ballist. Coef.	0.351	0.328	0.345	0.385	0.327	0.387	0.465	0.305	0.393
Part Number	1222	1415	1465	1608	1632	1638	1643	2026	2038
Box Count	50	50	50	50	50	50	50	50	50

Bullet Caliber & Type	30 GS Soft Point	338 GS Soft Point	35 GS Soft Point	375 GS Soft Point
Diameter	.308"	.338"	.358"	.375"
Weight (grs.)	180	250	250	285
Ballist. Coef.	0.416	0.431	0.335	0.354
Part Number	2063	2408	2455	2473
Box Count	50	50	50	50

AFRICAN GRAND SLAM

Bullet Caliber & Type	338 AGS Tungsten Solid	375 AGS Tungsten Solid	416 AGS Soft Point	416 AGS Tungsten Solid	45 AGS Soft Point	45 AGS Tungsten Solid
Diameter	338"	.375"	.416"	.416"	.458"	.458"
Weight (grs.)	275	300	400	400	500	500
Ballist. Coef.	0.291	0.258	0.381	0.262	0.285	0.277
Part Number	2414	2474	2475	2476	2485	2486
Box Count	25	25	25	25	25	25

HERCULES SMOKELESS SPORTING POWDERS

Twelve types of Hercules smokeless sporting powders are available to the handloader. These have been selected from the wide range of powders produced for factory loading to provide at least one type that can be used efficiently and economically for each type of ammunition. These include:

BULLSEYE® A high-energy, quick-burning powder especially designed for pistol and revolver. The most popular powder for .38 special target loads. Can also be used for 12 gauge-1 oz. shotshell target loads.

RED DOT® The preferred powder for light-to-medium shotshells; specifically designed for 12-gauge target loads. Can also be used for handgun loads.

GREEN DOT® Designed for 12-gauge medium shotshell loads. Outstanding in 20-gauge skeet loads.

UNIQUE® Has an unusually broad application from light to heavy shotshell loads. As a handgun powder, it is our most versatile, giving excellent performance in many light to medium-heavy loads.

HERCO® A long-established powder for high velocity shotshell loads. Designed for heavy and magnum 10-, 12-, 16- and 20-gauge loads. Can also be used in high-performance handgun loads.

BLUE DOT® Designed for use in magnum shotshell loads, 10-, 12-, 16-, 20- and 28-gauge. Also provides top performance with clean burning in many magnum handgun loads.

HERCULES 2400® For use in small-capacity rifle cartridges and .410-Bore shotshell loads. Can also be used for large-caliber magnum handgun cartridges.

RELODER® SERIES Designed for use in center-fire rifle cartridges. Reloder 7, 12, 15, 19 and 22 provide the right powder for the right use. From small capacity to magnum loads. All of them deliver high velocity, clean burn, round-to-round consistency, and economy.

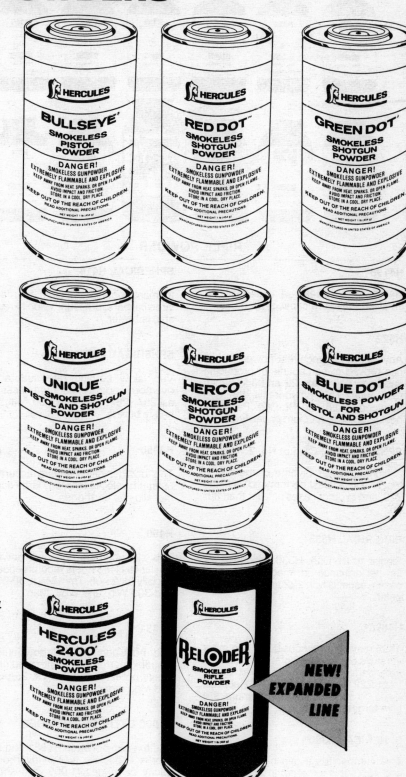

PACKAGING

POWDER	1-LB CANISTERS	4-LB CANISTERS	5-LB CANISTERS	8-LB KEG
Bullseye	●	●		●
Red Dot	●	●		●
Green Dot	●	●		●
Unique	●	●		●
Herco	●	●		●
Blue Dot	●		●	
Hercules 2400	●	●		●
Reloder Series	●		●	

HODGDON SMOKELESS POWDER

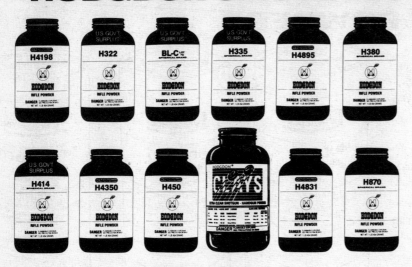

RIFLE POWDER

H4198

H4198 was developed especially for small and medium capacity cartridges.

H322

Any extruded bench rest powder which has proved to be capable of producing fine accuracy in the 22 and 308 bench rest guns. This powder fills the gap between H4198 and BL-C(2). Performs best in small to medium capacity cases.

SPHERICAL BL-C®, Lot No. 2

A highly popular favorite of the bench rest shooters. Best performance is in the 222, and in other cases smaller than 30/06.

SPHERICAL H335®

Similar to BL-C(2), H335 is popular for its performance in medium capacity cases, especially in 222 and 308 Winchester.

H4895®

4895 may well be considered the most versatile of all propellants. It gives desirable performance in almost all cases from 222 Rem. to 458 Win. Reduced loads, to as low as 3/5 of maximum, still give target accuracy.

SPHERICAL H380®

This number fills a gap between 4320 and 4350. It is excellent in 22/250, 220 Swift, the 6mm's, 257 and 30/06.

SPHERICAL H414®

In many popular medium to medium-large calibers, pressure velocity relationship is better.

SPHERICAL H870®

Very slow burning rate adaptable to overbore capacity Magnum cases such as 257, 264, 270 and 300 Mags with heavy bullets.

H4350

This powder gives superb accuracy at optimum velocity for many large capacity metallic rifle cartridges.

H450

This slow-burning spherical powder is similar to H4831. It is recommended especially for 25-06, 7mm Mag., 30-06, 270 and 300 Win. and Wby. Mag.

H4831®

The most popular of all powders. Outstanding performance with medium and heavy bullets in the 6mm's, 25/06, 270 and Magnum calibers.

H1000 EXTRUDED POWDER

Fills the gap between H4831 and H870. Works especially well in overbore capacity cartridges (1,000-yard shooters take note).

SHOTGUN AND PISTOL POWDER

HP38

A fast pistol powder for most pistol loading. Especially recommended for mid-range 38 specials.

CLAYS

A powder developed for 12-gauge clay target shooters. Also performs well in many handgun applications, including .38 Special, .40 S&W and 45 ACP. Perfect for 1¹/₈ and 1 oz. loads.
Now available:
Universal Clays. Loads nearly all of the straight-wall pistol cartridges as well as 12 ga. 1¹/₄ oz. thru 28 ga. ³/₄ oz. target loads.
International Clays. Perfect for 12 and 20 ga. autoloaders who want reduced recoil.

HS-6 and HS-7

HS-6 and HS-7 for Magnum field loads are unsurpassed, since they do not pack in the measure. They deliver uniform charges and are dense to allow sufficient wad column for best patterns.

H110

A spherical powder made especially for the 30 M1 carbine. H110 also does very well in 357, 44 Spec., 44 Mag. or .410 ga. shotshell. Magnum primers are recommended for consistent ignition.

H4227

An extruded powder similar to H110, it is the fastest burning in Hodgdon's line. Recommended for the 22 Hornet and some specialized loading in the 45-70 caliber. Also excellent in magnum pistol and .410 shotgun.

IMR SMOKELESS POWDERS

SHOTSHELL POWDER

Hi-Skor 700-X Double-Base Shotshell Powder. Specifically designed for today's 12-gauge components. Developed to give optimum ballistics at minimum charge weight (which means more reloads per pounds of powder). 700-X is dense, easy to load, clean to handle and loads uniformly.

PB Shotshell Powder. Produces exceptional 20 and 28-gauge skeet reloads; preferred by many in 12-gauge target loads, it gives 3-dram equivalent velocity at relatively low chamber pressures.

Hi-Skor 800-X Shotshell Powder. An excellent powder for 12-gauge field loads and 20 and 28-gauge loads.

SR-4756 Powder. Great all-around powder for target and field loads.

SR-7625. A fast-growing favorite for reloading target as well as light and heavy field loads in 4 gauges. Excellent velocity-chamber pressure.

IMR-4227 Powder. Can be used effectively for reloading .410-gauge shotshell ammunition.

RIFLE POWDER

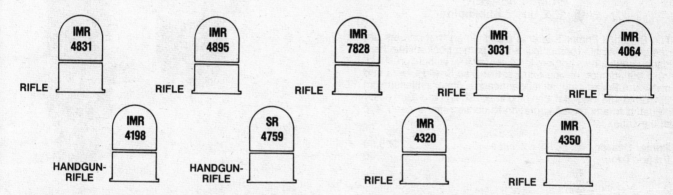

IMR-3031 Rifle Powder. Specifically recommended for medium-capacity cartridges.

IMR-4064 Rifle Powder. Has exceptionally uniform burning qualities when used in medium and large-capacity cartridges.

IMR-4198. Made the Remington 222 cartridge famous. Developed for small and medium-capacity cartridges.

IMR-4227 Rifle Powder. Fastest burning of the IMR Series. Specifically designed for the 22 Hornet class of cartridges.

SR-4759. Brought back by shooter demand. Available for cast bullet loads.

IMR-4320. Recommended for high-velocity cartridges.

IMR-4350 Rifle Powder. Gives unusually uniform results when loaded in Magnum cartridges.

IMR-4831. Produced as a canister-grade handloading powder. Packaged in 1 lb. canister, 8 lb. caddy and 20 lb. kegs.

IMR-4895 Rifle Powder. The time-tested standard for caliber 30 military ammunition; slightly faster than IMR-4320. Loads uniformly in all powder measures. One of the country's favorite powder.

IMR-7828 Rifle Powder. The slowest burning DuPont IMR canister powder, intended for large-capacity and magnum-type cases with heavy bullets.

PISTOL POWDER

PB Powder. Another powder for reloading a wide variety of centerfire handgun ammunition.

IMR-4227 Powder. Can be used effectively for reloading Magnum handgun ammunition.

Hi-Skor 700-X Powder. The same qualities that make it a superior powder contribute to its excellent performance in all the popular handguns.

Hi-Skor 800-X Powder. Good powder for heavier bullet handgun calibers.

SR-7625 Powder. For reloading a wide variety of centerfire handgun ammunition.

SR-4756. Clean burning with uniform performance. Can be used in a variety of handgun calibers.

FORSTER/BONANZA RELOADING TOOLS

CO-AX® BENCH REST® RIFLE DIES

Bench Rest Rifle Dies are glass hard for long wear and minimum friction. Interiors are polished mirror smooth. Special attention is given to headspace, tapers and diameters so that brass will not be overworked when resized. Sizing die has an elevated expander button which is drawn through the neck of the case at the moment of the greatest mechanical advantage of the press. Since most of the case neck is still in the die when expanding begins, better alignment of case and neck is obtained.

Bench Rest® Seating Die is of the chamber type. The bullet is held in alignment in a close-fitting channel. The case is held in a tight-fitting chamber. Both bullet and case are held in alignment while the bullet is being seated. Cross-bolt lock ring included at no charge.

Bench Rest® Die Set	**$58.00**
Full Length Sizer	26.50
Bench Rest Seating Die	32.00

PRIMER SEATER
With "E-Z-Just" Shellholder

The Bonanza Primer Seater is designed so that primers are seated Co-Axially (primer in line with primer pocket). Mechanical leverage allows primers to be seated fully without crushing. With the addition of one extra set of Disc Shell Holders and one extra Primer Unit, all modern cases, rim or rimless, from 222 up to 458 Magnum, can be primed. Shell holders are easily adjusted to any case by rotating to contact rim or cannelure of the case.

Primer Seater	**$56.00**
Primer Tube	5.00

PRIMER SEATER

CO-AX® INDICATOR

Bullets will not leave a rifle barrel at a uniform angle unless they are started uniformly. The Co-Ax Indicator provides a reading of how closely the axis of the bullet corresponds to the axis of the cartridge case. The Indicator features a spring-loaded plunger to hold cartridges against a recessed, adjustable rod while the cartridge is supported in a "V" block. To operate, simply rotate the cartridge with the fingers; the degree of misalignment is transferred to an indicator which measures in one-thousandths.

Price: Without dial	**$46.20**
Indicator Dial	54.60

FORSTER/BONANZA RELOADING TOOLS

ULTRA BULLET SEATER DIE

Forster's new Ultra Die is available in 51 calibers, more than any other brand of micrometer-style seater. Adjustment is identical to that of a precision micrometer—the head is graduated to .001″ increments with .025″ bullet movement per revolution. The cartridge case, bullet and seating stem are completely supported and perfectly aligned in a close-fitting chamber before and during the bullet seating operation.
Price: **$49.50**

CO-AX LOADING PRESS B-2

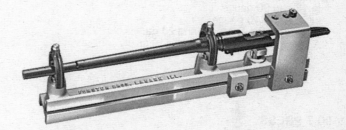

UNIVERSAL SIGHT MOUNTING FIXTURE

This product fills the exacting requirements needed for drilling and tapping holes for the mounting of scopes, receiver sights, shotgun beads, etc. The fixture handles any single-barrel gun—bolt-action, lever-action or pump-action—as long as the barrel can be laid into the "V" blocks of the fixture. Tubular guns are drilled in the same manner by removing the magazine tube. The fixture's main body is made of aluminum casting. The two "V" blocks are adjustable for height and are made of hardened steel ground accurately on the "V" as well as the shaft.
Price: **$312.00**

CO-AX® LOADING PRESS MODEL B-2

Designed to make reloading easier and more accurate, this press offers the following features: Snap-in and snap-out die change • Positive spent primer catcher • Automatic self-acting shell holder • Floating guide rods • Working room for right- or left-hand operators • Top priming device seats primers to factory specifications • Uses any standard $7/8″ \times 14$ dies • No torque on the head • Perfect alignment of die and case • Three times the mechanical advantage of a "C" press
Price: **$248.00**

BENCH REST POWDER MEASURE

BENCH REST POWDER MEASURE

When operated uniformly, this measure will throw uniform charges from $2^{1/2}$ grains Bullseye to 95 grains #4320. No extra drums are needed. Powder is metered from the charge arm, allowing a flow of powder without extremes in variation while minimizing powder shearing. Powder flows through its own built-in baffle so that powder enters the charge arm uniformly.
Price: **$91.00**

HORNADY

APEX SHOTSHELL RELOADER

This new and versatile shotshell reloader has all the features of a progressive press along with the control, accuracy, easy operation and low price tag of a single-stage loader. You can load one shell at a time or seven shells at once, turning out a fully loaded shell with every pull of the handle. Other features include: extra-large shot hopper, short linkage arm, automatic dual-action crimp die, swing-out wad guide, and extra-long shot and powder feed tubes.

Apex Shotshell Reloader (Automatic)
In 12 and 20 gauge $375.00
In 28 and .410 gauge 414.00
Basic Die Set in 12 and 20 gauge 140.00
Basic Die Set in 28 and .410 gauge 179.50
Apex-91 Shotshell Reloader (Standard)
In 12 and 20 gauge 142.00
In 28 and .410 gauge 159.00
Automatic Die Set in 12 and 20 ga. 60.00
Automatic Die Set in 28 and .410 ga. 77.00

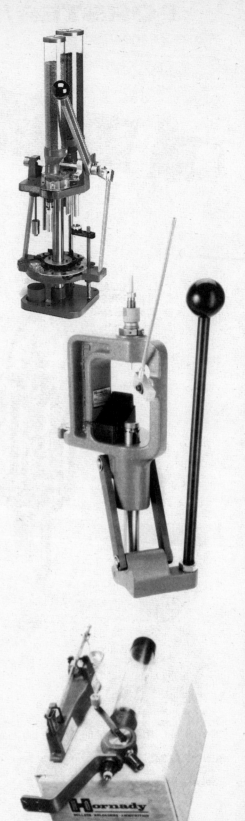

00-7 PRESS

- "Power-Pac" linkage multiplies lever-to-arm power.
- Frame of press angled 30° to one side, making the "O" area of press totally accessible.
- More mounting area for rock-solid attachment to bench.
- Special strontium-alloy frame provides greater stress resistance. Won't spring under high pressures needed for full-length resizing.

00-7 Press (does not include dies or shell holder) $105.50
00-7 Automatic Primer Feed (complete with large and small primer
tubes) 18.75

THE 00-7 PRESS PACKAGE
A reloading press complete with dies and shell holder

Expanded and improved to include Automatic Primer Feed. It sets you up to load many calibers and includes choice of a basic 00-7 complete with: • Set of New Dimension Dies • Primer catcher • Removable head shell holder • Positive Priming System • Automatic Primer Feed.

00-7 Package with Series I & II Dies (14 lbs.) $153.25
00-7 Package Series II Titanium Nitride (15 lbs.) 166.50
00-7 Kit with Series I & II Dies 314.95
00-7 Kit with Titanium Nitride Dies 329.00

THE HANDLOADER'S ACCESSORY PACK I

Here's everything you need in one money-saving pack. It includes: • Deluxe powder measure • Powder scale • Two non-static powder funnels • Universal loading block • Primer turning plate • Case lube • Chamfering and deburring tool • 3 case neck brushes • Large and small primer pocket cleaners • Accessory handle. Plus one copy of the *Hornady Handbook of Cartridge Reloading*.

Handloader's Accessory Pack I No. 030300 . . . . $169.25

HORNADY

TRIMMER PACKAGE

Combines Hornady's Case Trimmer with the new Metric Caliper and Steel Dial Caliper, which measures case and bullet lengths plus inside/outside diameters. Made from machined steel, the caliper provides extremely accurate measurements with an easy-to-read large dial gauge.

Trimmer Package $94.00

NEW DIMENSION RELOADING DIES

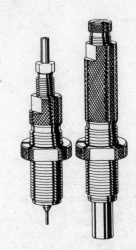

Features an Elliptical Expander that minimizes friction and reduces case neck stretch, plus the need for a tapered expander for "necking up" to the next larger caliber. Other recent design changes include a hardened steel decap pin that will not break, bend or crack even when depriming stubborn military cases. A bullet seater alignment sleeve guides the bullet and case neck into the die for in-line benchhrest alignment. All New Dimension Reloading Dies include: collar and collar lock to center expander precisely; one-piece expander spindle with tapered bottom for easy cartridge insertion; wrench flats on die body, Sure-Loc™ lock rings and collar lock for easy tightening; and built-in crimper.

New Dimension Reloading Dies:
Series I Two-die Rifle Set $22.90
Series I Three-die Rifle Set 25.50
Series II Three-die Pistol Set (w/Titanium Nitride) 34.35
Series III Two-die Rifle Set 29.85
Series IV Custom Die Set 52.65

PRO-JECTOR PRESS PACKAGE

- Includes Pro-Jector Press, set of New Dimension dies, automatic primer feed, brass kicker, primer catcher, shell plate, and automatic primer shut-off
- Just place case in shell plate, start bullet, pull lever and drop powder. Automatic rotation of shell plate prepares next round.
- Fast inexpensive changeover requires only shell plate and set of standard ⁷/₈ × 14 threaded dies.
- Primes automatically.
- Power-Pac Linkage assures high-volume production even when full-length sizing.
- Uses standard powder measures and dies.

Series I & II $370.20
Seriess II Titanium Nitride Dies 382.65
Extra Shell Plates 21.15
Pro-Jector Kit with Series I & II Dies 533.00
Kit Series II with Titanium Nitride Dies 545.30

MODEL 366 AUTO SHOTSHELL RELOADER

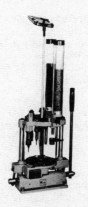

The 366 Auto features full-length resizing with each stroke, automatic primer feed, swing-out wad guide, three-stage crimping featuring Taper-Loc for factory tapered crimp, automatic advance to the next station and automatic ejection. The turntable holds 8 shells for 8 operations with each stroke. The primer tube filler is fast. The automatic charge bar loads shot and powder. Right- or left-hand operation; interchangeable charge bushings, die sets and Magnum dies and crimp starters for 6 point, 8 point and paper crimps.

Model 366 Auto Shotshell Reloader:
12, 20, 28 gauge or .410 bore $435.50
Model 366 Auto Die Set 86.50
Auto Advance 43.80
Swing-out Wad Guide & Shell Drop Combo $180.00

LYMAN BULLET SIZING EQUIPMENT

MAG 20 ELECTRIC FURNACE

The MAG 20 is a new furnace offering several advantages to cast bullet enthusiasts. It features a steel crucible of 20-pound capacity and incorporates a proven bottom-pour valve system and a fully adjustable mould guide. The improved design of the MAG 20 makes it equally convenient to use the bottom-pour valve, or a ladle. A new heating coil design reduces the likelihood of pour spout "freeze." Heat is controlled from "Off" to nominally 825° F by a calibrated thermostat which automatically increases temperature output when alloy is added to the crucible. A pre-heat shelf for moulds is attached to the back of the crucible. Availalbe for 100 V and 200 V systems.

Price: 110 V **$269.95**
220 V **270.00**

BULLET MAKING EQUIPMENT

Deburring Tool
Lyman's deburring tool can be used for chamfering or deburring of cases up to 45 caliber. For precise bullet seating, use the pointed end of the tool to bevel the inside of new or trimmed cases. To remove burrs left by trimming, place the other end of the deburring tool over the mouth of the case and twist. The tool's centering pin will keep the case aligned . . **$14.00**

Mould Handles
These large hardwood handles are available in three sizes single-, double- and four-cavity.
Single-cavity handles (for small block, black powder and specialty moulds; 12 oz.) **$24.95**
Double-cavity handles (for two-cavity and large-block single-cavity moulds; 12 oz.) **24.95**
Four-cavity handles (1 lb.) **28.95**

Rifle Moulds
All Lyman rifle moulds are available in double cavity only, except those moulds where the size of the bullet necessitates a single cavity (12 oz.) **$51.95**

Hollow-Point Bullet Moulds
Hollow-point moulds are cut in single-cavity blocks only and require single-cavity handles (9 oz.) **$51.95**

Shotgun Slug Moulds
Available in 12 or 20 gauge; do not require rifling. Moulds are single cavity only, cut on the larger double-cavity block and require double-cavity handles (14 oz.) **$51.95**

Pistols Moulds
Cover all popular calibers and bullet designs in double-cavity blocks and, on a limited basis, four-cavity blocks.
Double-cavity mould block **$51.95**
Four-cavity mould block **79.95**

Lead Casting Dipper
Dipper with cast-iron head. The spout is shaped for easy, accurate pouring that prevents air pockets in the finished bullet **$14.00**

Gas Checks
Gas checks are gilding metal caps which fit to the base of cast bullets. These caps protect the bullet base from the burning effect of hot powder gases and permit higher velocities. Easily seated during the bullet sizing operation. Only Lyman gas checks should be used with Lyman cast bullets.

22 through 35 caliber (per 1000) **$25.95**
375 through 45 caliber (per 1000) **29.95**
Gas check seater **7.95**

Lead Pot
The cast-iron pot allows the bullet caster to use any source of heat. Pot capacity is about 8 pounds of alloy and the flat bottom prevents tipping **$14.00**

Universal Decapping Die
Covers all calibers .22 through .45 (except .378 and .460 Weatherby). Can be used before cases are cleaned or lubricated. Requires no adjustment when changing calibers; fits all popular makes of $7/8 \times 14$ presses, single station or progressive, and is packaged with 10 replacement pins   **$11.50**

UNIVERSAL CARBIDE FOUR-DIE SET

Lyman's new 4-die carbide sets allow simultaneous neck expanding and powder charging. They feature specially designed hollow expanding plugs that utilize Lyman's 2-step neck-expansion system, while allowing powder to flow through the die into the cartridge case after expanding. Includes taper crimp die. All popular pistol calibers. **$49.95**

LYMAN RELOADING TOOLS

MAG TUMBLER

This new Mag Tumbler features an industrial strength motor and large 14-inch bowl design. With a working capacity of 2¾ gallons, it cleans more than 1,500 pistol cases in each cycle. The Mag Tumbler is also suitable for light industrial use in deburring and polishing metal parts. Available in 110V or 220V, with standard on/off switch.

Mag Tumbler $279.95
Mag AutoFlo 299.95

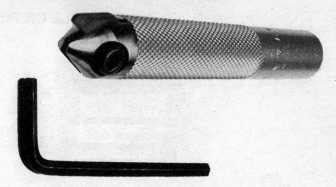

"INSIDE/OUTSIDE" DEBURRING TOOL

This unique new tool features an adjustable cutting blade that adapts easily to any rifle or pistol case from 22 caliber to 45 caliber with a simple hex wrench adjustment. Inside deburring is completed by a conical internal section with slotted cutting edges, thus providing uniform inside and outside deburring in one simple operation. The deburring tool is mounted on an anodized aluminum handle that is machine-knurled for a sure grip.

Deburring Tool $14.95

TUBBY TUMBLER

This popular tumbler now features a clear plastic "see thru" lid that fits on the outside of the vibrating tub. The Tubby has a polishing action that cleans more than 100 pistol cases in less than two hours. The built-in handle allows easy dumping of cases and media. An adjustable tab also allows the user to change the tumbling speed for standard or fast action.

Tubby Tumbler $79.95

MUZZLELOADERS' CASTING KIT

Designed especially to meet the needs of blackpowder shooters, this new kit features Lyman's combination round ball and maxi ball mould blocks. It also contains a combination double cavity mould, mould handle, mini-mag furnace, lead dipper, bullet lube, a user's manual and a cast bullet guide. Kits are available in 45, 50 and 54 caliber.

Muzzleloaders' Casting Kit $99.95

LYMAN RELOADING TOOLS

FOR RIFLE OR PISTOL CARTRIDGES

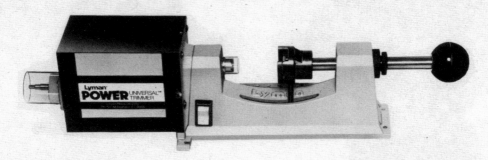

POWER CASE TRIMMER

The new Lyman Power Trimmer is powered by a fan-cooled electric motor designed to withstand the severe demands of case trimming. The unit, which features the Universal® Chuckhead, allows cases to be positioned for trimming or removed with fingertip ease. The Power Trimmer package includes Nine Pilot Multi-Pack. In addition to two cutter heads, a pair of wire end brushes for cleaning primer pockets are included. Other features include safety guards, on-off rocker switch, heavy cast base with receptacles for nine pilots, and bolt holes for mounting on a work bench. Available for 110 V or 220 V systems.

Prices: 110 V Model **$199.95**
220 V Model **210.00**

ACCULINE OUTSIDE NECK TURNER
(not shown)

To obtain perfectly concentric case necks, Lyman's Outside Neck Turner assures reloaders of uniform neck wall thickness and outside neck diameter. The unit fits Lyman's Universal Trimmer and AccuTrimmer. In use, each case is run over a mandrel, which centers the case for the turning operation. The cutter is carefully adjusted to remove a minimum amount of brass. Rate of feed is adjustable and a mechanical stop controls length of cut. Mandrels are available for calibers from .17 to .375; cutter blade can be adjusted for any diameter from .195″ to .405″.

Outside Neck Turner w/extra blade, 6 mandrels . . . **$29.95**
Outside Neck Turner only **19.95**
Individual Mandrels **4.50**

STARTER KIT

Includes "Orange Crusher" Press, loading block, case lube kit, primer tray, Model 500 scale, powder funnel and Lyman Reloading Handbook.

Starter Kit **$199.95**

LYMAN "ORANGE CRUSHER" RELOADING PRESS

The only press for rifle or pistol cartridges that offers the advantage of powerful compound leverage combined with a true magnum press opening. A unique handle design transfers power easily where you want it to the center of the ram. A 4½-inch press opening accommodates even the largest cartridges.

"Orange Crusher" Press:
With Priming Arm and Catcher **$109.95**

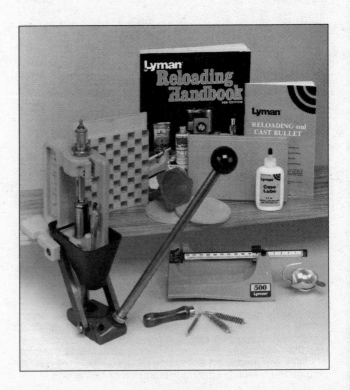

STARTER KIT

LYMAN RELOADING TOOLS

T-MAG TURRET RELOADING PRESS

With the T-Mag you can mount up to six different reloading dies on our turret. This means you can have all your dies set up, precisely mounted, locked in and ready to reload at all times. The T-Mag works with all $7/8 \times 14$ dies. The T-Mag turret with its quick-disconnect release system is held in rock-solid alignment by a $3/4$-inch steel stud.

Also featured is Lyman's Orange Crusher compound leverage system. It has a longer handle with a ball-type knob that mounts easily for right- or left-handed operation.

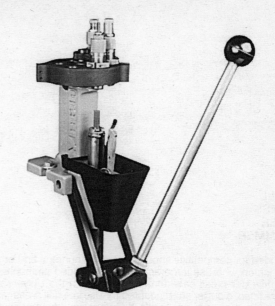

T-Mag Press w/Priming Arm & Catcher **$142.95**
    Extra Turret Head **19.95**

Also available:
EXPERT KIT that includes T-MAG Press, Universal Case Trimmer and pilot Multi-Pak, Model 500 powder scale and Model 50 powder measure, plus accessories.
    Available in calibers 9mm Luger, 38/357, 44 Mag., 45 ACP and 30-06 . . . . **$399.95**

ELECTRONIC SCALE MODEL LE: 1000

Accurate to $1/10$ grain, Lyman's new LE: 1000 measures up to 1000 grains of powder and easily converts to the gram mode for metric measurements. The push-botton automatic calibration feature eliminates the need for calibrating with a screwdriver. The scale works off a single 9V battery or AC power adaptor (included with each scale). Its compact design allows the LE: 1000 to be carried to the field easily. A sculpted carrying case is optional. 110 Volt or 220 Volt.

Model LE: 1000 Electronic Scale **$359.95**

PISTOL ACCUMEASURE

Lyman's Pistol AccuMeasure uses changeable brass rotors pre-drilled to drop precise charges of ball and flake pistol propellants (the tool is not intended for use with long grain IMR-type powders). Most of the rotors are drilled with two cavities for maximum accuracy and consistency. The brass operating handle, which can be shifted for left or right hand operation, can be removed. The Pistol AccuMeasure can be mounted on all turret and single station presses; it can also be hand held with no loss of accuracy.

Pistol AccuMeasure w/3-rotor starter kit **$33.95**

Also available:
AMMO HANDLER KIT that includes every tool
(except reloading press) needed to produce
high-quality ammunition **$174.95**
ROTOR SELECTION SET including 8 dual-cavity rotors and 4 single-cavity units. Enables reloaders to throw a variety of charges for all pistol calibers through 45 . . . . **$49.95**

LYMAN RELOADING TOOLS

DRILL PRESS CASE TRIMMER

Intended for competitive shooters, varmint hunters, and other sportsmen who use large amounts of reloaded ammunition, this new drill press case trimmer consists of the Universal™ Chuckhead, a cutter shaft adapted for use in a drill press, and two quick-change cutter heads. Its two major advantages are speed and accuracy. An experienced operator can trim several hundred cases in a hour, and each will be trimmed to a precise length.

Drill Press Case Trimmer $49.95

AUTO TRICKLER (not shown)

This unique device allows reloaders to trickle the last few grains of powder automatically into their scale powder pans. The Auto-Trickler features vertical and horizontal height adjustments, enabling its use with both mechanical and the new electronic scales. It also offers a simple push-button operation. The powder reservoir is easily removed for cleaning. Handles all conventional ball, stick or flare powder types.

Auto-Trickler $39.95

ACCU TRIMMER

Lyman's new Accu Trimmer can be used for all rifle and pistol cases from 22 to 458 Winchester Magnum. Standard shellholders are used to position the case, and the trimmer incorporates standard Lyman cutter heads and pilots. Mounting options include bolting to a bench, C-clamp or vise.

Accu Trimmer w/9-pilot multi-pak $42.95

UNIVERSAL TRIMMER WITH NINE PILOT MULTI-PACK

This trimmer with patented chuckhead accepts all metallic rifle or pistol cases, regardless of rim thickness. To change calibers, simply change the case head pilot. Other features include coarse and fine cutter adjustments, an oil-impregnated bronze bearing, and a rugged cast base to assure precision alignment and years of service. Optional carbide cutter available. Trimmer Stop Ring includes 20 indicators as reference marks.

Trimmer less pilots **$68.95**
Extra pilot (state caliber) 3.50
Replacement carbide cutter 46.95
Trimmer Multi-Pack (incl. 9 pilots: 22, 24, 27, 28/7mm, 30, 9mm, 35, 44 and 45A 73.95
Nine Pilot Multi-Pack 9.95

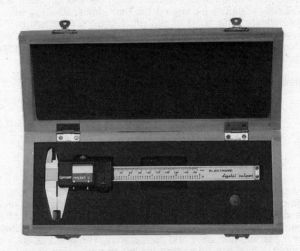

ELECTRONIC DIGITAL CALIPER

Lyman's new 6″ electronic caliper gives a direct digital readout for both inches and millimeters and can perform both inside and outside depth measurements. Its zeroing function allows the user to select zeroing dimensions and sort parts or cases by their plus or minus variation. The caliper works on a single, standard 1.5 volt silver oxide battery and comes with a fitted wooden storage case.

Electronic Caliper $99.95

MEC SHOTSHELL RELOADERS

MODEL 600 JR. MARK 5
$151.81

This single-stage reloader features a cam-action crimp die to ensure that each shell returns to its original condition. MEC's 600 Jr. Mark 5 can load 8 to 10 boxes per hour and can be updated with the 285 CA primer feed. Press is adjustable for 3″ shells. Die sets are available in all gauges at: **$57.00**

MODEL 650
$298.54

This reloader works on 6 shells at once. A reloaded shell is completed with every stroke. The MEC 650 does not resize except as a separate operation. Automatic Primer feed is standard. Simply fill it with a full box of primers and it will do the rest. Reloader has 3 crimping stations: the first one starts the crimp, the second closes the crimp, and the third places a taper on the shell. Available in 12, 16, 20 and 28 gauge and .410 bore. No die sets are available.

MODEL 8567 GRABBER
$428.28

This reloader features 12 different operations at all 6 stations, producing finished shells with each stroke of the handle. It includes a fully automatic primer feed and Auto-Cycle charging, plus MEC's exclusive 3-stage crimp. The "Power Ring" resizer ensures consistent, accurately sized shells without interrupting the reloading sequence. Simply put in the wads and shell casings, then remove the loaded shells with each pull of the handle. Optional kits to load 3″ shells and steel shot make this reloader tops in its field. Resizes high and low base shells. Available in 12, 16, 20, 28 gauge and .410 bore. No die sets are available.

MODEL 8120
SIZEMASTER
$228.75

Sizemaster's "Power Ring" collet resizer returns each base to factory specifications. This new generation resizing station handles brass or steel heads, both high and low base. An 8-fingered collet squeezes the base back to original dimensions, then opens up to release the shell easily. The E-Z Prime auto primer feed is standard equipment. Press is adjustable for 3″ shells and is available in 12, 16, 20, 28 gauge and .410 bore. Die sets are available at: **$85.26 ($100.00 in 10 ga.)**.

MEC RELOADING

MEC 8462 SPINDEX STAR CRIMP HEADS
(not shown)

Dual purpose 6 & 8 fold Spindex Kit in 12, 16 and 20 gauge. **$4.65**
In 10, 28 gauge and .410 bore 4.08

Additional MEC Accessories:
301L 13X BH & Cap Assembly **$3.99**
8300 Wad Finger Ptlc. 1.24
8042 Magnum Container 5.68
15CA E-Z Pak Assembly 6.99

E-Z PRIME "S"

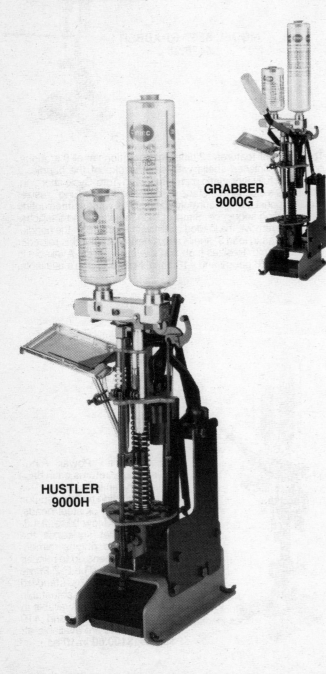

GRABBER 9000G

HUSTLER 9000H

E-Z PRIME "S" AND "V"
AUTOMATIC PRIMER FEEDS

From carton to shell with security, these primer feeds provide safe, convenient primer positioning and increase rate of production. Reduce bench clutter, allowing more free area for wads and shells.

- Primers transfer directly from carton to reloader, tubes and tube fillers
- Positive mechanical feed (not dependent upon agitation of press)
- Visible supply
- Automatic. Eliminate hand motion
- Less susceptible to damage
- Adapt to all domestic and most foreign primers with adjustment of the cover
- May be purchased separately to replace tube-type primer feed or to update your present reloader

E-Z Prime "S" (for Super 600, 650) or
E-Z Prime "V" (for 600 Jr. Mark V & VersaMEC) . . . **$37.07**

MEC 9000 SERIES SHOTSHELL RELOADER

MEC's 9000 Series features automatic indexing and finished shell ejection for quicker and easier reloading. The factory set speed provides uniform movement through every reloading stage. Dropping the primer into the reprime station no longer requires operator "feel." The reloader requires only a minimal adjustment from low to high brass domestic shells, any one of which can be removed for inspection from any station.

MEC 9000H Hustler **$1256.26**
MEC 9000G Grabber 520.00

MTM

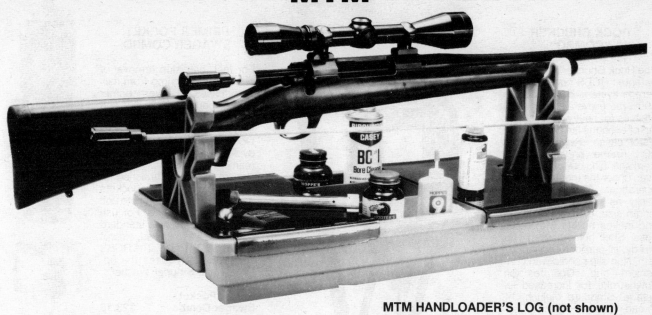

PORTABLE RIFLE MAINTENANCE CENTER

Holds rifles and shotguns for easy cleaning and maintenance (can also be used as a shooting rest). Features gun forks with built-in cleaning rod holders; sliding see-through dust covers; tough polypropylene material; fits conveniently on top of Case-Gard A-760.

Price: **$29.15**

50 ROUND HANDGUN AMMO BOXES

Designed with the shooter in mind, these 50-round ammo boxes feature a new "Step Design" on the partitions inside (for "E-Z" ammo extraction). The specially grooved lid is designed to match up with the feet on the bottom so that they nest into each other. Each box is supplied with its own label for recording custom loads.

Price: **$1.40**

MTM HANDLOADER'S LOG (not shown)

Space is provided for 1,000 entries covering date, range, group size or score, components, and conditions. Book is heavy-duty vinyl, reinforced 3-ring binder.

HL-74 . . . . **$9.50**
HL-50 (incl. 50 extra log sheets) **4.20**

CASE-GARD 100 AMMO CARRIER FOR SKEET AND TRAP (not shown)

The MTM™ Case-Gard® 100-round shotshell case carries 100 rounds in 2 trays; or 50 rounds plus 2 boxes of factory ammo; or 50 rounds plus sandwiches and insulated liquid container; or 50 round with room left for fired hulls. Features include:
* Recessed top handle for easy storage.
* High-impact material supports 300 pounds, and will not warp, split, expand or contract.
* Dustproof and rainproof.
* Living hinge guaranteed 3 years.
* Available in deep forest green.

S-100-12 (12 gauge) **$16.00**
S-100-20 (20 gauge) **16.00**

FUNNELS

MTM Benchrest Funnel Set is designed specifically for the bench-rest shooter. One fits 222 and 243 cases only; the other 7mm and 308 cases. Both can be used with pharmaceutical vials popular with bench-rest competitors for storage of pre-weighed charges. Funnel design prevents their rolling off the bench.

MTM Universal Funnel fits all calibers from 222 to 45.
UF-1 . . . . **$2.87**

Patented MTM Adapt 5-in-1 Funnel Kit includes funnel, adapters for 17 Rem., 222 Rem. and 30 through 45. Long drop tube facilitates loading of maximum charges: 222 to 45.
AF-5 . . . . **$4.14**

RCBS RELOADING TOOLS

ROCK CHUCKER "COMBO"

The Rock Chucker Press, with patented RCBS compound leverage system, delivers up to 200% more leverage than most presses for heavy-duty reloading of even the largest rifle and pistol cases. Rugged, Block "O" Frame prevents press from springing out of alignment even under the most strenuous operations. It case-forms as easily as most presses full-length size; it full-length sizes and makes bullets with equal ease. Shell holders snap into sturdy, all-purpose shell holder ram. Non-slip handle with convenient grip. Operates on downstroke for increased leverage. Standard $7/8$-inch$\times14$ thread.

Rock Chucker Press
(Less dies) $131.50

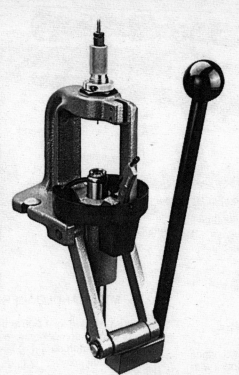

PRIMER POCKET SWAGER COMBO

For fast, precision removal of primer pocket crimp from military cases. Leaves primer pocket perfectly rounded and with correct dimensions for seating of American Boxer-type primers. Will not leave oval-shaped primer pocket that reaming produces. Swager Head Assemblies furnished for large and small primer pockets no need to buy a complete unit for each primer size. For use with all presses with standard $7/8$-inch$\times14$ top thread, except RCBS "A-3" Press. The RCBS "A-2" Press requires the optional Case Stripper Washer.

Primer Pocket Swager Combo $23.15

ROCK CHUCKER MASTER RELOADING KIT

For reloaders who want the best equipment, the Rock Chucker Master Reloading Kit includes all the tools and accessories needed. Included are the following: • Rock Chucker Press • RCBS 505 Reloading Scale • Speer Reloading Manual #11 • Uniflow Powder Measure • RCBS Rotary Case Trimmer-2 • deburring tool • case loading block • Primer Tray-2 • Automatic Primer Feed Combo • powder funnel • case lube pad • case neck brushes • fold-up hex ket set.

Rock Chucker Master Reloading Kit $349.74

PRIMER POCKET BRUSH COMBO

A slight twist of this tool thoroughly cleans residue out of primer pockets. Interchangeable stainless steel brushes for large and small primer pockets attach easily to accessory handle.

Primer Pocket Brush Combo $12.07

RCBS RELOADING TOOLS

RELOADER SPECIAL-5

This RCBS Reloader Special-5 Press is the ideal setup to get started reloading your own rifle and pistol ammo from 12 gauge shotshells and the largest Magnums down to 22 Hornets. This press develops ample leverage and pressure to perform all reloading tasks including: (1) resizing cases their full length; (2) forming cases from one caliber into another; (3) making bullets. Rugged Block "O" Frame, designed by RCBS, prevents press from springing out of alignment even under tons of pressure. Frame is offset 30° for unobstructed front access, and is made of 48,000 psi aluminum alloy. Compound leverage system allows you to swage bullets, full-length resize cases, form 30-06 cases into other calibers. Counter-balanced handle prevents accidental drop. Extra-long ram-bearing surface minimizes wobble and side play. Standard 7/8-inch-14 thread accepts all popular dies and reloading accessories.

Reloader Special-5
(Less dies) **$102.40**

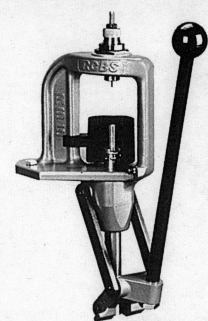

RELOADER SPECIAL-5

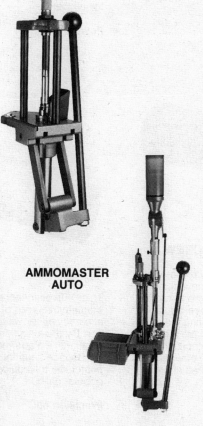

AMMOMASTER

AMMOMASTER AUTO

AMMOMASTER RELOADING SYSTEM

The AmmoMaster offers the handloader the freedom to configure a press to his particular needs and preferences. It covers the complete spectrum of reloading, from single stage through fully automatic progressive reloading, from .32 Auto to .50 caliber. The **AmmoMaster Auto** has all the features of a five-station press.

AmmoMaster **$177.08**
AmmoMaster Auto **403.64**

RELOADING SCALE MODEL 5-0-5

This 511-grain capacity scale has a three-poise system with widely spaced, deep beam notches to keep them in place. Two smaller poises on right side adjust from 0.1 to 10 grains, larger one on left side adjusts in full 10-grain steps. The first scale to use magnetic dampening to eliminate beam oscillation, the 5-0-5 also has a sturdy die-cast base with large leveling legs for stability. Self-aligning agate bearings support the hardened steel beam pivots for a guaranteed sensitivity to 0.1 grains.

Model 5-0-5 . . . . **$74.20**

RELOADING SCALE MODEL 10-10

Up to 1010 Grain Capacity
Normal capacity is 510 grains, which can be increased, without loss in sensitivity, by attaching the included extra weight.

Features include micrometer poise for quick, precise weighing, special approach-to-weight indicator, easy-to-read graduations, magnetic dampener, agate bearings, anti-tip pan, and dustproof lid snaps on to cover scale for storage. Sensitivity is guaranteed to 0.1 grains.

Model 10-10 Scale **$114.33**

RCBS RELOADING TOOLS

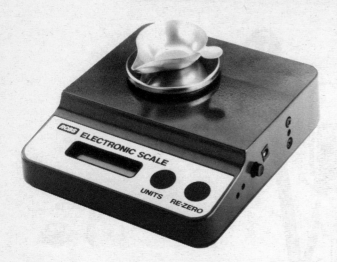

ELECTRONIC SCALE

This new RCBS Electronic Scale brings solid state electronic accuracy and convenience to handloaders. The LCD digital readings are ideal for weighing bullets and cases. The balance gives readings in grains, from zero to 500. The tare feature allows direct reading of the sample's weight with or without using the scale pan. The scale can be used on the range, operating on 8 AA batteries (approx. 50 hours).

Electronic Scale **$395.00**

POWDER CHECKER

Operates on a free-moving rod for simple, mechanical operation with nothing to break. Standard $^7/_8 \times 14$ die body can be used in any progressive loader that takes standard dies. Black oxide finish provides corrosion resistance with good color contrast for visibility.

Powder Checker **$22.76**

UPM MICROMETER ADJUSTMENT SCREW

Handloaders who want the convenience of a micrometer adjustment on their Uniflow Powder Measure can now add that feature to their powder measure. The RCBS Micrometer Adjustment Screw fits any Uniflow Powder Measure equipped with a large cylinder. It is easily installed by removing the standard metering screw, lock ring and bushing, which are replaced by the micrometer unit. Handloaders may then record the micrometer reading for a specific charge of a given powder and return to that setting at a later date when the same charge is used again.

UPM Micrometer Adjustment Screw **$32.64**

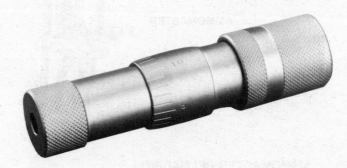

PRECISION MIC

This "Precisioneered Cartridge Micrometer" provides micrometer readings of case heads to shoulder lengths, improving accuracy by allowing the best possible fit of cartridge to chamber. By allowing comparison of the chamber to SAAMI specifications, it alerts the handloader to a long chamber or excess headspace situation. It also ensures accurate adjustment of seater die to provide optimum seating depth. Available in 19 popular calibers.

Precision MIC **$36.60**

REDDING RELOADING TOOLS

MODEL 721
"THE BOSS" PRESS

This "O" type reloading press features a rigid cast iron frame whose 36° offset provides the best visibility and access of comparable presses. Its "Smart" primer arm moves in and out of position automatically with ram travel. The priming arm is positioned at the bottom of ram travel for lowest leverage and best feel. Model 721 accepts all standard $^7/_8$-14 threaded dies and universal shell holders.

Model 721 "The Boss" $109.50
    With Shellholder and 10A Dies 139.50

Also available:
Boss Pro-Pak Deluxe Reloading Kit. Includes Boss Reloading Press, #2 Powder and Bullet Scale, Powder Trickler, Reloading Dies, and more $288.30

ULTRAMAG MODEL 700

Unlike other reloading presses that connect the linkage to the lower half of the press, the Ultramag's compound leverage system is connected at the top of the press frame. This allows the reloader to develop tons of pressure without the usual concern about press frame deflection. Huge frame opening will handle 50 × 3$^1/_4$-inch Sharps with ease.

No. 700 Press, complete $244.50
No. 700K Kit, includes shell holder and one set of dies 274.50

METALLIC TURRET RELOADING PRESS
MODEL 25

Extremely rugged, ideal for production reloading. No need to move shell, just rotate turret head to positive alignment. Ram accepts any standard snap-in shell holder. Includes primer arm for seating both small and large primers.

No. 25 Press, complete $249.00
No. 25K Kit, includes press, shell holder, and one set of dies 279.00

REDDING RELOADING TOOLS

MASTER POWDER MEASURE MODEL 3

Universal- or pistol-metering chambers interchange in seconds. Measures charges from 1/2 to 100 grains. Unit is fitted with lock ring for fast dump with large "clear" plastic reservoir. "See-thru" drop tube accepts all calibers from 22 to 600. Precision-fitted rotating drum is critically honed to prevent powder escape. Knife-edged powder chamber shears coarse-grained powders with ease, ensuring accurate charges.

No. 3 Master Powder Measure
(specify Universal- or Pistol-
Metering chamber) . . . . . . **$ 94.50**
No. 3K Kit Form, includes both
Universal and Pistol
chambers **115.50**
**No. 3-12 Universal or Pistol
chamber** **24.00**

MATCH GRADE POWDER MEASURE MODEL 3BR

Designed for the most demanding re-loaders—bench rest, silhouette and var-mint shooters. The Model 3BR is un-matched for its precision and repeatability. Its special features include a powder baffle and zero backlash mi-crometer.

No. 3BR with Universal or Pistol
Metering Chamber **$124.50**
No. 3 BRK includes both meter-
ing chambers **156.00**
No. 3-30 Benchrest metering
chambers (fit only 3BR) **36.00**

COMPETITION MODEL BR-30 POWDER MEASURE
(not shown)

This powder measure features a new drum and micrometer that limit the overall charging range from a low of 10 grains (depending on powder density) to a maximum of approx. 50 grains. For serious competitive shooters whose loading re-quirements are between 10 and 50 grains, this is the measure to choose. The diameter of Model 3BR's metering cavity has been reduced, and the metering plunger on the new model has a unique hemispherical or cup shape, creating a powder cavity that resembles the bottom of a test tube. The result: irregular powder setting is alleviated and charge-to-charge uniformity is enhanced.

Competition Model BR-30 Powder Measure **$148.50**

MASTER CASE TRIMMER MODEL 1400

This unit features a universal collet that accepts all rifle and pistol cases. The frame is solid cast iron with storage holes in the base for extra pilots. Both coarse and fine adjustments are provided for case length.

The case-neck cleaning brush and primer pocket cleaners attached to the frame of this tool make it a very handy addition to the reloading bench. Trimmer comes complete with:
• New speed cutter shaft
• Six pilots (22, 6mm, 25, 270, 7mm and 30 cal.)
• Universal collet
• Two neck cleaning brushes (22 thru 30 cal.)
• Two primer pocket cleaners (large and small)

No. 1400 Master Case Trimmer complete **$79.50**
No. 1500 Pilots **3.30**

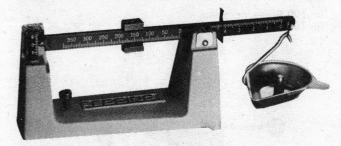

STANDARD POWDER AND BULLET SCALE MODEL RS-1

For the beginner or veteran reloader. Only two counterpoises need to be moved to obtain the full capacity range of 1/10 grain to 380 grains. Clearly graduated with white numerals and lines on a black background. Total capacity of this scale is 380 grains. An over-and-under plate graduate in 10th grains allows checking of variations in powder charges or bullets without further adjustments.

Model No. RS-1 . . . . **$43.50**

Also available: **Master Powder & Bullet Scale.** Same as stan-dard model, but includes a magnetic dampened beam swing for extra fast readings. 505-grain capacity **$64.50**

Reference

THE SHOOTER'S BOOKSHELF

The following is a current listing of recently published titles of special interest to shooters and gun enthusiasts. Most of these books can be found at your local library, bookstore or gunshop. If not available, contact the publisher directly. For a complete listing of in-print titles covering all subjects of interest to shooters, use the *Subject Guide to Books in Print,* which is updated annually and is available at most public libraries. The following entries are listed alphabetically by author and include year of publication, number of pages, publisher and retail price.

ARMS AND ARMOR

Benson, Ragnar. **Ragnar's Big Book of Homemade Weapons: Building and Keeping Your Arsenal Secure.** (Illus.). 288 p. 1992. Paladin Press. pap. $25.00

Hogg, Ian. **Jane's Infantry Weapons 1992–1993.** (Illus.). 1992. Jane's Infantry Group. ltd. ed. $225.00

Rice, Rodney. **One Hundred One Weapons for Women: Implement Weaponry.** (Illus.). 128 p. 1992. RiJo Productions. $10.95

BALLISTICS

Chinni, Michael, ed. **Ballistics Simulation Two.** 72 p. 1991. Soc. Computer Sim. pap. $32.00

DECOYS

Burk, Bruce. **Decorative Decoy Designs,** Vol. 3: Geese and Swans. (Illus.). 64 p. 1991. Stackpole. pap. $49.95

Kangas. **Collector's Guide to Decoys.** (Illus.). 232 p. 1992. Wallace-Homestead. pap. $17.95

DEER HUNTING

Rue, Leonard & Rue, Leonard L. III. **Whitetails: Answers to All Your Questions on Life Cycle, Feeding Patterns, Antlers, Scrapes & Rubs, Behavior During the Rut & Habitat.** (Illus.). 283 p. 1991. Stackpole. pap. $32.95

Smith, Richard. **Deer Hunting, 2d ed.** (Illus.). 272 p. 1991. Stackpole. pap. $14.95

ELK HUNTING

Robb, Bob. **Elk Hunting with the Experts.** (Illus.). 1993. Wolfe Pub. Co. pap. $16.95

van Zwoll, Wayne. **Elk Rifles, Cartridges & Hunting Tactics.** (Illus.). 1992. Wolfe Pub. Co. pap. $24.95

FIREARMS—CATALOGS

Blue Book of Gun Values, 13th ed. (Illus.). 1088 p. 1992. Blue Book Pubns. pap. $19.95

Gun Trader's Guide, 16th ed. (Illus.). 528 p. 1993. Stoeger Pub. Co. pap. $18.95

Lewis, Jack. **Gun Digest Book of Modern Gun Values, 9th ed.** (Illus.). 544 p. 1993. DBI. pap. $20.95

Schwing, Ned, et al. **Standard Catalog of Firearms, 2d ed.** (Illus.). 700 p. 1992. Krause Pubns. $24.95

FIREARMS—GENERAL

Adams, Rob. **World's Most Powerful Rifles & Guns.** 1991. Book Sales Inc. pap. $12.98

Adams, James. **Bull's Eye: The Assassination & Life of Supergun Inventor Gerald Bull.** 1992. Times Books. $22.50

Ball's Patent Repeating & Single-Loading Firearms. repr. of 1866 ed. Pioneer Press. pap. $2.00

Component Parts: Stevens Rifles, Shotguns, Pistols. Pioneer Press. pap. $2.50

Component Parts Price List of Marlin Rifles, Shotguns. Pioneer Press. pap. $2.50

Foss, Joe & Brennan, Mathew. **Top Guns.** 480 p. 1992. PB. pap. $5.99

Kasler, Peter A. **Glock: The New Wave in Combat Handguns.** (Illus.). 304 p. 1992. Paladin Press. pap. $25.00

Konig, Klaus-Peter & Hugo, Martin. **Nine Millimeter Parabellum: The History & Development of the World's 9mm Pistols & Ammunition.** (Illus.). 304 p. 1992. Schiffer. $39.95

Marshall, Evans & Sanow, Edwin J. **Handgun Stopping Power: The Definitive Study.** (Illus.). 240 p. 1992. Paladin Press. $39.95

Ramos, J. M. **Forty-Five Caliber ACP Super Guns: Modified .45 Autos for Competition Hunting & Personal Defense.** (Illus.). 144 p. 1991. Paladin Press. pap. $20.00

Ravenshear, Kit. **Simplified V-Springs: A Guncraftsmanship Manual.** 1991. Pioneer Press. pap. $2.00

van Zwoll, Wayne. **America's Great Gunmakers.** (Illus.). 288 p. 1992. Stoeger Pub. Co. pap. $16.95

FIREARMS—HISTORY

Gresham, Grits & Gresham, Toni. **Weatherby: The Man, the Gun, the Legend.** (Illus.). 304 p. 1992. Cane River AK. $24.95

Thomas, H. H. **The Story of Allen & Wheelock Firearms.** repr. of 1965 ed. 1991. Pioneer Press. pap. $9.00

FIREARMS—LAWS & LEGISLATION

Fine, J. David. **Gun Laws: Proposals for Reform.** 100 p. 1988. W. W. Gaunt. pap. $16.50

Gottlieb, A. M. **The Rights of Gun Owners,** rev. ed. 235 p. 1991. Merrill Press. pap. $9.95

Gun Rights Fact Book 1992. Gordon Press. ltd. ed. $250.00

La Rosa, Benedict. **Gun Control: A Historical Perspective.** 14 p. 1992. Candlestick. pap. $2.50

Restricting Handguns: The Case Against Gun Control Legislation. 1992. Gordon Press. ltd. ed. $75.00

Zimring, Franklin, & Hawkins, Gordon, eds. **Citizens Guide to Gun Control.** 1992. Macmillan. pap. $14.95

GAME & GAME BIRDS

Elliott, Charles. **Turkey Hunting with Charles Elliott.** (Illus.). 288 p. 1991. Bookmark GA. pap. $14.95

Streeter, Larry. **Eating Wild Game.** 188 p. 1991. Great Blue Heron. $19.95

GUNSHOT WOUNDS

Gunshot Injuries: A Guide for Medical Care Workers, Law Enforcement Officers, Forensic Pathologists, Students of Firearms & Workers in the Legal Profession. 1992. Gordon Press. $8.00

GAME COOKERY
Dalton, Diane & Dalton, Nicholas. **The Venison Cook: 106 Imaginative Recipes.** (Illus.). 128 p. 1991. Trafalgar. $24.95

Hayes, James J. **How to Cook a Deer—& Other Critters: A Game Cookbook for Men.** (Illus.). 160 p. 1991. Country Pub. Inc. pap. $14.95

Lamagna, Joseph. **The Wild Game Cookbook for Beginner & Expert, 2d ed.** (Illus.). 112 p. 1991. Delancey Press PA pap. $9.95

Lund, Duane. **Sauces, Seasonings & Marinades for Fish & Wild Game.** 1991. Adventure Pubns. pap. $7.95

HUNTING (see also *Deer Hunting*)
Erwin, Bauer. **Waterfowler's Bible.** 1989. D-day. pap. $7.95

Johns, Dena. **Hunting Quotations: 200 Years of Writings on the Philosophy, Culture & Experience.** 240 p. 1992. Vantage. $29.95

HUNTING—AFRICA
Capstick, Peter H. **The African Adventures: A Return to the Silent Places.** 288 p. 1992. St. Martins. $22.95

Sanchez, Tony. **Hunting in Tanzania: A Collection of Hunting Stories Covering the Country of Tanzania from 1889-1900.** (Illus.). 384 p. 1991. Safari Press. $125.00

HUNTING—NORTH AMERICA
Sheehan, Lawrence, et al. **The Sporting Life: A Passion for Hunting and Fishing.** (Illus.). 1992. Crown Pub. pap. $4.00

Spinks, J.L. **Hunting & Fishing Military Lands.** (Illus.). 256 p. 1991. Stackpole. pap. $16.95

Rutledge, Archibald. **Hunting & Home in the Southern Heartland: The Best of Archibald Rutledge** (James Casada, ed.). 256 p. 1992. U. of S.C. Press. pap. $19.95

HUNTING WITH BOW AND ARROW
Schuh, Dwight. **Fundamentals of Bowhunting.** 192 p. 1991. Stackpole. pap. $14.95

KNIVES
Houston, C. **The Official Price Guide to Collector Knives, 10th ed.** 1991. Ballantine. pap. $14.95

Levine, Bernard. **Levine's Guide to Knives & Their Values, 3d ed.** (Illus.). 512 p. 1993. DBI. pap. $24.95

Lewis, Jack & Combs, Roger. **Gun Digest Book of Knives, 4th ed.** (Illus.). 256 p. 1992. DBI. pap. $15.95

PISTOLS
Dance, Tom. **High Standard: A Collector's Guide to the Hamden & Hartford Target Pistols.** (Illus.). 192 p. 1991. A. Mowbray. pap. $24.00

Gangarosa, Gene, Jr. **P-38 Automatic Pistol: The First Fifty Years.** (Illus.). 272 p. 1993. Stoeger Pub. Co. pap. $16.95

Hogg, Ian, & Weeks, John. **Pistols of the World, 3d ed.** (Illus.). 320 p. 1992. DBI. pap. $18.95

Petty, Charles E. **High Standard Automatic Pistols, 1932-1950.** Gun Room. Price not set.

RELOADING
Grennell, Dean. **ABCs of Reloading, 5th ed.** (Illus.). 288 p. 1993. DBI pap. $18.95

REVOLVERS
Dougan, John C. **Know Your Ruger Single Action: The Second Decade (1963–1973).** (Illus.). 144 p. 1992. Blacksmith. $29.95

—**Compliments of Col. Ruger: A Study of Factory Engraved Single Action Revolvers.** (Illus.). 1993 Wolfe Pub. Co. $46.50

RIFLES
Adam, Rob. **World's Most Powerful Rifles & Guns.** 1991. Book Sales. pap. $12.98

Allen, Desmond W. **First Arkansas Confederate Mounted Rifles.** (Illus.). 104 p. 1988. Arkansas Res. pap. $16.00

Fadala, Sam. **Legendary Sporting Rifles.** (Illus.). 288 p. 1992. Stoeger Pub. Co. pap. $16.95

—**Rifle Guide.** (Illus.). 286 p. 1993. Stoeger Pub. Co. pap. $16.95

Stetzer, L. Gordon, Jr. **The Compleat Muzzleloader.** (Illus.). 128 p. 1992. Mountain Press. pap. $15.00

Walter, John. **Rifles of the World.** (Illus.). 320 p. 1993. DBI. pap. $19.95

Zogbi, Dennis M. **Rifle Markets in the U.S.: Statistical Analysis, 1991–1995: Bolt Action, Single Shot, Lever Action, Autoloader & Pump Action.** 150 p. 1991. Paumanok Pubns. lib. bdg. $195.00

SHOTGUNS
Lewis, Jack, ed. **Shotgun Digest, 4th ed.** (Illus.). 256 p. 1993. DBI. pap. $16.95

Wood, J.B. **Gun Digest Book of Firearms Assembly & Disassembly, Part 5: Shotguns,** rev. ed. (Illus.). 480 p. 1992. DBI. pap. $17.95

SPORTING CLAYS
Scherer, Ed. **Ed Scherer on Sporting Clays.** (Illus.). 200 p. 1993. Wolfe Pub. Co. pap. $29.95

WILDLIFE CONSERVATION & PRESERVATION
Evers, David C. **A Guide to Michigan's Endangered Wildlife.** (Illus.). 120 p. 1992. U. of Mich. Press. pap. $12.95

Wildlife of America. 1991. Outlet Book Co. $19.99

Heintzelman, Donald. **The Wildlife Protectors Handbook.** (Illus.). 208 p. 1992. Capra Press. pap. $9.95

Payne, Neil F. **Wildlife Habitat Management of Wetlands.** 250 p. 1991. McGraw-Hill. Price on request.

WINCHESTER RIFLES
Canfield, Bruce. **A Collector's Guide to Winchester in the Service.** (Illus.). 192 p. 1991. A. Mowbray. $38.00

WATERFOWL (see also *Game & Game Birds*)
Grinnell, George B. **American Duck Shooting.** (Illus.). 640 p. 1991. Stackpole. pap. $17.95

DIRECTORY OF MANUFACTURERS AND SUPPLIERS

The following manufacturers, suppliers and distributors of firearms, ammunition, reloading equipment, sights, scopes and accessories all appear with their products in the catalog and/or "Manufacturers Showcase" sections of this edition of SHOOTER'S BIBLE.

Action Arms, Ltd. (Brno handguns, rifles, Timber Wolf rifle, scopes)
P.O. Box 9573
Philadelphia, Pennsylvania 19124
(215) 744-0100

Aimpoint (sights, scopes, mounts)
203 Elden Street, Suite 302
Herndon, Virginia 22070
(703) 471-6828

American Arms (handguns, rifles, black powder, Franchi shotguns)
715 E. Armour Road
N. Kansas City, Missouri 64116
(816) 474-3161

American Derringer Corp. (handguns)
127 North Lacy Drive
Waco, Texas 76705
(817) 799-9111

American Military Arms Corp. (Iver Johnson rifles)
2202 Redmond Road
Jacksonville, Arkansas 72076
(501) 982-1633

Americase (carrying cases)
P.O. Box 271
Waxahachie, Texas 75165
(800) 880-3629

Anderson Mfg. Co. (scopecovers)
2741 N. Crosby Rd.
P.O. Box 2640
Oak Harbor, Washington 98277
(206) 675-7300

Anschutz (handguns, rifles)
Available through Precision Sales International

Arcadia Machine & Tool Inc. (AMT handguns, rifles)
6226 Santos Diaz Street
Irwindale, California 91702
(818) 334-6629

Armes de Chasse (Francotte rifles and shotguns; AYA shotguns)
P.O. Box 827
Chadds Ford, Pennsylvania 19317
(215) 388-1146

Armsport, Inc. (black powder)
3590 NW 49th Street, P.O. Box 523066
Miami, Florida 33142
(305) 635-7850

A-Square Company Inc. (rifles)
One Industrial Park
Bedford, Kentucky 40006
(502) 255-7456

Astra (handguns)
Available through European American Armory

Auto-Ordnance Corp. (handgun, rifles)
Williams Lane
West Hurley, New York 12491
(914) 679-7225

AYA (shotguns)
Available through Armes de Chasse

Bausch & Lomb (scopes)
See Bushnell (Division of)

Beeman Precision Arms, Inc. (imported handguns, rifles, scopes, mounts)
3440 Airway Drive
Santa Rosa, California 95403-2040
(707) 578-7900

Bell & Carlson, Inc. (rifle stocks)
509 North 5th
Atwood, Kansas 67730
(913) 626-3204

Benelli (shotguns)
Available through Heckler & Koch

Beretta U.S.A. Corp. (handguns, shotguns)
17601 Beretta Drive
Accokeek, Maryland 20607
(301) 283-2191

Bernardelli (shotguns)
Available through Magnum Research

Bersa (handguns)
Available through SGS Importers International

Blaser USA, Inc. (rifles)
c/o Autumn Sales, Inc.
1320 Lake Street
Fort Worth, Texas 76102
(817) 335-1634

Blount, Inc. (RCBS reloading equipment, Speer and CCI bullets, Weaver sights)
P.O. Box 856
Lewiston, Idaho 83501
(208) 746-2351

Bonanza (reloading tools)
See Forster Products

Brno (handguns, rifles)
Available through Action Arms

Browning (handguns, rifles, shotguns)
Route One
Morgan, Utah 84050
(801) 876-2711

Burris Company, Inc. (scopes, mounts)
331 East Eighth Street, P.O. Box 1747
Greeley, Colorado 80632
(303) 356-1670

Bushnell (scopes)
Division of Bausch & Lomb
300 North Lone Hill Avenue
San Dimas, California 91773
(714) 592-8000

Butler Creek Corp. (stocks, scope covers, slings)
290 Arden Drive
Belgrade, Montana 59714
(800) 423-8327

Charter Arms Corp. (handguns)
430 Sniffens Lane
Stratford, Connecticut 06497
(203) 377-8080

Choate Machine & Tool Co. (gun stocks, grips)
P.O. Box 218
Bald Knob, Arkansas 72010
(501) 724-6193

Churchill (shotguns)
Available through Ellett Brothers, Inc.

Clifton Arms (custom rifles)
P.O. Box 1471
Medina, Texas 78055
(210) 589-2666

Colt's Manufacturing Co., Inc. (handguns, rifles)
P.O. Box 1868
Hartford, Connecticut 06144-1868
(203) 236-6311

Connecticut Valley Classics
12 Taylor Lane
P.O. Box 2068
Westport, Connecticut 06880
(203) 435-4600

Coonan Arms (handguns)
830 Hampden Ave.
St. Paul, Minnesota 55114
(612) 646-0902

CVA (black powder guns)
5988 Peachtree Corners East
Norcross, Georgia 30071
(404) 449-4687

Daewoo (handguns)
Available through Davidson's

Dakota (handguns, rifles)
Available through E.M.F. Co., Inc.

Dakota Arms, Inc. (rifles)
HC 55, Box 326
Sturgis, South Dakota 57785
(605) 347-4686

Davidson's (Daewoo pistols)
2703 High Point Road
Greensboro, North Carolina 27403
800-367-4867

Davis Industries (handguns)
15150 Sierra Bonita Lane
Chino, California 91710
(714) 597-4726

Dixie Gun Works (black powder guns)
Reelfoot Avenue, P.O. Box 130
Union City, Tennessee 38261
(901) 885-0561

Dynamit Nobel/RWS (Rottweil shotguns)
105 Stonehurst Court
Northvale, New Jersey 07647
(201) 767-1995

Eagle Arms Inc. (rifles)
131 East 22nd. Avenue, P.O. Box 457
Coal Valley, Illinois 61240
(309) 799-5619

Ellett Brothers, Inc. (Churchill rifles, shotguns)
P.O. Box 128
Chapin, South Carolina 29036
(803) 345-3751

E.M.F. Company, Inc. (Dakota handguns, black powder)
1900 East Warner Avenue 1-D
Santa Ana, California 92705
(714) 261-6611

Erma (handguns)
Available through Precision Sales

Euroarms of America Inc. (black powder guns)
1501 Lenoir Drive, P.O. Box 3277
Winchester, Virginia 22601
(703) 662-1863

European American Armory (Astra handguns, E.A.A. handguns, rifles, shotguns)
P.O. Box 3498, Bright Station
Hialeah, Florida 33013
(305) 688-4442

Feather Industries, Inc. (rifles)
2300 Central Avenue, Unit K
Boulder, Colorado 80301
(303) 442-7021

Federal Cartridge Corporation (Federal/Norma ammunition, bullets, primers, cases)
900 Ehlen Drive
Anoka, Minnesota 55303-7503
(612) 422-2840

Ferlib (shotguns)
Available through W. L. Moore & Co.

Fiocchi
Route 2, Box 90-8
Ozark, MO 65721
(417) 725-4118

Forster Products (Bonanza and Forster reloading)
82 East Lanark Avenue
Lanark, Illinois 61046
(815) 493-6360

Fort Knox Security Products (gun cabinets and safes)
1051 N. Industrial Park Rd.
Orem, Utah 84057
(801) 224-7233

Franchi (shotguns)
Available through American Arms

Francotte (rifles and shotguns)
Available through Armes de Chasse

Freedom Arms (handguns)
One Freedom Lane, P.O. Box 1776
Freedom, Wyoming 83120
(307) 883-2468

Garbi (shotguns)
Available through W. L. Moore & Co.

Gibbs Rifle Co. (Parker-Hale rifles and black powder rifles)
Cannon Hill Industrial Park
Hoffman Road
Martinsburg, West Virginia 25401
(304) 274-0458

Glaser Safety Slug, Inc. (ammunition and gun accessories)
P.O. Box 8223
Foster City, California 94404
(415) 345-7677

Glock, Inc. (handguns)
6000 Highlands Parkway
Smyrna, Georgia 30082
(404) 432-1202

Gonic Arms (black powder rifles)
134 Flagg Road
Gonic, New Hampshire 03839
(603) 332-8457

Grendel, Inc. (handguns)
P.O. Box 560909
Rockledge, Florida 32956
(407) 636-1211

Gun South Inc. (Merkel shotguns, Steyr Mannlicher rifles)
108 Morrow Ave., P.O. Box 129
Trussville, Alabama 35173
(205) 655-8299

Carl Gustaf (rifles)
Available through Precision Sales Int'l

Hammerli U.S.A. (handguns)
19296 Oak Grove Circle
Groveland, California 95321
(209) 962-5311

Harrington & Richardson (handguns, rifles, shotguns)
Industrial Rowe
Gardner, Massachusetts 01440
(508) 632-9393

Harris Engineering Inc. (bipods and adapters)
Barlow, Kentucky 42024
(502) 334-3633

Hastings Barrels (muzzle brakes)
P.O. Box 224
Clay Center, Kansas 67432

Heckler & Koch (handguns, rifles, Benelli shotguns)
21480 Pacific Boulevard
Sterling, Virginia 22170-8903
(703) 450-1900

Hercules Inc. (powder)
Hercules Plaza
Wilmington, Delaware 19894
(302) 594-5000

Heritage Manufacturing (handguns)
4600 NW 135 St.
Opa Locka, Florida 33054
(305) 685-5966

Heym (rifles)
Available through JagerSports

Hodgdon Powder Co., Inc. (gunpowder)
6231 Robinson, P.O. Box 2932
Shawnee Mission, Kansas 66201
(913) 362-9455

Hornady Manufacturing Company (reloading, ammunition)
P.O. Box 1848
Grand Island, Nebraska 68802-1848
(308) 382-1390

IGA Shotguns
Available through Stoeger Industries

IMR Powder Company (gunpowder)
R.D. 5, Box 247E
Plattsburgh, New York 12901
(518) 561-9530

Imperial Magnum Corp. (rifles)
P.O. Box 306
Osoyoos, B.C., Canada V0H 1V0
(604) 495-3131

InterAims (sights)
Available through Stoeger Industries

Interarms (handguns, shotguns and rifles, including Mark X, Rossi, Star, Walther, Norinco, Whitworth)
10 Prince Street
Alexandria, Virginia 22314
(703) 548-1400

Ithaca Gun (shotguns)
891 Route 34B
King Ferry, New York 13081
(315) 364-7182

Iver Johnson/AMAC (handguns, rifles)
Available through American Military Arms Corp.

JagerSports (Heym and Voere rifles)
1 Wholesale Way
Cranston, Rhode Island 02920
(401) 944-9682

Jarrett Rifles Inc. (custom rifles and accessories)
383 Brown Road
Jackson, South Carolina 29831
(803) 471-3616

K.B.I., Inc. (handguns, shotguns, rifles, black powder)
P.O. Box 6346
Harrisburg, Pennsylvania 17112
(717) 540-8518

K.D.F. Inc. (rifles)
2485 Highway 46 North
Seguin, Texas 78155
(512) 379-8141

Krieghoff International Inc. (rifles, shotguns)
337A Route 611, P.O. Box 549
Ottsville, Pennsylvania 18942
(215) 847-5173

Lakefield Arms Ltd. (rifles)
P.O. Box 129
Lakefield, Ontario K0L 2H0
Canada

L.A.R. Manufacturing, Inc. (Grizzly handguns)
4133 West Farm Road
West Jordan, Utah 84084
(801) 255-7106

Leupold & Stevens, Inc. (scopes, mounts)
P.O. Box 688
Beaverton, Oregon 97075
(503) 646-9171

Llama (handguns)
Available through SGS Importers International

Lyman Products Corp. (black powder guns, sights, reloading tools)
Route 147
Middlefield, Connecticut 06455
(203) 349-3421

Magnum Research Inc. (Desert Eagle handguns and Bernardelli shotguns)
7110 University Avenue N.E.
Minneapolis, Minnesota 55432
(612) 574-1868

Magtech Recreational Products (shotguns)
5030 Paradise Rd., Ste C-211
Las Vegas, Nevada 89119
(702) 795-7191

Mark X (rifles)
Available through Interarms

Marlin Firearms Company (rifles, shotguns)
100 Kenna Drive
North Haven, Connecticut 06473
(203) 239-5621

Marocchi (Avanza shotguns)
Available through Precision Sales

Mauser/Precision Imports, Inc. (Mauser handguns, rifles)
5040 Space Center Drive
San Antonio, Texas 78218
(512) 666-3033

Maverick Arms, Inc. (shotguns)
Industrial Blvd., P.O. Box 586
Eagle Pass, Texas 78853
(512) 773-9007

McMillan Gun Works (handguns, rifles)
302 W. Melinda Drive
Phoenix, Arizona 85027
(602) 582-9627

MEC Inc. (reloading tools)
% Mayville Engineering Co.
715 South Street
Mayville, Wisconsin 53050
(414) 387-4500

Merkel (shotguns)
Available through Gun South Inc.

Millett Sights (sights and mounts)
16131 Gothard Street
Huntington Beach, California 92647
(714) 842-5575

Mitchell Arms (handguns, black powder, rifles)
3400-1 West MacArthur Blvd.
Santa Ana, California 92704
(714) 957-5711

M.O.A. Corp (handguns)
P.O. Box 185
Dayton, Ohio 45404
(513) 456-3669

Modern Muzzle Loading Inc. (black powder guns)
P.O. Box 130, 234 Airport Rd.,
Centerville, Iowa 52544
(515) 856-2623

William L. Moore & Co. (Garbi, Ferlib, Rizzini and Piotti shotguns)
31360 Via Colinas, No. 109
Westlake Village, California 91361
(818) 889-4160

O.F. Mossberg & Sons, Inc. (shotguns)
7 Grasso Avenue
North Haven, Connecticut 06473
(203) 288-6491

MTM Molded Products (reloading tools)
3370 Obco Court
Dayton, Ohio 45414
(513) 890-7461

Navy Arms Company, Inc. (handguns, black powder guns, replicas)
689 Bergen Boulevard
Ridgefield, New Jersey 07657
(201) 945-2500

New England Firearms Co., Inc. (handguns, rifles, shotguns; Harrington & Richardson handguns and shotguns)
Industrial Rowe
Gardner, Massachusetts 01440
(508) 632-9393

Nikon Inc. (scopes)
1300 Walt Whitman Road
Melville, New York 11747
(516) 547-4200

Norinco (rifles)
Available through Interarms

Norma (ammunition, gunpowder, reloading cases)
Available through Federal Cartridge Corp.

North American Arms (handguns)
1800 North 300 West
P.O. Box 707
Spanish Fork, Utah 84660
(800) 821-5783

North American Shooting Systems/NASS (rifles)
See Imperial Magnum Corp.

Nosler Bullets, Inc. (bullets)
P.O. Box 671
Bend, Oregon 97709
(503) 382-3921

Nygord Precision Products (Unique handguns, rifles)
P.O. Box 8394
La Crescenta, California 91224
(818) 352-3027

Olin/Winchester (ammunition, primers, cases)
427 North Shamrock
East Alton, Illinois 62024
(618) 258-2000

Pachmayr Ltd. (recoil pads, handgun grips, sights, swivels)
1875 South Mountain Avenue
Monrovia, California 91016
(818) 357-7771

Para-Ordnance (handguns)
3411 McNicoll Avenue
Scarborough, Ontario, Canada M1V 2V6
(416) 297-7855

Parker-Hale (rifles)
Available through Navy Arms

Parker Reproduction (shotguns)
124 River Road
Middlesex, New Jersey 08846
(908) 469-0100

Pentax (scopes)
35 Inverness Drive East
Englewood, Colorado 80112
(303) 799-8000

Perazzi U.S.A. (shotguns)
1207 S. Shamrock Ave.
Monrovia, California 91016
(818) 303-0068

Piotti (shotguns)
Available through W.L. Moore & Co.

Precision Sales International (Anschutz pistols and rifles, Carl Gustaf rifles, Marocchi shotguns; Erma pistols)
P.O. Box 1776
Westfield, Massachusetts 01086
(413) 562-5055

Precision Sports ("600 Series" shotguns)
P.O. Box 5588
Cortland, New York 13045
(607) 756-2851

Quality Firearms (QFI) (handguns)
See Heritage Manufacturing

RCBS, Inc. (reloading tools)
See Blount, Inc.

Redding Reloading Equipment (reloading tools)
1089 Starr Road
Cortland, New York 13045
(607) 753-3331

Redfield (scopes)
5800 East Jewell Avenue
Denver, Colorado 80224-2303
(303) 757-6411

Remington Arms Company, Inc. (handguns, rifles, shotguns, ammunition, primers)
1007 Market Street
Wilmington, Delaware 19898
(302) 773-5291

Rizzini (shotguns)
Available through W. L. Moore & Co.

Rossi (handguns, rifles, shotguns)
Available through Interarms

Rottweil (shotguns)
Available through Dynamit Nobel/RWS

Ruger (handguns, rifles, shotguns, black powder guns)
See Sturm, Ruger & Company, Inc.

Ruko Products, Inc. (Armscor rifles)
P.O. Box 1181
Buffalo, New York 14240-1181
(416) 826-9192

RWS/Diana (rifles)
See Dynamit Nobel

Sako (rifles, actions, scope mounts)
Available through Stoeger Industries

J. P. Sauer & Sohn (rifles)
P.O. Box 37669
Omaha, Nebraska 68137
(402) 339-3530

Savage Arms (rifles, shotguns)
Springdale Road
Westfield, Massachusetts 01085
(413) 568-7001

Schmidt and Bender (scopes)
Schmidt & Bender U.S.A.
P.O. Box 134
Meriden, New Hampshire 03770
(800) 468-3450

SGS Importers International Inc. (Bersa and Llama handguns)
1907 Highway 35
Ocean, New Jersey 07712
(908) 531-9424

Shiloh Rifle Mfg. Co., Inc. (Shiloh Sharps black powder rifles)
P.O. Box 279, Industrial Park
Big Timber, Montana 59011
(406) 932-4454

Shooting Systems Group, Inc. (gun holsters, cases)
1075 Headquarters Park
Fenton, Missouri 63026
(314) 343-3575

Sierra Bullets (bullets)
P.O. Box 818
1400 West Henry St.
Sedalia, Missouri 65301
(800) 223-8799

Sigarms Inc. (Sig Sauer handguns)
Corporate Park
Exeter, New Hampshire 03833
(603) 772-2302

Simmons Outdoor Corp. (scopes)
14530 SW 119th Ave.
Miami, Florida 33186
(904) 878-5100

Sinclair International Inc. (carbide primer pocket uniformer)
2330 Wayne Haven Street
Fort Wayne, Indiana 46803
(219) 493-1858

SKB Shotguns (shotguns, Nichols Scopes)
4325 South 120th Street
P.O. Box 37669
Omaha, Nebraska 68137
(402) 339-3530

Smith & Wesson (handguns)
2100 Roosevelt Avenue
Springfield, Massachusetts 01102-2208
(413) 781-8300

Speer (bullets)
See Blount, Inc.

Springfield Inc. (handguns, rifles)
25144 Ridge Rd.
Colona, Illinois 61241
(309) 441-6002

Star (handguns)
Available through Interarms

Steyr-Mannlicher (rifles)
Available through Gun South Inc.

Stoeger Industries (Sako rifles, IGA shotguns, Tikka rifles, shotguns; InterAims sights; mounts, actions)
55 Ruta Court
South Hackensack, New Jersey 07606
(201) 440-2700

Sturm, Ruger and Company, Inc. (Ruger handguns, rifles, shotguns)
Lacey Place
Southport, Connecticut 06490
(203) 259-7843

Swarovski American (scopes)
2 Slater Road
Cranston, Rhode Island 02920
(401) 942-3380

Swift Instruments, Inc. (scopes and mounts)
952 Dorchester Avenue
Boston, Massachusetts 02125
(617) 436-2960

Tasco (scopes and mounts)
7600 N.W. 26th Street
Miami, Florida 33122
(305) 591-3670

Taurus International, Inc. (handguns)
16175 N.W. 49th Avenue
Miami, Florida 33014
(305) 624-1115

Thompson/Center Arms (handguns, rifles, black powder guns, scopes)
Farmington Road, P.O. Box 5002
Rochester, New Hampshire 03867
(603) 332-2394

Tikka (rifles, shotguns)
Available through Stoeger Industries

Traditions, Inc. (black powder guns)
P.O. Box 235
Deep River, Connecticut 06417
(203) 526-9555

Trius Products, Inc. (traps, clay targets)
221 South Miami Avenue, P.O. Box 25
Cleves, Ohio 45002
(513) 941-5682

Uberti USA, Inc. (handguns, rifles, black powder rifles and revolvers)
362 Limerock Rd., P.O. Box 469
Lakeville, Connecticut 06039
(203) 435-8068

Ultra Light Arms Company (rifles, black powder rifles)
214 Price Street, P.O. Box 1270
Granville, West Virginia 26534
(304) 599-5687

Unique (handguns, rifles)
Available through Nygard Precision Products

U.S.A. Magazines (clips)
P.O. Box 39115
Downey, California 90241
(310) 921-0599

U.S. Repeating Arms Co. (Winchester rifles, shotguns)
275 Winchester Avenue
New Haven, Connecticut 06511
(203) 789-5000

Voere (rifles)
Available through JagerSports

Walther (handguns, rifles)
Available through Interarms

Weatherby, Inc. (rifles, shotguns, scopes, ammunition)
2781 Firestone Boulevard
South Gate, California 90280
(213) 569-7186

Weaver (scopes, mount rings)
See Blount, Inc.

Wesson Firearms Co., Inc. (handguns)
Maple Tree Industrial Center, Route 20
Wilbraham Road
Palmer, Massachusetts 01069
(413) 267-4081

Whitworth (rifles)
Available through Interarms

Wichita Arms (handguns)
P.O. Box 11371
Wichita, Kansas 67211
(316) 265-0661

Wideview Scope Mount Corp. (mounts, rings)
26110 Michigan Avenue
Inkster, Michigan 48141
(313) 274-1238

Wildey Inc. (handguns)
P.O. Box 475
Brookfield, Connecticut 06804
(203) 355-9000

Williams Gun Sight Co. (sights, scopes, mounts)
7389 Lapeer Road, P.O. Box 329
Davison, Michigan 48423
(313) 653-2131

Winchester (ammunition, primers, cases)
See Olin/Winchester

Winchester (domestic rifles, shotguns)
See U.S. Repeating Arms Co.

Winslow Arms Co. (rifles)
P.O. Box 783
Camden, South Carolina 29020
(803) 432-2938

Zeiss Optical, Inc. (scopes)
1015 Commerce Street
Petersburg, Virginia 23803
(804) 861-0033

GUNFINDER™

To help you find the model of your choice, the following list includes each gun found in the catalog section of SHOOTER'S BIBLE 1994. A supplemental listing of **Discontinued Models** and the **Caliberfinder** follow immediately after this section.

HANDGUNS

PISTOLS

Action Arms/Brno
Models CZ-75 Standard & Compact, Model
CZ-83, Model CZ-85 98

American Arms
Models CX-22, P-98 classic, PK-22 99

American Derringer
Models 1, 2, 3, 7, 10, 11, Lady Derringer,
Double Action 38 Derringer 100
Models 4, 6, Semmerling LM-4, Alaskan
Survival, Cop & Mini-Cop Derringers 101
125th Anniversary Double Derringer (1866–
1991) 101

AMT
1911 Government 102
AMT 380 Backup II 102
45 ACP Longslide 102
On Duty Double Action 102
Automag II, III & IV 103

Anschutz
Exemplar, Exemplar XIV 104
Exemplar Hornet 104

Astra
Model A-70, Model A-75 125
Model A-100 125

Auto-Ordnance
Model 1911A-1 Thompson, Pit Bull 105
Model 1911 "The General," Duo-Tone 105
Model 1927 A-5 105
WWII Parkerized Pistol 105

Beretta
Model 21 106
Model 84F 106
Model 85F 107
Model 86 107
Model 87 107
Model 89 Target 107
Models 92D, 92F, 92FS & 92F-EL 108
Model 96 108
Model 950 BS 106

Bersa
Thunder 9 DA 109
Model 23 DA 109
Model 83 DA 109
Models 85 & 86 109

Browning
9mm Hi-Power 110
Model BDM 9mm 110
Buck Mark 22 Series 111
Model BDA-380 111

Colt
Double Eagle MK Series 90 114
Combat Commander MK Series 80 114
Model M1991-AT 114
Lightweight Commander 114
Gold Cup National Match 115
Government Model Series 80 115
Government Model 380 Auto/Pocketlite 115
Delta Elite & Delta Gold Cup 116
Mustang 380 116
Officer's 45 ACP 116
Colt All American Model 2000 117

Coonan Arms
"Cadet" Compact Model 120
Coonan 357 Magnum 120

Daewoo Model DP51 9mm 121

Davis
Model D-Series Derringers 121
Model P-32 121
Model P-380 121

Erma
Model ESP 85A Sporting 124

European American Armory
Big Bore Bounty Hunter SA 127
Windicator DA 127
Witness Basic 126
Witness Subcompact 126
Witness Gold Team 126

Glock
Model 17 129
Model 17L Competition 129
Model 19 Compact 129
Models 20, 21 and 22 129
Model 23 Compact 129

Grendel
Model P-12 130
Models P-30, P-30M 130

Hammerli
Model 160 Free 131
Model 162 Electronic 131
Model 208S Target 131
Model 212 Target Pistol 131
Model 280 Sports 130

Heckler & Koch
Model HK USP 132
Models P7M8 & P7M10 Self-Loading 133
Model P7K3 133
Model SP 89 133

Heritage Mfg
Eagle Semiauto 134

KBI
Model PSP-25 135
FEG Models PJK-SHP & PMK 380 135

L.A.R.
Mark I & Mark 4 Grizzly 136
Grizzly Win. Mag. 136
Grizzly 50 Mark 5 136

Llama
Small-Frames 138
Compact Models 139
Large-Frame Auto 139
Model M-82 9mm 139

Magnum Research
Desert Eagle Mark I, VII 140
Desert Eagle Magnums 140
Lone Eagle Single Shot 141
Mountain Eagle & Baby Eagle 141

Mauser
Models 80-SA, 90-DA & 90-DAC 142

McMillan
Wolverine 143

Mitchell Arms
Pistol Parabellum '08 Luger 144
High Standard Models 144

M.O.A.
Maximum 145

Navy Arms
TT-Olympia 145

Para-Ordnance
Model P12·45 Compact 148

Remington
Model XP-100 Bolt Action Models 148
Model XP-100 Long-Range Customs 148

Ruger
Model P-Series 154
Mark II Models 155
Mark II Bull Barrel & 22/45 156

Sig Sauer
Model P220 "American" 157
Model P225 157
Model P226 157
Model P228 158
Model P229 158
Model 230 SL 158

Smith & Wesson
Model 41 162
Model 52 162
Model 411 161
Model 422 162
Model 915 161
Model 1000 Series 160
Model 2213/2214 Sportsman 162
Model 3900 Compact Series 159
Model 4000 Series 160
Model 4500 Series 160
Model 5900 Series 161
Model 6900 Compact Series 159

Springfield
Model 1911-A1 Models 171
Model P9 DA 171

Star
Models 31P & 31 PK 172
Models M40, M43, and M45 Firestars 172

Taurus
Model PT 22 172
Models PT 92 & PT 99 173
Model PT 92C 173
Model PT 58 173
Model PT 908 174
Models PT 100 & 101 174

Thompson/Center
Contender Bull & Octagon Barrels 179
Contender "Super 14" & "Super 16" 179
Contender Hunter 179

A. Uberti
1871 Rolling Block Target 180

Unique
Model DES 69U 181
Model Int'l Silhouette 181
Model DES 2000U 181

Walther
Models PPK & PPK/S 182
Model TPH Double Action Automatics 182
Model P-5 DA & Compact 183
Model PP 183
Model P-88 DA & Compact 183
Model P-38 DA & Commemorative 183
GSP Match 184
OSP Match Rapid Fire 184

CVA

1858 Remington Army Steel Frame	386
1858 Remington Target	386
Walker	386
New Model Pocket Remington	386
1861 Navy Brass-Framed	387
1851 Navy Brass-Framed	387
Sheriff's Model	387
1860 Army	387
Wells Fargo Model	388
Remington Bison	388
Third Model Dragoon	388
Pocket Police	388

Dixie

Remington 44 Army	395
1860 Army	395
Navy Revolver	395
Spiller & Burr	395
"Wyatt Earp"	395
RHO200 Walker	395
RHO301 Third Model Dragoon	396

EMF

Sheriff's Model 1851	402
Model 1860 Army	402

Model 1862 Police	402
Second Model 44 Dragoon	402

Euroarms

Rogers & Spencer (Model 1005)	406
Rogers & Spencer Army (Model 1006)	406
Rogers & Spencer (Model 1007)	406
Remington 1858 New Model Army	406

Mitchell Arms

1851 Colt Navy	409
Remington New Model Army	409
1860 Colt Army	409
Remington "Texas" Model	409

Navy Arms

1862 Police	411
Lemat (Army, Navy, Cavalry)	411
Colt Walker 1847	411
Rogers & Spencer	411
Reb Model 1860	412
Army 1860	412
1851 Navy "Yank"	412
Stainless Steel 1858 Remington	413
Target Model Remington	413
Deluxe 1858 Remington-Style	413
Remington New Model Army	413
Army 60 Sheriff's	413

A. Uberti

1st, 2nd & 3rd Model Dragoons	434
1861 Navy	434
Walker	434
1851 Navy	434
1860 Army	434
1858 Remington Army 44	435
Paterson	435

SHOTGUNS

CVA

Trapper Single Barrel	394
Classic Turkey Double Barrel	394

Dixie

Double Barrel Magnum	398

Euroarms

Single-Barreled Magnum Cape	403

Navy Arms

Model T&T	421
Mortimer Flintlock	421
Fowler	421
Steel Shot Magnum	421

Thompson/Center

New Englander	426

DISCONTINUED MODELS

The following models, all of which appeared in the 1993 edition of SHOOTER'S BIBLE, have been discontinued by their manufacturers or are no longer imported by U.S. distributors or are now listed under a new manufacturer/distributor.

HANDGUNS

AMT Javelina

Astra Now distributed by **European American Armory**

Beeman
Models MP-08 & P-08
Korth Semiauto
Unique Models 2000-U & 69U now listed under "Unique"
Hammerli models now listed under **Hammerli U.S.A.**

Charter Arms
Model 357 Magnum Bulldog Tracker
Pathfinder
Pit Bull

KBI Model 941 Jericho

Llama
Model M-87
Duo-Tone Models

Mitchell Arms
Models 1875 and 1890 Remington

QFI (now distributed by **Heritage**)
Model 722TP Silhouette
Model SA 25
Plains Rider SA
Victory MC5 pistol

Ruger
Blackhawk models
Super Blackhawk Hunter

Smith & Wesson
Model 16 Magnum Masterpiece
Model 29 Classic DX
Model 642 Centennial Airweight

Springfield Armory (now listed as **Springfield Inc.**)
Model 1911-A2 SASS
"R" Series pistols

Taurus
Model 73
Model PT 99

Dan Wesson
Action Cup/PPC
Gold Series

RIFLES

Browning Model 52 Ltd. Ed.

Heym (now distributed by **JagerSport**)
Classic Safari Series
Classic Sporter, Trophy
Drilling Models 33 and 37
Model SR20 Alpine Series

Remington
Model 700 ADL Deluxe
Model 700 Custom "KS" Mountain Rifle LWT
Model Seven Custom "KS" LWT

Sako
Deluxe
PPC Hunter
Whitetail/Battue

Steyr-Mannlicher Classic Model

Thompson/Center Hunter Model

Walther UIT Match

Weatherby
Classicmark I & II (now listed as Classicmark models)
Mark V Fibermark

Winchester
Models 70 LWT Wincam and Win-Tuff

SHOTGUNS

American Arms
Black Magic Series (Game, Trap, Skeet)

Armsport
Models 1050/1053
Models 2699/2700, 2717
Models 2730-2765
Model 2900

Benelli
Montefeltro Super 90 Slug Gun

Beretta
Models 686/687 English Course Sporting Clays

Bernardelli
Hemingway Deluxe SS LWT
Roma 6E SS

Chapuis Imperial Ultra

Churchill
Monarch
Windsor IV

Heym (now listed under **JagerSport**)
Safety Model 22 Shotgun/Rifle

Mossberg
Model 835 "NWTF" Ulti-Mag
Model 5500 MKII

Remington
Model 11-87 SP Magnum
Model 11-87 NWTF Turkey

Savage Model 312 Series

Winchester
Model 1300 Series III
Model 1300 Pistol Grip Defender

BLACK POWDER

CVA
Apollo 90 Percussion Rifle
Colonial Pistol
Pennsylvania Long Rifle
Squirrel Rifle

Freedom Arms
Competition Model
Silhouette Model

Navy Arms Rigby-Style Target Rifle

CALIBERFINDER™

How to use this guide: To find a 22LR handgun, look under that heading in the **Handguns** section below. You'll find several models of that description, including the Beretta Model 21. Turn next to the **Gunfinder** section and locate the heading for **Beretta** (pistols, in this case). Beretta's **Model 21,** as indicated, appears on p. 106.

HANDGUNS

17 Rem
Thompson/Center Contender "Super 14"

22LR
American Arms Models CX, PK & PX, Model P-98
American Derringer Models 1, 2 and 7
Anschutz Exemplar and Exemplar XIV
Beretta Model 21, Model 87, Model 89
Bersa Model 23
Browning Buck Mark 22 Series
Charter Arms Off-Duty
Davis Model D-22
EMF/Dakota Dakota Target, Hartford Scroll Engraved Single Action Revolver
Erma ESP 85A Sporting Pistol, Model 772 Match
European American Armory Windicator DA
Freedom Arms Model 252
Hammerli Models 160 Free Pistol, 162 Electronic, 208S Target Pistol, 212 Target, 280 Sport Pistol
Harrington & Richardson Sportsman 999
Heckler & Koch Model P7K3
Heritage Rough Rider SA
Llama Automatic (Small Frame), Comanche
Magnum Research Mountain Eagle
Mitchell Arms High Standard Pistols
Navy Arms Model TT-Olympia
New England Firearms Standard Revolver, Ultra Revolver
North American Arms Mini-Revolvers and Mini-Master Series
Rossi Model 515
Ruger New Model Single-Six, Mark II Pistols, Model SP101 Revolver, Bisley SA Target
Smith & Wesson Models 17, 41, 63, 422
Taurus Models 94, 96, PT 22
Thompson/Center Contender and "Super 14"
A. Uberti 1871 Rolling Block Target Pistol
Unique Models DES 69U, Int'l Silhouette
Walther Models GSP, Model PP DA, TPH DA
Wichita Arms International

22 Rimfire Magnum
American Derringer Model 1, Model 7, Cop & Mini-Cop DA Derringer
AMT 22 Automag II
European American Armory Windicator DA
Grendel Model P-30
Taurus Model 941
Dan Wesson 22 Rimfire Magnum, Silhouette
Wichita Arms International

22 Short
Harrington & Richardson Sportsman 999
New England Firearms Standard
Unique Model DES 2000U
Walther OSP Match Rapid Fire

22 Hornet
Anschutz Exemplar Hornet
Magnum Research Lone Eagle SS
MOA Maximum
Thompson/Center Contender
Uberti 1871 Rolling Block Target Pistol

22 Win. Mag.
Davis Model D-22
Heritage Rough Rider SA
Magnum Research Lone Eagle SS
New England Firearms Ultra Revolver
North American Mini-Revolvers and Mini-Master Series
Smith & Wesson Model 651
Thompson/Center Contender
Uberti 1871 Rolling Block Target Pistol
Dan Wesson 22 Win. Mag. Revolvers

22-250
Magnum Research Lone Eagle SS
Remington Model XP-100 LR and Custom Repeater

223 Remington
Magnum Research Lone Eagle SS
Remington Model XP-100, XP-100R Hunter, Long-Range Custom Repeater and XP-100 Silhouette Target Pistols
Thompson/Center Contender, Hunter and "Super 14"

223 Rem. Comm. Auto
American Derringer Model 1
Thompson/Center Contender Models and "Super 14"

6mm BR
Remington XP-100 Long-Range Custom

243
Magnum Research Lone Eagle SS

25 Auto
American Derringer Model 2
Beretta Model 21, Model 950BS
Davis Model D-22 Derringer
KBI/Kassnar Model PSP-25
Walther Model TPH

7mm BR
Remington Model XP-100 and XP-100 Hunter Target Pistols

7mm T.C.U.
Thompson/Center Contender, "Super 14"

7mm-08
Magnum Research Model Lone Eagle SS
Remington Model XP-100 Silhouette, Long-Range Custom and Hunter

7-30 Water
Thompson/Center Contender, Hunter
Wichita Arms International

30 Carbine
American Derringer Model 1
AMT Automag III
EMF/Dakota Model 1873
Ruger Model Blackhawk SA

30-30 Win.
Magnum Research Lone Eagle SS
Thompson/Center Contender, Hunter
Wichita Arms International

308 Win.
Remington XP-100 Long-Range Custom and Custom Repeater
Wichita Arms Silhouette

32 Mag.
American Derringer Models 1, 3 & 7, Lady Derringer
Charter Arms Bonnie & Clyde
Ruger Model SP101, Bisley SA Target, New Model Single Six
Dan Wesson Six-Shot

32 Auto
American Derringer Model 2
Davis Models D-22 and P-32
Walther Model PP Double Action

32 H&H Mag.
Wichita International

32 H&R
Charter Arms Police Undercover
European American Armory Windicator DA
New England Firearms Lady Ultra Revolver
Ruger New Model Single-Six SSM
Taurus Model 741

32 S&W Long
American Derringer Models 1, 2, 3, 7 and Lady Derringer, Cop
Smith & Wesson Model 52

32 S&W Wadcutter
Erma ESP 85A Sporting Pistol, Model 773 Match
Hammerli Model 280 Sport Pistol
Walther Model GSP Match

32-20
American Derringer Model 1
EMF/Dakota Model 1873, Hartford Models
Thompson/Center Contender

35 Remington
Magnum Research Lone Eagle SS
Remington Model XP-100, XP-100R Hunter, Long-Range, Custom Repeater and XP-100 Silhouette Target Pistols
Thompson/Center Hunter

357 Mag.
American Arms Regulator SA
American Derringer Models 1, 6, 38 DA and Cop Double Derringers
Colt King Cobra, Python
Coonan Arms 357 Magnum, Cadet Compact
EMF/Dakota Target, Model 1873, Model 1873 Dakota SA, 1875 Outlaw, 1890 Remington Police, Hartford Scroll Engraved SA
Erma Model 777 Sporting Revolver
European American Armory Big Bore Bounty Hunter, Windicator DA

Freedom Arms Model 353, Competition Models
L.A.R. Grizzly Mark I
Llama Comanche
Magnum Research Desert Eagle
Mitchell Arms SA Army revolvers
Rossi Model 971
Ruger Model GP-100, Model SP101, Bisley, Vaquero
Smith & Wesson Models 13, 19, 27, 65, 66, 586
Taurus Models 65, 66, 669, 689
Thompson/Center Contender
Uberti 1871 Rolling Block Target Pistol, 1873 Cattleman Quick Draw, 1875 Remington Army Outlaw, Buckhorn SA
Unique Model Int'l Silhouette
Dan Wesson 357 Mag., 357 Super Mag., Fixed Barrel
Wichita Arms International

357 Maximum

American Derringer Model 1
Thompson/Center Contender, Hunter
Dan Wesson 357 Super Mag.

358 Winchester

MOA Maximum

38 Special

American Derringer 1, 3, 7, 11, Lady Derringer, DA 38 and Cop Double Derringers
Charter Arms Police Undercover, Off-Duty, Undercover 38 Special, Bonnie & Clyde
Colt King Cobra DA, Python Premium DA, Detective Special
European American Armory Windicator DA
Heritage Sentry DA
Rossi Models 68, M88, 851
Ruger Model SP101
Smith & Wesson Models 442, 649, LadySmith
Taurus Models 80, 82, 83, 85, 86
Dan Wesson 38 Special, Model 738P, Fixed Barrel

380 Auto

American Derringer Models 1 and 7
AMT Model 380 Backup II
Beretta Model 84F, 85, 86
Bersa Model 83 DA, Model 85
Brno Model CZ-83
Browning Model BDA-380
Colt Government Model, Mustang, Mustang Plus II, Mustang Pocket Lite 380
Davis P-380
Grendel Model P-12
Heckler & Koch Model P7K3
Heritage Eagle
KBI/Kassnar FEG Model PMK-380
Llama Automatic (Small Frame)
Sig Sauer Model 230 SL
Taurus Model PT 58
Walther Model PPK & PPK/S, Model PP DA

38 Super

American Derringer Model 1
Auto-Ordnance Model 1911A-1 Thompson
Colt Combat Commander MK Series 80, Government Model Series 80
European American Armory Witness Gold Team
Llama Large Frame Auto Pistols
McMillan Wolverine
Sig Sauer Model 220 "American"
Springfield Armory Model 1911-A1 Standard

38 S&W

Smith & Wesson Models 10, 13, 14, 15, 36, 38, 49, 52, 60, 64, 65 and 640 Centennial

38-40

EMF/Dakota Model 1873, Hartford Model
Uberti 1873 Cattleman Quick Draw

9mm Luger

American Derringer Model 1, Model DA 38 Double Derringer
AMT On Duty DA Pistol
Brno Model CZ-75 Standard and Compact, CZ-85
Browning Model BDM Double Action
Heckler & Koch Model SP 89
Mauser Pistols

9mm Win. Mag.

AMT Automag III

9mm Parabellum

American Derringer Semmerling LM-4
Auto Ordnance Model 1911A-1 Thompson
Beretta Model 92F
Bersa Thunder 9 DA
Brno Model CZ-75 & CZ-85
Browning 9mm Hi-Power
Colt All-American Model 2000
Daewoo Model DP51
European American Armory Astra Models A-70, A-75, A-100, Witness Subcompact/Gold Team
Glock Models 17, 17L Competition, Model 19 Compact
Heckler & Koch Models SP89, HK USP
KBI/Kassnar Model PJK-9HP
Llama Automatics (Compact and Large Frame), Model M-82
Magnum Research Baby Eagle
McMillan Wolverine
Mitchell Arms Pistol Parabellum '08
Ruger Model SP101, P-Series
Sig Sauer Models 220, 225, 226, 228
Smith & Wesson Model 915, Model 940 Centennial, Third Generation Pistols (Model 3900 Compact Series, 5900 and 6900 Compact Series)
Springfield Model 1911-A1 Standard, Model P9 DA
Star Models 31P, 31PK, M43 Firestar
Taurus Models PT92, PT-92C, PT99, PT-908
Walther Models P-38, P-88 DA, P-5 DA

10mm

American Derringer Model 1
AMT Automag IV
Auto-Ordnance Model 1911-A1 Thompson
Colt Delta Elite, Delta Gold Cup, Double Eagle
Glock Model 20
L.A.R. Grizzly Mark I
McMillan Wolverine
Smith & Wesson Model 1000 Series

10mm Auto

Colt Double Eagle MK Series 90

40 S&W

American Derringer Model 1, 38 DA Derringer
AMT On Duty DA Pistol
Auto-Ordnance Model 1911A-1
Browning Hi-Power
Colt Double Eagle Officer's and Combat Commander, Government Model MK Series 80
European American Armory Astra Models A-70, A-75, A-100, Witness Subcompact/Gold Team
Heckler & Koch Model P7M10, Model HK USP
Llama Compact and Large Frame Pistols, Model M-82
Magnum Research Baby Eagle
Sig Sauer Model P229
Smith & Wesson Model 4000 Series, Model 411
Springfield Model P9 DA
Star Models 31P & 31PK, M40 Firestar
Taurus Model 100/101

40 Auto

Beretta Model 96
Ruger P-Series

41 Mag.

American Derringer Model 1
Magnum Research Desert Eagle
Ruger Model Bisley, Vaquero
Smith & Wesson Models 57, 657
Dan Wesson 41 Mag. Revolvers

41 Action Express

Magnum Research Baby Eagle

.410

American Derringer Models 1, 4 and 6
Thompson/Center Contender Super "16"

44 Magnum

American Derringer Model 1
Colt Anaconda
Freedom Arms Casull Premier & Field Grades, Competition Models
L.A.R. Grizzly Mark 4
Llama Super Comanche
Magnum Research Desert Eagle
Mitchell Arms SA Army Model Revolvers
Ruger Redhawk, Model Bisley, Super Blackhawk SA, Super Redhawk DA, Bisley SA Target
Smith & Wesson Model 29 and 629
Thompson/Center Contender, Hunter
Uberti Buckhorn SA
Unique Model Int'l Silhouette
Dan Wesson 44 Mag. Revolvers

44 Special

American Derringer Models 1, 7
Charter Arms Bulldog Pug 44 Special
Colt Anaconda
EMF/Dakota Hartford Models
Rossi Model 720
Smith & Wesson Model 629
Taurus Model 431 & 441
Uberti 1873 Cattleman Quick Draw

44-40

American Arms Regulator SA
American Derringer Model 1
Colt Single Action Army
EMF/Dakota Models 1873, 1873 Dakota SA, 1875 Outlaw, 1890 Remington Police, Hartford Scroll Engraved SA, Hartford Model
Navy Arms 1873 SA
A. Uberti 1873 Cattleman Quick Draw, 1875 Remington Army Outlaw, Buckhorn SA

445 Supermag

Dan Wesson 445 Supermag

45 Auto

American Derringer Models 1, 4, 6, 10 Semmerling LM-4
AMT Longslide & Government Models, On Duty DA Pistol
Auto-Ordnance Model 1911A-1 Thompson, Model 1911 "The General," Model 1927A-5
Colt Combat Commander, Lightweight Commander, Gold Cup National Match, Officer's ACP, Government Model, Double Eagle, Combat Elite MKIV Series 80, Model 1991A1
European American Armory Astra Models A-70, A-75, A-100
Glock Model 21
L.A.R. Grizzly Mark I
Llama Automatics (Large and Compact Frames)
McMillan Wolverine

Para-Ordnance Models P12 & P14
Ruger P-Series, Model P220
Sig Sauer Model 220 "American"
Smith & Wesson Third Generation (Model 4500 Series), Model 625-2
Springfield Armory Model 1911-A1 Standard, Model P9 DA, Model M45 Firestar
Uberti 1873 Cattleman Quick Draw, 1875 Army SA Outlaw, Pin Gun

45 Colt

American Arms Regulator SA
American Derringer Models 1, 4, 6, 10
Colt Single Action Army Revolver, Anaconda
EMF/Dakota Target, Models 1873, 1873 Dakota SA, 1875 "Outlaw," Model 1890 Remington Police, Scroll Engraved SA, Hartford Models (Cavalry Colt, Artillery)
Mitchell Arms SA Army Model Revolvers
Navy Arms 1873 SA and 1895 Calvary & Artillery
Ruger Model Bisley, Vaquero
Thompson/Center Contender Super "16"
Uberti 1871 Rolling Block Target Pistol, 1873 Cattleman Quick Draw, 1875 Remington Army Outlaw, Buckhorn SA

45 Win. Mag.

AMT Automag IV
American Derringer Model 1
L.A.R. Grizzly Mark I
Wildey Pistols

454 Casull

Freedom Arms Casull Premier & Field Grades, Silhouette and Competition Models

45-70 Government

American Derringer Models 1, 4
Thompson/Center Hunter

475 Wildey Mag.

Wildey Pistols

50 Mag. AE

L.A.R. Grizzly 50 Mark 5

RIFLES

CENTERFIRE BOLT ACTION

STANDARD CALIBERS

17 Bee

Francotte Bolt Action

17 Rem.

Remington Model 700 ADL, BDL, Model Seven
Sako Deluxe, Hunter Lightweight, Varmint
Ultra Light Model 20 Series
Winslow Varmint

22 Hornet

Brno Model CZ-527
Ultra Light Model 20 Series

220 Swift

McMillan Varminter
Remington Model 700 VS Varmint
Ruger Model M-77R, M-77V Varmint, M-77 Mark II HB

22 PPC

Ruger M-77 HB
Sako PPC Varmint/BR

222 Rem.

Brno Model CZ-527
Francotte Bolt Action
Remington Model 700 ADL, BDL, Ltd. Classic, Varmint Special (wood)
Sako Deluxe, Hunter Lightweight, Varmint
Steyr-Mannlicher Model SL, Varmint
Ultra Light Model 20 Series

223 Rem.

Brno Model CZ-527
Browning A-Bolt Short Action
JagerSports Voere Model VEC91
Jarrett Lightweight Varmint
Mark X Barreled Actions, Mini-Mark X
McMillan Varminter
Remington Models 700 ADL, BDL, BDL Stainless, Varmint Special, Model Seven
Ruger M-77 RL, M-77 Mark II HB, All-Weather, M-77 R
Sako Deluxe, Hunter Lightweight, Varmint
Savage Model 110 Series, Model 112FV & 116FSS
Steyr-Mannlicher Model SL, Varmint
Tikka Continental, New Generation, Premium Grade
Ultra Light Model 20 Series
Weatherby Vanguard Classic, Weatherguard
Winchester Models 70 Featherweight, Lightweight, Ranger, Sporter, Varmint

22-250

Blaser Model R84
Browning Short Action A-Bolt
European American Armory Sabatti Rover 870
KDF Model K15
Mark X Barreled Actions, Viscount Sporter, Whitworth Express
McMillan Classic, and Stainless Sporters, Talon Sporter, Varminter
Parker-Hale Models M81, 1000 Clip, 1100 LWT, 1200, 2100 Midland
Remington Model 700 ADL, BDL, CS, Varmint Special
Ruger Model 77R, M-77 Mark II HB
Sako Deluxe, Hunter Lightweight, LS, Left-Handed Models, Varmint
Savage Model 110 Series, Model 112FV
Steyr-Mannlicher Sporter Model L, Varmint
Tikka Continental, New Generation, Premium Grade
Ultra Light Model 20 Series
Weatherby Mark V Classicmark, Deluxe, Vanguard VGX, Varmintmaster
Winchester Model 70 Featherweight, Lightweight, Ranger, Sporter, Varmint
Winslow Basic

243 Win.

Blaser Model R84
Brno Model ZKK 601
Browning A-Bolt Short Action
Clifton Arms Scout
European American Armory Sabatti Rover 870
Francotte Bolt Action
KDF Model K15
Mark X Barreled Actions, Viscount Sporter, Whitworth Express
Mauser Model 66 & 99 Standard
McMillan Benchrest, Classic, Standard & Stainless Sporters, Talon, Varminter
Parker-Hale Models M81, 1000 Clip, 1100 LWT, 1200 Super, 2100 Midland, 1300C Scout
Remington Model Seven, Models 700 ADL, BDL, BDL European, BDL SS, CS, LS, Mountain, Varmint Special, 7400, 7600
Ruger M-77 Mark II HB & All-Weather, M-77RS, M-77RL, M-77RSI, M-77R

Sako

Sako Classic, Deluxe, Hunter Lightweight, Left-Handed Models, LS, Mannlicher-Style Carbine, Model TRG-S, Varmint
Savage Models 110 Series, Model 116FSS
Steyr-Mannlicher Models Luxus, SSG, Sporter L, Varmint
Tikka Continental, New Generation, Premium Grade
Ultra Light Model 20 Series
Weatherby Vanguard Classic, VGX, Weatherguard
Winchester Models 70 Featherweight, Lightweight, Ranger and Ranger Youth, Sporter, Varmint
Winslow Basic

244 Rem.

Winslow Basic

6mm BR

McMillan Benchrest Rifle, Classic & Talon Sporters

6mm Rem.

Blaser Model R84
KDF Model K15
McMillan Benchrest, Classic, Stainless & Talon Sporters, Varminter
Parker-Hale Models 81, 1000 Clip, 1100 LWT, 1200 Super, Model 2100 Midland
Remington Model Seven, Models 700 ADL, BDL, BDL SS, Varmint Special
Ruger Model M-77 Varmint
Steyr-Mannlicher Sporter Model L
Ultra Light Model 20 Series

6mm PPC

McMillan Benchrest
Ruger M-77 Mark II HB
Sako PPC Varmint, BR/Varmint

250-3000 Savage

Savage Model 110
Ultra Light Model 20 Series
Weatherby Mark V Whitetail Ltd. Ed.

25-06

Blaser Model R84
Browning A-Bolt
European American Armory Sabatti Rover 870
K.D.F. Model K15
Mark X Barreled Actions, Viscount Sporter, Whitworth, Mauser System Actions
Mauser Model 99 Standard
McMillan LA Classic, Stainless Sporters, Talon Sporter, Varminter
Remington Models 700 ADL, BDL, BDL SS, Mountain
Ruger Models 77RS, 77R
Sako Deluxe, Fiberclass, Hunter Lightweight, LS, Left-Handed Models
Sauer Model 90
Savage Model 110 Series
Ultra Light Model 24 Series
Winchester Model 70 Sporter
Winslow Basic

257 Ackley

Ruger Model M-77RL Ultra Light
Ultra Light Model 20 Series

257 Roberts

Browning A-Bolt Short Action
Dakota Arms Model 76 Classic
Remington Model 700 Mountain
Ruger Model M-77R Varmint
Ultra Light Model 20 Series
Winslow Basic

270 Win.

Blaser Models R84
Brno Model ZKK 600, CZ-537
Browning A-Bolt
Dakota Arms Model 76 Classic
European American Armory Sabatti Rover 870
Francotte Bolt Action
Carl Gustaf Model 2000
KDF Model K15
Mark X Viscount Sporter, Whitworth, Barreled Actions, Mauser System Actions
Mauser Models 66 & 99 Standard
McMillan Alaskan LA, Classic LA & Stainless Sporters, Talon Sporter, Titanium Mountain
Parker-Hale Models M81, 1000 Clip, 1100 LWT, 1200 Super, 2100 Midland
Remington Model 700 ADL & BDL, BDL SS, BDL European, CS, Mountain, 7400, 7600
Ruger Model M77R & 77RS, RL Ultralight, 77RSI, International, 77R, M77, All-Weather, M77 Deluxe
Sako Classic, Deluxe, Fiberclass, Hunter Lightweight, LS, Mannlicher-Style Carbine, Left-Handed Models, Model TRG-S
Sauer 90
Savage Model 110 Series, Model 114CU & 116FSS
Steyr-Mannlicher Luxus Model M (Sporter & Professional)
Tikka New Generation, Premium Grade, Whitetail/Battue
Ultra Light Model 24 Series
Unique Model TGC
Weatherby Models Mark V Alaskan, Classicmark, Sporter, Weathermark; Vanguard Alaskan, Classic, VGX, Weatherguard
Winchester Models 70 Featherweight, Lightweight, Ranger, Sporter, Super Grade, Winlite
Winslow Basic

280 Rem.

Blaser Models R84
Browning A-Bolt
Dakota Arms Model 76 Classic
KDF Model K15
McMillan Alaskan LA, Classic LA & Stainless Sporters, Talon Sporter, Titanium Mountain
Remington Models 700 ADL, 700 BDL, BDL European, BDL SS, CS, Mountain 7400, 7600
Ruger Model M-77R, M-77 All-Weather
Sako Deluxe, Fiberclass, Hunter, LS, Left-Handed Models
Winchester Models 70 Featherweight, Lightweight, Super Grade, Winlite
Winslow Basic

280 IMP

Jarrett Standard Hunting

284 Win.

Browning A-Bolt Short Action
McMillan Classic, Stainless & Talon Sporters
Ultra Light Model 20 Series
Winslow Basic

7mm Ackley

Ultra Light Model 20 Series

7mm BR

McMillan Classic, Stainless and Talon Sporters

7mm Express

Ultra Light Model 24 Series

7mm Mauser

Brno Model ZKK 600
Remington Model 700 Mountain
Ultra Light Model 20 Series
Winslow Basic

7mm STW

Jarrett Model 3

7mm-08

Browning A-Bolt Short Action
Clifton Arms Scout
McMillan Varminter, Talon, Classic & Stainless Sporters, National Match
Remington Model Seven, Models 700 ADL, BDL, BDL European, BDL SS, CS, Mountain and Varmint
Sako Deluxe, Hunter Lightweight, LS, Varmint, Model TRG-S, Left-Handed Models
Savage Model 110 Series
Ultra Light Model 20 Series
Unique Model TGC
Weatherby Vanguard Classic, Weatherguard
Winchester Model 70 Featherweight

30-06

A-Square Caesar and Hannibal
Blaser Model R84
Brno Model ZKK 600, CZ-537
Browning A-Bolt
Clifton Arms Scout
Dakota Arms Model 76 Classic
European American Armory Sabatti Rover 870
Francotte Bolt Action
Carl Gustaf Model 2000
K.D.F. Model K15
Mark X Viscount Sporter, Whitworth, Barreled Action, Mauser System Actions
Mauser Models 66 & 99 Standard
McMillan Alaskan LA, Classic & Stainless Sporters LA, Talon Sporter, Titanium Mountain
Parker-Hale Models M81 Classic, 1000 Clip, 1100 Lightweight, 1200 Super, 2100 Midland
Remington Models 700 ADL, BDL, BDL European, BDL SS, CS, Mountain, 7400, 7400 Carbine, 7600
Ruger Model M-77RS, 77RLS & 77RL Ultra Light, 77RSI International, 77R, M-77 All-Weather, M-77 Deluxe
Sako Classic, Deluxe, Mannlicher-Style Carbine, Fiberclass, Hunter Lightweight, LS, Left-Handed Models, Model TRG-S
Sauer Model 90
Savage Model 110 Series, Model 114CU & 116FSS
Steyr-Mannlicher Models M (Sporter & Professional), Luxus M
Tikka New Generation, Premium Grade, Whitetail/Battue
Ultra Light Model 24 Series
Unique Model TGC
Weatherby Mark V Classicmark, Deluxe, Lazermark, Sporter, Weathermark; Vanguard Alaskan, Classic, VGX, Weatherguard
Winchester Models 70 Featherweight, Lightweight, Ranger, Sporter, Super Grade, Winlite
Winslow Basic

30-06 Carbine

Remington Models 7400 and 7600 Carbines

300 Savage

Savage 110 Series
Ultra Light Model 20 Series

308 Win.

Brno Model ZKK-601, CZ-537
Browning A-Bolt Short Action
Clifton Arms Scout
European American Armory Sabatti Rover 870
Francotte Bolt Action
Carl Gustaf Model 2000
KDF Model K15
Mark X Barreled Action, Mauser System Actions, Viscount Sporter, Whitworth
Mauser Models 66, 86 & 99 Standard
McMillan Benchrest, Classic & Stainless Sporters, National Match, Talon Sporter, Varminter
Parker-Hale Models M81, M-85 Sniper, 1000 Clip, 1100 LWT, 1200 Super, Model 1300C, 2100 Midland
Remington Models Seven, 700 ADL, BDL, BDL Stainless, BDL European, 700 CS, Mountain, Varmint Special, 7400, 7600
Ruger Models 77RSI International, M-77 Mark II, M-77RS, M-77RL Ultra Light, M-77 All Weather, M-77R
Sako Deluxe, Hunter Lightweight, LS, Left-Handed Models, Mannlicher-Style Carbine, TRG-21, Varmint
Savage Model 110 Series
Steyr-Mannlicher Luxus L, Match UIT, Sporter L, SSG, Varmint
Tikka Continental, New Generation, Premium Grade, Whitetail/Battue
Ultra Light Model 20 Series
Unique Model TGC
Weatherby Vanguard Classic, Weatherguard
Winchester Model 70 Featherweight, Lightweight, Ranger Youth, Varmint
Winslow Basic

35 Whelen

Remington Models 700 ADL & BDL, 7400, 7600

358 Win.

Ultra Light Model 20 Series
Winslow Basic

MAGNUM CALIBERS (RIFLE)

222 Rem. Mag.

Steyr-Mannlicher Model Sporter (SL)
Ultra Light Model 20 Series

224 Weatherby Mag.

Weatherby Mark V Deluxe, Lazermark, Varmintmaster

240 Weatherby Mag.

Weatherby Mark V Classicmark, Deluxe, Lazermark

257 Weatherby/Roberts

Blaser Model R84
Mauser Model 99
Weatherby Mark V Alaskan, Classicmark, Deluxe, Lazermark, Sporter, Weathermark
Winslow Basic

264 Win. Mag.

Blaser Model R84
Ultra Light Model 26 Series
Winchester Model 70 Sporter
Winslow Basic

270 Weatherby Mag.

K.D.F. Model K15
Mauser Model 99

Weatherby Mark V Alaskan, Classicmark, Deluxe, Lazermark, Sporter, Weathermark; Vanguard VGX
Winslow Basic

7mm Imp. Mag.

Imperial Bolt Action

7mm Rem./Wby. Mag.

A-Square Caesar and Hannibal
Blaser Model R84
Browning A-Bolt
Dakota Arms Model 76 Classic
European American Armory Sabatti Rover 870
Carl Gustaf Model 2000
K.D.F. Model K15
Mark X Viscount Sporter, Barreled Action, Mauser System Actions, Mark X Whitworth
Mauser Model 66 & 99
McMillan Alaskan MA, Classic MA & Stainless MA Sporters, Long Range Rifle, Talon Sporter, Titanium Mountain
Remington Models 700 ADL, BDL, BDL European, BDL SS, CS
Ruger Models M-77RS, 77R, M-77 All-Weather, M-77 Deluxe
Sako Classic, Deluxe, Fiberclass, Hunter Lightweight, LS, Left-Handed Models, Model TRG-S
Sauer Model 90
Savage Model 110 Series, Model 114 CU & 116 FSS
Steyr-Mannlicher Luxus S, Sporter S & ST
Tikka New Generation, Premium Grade, Whitetail/Battue
Ultra Light Model 26 Series
Unique Model TGC
Weatherby Mark V Alaskan, Classicmark, Deluxe, Lazermark, Sporter, Weathermark; Vanguard Alaskan, Classic, VGX, Weatherguard
Winchester Model 70 Featherweight, Sporter, Super Grade, Winlite
Winslow Basic

8mm Rem. Mag.

A-Square Caesar and Hannibal
Remington Model 700 Safari Grade

300 Phoenix

McMillan Long Range, Safari, 300 Phoenix

300 Weatherby Mag.

A-Square Caesar and Hannibal
Blaser Model R 84
KDF Model K15
Mauser Models 66 & 99
McMillan Alaskan MA, Classic MA & Stainless MA Sporters, Safari and Talon Sporter
Remington Model 700 BDL SS, CS
Sako Deluxe, Hunter Lightweight
Sauer Model 90
Weatherby Mark V Alaskan, Classicmark, Deluxe, Lazermark, Sporter, Weathermark; Vanguard VGX
Winslow Basic

300 Win. Mag.

A-Square Caesar and Hannibal
Blaser Model R 84
Brno Model ZKK 602
Browning A-Bolt
Dakota Arms Model 76 Classic & Safari
European American Armory Sabatti Rover 870
Carl Gustaf Model 2000
KDF Model K15
Mark X Mauser System Actions, Barreled Action, Viscount Sporter, Whitworth
Mauser Model 66, 99

McMillan Alaskan, Classic MA & Stainless MA Sporters, Long Range Rifle, Safari, Talon Sporter, Titanium Mountain
Remington Models 700 ADL, BDL, BDL SS, Safari
Ruger M-77R, M-77RS, M-77 All-Weather
Sako Deluxe, Fiberclass, Left-Handed Models, Hunter Lightweight, LS, Model TRG-S
Sauer Model 90
Savage Model 110 Series, 114CU & Model 116FSS
Steyr-Mannlicher Model S/T & Sporter S & ST Models
Tikka New Generation, Premium Grade, Whitetail Battue
Ultra Light Model 26 Series
Unique Model TGC
Weatherby Mark V Alaskan, Sporter, Weathermark; Vanguard VGX
Winchester Model 70, Featherweight, Sporter, Super Grade, Winlite
Winslow Basic

300 H&H

A-Square Caesar and Hannibal
McMillan Alaskan MA, Classic MA & Stainless MA Sporters, Safari, Talon Sporter
Winchester Model 70 Sporter
Winslow Basic

300 & 311 Imp. Mag.

Imperial Bolt Actions

308 Norma

Winslow Basic

338 Lapua

Heym Model Express
McMillan Long Range, Safari

338 Win. Mag.

A-Square Caesar and Hannibal
Blaser Model R84
Browning A-Bolt
Dakota Arms Model 76 Classic, Safari
European American Armory Sabatti Rover 870
KDF Model K15
Mauser Model 99
McMillan Classic MA & Stainless MA Sporters, Talon Sporter & Safari
Remington Model 700 ADL, BDL, BDL SS
Ruger Model 77R, M-77RS, M-77 All-Weather, M-77 Deluxe
Sako Carbine, Deluxe, Hunter Lightweight, Fiberclass, Left-Handed Models, LS, Safari Grade, Model TRG-S
Sauer Model 90
Savage Model 110 Series, Model 116FSS & 116FSK "Kodiak"
Tikka New Generation, Premium Grade, Whitetail/Battue
Weatherby Vanguard VGX; Mark V Alaskan, Sporter, Weathermark
Winchester Model 70 Sporter, Super Grade, Winlite
Winslow Basic

340 Weatherby Mag.

A-Square Caesar and Hannibal
McMillan Alaskan MA, Classic MA & Stainless MA Sporters, Safari and Talon Sporter
Weatherby Mark V Alaskan, Classicmark, Deluxe, Lazermark, Sporter, Weathermark

350 Rem. Mag.

Clifton Arms Scout
McMillan Varminter, Talon Sporter

35 Whelen

Remington Model 700 ADL, BDL, Models 7400 & 7600

358 Win./Norma

McMillan Alaskan MA
Winslow Basic

375 H&H

A-Square Caesar and Hannibal
Blaser Model R84
Brno Model ZKK 602
Browning A-Bolt and Composite Stalker
Dakota Arms Model 76 Safari, Classic
Francotte Bolt Action
Heym Model Express
KDF Model K15
Mark X Barreled Action, Whitworth Express
Mauser Model 66 Safari & 99
McMillan Alaskan MA, Classic MA & Stainless MA Sporters, Safari, Talon Sporter
Parker-Hale Model M81 African, 1100M African
Remington Model 700 Safari Grade
Ruger 77 Magnum
Sako Deluxe, Fiberclass, Hunter Lightweight, LS, Left-Handed Models, Mannlicher-Style Carbine, Safari Grade, Model TRG-S
Sauer Model 90
Steyr-Mannlicher Models S & S/T
Weatherby Mark V Alaskan, Classicmark, Sporter, Weathermark
Winslow Basic

375 Weatherby

A-Square Caesar and Hannibal

378 Win./Wby. Mag.

A-Square Hannibal
Heym Express
McMillan Safari
Weatherby Mark V Classicmark, Deluxe, Lazermark

404 Jeffery

McMillan Safari
Ruger 77 Magnum

411 KDF

KDF Model K15

416 Rem./Weatherby Mag.

A-Square Caesar and Hannibal
McMillan Alaskan MA, Classic MA & Stainless MA Sporters, Safari, Talon Sporter
Remington Model 700 Safari Grade
Sako Deluxe, Fiberclass, Hunter Lightweight, Laminated Stock Models, Left-Handed Models, Safari Grade
Weatherby Mark V Classicmark, Deluxe, Lazermark

416 Rigby

A-Square Hannibal
Francotte Bolt Action
Heym Express
McMillan Safari
Ruger 77 Magnum

416 Taylor & Hoffman

A-Square Caesar and Hannibal

425 Express

A-Square Caesar and Hannibal

450 Ackley

A-Square Caesar and Hannibal
Heym Express

458 Win. Mag.

A-Square Caesar & Hannibal
Brno Model ZKK-602
Dakota Arms Model 76 Classic, Safari
KDF Model K15
Krieghoff Ulm & Teck
Mark X Barreled Action, Whitworth Express
Mauser Model 66 Safari
McMillan Safari
Parker-Hale Model 1100M African
Remington Model 700 Safari Grade
Ruger 77 Magnum
Sauer Safari, Model 90
Steyr-Mannlicher Model S & S/T
Winslow Basic

460 Win./Weatherby Mag.

A-Square Hannibal
Francotte Bolt Action
Heym Express
McMillan Safari
Weatherby Mark V Classicmark, Deluxe, Lazermark

500 N.E.

Heym Express

505 Gibbs

Francotte Bolt Action

600 N.E.

Heym Express 600

CENTERFIRE LEVER ACTION

218 Bee

Marlin Model 1894 Classic

22LR

A. Uberti Model 1866 Sporting, Model 1866 Yellowboy Carbine, Model 1871 Rolling Block Baby Carbine

22 Hornet

A. Uberti Model 1871 Rolling Block Baby Carbine

22 Magnum

A. Uberti Model 1866 Sporting & Yellowboy Carbine, Model 1871 Rolling Block Baby Carbine

222 Rem./223 Rem.

Browning Model 81 BLR

22-250

Browning Model 81 BLR

243 Win.

Browning Model 81 BLR
Savage Model 99C

25-20 Win.

Marlin Model 1894 Classic

270

Browning Model 81 BLR LA

284 Win.

Browning Model 81 BLR

7mm-08

Browning Model 81 BLR

7mm Mag.

Browning Model 81 BLR LA

7-30 Waters

Winchester Model 94 Standard Walnut

307 Win.

Winchester Model 94 Big Bore Walnut

308 Win.

Browning Model 81 BLR
Savage Model 99C

30-30 Win.

Marlin Models 30AS, 336CS
Winchester Models 94 Ranger, Walnut, Win-Tuff

30-06

Browning Model 81 BLR LA

32 Win.

Winchester Model 94 Standard Walnut

32-20 Win.

Marlin Model 1894 Classic

35 Rem.

Marlin Model 336CS

356 Win.

Winchester Model 94 Big Bore Walnut

357 Mag.

Marlin Model 1894CS
Mitchell Arms 1873 Winchester
Rossi Puma Models M92 SRS & SRC
Uberti Models 1871 Rolling Block Baby Carbine, Model 1873 Sporting & Carbine
Winchester Model 94 Trapper Walnut Carbine

38 Special

EMF Model 1866 Yellow Boy Rifle/Carbine
Marlin Model 1894CS
Rossi Puma Models M92 SRS & M92 SRC
A. Uberti 1866 Sporting, Model 1866 Yellowboy Carbine

44 Special

Marlin Model 1894S
Winchester Model 94 Trapper Walnut Carbine, Wrangler

44 Rem. Mag.

Marlin Model 1894S
Rossi Puma Model M65 SRC
Winchester Model 94 Trapper Walnut Carbine, Wrangler

444 Marlin

Marlin Model 444SS

44-40

EMF Model 1866 Yellow Boy Rifle/Carbine
Mitchell Arms 1858 Henry, 1866 and 1873 Winchesters
Navy Arms 1866 Yellowboy (rifle & carbine), Henry Military, Iron Frame & Trapper Models, 1873 Winchester-Style Rifle
Uberti Model 1866 Sporting, Yellowboy Carbine, Model 1873 Sporting & Carbine, Henry Rifle & Carbine

45 Colt

EMF Model 1866 Yellow Boy Rifle/Carbine, 1873 Sporting, Carbine

Marlin Model 1894S
Mitchell Arms 1873 Winchester
Navy Arms 1873 Rifle, Sharps Cavalry Carbine
Uberti Model 1866, Model 1866 Yellowboy Carbine & Sporting, Model 1873 Sporting & Carbine, Henry
Winchester Model 94 Trapper Walnut Carbine

45-70 Government

Browning Model 1886 Carbine
Marlin Model 1895SS

SINGLE SHOT

17 Rem.

Thompson/Center Contender

218 Bee

Ruger No. 1B Standard, No. 1S Medium Sporter

22 S, L, LR

Dakota Arms Model 10
Thompson/Center Contender

22 BR Rem.

Remington Model 40-XBBR Bench Rest

22 Hornet

New England Firearms Handi-Rifle
Ruger No. 1B Standard
Thompson/Center Contender

220 Swift

Remington Model 40XB Rangemaster
Ruger No. 1V Special Varminter, No. 1B Standard

222 Rem.

Remington Models 40-XB Bench Rest, Rangemaster

222 Rem. Mag.

Remington Model 40-XBBR

22-250 Rem.

Browning Model 1885
Remington Model 40-XB Rangemaster
Ruger No. 1B Standard, Special Varminter

223

Browning Model 1885
Harrington & Richardson Ultra Single Shot Varmint
Jarrett Varmint
New England Firearms Handi-Rifle
Remington Model 40-XBBR Bench Rest, Rangemaster
Ruger No. 1B Standard, No. 1V Special Varminter
Thompson/Center Contender

243 Win.

New England Firearms Handi-Rifle
Remington Model 40-XB Rangemaster
Ruger No. 1A Light Sporter, No. 1B, No. 1 RSI International Standard

25-06

Remington Model 40-XB Rangemaster
Ruger No. 1V Special Varminter, No. 1B Standard

6mm PPC

Ruger No. 1V Special Varminter

6mm BR Rem.

Remington Model 40-XBBR Bench Rest, Rangemaster

6mm Rem.

Remington Model 40-XB Rangemaster
Ruger No. 1B Standard, No. 1V Special Varminter

257 Roberts

Ruger No. 1B Standard

270 Weatherby

Ruger No. 1B Standard

270 Win.

Browning Model 1885
New England Firearms Handi-Rifle
Ruger No. 1A Light Sporter, No. 1B Standard,
 RSI International

280 Rem.

Ruger No. 1B Standard

30-06

Browning Model 1885
Remington Model 40XB Rangemaster
Ruger No. 1A Light Sporter, No. 1B Standard,
 RSI International

300 Weatherby Mag.

Ruger No. 1B Standard

300 Win. Mag.

Remington Model 40-XB Rangemaster
Ruger No. 1B Standard, No. 1S Medium Sporter

30-30 Win.

New England Firearms Handi-Rifle
Thompson/Center Contender

308 Win.

Remington Model 40-XBBR

7mm BR Rem.

Remington Model 40-XB Rangemaster

7mm Rem. Mag.

Browning Model 1885
Remington Model 40-XB Rangemaster
Ruger No. 1S Medium Sporter

338 Win. Mag.

Ruger No. 1S Medium Sporter, No. 1B Standard

375 H&H

Ruger No. 1H Tropical
Thompson/Center Contender

404 Jeffery

Ruger No. 1H Tropical

416 Rem./Rigby

Ruger No. 1H Tropical

45-70 Govt.

Browning Model 1885
Navy Arms No. 2 Creedmoor Target, Remington
 Style Rolling Block Buffalo, Sharps Cavalry
 Carbine
New England Firearms Handi-Rifle
Ruger No. 1S Medium Sporter

458 Win. Mag.

Ruger No. 1H Tropical

AUTOLOADING

22 LR

AMT Lightning and Small Game Hunting Rifle
Auto-Ordnance Thompson Model 1927-A3
Eagle Arms Model EA-15
Lakefield Model 64B
Mitchell Arms Models M-16A1 & CAR-15
Norinco Model 22ADT
Ruger 10/22 Carbine, Sporter & Stainless Models

223 Rem.

Colt Sporter Lightweight and Sporter Competition,
 Match H-Bar, Target Gov't Models
Ruger Mini-14, Mini-14 Ranch
Steyr-Mannlicher Aug S.A.

243 Win.

Browning BAR Semiauto

270 Win./Wby

Browning BAR Semiauto

30 Carbine

Iver Johnson M-1 Carbine

300 Win. Mag.

Browning BAR Semiauto

30-06

Browning BAR Semiauto

308 Win.

Heckler & Koch Models SR-9, SR-9 Target and
 PSG-1 Marksman's
Mauser Model 86 Precision
Springfield MIA Standard, Match; MIA-A1 Bush

338 Win. Mag.

Browning BAR Semiauto

45 Auto

Auto-Ordnance Thompson Models M1, 1927A1
Marlin Model 45

7mm Rem. Mag.

Browning BAR Semiauto

7.62X39

Navy Arms Cowboy's Companion
Ruger Mini-30

9mm

Colt Sporter Lightweight
Feather Model AT-9
Iver Johnson M-1 Carbine
Marlin Model 9 Camp

10mm

Auto-Ordnance Model 1927-A1

RIMFIRE BOLT ACTION

22 S, L, LR

Anschutz Match 64 Sporters: Models 1416D,
 1418D, 1516D, 1518D, 54.18S, 54.18S-REP,
 64MS, 1907, 1910, 1911, 1913, Model 1700
 Custom & Bavarian, Achiever, Biathlon Models
 1450B and 1827 B/BT
Beeman/Weihrauch Models HW 60M Smallbore,
 HW 60J-ST, HW 660 Match
Beeman/FWB Model 2600
Brno Model ZKM-452
Browning Model A-Bolt 22

Dakota Arms Sporter
European American Armory HW 660 Match and
 Target
Lakefield Sporting Models 90B, 91T & 91TR,
 92S, Mark I, Mark II
Marlin Models 15YN "Little Buckaroo," 25N, 880,
 881, Model 2000 Target
Mauser Models 107, 201
Norinco Model JW-15 "Buckhorn"
Remington Models 40-XR, 541-T
Ruger Model 77/22RS
Ruko Model M14P
Ultra Light Arms Model 20 RF
Unique Model T Dioptra Sporter, UIT Standard,
 T/SM Silhouette

22 Hornet

Anschutz Model 1700 Bavarian and 1700D
 Custom & Classic
Brno Model CZ-527

22 Magnum

Anschutz Model 1700 Bavarian, 1700D Custom,
 Match 64 Sporters
Ruger Model K77 Varmint

22 WMR

Marlin Models 25MN, 882, 882L, 883, 883SS
Mauser Model 201
Ruko Model M1500

222/223 Rem.

Anschutz Model 1700 Bavarian, Custom and
 1700D Classic
Beeman/Weihrauch Model HW 60J-ST
Brno Model CZ-527

7.62mm NATO

Remington Model 40-XC KS

RIMFIRE AUTOLOADING

22 S, L, LR

Anschutz Model 525
Browning Model 22 (Grades I & VI)
Feather Model AT-22 & F2 AT-22
Marlin Models 60, 70HC, 70P, 990L, 995
Remington Model 522 Viper, Model 552 BDL
 Deluxe Speedmaster
Ruger Model 10/22
Ruko Model M20P

22 Win. Mag.

Marlin Models 882L, 922 Mag.

RIMFIRE LEVER ACTION

22 S, L, LR

Browning Model BL-22 (Grades I & II)
Marlin Models 39TD, Golden 39AS
Winchester Model 9422

22 WMR Mag.

Winchester Model 9422

44

Navy Arms Henry Military and Iron Frame (rifles
 and carbines)

RIMFIRE PUMP ACTION

22 S, L, LR

Remington Model 572 BDL Deluxe Fieldmaster
Rossi Models M62 SAC & SA

DOUBLE RIFLES

| 308 |

Krieghoff Models Ulm & Teck

| 30-06 |

Heym Model 88B Safari and Side-by-Side
Krieghoff Models Ulm & Teck

| 300 Win. Mag. |

Krieghoff Models Ulm & Teck

| 9.3 X 74R |

Heym Model 88B
Tikka Model 412S

| 375 H&H |

Heym Model 88B Safari
Krieghoff Model Ulm

| 458 Win. |

Heym Model 88B Safari
Kreighoff Models Ulm & Teck

| 470 N.E. |

Heym Model 88B Safari

| 500 N.E. |

Heym Model 88B Safari

RIFLE/SHOTGUN COMBOS

| 22 LR |

Savage Model 24F

| 22 Hornet/12 ga. |

Savage Model 24F (20 ga. also)

| 223 Rem./12 ga. |

Savage Model 24-F (20 ga. also)

| 30-30/12 ga. |

Savage Model 24F (20 ga. also)

BLACK POWDER

HANDGUNS

| 30 |

Gonic Arms Model GA-90

| 31 |

CVA New Model Pocket Remington, Wells Fargo
Model, Vest Pocket Derringer

| 36 |

American Arms 1851 Colt Navy
Armsport Models 5133, 5136, 5154
CVA Models 1851 & 1861 Navy Brass-Framed
Revolvers, Sheriff's Model, Pocket Police
Dixie Navy Revolver, Spiller & Burr Revolver
EMF 1851 Sheriff's Model, Model 1862 Police
Euroarms 1851 Navy & Navy Confederate
Revolver
Mitchell Arms 1851 Colt Navy, Remington
"Texas" Model, General Custer's Remington
New Model Army
Navy Arms 1851 Navy "Yank" Revolver, 1862
Police Revolver, Reb Model 1860, Army 1860
Sheriff's Model
A. Uberti 1851 &1861 Navy, 1858 Navy, Paterson

| 38 |

Dixie Pedersoli Mang Target Pistol
Gonic Arms Model GA-90

| 41 |

Dixie Abilene & Lincoln Derringers

| 44 |

American Arms 1847 Walker, 1858 Remington
Army and Army SS Target, 1860 Colt Army
Armsport Models 5120, 5133, 5136, 5138, 5139,
5140, 5145, 5152, 5153
CVA 1861 Navy Brass-Framed, 1860 Army
Revolvers, Walker, Third Model Dragoon,
Remington Bison, 1858 Remington Target
Model and Army Steel Frame Revolver (also
Brass Frame)
Dixie Pennsylvania Pistol, Remington Army
Revolver, Third Model Dragoon, Walker
Revolver, Wyatt Earp Revolver
EMF Model 1860 Army, Second Model 44
Dragoon
Euroarms Rogers & Spencer Models 1005, 1006
& 1007, 1851 Navy, Remington 1858 New
Model Army
Gonic Arms Model GA-90
Mitchell Arms 1851 Colt Navy, 1860 Colt Army
Model, Remington "Texas" Model, General
Custer's Remington New Model Army
Navy Arms Colt Walker 1847, 1851 Navy Yank
Revolver, Reb Model 1860 Revolver, 1860
Army Revolver, Army 60 Sheriff's Model,
Rogers & Spencer Revolver, Target Model
Remington Revolver, Stainless Steel 1858
Remington, Remington New Model Army,
LeMat Revolvers, Le Page Flintlock/Percussion
& Cased Sets
Uberti 1st, 2nd & 3rd Model Dragoon, Walker,
1858 Remington Target, 1860 Army

| 45 |

CVA Philadelphia Derringer, Siber Target Pistol
Dixie LePage Dueling Pistol, Pedersoli English
Dueling Pistol
Gonic Arms Model GA-90
Traditions William Parker Pistol, Pioneer Pistol,
Trapper Pistol

| 50 |

CVA Kentucky Pistol, Hawken Pistol
Thompson/Center Scout Pistol
Traditions Trapper Pistol, William Parker Pistol,
Whitetail (rifle & carbine)

| 54 |

Thompson/Center Scout Pistol

| 58 |

Navy Arms Harpers Ferry Pistol

RIFLES & CARBINES

| 30 |

Gonic Arms Model GA-87

| 32 |

CVA Varmint
Dixie Tennessee Squirrel
Navy Arms Pennsylvania Long

| 36 |

Traditions Frontier Scout

| 38 & 44 |

Gonic Arms Model GA-87

| 44-40 |

Dixie Winchester '73 Carbine

| 45 |

Dixie Hawken, Kentuckian, Pedersoli
Waadtlander, Pennsylvania, Tryon Creedmoor
Gonic Arms Model GA-87
Navy Arms Pennsylvania Long
Thompson/Center Hawken, White Mountain
Carbine
Traditions Frontier, Frontier Scout, Pennsylvania,
Ultra Light Arms Model 90
White Model Super 91 and "G" Series

| 451 |

Navy Arms Tryon Creedmoor
Parker-Hale Volunteer Rifle, Whitworth Military
Target & Sniper Rifles

| 45-70 |

Shiloh Sharps Model 1874 Sporting Rifle #1 &
#3/Business/Military/"Civilian" Carbine

| 45-90 |

Shiloh Sharps Model 1874 Sporting #1 & #3;
Model 1874 Business/"Civilian" Carbine

| 45-120 |

Shiloh Sharps Model 1874 Sporting #1 & #3,
Business

| 50 |

American Arms Hawkeye
CVA Kentucky, Stalker and Sierra Stalker,
Tracker Carbine, Bushwacker, St. Louis
Hawken, Apollo Carbelite, Sporter & Shadow,
Express Double Rifle & Carbine, Frontier &
Hunter Carbine, Plainsman, Trophy Carbine
Dixie Hawken, In-Line Carbine, Tennessee
Mountain
Gonic Arms Model GA-87 Rifle, GA-93 Carbine
Lyman Deerstalker Rifle and Carbine, Great
Plains, Trade Rifle
Modern Muzzleloading Knight MK-85 Series,
Model BK-92 Black Knight
Navy Arms Ithaca-Navy Hawken, Japanese
Matchlock, Smith Carbine
Thompson/Center Hawken, New Englander,
Pennsylvania Hunter, Renegade, Renegade
Hunter, Scout Carbine, White Mountain Carbine
Traditions Buckskinner Carbine, Deerhunter,
Frontier Scout, Frontier (rifle & carbine),
Hawken, Hawken Woodsman, Pennsylvania,
Pioneer, Trophy
Uberti Santa Fe Hawken
Ultra Light Arms Model 90
White Model Super 91 and "G" Series

| 50-70 | | 50-90 | | 50-140 |

Shiloh Sharps Model 1874 Business, Sporting #1
& #3, Military

| 54 |

American Arms Hawkeye
CVA Apollo Carbelite & 90 Shadow, Express
Double Barrel, Frontier Hunter Carbine, St.
Louis Hawken, Stalker (rifle & carbine), Trophy
Carbine
Dixie Hawken, In-Line Carbine
Euroarms 1803 Harpers Ferry, 1841 Mississippi
Gonic Arms Model GA-87
Lyman Deerstalker Rifle, Great Plains, Trade Rifle
Modern Muzzleloading Knight MK-85 Series, BK-
92 Black Knight
Navy Arms 1803 Harpers Ferry, 1841 Mississippi,
Mortimer Flintlock, Sharps Cavalry Carbine

Shiloh Sharps Model 1863 Sporting
Thompson/Center Hawken, New Englander, Renegade, Renegade Hunter, Scout Carbine, White Mountain Carbine
Traditions Hawken, Hawken Woodsman, Hunter, Pioneer, Trophy
Uberti Sante Fe Hawken
White "G" Series

| 577 |

Parker-Hale 1853 & 1858 Enfields, 1861 Enfield Musketoon

| 58 |

Dixie 1858 Two-Band Enfield rifle, U.S. Model 1861 Springfield, Mississippi, 1862 Three-Band Enfield Rifle Musket, 1863 Springfield Civil War Musket

Euroarms Model 2260 London Armory Company Enfield 3-Band Rifle Musket, Models 2270 and 2280 London Armory Company Enfield Rifled Muskets, Model 2300 Cook & Brother Confederate Carbine, J. P. Murray Carbine, 1861 Springfield, 1863 Zouave, C. S. Richmond Musket
Navy Arms Mississippi Model 1841, 1853 Enfield Rifle & Musket, 1861 Enfield Musketoon, 1861 Springfield, 1862 C.S. Richmond, 1863 Springfield, J.P. Murray Carbine
Thompson/Center Big Boar Caplock

| 69 |

Dixie U.S. Model 1816 Flintlock Musket
Navy Arms 1816 M.T. Wickham Musket

| 75 |

Dixie Second Model Brown Bess Musket
Navy Arms Brown Bess Musket & Carbine

SHOTGUNS (Black Powder)

CVA Trapper Single Barrel & Classic Turkey Double Barrel (12 ga.)
Dixie Double Barrel Magnum (12 ga.)
Euroarms Model 2295 Magnum Cape (single barrel)
Navy Arms Model T&T, Fowler (12 ga.), Mortimer Flintlock 12 ga., Steel Shot Magnum 10 ga.
Thompson/Center New Englander